MANUAL OF HOUSING/ PLANNING AND DESIGN CRITERIA

Joseph DeChiara
and
Lee Koppelman

Prentice-Hall, Inc. / Englewood Cliffs, N. J.

Prentice-Hall International, Inc., *London*
Prentice-Hall of Australia, Pty. Ltd., *Sydney*
Prentice-Hall of Canada, Ltd., *Toronto*
Prentice-Hall of India Private Ltd., *New Delhi*
Prentice-Hall of Japan, Inc., *Tokyo*

© 1975 by

Prentice-Hall, Inc.
Englewood Cliffs, N.J.

Second Printing . . . . . August, 1975

Library of Congress Cataloging in Publication Data

De Chiara, Joseph
  Manual of housing/planning and design criteria.

  Includes bibliographical references.
  1.   Housing surveys—Handbooks, manuals, etc.
2. Cities and towns—Planning—Handbooks, manuals, etc.
I. Koppelman, Lee, joint author. II. Title.
HD7287.5.D4   309.2′62   74-3049
ISBN 0-13-553529-8

Printed in the United States of America

To

Edith and Connie

PREFACE

The general aim of this book is to afford those interested in the planning for housing—whether they be students, teachers, practitioners, advocates, or consumers—a reference of current procedures, designs, and standards. Although the primary emphasis is on graphical and pictorial presentation, textual material is included to ensure comprehensive treatment of the subject.

We wish to acknowledge the generous support and courtesy of the many agencies, practitioners, and publications in allowing the use of their material. In particular we are indebted to Mr. Edward Logueand of the New York State Urban Development Corpo-

ration, Mr. Timothy McInerney of the Long Island Builders Institute, and Dr. Karl A. Baer, Chief Librarian of the National Association of Home Builders for their technical assistance.

In addition, we are appreciative of the friendly spirit and willingness to make their works available to us by the following architects: Conklin and Rossant; Davis Brody and Associates; Gruzen and Partners; and Paul Friedberg & Associates.

Joseph DeChiara
Lee K. Koppelman

CONTENTS

Preface .... *i*

A   Housing Studies 1

B   General Planning Considerations 49

C   Neighborhood Organization 99

D   Community Facilities 169

E   Site Considerations 243

F   Types of Housing 289

G   Types of Apartments 373

H   Housing Controls 459

I   Governmental Programs 515

Index 546

HOUSING STUDIES

A

A-1   Introduction
A-2   Housing Study
A-3   Population Study
A-4   Community Renewal Study–EDP
A-5   Housing Census Reports
A-6   Census Items, 1970
A-7   Population Data, Tract Report
A-8   Housing Data, Tract Report
A-9   Population Projection
        Apportionment Method
A-10   Population Projection
        Migration–Natural Increase Method
A-11   Population Projection
        Mathematical Method
A-12   Required Housing Element
A-13   Housing Element Case Study
A-14   Deficient Housing Units

A-15   Housing of Welfare Recipients
A-16   Design Prototype
        Introduction
A-17   Design Prototype
        Existing Land Use
A-18   Design Prototype
        Proposed Land Use
A-19   Design Prototype
        Existing Neighborhood Pattern
A-20   Design Prototype
        Proposed Neighborhood Pattern
A-21   Design Prototype
        Community Pattern
A-22   Design Prototype
        Regional Pattern
A-23   Design Prototype
        Conclusions
Bibliography

Introduction

Community planning often fails in concept, plan development and eventual execution due to the lack of attention paid to housing as a major and specific element of land use. Although programs and design methods discussed elsewhere in this book are applicable towards this end, e.g., codes, federal programs, and design examples, it is essential that specific methodologies and techniques be utilized in the comprehensive analysis and plan formulation of the communities' existing and projected housing needs. This is a particularly relevant subject due to the new H.U.D. requirements concerning housing elements. It is therefore the intent of this chapter to explore a suitable approach for the carrying out of a housing study. The contents are by no means all-inclusive nor the only approach. Yet it is one that has been developed as a working model for a regional area covering 1,200 square miles with a current population of 2½ million and a wide range of housing types and conditions in urban, semiurban and rural settings. The study has already led to partial implementation of the regional plan geared for an eventual 3.3 million people by the year 1985.

In essence a housing study should encompass inventories, analyses and projections of housing by quantity, quality, and type related to existing and projected demographic conditions. It should also include programs, recommendations and design criteria for implementation. Therefore the initial phases of a housing study may be conducted in tandem. Namely, the inventory and analysis of existing units can be carried out in conjunction with detailed studies of the existing and proposed population by number, age, race, family size and income. This latter data allows for an evaluation of current matching or, more to the point, mismatching of need to supply, and future demand by type and cost. The housing data gleaned in the inventory stage will uncover the need for remedial action, the extent of need for replacement units by type, and perhaps some insight into the required measures for the elimination of existing problems and the prevention of recurrence. This quantification stage is then followed by the design phase or "housing plan" indicating the distribution by type and location of the eventual housing inventory. Figures A-1-1 and A-1-2 summarize the flow patterns in the conduct of such work. Figure A-1-3 depicts the combination of housing and demographic analysis suitable for a computerized system that may be applied for a community renewal program for a single neighborhood up to a regional area.

One of the great sources of data on housing and population is available from the United States Bureau of the Census. Section A-6 contains a summary of the reports available from the 1970 census. Other sources of historic and existing conditions may be obtained from state and local housing agencies, utility companies, local building and planning departments, and health and welfare agencies. Sections A-9, A-10 and A-11 contain brief explanations of techniques used in making population projections.

This is followed by a discussion of the housing element planning requirement as contained in the Housing Act of 1968. In order to provide a working example of a complete housing element, the balance of the chapter starting with Section A-13 contains a case study of the Nassau-Suffolk Regional Board's housing study, including a prototype plan that incorporates the results of the quantitative analysis with a design solution. This study was one of the first housing elements completed in the United States as part of the "701" planning program and was cited by H.U.D.

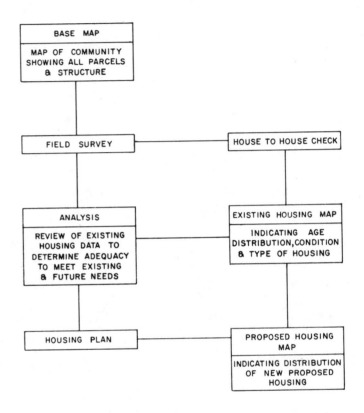

A-1-1   Generalized Housing Study Flow Pattern

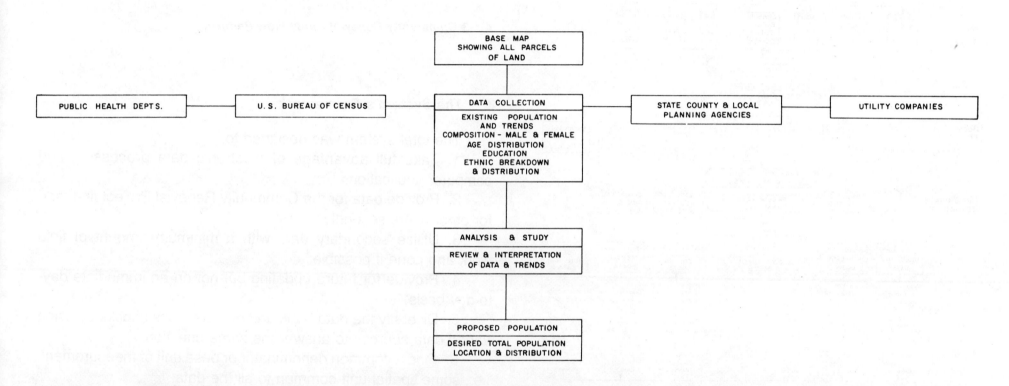

A-1-2 Generalized Population Study Flow Pattern

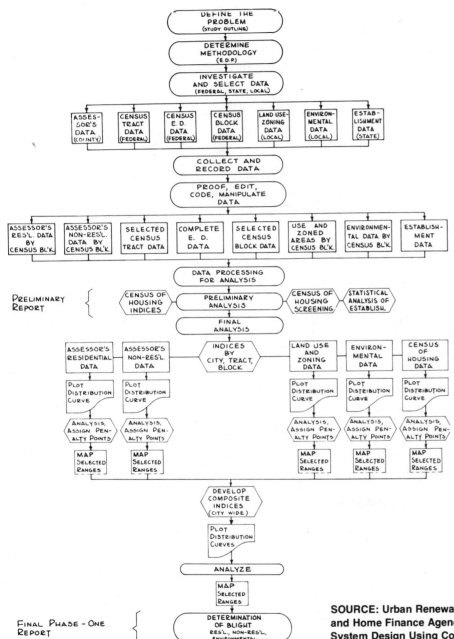

A-1-3 Community Renewal Study Flow Pattern

The System's Framework

The total system was designed to:

1. Take full advantage of electronic data processing and computer applications.

2. Provide data for the Community Renewal Project first, and for other users secondly.

3. Utilize secondary data with a minimum amount of field work and none if possible.

4. Provide for future updating but not on an immediate day-to-day basis.

5. Diversify the data bank and provide cross checks by using varied data sources to answer the same question.

6. Find a common denominator or base unit of measurement, i.e., some spatial unit common to all the data.

7. Provide a data recall and graphical display system capable of operation by the user without consulting with or hiring an experienced programmer or computer technician.

SOURCE: Urban Renewal Service, Urban Renewal Administration Housing and Home Finance Agency, Washington, D.C.—1962 Spokane C.R.P. Data System Design Using Computer Graphics in Community Renewal.

PUBLICATION AND COMPUTER SUMMARY TAPE PROGRAM

The results of the 1970 Census of Population and Housing are being issued in the form of printed reports, microfiche copies of the printed reports, computer summary tapes, computer printouts, and microfilm. Listed below are short descriptions of the final report series as currently planned. More detailed information on this program can be obtained by writing to the Publications Distribution Section, Bureau of the Census, Washington, D.C. 20233.

Housing Census Reports

Volume I.
HOUSING CHARACTERISTICS FOR STATES, CITIES, and COUNTIES

This volume will consist of 58 "parts"—number 1 for the United States, numbers 2 through 52 for the 50 States and the District of Columbia in alphabetical order, and numbers 53 through 58 for Puerto Rico, Guam, Virgin Islands, American Samoa, Canal Zone, and Trust Territory of the Pacific Islands, respectively. Each part, which will be a separate clothbound book, will contain two chapters designated as A and B. Each chapter (for each of the 58 areas) will first be issued as an individual paperbound report in two series designated as HC(1)-A and B, respectively.

- Series HC(1)-A.
  ### GENERAL HOUSING CHARACTERISTICS

Statistics on tenure, kitchen facilities, plumbing facilities, number of rooms, persons per room, units in structure, mobile home, telephone, value, contract rent, and vacancy status are presented for some or all of the following areas: States (by urban and rural residence), standard metropolitan statistical areas (SMSA's), urbanized areas, places of 1,000 inhabitants or more, and counties.

- Series HC(1)-B.
  ### DETAILED HOUSING CHARACTERISTICS

Statistics are presented on a more detailed basis for the subjects included in the Series HC(1)-A reports, as well as on such additional subjects as year moved into unit, year structure built, basement, heating equipment, fuels, air conditioning, water and sewage, appliances, gross rent, and ownership of second home. Each subject is shown for some or all of the following areas: States (by urban, rural-nonfarm, and rural-farm residence), SMSA's, urbanized areas, places of 2,500 inhabitants or more, and counties (by rural and rural-farm residence).

Volume II.
METROPOLITAN HOUSING CHARACTERISTICS

These reports, also designated as Series HC(2), will cover most of the 1970 census housing subjects in considerable detail and cross-classification. These will be one report for each SMSA, presenting data for the SMSA and its central cities and places of 50,000 inhabitants or more, as well as a national summary report.

Volume III.
BLOCK STATISTICS

One report, under the designation Series HC(3), is issued for each urbanized area showing data for individual blocks on selected housing and population subjects. The series also includes reports for the communities outside urbanized areas that have contracted with the Census Bureau to provide block statistics from the 1970 census.

Volume IV.
COMPONENTS OF INVENTORY CHANGE

This volume will contain data on the disposition of the 1960 inventory and the source of the 1970 inventory, such as new construction, conversions, mergers, demolitions, and other additions and losses. Cross-tabulations of 1970 and 1960 characteristics for units that have not changed and characteristics of the present and previous residence of recent movers will also be provided. Statistics will be shown for 15 selected SMSA's and for the United States and regions.

Volume V.
RESIDENTIAL FINANCE

This volume will present data regarding the financing of privately owned nonfarm residential properties. Statistics will be shown on amount of outstanding mortgage debt, manner of acquisition of property, homeowner expenses, and other owner, property, and mortgage characteristics for the United States and regions.

Volume VI.
ESTIMATES OF "SUBSTANDARD" HOUSING

This volume will present counts of "substandard" housing units for counties and cities, based on the number of units lacking plumbing facilities combined with estimates of units with all plumbing facilities but in "dilapidated" condition.

Volume VII.
SUBJECT REPORTS

Each report in this volume will concentrate on a particular subject. Detailed information and cross-classifications will generally be provided on a national and regional level; in some reports, data for States or SMSA's may also be shown. Among the subjects to be covered are housing characteristics by household composition, housing of minority groups and senior citizens, and households in mobile homes.

Population Census Reports

Volume I.
CHARACTERISTICS OF THE POPULATION

This volume will consist of 58 "parts"—number 1 for the United States, numbers 2 through 52 for the 50 States and the District of Columbia in alphabetical order, and numbers 53 through 58 for Puerto Rico, Guam, Virgin Islands, American Samoa, Canal Zone, and Trust Territory of the Pacific Islands, respectively. Each part, which will be a separate clothbound book, will contain four chapters designated as A, B, C, and D. Each chapter (for each of the 58 areas) will first be issued as an individual paperbound report in four series designated as PC(1)-A, B, C, and D, respectively. The 58 PC(1)-A reports will be specially assembled and issued in a clothbound book, designated as Part A.

- Series PC(1)-A.
  ### NUMBER OF INHABITANTS

Final official population counts are presented for States, counties by urban and rural residence, SMSA's, urbanized areas, county subdivisions, all incorporated places, and unincorporated places of 1,000 inhabitants or more.

■ Series PC(1)-B
**GENERAL POPULATION
CHARACTERISTICS**

Statistics on age, sex, race, marital status, and relationship to head of household and presented for States, counties by ruban and rural residence, SMSA's, urbanized areas, county sub-divisions, and places of 1,000 inhabitants or more.

■ Series PC(1)-C.
**GENERAL SOCIAL AND
ECONOMIC CHARACTERISTICS**

Statistics are presented on nativity and parentage, State or county of birth, Spanish origin, mother tongue, residence 5 years ago, year moved into present house, school enrollment (public or private), years of school completed, vocational training, number of children ever born, family composition, disability, veteran status, employment status, place of work, means of transportation to work, occupation group, industry group, class of worker, and income (by type) in 1969 of families and individuals. Each subject is shown for some or all of the following areas: States, counties (by urban, rural-nonfarm, and rural-farm residence), SMSA's, urbanized areas, and places of 2,500 inhabitants or more.

■ Series PC(1)-D.
DETAILED CHARACTERISTICS

These reports will cover most of the subjects shown in Series PC(1)-C, above, presenting the data in considerable detail and cross-classified by age, race, and other characteristics. Each subject will be shown for some or all of the following areas: States (by urban, rural-nonfarm, and rural-farm residence), SMSA's, and large cities.

**Volume II.
SUBJECT REPORTS**

Each report in this volume, also designated as Series PC(2), will concentrate on a particular subject. Detailed information and cross-relationships will generally be provided on a national and regional level; in some reports, data for States or SMSA's will also be shown. Among the characteristics to be covered are national origin and race, fertility, families, marital status, migration, education, unemployment, occupation, industry, and income.

Joint Population-Housing Reports

**Series PHC(1).
CENSUS TRACT REPORTS**

This series will contain one report for each SMSA, showing data for most of the population and housing subjects included in the 1970 census.

**Series PHC(2).
GENERAL DEMOGRAPHIC TRENDS
FOR METROPOLITAN AREAS,
1960 to 1970**

This series consists of one report for each State and the District of Columbia, as well as a national summary report presenting statistics for the State and for SMSA's and their central cities and constituent counties. Comparative 1960 and 1970 data is shown on population counts by age and race and on such housing subjects as tenure, plumbing facilities, value, and contract rent.

**Series PHC(3).
EMPLOYMENT PROFILES OF
SELECTED LOW-INCOME AREAS**

This series will consist of approximately 70 reports, each presenting statistics on the social and economic characteristics of the residents of a particular low-income area. The data relates to low-income neighborhoods in 54 cities and seven rural poverty areas. Each report will provide statistics on employment and unemployment, education, vocational training, availability for work, job history, and income, as well as on value or rent and number of rooms in the housing unit.

U.S. DEPARTMENT OF COMMERCE FIELD OFFICES

Publications of the Bureau of the Census may be ordered from any field office listed below.

Albuquerque, N. Mex. 87101, Room 316, U.S. Courthouse
Anchorage, Alaska 99501, 412 Hill Building
Atlanta, Ga. 30309, 1401 Peachtree St. N.E.

Baltimore, Md. 21202, 415 U.S. Customhouse
Birmingham, Ala. 35205, 908 South 20th St.
Boston, Mass. 02203, Room 510, John F. Kennedy Fed. Bldg.
Buffalo, N.Y. 14203, 117 Ellicott St.

Charleston, S.C. 29403, 334 Meeting St.
Charleston, W. Va. 25301, 500 Quarrier St.
Cheyenne, Wyo. 82001, 2120 Capital Ave.
Chicago, Ill. 60604, 219 South Dearborn St.
Cincinnati, Ohio 45202, 550 Main St.
Cleveland, Ohio 44114, Room 600, 666 Euclid Ave.

Dallas, Tex. 75202, 1114 Commerce St.
Denver, Colo. 80202, Room 161, New Customhouse
Des Moines, Iowa 50309, 210 Walnut St.
Detroit, Mich. 48226, 445 Federal Bldg.

Greensboro, N.C. 27402, 258 Federal Bldg.

Hartford, Conn. 06103, 450 Main St.
Honolulu, Hawaii 96813, 1015 Bishop St.
Houston, Tex. 77002, 201 Fannin Street

Jacksonville, Fla. 32202, 400 West Bay St.

Kansas City, Mo. 64106, 601 East 12th St.

Los Angeles, Calif. 90024, 11000 Wilshire Blvd.

Memphis, Tenn. 38103, 147 Jefferson Ave.
Miami, Fla. 33130, 25 West Flagler St.
Milwaukee, Wis. 53203, 238 West Wisconsin Ave.
Minneapolis, Minn. 55401, 110 South Fourth St.

New Orleans, La. 70130, 610 South St.
New York, N.Y. 10007, 26 Federal Plaza, Foley Sq.

Philadelphia, Pa. 19107, 1015 Chestnut St.
Phoenix, Ariz. 85025, 230 North First Ave.
Pittsburgh, Pa. 15222, 1000 Liberty Ave.
Portland, Oreg. 97204, 520 S.W. Morrison St.

Reno, Nev. 89502, 300 Booth St.
Richmond, Va. 23240, 400 North 8th St.

St. Louis, Mo. 63103, 1520 Market St.
Salt Lake City, Utah 84111, 125 South State St.
San Francisco, Calif. 94102, 450 Golden Gate Ave.
San Juan, P.R. 00902, Post Office Bldg.
Savannah, Ga. 31402, 125-29 Bull St.
Seattle, Wash. 98104, 909 First Avenue

Subject Items Included in the 1970 Census

(Percents indicate size of sample for which the question is asked; 100 percent is complete coverage)

Population items
100 percent .... Relationship to head of household
Color or race
Age
Sex
Marital status
20 percent .... State or country of birth
Years of school completed
Employment status
Hours worked last week
Weeks worked in 1969
Last year in which worked
Occupation, industry, and class of worker
Activity 5 years ago
Income in 1969
15 percent .... Country of birth of parents
Mother tongue
Year moved into this house
Place of residence 5 years ago
School or college enrollment (public or
  private)
Veteran status
Place of work
Means of transportation to work
5 percent .... Mexican or Spanish origin or descent
Citizenship
Year of immigration
When married
Vocational training completed
Presence and duration of disability
Occupation-industry 5 years ago
Housing items
100 percent .... Number of units at this address
Telephone
Private entrance to living quarters
Complete kitchen facilities
Rooms
Water supply
Flush toilet
Bathtub or shower
Basement
Tenure
Commercial establishment on property
Value

9

Contract rent
Vacancy status
Months vacant
20 percent .... Components of gross rent
Heating equipment
Year structure built
Number of units in structure and whether
  a trailer
Farm residence
15 percent .... Source of water
Sewage disposal
Bathrooms
Air conditioning
Automobiles
5 percent .... Stories, elevator in structure
Fuel—heating, cooking, water heating
Bedrooms
Clothes washing machine
Clothes dryer
Dishwasher
Home food freezer
Television
Radio
Second home

General Characteristics of the Population

Census Tracts

RACE

    All persons ....
    White ....
    Negro ....
       Percent Negro ....

AGE BY SEX

    Male, all ages ....
Under 5 years ....
  3 and 4 years ....
5 to 9 years ....
  5 years ....
  6 years ....
10 to 14 years ....
  14 years ....
15 to 19 years ....
  15 years ....
  16 years ....
  17 years ....
  18 years ....
  19 years ....
20 to 24 years ....
  20 years ....
  21 years ....
25 to 34 years ....
35 to 44 years ....
45 to 54 years ....
55 to 59 years ....
60 to 64 years ....
65 to 74 years ....
75 years and over ....

    Female, all ages ....
Under 5 years ....
  3 and 4 years ....
5 to 9 years ....
  5 years ....
  6 years ....
10 to 14 years ....
  14 years ....
15 to 19 years ....

15 years ....
16 years ....
17 years ....
18 years ....
19 years ....
20 to 24 years ....
  20 years ....
  21 years ....
25 to 34 years ....
35 to 44 years ....
45 to 54 years ....
55 to 59 years ....
60 to 64 years ....
65 to 74 years ....
75 years and over ....

RELATIONSHIP TO HEAD OF HOUSEHOLD

    All persons ....
In households ....
  Head of household ....
    Head of family ....
    Primary individual ....
  Wife of head ....
  Other relative of head ....
  Not related to head ....
In group quarters ....
Persons per household ....

TYPE OF FAMILY AND NUMBER OF OWN CHILDREN

    All families ....
With own children under 18 years ....
  Number of children ....

    Husband-wife families ....
With own children under 18 years ....
  Number of children ....
    Percent of total under 18 years ....

    Families with other male head ..
With own children under 18 years ....
  Number of children ....

Families with female head.........
With own children under 18 years ....
Number of children ....
Percent of total under 18 years ....
Persons under 18 years.........................

MARITAL STATUS

Male, 14 years old and over......
Single...
Married ....
Separated ....
Widowed...
Divorced ....

Female, 14 years old and over..
Single...
Married ....
Separated ....
Widowed...
Divorced ....

Social Characteristics of the Population

Census Tracts

NATIVITY, PARENTAGE, & COUNTRY OF ORIGIN

All persons...............................
Native of native parentage.....................
Native of foreign or mixed parentage .....
Foreign born..

Foreign stock............................
United Kingdom....................................
Ireland (Eire).......................................
Sweden..
Germany...
Poland ....
Czechoslovakia ....
Austria ....
Hungary ....
U.S.S.R..
Italy..

Canada...
Mexico ....
Cuba...
Other America ....
All other and not reported ....

Persons of Spanish language ......
Other persons of Spanish surname...
Persons of Spanish mother tongue..
Persons of Puerto Rican birth or parentage...

SCHOOL ENROLLMENT

Enrolled persons, 3 to 34 years old ....
Nursery school..............................
Public ....
Kindergarten ....
Public ....
Elementary....................................
Public ....
High school ....
Public ....
College...
Percent enrolled in school by age:
16 and 17 years......................
18 and 19 years......................
20 and 21 years......................
22 to 24 years........................
25 to 34 years........................
Percent 16 to 21 years not high school graduates and not enrolled in school ....

YEARS OF SCHOOL COMPLETED

Persons, 25 years old and over
No school years completed.....................
Elementary: 1 to 4 years......................
5 to 7 years......................
8 years.............................
High school: 1 to 3 years......................
4 years............................
College: 1 to 3 years......................
4 years or more ....
Median school years completed ....
Percent high school graduates ....

CHILDREN EVER BORN

Women, 35 to 44 years old ever married...............................
Children ever born..................................
Per 1,000 women ever married..........

RESIDENCE IN 1965

Persons, 5 years old and over, 1970...
Same house as in 1970.........................
Different house:
In central city of this SMSA ....
In other part of this SMSA..................
Outside this SMSA ....
North and West................................
South ....
Abroad..

MEANS OF TRANSPORTATION AND PLACE OF WORK

All workers ....
Private auto: Driver ....
Passenger.......................
Bus or streetcar....................................
Subway, elevated train, or railroad.........
Walked to work.....................................
Worked at home....................................
Other...
Inside SMSA..
A city central business district............
Balance of A city...............................
Balance of A County..........................
B County ....
C County ....
D County ....
E County ....
F County ....
G County..
H County..
I County ....
J County...
K County ....
Outside SMSA......................................
Place of work not reported.....................

Labor Force Characteristics of the Population

Census Tracts

EMPLOYMENT STATUS

Male, 16 years old and over......
Labor force..
Percent of total ....
Civilian labor force ....
Employed ....
Unemployed ....
Percent of civilian labor force.......
Not in labor force..................................
Inmate of institution ....
Enrolled in school ....
Other under 65 years ....
Other 65 years and over ....

Male, 16 to 21 years old............
Not enrolled in school ....
Not high school graduates.................
Unemployed or not in labor force....

Female, 16 years old and over..
Labor force..
Percent of total ....
Civilian labor force ....
Employed ....
Unemployed ....
Percent of civilian labor force.......
Not in labor force..................................
Married women, husband present ....
In labor force....................................
With own children under 6 years........
In labor force.................................

OCCUPATION

Total employed, 16 years old and over..
Professional, technical and kindred workers...
Health workers...................................
Teachers, elementary and secondary schools..

11

Managers and administrators, except farm ....
   Salaried..
   Self-employed in retail trade...............
Sales workers...
   Retail trade ....
Clerical and kindred workers.................
Craftsmen, foremen, and kindred workers ....
   Construction craftsmen.......................
   Mechanics and repairmen ....
Operatives, except transport..................
Transport equipment operatives ....
Laborers, except farm ....
Farm workers...
Service workers.......................................
   Cleaning and food service workers.....
   Protective service workers...................
   Personal and health service workers ..
Private household workers......................

Female employed, 16 years old and over.......................................
Professional, technical, and kindred workers..
   Teachers, elementary and secondary schools...
Managers and administrators, except farm ....
Sales workers...
Clerical and kindred workers.................
   Secretaries, stenographers, and typists ....
Operatives, including transport ....
Other blue-collar workers.......................
Farm workers ....
Service workers, except private household...
Private household workers......................

INDUSTRY

Total employed, 16 years old and over...
Construction ....
Manufacturing..
   Durable goods ....
Transportation ....

Communications, utilities, and sanitary services...
Wholesale trade ....
Retail trade ....
Finance, insurance, and real estate........
Business and repair services..................
Personal services ....
Health services ....
Educational services ....
Other professional and related services .
Public administration ....
Other industries ....

CLASS OF WORKER

Total employed, 16 years old and over...
Private wage and salary workers............
Government workers.................................
   Local government workers ....
Self-employed workers............................
Unpaid family workers.............................

Income Characteristics of the Population

Census Tracts

INCOME IN 1969 OF FAMILIES AND UNRELATED INDIVIDUALS

All families...................................
Less than $1,000....................................
$1,000 to $1,999 ....
$2,000 to $2,999 ....
$3,000 to $3,999 ....
$4,000 to $4,999 ....
$5,000 to $5,999 ....
$6,000 to $6,999 ....
$7,000 to $7,999 ....
$8,000 to $8,999 ....
$9,000 to $9,999 ....
$10,000 to $11,999 ....
$12,000 to $14,999 ....
$15,000 to $24,999 ....
$25,000 to $49,999 ....
$50,000 or more.....................................

Median income..
Mean income...
Families and unrelated individuals..........
   Median income ....
   Mean income ....
Unrelated individuals..............................
   Median income ....
   Mean income ....

TYPE OF INCOME IN 1969 OF FAMILIES

All families....................................
With wage or salary income...................
   Mean wage or salary income ....
With nonfarm self-employment income...
   Mean nonfarm self-employment income ....
With farm self-employment income.........
   Mean farm self-employment income ...
With Social Security income ....
   Mean Social Security income..............
With public assistance or public welfare income ....
   Mean public assistance or public welfare income.......................................
With other income ....
   Mean other income.............................

RATIO OF FAMILY INCOME TO POVERTY LEVEL

Percent of families with incomes:
   .50 to .74...
   .75 to .99...
   1.00 to 1.24.......................................
   1.25 to 1.49.......................................
   1.50 to 1.99.......................................
   2.00 to 2.99.......................................
   3.00 or more......................................

INCOME BELOW POVERTY LEVEL

Families ....
   Percent of all families.......................
   Mean family income...........................
   Mean income deficit...........................

Percent receiving public assistance income...
Mean size of family.................................
With related children under 18 years ..
   Mean number of related children under 18 years ....
With related children under 6 years ....
   Mean number of related children under 6 years ....
Families with female head.................
   With related children 18 years........
   Mean number of related children under 18 years..........................
   With related children under 6 years.
   Percent in labor force ....
   Mean number of related children under 6 years.............................

Family heads......................................
   Percent 65 years and over..................
   Civilian male heads under 65 years....
   Percent in labor force.....................

Unrelated individuals ....
   Percent of all unrelated individuals..
   Mean income ....
   Mean income deficit.............................
   Percent receiving public assistance income...
   Percent 65 years and over...............

Persons ....
   Percent of all persons.......................
   Percent receiving Social Security income...
   Percent 65 years and over...............
   Percent receiving Social Security income ....
   Related children under 18 years ....
   Percent living with both parents.......

Households ....
   Percent of all households ....
   Owner occupied...................................
   Mean value of unit ....
   Renter occupied...................................
   Mean gross rent...............................
   Percent lacking some or all plumbing facilities..

General and Social Characteristics of the Negro Population: 1970

Census Tracts with 400 or More Negro Population

AGE BY SEX

Male, all ages ....
Under 5 years.................................
  3 and 4 years.....................................
5 to 9 years...................................
  5 years ....
  6 years ....
10 to 14 years ....
  14 years ....
15 to 19 years ....
  15 years ....
  16 years ....
  17 years ....
  18 years ....
  19 years ....
20 to 24 years ....
  20 years ....
  21 years ....
25 to 34 years ....
35 to 44 years ....
45 to 54 years ....
55 to 59 years ....
60 to 64 years ....
65 to 74 years ....
75 years and over ....

Female, all ages ....
Under 5 years.................................
  3 and 4 years.....................................
5 to 9 years ....
  5 years ....
  6 years ....
10 to 14 years ....
  14 years ....
15 to 19 years ....
  15 years ....
  16 years ....
  17 years ....
  18 years ....

  19 years...
20 to 24 years ....
  20 years ....
  21 years ....
25 to 34 years ....
35 to 44 years ....
45 to 54 years ....
55 to 59 years ....
60 to 64 years ....
65 to 74 years ....
75 years and over ....

RELATIONSHIP TO HEAD OF HOUSEHOLD

All persons ....
In households................................
  Head of household ....
    Head of family.............................
    Primary individual........................
  Wife of head ....
  Other relative of head....................
  Not related to head.........................
In group quarters.............................
Persons per household ....

TYPE OF HOUSEHOLD

All households ....
Male primary individual ....
Female primary individual ....
Husband-wife households..................
Households with other male head ....
Households with female head...............

SCHOOL ENROLLMENT

Persons, 16 to 21 years old ......
Not attending school ....
  Not high school graduates.................
    Percent of total............................

YEARS OF SCHOOL COMPLETED

Persons, 25 years old and over
No school years completed.................

Elementary: 1 to 4 years.....................
          5 to 7 years.....................
          8 years......................
High school: 1 to 3 years.....................
          4 years ....
College: 1 to 3 years.................
          4 years or more ....
Median school years completed ....
Percent high school graduates ....

RESIDENCE IN 1965

Persons, 5 years old and over, 1970..............................
Same house as in 1970.....................
Different house:
  In central city of this SMSA................
  In other part of this SMSA.................
  Outside this SMSA........................
    North and West..........................
    South..................................
Abroad.......................................

Economic Characteristics of the Negro Population: 1970

Census Tracts with 400 or More Negro Population

EMPLOYMENT STATUS AND OCCUPATION

Male, 16 years old and over ......
Labor force...................................
  Civilian labor force.........................
    Employed ....
    Unemployed ....
Not in labor force.............................

Female, 16 years old and over..
Labor force ....
  Civilian labor force.........................
    Employed ....
    Unemployed ....
Not in labor force.............................
Married women in labor force, husband present..

With own children under 6 years.........

Total employed, 16 years old and over....................
Professional, technical, and kindred workers ....
Managers and administrators, except farm...
Sales workers................................
Clerical and kindred workers................
Craftsmen, foremen, and kindred workers ....
Operatives, except transport................
Transport equipment operatives ....
Laborers, except farm ....
Farm workers ....
Service workers, except private household ....
Private household workers...................

Female employed, 16 years old and over....................
Professional, technical, and kindred workers ....
Managers and administrators, except farm...
Sales workers................................
Clerical and kindred workers................
Operatives, including transport ....
Other blue-collar workers....................
Farm workers ....
Service workers, except private household ....
Private household workers...................

FAMILY INCOME IN 1969

All families..............................
Less than $1,000.............................
$1,000 to $1,999............................
$2,000 to $2,999............................
$3,000 to $3,999............................
$4,000 to $4,999............................
$5,000 to $5,999............................
$6,000 to $6,999............................
$7,000 to $7,999............................
$8,000 to $8,999............................
$9,000 to $9,999............................
$10,000 or more.............................

Median income: Families ....
　　　　　　Families and unrelated
　　　　　　individuals....................

**RATIO OF FAMILY INCOME
TO POVERTY LEVEL**

Percent of families with incomes:
　Less than .50 of poverty level ....
　.50 to .74...............................
　.75 to .99...............................
　1.00 to 1.24.............................
　1.25 to 1.49.............................
　1.50 to 1.99.............................
　2.00 or more ....

INCOME BELOW POVERTY LEVEL

Families.................................
　Percent of all families.......................
　Mean family income.........................
　Mean income deficit..........................
　Percent receiving public assistance
　　income..................................
　Mean size of family........................
　With related children under 18 years ..
　　Mean number of related children
　　　under 18 years ....
　With related children under 6 years ....
　　Mean number of related children
　　　under 6 years ....
　Families with female head.................
　　With related children under 18 years
　　　Mean number of related under
　　　children under 18 years............
　　With related children under 6 years.
　　　Percent in labor force.................
　　　Mean number of related children
　　　　under 6 years........................
Family heads.............................
　Percent 65 years and over.................
　Civilian male heads under 65 years....
　　Percent in labor force.....................
Unrelated individuals......................
　Percent of all unrelated individuals..
　Mean income ....
　Mean income deficit.........................
　Percent receiving public assistance
　　income..................................

Percent 65 years and over.................
Persons ....
　Percent of all persons.....................
　Percent receiving Social Security
　　income................................
　Percent 65 years and over.................
　　Percent receiving Social Security
　　　income...............................
　Related children under 18 years ....
　　Percent living with both parents......
Households..............................
　Percent of all households ....
　Owner occupied...........................
　　Mean value of unit ....
　Renter occupied...........................
　　Mean gross rent..........................
　Percent lacking some or all plumbing
　　facilities...............................

General and Social Characteristics of Persons of Spanish Language: 1970

**Census Tracts with
400 or More Persons
of Spanish Language**

AGE BY SEX

Male, all ages ....
Under 5 years.................................
　3 and 4 years..............................
5 to 9 years ....
　5 years...................................
　6 years...................................
10 to 14 years ....
　14 years..................................
15 to 19 years ....
　15 years..................................
　16 years..................................
　17 years..................................
　18 years..................................
　19 years..................................
20 to 24 years ....
　20 years..................................
　21 years..................................
25 to 34 years ....
35 to 44 years ....
45 to 54 years ....
55 to 59 years ....
60 to 64 years ....
65 to 74 years ....
75 years and over ....

Female, all ages ....
Under 5 years.................................
　3 and 4 years..............................
5 to 9 years ....
　5 years...................................
　6 years...................................
10 to 14 years ....
　14 years ....
15 to 19 years ....
　15 years..................................
　16 years..................................
　17 years..................................
　18 years..................................
　19 years..................................

20 to 24 years ....
　20 years..................................
　21 years..................................
25 to 34 years ....
35 to 44 years ....
45 to 54 years ....
55 to 59 years ....
60 to 64 years ....
65 to 74 years ....
75 years and over ....

**RELATIONSHIP TO HEAD OF
HOUSEHOLD**

All persons...............................
In households................................
　Head of household ....
　　Head of family ....
　　Primary individual.........................
　Wife of head ....
　Other relative of head......................
　Not related to head.........................
In group quarters...........................
Persons per household ....

TYPE OF HOUSEHOLD

All households..........................
Male primary individual ....
Female primary individual ....
Husband-wife households.....................
Households with other male head ....
Households with female head...............

SCHOOL ENROLLMENT

Persons, 16 to 21 years old ......
Not attending school ....
　Not high school graduates.................
　　Percent of total............................

YEARS OF SCHOOL COMPLETED

Persons, 25 years old and over
No school years completed...................

Elementary: 1 to 4 years.........................
5 to 7 years.........................
8 years.............................
High school: 1 to 3 years.........................
4 years.............................
College: 1 to 3 years.........................
4 years or more ....
Median school years completed ....
Percent high school graduates ....

Economic Characteristics of Persons of Spanish Language: 1970

Census Tracts with 400 or More Persons of Spanish Language

EMPLOYMENT STATUS AND OCCU-PATION

Male, 16 years old and over .....
Labor force ....
Civilian labor force................................
Employed ....
Unemployed ....
Not in labor force..

Female, 16 years old and over ..
Labor force ....
Civilian labor force................................
Employed ....
Unemployed ....
Not in labor force..
Married women in labor force, husband present...
With own children under 6 years.........

Total employed, 16 years old and over...............................
Professional, technical, and kindred workers ....

Managers and administrators, except farm...
Sales workers...
Clerical and kindred workers....................
Craftsmen, foremen, and kindred workers ....
Operatives, except transport....................
Transport equipment operatives ....
Laborers, except farm ....
Farm workers ....
Service workers, except private household ....
Private household workers........................

Female employed, 16 years old and over.....................................
Professional, technical, and kindred workers ....
Managers and administrators, except farm...
Sales workers...
Clerical and kindred workers....................
Operatives, including transport ....
Other blue-collar workers.........................
Farm workers ....
Service workers, except private household ....
Private household workers........................

RESIDENCE IN 1965

Persons, 5 years old and over, 1970..
Same house as in 1970.........................
Different house:
In central city of this SMSA................
In other part of this SMSA.................
Outside this SMSA ....
North and West.......................
South ....
Abroad...

FAMILY INCOME IN 1969

All families..............................
Less than $1,000.....................................
$1,000 to $1,999......................................
$2,000 to $2,999......................................
$3,000 to $3,999......................................
$4,000 to $4,999......................................
$5,000 to $5,999......................................
$6,000 to $6,999......................................
$7,000 to $7,999......................................
$8,000 to $8,999......................................
$9,000 to $9,999......................................
$10,000 or more.......................................
Median income: Families ....
Families and unrelated individuals....................

RATIO OF FAMILY INCOME TO POVERTY LEVEL

Percent of families with incomes:
Less than .50 of poverty level.............
.50 to .74..
.75 to .99..
1.00 to 1.24..
1.25 to 1.49..
1.50 to 1.99..
2.00 or more ....

INCOME BELOW POVERTY LEVEL

Families...
Percent of all families......................
Mean family income..........................
Mean income deficit...........................
Percent receiving public assistance income..
Mean size of family...........................
With related children under 18 years ..
Mean number of related children under 18 years ....
With related children under 6 years ....
Mean number of related children under 6 years ....
Families with female head..................
With related children under 18 years
Mean number of related children

under 18 years.........................
With related children under 6 years.
Percent in labor force.................
Mean number of related children under 6 years.........................
Family heads..
Percent 65 years and over...............
Civilian male heads under 65 years....
Percent in labor force...................
Unrelated individuals...........................
Percent of all unrelated individuals..
Mean income ....
Mean income deficit............................
Percent receiving public assistance income..
Percent 65 years and over................
Persons ....
Percent of all persons.....................
Percent receiving Social Security income..
Percent 65 years and over...............
Percent receiving Social Security income..
Related children under 18 years ....
Percent living with both parents.......
Households..
Percent of all households ....
Owner occupied..................................
Mean value of unit ....
Renter occupied..................................
Mean gross rent.............................
Percent lacking some or all plumbing facilities..

Occupancy, Utilization, and Financial Characteristics of Housing Units

Census Tracts

All housing units ....
    Vacant—seasonal and migratory ....

All year-round housing units ....

TENURE, RACE, AND VACANCY STATUS

Owner occupied ....
    Cooperative and condominium ....
    White ....
    Negro ....
Renter occupied ....
    White ....
    Negro ....
Vacant year-round...............................
    For sale only ....
      Vacant less than 6 months ....
      Median price asked.......................
    For rent ....
      Vacant less than 2 months ....
      Median rent asked ....
    Other...

LACKING SOME OR ALL PLUMBING FACILITIES

All units ....
Owner occupied ....
    Negro ....
Renter occupied ....
    Negro ....
Vacant year-round................................
    For sale only ....
    For rent ....

COMPLETE KITCHEN FACILITIES AND ACCESS

Lacking complete kitchen facilities..........
Access only through other living quarters

ROOMS

1 room ....
2 rooms ....
3 rooms ....
4 rooms ....
5 rooms ....
6 rooms ....
7 rooms ....
8 rooms ....
9 rooms or more..........................
Median.......................................
    All occupied housing units ......

PERSONS

1 person ....
2 persons...................................
3 persons...................................
4 persons...................................
5 persons...................................
6 persons or more.........................
Median, all occupied units.....................
Median, owner occupied units ....
Median, renter occupied units................
Units with roomers, boarders, or lodgers

PERSONS PER ROOM

1.00 or less................................
1.01 to 1.50 ....
1.51 or more..............................
Units with all plumbing facilities—1.01 or more ....

VALUE

    Specified owner-occupied units
Less than $5,000...................................
$5,000 to $7,499 ....
$7,500 to $9,999 ....
$10,000 to $14,999 ....
$15,000 to $19,999 ....
$20,000 to $24,999 ....

$25,000 to $34,999 ....
$35,000 to $49,999 ....
$50,000 or more.................................
Median...

CONTRACT RENT

    Specified renter-occupied units
Less than $30......................................
$30 to $39 ....
$40 to $59 ....
$60 to $79 ....
$80 to $99 ....
$100 to $149 ....
$150 to $199 ....
$200 to $249 ....
$250 or more......................................
No cash rent......................................
Median..

Structural, Equipment, and Financial Characteristics of Housing Units

Census Tracts

All year-round housing units ....

UNITS IN STRUCTURE

1 (includes mobile home or trailer) ....
2..
3 and 4 ....
5 to 49 ....
50 or more..

YEAR STRUCTURE BUILT

1969 to March 1970 ....
1965 to 1968 ....
1960 to 1964 ....
1950 to 1959 ....
1940 to 1949 ....
1939 or earlier....................................

HEATING EQUIPMENT

Steam or hot water..............................

Warm air furnace.................................
Built-in electric units ....
Floor, wall, or pipeless furnace..............
Other means or not heated...................

BASEMENT

All units with basement.........................
One-family houses with basement.........

SELECTED EQUIPMENT

With more than 1 bathroom ....
With public water supply ....
With public sewer................................
With air conditioning............................
    Room unit(s) ....
    Central system................................
    All occupied housing units ....

YEAR MOVED INTO UNIT

1968 to March 1970 ....
1965 to 1967 ....

1960 to 1964 ....
1950 to 1959 ....
1949 or earlier.......................................

AUTOMOBILES AVAILABLE

1..
2..
3 or more..
None..

GROSS RENT

Specified renter-occupied units
Less than $40..
$40 to $59 ....
$60 to $79 ....
$80 to $99 ....
$100 to $149 ....
$150 to $199 ....
$200 to $249 ....
$250 or more...
No cash rent..
Median...

Occupancy, Utilization, and Financial Characteristics of Housing Units with Negro Head of Household

Census Tracts with 400 or More Negro Population

All occupied housing units ....

TENURE AND PLUMBING

Owner occupied ....
  With all plumbing facilities ....
Renter occupied ....
  With all plumbing facilities ....

ROOMS

1 room ....

GROSS RENT AS PERCENTAGE OF INCOME BY INCOME

Specified renter-occupied units
Less than $5,000......................................
  Less than 20 percent..........................
  20 to 24 percent ....
  25 to 34 percent ....
  35 percent or more.............................
  Not computed ....
  Median...
$5,000 to $9,999......................................
  Less than 20 percent..........................
  20 to 24 percent ....
  25 to 34 percent ....
  35 percent or more.............................
  Not computed ....
  Median...
$10,000 to $14,999 ....
  25 percent or more.............................
  Not computed ....
  Median...
$15,000 or more.......................................
  25 percent or more.............................
  Not computed ....
  Median...

2 rooms ....
3 and 4 rooms ....
5 and 6 rooms ....
7 rooms or more......................................
Median..

PERSONS

1 person ....
2 and 3 persons ....
4 and 5 persons ....
6 persons or more...................................
Median..
Units with roomers, boarders, or lodgers

PERSONS PER ROOM

1.00 or less..
1.01 to 1.50 ....
1.51 or more..
Units with all plumbing facilities—1.01 or more ....

VALUE

Specified owner-occupied units
Less than $5,000....................................
$5,000 to $9,999 ....

Structural, Equipment, and Financial Characteristics of Housing Units with Negro Head of Household

Census Tracts with 400 or More Negro Population

All occupied housing units ......

UNITS IN STRUCTURE

1 (includes mobile home or trailer) ....
2 to 4 ....
5 or more...

YEAR STRUCTURE BUILT

1960 to March 1970.............................
1950 to 1959 ....
1949 or earlier.......................................

SELECTED EQUIPMENT

With air conditioning...............................
With more than 1 bathroom ....
With central or built-in heating system....
With public water supply ....
With public sewer....................................
With automobile(s) available...................
  1...
  2 or more..

$10,000 to $14,999 ....
$15,000 to $19,999 ....
$20,000 to $34,999 ....
$35,000 or more.....................................
Median..

CONTRACT RENT

Specified renter-occupied units
Median..

YEAR MOVED INTO UNIT

1968 to March 1970.............................
1960 to 1967 ....
1959 or earlier.......................................

GROSS RENT

Specified renter-occupied units
Less than $40...
$40 to $59..
$60 to $79..
$80 to $99..
$100 to $149..
$150 to $199..
$200 or more..
No cash rent...
Median..

GROSS RENT AS PERCENTAGE OF INCOME BY INCOME

Less than $10,000..................................
  25 percent or more.............................
  35 percent or more.............................
  Not computed ....
  Median...

Characteristics of Housing Units with Household Head of Spanish Language

(Same data items as shown in the 2 preceding tables)

POPULATION PROJECTION—APPORTIONMENT METHOD

Projections Based on Relationships of Population Growth in an Area to Growth in Other Areas

Population growth in an area or community is usually more closely related to or affected by economic and population changes in the economic region or State in which it lies. Future population changes in those larger areas may have an important influence on growth or decline in the smaller area. Hence, past relationships between population growth in an area or community and that of its economic region or State are valuable guides for projection of the local population. If logically founded population projections for the nation, State or economic region are available, projections for the area or community can be derived directly therefrom.

Statistical Projections Based on Relative Rates of Past Growth

Statistical projections of the relationships of population growth in a particular area to growth in other areas can be made in various ways. The simplest procedure is to compute the percentages that the population of the particular area represented of the population of its economic region, its State, and the nation in past census years, and plot them on graph paper. The line or curve of these percentages can then be projected to the forecast date by techniques similar to those for projections of population growth curves described for mathematical methods.

Applying the projected percentages to population projection figures for the nation, the State, or the economic region will produce numerical projections of the population of the area for applicable forecast dates. If projections for the larger areas are not available, or are considered unreliable, the forecaster can make his own projections for them.

Purely statistical projections made by this method should be used with caution. Former relationships between population growth in the area under consideration and that in other areas may suddenly change. Moreover, the economic and social forces that cause births and migration to increase, or decline, nationally exert differing effects at different times on particular areas. Some areas have shown fairly consistent trends between their population growth and that of their region, State, or the nation. Others have shown divergent or erratic relationships to population changes in the larger areas. For these, this method appears less valid than for areas exhibiting more consistent trends. A recent evaluation of this method finds it of limited value for forecasting the populations of isolated cities.

On the other hand, these procedures have several advantages over method 1. The factors affecting population growth in the area or community may be more clearly visualized and appraised with a knowledge of its past relationships to growth in its economic region, State, and the nation than if these relationships have not been studied. It may be easier to foresee and evaluate the effects of new conditions that may change past relationships than it would be to appraise the prospects for future growth in the area irrespective of the rate of growth in other areas. Population projections for the nation and for states have generally been closer to the mark than those for smaller areas or communities. By trying in their projections with those for the larger area, the range for error may be lessened.

Projections made by this method are also valuable as guides and checks in establishing projections developed by other procedures.

Sample Apportionment Method

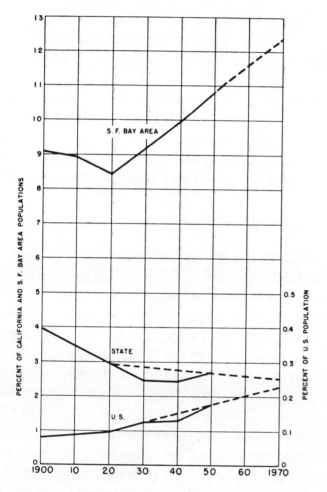

Santa Clara county population as a percent of population of San Francisco Bay area, of California, and of the United States, 1900-1950, with illustrative projections to 1970.

SOURCE: Van Beuren Stanbery, Better Population Forecasting for Areas and Communities. U.S. Dept. of Commerce, Wash. D.C.

PROJECTIONS OF NET MIGRATION AND OF NATURAL INCREASE

Population forecasts are frequently obtained by making separate but related projections of net migration and of natural increase and adding the figures. Because migration affects the number of births and deaths in an area, projections of net migration are made before those for natural increase.

Migration Projections

Logically founded projections of net migration can be developed from study of net migration in the area in the past and the conditions causing people to move into or out of it.

The direction and approximate volume and composition of net migration into or out of the area during recent decades are first determined.

Changes that have occurred, or appear likely to occur, in the conditions and relationships affecting migration in the area are considered. Finally, the probable effects of such changes on net migration during the forecast period are reviewed and appraised.

With these analyses and appraisals, it is usually possible to develop reasonable high and low projections for net migration. At least, they provide some indication whether net migration during the next decade may be expected to be about the same as, or larger or smaller than, that of the preceding decade.

Natural Increase Projections

Projections of natural increase are made by a variety of techniques. Some of them produce approximate figures while others give more precise results. Principal factors to be considered are the racial, sex, and age composition of the area population, and its future birth and death rates.

The most precise, but also the most laborious, procedure is the "cohort-survival" technique. Briefly, this is as follows:

The survivors of the resident population of each sex on the forecast date are first computed for each 5-year or 10-year age group from age-specific mortality tables and trends.

The total net migration projection for the area to the forecast date is then distributed by sex and by age, and added to, or subtracted from, the figures for the surviving residents in the corresponding age groups. It should be noted that the sex and age characteristics of the migrant population are usually quite different from those of the resident populations of the areas from which they move or in which they settle. The sex and age distribution of net migrations into or out of the particular area or its State during recent decades therefore should be carefully analyzed and used as guides in estimating the sex and age distribution of the projected net migration.

Birth rates by age of mother during the forecast period are then projected or assumed. The expected number of births is then obtained by multiplying the assumed age-specific birth rates by the average number of women in each 5-year age group within the child-bearing ages during the forecast period. This average figure is usually obtained by adding the number of women at the beginning and end of the forecast period in each 5-year age group, and dividing by two. The survivors of those births on the forecast date are then computed by using death rates of young children. As the number of male births usually exceeds the number of female births in the ratio of about 105 or 106 to 100, this should be taken into account in precise calculations.

The cohort-survival procedure does not directly measure natural increase itself. Instead, the population projection is obtained by adding the survivors of the resident population, the expected net migration, and the survivors of babies born to former residents and to newcomers during the period. If the net migration is outward, the estimate of births is reduced because of the smaller average number of women in the child-bearing ages. Since most of the migrants are between ages 20-45 years, when they move, net out-migration tends to reduce the crude birth rate also. Further refinements, such as allowances for births to in-migrant women who die during the period, are sometimes included in the calculations.

This is being relied on more and more for population projections. For most areas and communities, it should yield better forecasts than other methods, particularly for projections not exceeding two decades.

This method takes into account the size of the area's population at the beginning of the forecast period, and the effects of a population of that size on future births, deaths, and migration. Other methods do not provide as accurate measures of the effects of changes in the size of the population from decade to decade.

MATHEMATICAL PROJECTIONS

1. The simplest mathematical procedure is to compute the average numerical population change per decade in the past, and then to project this numerical increase into the future. This is called an "arithmetical projection," and it should produce the same result as a straight-line graphic projection on plain coordinate paper.

To illustrate, from 1900 to 1950 the population of California increased an average of 1,823,000 per decade; assuming the same numerical increase, the population, which was 10,586,000 in 1950, would be 12,409,000 in 1960, and 14,232,000 in 1970.

2. Another simple method is to compute the average rate of population change for the area per decade in the past, and then project this average rate, or percent change, into the future. This is called a "geometric projection," and corresponds to a graphic projection on semilogarithmic paper.

For example, the average rate of increase per decade of the population of California during 1900-50 was approximately 49 percent. Projecting this average rate gives a population of 15,773,000 in 1960, and 23,502,000 in 1970.

3. A more refined procedure is to plot the curve of past population growth on a semilogarithmic scale and then to develop by the method of least squares an exponential equation that best fits the past curve. From this equation the size of the population in future years can readily be computed.

4. Another technique is to fit some other mathematical curve, such as the "logistic" curve, to the curve of past population growth of the area, and then to determine the size of the future population therefrom.

The logistic curve is based on a "law of growth in a limited area" propounded and mathematically developed by P.F. Verhulst in 1838. It is shaped like an elongated and flattened letter S.

The logistic curve implies a constantly decreasing rate of increase per amount of population per unit of time after the initial increment of increase. Its validity for areas subject to net immigration that might accelerate for a time the rate of increase relative to the size of the population is questionable.

The advantage of graphic or mathematical projections is that they are the easiest to make. They generally are better suited to areas that have had relatively constant changes per decade in the size of their populations, and for which no marked changes from past trends appear likely, than for areas subject to rapid or erratic fluctuations in population. Obviously, they should be more dependable for short-term projections of 5 to 10 years than for longer projections.

The weakness of such projections is that they are founded on the assumption that the factors and conditions that produced population growth or decline in the area in the past will continue unchanged and will have the same effects in the future, or that they are derived from an assumed curve of population growth. In view of the changes that have recently taken place in fertility, mortality, and migration trends, projections of this kind are becoming less reliable.

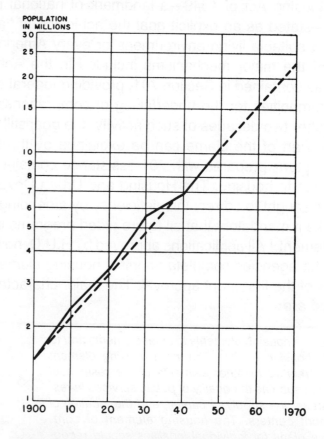

Growth of California Population, 1900-1950, with Geometrical Projection to 1970.

SOURCE: Van Beuren Stanbery, Better Population Forecasting for Areas and Communities. U.S. Dept. of Commerce, Wash. D.C.

As indicated before, graphic and mathematical projections are useful, however, as rough checks on those obtained by other methods. In the absence of other data and analyses, an arithmetical projection might be used as a probable minimum forecast, and a geometrical projection as a maximum figure.

REQUIRED HOUSING ELEMENT

The Housing Act of 1949—a landmark of national planning legislation—stated as an explicit goal the achieving of "a decent home and a suitable living environment for every American family." One of the major mechanisms included in the Act for this purpose was contained in Section 701, providing federal grants to eligible communities for the undertaking of comprehensive planning. Yet, after two decades of such activity, the goal still remains unattained. Part of the blame can be explained by the fact that most of the plans prepared with 701 assistance contained little if any reference to housing. The Housing and Urban Development Act of 1968 sought to correct this deficiency by amending Section 701 to make it mandatory that all future aided programs include a housing element.[1] All applications approved by H.U.D. now require that planning agencies complete an initial housing element within six months of the first grant approval. The major characteristics to be included are:

a. *Relation of the housing elements to other elements and to the larger housing market. The initial housing element should be related to other elements of the residential environment such as the quality of public services in residential areas, the supply of capital, and the location of employment centers. The housing element of comprehensive plans for individual localities should recognize the relationship of their housing supply and demand to the larger housing market.*

b. *Tailored to governmental responsibilities. The initial housing element must be tailored to the powers and activities of the Planning Agency and the political jurisdiction associated with it. Accordingly, an initial housing element prepared by a state Planning Agency should be different*

than those of a regional multijurisdictional Agency, such as a Council of Governments or a county.

c. *Recognition of unique needs in the area. The initial housing element should recognize the specific needs of the planning jurisdiction. The element should make reference to specific numbers, housing or housing-related needs of the locations, population, authorities, laws, etc. peculiar to the housing or housing-related needs of the planning area. Innovative approaches are strongly encouraged.*

d. *Emphasis on implementation. The initial housing element should be designed to achieve implementation of housing objectives. Planning for housing should take into account existing and needed resources and powers to implement proposals. Planning for housing should focus on eliminating obstacles to implementing housing proposals.*

e. *Low-income and minority needs. The initial housing element must consider the needs of all elements of society, but particular attention must be given to the housing problems and opportunities of those groups with least access to the housing market: the low- and moderate-income and minority groups.*

In order to achieve a satisfactory document, the housing study should contain the following components:[2]

a. *STATEMENT OF PROBLEMS (Guideline). This statement should consist of a preliminary identification and listing, according to importance of the housing and housing-related problems.*

b. *STATEMENT OF OBSTACLES (Guideline). This statement should consist of a preliminary identification and listing, according to importance of the obstacles to the solution of identified housing and housing-related problems.*

c. *STATEMENT OF OBJECTIVES (Guideline). This statement should consist of a preliminary presentation of annual housing and housing-related objectives covering a*

---

[1] *Comprehensive Planning Assistance Handbook I: Guidelines Leading to a Grant,* March 1969 (MD 6041.1), p. 6.

[2] Ibid., pp. 6, 13-18.

period of three to five years. Objectives should be related to the identified housing problems. To the extent possible, objectives should be stated in quantified terms and target dates should be set for their achievement.

d. *STATEMENT OF PLANNING ACTIVITIES (Requirement). This statement must consist of an identification of (1) previous planning activities related to housing undertaken by the Planning Agency during the preceding year, and (2) future planning activities related to housing to be undertaken over the next three to five years. Exception: In the case of cities and counties under 50,000 population, the time frame of the work program for housing should include a listing of activities such as surveys, analyses and the preparation of plans. Necessary manpower, costs and timing should be detailed. The specific activities of the work program should relate to identified housing and housing-related problems and be designed to accomplish specified objectives.*

e. *STATEMENT OF IMPLEMENTING ACTIONS (Guideline). This statement should consist of an identification of (1) previous implementation actions, both public and private, taken during the last year to implement housing programs or ameliorate housing problems, and (2) future implementation actions, both public and private, to be taken annually over the next three to five years.*

In order for an agency to continue its eligibility for additional assistance, every recipient must undertake the housing planning activities contained within the initial study. Several other suggested and required actions are also called for, including coordination between other planning elements and other planning agencies. However, the focus of this chapter is on housing studies so the following pages will concentrate on the substance, techniques and resource data useful in the development of housing plans and programs. A case study is included of the housing element of the Nassau-Suffolk Regional Comprehensive Plan as an example of an approach to housing planning. Although this program preceded the 1968 legislation, it nevertheless contained the major charac-

teristics and fulfilled both the recommended and required elements as noted in the previous pages.

NASSAU-SUFFOLK HOUSING ELEMENT—CASE STUDY

The study proceeds from a survey of housing inventory and demographic relationships to the more specific qualitative and quantitative aspects of deterioration and dilapidation. The inventory portion was reasonably straightforward, utilizing census data in conjunction with updated records gathered from local and State building, health and planning agencies. This included permits and certificates of occupancy issued subsequent to the prior census; and quantitative verification by comparison with the existing land-use maps and utility customer listings. The existing population was derived from the census data of 1960 and subsequent special annual census runs made by several of the towns extrapolated to the present by using natural-increase factors from the monthly health agencies (births over deaths) added to migration increases as determined from annual school census information, and new utility service counts. The utility counts are a measure of family units and may be converted to individuals by using an average family size multiplier. Population projections were made by using a cohort-survival method and other mathematical modes as shown in Sections A-9, A-10 and A-11.

As part of the Residential Market Analysis, a study was undertaken of deficient housing units in Nassau and Suffolk counties. The determination of housing condition was slightly more complex. Census data offers a base that must be verified by field examination as to external indications and subsequent additional blight between the general census and the time of study. Housing code violations, as recorded by health and building departments, were also correlated into this aspect of inventory. A special effort was made to determine the housing status of welfare recipients since it was felt that this segment of the community had unique problems. A summary of this study is included on the following pages.

1. What are the possible remedial actions for improving housing conditions?
2. What is the approximate extent of the need for replacement housing for people living in deficient housing units? What types of housing will be required (e.g., housing for the elderly)?
3. What measures should be instituted by various governmental levels and the private-housing industry to eliminate the housing problems that exist and prevent a repetition of these conditions?

Housing costs relative to market demands were examined and projection of housing needs according to type and cost, e.g., multifamily, single-family, low-cost, were made to the year 1985.

Design solutions were developed for general applicability to subdivision layout and for the improvement of deteriorating communities. A prototype is included in this chapter as an example of the methodologies involved. Emphasis was also placed on the problems of implementation. Twenty-six recommendations were made ranging from the initiation of an advisory housing projection service in each county planning agency to the establishment of a County Housing Agency with broad powers.

Of course, the entire housing element, which is a major integral part of the comprehensive planning process, must not be carried out as an arithmetic exercise. It must relate to a community-established set of goals. While placed at the end of this recitation, it should be stressed that this was the first determination made by the planning agency and its broadbased citizens committee. They are as follows:

A housing program should be directed to three goals:

1. *Adequate Housing for All–To stimulate a rate of housing construction adequate for an expanding population, and*
to provide a decent home for all residents regardless of age, income, or ethnic background, with maximum choice of rental or ownership, type and location.
2. *Eliminating Housing Deficiencies–To eliminate deficient housing and prevent future blight through the expansion of current programs and initiation of new programs for construction, rehabilitation, and demolition.*
3. *Livable Communities with Open Space–To encourage the development of communities with a balanced population, a variety of housing types, employment opportunities, park and recreation space, and an accessible town center with shopping and community facilities.*

Many programs directed at these goals already exist, such as fair-housing laws, public housing, rent subsidies, Federal and State financing assistance, and grants for urban renewal, code enforcement, community facilities, urban beautification, and open-space grants. The various existing Federal and State programs, which should be more widely used on Long Island, were woefully underfunded. To accomplish the above goals, however, new programs and strengthened administrative procedures are also needed. The policies and programs recommended herein are of two types: (1) those authorized by present laws; and (2) those that require new Federal or State laws and programs.

Poverty is a major cause of housing problems stemming from complex factors—racial discrimination, unemployment, lack of education, social maladjustment. While the focus of this study is on the improvement of housing, proposed actions should be closely related to programs in education, job training, medical care, and income maintenance.

THE EXTENT AND LOCATION OF DEFICIENT HOUSING UNITS

The 1960 Census of Housing comprises the most comprehensive source of data available for housing conditions. In order to gain an understanding of 1967 housing conditions, field surveys have been conducted. Field inspections were made by the staffs of the Nassau and Suffolk Planning Departments in all Enumeration Districts in which a significant amount of deficient housing was reported by the Census in 1960. Furthermore, areas were surveyed where significant downgrading of housing was suspected to have occurred since 1950. This survey utilized information provided primarily by the staffs of the Nassau and Suffolk Planning Departments, as well as the two County Health Departments, the staffs of the various poverty programs, and the existing municipal Master Plans and renewal studies. A-14-1 is a facsimile of the form used for the field survey.

Blight was found to exist in 1967 in 432 Census Enumeration Districts, of which 267 lie in Suffolk and 165 in Nassau County. Certain deteriorated areas have expanded significantly since 1960, and new pockets of blight have appeared. Census tracts with 100 or more deficient housing units in 1960 are identified,[3] as well as Enumeration Districts[4] where moderate or severe deficiencies were found in 1967 through the field survey.

Profile Areas

As a result of the vast amount of inadequate housing in Nassau and Suffolk Counties, an approach was developed in which the numerous types of housing problem areas were classified according to their dominant physical characteristics. Prototypes of each category, called "Profile Areas," were then selected for more intensive study. This method provides a reasonably detailed knowledge of certain representative areas, including the types of housing problems, the various processes of deterioration, and the social and economic background of the families living within these

areas. Such a pilot study, when complete, forms the basis for a conceptualization of the entire housing problem in Nassau and Suffolk Counties, as well as providing sufficient insight into the housing situation to permit the formulation of general programs for preventative and remedial action.

In categorizing and selecting areas, certain questions were first posed about the neighborhood as a whole and about the actual deficient units within the neighborhood. (The "neighborhood" usually included sound housing as well as dilapidated.)

1. *Was the neighborhood urban in character? If so, was it a central business district, a densely built-up residential suburb of New York City, a village of moderate density, or a hamlet?*
2. *Have any recent forces been evident that have caused or are causing a change in the character or quality of the neighborhood?*

Examples of this would be urban renewal, demolition due to highway construction, new subdivision activity, a dramatic change in the racial, economic, or other characteristics of the residents. Can anything be concluded about how the area was originally constructed—or has since been maintained?[5]

3. *What are the predominant land uses? Is there evidence of incompatibility? Some neighborhoods were predominantly single-family residential, some industrial, commercial, agricultural or resort-seasonal or contained large public or semipublic uses. Most areas contained several different uses and in such cases, the predominant types were all noted. Are these structures in mixed use? What is the zoning?*
4. *What is the density of development of the neighborhood?*

---

[3]"Deficient" housing units are defined as comprising the Census categories of "dilapidated," "deteriorating," and "sound" housing units lacking some or all plumbing facilities.

[4]An Enumeration District is the geographical area that could be canvassed by one Census enumerator. The size varies from 6 or 7 small blocks in densely populated sections of Nassau County to areas of about 15 square miles in rural Suffolk County.

[5]Census Tracts are composed of a group of Enumeration Districts. A Census Tract may include several neighboring communities, one of which contains over one hundred deficient housing units; the other none. Because of this, a community with no housing problems may nevertheless appear on the map as part of an area having units "with deficiencies."

A-14-1 Housing Survey Observations

Tract No:_____ N/S

E.D._____.

Community_____

Street and Number_____

Interview Team_____

Calls:

	1	2	3
Date			
Time			

DU Location (in building)_____

W/N/PR/Other_____

Condition:

	1	2	3	4	5
Building Exterior					
D.U.					

Lot Condition: clean and good____, poor____, debris____

Structure Type:

1 Family_____ 2 Family_____

Multifamily: No. of DUs in Structure_____

Mixed Use: List uses by floor (including no. of DUs per floor)

	Uses	D.U.s
1st Floor	_____	_____
2nd Floor	_____	_____
3rd Floor	_____	_____

Basement: Yes_____ No_____

Used for dwelling? Yes_____ No_____

Number of Stories_____

Exterior Material:

Brick, wood, stone, or other durable material_____

Other (Specify)_____

	Yes	No
Well-maintained?	____	____
Waterproof	____	____

Year-round_____

Converted from seasonal use_____

Seasonal construction_____ (Built for use only in summer, no central heat, insulation, basement)

Is it predominantly vacant? Is there overcrowding on the land?

5. *Are there adverse environmental factors present? Specific note was made of homes adjacent to railroads, dumps, large incinerators, heavy industry, or any other major producer of noise, smoke, fumes, etc.*
   The maintenance of the neighborhood as a whole was checked. Was there dumping on vacant lots? Did the neighborhood as a whole seem well-maintained—a place where residents took pride in their homes?

6. *Were there adequate public and service facilities nearby, such as parks, schools, shopping? Any public transportation? Is the garbage collected, or do residents have to carry it to the dump themselves?*

7. *What was the condition of the streets and were there adequate utilities? Does the street layout ignore topography or are there excessive streets wasting valuable land? Were the streets paved? In need of repairs? Were the edges finished? In urban areas, were there sidewalks and street trees? Was there storm drainage, sewers, street lights? Were the streets congested, narrow, crowded with parked cars?*

Categorization of Areas

The field surveys, and the answers to the questions above, led to preliminary categorization of types of areas. Within each category there are, of course, ranges in area and the degree of substandard conditions. Profile Areas have been chosen to illuminate these categories. At this point in the study, three Profile Area analyses are presented; later, a Profile Area will be discussed for each category.

1. Core Areas

Deterioration adjacent to or around the central business district is found in many older centers, whether they may be in small villages or serve as the business center for larger areas. Many of these are the focus of urban-renewal pro-

jects. For the most part, these are relatively small in area, although they may in some cases house many hundreds of families. They are characterized by aging structures, obsolete building forms with outmoded uses, the adverse influence of industry and commerce, with attendant heavy automotive traffic.

2. Suburban Developments

In some large sections of postwar one-family housing developments, either inadequate original construction or poor maintenance, or, in some cases, both have combined to create a unique but nevertheless seriously spreading form of blight.

3. Premature Land Subdivisions

Generally, further out on the Island are vast areas of scattered housing in premature land subdivisions that are still predominantly vacant and where one finds year-round and seasonal homes of good quality intermixed with houses in need of repair or even dilapidated shacks. These areas also suffer from inadequate public facilities and services.

Many streets are unpaved and badly maintained. Residents complain that garbage collection service is infrequent, and police and fire protection inadequate. Frequently, there has been industrial intrusion into these areas, which has been a strong blighting factor.

4. Scattered Rural

Many farmhouses or houses scattered along the main and side roads outside the settled areas are aging, sagging, and generally deteriorating. Frequently, two or three such houses are clustered. Modernization, perhaps with Farm Security Administration aids, seems appropriate.

5. Housing for Migrants

Migrant "camps" for five or more persons, and accommodations for less than five, frequently found behind the farmer's house, have long been a problem, but are now improving as a result of greater awareness of the problem by farm groups and County Health Department regulations and inspection.

6. The Shacks

Homemade, makeshift housing, usually found in Negro ghettos, some of one or two units, some with up to 30-35 units, without adequate heat, water, sewage, garbage disposal. Often hovels, unfit for human occupancy, located off the main roads, hidden from view, frequently near dumps and junk yards. Without question most of these buildings should never have been built. Without question they should be razed, but low-rent replacement housing must first be available for the occupants who cannot afford decent housing as may be available to them on the private market.

7. Seasonal

Older resort communities along the south shore, somewhat newer settlements on lakes or ponds in the center of the Island, and a more scattered pattern on the north shore abound with homes built for seasonal use but now occupied on a year-round basis. The density of development may vary, but the older and poorly constructed houses in these areas have become a major problem requiring urgent attention throughout the Island.

Household Interviews

During the summer of 1967, 487 interviews were conducted with year-round residents of deficient housing units who were not welfare recipients.

The purpose of these household interviews was to develop some insight into the characteristics of people living in deficient housing in the Profile Areas of the Nassau-Suffolk region. However, the total county figures form a comparison to the study of the housing of welfare recipients—although the total data in this study was not a sample of the two counties but, rather, a sample of selected areas within the two counties. Similar data were gathered for both studies; however, the welfare study was based on caseworkers' knowledge of the families, whereas this study relied on interviews in the field, and excluded from the tabulation all seasonal residents and welfare recipients.

Not surprisingly, the households involved in both studies had many characteristics in common. The high proportion of nonwhite, generally Negroes—about half of the families in both studies —contrasted with the fact that nonwhites form less than four percent of the population of the Nassau-Suffolk region. Moreover, the concentrations of housing occupied by nonwhites is more overcrowded than housing occupied by whites. Finally, by any standard, nonwhites pay more for their housing than do whites in deficient areas.

A-14-2 is a facsimile of the form used in the household interview survey.

A-14-2 Housing Survey Interview

1. (Check one) Owner____Renter____

2. a. How long have you lived in this building?____ in this County?____
   b. Do you live here all year round? Yes____No____

   If not where do you live in the winter?_____

3. The Dwelling Unit:

   a. Total number of rooms____Bedrooms____

   b. Number of families in unit____

   c. Total number of persons in unit____

   d. Number of rooms in unit rented to nonfamily members____

   e. Heating facilities: Central_____
      Other (Specify)_____
      None_____

   f. Private kitchen: Yes____ No____

   g. Water supply: In Kitchen   In Bath

      Running hot _____ _____

      Cold only _____ _____

      None _____ _____

   h. Private flush toilet in unit?_____ If not, where?_____

   i. Private bath or shower in unit?_____ If not, where?_____

   j. Garbage disposal methods:

      Cans inside____Outside____Pick-ups per week____

   k. Electricity: Yes____No____

   l. Sewage: Public sewers____ Septic tank or cesspool ____Outhouse____

4. Where—in what location—does the head of the household work?_____

   Other employed family members?_____

5. How does he (do they) get to work?_____

6. Do you own a car?_____

7. Employment: (Fill out columns 1 through 4 for each person living in dwelling unit whether employed or not)

1	2	3	4	5	6		
All Members of Household (list by relationship to head)	Sex	Age	Employment Status*	Occupation	Yearly Income of Each Member Before Deductions, from		
					Wages & Salaries	Social Security & Pensions	All other sources incl. Welfare

*Use the following code:

1. Regularly employed
2. Seasonal, occasional, or temporary employment
3. Unemployed but looking for a job.
4. Retired (and over 65).
5. Not working because underage.
6. Other unemployable or not interested.
7. On welfare

8. OWNERS ONLY

What is your average expense for the following housing items?

(If item is not applicable indicate "N/A")

a. Total mortgage payment. Indicate if any
items below are included in this payment.   _____

b. Monthly cost of home improvement loan (if any)   _____

c. Heating (per year)   _____

d. Water, Gas, Electricity (per month)   _____

e. Taxes (per year)   _____

f. Insurance (per year)   _____

g. Repairs or improvements made in recent
years (not covered in 11b)   Cost

_____   _____

_____   _____

_____   _____

_____   _____

9. OWNERS ONLY

Total rental income_____(per month)

From: rental unit, in case of 2- or more family dwelling_____

rooms in dwelling united rented to boarders:____rooms

10. TENANTS ONLY

a. Rent paid monthly   _____

b. Gas, Electricity and other Utilities   _____

c. Total   _____

11. a. What services are needed in your neighborhood?

	Need	Don't Care	Don't Need
Roads (paved, improved)			

	Need	Don't Care	Don't Need
Schools			
Parks			
Sewers			
Public transportation			
Other			

b. Do you like living in this house? Yes____ No____

Why?_____

_____

12. a. In what ways do you think the neighborhood is changing from what it was when you first moved here?

_____

_____

_____

b. Do you think these changes are for the: better _____

worse _____

no opinion _____

13. Other Comments:

HOUSING OF WELFARE RECIPIENTS

Introduction

Our system of public assistance is now 30 years old and has obvious faults. The standards of need set by many states are unrealistically low; benefits are further restricted by excessively stringent eligibility conditions. In some respects the system perpetuates dependency.

1. State standards of need are miserably low. In 18 states a family of 4 is presumed able to manage for a month on

$45 per person—or less. And in many states, actual payments average below their own standards of need.

It is time to raise payments toward more acceptable levels. . .

2. *With minor exceptions, payments under public assistance are reduced for dollar of earnings by the recipient, removing any incentive to accept part-time work. We should encourage self-help, not penalize it.*

It is time to put an end to this 100 percent tax on the earnings of those on public assistance. . .

3. *Many recipients of public assistance are capable of receiving training that would ultimately make them self-supporting.*

. . .all states receiving Federal support under Aid to Families with Dependent Children (should be required) to cooperate in making Community Work and Training available for the unemployed parents of dependent children.

The above is quoted from the Economic Report of the President, which was delivered by President Johnson to the Congress on January 26, 1967.

In this same report, President Johnson called for changes in the Public Assistance Laws, as well as for other programs designed to help the disadvantaged.

For those who will be unable to earn adequate incomes, there must be help—most of all for the benefit of children, whose misfortune to be born poor must not deprive them of future opportunity . . .

Wherever the poor and disadvantaged are concentrated, intensive and coordinated programs to break the cycle of deprivation and dependency must continue and be reinforced . . .

The following report on the Nassau-Suffolk counties' welfare population emphasizes their housing needs. This is only one part of the total "package" of goods and services required by welfare recipients to give them the opportunity to break out of what has often been called the "vicious cycle of poverty." But adequate housing is probably one of the most important single factors for improving living standards for the welfare population.

Adequate housing for the welfare population also benefits the entire community. Once blight begins, natural market forces quicken the decay over large areas as the deterioration of a neighborhood weakens incentives for homeowner and landlord to maintain their property. By eliminating blighted areas that could spread and downgrade areas of standard housing, the value of property in the entire community is supported.

It is obvious that the solutions to the problems of housing blight and adequacy of welfare payments requires efforts on national, regional, and state levels, as local governments do not have the financial and manpower resources or the legal powers to bring about the changes that are required. However, the posture of local governments in dealing with the requirements of the welfare population should take advantage of any commitments the Federal Government has made or is considering.

Following are a few of the specific proposals made by the President of the United States in his January 1967 Economic Report that related to methods of assisting welfare recipients and areas of blighted housing.

1. *A commission was appointed " . . .to work with the Department of Housing and Urban Development to examine problems of codes, zoning, taxation, and development standards and to recommend ways to increase the supply of low-cost housing . . ."*
2. *Increased appropriations for " . . .Federal aid for water and sewer projects, open land conservation, and urban mass transportation . . ." will be sought.*

3. *"Federal programs for fiscal 1968 will assist in construction or renovation of 165,000 housing units for the urban poor, the elderly, and the handicapped. The Rent Supplement program will contribute to this goal."*

Other Federal and State programs should be analyzed to determine if Nassau and Suffolk counties can qualify for assistance.

Closely related to the problems of providing adequate housing for welfare recipients is the problem of racial discrimination in housing markets. In 1966, the Annual Report of the Council of Economic Advisors described the problem as follows:

Negroes are . . . at a disadvantage in the housing market. Many Negroes live in substandard housing because their incomes are low; but others are forced to do so by direct discrimination. While 57 percent of nonwhite households with annual incomes of less than $4,000 live in substandard housing, only 27 percent of whites at these same income levels live in such housing. Among households with more than $4,000 a year, 6 percent of the white families live in substandard housing, compared with 20 percent for nonwhite families. Discrimination in housing forces Negroes to pay higher rents and in many places to attend inferior schools. The President has announced that he will ask for legislation to prevent discrimination in private sales or rental of housing.

In New York State, the legislation to prevent discrimination in private sales or rental of housing is stronger than in most other states.

However, as the report will show, the housing supplied to white welfare recipients in Nassau and Suffolk counties is generally superior to the housing supplied to nonwhites and overcrowding of nonwhites is substantially higher. In addition to the social costs that the entire community, white and nonwhite, must bear, there are needless financial costs the entire community bears. Briefly, these relate to welfare department rental payments for substandard housing that could not be rented on the commercial market at similar prices.

The study of the housing characteristics of recipients of Public Welfare was undertaken in response to the concerns expressed by representatives of the Nassau and Suffolk Regional Planning Board. These representatives reported several difficult problems regarding the housing of the welfare caseload. They are:

1. The scarcity of adequate housing for all recipients, but especially for families with children, and especially for Negro families.

2. The overcrowding of families resulting from the unavailability of larger accommodations, and the lack of private kitchen and bath facilities.

3. The high cost of housing, especially rental housing, on which the majority of the caseload is dependent. In addition, it was also suspected that the cost of housing is higher for Negro recipients than for white recipients.

4. The poor quality of housing available to recipients.

All of the housing problems listed above were thought to be more serious in Nassau than in Suffolk.

Purpose

The study, then, was designed to determine the existence and the scope of the problems outlined above. And since both Departments maintain current statistics on their caseloads, they were an excellent source of updated data on the housing of families from the low-income group. Further, it is a fairly safe assumption that welfare recipients are representative of a sizable segment of the low-income group at least in their need for cheap and adequate housing. Included in the study were questions designed to determine some of the social characteristics of the welfare population, in order to discover whether these would indicate any special housing needs.

Methodology

The study was performed by using a 5 percent random sample of the caseload of each caseworker in the Public Assistance Division of the two Welfare Departments. In each case, the types of relief covered were Old Age Assistance, Aid to Disabled, Aid to the Blind, Aid to Dependent Children, and Home Relief. In Suffolk County the cases also included Medical Assistance in the home. The sample was drawn from the caseload that was being served in November, 1966. These cases constituted all the relief-in-the-home programs administered by these two departments, with the exception of the Medical Assistance in the home caseload for Nassau.

Caseloads are assigned by geographical area in both departments. Welfare Department caseworkers were instructed to choose every 20th name in their alphabetical file and to fill out forms showing the social characteristics and housing characteristics of each household head. (A sample form and instructions to each caseworker follow in A-15-1.)

Information supplied on the form was derived from the case record except for questions 12, 15, and 17, which required a judgment by the caseworker based on his knowledge of the case. Detailed instructions were given to each caseworker to enable consistent sampling. They are included on the following pages.

The terms "case" or "household head" refer to either a head of a family or an individual living alone. A family consists of any case with two or more persons, whether adults or children. A single individual is an adult who does not share his housing accommodation with any other person. Cases described as Puerto Rican were defined as nonwhite, for the purposes of the study, because the housing problems of this group closely paralleled those of the Negro group.

At the time of the survey, the Nassau caseload was 8,084 excluding Medical Assistance. The sample size was 490 or 6.1 percent of the caseload. Two classes of cases were eliminated from the sample resulting in a reduction in sample size to 459, or 5.6 percent of the total caseload. The two cases that were eliminated were:

1. *Residents of public housing. Eight cases from the sample were in this category. They were excluded because it was assumed that housing size, quality and cost were acceptable according to government standards.*
2. *Cases residing rent-free with primary families. There were 23 cases in this category. They were eliminated because detailed housing information was not always known to the caseworker.*

The Suffolk County caseload was 7,883 including Medical Assistance at the time of the survey. The sample size for Suffolk was 417, and this was reduced to 392 or 5.0% of the total caseload, by excluding those cases residing rent-free with primary families. There was no occupied public housing in Suffolk County at the time of the survey.

A-15-1 Nassau-Suffolk Regional Planning Board Housing Survey of Welfare Recipients

NASSAU ____	SUFFOLK ____

Address_____ Apt. No._____ Post Office_____

Municipality_____ Neighborhood_____ Census Tract_____

DESCRIPTION OF HOUSING UNIT

1. Type: One Family ____
   Two Family ____
   Apartment ____
   Rooming House ____

2. No. of families sharing unit ____

3. Number of Rooms ____ Bedrooms ____

4. Occupied by: Owner ____
   Tenant ____

5. Heating Facilities: Central ____
   Other ____
   None ____

6. Private Kitchen: Yes ____ No ____

7. Water Supply:

	In Kitchen	In Bath
Running hot		
Cold only		
None		

8. Private flush toilet in unit: Yes ____ No ____

9. Private bath or shower in unit: Yes ____ No ____

10. Monthly rent or home payment for unit (excluding utilities) to nearest $_____
    If furniture is included, mark X ____

11. Monthly Utilities Cost: Heat $_____
    Gas $_____
    Electric $_____

12. Structural Condition of Unit: Sound ____ Deteriorated ____ Dilapidated ____

Remarks: _____
_____
_____

HOUSEHOLD DATA

13. Characteristics: White ____
    Negro ____
    Puerto Rican ____
    Other ____

14. Length of Residence:
    In housing unit
    In County

Yrs.	Mos.

15. Employment pattern of Head of household:
    Steady ____
    Temporary or Seasonal ____
    Unemployed ____
    Unemployable ____

16. Welfare Record: Chronic ____
    Temporary ____

17. Eligible for Public Housing: Yes ____ No ____

18.

Members of Household (list by relation- ship to head)	Sex	Age	Employment Status (Present)	Occupation	Monthly Income of Each Member (before deductions) From:		
					Wages and Salaries	Public Assis- tance Grants	All other Sources
Head							

Caseworker: Date:

The data supplied by each caseworker was reviewed by staff in the Welfare Departments before being submitted to the consultants. This data was then submitted to the Suffolk County Data Processing Center for coding, tabulation, and presentation in the form of tables designed by the consultants in association with the Nassau and Suffolk Welfare Departments.

Nassau-Suffolk Regional Planning Board
Housing Survey of Welfare Recipients

Instructions to Caseworkers

This sample survey of welfare recipients' housing conditions and costs is an important element of the Bi-County planning study currently underway. Your cooperation in assembling this data is, therefore, sincerely appreciated.

A. Selection of Sample

A sample of five cases is requested from each caseworker. This will result in a sample of 5% to 7% of the current welfare caseload. It is essential that this be a completely random and unbiased sample, which might best be achieved by dividing the number of cases you have on your roster by five and then using the resulting figure as the interval between cases to be selected (e.g. if you have 60 cases, the interval would be 12, and you would, therefore, pull every 12th case record from your file). When returning your completed forms, please indicate the total caseload from which they have been selected.

B. Location of Dwelling

The first section at the top of the form is for locational information. The name of the welfare recipient is not to be given, so there will be no disclosure of identity. Please check whether in Nassau or Suffolk County and fill in the Street Address, Apartment Number, and Post Office. Do not fill in the information on Municipality, Neighborhood, or Census Tract as this will be filled in by the planning staff.

C. Description of Housing Unit

Definition–the information requested applies to the housing unit within which the family resides. If it is located within a two-family or apartment structure, the words "unit" or "in unit" herein apply to the apartment or portion within which the subject family resides.

A. **Housing Unit** *is defined by the U.S. Census Bureau as "a house, an apartment or other group of rooms, or a single room ... when it is occupied or intended for occupancy as separate living quarters; that is, when the occupants do not live and eat with any other persons in the structure and there is either (1) direct access from the outside or through a common hall, or (2) a kitchen or cooking equipment for the exclusive use of the occupants of the unit. The occupants of a housing unit may be a family or other group of persons, or a person living alone."*

1. **Type**
   One-family *is a detached house, designed for occupancy by a single household.*

   Two-family *is a dwelling structure originally intended for occupancy by two families, whether side-by-side or on separate floors.*

   Apartment *is a unit in any multifamily structure.*

   Rooming House *is a structure in which rooms are rented out and there is shared use of kitchen and bath facilities.*

2. **Number of Families Sharing Unit**–*A family is a group of related individuals, together with any nonrelated boarders who share their household with them. If boarders are related, then they form a separate family.*

3. **Number of Rooms**–According to the U.S. Census, the number of rooms is the count of whole rooms used for living purposes, such as living rooms, dining rooms, bedrooms, kitchens, finished attic or basement rooms, recreation rooms, lodgers' rooms, and rooms used for offices by a person living in the unit. Not considered as rooms are bathrooms, halls, foyers, or vestibules; closets; alcoves; pantries; strip or pullman kitchens; laundry or furnace rooms; unfinished attics, basements, and other space used for storage; porches, unless they are permanently enclosed and suitable for year-round use; and offices used only by persons not living in the unit. A partially divided room, such as a dinette next to a kitchen or living room, is considered as a separate room if there is a partition from floor to ceiling. Rooms equipped with movable partitions from floor to ceiling are separate rooms. If a room is shared by occupants of more than one unit, it is included with the unit from which it is most easily reached.

Under Number of Bedrooms enter only rooms used exclusively for sleeping purposes.

4. a. **Occupied by Owner** means that the case reported is the owner of the housing unit. However, the owner need not be the head of the household. A dwelling may be owned even if it is mortgaged or not fully paid for, and includes a cooperative apartment unit.
   b. **Occupied by Tenant**–Any occupant other than an owner.

5. **Heating Facilities**
   a. **Central**–A single source of heat distributed throughout the housing unit by built-in equipment (pipes, ducts, registers, etc.)
   b. **Other**–Includes space heaters, whether vented or not, portable electric heaters, etc.
   c. **None**–No heating equipment of any kind.

6. **Private Kitchen**–Enter "yes" only if the unit has a stove, sink, and refrigerator for the exclusive use of the occupants of the housing unit. All other conditions should be entered as "no."

7. **Water Supply**–Indicate listed type of water facility and whether it exists in the kitchen and/or the bathroom.

8. **Private Flush Toilet in Unit**–Mark "yes" only if such a facility is provided within the housing unit, for the exclusive use of its occupants. A toilet shared with others or located outside the unit should be entered as "no."

9. **Private Bathtub or Shower in Unit**–"Yes" denotes the presence of such a facility within the housing unit for the exclusive use of its occupants.

10. **Monthly Rent**–Enter actual cash payment, plus the estimated value of all supplementary payments in kind, such as janitorial service. If any utilities are included, deduct them from this figure and list them in #11, below. For owner-occupied units, the house payment represents the monthly total of mortgage payments and all taxes. Add 10% for upkeep. If necessary, get yearly total and divide by 12.

    If furniture is included in rent, check box indicating same.

11. **Monthly Cost of Utilities**–
    a. **Heat**–Enter total annual fuel cost divided by 12. If unit is heated by gas, write in word "gas" and enter cost on next line.
    b. **Gas**–Enter the total annual gas bill for cooking, hot water heating, etc., divided by 12.
    c. **Electric**–The total annual electric bill divided by 12.

12. Sound housing is defined as that which has no defects, or only slight defects that normally are corrected during the course of regular maintenance. Examples of slight defects are: lack of paint; slight damage to porch or steps; slight wearing away of mortar between bricks or other masonry; small cracks in walls, plaster or chimney; cracked windows; slight wear on floors, doorsills, doorframes, window sills, or window frames; and broken gutters or downspouts.

    Deteriorating housing needs more repair than would be provided in the course of regular maintenance. Such housing has one or more defects of an intermediate nature that must be corrected if the unit is to continue to provide safe and adequate shelter. Examples of intermediate defects are: holes, open cracks, rotted, loose, or missing materials over a small area of the foundation, walls, roof, floors, or ceilings; shaky or unsafe porch, steps, or railings; several broken or missing window panes; some rotted or loose window frames or sashes that are no longer rainproof or windproof; broken or loose stair treads, or broken, loose, or missing risers, balusters, or railings on inside or outside stairs; deep wear on doorsills, doorframes, outside or inside steps or floors; missing bricks or cracks in the chimney that are not serious enough to be a fire hazard; and makeshift chimney, such as a stovepipe or other uninsulated pipe leading directly from the stove to the outside through a hole in the roof, wall, or window. Such defects are signs of neglect that lead to serious structural deterioration or damage if not corrected.

Dilapidated housing does not provide safe and adequate shelter and, in its present condition, endangers the health, safety, or well-being of the occupants. Such housing has either (1) one or more critical defects; (2) a combination of intermediate defects in sufficient number or extent to require considerable repair or rebuilding; or (3) is of inadequate original construction. The defects are either so critical or so widespread that the structure should be extensively repaired, rebuilt, or torn down.

Critical defects result from continued neglect or lack of repair or indicate serious damage to the structure. Examples of critical defects are: holes, open cracks, or rotted loose or missing material (clapboard siding, shingles, bricks, concrete, tile, plaster, or floorboards) over a large area of the foundation, outside walls, roof, chimney, or inside walls, floors, or ceilings; substantial sagging of floors, walls, or roofs; and extensive damage by storm, fire, or flood.

To be classified as dilapidated on the basis of intermediate defects, a housing unit must have such defects in sufficient number or extent that it no longer provides safe and adequate shelter. No set number of intermediate defects is required.

Inadequate original construction includes: shacks, huts, or tents, structures with makeshift walls or roofs, or built of packing boxes, scrap lumber, or tin; structures lacking foundations (walls rest directly on the ground); structures with dirt floors; and cellars, sheds, barns, garages, or other places not originally intended for living quarters and inadequately converted to such use.

D. Household Data

13. **Characteristics**–If there is any doubt, enter the response of the individuals concerned, as given to you.
14. **Length of Residence**–Approximations to the nearest six months will be satisfactory. Use the "months" column only for persons residing less than one year in the unit or in the community.
15. **Head of Household Employment Pattern**–The choices are self-explanatory and should be based on the caseworker's evaluation.
16. **Welfare Record**–The purpose of this question is to separately identify the portion of the caseload that is "rehabilitable" from that which, in all likelihood, will be in need of assistance for very long periods of time. Among the latter would be included the aged, the chronic invalids, single mothers with small children, etc.
17. **Eligible for Public Housing**–Generally, public housing authorities do not accept unmarried couples or persons with a record of offenses greater than misdemeanors. Of course, such decisions are based on close scrutiny and investigation, which is not possible in this survey. This question should, therefore, reflect the knowledge and judgment of the caseworker as to whether the recipient would be admitted if he or she applied for admission to a public housing project.
18. **Data on Individual Members of Household**
    a. Members of Household–Names are not to be given. Merely indicate the relationship to the head, i.e.

wife, son, daughter, sister, etc., or boarder if not related. Data requested in each column should be given for each individual, except where not applicable–e.g. a child who is not employed and, therefore, has no income and is included in the family public assistance grant.

b. Sex–M (male) or F (female).

c. Age–to nearest year.

d. Employment status–Select from alternatives provided in Question 15. Since the head of household is covered in that question, it is blanked out here.

e. Occupation–This should indicate the type of work and not the industrial classification of the firm for which the individual works. Please select your response from the 1960 U.S. Census of Population classification list, below, if possible:

1. Professional, technical and kindred workers.
2. Farmers and farm managers.
3. Managers, officials and proprietors, except farm.
4. Clerical and kindred workers.
5. Sales workers.
6. Craftsmen, foremen and kindred workers.
7. Operatives and kindred workers.
8. Private household workers.
9. Service workers, except private household.
10. Farm laborers and foremen.
11. Laborers, except farm and mine.

Detailed descriptions of these classifications are appended at the end of these instructions.

f. **Monthly Income of Each Member of Household**
These shall include current income, from all sources, before tax deductions.

i. Wages and Salaries–include wages, salary, pay from Armed Forces, commissions, tips, piece rate payments, and cash bonuses earned.

ii. Public Assistance Grants–include the total of all public assistance grants, including rental and utility allowances.

iii. All Other Sources–include self-employment income, net income from rents or receipts from roomers or boarders, social security benefits, pensions, veterans' payments, military allotments for dependents, unemployment insurance, contributions for support from persons who are not members of the household, alimony, and periodic receipts from insurance policies or annuities. If there is more than one family living in the household, draw a heavy line across the page between family groupings. Use an additional form if you need more lines.

Please sign form and indicate date. If you have any remarks that will assist in the evaluation of your entries or will clarify questions that have arisen in filling out the form, use the back of the form.

Thank you very much for your cooperation and assistance.

A DESIGN PROTOTYPE

To illustrate the potential of design and financing tools to improve housing and neighborhoods on Long Island, a prototype plan has been prepared for the North Amityville area. The study area includes both the housing problems and the housing opportunities common to many communities in Nassau and Suffolk. The pressures for growth in the region will call for increasing volumes of new residential construction. It is possible to meet a portion of this demand through carefully planned additions to and changes in fully or partially developed areas such as North Amityville.

Objectives

The objectives are to create a functional, well-defined and attractive community that:

1. contains a significantly greater number of housing units;

2. knits together desirable elements of existing, but unrelated, developments;

3. preserves the maximum number of existing homes and surrounds them with similar or compatible development;

4. provides a diversity of housing types;

5. provides housing opportunities for people of varying ages, incomes, and ethnic backgrounds;

6. contains a safe and efficient circulation pattern for pedestrian and vehicular traffic; and

7. includes a full range of community facilities.

Location

North Amityville is an unincorporated area located in the Town of Babylon in Suffolk County, about three miles from Great South Bay and about 40 miles and an hour's train ride east of Manhattan. The study area or "district" is roughly square, covers about three square miles, houses about 11,000 people, and is bounded by four roads of regional importance. Road access is provided largely by Sunrise Highway on the southern border of the district, and Southern State Parkway, which forms the northern district boundary. The Central Branch of the Long Island Railroad provides rail access. Immediately to the north of the district is Republic Airport recently proposed for a major transportation hub providing a regional air-rail-bus-truck interchange point. The projected increase in air traffic at Republic would require the closing of Zahn's Airport, thereby increasing the amount of land available for development.

Character

North Amityville is one of the poverty areas of Suffolk County. The existing development pattern is the result of scattered and haphazard growth. A high proportion of the land is flat and vacant,

including the remnants of subdivisions that were started but never completed. In some areas newly surfaced streets lead nowhere; elsewhere, rutted lanes serve residential developments. Many streets are littered with garbage and wrecked cars. Amidst all of this, new home construction is occurring in several places.

North Amityville is an area of contrast. In the northwest corner along Broadway (Route 110) is a large, intensively developed trailer camp. There are substandard, rural, homemade shacks in undeveloped sections. Scattered throughout the district, however, are attractive and substantial new homes. In more densely developed areas, many once sound homes have become dilapidated beyond rehabilitation. Near the center of the study area, several postwar developments of small, inexpensive homes have deteriorated and require inspection to identify code violations and necessary rehabilitation. Some areas, the largest of which is located east of Zahn's Airport, contain well-maintained, single-family homes in sound neighborhoods. Zahn's Airport forms a barrier. Although many of the 11,000 residents of the district are black, few blacks, if any, live east of Zahn's.

Sunrise Highway, the southern boundary of the district, serves as both a major artery and a commercial service road, but does not provide convenient shopping facilities for local residents. The commercial development in the interior of the area appears to be failing; many stores are doing a marginal business or are boarded up. Several semipublic or institutional uses—Zahn's Airport, a Catholic church and convent, a U.S. Army Nike Missile Site, and three cemeteries—occupy large tracts of relatively open land unavailable for public recreation. The amount of public recreation facilities is inadequate: three school playgrounds, one pool, and a small new park.

Residential (5 Dwelling units per acre)
Residential (8 Dwelling units per acre)
Trailer Park
School:
E - Elementary School
Jr. H - Junior High School
H - High School
Church
Cemetery
Community Facility
Commercial
Industry
Office
Governmental or Quasi-Governmental
Recreation and Open Space

Existing Land-Use Pattern

The district contains large tracts of open land. Much of it is simply vacant and undeveloped, but about one-eighth of the total land area is in semipublic or institutional uses. The largest such tract is Zahn's Airport, with about 150 acres. Immediately west of the airport is the large church property with about 95 acres, other major open-land uses are three cemeteries, three schools, and an Army installation. With the exception of the airport, these semipublic uses can be expected to remain in the future, and add an important dimension to the openness the district now displays. Total vacant areas are also scattered throughout the district, and range in size from several acres to a few thousand square feet.

While some industry has logically developed near the Long Island Railroad, other industrial and warehousing uses are spotted throughout the district. Commercial development has little relation to community patterns. Most of it is strung out along major boundary roads where it contributes to traffic problems.

The only multifamily development is a garden apartment complex, still under construction, located on the northern boundary of the district near Southern State Parkway. Other residences are single-family houses, with the exception of a trailer camp in the northwest corner of the study area.

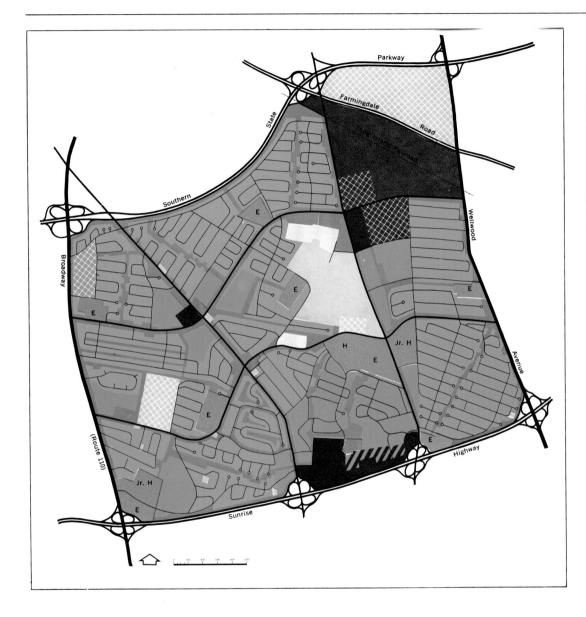

Proposed Land-Use Pattern

The proposed land-use pattern would provide for a community of 25,000 people which is more than twice the total now living in the district. Housing accommodations would be of many types, including single-family homes, townhouse clusters, garden apartments, and a few high-rise apartments. Thus the community would provide for a wide range of housing needs. Housing density would be highest in and near the commerical and community centers. Overall residential density would be increased from 1.4 to about 3.2 families per acre, a comparatively low density for a built-up area of mixed housing types.

The district plan includes recommendations for development of Zahn's Airport—a major land resource in this area. However, the transformation of North Amityville from an amorphous area into a coherent community does not depend on the recommended redevelopment of the airport site.

The existing industrial park in the vicinity of the Long Island Railroad would be expanded to comprise an industrial and office employment center for the growing community. The small light industrial area along Sunrise Highway would be retained.

A major commercial center would be located along Sunrise Highway, to provide shopping facilities and a community center. Two smaller centers would be located at major intersections of the road network to provide local neighborhood shopping; these centers would also contain community facilities and a church. The center related to the employment area would serve both employees and the surrounding neighborhood.

Elementary schools would be dispersed throughout the district to provide an educational and cultural focus for each neighborhood. The high school, a junior high, and an elementary school would be grouped in the center of the district as the major educational, cultural, and recreational complex.

Open space other than active recreational areas would be in the form of narrow strip parks located throughout the community. These would serve as a pedestrian network to link homes with shopping and district activities, as well as providing a close relationship between homes and a natural setting.

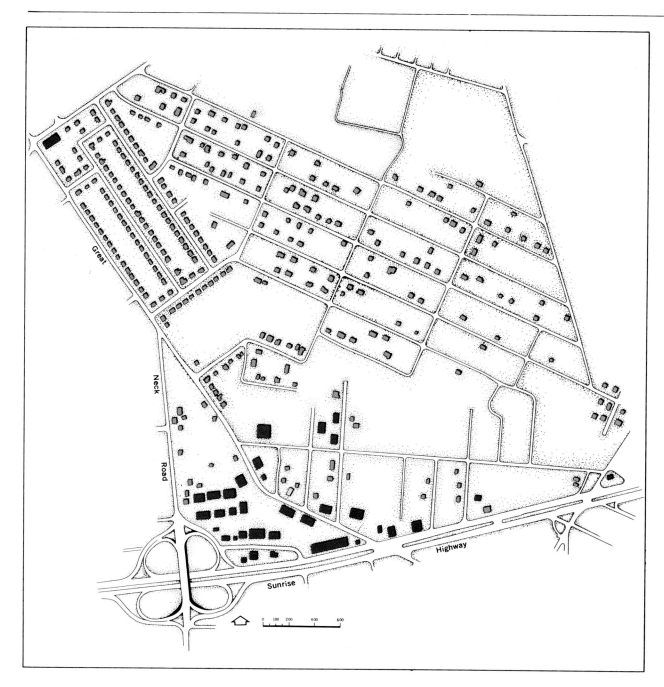

Existing Neighborhood Pattern

The major physical deficiencies of the district are all contained in the neighborhood selected for further study. The inefficient road network of the present district of North Amityville affects the character of this neighborhood. At the neighborhood level there is no separation of local and through traffic, and there are troublesome intersections between minor local streets and major arteries.

The large open spaces located here serve no public purpose and are difficult to utilize because of their lack of relation to the road network. Although some houses are new or in good repair, most residential structures are in some stage of deterioration. In general, the houses near Sunrise Highway, which are intermixed with industrial and commercial uses, are in the worst structural condition. In the northwest corner of the neighborhood a postwar subdivision of inexpensive homes has seriously deteriorated. While probably not requiring demolition, this area is in need of a strict code enforcement program. The land abutting Sunrise Highway is used for an array of highway commercial uses, which are physically unrelated to adjacent homes, and which do not market the type of merchandise likely to provide a community focus.

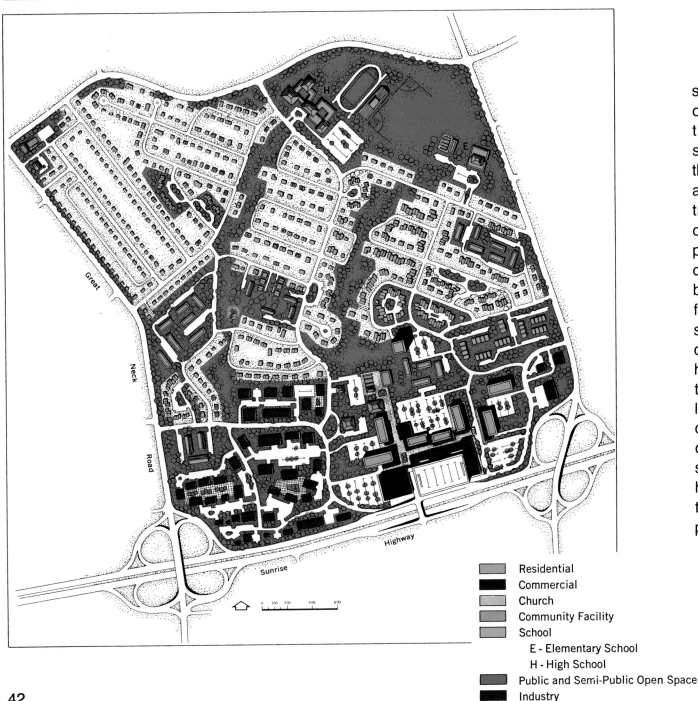

Residential

Commercial

Church

Community Facility

School

   E - Elementary School

   H - High School

Public and Semi-Public Open Space

Industry

Proposed Neighborhood Pattern

The major road network would be shifted to conform to the grid pattern of the total community, and a pedestrian system of interlinked open spaces and pathways would connect the educational complex, town center and all residential areas. The industrial development in the southwest corner would be slightly expanded to provide more local employment; access by public transportation would be improved. A town center (seldom found on Long Island) would contain shopping, community administration, cultural and recreational facilities and housing. It would have direct access to Sunrise Highway and direct vehicular connections to the proposed mirror center south of the highway. The town center would contain a number of six-story and three-story apartment houses; a single high-rise apartment tower would serve as a visual focal point for the entire community.

Community Pattern

Restructuring the area south of Sunrise Highway to mirror the proposed development pattern of North Amityville would create a total community of about 50,000 people.

The two shopping centers would be tied across the highway by a pedestrian and vehicular overpass, and the combined facilities of the two centers would serve as the town center of this community. Office and industrial employment areas for the total community are shown on the accompanying plan, concentrated along the peripheral high-speed roadways. Educational facilities would be dispersed throughout the community to create neighborhood focal points; each resident would be within walking distance of a local elementary school. A local bus system could operate within walking distance of every resident, and connect the regional intercommunity public transport system and town center with the industrial areas and the remainder of the community.

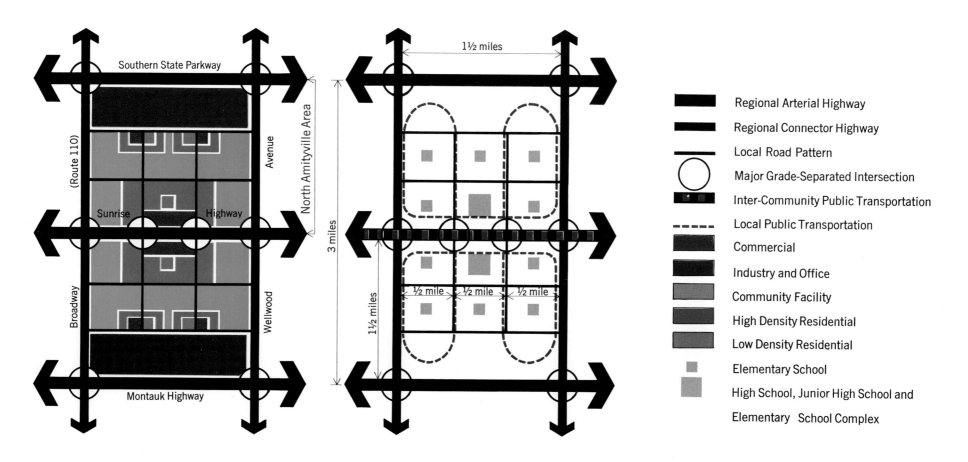

Land Use Pattern

Educational and Transportation Pattern

Legend:

- Regional Arterial Highway
- Regional Connector Highway
- Local Road Pattern
- Major Grade-Separated Intersection
- Inter-Community Public Transportation
- Local Public Transportation
- Commercial
- Industry and Office
- Community Facility
- High Density Residential
- Low Density Residential
- Elementary School
- High School, Junior High School and Elementary School Complex

Regional Pattern

The proposed plan for the district has been conceived in light of a repeatable pattern that reasonably applies to Long Island as a whole. The community pattern, expanded on a grid of roads, might avoid some of the problems of existing towns. The larger regional pattern of Long Island is essentially linear, and one development pattern that appears to fit the requirements of this region is a "ladder" grid with an emphasis on east-west movement. Such a grid, presented in the accompanying diagram, was used as the basis for the North Amityville scheme. It would provide for an orderly layout of communities and districts with generally simple and obvious lines of communication.

The heaviest pressure for development would be expected near the major east-west roads. By relating future growth to such routes, it is probable that an economical balance would be obtained between capital investment in roads and an improved regional development pattern. In transportation terms, such a regional pattern consists of the following major elements: two longitudinal high-speed roads; one spine road for movement between communities, and secondary routes for local movements. The spine road is intended for public transport, probably high-speed buses, to operate on it without serious conflict with demands from private cars and trucks.

The object of this type of structure is a linear strip of economically and socially balanced, identifiable communities that are all interdependent. Major regional centers should logically develop near the points where these east-west strips of development intersect major north-south routes.

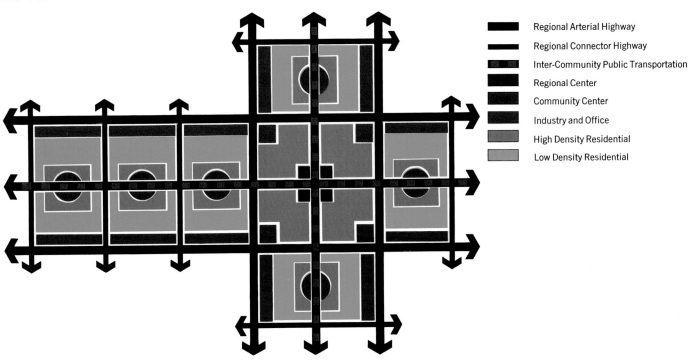

- Regional Arterial Highway
- Regional Connector Highway
- Inter-Community Public Transportation
- Regional Center
- Community Center
- Industry and Office
- High Density Residential
- Low Density Residential

THE THREE HOUSING GOALS

The North Amityville design prototype illustrates the potential of many Long Island communities through the judicious utilization of various state and federal programs. A major goal of the design plan was, to the maximum extent, the retention of the existing community fabric. New housing, new schools, new streets, new facilities of all kinds have been woven into the area without causing a major disruption of people, their homes, or their community facilities. At the same time, however, the physical recommendation of the plan provides the opportunity for meaningful economic and racial integration.

The three housing goals established earlier in this chapter have been met in the North Amityville design study as follows:

1. Adequate housing for all has been achieved by retaining the good housing that exists, while at the same time providing opportunities for the increasing numbers of low- and moderate-income families of all races and ages.

2. Housing deterioration has been eliminated in the design plan without eliminating the area's neighborhoods. In fact, by removing only the worst housing and by maintaining or rehabilitating a maximum number of existing homes, the North Amityville depicted in the plan offers residents a better place to live.

3. A more livable community has been created with increased employment, new community facilities and services, parks and open space near each home, and greater opportunities for easy and cheap travel between employment centers and places of residence.

This community, unlike any existing today on Long Island, has been created without eliminating an existing community. It will, however, require the use of a combination of most existing governmental assistance programs as well as new programs and administrative agencies.

PREVENTIVE AND DIAGNOSTIC ACTION

The previous paragraphs deal with corrective action necessary after blight has occurred. But there are preventative tools, available at county, town, and village levels, that can be used before, during, and after construction.

Before Construction—Zoning and subdivision regulations control land use, density and site design. Zoning is a city, town, and village responsibility although some proposed changes must be submitted to the County Planning Boards for review. Subdivision regulations can be enacted by cities, towns, and villages.

During Construction—City, town and village building, plumbing, and electrical codes control materials and set specifications.

After Construction—Housing, health, and fire codes require maintenance of set physical and occupancy standards. The County Health Departments inspect and license temporary housing including farm labor camps and, in response to complaints, inspect additional thousands of residences each year. (In 1967, the Suffolk County Department of Health inspected housing in North Bellport and Wyandanch.) The Social Services Departments and, in Nassau County, the Fire Marshall's office, also make inspections. The three Nassau towns and two cities have adopted housing codes, as have four of the ten Suffolk towns and several villages in both counties; only one municipality has more than two inspectors.

Further controls for maintaining quality after construction might include the licensing of rental units, with reinspection required for each change of tenancy. A license fee would cover the cost of the additional inspection personnel. Absentee landlords can be required to name a responsible local agent who can be held accountable.

It is often hard to diagnose why one neighborhood succeeds while another fails, but the symptoms of failure are clear. There is the lack of care—lack of care by a resident who doesn't repair broken screens, doesn't mow the grass, doesn't even take his daughter's doll off the roof. While he may isolate his yard with an expensive chain link fence and warn the world of his vicious dog, his house is assembled of scraps of lumber and tar paper, and doors scavenged from the dump. His garden is planted with abandoned cars and refrigerators.

There is the lack of care by government, which doesn't collect garbage or refuse, provide street lights, maintain streets, or provide adequate police and fire protection.

Recipes for producing sound neighborhoods are complex, and planning to rescue a troubled neighborhood may require additional ingredients—extra imagination, effort, and money. Following are four basic needs:

1. Good Planning and Zoning. Jobs and people should be located where they can find each other, yet not be mutually harmful. A worker should be able to get to his job quickly and cheaply, but not worry that trucks rumbling past his house will endanger his children.

2. Community Centers and Open Space. Children need to play, walk, and run. Teens require places to congregate, show off, be athletic, be themselves. Adults who are lonely and isolated by responsibilities for children or by the defeats of life need facilities. Within easy and safe walking distance should be: a day-care center, homemaker classes, a teenage center, athletic facilities, a library, ball fields, an old-age center, community meeting places, and parks.

3. Good Governmental Services. The poor as well as the rich require paved roads, curbs, street lights and trees, public water and sewers, adequate fire and police protection, and garbage collection.

4. Integration. Communities should have both an ethnic and an economic heterogeneity.

A Planned Community[6]

How is such a community achieved? How can woods, scrub pines, beaches, and berry bushes be saved? How can a small boy be given a chance to wander safely, to observe nature, to be thrilled by frogs and wild flowers?

Suppose that instead of 15,000 square feet (about a third of an acre) the lot had 10,000 square feet (about a quarter-acre). The house might be a little closer to neighbors—"clustered"—but there would be a little less road to pay taxes for, fewer feet of water and

Community Plan

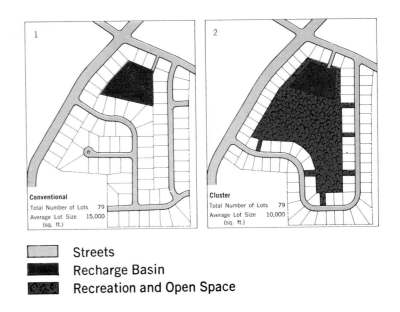

Streets
Recharge Basin
Recreation and Open Space

[6]This 35-acre subdivision is now under construction in Brookhaven. There is little usable open space. Roads and utilities cost about $3,600 per house.

sewer pipes, and less grass to mow.[7] By combining the 5,000 square feet saved with similar savings of several neighbors, a large park could be created. Both the original house purchase price and the annual taxes might be less.

The acres saved could be used for a park and open space system, with green walkways behind houses connected to schools, community centers, and "downtown." Areas of scenic and recreation value could be saved for enjoyment, as areas that are the least desirable for homes are frequently the most scenic.

No one would drive past homes unless he had business in the neighborhood, for local streets would not be shortcuts to someplace else. Bounding each small neighborhood would be collector streets tying neighborhoods and "downtown" together; roads would connect "downtown" with the next town as well as major arterial highways.

Homes in the neighborhood would not be identical. Bordering the through streets would be apartments. On scattered sites there might be two-family houses or groups of row houses, offering each family a small plot of private land, but less costly than a detached one-family house. Prefabricated, mass-produced housing, evolving from both mobile homes and experiments such as Habitat, would house low- and moderate-income families.

Such a concept, though best embodied in a "new town," can serve as the model for new subdivisions or infilling of existing development as in the North Amityville design prototype.

BIBLIOGRAPHY

Housing Studies

FHA Techniques of Housing Market Analysis (Washington, D. C., Department of H.U.D., January 1970).

Residential Market Analysis (Hauppauge, N.Y., Nassau-Suffolk Regional Planning Board, September 1967) Volume I.

Residential Market Analysis (September 1968) Volume II.

Housing–Better Homes for Better Communities (October 1968).

Population Studies

Hauser, P.M., and Duncan O. D. *The Study of Population* (Chicago, The University of Chicago Press, 1959).

Building the American City (Washington, D. C., Report of the National Commission on Urban Problems . . ., December 1968).

Urban Housing Needs Through the 1980s: An Analysis and Projection (Washington, D. C., Prepared for the National Commission on Urban Problems, Research Report, No. 10, 1968).

General Housing Characteristics: United States Summary, 1970 Census of Housing (Washington, D. C., U. S. Department of Commerce, Dec. 1971) pp. App. 11-12.

---

[7]By clustering the same number of houses, 14½ acres of open space are gained. Road and utility costs are reduced to about $3,000 per house.

GENERAL PLANNING CONSIDERATIONS

B

B-1   Types of Planning Units
B-2   Location
B-3   Compatibility of Other Land
       Uses with Housing
B-4   Accessibility Criteria for
       Various Destinations
B-5   Relationship of Employment
       Facilities to Housing Site
B-6   Relationship of Central
       Facilities to Housing Site
B-7   Relationship of Recreational and
       Cultural Facilities to Housing Site
B-8   Topographic Considerations of
       Housing Site
B-9   Inland and Shore Considerations
       of Housing Sites

B-10   Site Configuration
B-11   Site Comparison–Checklist
B-12   Utilities
B-13   Pollution Factors
B-14   Air Rights–Residential Development
B-15   Development Over Water
B-16   Residential Density
B-17   Density Ranges
B-18   Density Measures
B-19   Density/Open Space Standards
B-20   Land-use Intensity
B-21   Types of Occupancy
B-22   Family Cycle
B-23   Types of Neighborhoods

Introduction

This chapter covers the external characteristics in which residential development takes place. It ranges from the very general topics of community settings and related criteria, such as: location, accessibility, facilities; to physical concerns of topography, site configuration and development over water; and closes with population-related data concerning density ranges and measures, family cycle housing patterns, and types of occupancy.

PLANNING UNITS—TYPES AND FUNCTIONS

Types of Planning Units

In planning a system of interrelated areas and facilities, each type of geographic area—neighborhood, community, school district, city, county, region, state, and nation—must be considered. In some instances, the entire state must be included and, when accessible, areas and facilities provided by the Federal Government must be taken into account.

The Neighborhood

The neighborhood is a residential area with homogeneous characteristics, of a size comparable to that usually served by an elementary school. A typically ideal neighborhood for planning purposes would be an area three-fourths of a mile to a mile square and containing about six to eight thousand people.

Neighborhoods occur in various shapes and sizes. Population densities vary from a few thousand to many thousands per square mile and there is also a wide variation in the numbers of children. Therefore, each neighborhood must be studied carefully. Because most residents live within a short distance of the school or playground, they walk to it and tend to use it frequently, often for shorter periods than in the centers planned for a larger geographic unit.

The Community

The community is a section of a city, primarily a residential area. It usually represents the service area of a high school, contains a large business center and commonly constitutes a section of the city measuring two or three miles across. It can be thought of as a "community of neighborhoods" because it is usually composed of three to five neighborhoods. Consequently, the population varies, but on the average is three to five times that of a neighborhood, or from twenty thousand to forty thousand people. It may have a less pronounced homogeneity than the neighborhood, but should not be so dissimilar as to make unified planning impossible. If the dissimilarities are pronounced, the community may need to be subdivided for planning.

The City or School District

The area designated as the city, town, borough, or village lends itself to the provision of areas and facilities for use by the entire population of the political subdivision. Major parks, golf courses, camps, museums, and botanical gardens, which cannot be provided in each neighborhood and community, are typical city-wide areas. In small localities comprising one community and with a single high school, city-wide planning is largely comparable with planning for a single community as described above, although some facilities commonly provided in larger city-wide areas are included.

School districts vary widely in size and population, but district-wide school planning involves primarily neighborhoods and communities. Some of the large school districts provide district-wide facilities for an outdoor education-recreation complex, interscholastic activities, consolidated educational programs, and some type of post-high school center or community college for day pupils.

51

Larger Units

The county or the region, which is a geographic area that sometimes includes parts of more than one county, is increasingly used as a unit for planning. Many such planning units are located in close proximity to a metropolitan city and include both the city and the surrounding region. Others are primarily rural in nature and are composed primarily of unincorporated areas. Planning on a regional or district basis lends itself to the provision of extensive properties usable for family outings, winter and water sports, and other activities requiring large land and water areas. Since these properties are distant from dense population centers, people require transportation in order to reach them and, consequently, tend to use them less frequently but for longer periods than is true of the areas in the smaller planning untis. The increase in state-wide planning makes it important that plans developed for smaller geographic units take into account existing and proposed facilities for state-wide use.

Unit Relationships

Even though area and facility planning is done for various geographic units and political subdivisions and involves a great variety of school and recreational properties, there is a relationship among the resultant plans. The areas and facilities provided in one unit or subdivision often influence the need for them elsewhere. Areas and facilities in the larger units supplement those in the smaller ones and are used by the people living in all these subdivisions. Therefore, cooperation among the agencies involved in planning at different levels is essential in order to achieve coordinated programs.

LOCATION

In planning a housing development, a careful study and analysis of all the factors that eventually determine rentals or sales must be made. Land costs, building costs, operating and maintenance expenses, taxes, insurance rates, interest rates, and all other items that enter into the cost of producing the rental property and maintaining the services of shelter for which it is planned, must sum up to a figure consistent with the rental income expectancy of the completed property.

In order to be acceptable, a housing development must meet certain fundamental requisites with respect to location and planning. First, the project should be located in or near a city or town where there is a definite prospect of continuing demand for housing at the proposed rental rates; it should be located in a neighborhood where the possibilities of future deterioration are at the minimum; and the site itself should be suitable for the development of a project of the type and magnitude contemplated. Second, the plans of the entire development should embody qualities of design and construction in terms of open space, lawns and planting, light and air, convenience and privacy of the dwelling units, and other amenities of family living, to the end that appeal may be enhanced and the factors of obsolescence may be minimized.

Rental income or selling price, to a great extent limited by the conditions prevailing in the market, are the controlling factors in the planning of a project. A fair return on the investment is assured only when costs, both construction and operating, are geared to the rental income expectancy. Planning affects not only the original cost of construction, but also, and equally important, the cost of operating and maintaining the property. But planning alone cannot be relied upon as the sole means of attaining these goals, nor is it to be inferred that, under varying conditions and circumstances, a given plan will result in the same rental rate. Experience has indicated, however, that under similar conditions of land costs, financing costs, and taxes, certain types of planning permit lower rentals than do other types. When the fullest possible advantage is taken of economies of layout and construction, less rental income is required to sustain a given project.

In the search for methods of reducing building and operating costs, there are certain essentials that must not be sacrificed. Substantial, well-built structures, located in good residential neighborhoods, with adequate space and equipment must be provided. A garden environment with play space for children is desirable, and ordinarily will be required. Plans must provide for light and ventilation, and each unit should incorporate the highest attainable degree of privacy and other amenities of family living. There must be adequate provision for automobiles, either in garages or parking spaces. Due attention must be given to the problem of servicing the dwelling units and the removal of waste.

B-3 COMPATIBILITY OF OTHER LAND USES WITH HOUSING

LISTING	GENERAL DESCRIPTION	COMPATIBILITY WITH HOUSING
Parks and Playgrounds		Desirable
Elementary School		Desirable
Churches and Synagogues		Desirable
Housing in Good Condition		Desirable
Local Shopping		Desirable
Medical Facilities		Desirable
Stores or Shops		Acceptable
Highway with Buffer Strips.		Acceptable
Housing in Fair Condition		Acceptable
Industrial Park		Acceptable
High School		Acceptable
Industrial Uses—Not Properly Screened		Not Acceptable
Airports		Not Acceptable
Highway without Buffer Strips		Not Acceptable
Warehouses, Railroad Tracks and Yards		Not Acceptable
Deteriorated or Dilapidated Housing		Not Acceptable

WATERTOWN EAST DEVELOPMENT

M. Paul Friedberg & Associates

B-4 ACCESSIBILITY CRITERIA FOR VARIOUS DESTINATIONS

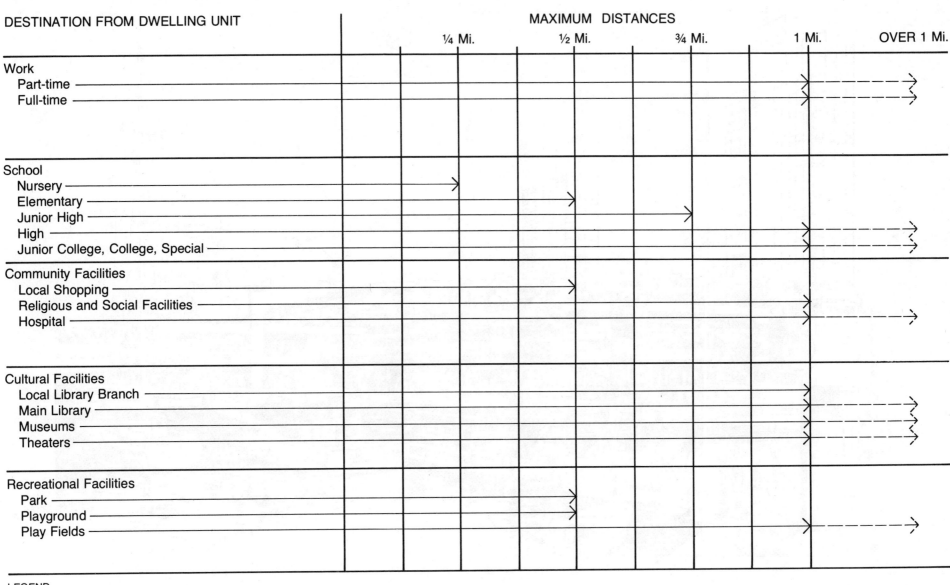

DESTINATION FROM DWELLING UNIT	MAXIMUM DISTANCES				
	¼ Mi.	½ Mi.	¾ Mi.	1 Mi.	OVER 1 Mi.
Work					
Part-time					→ →
Full-time					→ →
School					
Nursery	→				
Elementary		→			
Junior High			→		
High				→	→
Junior College, College, Special				→	→
Community Facilities					
Local Shopping		→			
Religious and Social Facilities				→	
Hospital				→	→
Cultural Facilities					
Local Library Branch				→	
Main Library				→	→
Museums				→	→
Theaters				→	→
Recreational Facilities					
Park			→		
Playground			→		
Play Fields				→	→

LEGEND

————————→ MAXIMUM WALKING DISTANCE

— — — — —→ RIDING DISTANCE (CAR OR PUBLIC TRANSPORTATION)

Accessibility of Employment Facilities

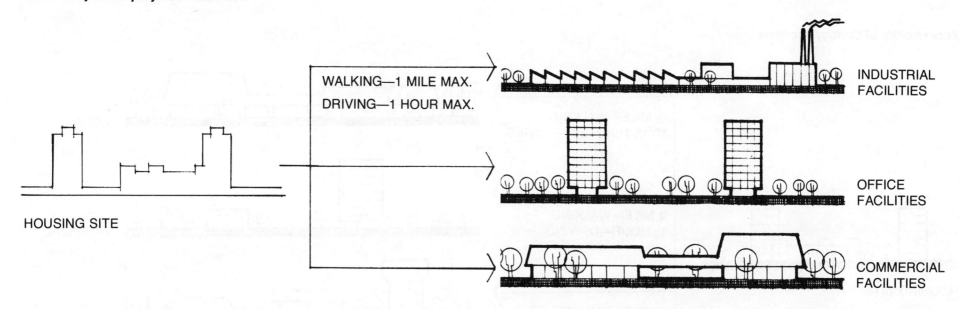

WALKING—1 MILE MAX.

DRIVING—1 HOUR MAX.

INDUSTRIAL FACILITIES

OFFICE FACILITIES

COMMERCIAL FACILITIES

HOUSING SITE

The selection of the community in which to build is the first problem confronting the sponsor of a project. To be acceptable, a project must be located in or near a city or town where there are adequate sources of employment, preferably in diversified occupations rather than in one or a few principal industries. Above all, it must be located in an economically stable community where there is evidence of a definite and continuing demand for housing at rentals sufficient to cover the requirements of the project as a sound business enterprise.

Within a given community, a location meriting approval should be readily accessible to places of employment and satisfactory transportation facilities should be available. It should be conveniently situated with respect to schools, churches, shopping centers, and the recreational facilities of the community. The site must be suitable for residential development, free from the hazards of floods, fog, smoke, noxious odors, nuisance industries, and the like. It must be located in a neighborhood where zoning or other types of protective regulation will permit the sort of development contemplated, and it must conform with city, county, or regional planning where such planning is in force.

Accessibility of Central Facilities

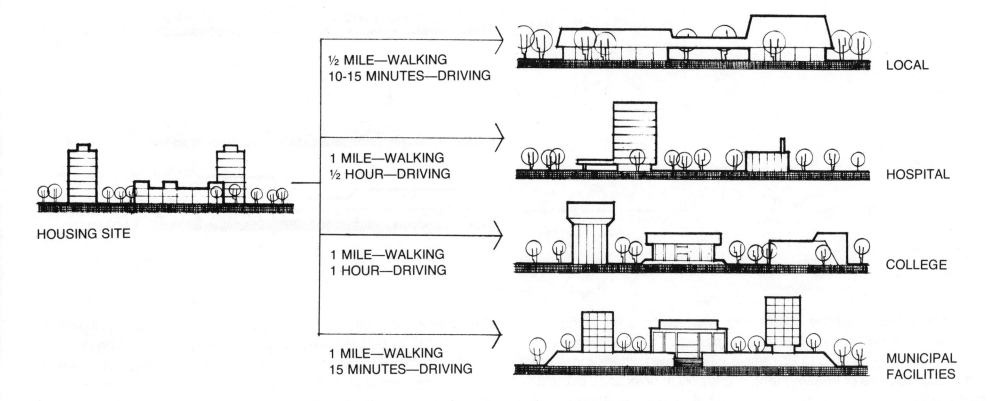

HOUSING SITE

½ MILE—WALKING
10-15 MINUTES—DRIVING

1 MILE—WALKING
½ HOUR—DRIVING

1 MILE—WALKING
1 HOUR—DRIVING

1 MILE—WALKING
15 MINUTES—DRIVING

LOCAL

HOSPITAL

COLLEGE

MUNICIPAL
FACILITIES

Accessibility of Recreational and Cultural Facilities

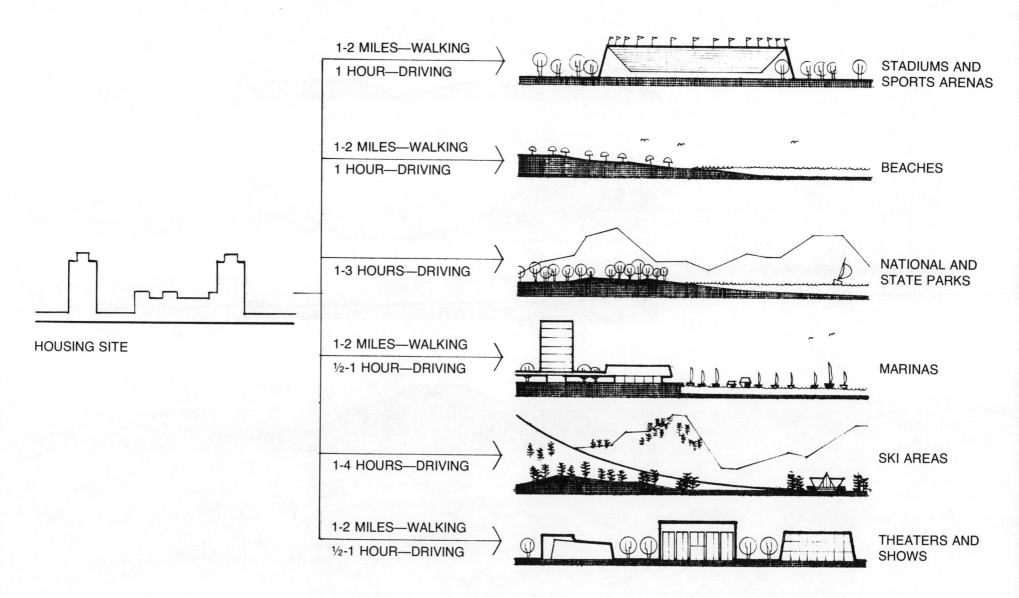

HOUSING SITE

1-2 MILES—WALKING
1 HOUR—DRIVING
STADIUMS AND SPORTS ARENAS

1-2 MILES—WALKING
1 HOUR—DRIVING
BEACHES

1-3 HOURS—DRIVING
NATIONAL AND STATE PARKS

1-2 MILES—WALKING
½-1 HOUR—DRIVING
MARINAS

1-4 HOURS—DRIVING
SKI AREAS

1-2 MILES—WALKING
½-1 HOUR—DRIVING
THEATERS AND SHOWS

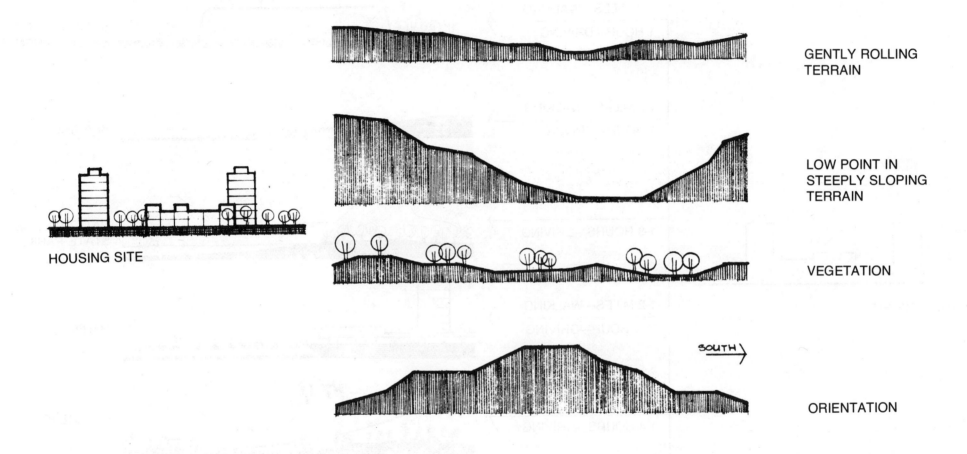

HOUSING SITE

GENTLY ROLLING TERRAIN

LOW POINT IN STEEPLY SLOPING TERRAIN

VEGETATION

SOUTH

ORIENTATION

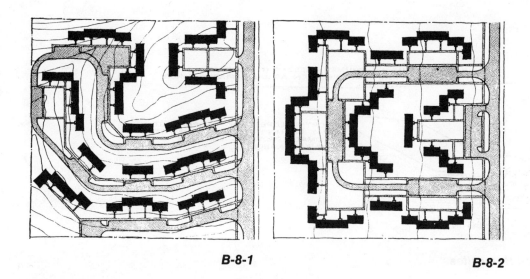

B-8-1

B-8-2

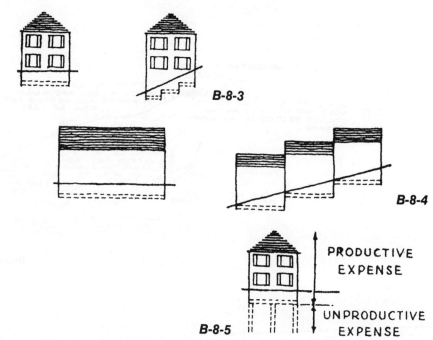

B-8-3

B-8-4

B-8-5

PRODUCTIVE EXPENSE

UNPRODUCTIVE EXPENSE

1. *A gently sloping site is preferable to one presenting serious topographical difficulties.* This will be apparent by an examination of figures B-8-1 and B-8-2 in which the same area has been assumed in both cases, the same access streets, and the same number of dwelling units, but with different topography. A study of these plans will make it evident that in figure B-8-1 there is a greater likelihood of expensive cut and fill. The steep slope also requires added provision for surface drainage to prevent heavy accumulation of rain water. Culverts and large-sized storm sewers may be required to remove it.

If the buildings are on a steep slope, they may be more costly because of added exterior walls (figure B-8-3). This is especially true where basements are omitted.

Where a long building runs perpendicular to the contours, it may be necessary to vary the floor and roof levels (figure B-8-4). This means added costs of roof and finishing the stepped gable ends.

A comparison of the two plans in figures B-8-1 and B-8-2 will also demonstrate the added flexibility of planning in the level site due to the unrestricted possibilities of placing the buildings. The difference in length and cost of road improvements to produce similar ease of access will also be apparent.

2. *Sites containing soft ground, heavy uncompacted fill, or outcroppings of rock should be avoided* (figure B-8-5). Preparation of the site to obviate these objectionable features is expensive and adds nothing to rental value.

3. *Choose a site where heavy-duty road construction will not be required.* The traffic tributary to the average housing development is not heavy and comparatively light hard-surfaced roads of moderate widths will suffice. If the needs of urban or through traffic require the construction of heavy-duty roads, either boundary or internal, at the expense of the project, an unproductive burden of cost is saddled on the enterprise.

4. *Sites remote from public roads and utilities are less desirable than those where these facilities are immediately available.* If roads and utilities must be brought from a great distance, low-priced land may prove to be prohibitive in final cost.

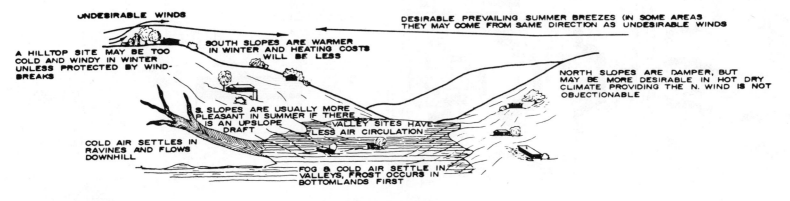

UNDESIRABLE WINDS

DESIRABLE PREVAILING SUMMER BREEZES (IN SOME AREAS THEY MAY COME FROM SAME DIRECTION AS UNDESIRABLE WINDS

A HILLTOP SITE MAY BE TOO COLD AND WINDY IN WINTER UNLESS PROTECTED BY WIND-BREAKS

SOUTH SLOPES ARE WARMER IN WINTER AND HEATING COSTS WILL BE LESS

NORTH SLOPES ARE DAMPER, BUT MAY BE MORE DESIRABLE IN HOT DRY CLIMATE PROVIDING THE N. WIND IS NOT OBJECTIONABLE

S. SLOPES ARE USUALLY MORE PLEASANT IN SUMMER IF THERE IS AN UPSLOPE DRAFT

VALLEY SITES HAVE LESS AIR CIRCULATION

COLD AIR SETTLES IN RAVINES AND FLOWS DOWNHILL

FOG & COLD AIR SETTLE IN VALLEYS, FROST OCCURS IN BOTTOMLANDS FIRST

Inland Homesites

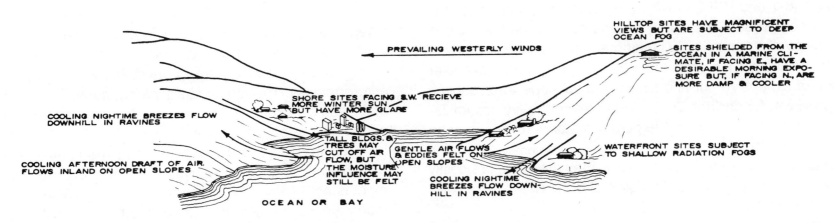

HILLTOP SITES HAVE MAGNIFICENT VIEWS BUT ARE SUBJECT TO DEEP OCEAN FOG

PREVAILING WESTERLY WINDS

SITES SHIELDED FROM THE OCEAN IN A MARINE CLIMATE, IF FACING E., HAVE A DESIRABLE MORNING EXPOSURE BUT, IF FACING N., ARE MORE DAMP & COOLER

SHORE SITES FACING S.W. RECIEVE MORE WINTER SUN BUT HAVE MORE GLARE

COOLING NIGHTTIME BREEZES FLOW DOWNHILL IN RAVINES

TALL BLDGS. & TREES MAY CUT OFF AIR FLOW, BUT THE MOISTURE INFLUENCE MAY STILL BE FELT

GENTLE AIR FLOWS & EDDIES FELT ON OPEN SLOPES

WATERFRONT SITES SUBJECT TO SHALLOW RADIATION FOGS

COOLING AFTERNOON DRAFT OF AIR FLOWS INLAND ON OPEN SLOPES

COOLING NIGHTTIME BREEZES FLOW DOWN-HILL IN RAVINES

OCEAN OR BAY

Shore Homesites

SOURCE: *Landscape Development*
Dept. of the Interior, Littleton, Colo.

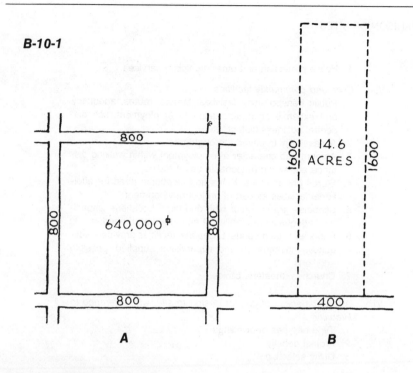

B-10-1

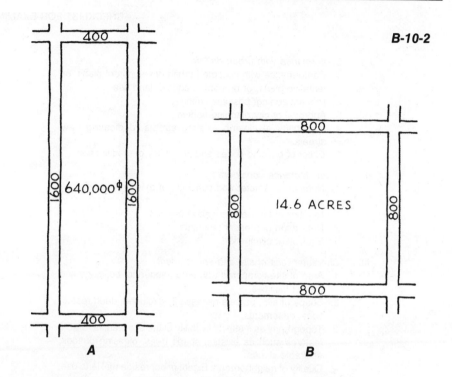

B-10-2

SITE CONFIGURATION

It will be evident from figure B-10-1 that case "A" will afford frontages toward which the building units may be faced, and little road development inside the site will be necessary. Case "B" with a narrow frontage and a depth of almost one-third of a mile, will of necessity require interior roads.

In this connection, it may be stated as a general principle that the narrow and deep site presents problems of site planning similar to the difficulties encountered in planning a single dwelling unit on a narrow and deep lot.

5. *Where surrounding roads must be constructed and paid for directly or by assessment, the site most nearly square is preferable.* This is a simple matter of geometry and is illustrated by figure B-10-2.

6. *Utilities.* The knowledge that utilities are available to a given site is insufficient evidence on which to proceed. The adequacy of such utilities to bear the added loads that will be created by the proposed project must be satisfactorily determined. If water mains and sewers must be replaced, they might as well not be there.

Where access to a sewerage system is not possible and septic tanks are resorted to, the site should be carefully studied to determine that:

(a) There will be an available disposal field of adequate area.

(b) The soil will absorb the outflow water from the tanks.

(c) Public authorities will approve such installation.

7. *Fire Protection.* Careful investigation should be made of the rate of fire insurance. If nonfireproof structures have been contemplated, the sponsors should investigate whether a differential in insurance cost would warrant the adoption of fireproof construction, or whether a different site should be chosen.

B-11 SITE COMPARISON—CHECKLIST

CHECKLIST FOR EXAMINATION AND COMPARISON OF SITES

I. *Conformance with urban pattern*
1. Conformance with accepted urban development plans, or tentative plans, or probable trends in land use.
2. Present zoning: possible changes.
3. Approval of city planning bodies.
4. Possibility of closing existing streets, dedicating new streets.
5. Effect of building codes and possibility of modification.

II. *Slum clearance considerations*
1. Number, character and condition of existing buildings on site.
2. Number of families housed at present.
3. Relocation of present residents.
4. Equivalent elimination.

III. *Characteristics of site and environment*
1. Area of site compared with area needed for buildings and project facilities.
2. Shape of site; parcels necessarily excluded; deed restrictions; easements.
3. Topography as it affects livability of the site plan; favorable features such as existing shade trees, pleasing outlook, desirable slopes.
4. Quality of neighborhood: Extent of nonresidential land use; suitability of neighborhood for dwelling type desired.
5. Effect of project on neighborhood.
6. Hazards: Possibility of flooding, slides or subsidence. Proximity to railroads, high-speed trafficways, high embankments, unprotected bodies of water; presence of insect or rodent breeding places; or high groundwater level that might cause dampness in building.
7. Nuisances: Nearness to industrial plants, railroads, switchyards, heavy-traffic streets, airports, etc., causing noise, smoke, dust, odor, vibrations.

IV. *Availability of special municipal services*
1. Garbage and rubbish collection.
2. Fire protection as affected by site location and street access.
3. Streets: lighting, cleaning, maintenance, snow removal, tree planting and maintenance, etc.
4. Police protection and other municipal services.

V. *Civic and community facilities*
1. Public transportation facilities: Means, routes, adequacy and expense of transportation to employment, schools, central business district, etc.
2. Accessibility to paved thoroughfares.
3. Amount and character of employment within walking distance and within reasonable travel radius.
4. Stores and markets: Kinds and locations; need for additional facilities as part of project development.
5. Schools—grade, junior high and high: Locations, capacities, adequacy; probability of enlargement, if needed.
6. Parks and playgrounds: Locations, facilities provided, adequacy, maintenance and supervision supplied; possible additions.
7. Churches, theaters, clinics.

VI. *Appropriateness of project design to site, with reference to livability*
1. Type or types of dwellings
2. Project density
3. Utility selection

VII. *Elements of project development cost*
1. Land costs, including site acquisition, expense, and unpaid special assessments.
2. Effect of soil conditions, topographic features, project density appropriate to the neighborhood, availability of utilities, extent of existing street improvements, recreational facilities and additions to be provided by municipality or utility companies, etc.
3. Building types, utility selection, site conditions, and requirements for nondwelling structures.

VIII. *Project maintenance and operating costs*
1. Differences in costs of utilities appropriate to the respective sites.
2. Differentials in grounds maintenance costs due to topography.
3. Differences in estimated payments in lieu of taxes.

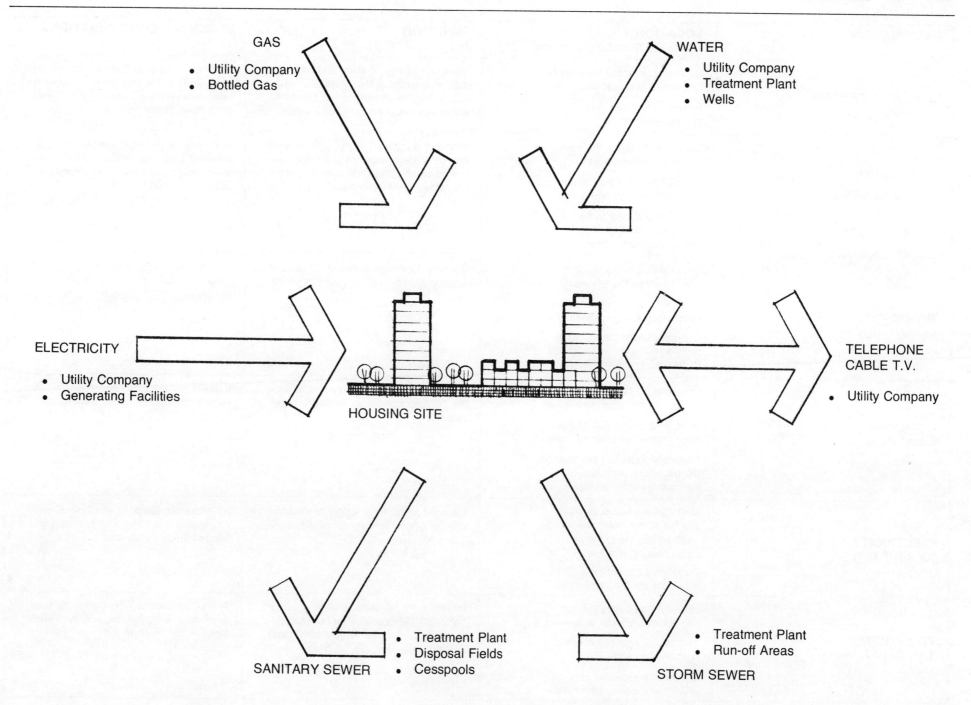

GAS
- Utility Company
- Bottled Gas

WATER
- Utility Company
- Treatment Plant
- Wells

ELECTRICITY
- Utility Company
- Generating Facilities

HOUSING SITE

TELEPHONE
CABLE T.V.
- Utility Company

SANITARY SEWER
- Treatment Plant
- Disposal Fields
- Cesspools

STORM SEWER
- Treatment Plant
- Run-off Areas

B-12 UTILITIES

DESIGNATION	LOCATION Within the Street Right of Way	FUNCTION	PLANNING CONSIDERATIONS
SANITARY SEWERS	Underground below the frost line and all other utilities. Between the water main and the storm sewer.	Intended to carry off water and other liquids containing organic materials, materials subject to decomposition and other waste, but not storm or surface water.	Essential to handle large volume of sewerage; if soil has poor absorption rate, sewers are necessary; local treatment plant can be utilized.
STORM SEWERS	Underground below the frost line and all other utilities. 21 to 22 ft. either side of the street right-of-way center line. Generally adjacent to the curb on narrow streets and under the roadway on wide streets.	Intended to carry off storm, surface, and any other clear water or liquid not containing organic materials or other materials subject to decomposition.	In built-up areas, storm water must be removed from site; in rural or suburban areas, storm water may drain to adjacent streams or lands.
WATER	Underground below the frost line but above the sewers. 20 to 30 ft. either side of the street right-of-way center line. Generally under the sidewalk on narrow streets and adjacent to the curb on wide streets.	Intended to deliver a supply of potable water to a community for public or private use.	An adequate and sustained supply of water is essential to any housing development.
GAS	Underground below the frost line but above water and sewer. 30 to 34 ft. either side of the street right-of-way center line. Generally under the sidewalk on narrow streets and adjacent to the curb on wide streets.	Intended to deliver a supply of combustible gas to a community for public or private use.	If gas is not available, electricity may be substituted; bottled gas is another alternative.
ELECTRICITY (CONDUIT)	Underground below the frost line but above water and sewer. 15 ft. either side of the street right-of-way center line. Generally adjacent to or under the roadway pavement.	Intended to deliver a supply of electrical energy to a community for public or private use.	An adequate source of electricity is critical; source should be able to supply expanded future needs also.
TELEPHONE, T.V. CABLE	Underground below the frost line but above water and sewer. 15 ft. either side of the street right-of-way center line. Generally adjacent to or under the roadway pavement.	Intended to facilitate and maintain a communication network for public or private use on an intra- or intercommunity basis.	These services are becoming increasingly more important; expansion of such facilities can be expected.

CLASSIFICATION	CAUSE	EFFECTS	SOLUTIONS

AIR, SMOKE, AND DUST	Incinerators
	Industry
	Vehicular Traffic
	Refuse Dumps
		Soiling of Property
		Nuisance
		Visibility Reduction
		Corrosion and Other Material
		  Decomposition
		Plant Damage
		Toxic Effects
		Health Hazards
		May Depreciate Property Value
			Use of:
			Cyclones
			Bag Filters
			Electrostatic Precipitators
			Washers, Etc.
			More Efficient Fuels
			Automotive Pollution-control
			  Devices

NOISE	Airports Industry Railroads Recreational Activities Trucks Vehicular Traffic	Nuisance Health Hazards May Depreciate Property Value	Use of: Landscaping as Buffer More Effective Vehicle Noise-control Devices Open-space Separation
ODOR	Disposal Areas Dumps Industry Sewage-treatment Plants Swamps	Nuisance May Indicate Other Air Pollution May Depreciate Property Value	Use of: Good Housekeeping Chemical Control Masking Counteractant Etc.
VISUAL	Buildings in Deteriorated Condition Overhead Wires Signs Poor Landscaping Poor Maintenance	Nuisance May Depreciate Property Value	Use of: Landscaping as Barrier Good Building and Property Maintenance Sensitive Selection of Advertising Graphics Concealment of Utility Lines High Standards of Landscaping

WATER	Industry
	Recreational Uses
	Polluted Streams and Lakes
		Soiling of Property
		Nuisance
		Corrosion and Other Material
		  Decomposition
		Wildlife Damage
		Health Hazards
		May Depreciate Property Value
			Use of:
			Controlled Discharge of
			  Waste and Chemicals

AIR RIGHTS

Air rights are simply rights to use the space above a particular area, without disturbing the primary use of the land itself. The most logical areas that lend themselves to such use are open or one-story uses, such as highways, railroads, streets, parking lots, and low structures.

Such use enables the land to be fully utilized. It brings a greater return to the owner and provides greater concentration of development.

In a time when land is becoming increasingly scarce, especially in urban areas, the use of air rights provides an important source of sites. In most cases, the uses will be different and the question of compatibility arises. Care must be taken to protect the individual functions so that they do not interfere with each other.

In recent years, by utilizing air rights, housing has been constructed or proposed over freeways, railroads, schools and commercial development.

From a planning standpoint, the utilization of such air rights would provide additional opportunity for necessary development in the community. It could provide greater concentration and efficient functional relationship of the different uses. Such air rights would also make property more valuable and thereby increase taxes on these properties.

Air rights would enable some community development to occur vertically rather than constantly to seek new horizontal expansion.

OVER HIGHWAYS

OVER RAILROADS

OVER INDUSTRIAL PLANTS

OVER SCHOOLS, POST OFFICES, ETC.

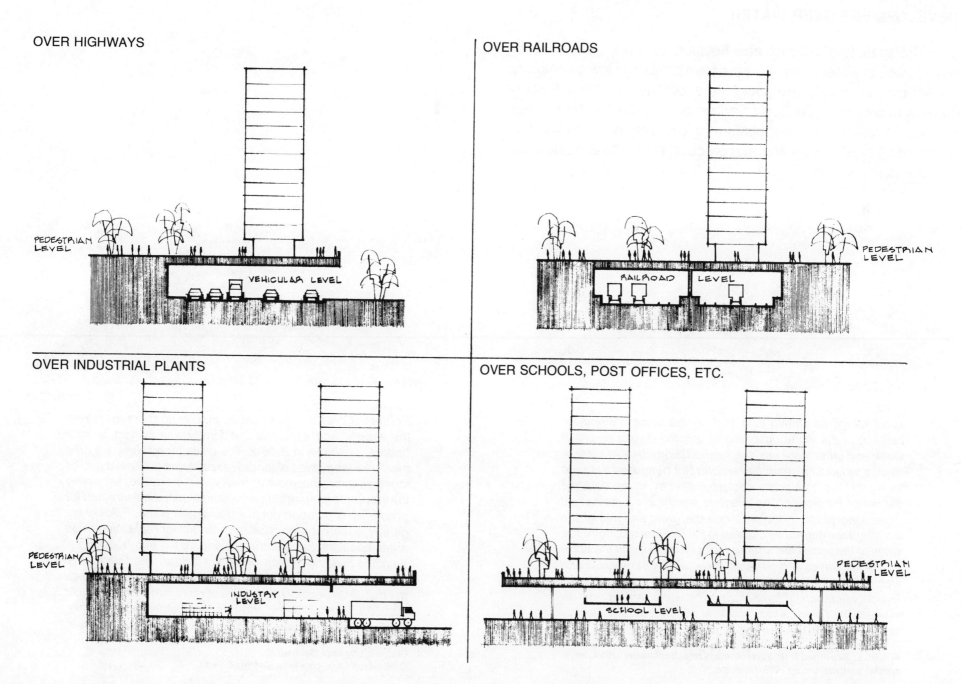

DEVELOPMENT OVER WATER

The scarcity of land for new housing sites has led to building over bodies of water. This takes the form of filling in low swamp and marshlands or simply extending the shoreline out into a body of water with proper fill. Recently, various proposals have been made that would create sufficient platform areas over water to build an entire city. Illustrated are the four practical methods as to how this can be achieved.

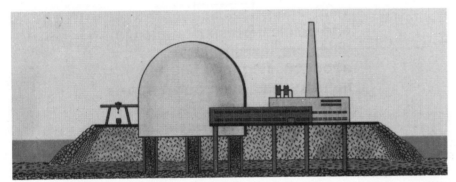

B-15-1

Land filing, as shown in B-15-1, is the basic method for building in the water. Involving simply the displacement of water and other materials, this method is practical at shallow depths when fill is readily available. But because fill is paid for by the cubic yard, the cost rises directly as the depth of the water increases. The island is used for a hypothetical generating plant; in this instance the great weights of the buildings are carried by caisson to the firm underbottom. The sides of the island are armored with stone to resist the abrasion of the waves and currents. An actual sixteen-acre island was built by Detroit Edison Co. for a power plant at Harbor Beach, Michigan, in Lake Huron. The water ranges from six to twenty feet deep, a very practical depth for fill. A protective breakwater runs behind the island.

SOURCE: Reprinted from *Fortune* magazine, September, 1969, by special permission; © 1969 Time, Inc.

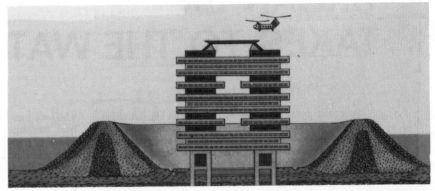

B-15-2

Polders of dry land are made by putting up dikes to restrain the waters, and exposing the former sea bottom or lake bottom, as shown in B-15-2. The dikes themselves are built much like long strips of landfill, except that they must be put together somewhat more carefully, with an eye to restraining the inevitable seepage. This seepage, sometimes treated for pollutants, is pumped out along with rain water. Polders are generally more economical than landfill for reclaiming large areas because less material is used. In the above example, an office building stands within the polder. The Dutch have seized more than 1,600,000 acres of land from the sea since the thirteenth century and today are reclaiming land for about $2,000 per acre. So far, the deepest polder in the Netherlands, near Rotterdam, is twenty-one feet below sea level.

Diagrams by Max Gschwind,
O. Winston Link, courtesy, Detroit Edison

B-15-3

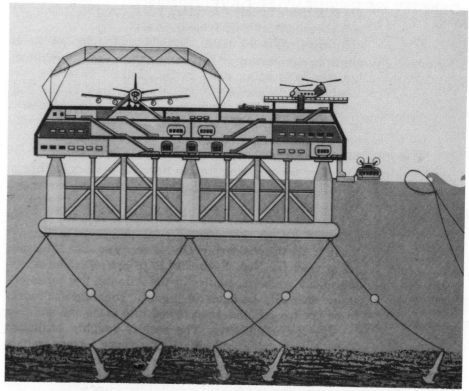

B-15-4

Piles are used to support many water structures, from the wooden poles on which most of Venice rests to the gigantic steel legs that support offshore oil-drilling platforms. Piles are made also of concrete, but whatever their material, they must be driven into firm bottom soil if, as in B-15-3, they are intended to hold up any kind of permanent structure. Piling has two important advantages over the methods shown on the preceding page. Structures can be erected at greater practical depths and instead of blocking normal water currents, they permit them to pass underneath. The deepest known fixed piling installation is an oil platform in 340 feet of water in the Gulf of Mexico. Freeport Sulphur Co.'s Caminada mine is located six miles off the Louisiana shore in fifty feet of water. A heated, insulated underwater pipeline was trenched into the Gulf floor to carry the molten sulphur to the mainland.

Floating structures have been designed to support airports as shown in B-15-4, oil rigs and housing projects. The most flexible form of building on water, floats can be moored at varying depths without increasing their cost and can be moved from one location to another. As a rule, floating structures cost more than other methods of building on water. They must be even stronger than most ships because they are not intended to ride with the force of the waves, but to resist it. B-15-4 illustrates two methods of improving seaworthiness. First, the flotation chambers that make the airport buoyant are submerged so that they will be below the greatest turbulence in storms, permitting waves to pass through a fairly open framework. Second, a protective breakwater of large bags, partially filled with water, is moored around the airport to absorb some of the force of the waves.

DENSITY OF RESIDENTIAL DEVELOPMENT

This section deals with selected methods of measuring the density of development within residential areas of a neighborhood, and of determining proper limits for such density.

Governing Criteria for Density

The intensity of land use should not be so great as to cause congestion of buildings or to preclude the amenities of good housing. Specifically, densities should be limited to provide:

a) adequate daylight, sunlight, air and usable open space for all dwellings;

b) adequate space for all community facilities;

c) a general feeling of openness and privacy.

Densities should have a reasonable relationship to land and improvement costs. Two types of density measurement are needed:

1) density measures for residential areas of the neighborhood (called residential or dwelling densities) to insure adequate open space, light and air for residential facilities;

2) density measures for the entire neighborhood (termed neighborhood densities), taking all land uses into account, to insure provision of adequate community facilities in relation to population load.

Site Planning Characteristics Reflected by Residential Density

The importance of density measurement as a planning tool arises from the fact that densities reflect with a certain degree of accuracy important characteristics of site planning. Densities show the crowding of people and structures on the land and the amount of open space available to the families. For example, the percent of land covered by buildings reflects in general the amount of open space available for gardens, children's play, outdoor living, the drying of laundry and the like.

Since densities bear an obvious relation to the spacing of buildings and their height, another important factor is measured by densities, namely the approximate amount of light and air admitted to dwellings.

Density standards are useful as a guide for preliminary design schemes, and for estimating population loads and required areas of land. Density measurements provide a uniform and objective method of comparison of site plans for general openness, amenity and livability.

Density standards have major value as controls in zoning ordinances, subdivision regulations and the like. Proper standards, carried out through competent design, give assurance that land crowding, encroachments on daylight and similar blight-inducing factors will be controlled.

It must be recognized that density figures, no matter how accurately computed, are but a crude index of the design quality of a site plan. Being rigid mathematical ratios for relatively large areas, they cannot properly reflect all factors of design. For example, suitable average densities for large tracts of land will not necessarily insure that buildings are not crowded together in some parts of the development area. The amount of open space established by density standards has limited meaning unless that space is properly distributed and designed for usability.

Good design practice can provide adequate open space for all outdoor functions of family life at relatively high densities. On the other hand, poor site planning may create land crowding and lack of usable open space even at low densities. In addition to meeting density standards, therefore, residential areas must also comply with all standards for spacing of structures, orientation and other features of site layout.

M. Paul Friedberg & Associates

Measures of Density

The intensity of residential use can be expressed by different types of density calculations, showing mathematical relationships between the area of a given piece of land and the population load or building bulk. Area measurements are usually given in acres, population load as number of persons or families, and building bulk in terms of ground area covered or total floor area. Thus, for example, population density is expressed as the number of persons (or families) per acre of land, or as acres of land per 1,000 persons, and dwelling density as the number of dwelling units per acre of land or as the number of acres (or square feet) of land per dwelling unit.

A complete discussion of the many methods of density measurement used for planning or regulatory purposes is beyond the scope of this book. A limited number of density factors relating to residential land use have been selected for further discussion on the basis that they seem to best reflect the characteristics of the site plan.

Net Dwelling Density: the number of dwelling units per acre of net residential land (land devoted to residential buildings and accessory uses on the same lots, such as informal open space, drives and service areas, but excluding land for streets, public parking, playgrounds and nonresidential buildings).[1]

Building Coverage: the proportion of net or gross residential land taken up by buildings.

Building Bulk (floor area ratio): the total floor area of all stories used for residential purposes, divided by the area of residential land.

Application of each of these measures of residential density is discussed in later paragraphs of this section.

Useful as they are in planning residential land, residential densities are not an adequate measure of land use in the neighborhood as a whole. Requirements as to light and air, for instance, can be met in terms of residential densities that may still overtax the available schools, playgrounds, streets or other community facilities. The building up of one tract after another on the basis of maximum residential densities alone, without regard for these neighborhood elements, will lead to most serious land crowding.

A further type of density measurement is therefore needed: *Neighborhood Density:* the number of dwelling units per acre of total neighborhood land (new residential land plus streets and land used for schools, recreation, shopping and other neighborhood community purposes).[2]

In addition to residential densities discussed in this chapter, neighborhood density standards must be met in order not to overload playgrounds, schools, and other community-, district- or city-wide facilities.

Net Dwelling Densities: Basis of Calculation

B-16-1 gives recommended area (net residential land) allowances per family with the various dwelling types.

For one- and two-family dwellings, only the recommended total lot area is shown. This is based on the sizes assumed below:

Dwelling Type	Lot size or equivalent (feet)	Net residential area per family (square feet)
a) One-family detached	60 x 100	6,000
b1) One-family semidetached	80 x 100 for two families	4,000
b2) Two-family detached	80 x 100 for two families	4,000
c1) One-family attached (row)	20 x 100 plus 40-foot side yard between each 10 units*	2,400
c2) Two-family semidetached	48 x 100 for two families	2,400

*Figures are for two-story, 25 foot minimum lot width is recommended.

---

[1]Gross dwelling density, a measurement much used in the past, is not employed in this section. Gross density is the number of dwelling units per acre of gross residential land (land as described above, plus bordering streets up to limited distances—ordinarily to the center of the street).

It is one purpose of this book to encourage replacement of the gross dwelling density concept by that of overall neighborhood density.

[2]Neighborhood land excludes nonneighborhood uses and unusable land within the neighborhood boundaries.

For multifamily dwellings, total land area is derived from its component parts: 1) area covered by buildings, 2) outdoor living space, 3) area for service, laundry drying, walks and setbacks, 4) off-street residential parking areas. These together constitute the net residential land area.

The area covered by multifamily buildings has been assumed on the basis of floor area allowances per family under normal contemporary design and construction practice, as shown below. Total floor area of buildings (including shared circulation space) is divided by the number of stories per building. Gross floor area per family is assumed to increase as height increases, because of the need for added interior service and circulation space.

Height of Building (stories)	Assumed Gross Floor Area (Square feet)	Area covered by Building—(Sq.Ft.)
2	870 per family	435 per family
3	870 per family	290 per family
6	870 per family	145 per family
9	945 per family	105 per family
13	945 per family	75 per family (approx)

Since floor areas may vary with local design practice for various types of multifamily dwellings, the figures above should be adjusted where necessary. The effect of such adjustments on B-16-1 and later tables should then be checked before these are applied to local plan solutions.

Allowances for outdoor living space in B-16-1 are based on established standards, and should be complied with. Areas for service, walks, setbacks and off-street parking are the most difficult to assess. The figures shown are based on generally accepted servicing and layout practice for different dwelling types. Off-street parking is calculated at 240 square feet per car, with 1/2 to 2/3 car per family (in multiple dwellings).

It is recognized that the figures given can serve only as a guide and that satisfactory design solutions may be achieved with different area allowances.

Net Dwelling Densities: One- and Two-Family Houses

B-16-2 translates the above lot sizes and other net residential area requirements into recommended net dwelling densities for one-, two- and multifamily dwellings.

Recommended lot sizes for one- and two-family houses will result in maximum densities of 7 units per net acre of residential land for detached one-family houses, and 12 units per acre for semidetached houses of this type. One-family row houses should not normally exceed 19 dwellings per net acre. Although higher densities for these dwelling types may be compatible with standards for light and air, it is doubtful whether densities beyond these maxima will permit sufficient flexibility in design to insure privacy and other amenities that should be obtained with one- and two-family dwellings.[3]

Although the above dwelling densities are approved as standard, lower densities (shown in B-16-2) should be the goal, especially in an unfavorable location. They will permit flexibility in site layout where poor topography reduces the amount of usable space attached to the house, or where larger than normal setbacks are needed for noise reduction. Lower densities are also desirable to permit increased lot widths for privacy.

Net Dwelling Densities: Multifamily Buildings

Apartment layout makes possible the shared use of service areas, approaches, playlots and other residential land by a number of families and thereby permits some reduction of area allowances per family as compared to layouts in individual lots. Greater sharing of outdoor areas is possible as the number of families increases.

[3]For instance, spacing standards for sunlight may require a minimum distance between facing rows of buildings of two times the height of the building. For one-story buildings this might permit a minimum of 20 feet between buildings. Yet 20 feet is too little to give an adequate sense of space or privacy in backyards, and cannot be considered acceptable.

B-16-1. ALLOCATION OF NET RESIDENTIAL LAND TO MAJOR DWELLING USES
Recommended Allowance per Family, by Dwelling Type and by Component Uses[a]

	Land Area: Square Feet Per Family[b]				
Dwelling Type	Total	Covered by Buildings	Outdoor Living[c]	Service, Walks and Setback	Off-Street Parking
One- and Two-Family (Individual Access and Services)					
1-family detached............................	6,000	varies	within	lot	area
1-family semidetached or 2-family detached }	4,000	varies	within	lot	area
1-family attached (row) or 2-family semidetached }	2,400	varies	within	lot	area
Mutifamily (Common Access and Services)					
2-story....................................	1,465	435	415	455	160
3-story....................................	985	290	315	220	160
6-story....................................	570	145	215	50	160
9-story....................................	515	105	215	35	160
13-story..................................	450	75	215	35	125

[a]The standards of this table apply only to net residential land. Plans for a development must comply, in addition, with neighborhood density standards for streets and community facilities.

[b]For basis of allowance, see text: Net Dwelling Densities: Basis of Calculation.

[c]Including playlot for small children.

Therefore, space allowances per family can be decreased somewhat for taller apartments housing a more concentrated population, without impairing livability.

It should also be remembered that the more stories a building has, the less ground area per family is covered by the building. Assuming, for instance, the same floor area for each family, a six-story apartment housing *x* families will cover only one-half of the ground covered by two three-story buildings housing (together) the

SOURCE: *Planning the Neighborhood*, by the American Public Health Association Committee on the Hygiene of Housing Public Administration Service, Chicago, Ill. 1960

B-16-2. NET DWELLING DENSITIES AND BUILDING COVERAGE
Recommended Standard Values, by Dwelling Type[a]

	Net Dwelling Density		Net Building Coverage
Dwelling Type	(Units per Acre of Net Residential Land)		(Percent of Net Residential Land Built Over)
	Standard: Desirable	Standard: Maximum	Standard: Maximum
One- and Two-Family			
1-family detached................	5	7	0
1-family semidetached or 2-family detached }	10	12	0
1-family attached (row) or 2-family semidetached }	16	19	30
Multifamily			
2-story	25	30	30
3-story	40	45	30
6-story	65	75	25
9-story	75	85	20
13-story	85	95	17

[a]In addition to meeting the standards of this table, plans for a development must comply with neighborhood density standards for streets and community facilities.

same number of families. These considerations permitting higher densities as the number of stories increases, without detriment to health or amenity, are reflected in the figures of B-16-2.

Densities of multifamily buildings should be kept within the desirable range of the table: from 25 units per net residential acre for two-story apartments to 85 dwellings per net residential acre for thirteen-story elevator apartments. Although somewhat higher densities may be attainable, it is doubtful whether satisfactory site layouts meeting all standards can be devised except under especially favorable conditions. In no case should net dwelling densities exceed the maximum figure shown in B-16-2.

Net Dwelling Densities in Relation to Population Densities

Dwelling densities have the limitation that they do not measure the exact population load on residential land. The number of persons per room is likely to decrease, and floor area per person is likely to increase, from low- to high-income families. If the dwelling count is to represent the actual population load, both the dwelling sizes (number of rooms per dwelling) and occupancy condition (number of persons per room) must be taken into account.

As far as housing environment is concerned, the number of persons per acre is particularly useful as an index of the population load on the various community facilities. For this reason, standards for population density are most usefully applied on a neighborhoodwide basis. However, population load has a direct effect on the amount of residential land required for multiple dwellings. Net population densities, therefore, are useful as a guide to residential land area requirements in multiple dwelling developments.[4] There has not been sufficient research to determine the exact population densities that conform to the required amount of usable open space. Population densities should under no circumstances be so high that the outdoor residential space requirements cannot be met.

Building Coverage

Building coverage is the proportion of net or gross residential land area taken up by buildings. Thus, for instance, 40 percent net coverage means that 40 percent of the residential land area is covered by buildings, leaving 60 percent in open land for residential outdoor uses.

While building coverage bears an obvious relationship to popu-

[4]Population density for new developments may be approximated by multiplying the net dwelling density by the average size of family (based on proposed dwelling size).

lation density, it is, nonetheless, a separate matter that must be considered on its own merits. Even if, by using low buildings, a low density is maintained, it is obvious that if these buildings cover too large a percentage of the land, insufficient outdoor space will remain for various uses conducive to health, and this lack of space may also result in inadequate arrangements for circulation.

Figures for building coverage are more tangible standards than those described for light and air and for other criteria that would affect building spacing, and are, therefore, useful in municipal regulation. However, such figures are a means of achieving an end, rather than the end itself. Poorly located buildings covering only 25 percent of the net residential land may easily admit less light to living and sleeping rooms than well-designed ones with 35 percent coverage. Coverage and height are closely interrelated, and can only be established in the process of design. At the present time, 20 percent to 30 percent coverage of land within property lines appears to be practical and to permit conformity with standards for light, air and open spaces. Controls that set maximum net coverages exceeding 35 percent may fail to provide sufficient open space and may lead to overcrowding of people on the land.

In our opinion, no designs for arrangement of multiple dwellings have yet been published that provide for adequate sunlight (at least in latitudes of the temperate zone) and at the same time show net building coverage in excess of 40 percent. The lower values in B-16-2 are believed in line with progressive current practice.

Net building coverage by itself is the crudest measure of residential density, and, unless it is related to building height and population density, it measures no more than the approximate overall amount of outdoor space available for gardens, children's play, adults' recreation, laundry drying, driveways, private garages, etc. The usability of outdoor space will depend on its good design, and the amount of space available to each family will depend on the population load put on the land.

Building Bulk (Floor Area Ratio)

The measurement of building bulk in terms of "floor area ratios" has been found so useful as a density control that it is being applied increasingly by planners both in the United States and Britain. The floor area ratio is a comparatively recent concept that requires a clear understanding.

Floor area ratio is the total floor area of all stories[5] used for residential purposes, divided by the area of residential land.

For example, a floor area ratio of 1.00 means that the combined floor area of buildings equals the residential land area. This corresponds to a building coverage of 25 percent by four-story buildings or a coverage of 50 percent by two-story buildings. A floor area ratio of 1.20 may mean that 30 percent of the area of the land is covered by four-story structures, or that 15 percent of the land is covered by eight-story structures.

Although in current zoning ordinances floor area ratios refer to net residential area, figures for floor area ratios are given here in relation to gross residential site areas (including land for streets), because, from the point of view of spacing buildings for sunlight and daylight penetration, it does not make any difference whether streets occupy some of the intervening open spaces.

Because floor area ratio establishes a mathematical relation between the land area, the floor area of the building and its height, it is considered among the most accurate indices for adequacy of light and air.[6] This becomes clear when floor area ratio is related to the spacing of buildings and their height. If, for instance, parallel rows of six-story buildings are spaced two and one-half times their height to permit proper sunlight admission, the floor area ratio must be approximately 1.14 with normal story height and depth of building.[7]

Based on similar computations, floor area ratios required to enable rows of buildings of different height to be spaced two and one-half times their height will range from 0.86 for three-story apartments[8] to 1.27 for nine-story elevator apartments. Apartments of thirteen stories will require a floor area ratio of 1.34.

If the above floor area ratios are used as density controls, they will generally assure adequate admission of sunshine, daylight and air to dwellings. However, residential areas should also meet standards for dwelling densities based on usability of residential land, and they must also comply with neighborhood densities.

It should also be noted that floor area ratios do not reflect population densities, because floor area per person varies (usually increasing as income increases). In order to measure population loads, an additional index of floor area per person should be used. This makes it impossible to relate density in terms of floor area ratios to population density.

---

[6]The mathematical relationship of floor area ratio to building coverage and height is expressed by the following formula:

$$F = \frac{G \times S}{L} = B \times S$$

F=Floor Area Ratio
G=Ground Area of Building
S=Number of Stories
L=Area of Land
B=Building Coverage (ground area of building divided by area of land)

[7]Assuming a 10-foot story height, the distance between buildings will be 2-1/2 x 60 feet equals 150 feet. If, furthermore, the buildings are assumed to be 35 feet deep, their coverage will be 35/185 or 19 percent. The floor area ratio will be the coverage times number of stories or 0.19 x 6 equals 1.14.

[8]Assumed height of stories: 10 feet per story for first six stories; 85 feet for nine stories; 122 feet for thirteen stories. Assumed depth of buildings: 35 feet.

---

[5]The ground area of the building multiplied by the number of stories gives the total floor area (except where there are setbacks in upper stories). For instance, the total floor area of a two-story building covering 800 square feet of ground is 1,600 square feet (2 x 800). For a four-story building having the same ground area of 800 square feet, the total floor area of all stories is 3,200 square feet (4 x 800).

Density Ranges

HOUSING TYPE	DENSITY IN DWELLING UNITS PER ACRE

Density axis markers: 5 10 15 20 25 30 35 40 45 50 55 60 65 70 75 80 85 90 95 100 105 110 115 120 125 130 135

Housing Type	Approximate Density Range (dwelling units per acre)
One- and Two-Family	
1-Family Detached	~5
1-Family Semidetached	~10
1-Family Attached	~15
2-Family Detached	~10
2-Family Semidetached	~15
Multifamily	
2 Story (Garden Apts.)	~25–30
3 Story	~40–45
6 Story	~65–75
9 Story	~75–85
13 Story	~85–95
18 Story	~95–105
24 Story	~105–115
25 Story and Over	

NOTE: All densities indicated are approximate
and should be used as a guide only.

B-18 DENSITY MEASURES

	AREA USER UNIT	PER UNIT OF LAND					OR	UNIT OF DWELLING AREA		
		Gross	Net	Open	Public	Private	Room	Dwelling Unit	Residential Floor Area	Lot Area
POPULATION										
Individuals	Persons	Acre	Acre	Acre	Acre	Acre	Room	Dwelling Unit	Sq. Ft.	Sq. Ft.
Families	Families	Acre	Acre	Acre	Acre	Acre	Room	Dwelling Unit	Sq. Ft.	Sq. Ft.
Households	Households	Acre	Acre	Acre	Acre	Acre	Room	Dwelling Unit	Sq. Ft.	Sq. Ft.
Permanent Residents	Residents	Acre	Acre	Acre	Acre	Acre	Room	Dwelling Unit	Sq. Ft.	Sq. Ft.
Temporary Residents	Transients	Acre	Acre	Acre	Acre	Acre	Room	Dwelling Unit	Sq. Ft.	Sq. Ft.
Temporary Residents	Daytime Users	Acre	Acre	Acre	Acre	Acre	Room	Dwelling Unit	Sq. Ft.	Sq. Ft.
Temporary Residents	Nighttime Users	Acre	Acre	Acre	Acre	Acre	Room	Dwelling Unit	Sq. Ft.	Sq. Ft.
Temporary Residents	Summer Users	Acre	Acre	Acre	Acre	Acre	Room	Dwelling Unit	Sq. Ft.	Sq. Ft.
Users According to Sex	Males	Acre	Acre	Acre	Acre	Acre	Room	Dwelling Unit	Sq. Ft.	Sq. Ft.
Users According to Sex	Females	Acre	Acre	Acre	Acre	Acre	Room	Dwelling Unit	Sq. Ft.	Sq. Ft.
AGE										
Preschool	Preschool-age Persons	Acre	Acre	Acre	Acre	Acre	Room	Dwelling Unit	Sq. Ft.	Sq. Ft.
School	School-age Persons	Acre	Acre	Acre	Acre	Acre	Room	Dwelling Unit	Sq. Ft.	Sq. Ft.
Elderly	Elderly Persons	Acre	Acre	Acre	Acre	Acre	Room	Dwelling Unit	Sq. Ft.	Sq. Ft.
ECONOMIC										
Occupation	Occupation Group (Doctors, Lawyers, etc.)	Acre	Acre	Acre	Acre	Acre	Room	Dwelling Unit	Sq. Ft.	Sq. Ft.
Employment Status	Employment Group (Blue-Collar Worker, etc.)	Acre	Acre	Acre	Acre	Acre	Room	Dwelling Unit	Sq. Ft.	Sq. Ft.
Income Level	Annual Income ($5,000, $10,000, etc.)	Acre	Acre	Acre	Acre	Acre	Room	Dwelling Unit	Sq. Ft.	Sq. Ft.
Homeowner	Homeowners	Acre	Acre	Acre	Acre	Acre	Room	Dwelling Unit	Sq. Ft.	Sq. Ft.
Tenant	Tenants	Acre	Acre	Acre	Acre	Acre	Room	Dwelling Unit	Sq. Ft.	Sq. Ft.
CULTURAL										
Ethnic Background	Descendant Group (Italians, Irish, etc.)	Acre	Acre	Acre	Acre	Acre				
Educational Level	Max. Ed. Attainment (High School Grads, etc.)	Acre	Acre	Acre	Acre	Acre				

Persons per Acre

No. of Persons	AREA IN ACRES					
	1/8	1/4	1/2	3/4	1	2
1	8	4	2	1.5	1	0.5
3	24	12	6	4.5	3	1.5
5	40	20	10	7.5	5	2.5
10	80	40	20	15	10	5
20	160	80	40	30	20	10
30	240	120	60	45	30	15
40	320	160	80	60	40	20
50	400	200	100	75	50	25
60	480	240	120	90	60	30
70	560	280	140	105	70	35
80	640	320	160	120	80	40
90	720	360	180	135	90	45
100	800	400	200	150	100	50
150	1200	600	300	225	150	75
200	1600	800	400	300	200	100

NOTE: To obtain number of families, divide by the number of persons in the average family in the community.

Families per Acre

No. of Families	AREA IN ACRES					
	1/8	1/4	1/2	3/4	1	2
1	8	4	2	1.5	1	0.5
3	24	12	6	4.5	3	1.5
5	40	20	10	7.5	5	2.5
10	80	40	20	15	10	5
20	160	80	40	30	20	10
30	240	120	60	45	30	15
40	320	160	80	60	40	20
50	400	200	100	75	50	25
60	480	240	120	90	60	30
70	560	280	140	105	70	35
80	640	320	160	120	80	40
90	720	360	180	135	90	45
100	800	400	200	150	100	50
150	1200	600	300	225	150	75
200	1600	800	400	300	200	100

NOTE: To obtain total number of persons, multiply by the average number of persons in the family.

Density Related to Lot Sizes

EFFECT OF VARIATION OF GROSS AND NET DENSITY ON THE OPEN SPACE STANDARD

Allocation of Column 4 between Housing and Open Space for various net densities in rooms per acre (Occupancy Rate–0.89)

Column a - acres of net residential area per 1,000 persons   Column b - acres of open space per 1,000 persons

Gross Density (persons per acre)	Land Area (acres per 1,000 persons)	Deduction for Schools, Shops, Roads, etc. (acres per 1,000 persons)	Balance available for Housing and Open Space (acres per 1,000 persons)	20 rooms per acre a	b	25 rooms per acre a	b	30 rooms per acre a	b	40 rooms per acre a	b	50 rooms per acre a	b	60 rooms per acre a	b	70 rooms per acre a	b	80 rooms per acre a	b	90 rooms per acre a	b	100 rooms per acre a	b	120 rooms per acre a	b	140 rooms per acre a	b	160 rooms per acre a	b	180 rooms per acre a	b	200 rooms per acre a	b
1	2	3	4	a	b	a	b	a	b	a	b	a	b	a	b	a	b	a	b	a	b	a	b	a	b	a	b	a	b	a	b	a	b
10	100.0	9.1	90.9	56.0	34.9	45.0	45.9	37.4	53.5	28.0	62.9	22.4	68.5	18.7	72.2	16.0	74.9	14.0	76.9	12.5	78.4	11.2	79.7	9.4	81.5	8.0	82.9	7.0	83.9	6.2	84.7	5.6	85.3
15	66.6	8.3	58.3			45.0	13.3	37.4	20.9	28.0	30.3	22.4	35.9	18.7	39.6	16.0	42.3	14.0	44.3	12.5	45.8	11.2	47.1	9.4	48.9	8.0	50.3	7.0	51.3	6.2	52.1	5.6	52.7
20	50.0	7.5	42.5					37.4	5.1	28.0	14.5	22.4	20.1	18.7	23.8	16.0	26.5	14.0	28.5	12.5	30.0	11.2	31.3	9.4	33.1	8.0	34.5	7.0	35.5	6.2	36.3	5.6	36.9
25	40.0	6.7	33.3							28.0	5.3	22.4	10.9	18.7	14.6	16.0	17.3	14.0	19.3	12.5	20.8	11.2	22.1	9.4	23.9	8.0	25.3	7.0	26.3	6.2	27.1	5.6	27.7
30	33.3	6.0	27.3									22.4	4.9	18.7	8.6	16.0	11.3	14.0	13.3	12.5	14.8	11.2	16.1	9.4	17.9	8.0	19.3	7.0	20.3	6.2	21.1	5.6	21.7
35	28.6	5.6	23.0											18.7	4.3	16.0	7.0	14.0	9.0	12.5	10.5	11.2	11.8	9.4	13.6	8.0	15.0	7.0	16.0	6.2	16.8	5.6	17.4
40	25.0	5.1	19.9													16.0	3.9	14.0	5.9	12.5	7.4	11.2	8.7	9.4	10.5	8.0	11.9	7.0	12.9	6.2	13.7	5.6	14.3
45	22.2	4.8	17.4															14.0	3.4	12.5	4.9	11.2	6.2	9.4	8.0	8.0	9.4	7.0	10.4	6.2	11.2	5.6	11.8
50	20.0	4.5	15.5																	12.5	3.0	11.2	4.3	9.4	6.1	8.0	7.5	7.0	8.5	6.2	9.3	5.6	9.9
55	18.2	4.2	14.0																			11.2	2.8	9.4	4.6	8.0	6.0	7.0	7.0	6.2	7.8	5.6	8.4
60	16.6	4.1	12.5																					9.4	3.2	8.0	4.5	7.0	5.5	6.2	6.3	5.6	6.9
65	15.4	3.9	11.5																							8.0	3.5	7.0	4.5	6.2	5.3	5.6	5.9
70	14.2	3.7	10.5																									7.0	3.5	6.2	4.3	5.6	4.9

*Sample Procedure for Determination of Land Use
Intensity, Floor and Building Areas, and Car Data*

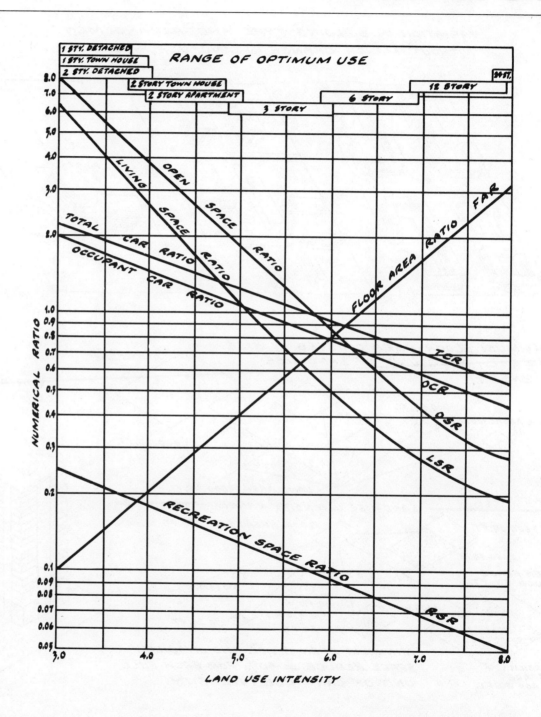

RANGE OF OPTIMUM USE

1 STY. DETACHED
1 STY. TOWN HOUSE
2 STY. DETACHED
2 STORY TOWN HOUSE
2 STORY APARTMENT
3 STORY
6 STORY
12 STORY
24 ST.

LIVING OPEN SPACE SPACE RATIO RATIO

TOTAL CAR RATIO

OCCUPANT CAR RATIO

FLOOR AREA RATIO FAR

TCR
OCR
OSR
LSR

RECREATION SPACE RATIO

RSR

NUMERICAL RATIO

LAND USE INTENSITY

SOURCE: *Design Manual–Family Housing*
Naval Facilities Engineering Command
Dept. of the Navy, Wash., D.C. 1967

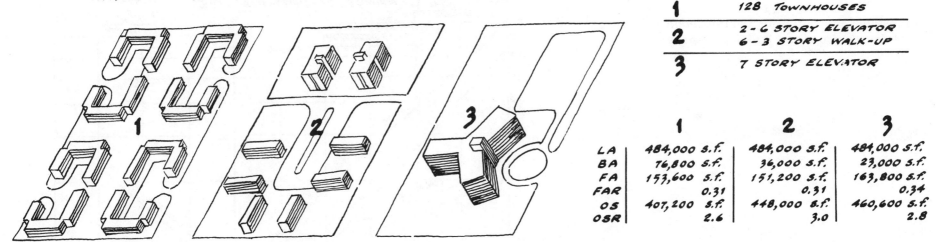

VARIATION IN BUILDING TYPE AND ARRANGEMENT
WITHOUT MAJOR CHANGE IN LAND-USE INTENSITY

1	128 TOWNHOUSES
2	2-6 STORY ELEVATOR 6-3 STORY WALK-UP
3	7 STORY ELEVATOR

	1	2	3
LA	484,000 s.f.	484,000 s.f.	484,000 s.f.
BA	76,800 s.f.	36,000 s.f.	23,000 s.f.
FA	153,600 s.f.	151,200 s.f.	163,800 s.f.
FAR	0.31	0.31	0.34
OS	407,200 s.f.	448,000 s.f.	460,600 s.f.
OSR	2.6	3.0	2.8

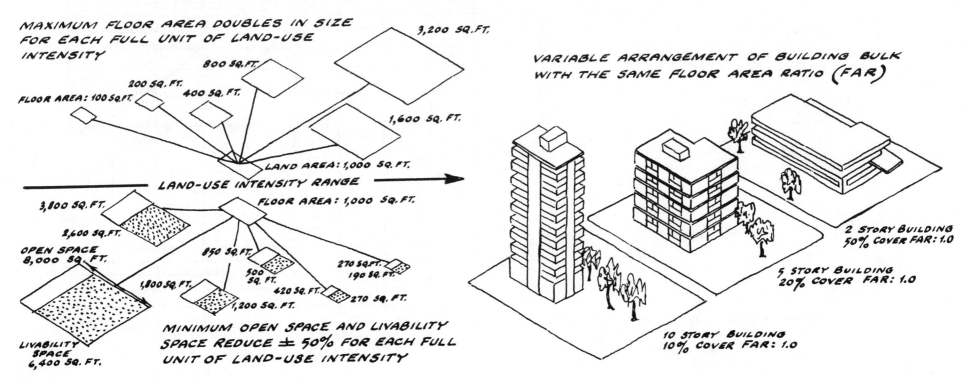

MAXIMUM FLOOR AREA DOUBLES IN SIZE
FOR EACH FULL UNIT OF LAND-USE
INTENSITY

3,200 SQ.FT.

800 SQ.FT.

200 SQ.FT.

400 SQ.FT.

FLOOR AREA: 100 SQ.FT.

1,600 SQ.FT.

LAND AREA: 1,000 SQ.FT.

LAND-USE INTENSITY RANGE →

FLOOR AREA: 1,000 SQ.FT.

3,800 SQ.FT.

2,600 SQ.FT.

OPEN SPACE
8,000 SQ.FT.

850 SQ.FT.

500 SQ.FT.

270 SQ.FT.
190 SQ.FT.

1,800 SQ.FT.

420 SQ.FT.

270 SQ.FT.

1,200 SQ.FT.

LIVABILITY
SPACE
6,400 SQ.FT.

MINIMUM OPEN SPACE AND LIVABILITY
SPACE REDUCE ± 50% FOR EACH FULL
UNIT OF LAND-USE INTENSITY

VARIABLE ARRANGEMENT OF BUILDING BULK
WITH THE SAME FLOOR AREA RATIO (FAR)

2 STORY BUILDING
50% COVER FAR: 1.0

5 STORY BUILDING
20% COVER FAR: 1.0

10 STORY BUILDING
10% COVER FAR: 1.0

LAND-USE INTENSITY

Definition of Terms

The definitions in this paragraph apply to terms used in LUI calculations. Under 4 and 6 below, read "outside faces of exterior walls" instead of "faces of exterior walls."

"1. Unusable Land. Land not beneficial to residential use due to location or character such as swamps, drainage ditches, ravines, dense woods, and swales, and utility strips when their presence renders land unusable for residential use.

"2. Nonresidential Land. Land used for such purposes as maintenance buildings, fire stations and community-use facilities such as swimming pools, baseball diamonds, tennis courts, or other developed sports areas. Boundaries for these facilities shall be established at exterior wall or fence faces or at the surfaced limits of parking or storage areas.

"3. Residential Land Area. Area within project boundaries, excluding unusable land and nonresidential land.

"4. Floor Area. The sum of area for residential use on the several floors of a living unit measured from the faces of the exterior walls; the floor area including halls, lobbies, stairways, and elevator shafts, interior storage areas, and the basement or lowest story to extent used for residential purposes. The floor area does not include relatively open exterior balconies, any garages or carports or any area used for mechanical equipment.

"5. Building Area. Consists of the floor area at ground level of all buildings occupying space within the residential land area. Included are any enclosed storage facilities, enclosed trash/garbage storage areas, garages, carports, whether partially or entirely open, covered porches, breezeways, etc. In making computations, con-

sideration should be given to the total ground area covered by enclosed building space. Areas are measured from the faces of the exterior line of omitted walls at the mean-grade level of each building. Fenced or otherwise enclosed patios are excluded from the computations as are all roof overheads.

"6. Car Movement Area. One-half of abutting streets plus on-site streets and roads, aprons, and drives to individual garages or carports where drives are too short for additional car storage.

"7. Open Car Storage Area. Parking courts and drives to individual garages and carports where drives are large enough for additional car storage. Excludes area of garages and carports included in computing Building Area and areas not surfaced for vehicular traffic, such as islands.

"8. Recreation Space. Livability space countable as recreation space. Open green area may be counted as recreation space if the space has minimum area of 10,000 square feet with an average dimension of not less than 100 feet and no dimension less than 50 feet. In those cases where project boundaries must be described artificially, and where perpetuity exists adjacent to these boundaries, areas with a maximum depth of 100 feet, beginning at a point 20 feet away from any residential wall containing windows on the ground floor, or beginning at the face of any windowless wall, may be included in the calculation of the recreation space. However, such recreation space outside of the project boundary is not considered within the project LUI computation.

"9. Number of Car Spaces. Including garages, carports, and driveways to individual garages or carports capable of parking one or two cars (normally 1.5 parking spaces per living unit will be provided, but this does not preclude a greater number where costs, criteria, or siting permit)."

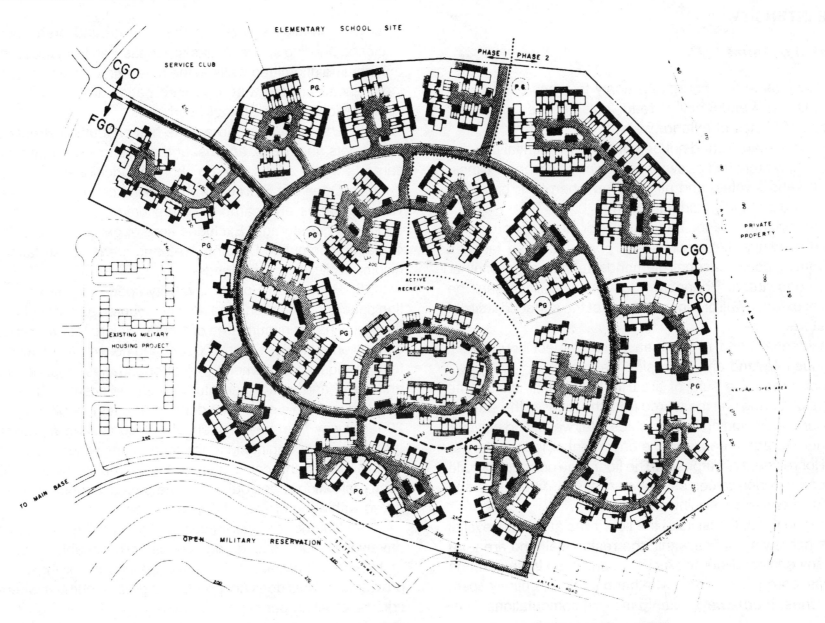

CAR MOVEMENT   CAR STORAGE

SOURCE: *Design Manual–Family Housing*
Naval Facilities Engineering Command
Dept. of the Navy, Wash., D.C. 1967

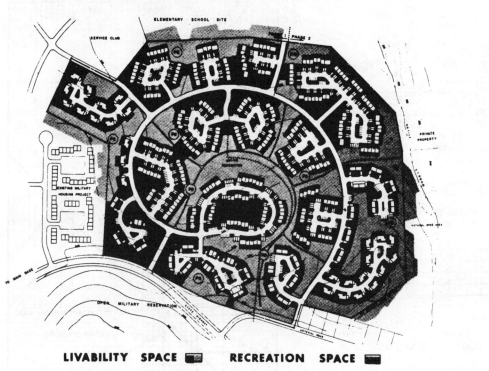

LIVABILITY SPACE ▨ RECREATION SPACE ▨

FLOOR AREA ■ BUILDING AREA ■

SOURCE: *Design Manual–Family Housing*
Naval Facilities Engineering Command
Dept. of the Navy, Wash., D.C. 1967

LAND USE INTENSITY COMPUTATIONS

Installation _____ FY _____ Occupant Category _____

A. PROJECT COMPOSITION:

HOUSE TYPE	TOTAL		PHASE I		PHASE II		FOLIO TYPE		TOTAL		PHASE I		PHASE II	
			NUMBER							TOTAL GROSS SQ. FT.					
	CGO	FGO	CGO	FGO	CGO	FGO			CGO	FGO	CGO	FGO	CGO	FGO
2 BR	27		20		7		I EM9	962 sq.ft.	25,974		19,240		6,734	
3 BR	121		66		55		I EM1	1136 sq.ft.	137,456		74,976		62,480	
3 BR	15		6		9		I EM4	1127 sq.ft.	16,905		6,762		10,143	
4 BR	89		51		38		I EM2	1333 sq.ft.	118,637		67,983		50,654	
4 BR	19		10		9		I CGO15	1617 sq.ft.	30,723		16,170		14,553	
3 BR		56		26		30	IV FGO8	1588 sq.ft.		88,928		41,288		47,640
4 BR		26		13		13	IV FGO7	1588 sq.ft.		46,800		23,400		23,400
4 BR														
Total	271	82	153	39	118	43			329,695	135,728	185,131	64,688	144,564	71,040

B. RATIOS

(Taken from curves for Land Use Intensity Standards.)

		REQUIRED FOR COMPUTED LUI			TOTAL		PHASE I		PHASE II	
			CGO	FGO	CGO	FGO	CGO	FGO	CGO	FGO
							ACTUAL FOR PROJECT			
Land-use Intensity (LUI)			xxxxxx		LUI 4.1	3.5	4.2	3.4	4.1	3.6
Floor Area Ratio (FAR)	Maximum FAR	0.22	0.14		FAR 0.22	0.14	0.23	0.13	0.20	0.15
Open Space Ratio (OSR)	Minimum OSR	3.50	5.20		OSR 3.86	6.20	3.42	6.68	4.33	5.77
Livability Space Ratio (LSR)	Minimum LSR	2.30	3.90		LSR 3.00	4.98	2.60	5.31	3.51	4.67
Recreation Space Ratio (RSR)	Minimum RSR	0.18	0.21		RSR 1.47	3.28	1.59	3.09	1.28	3.45
Car Ratio (CR)	Minimum CR	1.50	2.00		CR 1.65	2.34	1.60	2.41	1.71	2.28

C. COMPUTATION OF LUI AND RATIOS

(See Explanatory Notes)

ITEM			TOTAL		PHASE I		PHASE II	
			CGO	FGO	CGO	FGO	CGO	FGO
					AREAS (SQ. FT.) AND RATIOS			
1. Unusable Land			--	--	--	--	--	--
2. Non-residential Land			--	--	--	--	--	--
3. Residential Land Area (LA)			1,511,532	955,706	777,600	486,586	733,932	469,120
4. Floor Area (FA)			329,695	135,728	185,131	64,688	144,564	71,040
5. Floor Area Ratio (FAR)	FA ÷ LA		0.22	0.14	0.23	0.13	0.20	0.15
6. Building Area (BA)			252,317	113,814	144,237	54,769	108,080	59,045
7. Open space (OS)	LA — BA		1,259,215	841,892	633,363	431,817	625,852	410,075
8. Open Space Ratio (OSR)	OS ÷ FA		3.86	6.20	3.42	6.68	4.33	5.77
9. Car Movement Area			235,754	144,574	134,290	77,410	101,464	67,164
10. Open Car Storage Area			35,400	22,000	18,600	11,000	16,800	11,000
11. Livability Space (LS)	OS — (9 + 10)		988,061	675,318	480,473	343,407	507,588	331,911
12. Livability Space Ratio (LSR)	LS ÷ FA		3.00	4.98	2.60	5.31	3.51	4.67
13. Recreation Space			480,560	445,440	293,760	200,320	186,800	245,120
14. Recreation Space Ratio (RSR)	RS ÷ FA		1.47	3.28	1.59	3.09	1.28	3.45
15. Number of Living Units			271	82	153	39	118	43
16. Number of Car Spaces			448	192	246	94	202	98
17. Car Ratio (CR)	16 ÷ 15		1.65	2.34	1.60	2.41	1.71	2.28

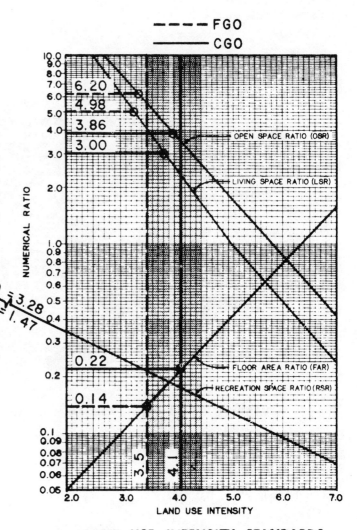

LAND USE INTENSITY STANDARDS

SOURCE: *Design Manual–Family Housing*
Naval Facilities Engineering Command
Dept. of the Navy, Wash., D.C. 1967

TYPE	OCCUPANCY RELATIONSHIP	LEGAL CONTROL	CHARACTERISTICS	PLANNING CONSIDERATIONS
RENTAL	TENANT	LEASE	An owner builds and finances the building or complex; the occupants rent their dwelling units (apartments); utilities, appliances and furnishings may be included in the rental charge; enclosed or open off-street parking may be provided at an additional charge to the tenant; maintenance and operating costs are almost always the responsibility of the owner; time of leases vary, but three years is most common; tenant families tend to be somewhat transient; rental projects are erected primarily for investment.	Tenants tend to be more transient than other types of occupants. Large apartments generate more children than small apartments. Smaller apartments will generally be occupied by single people, young married couples, or the elderly.
COOPERATIVE	TENANT	STOCK	Tenant-owner corporation owns the building or complex; tenants own stock in the building or complex in proportion to the value of their dwelling units; depending upon the lease conditions, a tenant-owner may sell his stock either back to the corporation or to a new tenant-owner when he moves; mortgage, operating, maintenance and any other costs for the building or complex are paid by the tenant-owner corporation.	Families have a vested interest, will tend toward a stable occupancy; greater interest and participation will occur both in project and community affairs.
CONDOMINIUM	OWNERSHIP	OWNERSHIP	A form of cooperative; occupant owns outright his dwelling unit upon which there are no restrictions as to sale, rental, or transfer; the owner-occupant is responsible for the mortgage (if he has one), operating, maintenance, and any other costs only insofar as they pertain to his dwelling unit; all spaces beyond the individually owned dwelling units are held in common ownership.	Owner will generally react as any homeowner in the community; since the unit is owned outright, the owner will invest additional funds for maintenance and upkeep; no control over buying and selling of units.

B-22 FAMILY CYCLE

Family Life Cycle

One of the basic factors in housing design is the continually changing family size, e.g., organization, composition, age, and size. As a result of this continuous change, the physical space requirements also change. Most often it is a gradual process over the years.

The conflict occurs with the ever-fluctuating family organization and the inflexible physical space they occupy at a particular period in time. For example, when a family needs an additional bedroom or more recreational space, it cannot easily increase or expand its space. This is possible with detached single-family houses, but becomes quite difficult to accomplish with any other type of living unit. In like manner, when the family is getting smaller, the physical space requirements will contract substantially. Again, a situation exists where the physical space does not match the family needs.

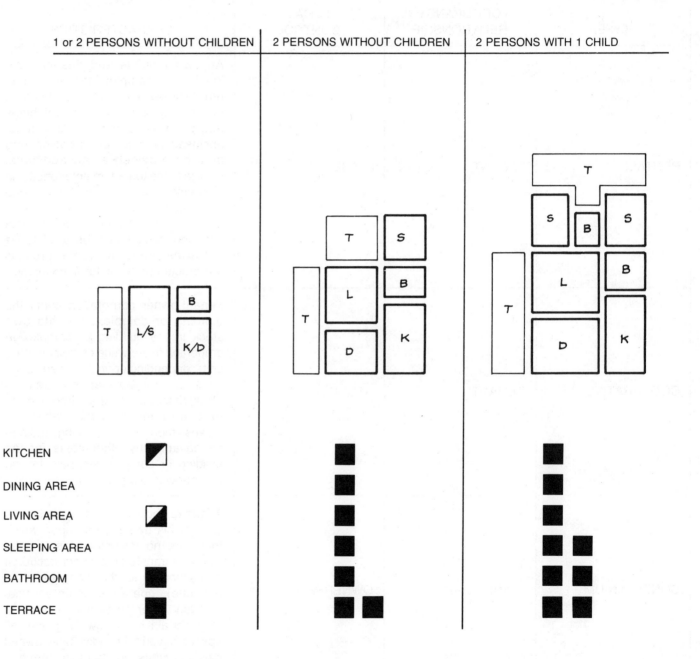

90

2 PERSONS WITH 2 CHILDREN	2 PERSONS WITH 1 CHILD	2 PERSONS WITHOUT CHILDREN	1 OR 2 PERSONS WITHOUT CHILDREN

TYPES OF NEIGHBORHOODS

A man's home is his castle. This is true whether the castle is the traditional single-family detached dwelling or a modern apartment high in the sky. It is true even if the castle is surrounded by a moat of uncut grass, a fleet of scooters, tricycles, and skates. But most families and individuals do not live entirely within their castles. They live on a street in a neighborhood.

What makes a neighborhood? In addition to individual homes, a neighborhood contains schools, churches, parks, and business centers. Some things are the result of joint effort—the streets, storm drainage system, water supply, electricity, telephone, power, gas, and the sewage disposal system. Even the street names and house addresses are a part of the neighborhood as well as of the individual residence. Postmen, milkmen, policemen, and deliverymen are a few of the inhabitants who work in the neighborhood but who do not live there. A man may live in his castle, but he does not live alone.

The first step in planning for housing is the determination of the location, size, and characteristics of the existing residential neighborhood. It is also important to know the location of potential residential areas and the potential market for residential housing.

It is important to know something about each of the residential areas in a neighborhood sense—in what ways the neighborhood is growing, declining, or changing character. This is not revealed entirely by exterior inspection. It is necessary to go beneath the surface and understand the underlying economic facts about the area. Is the type of home in this area suitable for modern accommodations? Some communities that were built as recently as the post-Korean period consist predominantly of two-bedroom units. Two-bedroom units have proven to be inadequate for the larger postwar family in some localities. Conversely, there are many older towns with houses of seven and eight bedrooms that are far too large for most families today. Does the neighborhood need rejuve-

nation through new building, or protection from commercialization and overcrowding?

What are the different types of neighborhoods, and what are their special needs? Residential neighborhoods may be broadly classified into five types.

At one end of the scale, there is the older neighborhood of fine old mansions that have survived several generations, perhaps dating from before the turn of the century. Here the homes and lots are large. Land and building values have remained consistently high for several generations. These neighborhoods were well laid out, the buildings well constructed. They have sturdily survived to this day, but what of their future? Among the dangers this kind of neighborhood may face are (1) overcrowding of structures (doubling up of families, conversion of homes to apartments), (2) undermaintenance of structures, (3) aging of public schools and utilities, and (4) commercialization of properties (partial conversion to business use).

What can help this type of older residential neighborhood? Zoning may help by preventing the incursion of new, adverse land uses such as manufacturing, commercial uses, and warehousing. Such uses are likely to appear in older residential neighborhoods located next to commercial areas. First, it is necessary to prevent this kind of land-use invasion by establishing a clearly defined boundary around the neighborhood and by permitting only residentially compatible uses. Zoning may help by providing a favorable climate for continued residential occupancy of the area. This may be done by recognizing that the older type of home found in the area may no longer be practical for modern accommodations, even if it is still structurally sound. What can be done if it is found, from real estate market analysis, that an older area is declining because of its inability to compete with the modern suburban home? It may be well to recognize the fact that such older areas are open to a greater threat from the introduction of commerical uses than they are from the introduction of different residential building types. It is sometimes better in such communities to permit scattered apartment clusters when individual older residences have deteriorated and have outlived their economic life.

A second general type of residential neighborhood is the moderately old single-family residential area. This is the residential area that was developed perhaps in the 1920s and early 1930s. Such areas are often characterized by spacious lots, two-level single-family detached dwellings, and detached garages. Often this type of neighborhood was originally a tract development created by a single realtor. It may have many advantages such as complete public facilities, a relatively modern school, and adequate park and playground property. It may also be further from the core of the community, so that it stands less chance of becoming mixed with industrial and commercial uses.

A third type of residential neighborhood is one that is in transition from residential to commercial uses. It is usually an older area, but new areas are also affected. It is a neighborhood that already has mixed land uses (some business or industrial as well as residential uses) and mixed residential building types (duplexes and apartments as well as single-family homes). Such neighborhoods are found both close to the downtown core and on the fringe of the community. In the very old area close to downtown where there has been no zoning protection, older residential homes may have been demolished for business and industrial uses in a haphazard pattern so that today homes are next door to businesses. In the newer, outlying areas, vacant land may have been developed at different times for different land uses, with modern residential tract developments going up next to older commercial and industrial establishments. The buildings of the transitional neighborhood are usually old and undermaintained. In some places, modern developments are pushing out older ones. In any case, the transitional neighborhood is changing, and the problem is to direct the change.

The fourth kind of residential neighborhood is the new residential neighborhood located in the outlying fringe areas—the emerging neighborhood. This neighborhood may be only partially developed at this point. Its problems often are merely ones of providing full public facilities such as streets, curbs, gutters, storm drainage, schools, and recreation areas. The emerging neighborhood with vacant land for development is often the place for a new type of urban development that permits the intermingling of different building types.

The fifth general type of neighborhood is the residential "remnant" neighborhood. Remnant neighborhoods are the residential "pockets" of two or three blocks that are found scattered throughout a community. Often these are the remaining segments of once-flourishing communities. Within almost all communities, there is a section "on the other side of the tracks" that is a small slum remnant of a once-thriving community. The district may be completely surrounded by industrial uses. Some blocks may have two or three kinds of land uses. This kind of residential pocket may be slated for ultimate redevelopment by either private or public uses over a long period of time.

What might be called a sixth "neighborhood," but is not really a neighborhood, is the isolated housing unit found scattered throughout the community. These residential fragments are generally not zoned for residential use. They are a part of the industrial or commercial area.

LOCATION

Location criteria include factors of health, safety, convenience, amenity, and economy, all related to a residential life-style. In general, three basic examinations for any housing site should be undertaken. These are:

1. the environmental setting

93

2. the neighborhood setting
3. the ancillary setting

The Environmental Setting

Residential communities should be compatible with the carrying capacity of the natural environment. This means that topography and soil conditions must be considered to insure the stability of the physical structures as well as to identify and preserve unique natural features for protection and preservation. In addition, the density of development should relate well to the availability of a continuous safe yield of potable water and to the capacity of the environment to absorb the soil and sewage waste of the community. Wind directions should be considered vis-a-vis potential smoke and fume pollution.

The Neighborhood Setting

Whether the new housing is to be built in an existing community, or is part of a newly created one, the primary awareness must be of the general neighborhood condition. In existing communities the significant indices include the age and condition of buildings, the relative stability and/or direction of growth, accessibility, the mix of housing types, and the existing nonresidential uses. In new communities the two major factors are accessibility and compatibility with the surrounding land uses.

The Ancillary Setting

The prime concern is the adequacy of community facilities for work, shopping, and community activity including education, recreation, religion, health services, and protection. The nonresidential uses should be in compatible settings, with sufficient buffers to insure protection from noise, air, and visual pollution. The following list typifies compatible and noncompatible uses.

It is not usually necessary or practical for all services to be within close physical proximity to the residential neighborhood. Therefore, accessibility in terms of convenience and safety is an important community feature. The following pages illustrate general standards and criteria for location, compatibility, and accessibility.

Compatibility

The neighborhood or immediate surrounding area must also be carefully considered with the new housing. The condition of structures and character of the neighborhood are significant indications. Most important to determine would be the prevailing trend of the neighborhood, for example: An existing "so-called" stable neighborhood may be deteriorating and on its way to becoming a slum area, or vice-versa. Since housing is expected to be economically viable for a 40-50 year period, the eternal factors acting upon a neighborhood are essential to identify.

Listed below are some general land uses and their degree of desirability as neighbors for a housing development:

Desirable	Acceptable	Not Acceptable
Parks and playgrounds	Stores or shops	Industrial uses, not properly screened.
Elementary schools	Highways with buffer strips	
Churches		Airports
Housing, in good condition	Housing, in fair condition	Highways without buffer strips
Local shopping	Industrial park	Warehouses
Medical facilities	High school	Railroad tracks and yards
		Deteriorated or dilapidated housing

Private Automobile

Currently the automobile is the most convenient way to travel. However, it is expensive and highly inefficient as a means of moving large numbers of people from their homes to work or other facilities. Automobiles require highways to get to a destination and once there need parking space. Both of these requirements commit large amounts of land that can be utilized more productively. Also, in recent years the automobile has become the major culprit in atmospheric pollution.

The table in section B-4 indicates the acceptable accessibility criteria for various destinations.

Accessibility

The housing development must have convenient routes of access to employment, shopping, institutional needs, and recreation. Location near major highways or public transportation is desirable.

The three methods of access are:
1. Walking
2. Public transportation
3. Private automobile

Walking

The simplest method of access to any facility would be by walking. Even though many facilities cannot be located within walking distance, effort should be made to have as many of the facilities used most frequently nearby.

A variation of walking is the use of bicycles. This greatly increases the range of accessibility but is still highly economical in time and money. Provisions should be made for the maximum utilization of bicycles within the housing development and the surrounding circulation network. This can be achieved by the use of special bike lanes parallel to the street or completely independent bikeways away from the vehicular traffic.

Public Transportation

Aside from walking, planners generally agree that mass transportation modes provide the most rational means of circulation within urban and suburban settings. This includes trains, buses, monorails, subways, minibuses, and many other variations. Public transportation is more efficient and can move greater numbers of people than any other means. Also, mass transportation uses less land for right-of-ways and reduces air pollution in sharp contrast to the automobile.

Necessary utilities must be readily available to the site if the development is to be built. These include water, sanitary and storm sewers, gas and electricity.

Water

The best source for water is to have a public water supply system. This usually means water of sufficient quantity and quality as to present no difficulties. However, if no public system exists, it will be necessary to provide a private system utilizing well water, if it is readily available. In dealing with detached houses, use of individual wells may be explored. Not only does the use of wells add cost but additional precautions are necessary to insure protection of the water system from contamination from septic tanks or sewers. In addition, storage tanks most likely will be required to meet the demand of peak-hour consumption, constant pressure and a two-hour fire protection reserve.

Sanitary Sewers

The best method is to have a public system available to connect with the new sewer lines. This will generally provide proper sewerage treatment and disposal at a distant plant. In lieu of a public system available, it will be necessary to provide a private self-contained package type of sewerage treatment plant. Despite the initial cost, this method is acceptable. Provisions should be made to hook up to a public system, if and when one does become available. The least recommended method is to use septic tanks. The reason against septic tanks is the possible contamination of nearby wells or of the water supply and the need for drainage fields. If the soil does not have proper percolation, this may seriously limit the use of the land.

Storm Sewers

Storm sewers are generally recommended to be separated from sanitary sewers. As with the other utilities, it is best that a public system of storm sewers exist. If none exists, discharge into adjacent lakes or streams may be satisfactory. Precautions are necessary to protect these natural water courses from becoming polluted. Permission to discharge into them may also be required from local and state authorities.

Electricity

An adequate supply of power both for present and for future use is essential. The amount of electricity used has steadily increased over the years and, from all indications, will continue to do so in the near future. Consultation and planning with local utility companies is recommended. Service lines should be placed underground to minimize disruptions from bad weather and to improve the visual aspects of the landscape.

Gas

Gas mains, if required, should be carefully located and protected from possible damage. Cost analysis should be made for installing new gas mains as opposed to utilizing an all-electric system.

The use of bottled gas is not recommended unless it is absolutely necessary.

Density

Density of residential development is the ratio of occupancy (dwellings, persons, families or habitable rooms, etc.) to land area (acre, hectare, or square mile, etc.). It can be expressed in different ways, according to the choice of terms for occupancy or land area. Of all measures of intensity, density is the one most commonly accepted as reflecting the livability of multifamily housing.

In the United States the most consistently used ratio is number of dwellings (or families) per acre. Usually no distinctions are made regarding the size of individual dwellings and/or number of persons occupying them. Project size acreage is generally expressed in net acres. Areas devoted to commercial activities, community facilities, public recreation, and major roads are excluded from net acreage computations but these are included in gross acre computations. The most frequent variation in the expression of density consists of substituting persons for dwellings. This is often used when the housing is not occupied by families of average size. For instance, in stating the density of a dormitory group, persons per acre is more meaningful than either dwelling units (since the latter are frequently single sleeping rooms) or families (which might consist of one person).

The two components of the density ratio, occupancy and size of site, are also meaningful when considered independently. Occupancy is a measure of activity on a site and is also significant in an appraisal of the adequacy of community facilities. The provision of schools, recreation space, shops, and similar facilities is directly related to number of persons. Site size, as a separate component, influences the quality of a housing project. While density can be described in a straightforward fashion, degrees of density are difficult to state in absolute terms. What constitutes high, medium, or low density is relative to a number of factors, namely a county's or city's tradition of residential development, location of housing, and building type. For example, high-density housing on the fringe of a city may be considered medium or even low density at its core. Fifteen dwelling units to the acre is regarded as high for single-family, detached structures, medium for row houses, and low for multistory structures.

Coverage

Coverage is the percentage of land occupied by structures. The higher the coverage, the less open land for outdoor recreation, gardens, parking spaces, and other needs.

Coverage is a somewhat misleading measure for large projects with a variety of building types because it is a percentage for the entire project and may not represent the coverage of any specific building group. It would be more accurate to measure coverage separately for each subarea of similar building types.

Floor Area Ratio

Floor area ratio is defined by the American Public Health Association as " . . . the total floor area of all stories used for residential purposes, divided by the area of residential land."[9] It is a measure of building bulk, and is often preferred over coverage because the latter fails to reflect above-ground development. On the other hand, floor area ratio does not reveal the amount of open space available on a site. A one-story building that covers 100 percent of a site and a two-story building that covers 50 percent of a site both have a floor area ratio of 1.0. Because neither floor area ratio nor coverage

[9]American Public Health Association—Committee on the Hygiene of Housing. Planning the Neighborhood. (Standards for Healthful Housing Series.) Edited by Allan A. Twichell. Chicago: Public Administration Service, 1960. p. 40.

alone describes the characteristics of residential development, they are often used in combination.

Since architects, to date, have not yet designed a truly flexible house that can expand and contract as the needs of the family change, the solution must be achieved in a different manner.

The only other solution to retain neighborhood stability is to provide, within the neighborhood, sufficient variety of living units that will enable most of the families to provide for their needs at different stages of their development (see Stein). The chief factors in planning for housing center around the "family" and the "household" rather than the individual. This results from the fact that the family represents the basic social unit in our society today and that a house or apartment is generally occupied by a "family."

The difference between a "household" and a "family," as used by the Census Bureau, is highly significant. A household is defined as all the persons who occupy a housing unit. A household includes the related family members and all the unrelated persons who share the housing unit. A "family" refers to a group of two persons or more related by blood, marriage, or adoption and residing together.

The rate of household formation in the United States has consistently been greater than the rate of population growth. This can be seen in the following table:

Comparison of Housing Formation and Rate of Population Growth, U.S. 1920-1970

	No. of Households	% Increase	Population	% Increase	Average Household Size
1920	17.6	24.5	74.1	—	4.2
1930	23.3	32.4	92.6	25.0	4.0
1940	27.7	19.1	110.5	9.5	3.67
1950	37.1	33.7	127.6	25.8	3.37
1960	47.5	11.6		10.1	3.33
1970	56.2	8.8			3.17

Source: U.S. Bureau of the Census

The rate of household formation is a highly important factor in housing demand. Also, most important for housing is that the average size of households in the United States has continually decreased. In 1920 the average household size was 4.2 persons but in 1970 it was reduced to 3.17 persons. The decrease in number of persons per household during the last decade resulted from an increase in the proportion of households maintained by both young and older adults living alone and from a decreased in the average number of children under 18 years of age per household.

Rental

The rental type of housing provides for less permanent type of occupancy. It also provides smaller housing units for newly married couples and for elderly people. The major criticism is that it provides transient-type occupancy with people who have no permanent roots to the community. However, it does give flexibility in providing a range of apartment types and sizes. The number of school-age children depends on the size of apartments.

Cooperative

This type of housing provides a type of occupancy that encourages participation in the operation of the project. It creates a sense of communal ownership and belonging to an identifiable group. It makes for permanent residency.

Condominium

This provides ownership of housing units with all its related considerations. It avoids all the maintenance chores, yet enables occupants to remain aloof of community participation. It is a relatively permanent form of occupancy. The number of school-age children depends on the size of apartments.

NEIGHBORHOOD ORGANIZATION

C

C-1   The Garden City–Ebenezer Howard
C-2   The Neighborhood Unit–Perry
C-3   The Neighborhood Concept–Variations
C-4   Radburn, N.J.
C-5   Neighborhood Unit
C-6   Neighborhood Densities
C-7   Physical Elements in the Organization
        of the Neighborhood
C-8   Basic Planning Unit
        Detached House/Dwelling Unit
C-9   Typical Floor/Apartment Building
C-10   Apartment Building Complex
        Cluster of Blocks
        Example

C-11   Neighborhood/Cluster of
        Neighborhoods
C-12   Subdivisions
        Land Subdivision Design
        Site Characteristics
        Street Layout
        Lot Layout
        Drainage and Streams
        Costs–Preliminary Plat
        Preliminary Plat
        Design Considerations
C-13   Lot Area per Gross Acre
C-14   Planned-unit Development
        Zoning
        Clusters

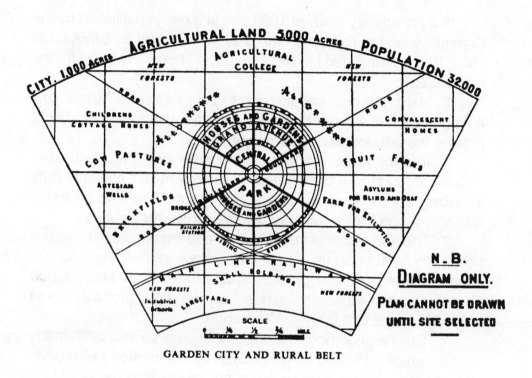

GARDEN CITY AND RURAL BELT

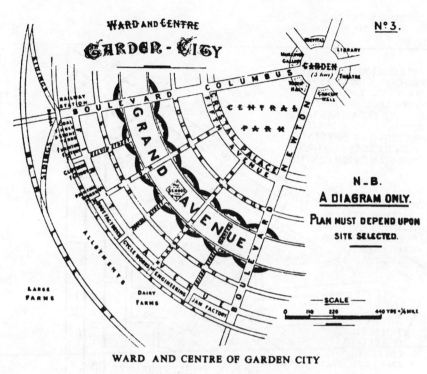

WARD AND CENTRE OF GARDEN CITY

Ward and Centre of Garden City

Total area of city	–6000 acres
Built-up area	–1000 acres
Permanent green belt	–5000 acres
Total population	–32,000 people

City Organization

Center-	civic buildings
1st Ring-	central park
2nd Ring-	housing of various types bisected by Grand Ave.
3rd Ring-	crystal palace or covered promenades
4th Ring-	factories and warehouses
Green belt-	permanent open space

Ebenezer Howard put forth his concept of a garden city in a book entitled *TOMORROW: A Peaceful Path to Real Reform* in 1898. The basic goal was to combine the advantages of town life with that of the country. He advocated the building of "towns designed for healthy living and industry of a size that makes possible a full measure of social life but not larger; surrounded by a rural belt; the whole of the land being in public ownership, or held in trust for the community."

SOURCE: Ebenezer Howard, *Garden Cities of Tomorrow*, Faber and Faber, London—1946.

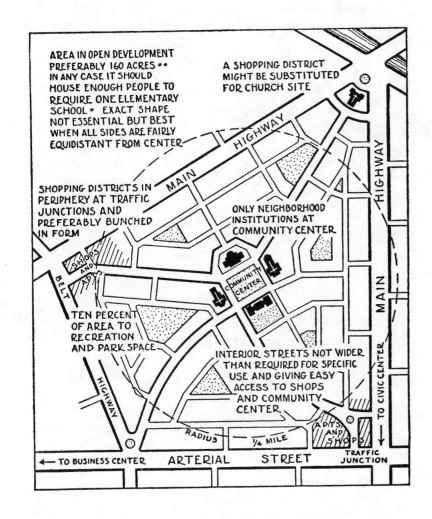

AREA IN OPEN DEVELOPMENT PREFERABLY 160 ACRES •• IN ANY CASE IT SHOULD HOUSE ENOUGH PEOPLE TO REQUIRE ONE ELEMENTARY SCHOOL • EXACT SHAPE NOT ESSENTIAL BUT BEST WHEN ALL SIDES ARE FAIRLY EQUIDISTANT FROM CENTER

A SHOPPING DISTRICT MIGHT BE SUBSTITUTED FOR CHURCH SITE

SHOPPING DISTRICTS IN PERIPHERY AT TRAFFIC JUNCTIONS AND PREFERABLY BUNCHED IN FORM

ONLY NEIGHBORHOOD INSTITUTIONS AT COMMUNITY CENTER

TEN PERCENT OF AREA TO RECREATION AND PARK SPACE

INTERIOR STREETS NOT WIDER THAN REQUIRED FOR SPECIFIC USE AND GIVING EASY ACCESS TO SHOPS AND COMMUNITY CENTER

HIGHWAY

MAIN

BELT

HIGHWAY

MAIN

TO CIVIC CENTER

SHOPS AND APTS

COMMUNITY CENTER

APTS AND SHOPS

RADIUS ¼ MILE

TRAFFIC JUNCTION

← TO BUSINESS CENTER ARTERIAL STREET

SOURCE: New York Regional Survey of New York and Its Environs—1929

In a preliminary study in 1926 and in a report published by the Committee on the Regional Plan of New York and Its Environs in 1929, Perry enunciated his Neighborhood Theory. Its basic principles were:

1. Major arterials and through traffic routes should not pass through residential neighborhoods. Instead, these streets should provide the boundaries of the neighborhood.

2. Interior street patterns should be designed and constructed through use of cul-de-sacs, curved layout and light-duty surfacing so as to encourage a quiet, safe, low-volume traffic movement and preservation of the residential atmosphere.

3. The population of the neighborhood should be that which is necessary to support its elementary school. (When Perry formulated his theory, this population was estimated at about 5,000 persons; current elementary school size standards probably would lower the figure to 3,000-4,000 persons.)

4. The neighborhood focal point should be the elementary school centrally located on a common or green, along with other institutions that have service areas coincident with the neighborhood boundaries.

5. The neighborhood would occupy an approximately 160 acres with a density of 10 families per acre. The shape would be such that no child would walk more than one-half mile to school.

6. The unit would be served by shopping facilities, churches, a library, and a community center located near the elementary school.

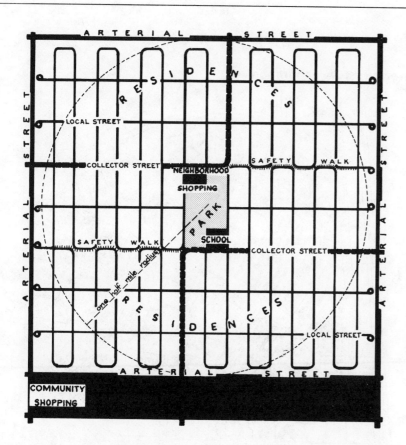

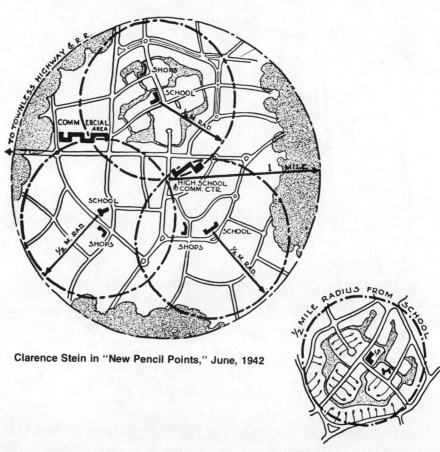

The Neighborhood Unit–Clarence Stein

Clarence Stein in "New Pencil Points," June, 1942

A sound area for living with:
1. *Adequate school and parks within a half-mile walk*
2. *Major streets around rather than through the neighborhood*
3. *Separate residential and nonresidential districts*
4. *Population large enough to support an elementary school, usually 5,000 to 10,000 people*
5. *Some neighborhood stores and services*

SOURCE: Reproduced from *Comprehensive Planning for The Whittier Neighborhood*, courtesy of Minneapolis City Planning Commission.

The elementary school is the center of the unit and within a one-half mile radius of all residents in the neighborhood. A small shopping center for daily needs is located near the school. Most residential streets are suggested as cul-de-sac or "dead-end" roads to eliminate through traffic, and park space flows through the neighborhood in a manner reminiscent of this Radburn plan.

The grouping of three neighborhood units is served by a high school and one or two major commercial centers, the radius for walking to these facilities being one mile.

General Plan Showing Neighborhoods

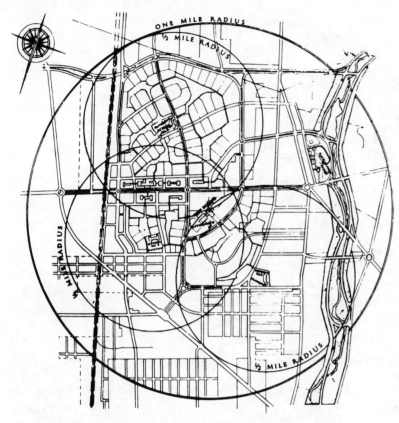

Northwest Neighborhood

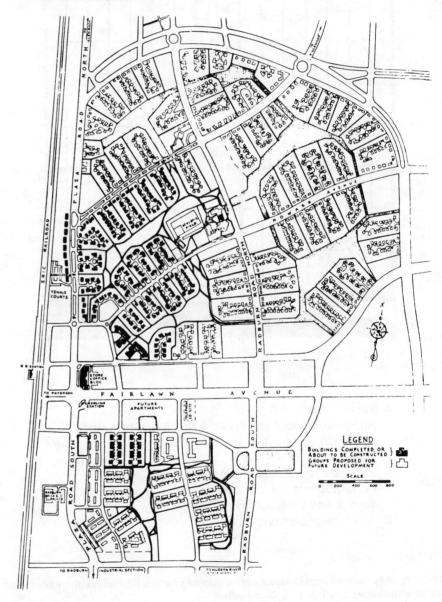

In their design of the suburb of Radburn in New Jersey, C.S. Stein and Henry Wright introduced a new approach to residential planning. They originated the superblock idea, the main feature of which is the separation of pedestrian and automobile traffic. At Radburn, houses are grouped around a series of cul-de-sacs that are linked by walkways with the park, the school, and the shops, all of which are located in the interior of the superblock. The superblock is considered an ideal solution to the circulation problem since it provides a means of locating the houses off the main road.

SOURCE: Clarence Stein, *Toward New Towns for America*, Reinhold Publishing Corp., New York—1957.

The illustration shows a typical cul-de-sac street employed at Radburn. Its characteristics may be summarized as follows: The short cul-de-sac acts as a service lane only; it provides vehicular access to houses and garages, permitting delivery and other services, and it also serves for most of the parking; footways located on the perimeter of each cul-de-sac house group serve as sidewalks. As opposed to established planning practices, houses have been "turned around," the living rooms, porches, and as many bedrooms as possible facing the gardens at the rear of dwellings, and kitchens and cellar storage, the service lane.

The dwellings are loosely disposed around the dead-end streets and, as a group, they show little of formal architectural discipline. The landscaping, judiciously planned, undoubtedly is the most important uniting element in the composition. Other uniting elements are the consistency in the use of building materials and the continuity in roof lines. Also, by joining houses by means of coupling their garages, the usual disorderly appearance of the free-standing houses in relation to each other has been eliminated and sufficient space left on either side of the buildings. The architectural informality of the Radburn cul-de-sac distinguishes it from the British dead-end street in which a formal correlation of the houses predominates.

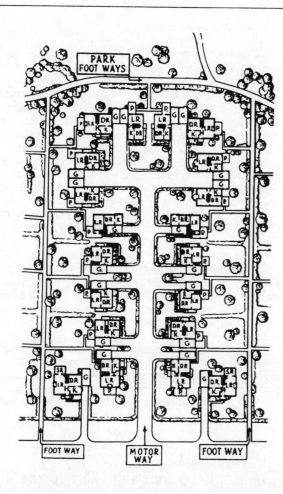

Plan of a typical "lane" at Radburn. The park in the center of the superblock is shown at the top; the motorways to the houses are at right angles to the park.

SOURCE: Clarence Stein, *Toward New Towns for America*, Reinhold Publishing Corp., New York—1957.

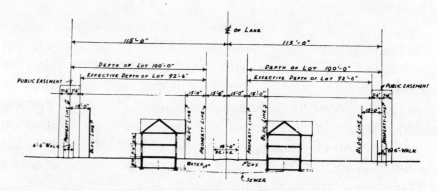

Typical transverse section of a "lane" in the first unit of Radburn.

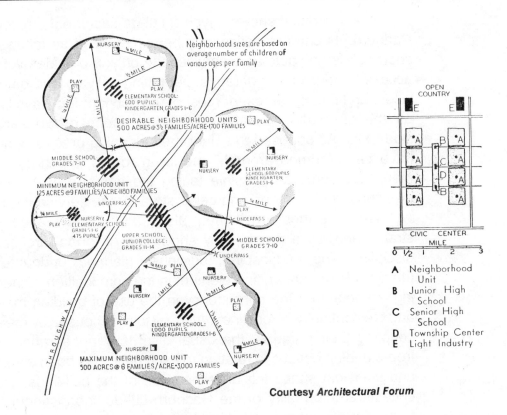

Neighborhood sizes are based on average number of children of various ages per family

DESIRABLE NEIGHBORHOOD UNITS
500 ACRES @ 3½ FAMILIES/ACRE=1700 FAMILIES

MINIMUM NEIGHBORHOOD UNIT
125 ACRES @ 9 FAMILIES/ACRE=1180 FAMILIES

MAXIMUM NEIGHBORHOOD UNIT
500 ACRES @ 6 FAMILIES/ACRE=3000 FAMILIES

Courtesy Architectural Forum

OPEN COUNTRY

CIVIC CENTER

MILE

0 ½ 1   2   3

A Neighborhood Unit
B Junior High School
C Senior High School
D Township Center
E Light Industry

A Neighborhood Unit by José Sert

This diagram illustrates an organization of neighborhood units suggested by José Sert. While some authorities have stated that the maximum walking distance from home to the elementary school should be one-half mile, this diagram indicates a maximum distance of about one-quarter mile, which is the standard accepted by a number of communities. In contrast to a population density of 20-25 persons assumed as a desirable average in many communities, Sert assumes a density of two or three times this number, which may account for the shorter walking distances he proposes from homes to the several schools in his scheme.

The elementary school occupies a central position in the neighborhood unit and a group of these units–six to eight in number––constitute a "township" with a population of between 56,000 and 80,000 people. A junior high school serves four neighborhoods; a senior high school serves the eight units; these facilities are situated within a "township center" surrounded by a "greenbelt." The neighborhood unit includes the elementary school, preschool play lots, playground, church, shopping center, library, and emergency clinic. The "township center" includes the junior and senior high schools, community auditorium and meeting rooms, concert hall, theaters, main shopping center, recreation and administrative center.

Traffic ways bypass the neighborhood units and connect them with the "civic center," which includes the regional facilities for administration, education, hotels, trade and recreation, and transportation stations on one side, and on the other side are the locations for light industrial plants. All these elements are separated from each other by "greenbelts," and the open countryside is accessible to all the people.

A NEIGHBORHOOD UNIT

N.L. Engelhardt, Jr., has presented a comprehensive pattern of the neighborhood as a component of the successively larger segments in a city structure. The neighborhood unit includes the elementary school, a small shopping district, and a playground. These facilities are grouped near the center of the unit so that the walking distance between them and the home does not exceed one-half mile. An elementary school with a standard enrollment of between 600 and 800 pupils will represent a population of about 1,700 families in the neighborhood unit.[1]

Two such units (3,400 families) will support a junior high school with a recreation center in conjunction; the walking distance does not exceed one mile from the center to the most remote home. Four units (6,800 families) will require a senior high school and a commercial center. It will also be an appropriate size for a major park and recreation area. This grouping of four neighborhood units forms a "community" with a population of about 24,000 people. The component parts of this community pattern are integrated, and such communities may be arranged in whatever combinations the sources of employment and communication to and from them may require.

[1]The School-Neighborhood Nucleus, N.L. Engelhardt, Jr., *Architectural Forum*, October 1943.

NEIGHBORHOOD CENTER

M. Paul Friedberg and Associates

McMillan, Griffis and Mileto, Architects

THE DENSITY TABLES: ORGANIZATION AND MEANING

C-6-1, 2, 3, 4 derive a range of what may reasonably be considered as maximum permissible neighborhood densities, subject to the limitations indicated in the paragraphs immediately following. Table C-6-1 is an illustrative calculation of land required per family for all neighborhood uses in a development of 5,000 persons. Net residential land allowances are combined with the community facilities requirements; addition to these of street allowances gives the total neighborhood land requirement. Table C-6-2 gives a total land requirement per family (based on similar calculations) for each size of neighborhood and each type of dwelling considered in this report. Tables C-6-3 and C-6-4 convert these data into neighborhood density allowances: families per acre and persons per acre, respectively.[2]

Assumptions Made; Limitations of the Data

Areas allowed for each type of land use conform to established recommendations. In all calculations, the most favorable conditions in regard to topography and usability of land have been assumed. Unusable land or land devoted to nonneighborhood uses has been excluded from the computations. If such land occurs within the neighborhood, its area must be deducted before these densities can be applied. Deductions must also be made for any unusual setbacks necessary at boundaries or other similar unspecified land allowances, including area required for an on-site community water supply or sewage disposal plant. For irregular or steep land, densities must be lowered.

In determining land requirements for some of the community facilities, certain assumptions had to be made, since there is no

[2]The fact that the proposed neighborhood density standards are given by type of dwelling unit in no way implies that neighborhoods composed of a single dwelling type are recommended. The tables are set up by dwelling type only because this method of presentation will permit the greatest freedom in the analysis of density limits. Table C-6-5 gives the method for calculating densities in a neighborhood with diversified dwelling types.

C-6-1 LAND AREA PER FAMILY FOR A NEIGHBORHOOD OF 5,000 PERSONS (1,375 FAMILIES)[a]
Illustrative Calculation of Basic Allowances, in Square Feet, by Type of Dwelling[b]

Dwelling Type	Net Residential		Streets Serving Dwellings[e]		Community Facilities		Streets Serving Com. Fac.[d]		Total	
One- or Two-Family Dwellings										
1-family detached	6,000	71%	1,800	22%	530	6%	110	1%	8,440	100%
1-family semidetached or 2-family detached	4,000	68	1,200	21	530	9	110	2	5,840	100
1-family attached (row) or 2-family semidetached	2,400	64	700	19	530	14	110	3	3,740	100
Multifamily Dwellings										
2-story	1,465	53	600	21	610	22	120	4	2,795	100
3-story	985	45	480	21	610	28	120	6	2,195	100
6-story	570	36	280	18	610	39	120	7	1,580	100
9-story	515	35	220	15	610	42	120	8	1,465	100
13-story	450	32	220	15	610	44	120	9	1,400	100

[a]Assumed: average family size 3.6 persons.

[b]Organization of this and later tables by dwelling types does not imply that a neighborhood should consist of one dwelling type alone. For neighborhoods of diversified dwelling types, see Table C-6-5.

[c]Allowance based on design factors. Will vary locally with volume of traffic, street widths, parking scheme, etc.

[d]Allowance is approximately 20 percent of area of community facilities.

C-6-2 LAND AREA PER FAMILY FOR NEIGHBORHOODS OF VARIOUS SIZES
Basic Allowance, in Square Feet, by Type of Dwelling and Population of Neighborhood[a]

Dwelling Type	Neighborhood Population				
	1,000 persons 275 families	2,000 persons 550 families	3,000 persons 825 families	4,000 persons 1,100 families	5,000 persons 1,375 families
	Square Feet per Family				
One- or Two-Family Dwellings					
1-family detached	9,060	8,600	8,520	8,460	8,440
1-family semidetached or 2-family detached	6,460	6,000	5,920	5,860	5,840
1-family attached (row) or 2-family semidetached	4,360	3,900	3,820	3,760	3,740
Multifamily Dwellings					
2-story	3,425	2,960	2,885	2,825	2,795
3-story	2,825	2,360	2,285	2,225	2,195
6-story	2,210	1,745	1,670	1,610	1,580
9-story	2,095	1,630	1,555	1,495	1,465
13-story	2,030	1,565	1,490	1,430	1,400

[a]Calculated as in Table C-6-1.

SOURCE: *Planning the Neighborhood* by the American Public Health Association Committee on the Hygiene of Housing, Public Administration Service, Chicago, Ill., 1960.

universal formula, for instance, for shopping center size or school size. Variables in these and similar factors must be determined locally. For this reason the proposed neighborhood densities cannot be considered as mandatory standards but can serve only as a guide. Increases above the recommended densities may be possible in some special situations; however, in general neighborhood densities should not be materially increased from those recommended unless there is ample proof that higher densities will not impair the livability of residential areas.

Effect of Design on Density

Whether the basic standards for a healthful environment can be met at a given density depends on the design of the project. Often, densities will have to be considerably lower to take care of special conditions. This might be the case where the recommended multiple use of facilities is impractical, where land is hilly, where streets are unusually wide, and so on. Or it may be possible to increase densities without lowering the basic standards where general conditions are exceptionally favorable and design is good. Use of balconies and roof gardens for part of the outdoor living area, use of underground car storage, etc. might permit somewhat higher densities than those recommended. Although the recommended densities are valid in normal cases, they are in no way intended to restrict the designer who can meet the essential standards at higher densities, nor can they be used as a substitute for good design.

Regardless of compliance with recommended densities, it is essential that all residential areas comply also with specific design recommendations and environmental standards.

IMPLICATIONS OF NEIGHBORHOOD DENSITY STANDARDS

While the density tables are presented only as a general

SOURCE: Planning the Neighborhood by the American Public Health Association Committee on the Hygiene of Housing, Public Administration Service, Chicago, Ill., 1960.

C-6-3 NEIGHBORHOOD DENSITY: FAMILIES PER ACRE[a]
Basic Allowance, by Type of Dwelling and Population of Neighborhood

Dwelling Type	1,000 persons 275 families	2,000 persons 550 families	3,000 persons 825 families	4,000 persons 1,100 families	5,000 persons 1,375 families
			Families per Acre		
One- or Two-Family Dwellings					
1-family detached	4.8	5.1	5.1	5.1	5.2
1-family semidetached or 2-family detached	6.8	7.3	7.4	7.4	7.5
1-family attached (row) or 2-family semidetached	10.0	11.2	11.4	11.6	11.7
Multifamily Dwellings					
2-story	12.7	14.7	15.1	15.5	15.6
3-story	15.5	18.5	19.1	19.6	19.9
6-story	19.7	25.0	26.1	27.1	27.6
9-story	20.8	26.8	28.0	29.2	29.8
13-story	21.5	27.8	29.2	30.5	31.2

[a]Calculated from land area allowances (square feet per family), Table C-6-2.

C-6-4 NEIGHBORHOOD DENSITY: PERSONS PER ACRE[a]
Basic Allowance, by Type of Dwelling and Population of Neighborhood

Dwelling Type	1,000 persons 275 families	2,000 persons 550 families	3,000 persons 825 families	4,000 persons 1,100 families	5,000 persons 1,375 families
			Persons per Acre		
One- or Two-Family Dwellings					
1-family detached	17	18	18	18	19
1-family semidetached or 2-family detached	24	26	27	27	27
1-family attached (row) or 2-family semidetached	36	40	41	42	42
Multifamily Dwellings					
2-story	46	53	54	56	56
3-story	56	66	69	71	72
6-story	71	90	94	98	99
9-story	75	96	101	105	107
13-story	77	100	105	110	112

[a]Calculated from Table C-6-3, assuming average family size of 3.6 persons.

guide, and it is recognized that local conditions will somewhat alter the limits recommended, these tables bring out certain fundamental relationships that will be little affected by local variants. These relationships cannot be overemphasized, for an outstanding weakness of American housing and community planning is the lack of reasonable density standards.

Total Range of Neighborhood Densities

C-6-3 and C-6-4 indicate that even for a neighborhood composed entirely of 13-story apartments, which is unlikely to occur and which is not recommended, the neighborhood density should not exceed 31 families or 112 persons per neighborhood acre. That densities greatly in excess of this figure have been achieved in recent developments of this type is generally due to skimping in one or more of the essentials: spacing of buildings for sunlight; adequate areas for juvenile and adult recreation; integral provision of schools, garages or car-parking space; and similar factors. It is to be doubted whether developments with these shortcomings will long maintain a favorable competitive position with respect to neighborhoods providing such necessities in reasonable measure.

For a neighborhood composed entirely of one-family detached houses, the neighborhood density should not exceed 5 families or 19 persons per neighborhood acre; and for one-family row houses, 12 families or 42 persons per neighborhood acre. Densities of the latter order are characteristic of much recent public housing.

Effect of Dwelling Types on Neighborhood Density

The foregoing tables indicate that neighborhood densities can rise as net residential densities increase without violating standards of healthful environment. A 5,000-person neighborhood developed with one-family houses requires approximately 8,400 square feet of neighborhood land per family as compared with 1,400 square feet per family for 13-story apartment dwellings (C-6-1). This is equivalent to a range of 5.2 to 31.2 families per neighborhood acre (C-6-3), or 19 to 112 persons per acre (C-6-4).

However, there is a diminishing return on increasing the height of buildings as a means of increasing density. By adding one story to 2-story multiple dwellings, approximately 5 additional families may be accommodated per acre of neighborhood land. Adding 4 stories to 9-story buildings, however, allows only two more families per acre.

One reason for this is that as density rises, community facilities require an increasing proportion of the total land. In a 5,000-person neighborhood of detached one-family houses, for example, community facilities and related streets require only 7 percent of the land; in a neighborhood of 13-story apartments, they require 53 percent of the land (C-6-1).

Thus, the difference between permissible net residential and neighborhood densities becomes conspicuously greater as densities increase. For one-family dwellings with a net density of 7 families per acre, the neighborhood density is 5.2 families per acre. For a neighborhood of 13-story buildings, however, with a net density of 95 families per acre, the neighborhood density is only 31.2 families per acre.

The great gap between net and neighborhood densities for multistory buildings emphasizes the importance of insuring that housing areas conform to standards for both types of densities.

Effect of Neighborhood Population on Densities

The tables indicate that permissible density increases not only with an increase in height of buildings but with an increase in total neighborhood population up to a 5,000-person neighborhood. For a development of 6-story apartments, the number of persons increases to 99 persons per acre for a neighborhood of 5,000 persons (C-6-4). This is due to the fact that maximum permissible population loads on parks and playgrounds are not reached with less than 4,000 to 5,000 persons. Therefore, highest densities may be reached in neighborhoods of 4,000 to 5,000 persons (1,100 to 1,375 families). Neighborhood densities beyond this point may

111

decrease, because some duplication of playgrounds and parks may be required for neighborhoods with larger population.

DENSITIES FOR NEIGHBORHOOD OF DIVERSIFIED DWELLING TYPES

The need for various kinds and sizes of dwellings to meet the needs of different families within a neighborhood cannot be too emphatically stressed. Neighborhood densities should always be visualized in terms of diversified dwelling types.

The designer may proceed on either of two bases: a) he may determine first the desired proportion of different dwelling types and compute the resulting neighborhood area and density; b) the density for a neighborhood may be set in advance by zoning regulations or other planning considerations, and the designer may determine the dwelling type combinations suited to the fixed neighborhood density.

The following examples illustrate how the density tables given in the previous section may be used in the two types of situations.

Neighborhood Area and Density for a Development of Mixed Dwelling Types

C-6-5 illustrates the method by which total land area and resultant density is arrived at for a neighborhood of 5,000 persons (1,375 families) with diversified dwelling types.

For illustrative purposes it is assumed that the distribution of family types to be housed follows the findings of the U.S. Census for all urban families. On this basis 52 percent of households would be families with minor children, and 48 percent would consist of adults only, in various combinations. According to recommendations for dwelling type selection, it would seem desirable to provide some form of one- or two-family dwellings for families with children, while apartments would be suitable for households consist-

C-6-5 LAND AREA AND DENSITY FOR A NEIGHBORHOOD OF 5,000 PERSONS (1,375 FAMILIES) WITH DIVERSIFIED DWELLING TYPES

Population Composition		Proposed Dwelling Type	Dwelling Units (Families)		Required Neighborhood Land Area	
Type of Family	Percent of Families		Percent	Number	Sq. Ft. per Family[a]	Total Acres
Families with minor children	52.0	1-family detached	26.0	357	8,440	69.0
		1-family row	26.0	357	3,740	30.3
Childless couples, single adults and other adult households	48.0	3-story apartments	20.0	275	2,195	13.8
		6-story apartments	28.0	386	1,580	14.0
Total	100.0		100.0	1,375		127.1
Resultant Neighborhood Density: 10.8 Families per Acre						

[a]Neighborhood land area requirements from Table C-6-2.

ing of adults. The developer proposes to house families with children in an equal proportion of one-family detached and one-family row houses, so that 26 percent of all dwellings (357 units) would be in each of these dwelling types. To meet the needs of families without children, the developer further desires to provide 20 percent of dwellings (275 units) in 3-story walk-up apartments (corresponding roughly to the proportion of childless couples) and the remaining 28 percent, or 386 units, in 6-story elevator apartments.

Total neighborhood land area requirements (in square feet per family) are now computed from C-6-2, separately for each group of dwellings. Since community facility space allowances vary with size of neighborhood and since we are dealing with a 5,000-person neighborhood, the figures of the last column of C-6-2 are used. These allowances include net residential land requirements for each dwelling type together with prorated areas for community facilities and streets.

Thus, one-family detached houses require 8,440 square feet per family of neighborhood land, one-family row houses 3,740 square feet, etc. On this basis the total area needed for all neighborhood land uses is 127 acres and the resultant neighborhood density is 10.8 families per acre.

It should be noted that U.S. Census data for urban families was used as a basis for illustrative purposes only and that in each

SOURCE: Planning the Neighborhood by the American Public Health Association Committee on the Hygiene of Housing, Public Administration Service, Chicago, Ill., 1960.

instance local population figures should be analyzed for family-type distribution and for the selection of appropriate dwelling types.

Dwelling Type Combinations for a Given Neighborhood Density

When legal regulations or other planning considerations fix overall neighborhood density, the developer is free to use any suitable combination of dwelling types that produces the given neighborhood density, as long as the individual residential portions conform to net density requirements for the selected dwelling types. There is considerable leeway within a given neighborhood density. For instance, in a neighborhood of 5,000 persons (approximately 1,375 families) with a neighborhood density limited to 12 families per acre, the following dwelling type combinations are among the possible choices:[3]

a) 1,300 units in 1-family row houses
   75 units in 3-story multifamily buildings
b) 175 units in 1-family detached houses
   600 units in 1-family row houses
   600 units in 3-story multifamily buildings
c) 375 units in 1-family detached houses
   200 units in 1-family row houses
   800 units in 13-story multifamily buildings

Most zoning ordinances do not recognize the need for diversifying dwelling types within neighborhoods. However, some recently adopted ordinances permit the establishment of "special planning districts" in which dwelling types may be diversified, subject to the approval of the overall plan by the city planning commis-

sion. Wherever possible, planning agencies should set neighborhood densities to permit suitable diversification of dwelling types, in accordance with recommendations made for dwelling type selection.

RANGE OF NEIGHBORHOOD SIZES

Determination of Neighborhood Area and Population

The neighborhood size at which all the requirements for neighborhood facilities can be met is based on the following factors:

a) Population that will support an elementary school and other neighborhood community facilities;
b) Area that will meet accessibility standards (walking distance to community facilities);
c) Area that will accommodate the necessary dwellings and community facilities, in accordance with space requirements;
d) City planning and administrative considerations that may modify theoretical size within the maximum limits. The most important of these are conformity to appropriate physical boundaries and choice of neighborhood density to avoid excessive multiplication of facilities within a small area.

The size of a neighborhood is expressed in two ways: the population and the geographic area. The upper and lower limits for population are set by the capacity of the elementary school. The maximum extent of the area is fixed mainly by walking distance to school and other community facilities. Since density is the ratio of population to area, two of these variables will determine the third. Therefore, population or area within the above limits will depend on desirable densities. C-6-6 indicates neighborhood areas based on maximum neighborhood densities for different dwelling types.

---

[3]For 1,375 dwellimgs at an overall density of 12 families per acre, a total neighborhood area of 115 acres is required. Dwelling type combinations are calculated on the basis of densities given in Column 5, C-6-3, as follows: 300 row houses at a density of 11.7 families per acre require 111.0 acres of neighborhood land. Four acres of neighborhood land are left available. The remaining 75 families can be accommodated in 3-story multiple dwellings at a density of 19.9 families per acre and will require 3.8 acres. Similar computations give distribution of dwelling types under b) and c) above.

C-6 NEIGHBORHOOD DENSITIES

C-6-6 NEIGHBORHOOD AREA DERIVED FROM NEIGHBORHOOD DENSITY ALLOWANCES[a]
Acres in All Neighborhood Uses, by Type of Dwelling and Population of Neighborhood

| Dwelling Type | Neighborhood Population | | | | |
	1,000 persons 275 families	2,000 persons 550 families	3,000 persons 825 families	4,000 persons 1,100 families	5,000 persons 1,375 families
One-or Two-Family Dwellings		Acres in All Neighborhood Uses			
1-family detached............................	57	108	162	213	265 Within
1-family semidetached or 2-family detached }	40	75	111	149	¼-½ 183 mile radius
1-family attached (row) or 2-family semidetached }	28	49	73	95	116
Multifamily Dwellings					
2-story	22	38	55	71	88 Less than
3-story	18	29	43	56	69 ¼-mile
6-story	14	22	32	41	50 radius
9-story	13	21	30	38	46
13-story	13	19	28	36	44

[a]Calculated from Table C-6-3.

C-6-7 NEIGHBORHOOD SIZE AND DENSITY RELATED TO SCHOOL SERVICE AREA
By Neighborhood Density and Population Supporting an Elementary School

| Neighborhood Density | Neighborhood Population | | |
	2,000 persons[a] 550 families	4,250 persons[b] 1,200 families	8,250 persons[c] 2,300 families
Families per Acre		Acres in All Neighborhood Uses	
5.............................	110	240	460
7.............................	79	170	330 Within
9.............................	61	135	260 ¼-½
11...........................	50	110	210 mile
15...........................	36	80	150 radius
20...........................	27[d]	60	115
25...........................	22[d]	48	92 Less than
30...........................	18[d]	40	77 ¼-mile
35...........................	16[d]	35	66 radius

[a]Population required for a 6- or 8-grade school containing 1 classroom per grade.
[b]Population required for a school containing 1 classroom per semester-grade (2 classrooms per grade).
[c]Population required for a school containing 2 classrooms per semester-grade.
[d]Units of less than 30 acres are apt to require duplication of public facilities beyond practical economic limits. Therefore, such small units are considered unlikely except in the case of redevelopment projects.

SOURCE: Planning the Neighborhood by the American Public Health Association Committee on the Hygiene of Housing, Public Administration Service, Chicago, Ill., 1960.

Effect of Accessibility Standards on Neighborhood Area

Assuming a fairly central location of the school and other community facilities, an area of 126 acres will be equivalent to ¼-mile radius of accessibility. An area of 500 acres will correspond to ½-mile radius.

Within these geographic limits of accessibility the area of the neighborhood will depend on densities and dwelling types in relation to the population housed (C-6-7).

A 5,000-person neighborhood can arrange from 44 acres for a 13-story building development to 265 acres for a single-family detached-house development. Calculations of required acreage indicate that all neighborhoods of 5,000 persons or less, developed predominately with row or multifamily structures, will contain less than 126 acres, the area equivalent to ¼-mile radius of accessibility. Developments composed of detached or semidetached houses will contain less than 500 acres, the area equivalent to ½-mile radius of accessibility, and will in general fall below 222 acres, equivalent to ⅓-mile radius.

It appears, therefore, that the desirable standard of ¼-mile radius is practicable for all except neighborhoods of detached or semidetached one-family houses. The distance from the farthest house to the school and other community facilities need seldom exceeds ⅓ mile even in low-density developments.

Effect of School Capacity on Neighborhood Population and Area

An analysis of the population supporting normal sizes of elementary schools, in terms of different density distributions, gives the ranges of neighborhood areas shown in C-6-7. For a school with only one classroom per grade, neighborhood areas will range from 16 to 110 acres. Even at the low density of 5 families per acre, the area will not exceed ¼-mile radius. At high densities the service areas will be so small as to be economically inefficient. A school with two classrooms per grade, which is supported by about 4,300 persons, can serve an area within ¼-mile radius for moderate to high densities (11 to 35 families per acre) and the neighborhood will not exceed 240 acres, equivalent to slightly more than ⅓-mile radius, even at low densities.

It appears, therefore, that a 4,000- to 5,000-person neighborhood offers certain advantages as a planning unit. In the first place, it makes for efficient use of land since, as outlined in previous sections, population concentration above these figures may require duplication of some community facilities. Second, the 4,000- to 5,000-person neighborhood supports a school of the size recommended by many educational authorities. Third, the geographic area will not exceed the desirable ¼-mile radius of accessibility, except for low densities, in which case the farthest dwellings will only be slightly more than ⅓-mile distant from the school.

Among additional considerations that may modify neighborhood sizes based on school capacity, accessibility of community facilities and densities, the following should be noted in particular.

Suitable Size for Residents' Participation

No scientific data exists as to the neighborhood size most suitable for resident participation in neighborhood activities and for the creation of a sense of neighborhood living. However, the general consensus, based on evaluation of existing neighborhood developments and small towns, indicates that many more than 5,000 persons is too large for a single neighborhood under normal circumstances.

This fact in no way precludes the development of appropriate housing areas for a larger population. It merely implies that in those cases, consideration should be given to the possibility of dividing such areas into several neighborhoods, just as it may be advisable to incorporate a number of smaller developments into a single neighborhood.

Suitable Area for Administration

Administrative practices of local government may considerably affect the size of the neighborhood area. Neighborhoods at high densities of 30 families or more per acre, supporting a small elementary school (1 classroom per grade), may be contained in less than 20 acres, and still meet density and population requirements. However, municipal funds for schools, playgrounds, etc. are limited. Multiplication of such facilities within a small area is apt to overburden municipal finances and thereby affect the adequacy of the facilities. It is, therefore, considered unlikely that neighborhood units of less than 30 acres will in the long run be considered desirable by city officials, except for redevelopment projects in extremely high-density areas.

SOURCE: Planning the Neighborhood by the American Public Health Association Committee on the Hygiene of Housing, Public Administration Service, Chicago, Ill., 1960.

Neighborhood Organization

Residential Element	Area Served (radius in ft. or mi.)	Number of Families Served	Types of Open Space and Community Facilities Required	Plan Relationships
Single-family detached home	0-40 ft.	1	Patio, outdoor recreation area, family room	
Single dwelling unit in a multi-unit building	0-40 ft.	1	Terrace or balcony, open corridor, outdoor living room	
Typical floor in a multi-unit building	40-200 ft.	4-10	Enclosed play space, enclosed sitting area	
Apartment building	200-400 ft.	10-150	Outdoor areas for play and sitting, roof deck, pool, community room, tot lot	
Complex of apartment buildings or a residential block or street	400-800 ft.	30-500	Outdoor areas for play and sitting, pool or pools, small community building	
Hamlet or cluster of blocks	800-4000 ft.	90-1,500	Outdoor areas for sports, play (playground) and sitting, pool or pools, community building	
Single neighborhood	¼-½ mi.	1,000-5,000	Play field (sports), playground, sitting and picnic areas, pools, large community building	
Cluster of neighborhoods	½-2 mi.	3,000-15,000	Play fields, playgrounds, sitting and picnic areas possibly with a lake, pools, recreation and community center	

Single-family Detached Home

Single Dwelling Unit (in a Multiunit Building)

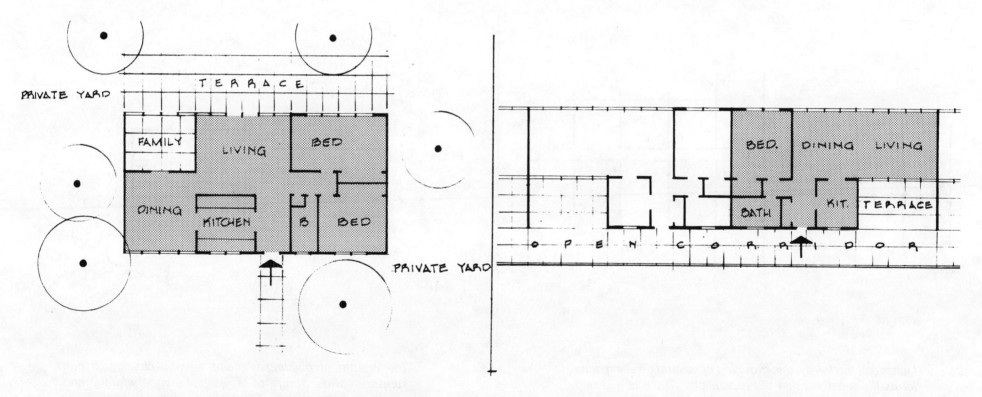

The single-family house and the single apartment unit are the basic planning units containing the family as a social entity. The type and character of this basic planning unit play a strong part in establishing the nature and quality of the community as a whole.

Cluster

Typical Floor (in a Multiunit Building)

Apartment Building (Roof and Ground Plan Shown)

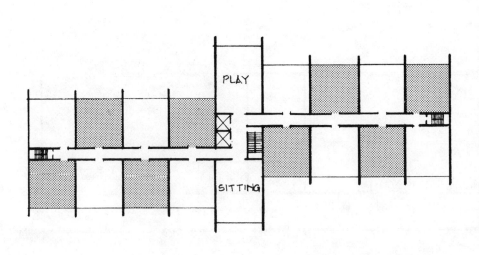

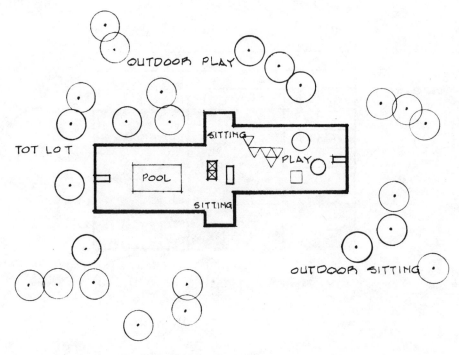

Outside of the family, this grouping of several dwelling units forms the most intimate of associations. There is a strong personal identification among all individuals. Physical proximity is an important element.

The apartment building contains several clusters. It can support a wider range of facilities. Personal identity and close proximity are significant in this relationship.

Complex of Apartment Buildings

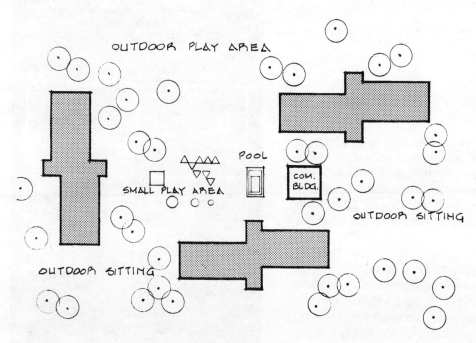

Hamlet or Cluster of Blocks

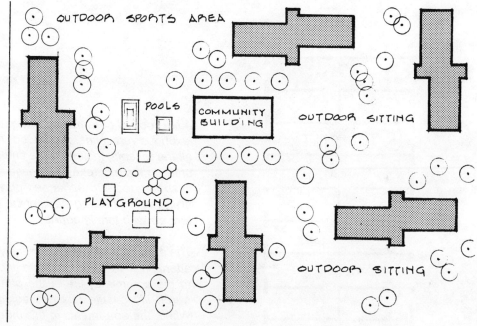

As the grouping becomes larger, relationships are more selective and based on special interests. Less personal contact and physical proximity.

This grouping is similar to a neighborhood, except in number. It contains a wide range of families. There is limited personal contact and a wider assortment of facilities.

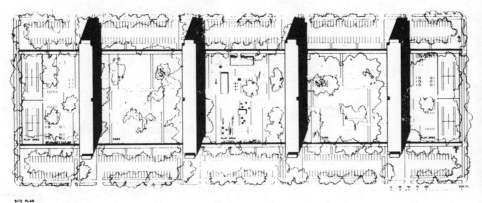

SITE PLAN

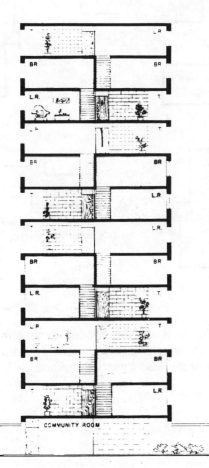

COMMUNITY ROOM

A full flood of **community living** is in this imaginative design for a luxurious vertical neighborhood. All ground floor area is for use of all the tenants, including the enclosed first floor of the apartment units. In the plot for four of these apartment units, communal land is subtended into parks and play areas, and fenced by parking areas down the long sides of the rectangular plot. Short ends are fenced with tennis courts.

The architects of this apartment type also gave deep and obvious attention to the more intimate undertow of **family life**, in addition to the community life of the ground level, and the intermediate porch life on the terraces adjoining the sidewalks in the sky. Within the apartments in this ingenious design the family can be alone without being closed in; and even in the one-bedroom apartments there is the duplex arrangement, guaranteeing further privacy. Three-bedroom and one-bedroom apartments are created simply by transferring proprietorship of one of the two bedrooms in the basic arrangement.

Project by Leinweber, Yamasaki & Hellmuth, Architects

TYPICAL 2 BEDROOM UNITS

TYPICAL 2 BEDROOM UNITS

TYPICAL 1 & 3 BEDROOM UNITS

0 5 10 15 20 FT

CORRIDOR

TYPICAL 1 & 3 BEDROOM UNITS

Single Neighborhood

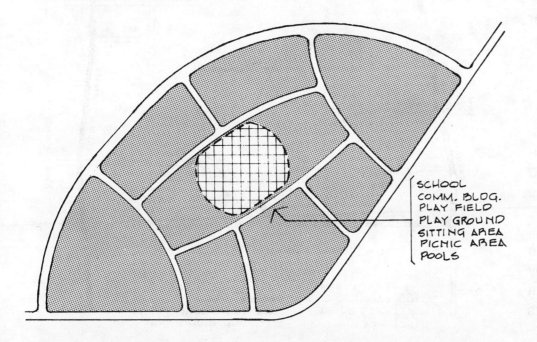

SCHOOL
COMM. BLDG.
PLAY FIELD
PLAY GROUND
SITTING AREA
PICNIC AREA
POOLS

Cluster of Neighborhoods

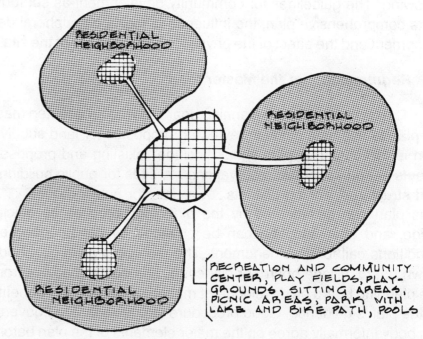

RECREATION AND COMMUNITY
CENTER, PLAY FIELDS, PLAY-
GROUNDS, SITTING AREAS,
PICNIC AREAS, PARK WITH
LAKE AND BIKE PATH, POOLS

Sufficiently large to support an elementary school, local shopping, and a range of recreational facilities. It is small enough with which to personally identify, yet large enough to sustain a variety of interests and friendships.

It is a major planning tool in organizing larger physical areas.

Contains adequate number of people to support a full range of educational, social, and economic facilities. May be considered a small town or village.

121

Good subdivision requires the recognition and evaluation of the elements that will be of significance in creating functional, well-balanced and esthetically pleasing communities. In addition to requiring technical skill in laying out the subdivision, the creation of satisfactory development is also predicated on achieving coordinated action on the parts of the subdivision developer, planning board and other municipal officials.

The general determinants of subdivision design include the following: The guidelines for community development as set forth in its comprehensive plan; the influence of existing peripheral development and the effect of the physical characteristics of the site.

Requirements of the Master Plan

The desirability of the planning board having an adopted master plan to use as a guide in reviewing proposals for land subdivision is obvious. This plan should include "existing and proposed streets . . . parks, public reservations . . . sites for public buildings and structures, zoning districts . . . routes for public utilities. . . ." This plan can be adopted by the planning board as its official guide, and after adoption can be changed by the board when conditions call for its amendment. The municipal governing body (town board, village board, or city council) in seeking advice from the planning board on development matters will obtain the benefits of the plan's guidance. Good procedure suggests that the governing body informally agree on the major elements of the plan before it is adopted by the planning board so that it will reflect the views of the elected officials in the community.

The board can refuse approval to a layout that is not properly related to the street layout shown on the master plan and provides the board with its most important tool for implementing the street system planned for the community. More extensive use of this power in the past could have corrected many errors in street layout now obvious to planners and laymen.

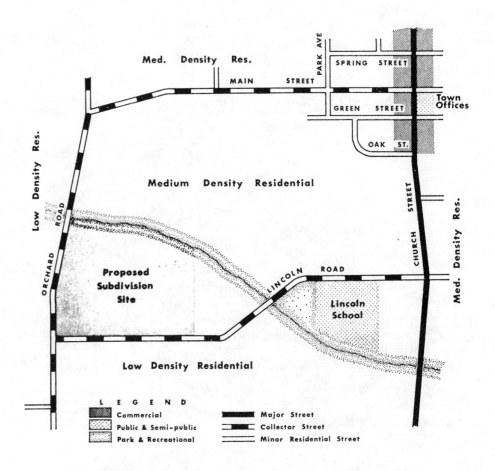

C-12-1 A portion of a town master plan with the location of a proposed subdivision site superimposed thereon.

SOURCE: Control of Land Subdivision—1968. Office of Planning Coordination, State of New York.

C-12-2 Some Alternative Ways of Achieving Open Space

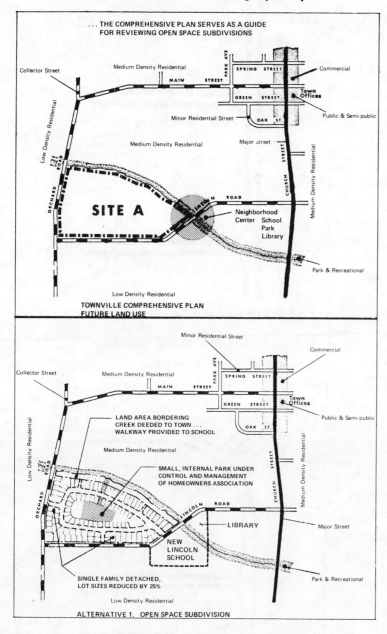

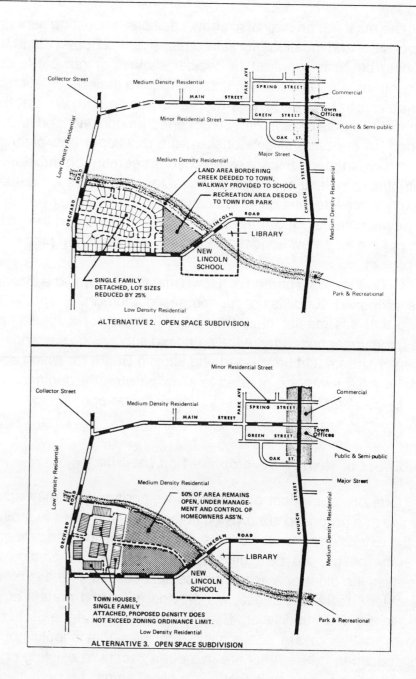

SOURCE: Open Space Subdivisions, NYS—Office of Planning Services

The master plan may also show additions to existing park and school sites and locations for future parks and schools. Since the planning board is required to decide whether or not parks and playgrounds are needed, and if so, to require their reservation by the developer, the park and playgrounds shown on the community's master plan can be obtained (in part) as land is subdivided. In the case of school sites, the developer and planning board have in many instances reached agreement on substantial contributions of land at reasonable cost (or no cost) as a means of helping to provide the schools necessary to serve large new housing developments. More than one developer has found the provision of land for a new school a valuable sales aid when promoting his project.

C-12-1 shows a portion of a town master plan with the location of a proposed subdivision superimposed thereon. It should be noted that this master plan shows the location for a future park along the upper boundary of the proposed subdivision site and two collector streets (Orchard Road and Lincoln Road) for which additional rights-of-way are needed to allow for street widenings.

C-12-2 shows alternate ways of achieving open space.

Effect of Nearby Development on the Site

One obvious effect of existing development that may adjoin the site of a proposed subdivision comes from the need to provide for the extension of roads from the adjoining area into the new one. In some cases, the new development will need to employ the streets in the older one as the means of access to it, and in others the older subdivision streets will provide a second means of access to the new subdivision. Experience throughout the State has shown that there are some basic principles that should not be violated when new streets are laid out adjacent to existing ones. One of these principles is that no "reserve strips" be permitted at

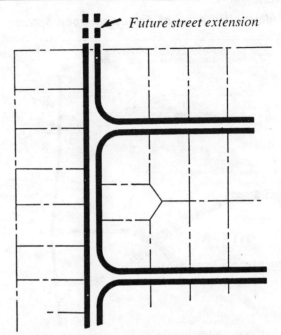

Future street extension

C-12-3   Provision for future street extension

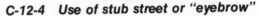

C-12-4   Use of stub street or "eyebrow"

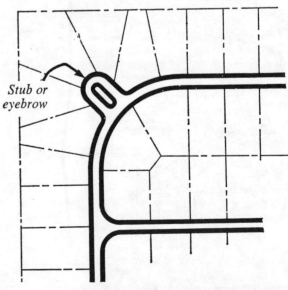

Stub or eyebrow

SOURCE: Control of Land Subdivision—1968. Office of Planning Coordination, State of New York.

the end of a street so as to prohibit future access into land beyond it. The need for convenient traffic circulation throughout a community makes this protective device an obsolete method of providing "privacy" for a particular subdivision. Another principle is that the main means of access to a large new subdivision (say more than ten lots) should be provided from a street designed to carry a fairly high traffic load and should not be provided through a local street designed only for light traffic. If the community does not have a master plan that shows how these traffic routes are to be laid out and coordinated as the area is developed, common sense will often indicate where through traffic or collector-street traffic is best routed. The planning board that has a master plan for traffic circulation will be in a better position to make sure that both new and existing development is not devalued by heavy or high-speed traffic.

When the subdivision design requires that a proposed street be continued to the edge of a presently undeveloped area to make provision for its future extension, it is desirable to require a *temporary* turnaround at the end of the street to allow for convenient vehicular movement. Such excess right-of-way that may be required for the temporary turnaround can revert to the abutting lots when the street is extended.

Unless there is an existing or proposed street to be extended, it is generally undesirable to terminate a street at a property line (See C-12-3). The problem of providing street access to the corner of a property can be solved by the provision of a short stub or "eyebrow" around which usable lots can be created (See C-12-4).

When the new subdivision lies next to an area already provided with public services and utilities, the extension of these becomes an important factor in the layout. Water mains and hydrants can usually follow streets without serious problems, unless a significantly higher elevation is involved, which may call for some adjustment in water pressure. Gas mains are a similar utility, with pressure rarely a problem. Sanitary sewers, however, normally rely on gravity flow, and the grades of streets will very definitely affect the adequacy and cost of this service. In many cases, it is necessary to provide a sanitary sewer easement across lots to make the system workable. (It is good practice to have such easements follow lot lines where possible.) Pumping sewage should be avoided and in some areas will not be approved by health authorities. Storm water drainage is a comparable service: it requires careful analysis to relate its requirements to the street system, the slope of the individual lot, and the location of buildings.

Storm water drainage will need to be routed to some point or points at the boundary of the subdivision where it can be safely carried away (in some few cases the subdivision may include its own drainage "sump"). Where this water leaves the developer's property is a crucial design matter and in the past has caused a great deal of argument among landowners and often has been responsible for costly improvements by the municipality itself. Developments increase water run-off because the new lawns, roofs, driveways, and paved streets are less absorbent than vacant or farm land. This will increase loads on storm drains downstream, and means that the developer, adjoining owner and municipality will have to cooperate in providing solutions. A master plan can include proposals for handling storm drainage on a long-term and coordinated basis and thus provide the planning board and developer with a guide to the solution of drainage problems.

Other connecting utilities and services needing study at the time of subdivision approval are electric power and street lighting, fire alarm boxes, street signs, and sidewalks.

The relation of the subdivision to a nearby school or park should be studied. Persons going to the park or children walking to school should be given a convenient and safe route, and the needs of persons who will be living in the future on land beyond the present subdivision itself will also require study. Again, a master plan will identify these needs and show how they can be met in the design of the new subdivision.

Effect of the Physical Characteristics of the Site

The effect of an area's physical characteristics is one of the most important factors to be considered in the design of any subdivision. When these characteristics are ignored, costs can go up and long-term values will be endangered. When selecting land for development, careful consideration should be given to its slope, drainage and soils. In many cases these factors become so important that they will, in effect, dictate the type of development that is practical. A common example of this is the case where the site under consideration has a very steep slope, which makes intensive one-family housing impractical because of the cost involved in making small lots actually usable.

The developer should take advantage of trained engineering, surveying, and site design services when he begins to plan the layout of the subdivision. The engineer will normally need to make some sort of *topographic map* his basic tool in laying out streets at acceptable grades and in providing a storm water drainage system that is adequate. A topographic map shows the elevations of the site by use of contour lines and usually includes information about watercourses, rock outcrops, and the other physical features of the site. Since the developer will normally need this type of map to make his plans, the planning board may reasonably require the subdivider to supply it as part of his submission for planning board review. Many communities specify in their subdivision regulations that a topographic map be used as a basis for preparation of the subdivider's preapplication sketch (See C-12-23) and preliminary plat (See C-12-24). Where the land is steep, the topographic map will tell how steep it is and will show where roads should not be built. Where land is very flat, the topographic map will show where there is a need for careful design of the drainage system to avoid future flooding or stagnant water.

Specific data or information based on local experience or special study in the area of the site will be needed to show how the water table, type of soils, and underground rock structure will affect the proposed development. If the site is not to be served by water mains or a collective sewerage system, this type of data becomes absolutely essential, and it will be required by health authorities before they will approve any plans. It will also help the developer and planning board to decide on the most practical type of road system, since surface or subsurface rock can add greatly to the cost of road building, pipe laying, and building foundation works. A high water table may be equally difficult to handle.

Recent developments in aerial photography permit much of this kind of data to be obtained from air photos with a minimum of ground survey work. For large tracts, aerial photgraphy will usually be a cheaper method of obtaining topographic and other information than detailed field work on the ground.

One of the most valuable characteristics of a site is the view it may have across neighboring lands or to the horizon. The property with a good view is desirable if the view is pleasing and the lot and houses are laid out to make use of the view. There are many examples of excellent views being wasted when the developer fails to locate the streets and houses in the way that will allow residents actually to see the view. While a planning board is not in the business of designing individual house layouts, it often can persuade the builder to use this valuable resource more fully. When the view is toward visually unattractive commercial or industrial areas, the lot layout should be modified to minimize this effect.

A common complaint about new subdivisions, particularly those that have a large number of new lots and houses, is that they are barren of trees. The preservation of existing healthy and well-suited trees that are already on the site is important in order to keep them as a future asset. Trees increase the value of the lots, as they make the new subdivision more attractive from the beginning. Many builders have found that good trees increase the market price of the lot or house by more than the saving obtained from "clean-sweep" bulldozing. In preserving trees it is important to realize that all trees have a limited useful life: many a handsome forest tree is actually nearing the end of its life and should be removed. The advice of a trained forester or landscape architect will be helpful in these matters. The planning board may require street trees as part of the improvements to be provided by the developer.

If the site under consideration has watercourses, or ponds, or other terrain features that can contribute to the beauty of its layout, it is well to take care to see that as much as possible of these gifts of nature is preserved. A planning board and developer should be able to maximize the use of these resources without unduly restricting the use of the property, as the solutions are usually matters of design detail rather than major land use.

Many sites for new subdivisions have formerly been active farms or had other rural uses that leave on the land, when they are abandoned, certain man-made features that can be turned to advantage at the time of subdivision. Examples of these are stone walls, fences, orchards, ponds, lanes, avenues of trees, and ornamental landscaping. Contrariwise, some of the existing man-made features may be a hindrance to an attractive subdivision, such as the existing buildings on the site, which may be obsolescent or out of character with the new buildings proposed. Old dwellings in this situation are likely to cause zoning variance problems, owing to their bulk, which will tend to make them unusable except for a multifamily purpose (or perhaps a nursing home, fraternal club, or even a commercial use.) These uses in a new one-family area are a devaluating factor in many cases and a good rule to follow under such conditions is to remove them and employ the site for a new use.

Street and Lot Layout

The prime function of residential streets is to provide access to individual properties to accommodate their prospective traffic

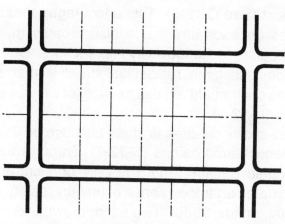

C-12-5 A rectangular or grid street pattern

and to allow the convenient entry of fire-fighting, snow-removal and other road maintenance equipment. Streets should also be logically related to the topography and be coordinated into a system whereby each street performs the function for which it is intended.

The function that a street is intended to serve will determine both its right-of-way width and its pavement width. A minor residential street that serves a relatively low-density residential area may need less pavement width than if the same street served higher concentrations of residential development. This results from both the higher volumes of traffic on the street and from the resultant higher incidence of on-street parking. Collector streets and major streets carry progressively higher amounts of traffic than minor residential streets. This fact must be reflected in the criteria used for determining the street cross section. Other considerations affecting street right-of-way width are sidewalks, planting strips and utilities, including street lights and fire hydrants.

The volume and speed of vehicular traffic on a street can be influenced by its particular design. An undifferentiated rectangular or grid street pattern usually does not include a collector or secondary street system and tends to make each local street as important as the next (See C-12-5). This encourages through traffic at higher speeds on each street and also creates many potential traffic conflict points at the four-way intersections. One of the most trouble-free designs for a residential street is that of a "loop," which provides convenient access to each lot without encouraging through traffic (C-12-6).

The dead-end or cul-de-sac street can also be used to advantage in residential subdivisions (C-12-7). Through traffic is completely eliminated because there is only one entrance into the street. This creates an added sense of privacy, safety and value to the lots fronting on this street. Two major drawbacks of cul-de-sac streets are that access to the interior lots can be impeded by a blockage at the open end and that traffic at the open end can become undesirably high if the street is too long and access to a large number of homes is provided. These streets should have paved turnarounds at their closed ends that are wide enough to permit vehicles to negotiate the turn without the need for backing.

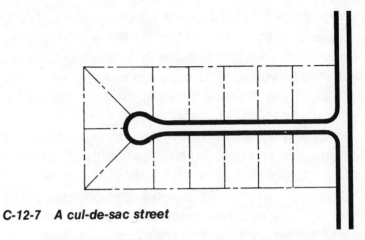

C-12-7 A cul-de-sac street

When residential development occurs along major streets and other highly travelled traffic arteries, special consideration must be given to its design. Lots should not front directly on or have direct access to such streets (C-12-8). When this occurs, the efficiency of these streets is reduced and they are no longer able to adequately perform the function for which they were designed. This problem can usually be solved by either building a marginal access street (C-12-9) or backing the lots up to the major street (C-12-10). The marginal access street provides frontage for the individual lots and greatly reduces the number of points of access to the major street. When the landscaped buffer strip is provided between the marginal access street and the major street, the traffic noise will be reduced and a more private environment created. Unless care is taken in designing the marginal access street, it may cause more traffic conflict at its entrances and exits than it is intended to solve. By maintaining a minimum safe distance between these entrances and exits and other intersections most of this traffic conflict can be avoided.

In cases where lots can be backed onto a major street, the land-use conflict can be reduced by requiring a landscaped buffer zone between the major street and the rear property line. In addition, a fence along the rear property line can provide for more privacy and a safer backyard.

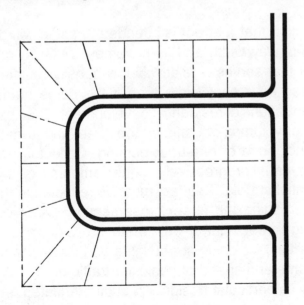

C-12-6 A loop street

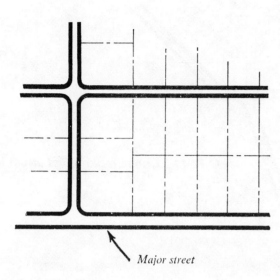

C-12-8 The practice of fronting lots directly on a major street is undesirable

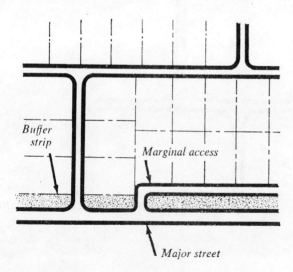

C-12-9 Use of a buffer strip and marginal access street is more desirable

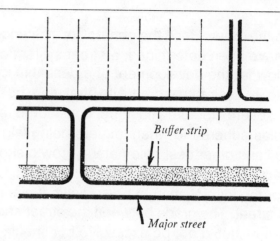

C-12-10 Use of a buffer strip when backing lots on a major street is desirable

Intersections are another important element of street design. When improperly designed, street intersections become potential traffic hazards. Streets should intersect at right angles (C-12-12) and not at acute angles (C-12-11). The center lines of offset street intersections should be far enough apart so that traffic is deterred from cutting diagonally across them. Intersections should occur on straight sections of street instead of on curves, and should have gentle grades rather than steep slopes. Four-way intersections should be avoided except at the crossing of collector or major streets where traffic-control devices are utilized.

The blocks that make up a subdivision are inherently related to the street patterns. Although the number of intersections should be kept to a minimum, it is necessary to limit block length in order to permit adequate vehicular and pedestrian circulation within the subdivision. In situations where excessive block lengths are unavoidable, such as under unusual topographic or drainage conditions, a right-of-way or easement for pedestrians should be provided across the block to break up its excessive length.

The lot layout and street arrangement in a subdivision are so closely interrelated that one cannot be planned without considering its effect on the other. Once the general lot size and dimension requirements have been determined, a street system can then be designed to allow for the development of a desirable lot layout. In order to create a desirable home site that can be developed economically, several factors must be considered and certain general principles adhered to when lots are being laid out.

Good trees and other desirable natural growth should be preserved and the amount of grading kept to a minimum. Generally, it is preferable for the lot elevation to be somewhat higher than that of the abutting street. The grade between the street and the house location on the lot should not be excessive but should be enough to provide good surface drainage to the street and subsequently to a storm drainage system. Each lot should provide a desirable building site that allows adequate space for side yards and a driveway. It should be deep enough to allow for proper building setback and provide some space for outdoor activities.

The size and shape of the individual lot is often influenced by the type and size of dwelling contemplated for the development. This is especially true when the subdivider is also the home builder. Rectangular lots are generally the most usable. However, topography, street layout and the shape of the original parcel often necessitate creation of lots that are not rectangular. When this occurs, odd-shaped lots with excessive jogs and corners should be avoided (C-12-13). Whenever possible, side lot lines should be perpendicular to straight streets or radial to curved streets (C-12-14). Corner lots that are too small do not provide an adequate building site (C-12-15). Generally, corner lots should be larger than interior lots to allow for required setback from each street and provide a more usable backyard (C-12-16).

When developing an odd-shaped parcel of land fronting on an existing road, creation of excessively deep lots should be avoided (C-12-17). Use of a short cul-de-sac street can often facilitate development of the parcel into more desirable lots (C-12-18).

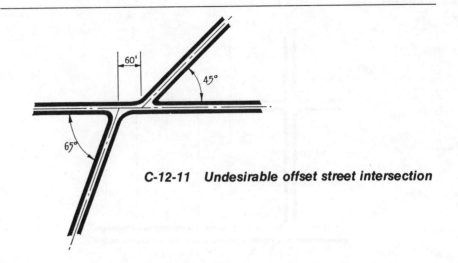

C-12-11   Undesirable offset street intersection

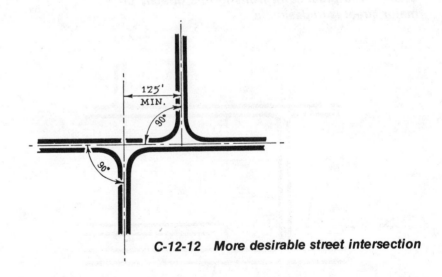

C-12-12   More desirable street intersection

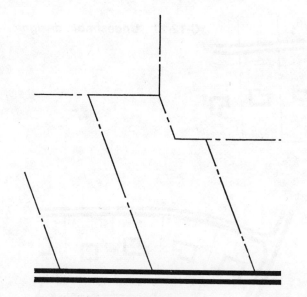

C-12-13 Undesirable lot layout

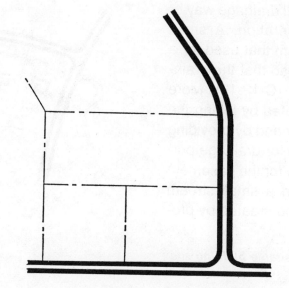

C-12-15 Undesirable corner lot arrangement

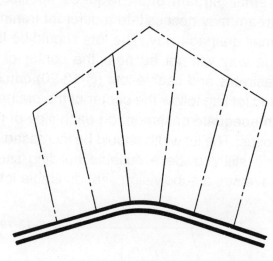

C-12-17 Excessively deep lots

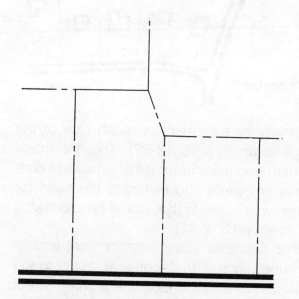

C-12-14 More desirable lot layout

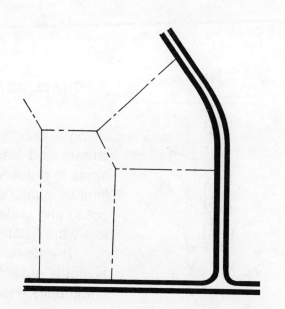

C-12-16 More desirable corner lot arrangement

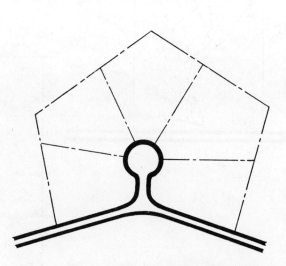

C-12-18 More desirable lots

A subdivision site that is traversed by a small drainage way or a small stream often requires special consideration. A small stream may necessitate a different treatment from that used for a small drainage way. The lots should be laid out so that the drainage way will not be near the center of the lot (C-12-19). More desirable and usable lots (C-12-20) can be created by letting the side lot line follow the center of the drainage way and by providing an adequate easement on each side of this line for drainage purposes. The lot width should be increased to allow for the easement and still provide a suitable building site. When a small stream traverses a subdivision site, desirable lots can be created by pro-

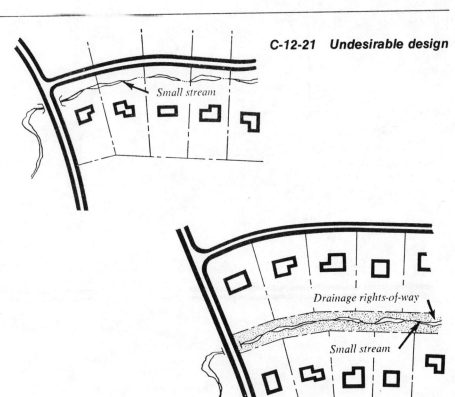

C-12-21   *Undesirable design*

C-12-22   *More desirable design*

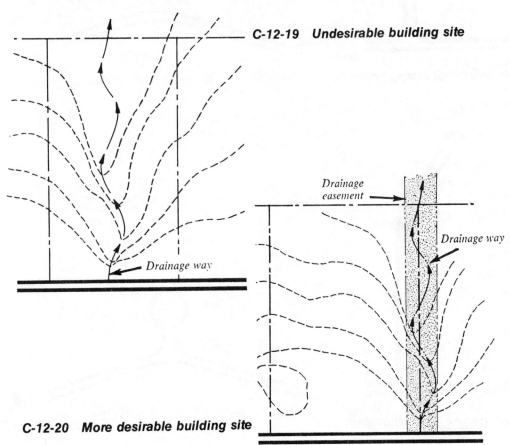

C-12-19   *Undesirable building site*

C-12-20   *More desirable building site*

viding a drainage right-of-way or easement on each side of the stream and backing the lots up to it (C-12-22). This treatment tends to preserve the stream bed in its natural state, provide continuous public or private open space and eliminate the need for costly and undesirable driveway culverts that would be required if lots were fronted on the stream (C-12-21).

The development of a desirable street arrangement and lot layout is essential if the subdivision is to become an asset to the community. However, this alone is not enough. Adequate street improvements, utilities and drainage facilities must be installed and certain community facilities provided.

Controlling the Cost of Improvements

Subdividers can be required to provide for acceptable street improvements in their subdivisions. If the proper standards of design have been used, and the highest quality of contruction maintained, the original cost and annual upkeep will, over the long run, prove cheaper than cutting original costs by inadequate design and construction. A low-cost street base and pavement, while reducing the developer's cost for an improved lot will last only a few years, and the new taxpayers will join in paying the costs of future reconstruction or expensive annual maintenance.

The subdivider's provision of street lights, fire hydrants, fire alarm boxes, trees, and other items can be referred to the local officials involved for their approval. Private utility mains should be approved by the companies that will provide the service.

Many subdivision layouts are not carefully designed to insure the most economical provision of street improvements. In fact, many planning boards have redesigned layouts to cut the length of street without sacrificing lots, a fact that points up the usefulness to the developer of obtaining experienced design assistance. Specific examples of uneconomic layout include excessive street pavement due to short blocks, excessive road construction costs due to steep grades requiring cuts, poor lot layouts resulting in unsalable lots such as corner lots too small, odd-shaped lots without a good building site, and the improper use of wet area, rock area, or land otherwise poorly suited to development.

Experience indicates that time and money spent, by both developer and planning board at the beginning of a development, on experienced technical assistance and complete site analysis will save money during construction and after completion. Rigorous application of the proper standards for improvements will return dividends in lower maintenance costs, greater contentment among the new residents, fewer burdens on the local municipal budget for the improvements finally needed, and a quality of development that will show higher and more stable tax values.

Controlling Maintenance Costs

Proper layout of the new subdivision will obtain the most value for the least amount of street. This will reduce overall street maintenance costs—such as resurfacing, snow plowing, street cleaning, catch basin cleaning, hydrant and street light service, to name a few. Other direct savings will accrue to delivery vehicles through a reduction of the length of trip. Garbage and rubbish collections are similarly affected. In addition to street length, street grade will affect maintenance and servicing costs. Steep grades can force heavy vehicles to take circuitous routes, and can cause hazards amounting to virtual road blocks during adverse weather conditions. The cumulative savings by individuals from proper layout can amount to an impressive sum over a period of years.

Preliminary Plat

Experience indicates that it is generally not advisable for the subdivider to attempt to present a fully completed subdivision plat to the planning board before submitting a less detailed (and less costly) preliminary map for the board's review. There are usually changes needed after the subdivider and board go over the proposal, and making these changes at the preliminary stage can save costs. Because of this, a "preliminary plat" procedure is specified in many regulations. Town law makes provision for a town planning board to continually approve, with or without modifications, or disapprove a "preliminary plat."

At this preliminary stage, the subdivider is usually expected to present a carefully worked out plan for the development of the site, but is not required to finalize this in expensive drawings. The preliminary plat (C-12-24) should be at a suitable scale with accurate drafting so that all of the characteristics of the final plat can be anticipated. Many boards require considerable supplementary data at this stage in addition to the developer's plan. Some of these supplementary requirements may be:

1. Affidavit by owner consenting to the application and submitting proof of ownership.
2. Locational sketch showing how the proposed subdivision fits into the area around it.
3. Preliminary plans and specifications for road construction, drainage, utilities, and other improvements.
4. Temporary stakes along center lines of roads to facilitate board's field inspection.
5. Comments by Health Department officials on feasibility of water supply and sanitary wastes disposal.
6. Comment by county, state, and federal agencies relating to public rights-of-way and sites for public development where applicable.

Due to the detailed nature of the information required for the consideration of a preliminary plat, many regulations offer a "pre-application conference" procedure to the subdivider where he is given opportunity to discuss his project with the board in order to determine its requirements before engaging technical help. This is a practical necessity where the project is a large one or where the developer is new in the community. C-12-23 shows a pre-application sketch used by the subdivider when discussing his project with the planning board and suggested modifications and additional requirements were noted thereon by the board.

The action of the planning board, after its review of the subdivider's preliminary plat, should be such as to avoid any inference that the subdivider has, in fact, received approval of a *plat*, since this can be given only after a public hearing as required by law.

It is recommended that the board's action, including any changes it deems necessary before its final approval, be given to the subdivider in writing and be entered in its record. A written communication from the board to the subdivider is the most practical method of assuring that all parties have a clear understanding of the board's position at this stage.

For example, in taking action on the preliminary plat shown in C-12-24, the planning board granted "conditional approval" subject to elimination of the four-way intersection by use of cul-de-sac and satisfactory adjustment of the lot layout.

Health Department Approval

Prior to the preparation of a final subdivision plat drawing, the applicant should check its design with the appropriate health department, so that the plat presented to the planning board for its approval will also be acceptable to the health officer and thus be suitable for filing with the county clerk.

Health officers recommend that subdividers engage engineering assistance for advice on the water supply and sewerage aspects of land proposed for development. In turn, engineers are encouraged to discuss their projects with the district health engineer prior to the preparation of detailed plans, since health requirements often necessitate changes in proposals, particularly with respect to the size of lots when individual sewerage systems are involved.

If water supply, other than a well for each lot, is proposed, the developer may need the approval of a local water district, or county or state authorities.

The Subdivision Plat

After the preliminary plat has been brought into acceptable shape and health department requirements have been met, the subdivider is ready to apply for final approval of his project. At this stage, many localities require a formal application (which may be supplementary to that required for the preliminary plat), an affidavit of ownership, and the payment of application fees. C-12-25 shows a subdivision plat.

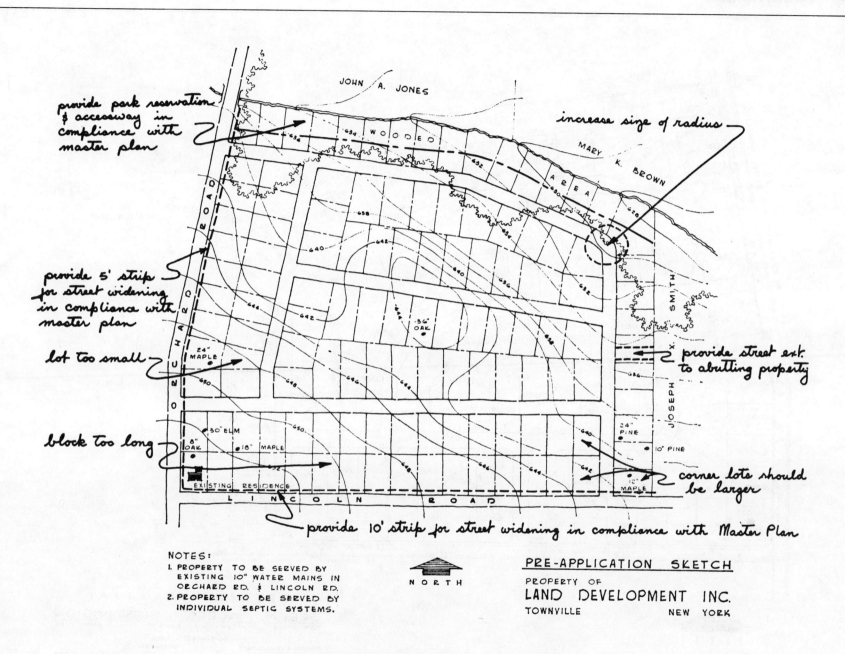

C-12-23 A preapplication sketch of a subdivision
with the planning board's review comments added

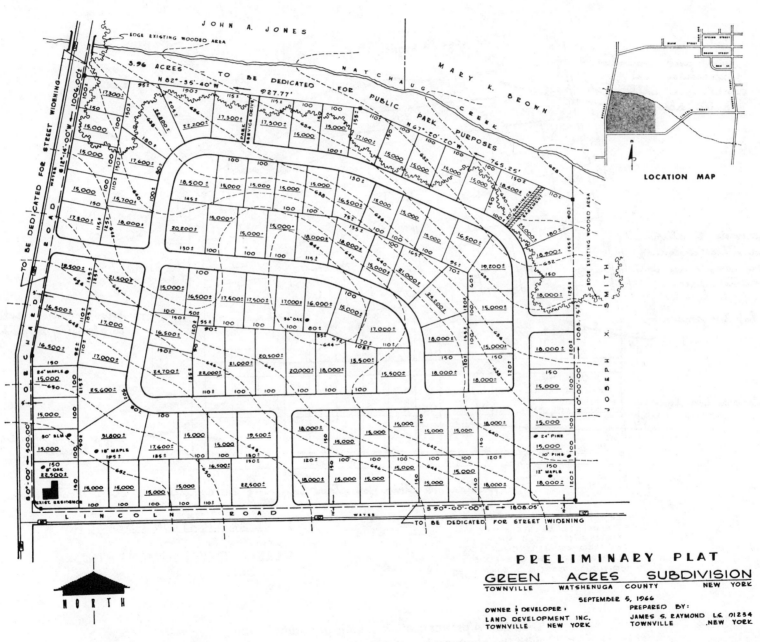

C-12-24 A preliminary plat

LOCATION MAP

■ STONE MONUMENT

1" O.D. IRON LOT PINS TO BE
INSTALLED AT ALL LOT CORNERS

Refer to Subdivision Application Number **78**
on file with the Townville Planning Board
for all correspondence and additional data
relative to approval of this plat.

Approved By
THE TOWN PLANNING BOARD
Town of Townville
Watshenuga County New York

Allan B. O'Brien   Dec. 14, 1966
chairman   date

WATSHENUGA COUNTY DEPARTMENT OF HEALTH

This is to certify that the proposed arrangements
or water supply and sewerage for **GREEN ACRES SUBD.**
in the Town of Townville are approved subject to the
conditions listed in letter of this date, and in
accordance with Article X of the Watshenuga County
Sanitary Code. Consent is hereby given for the filing
of this map in the office of the County Clerk.

Date Dec. 13, 1966   Carl H. Trued M.D.

by R.T. Dunn C.E. & P.E.   Director, Division
                            Environmental Health
                            Service

subdivision   plat

Green   Acres   Subdivision

TOWNVILLE   WATSHENUGA COUNTY   NEW YORK

NOVEMBER 2, 1966

Owner & Developer: Prepared By:
LAND DEVELOPMENT INC.   JAMES S. RAYMOND L.S. 01234
TOWNVILLE   NEW YORK   TOWNVILLE   NEW YORK

C-12-25   A subdivision plat

137

Discourage Heavy Through Traffic

Minor streets should be so arranged as to make fast through travel impossible. Rapidly moving traffic on local residential streets results in an undue number of accidents and also unnecessarily increases the cost of pavement construction and maintenance.

The mixture of local and through traffic on a residential street creates a condition that tends toward a doubtful policy as to land use and neighborhood growth. Where lots have unlimited and direct access to a heavy traffic street there is a constant threat that the restrictive covenants and zoning ordinance may be broken down by pressure to convert detached dwelling lots into income properties.

The upper illustration at the right shows poor street planning that results in unfavorable conditions.

BAD 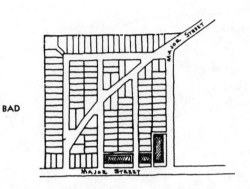 GOOD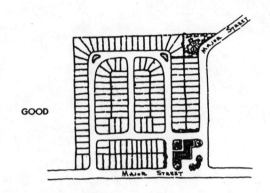

Plan for Extension of Major Streets

In the development of a large subdivision, the relationship of the tract to the master city plan of a community, if such exists, should be ascertained. It is obvious that proposed major streets, transportation, recreation, and public utilities should be considered in planning a new segment of the city.

Where no official plans exist, however, provisions should be made for projecting major streets through the subdivision that now end at the boundary of the tract.

When major traffic streets are not planned as part of the subdivision, lots may be sold and houses built in the path of a future trafficway. Either the development of a through street is blocked or opening of the street later is an unnecessary expense.

BAD 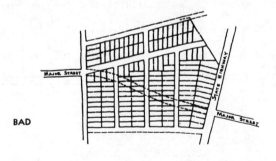 GOOD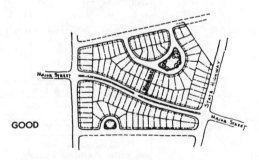

SOURCE: *Planning Profitable Neighborhoods*, FHA Technical Bulletin #7, Washington, D.C.—1933

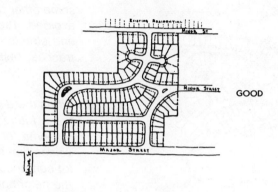

Traffic Should Flow Toward Thoroughfares

When traffic does not flow toward main thoroughfares, it causes an unnecessary use of local streets in order to reach the main trafficways. This excessive use of residential streets causes an added expense of pavement construction and maintenance. Local streets that carry unnecessary traffic form definite hazards to pedestrians and children.

The street design of a subdivision should be carefully planned to provide for all traffic demands and at the same time create a street arrangement that will make an attractive neighborhood. This will generally produce fewer streets than one that cuts up the land into numerous rectangles without consideration of proper traffic routing.

A monotonous street system of this type is generally extravagant, producing more streets than are needed.

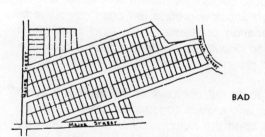

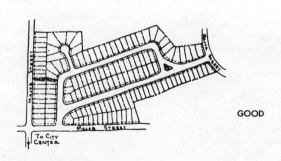

Minor Streets Should Enter Major Streets At Right Angles

Streets should intersect each other as nearly at right angles as is practicable, and the number of streets converging upon a single point should be kept at a minimum. All minor streets approaching a major thoroughfare at acute angles should be turned so that for a distance of about 100 feet they will be at right angles to the major street.

When minor streets join a thoroughfare at raking angles, visibility is greatly impaired for both motorists and pedestrians. Drivers are also tempted to turn in and out of such streets without greatly reducing their speed.

The sketch plans at the left illustrate how hazardous traffic intersections can be improved by correct plotting to obtain streets crossing at right angles.

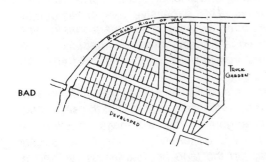

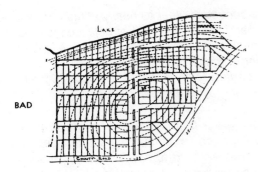

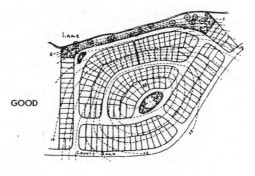

Avoid Planning of Dead-end Streets

The practice has been, in the past, to place dead-end streets against railroad rights-of-way, open country, or some other permanent or temporary barrier. This should be avoided. The remote possibility, in many cases, of dead-end streets connecting with future streets in an adjoining tract has resulted in blighted property in that particular locality.

When there is a possibility of the street going on through, at some future time, the lot at the end of the street may be reserved for a given time and not sold or built on. If it develops that the street connection will not be necessary, the lot can become a building site and complete the design of the neighborhood. When conditions make it impractical to avoid a dead-end street, it should be terminated by a turn-around. This circle should have a diameter of at least 100 feet and be at least the depth of one lot from the boundary line of the tract.

Streets Should Fit Contours of Irregular Land

When ground levels of a tract vary considerably, streets should be laid out to conform to natural conditions. Observations as to high and low ground are often adequate to determine the location of streets. If the land is rough, a topographical map should be made to obtain a complete representation of ground conditions.

Streets laid out to fit the contours of the land will avoid excessive grades and reduce construction cost. A subdivision plan based upon the topography of the site not only makes possible a better-designed development, but also makes the installation of utilities more economical.

In locating streets, consideration should be given to the size and shape of lots and blocks in order to obtain the best use of the land.

Short Blocks Are Not Economical

These sketches contrast two types of local street design —one, an example of the rigid gridiron pattern, the other planned to meet the requirements of local access and circulation.

Short blocks increase initial construction costs because of the large number of cross streets, and also increase traffic hazards and travel time through such districts. In the lower plan, better-shaped lots are secured and those facing the State highway are protected by a park strip. This plan also provides a local shopping center and a school site.

The platting of suburban residential blocks up to 1,300 feet in length by two lot-depths wide, bounded by streets that are adjusted to topographic and traffic requirements, is recommended as being most economical.

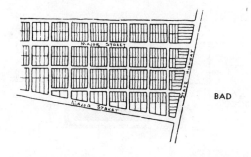

BAD

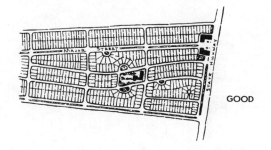

GOOD

Long Blocks Require Crosswalks Near Center

The use of crosswalks through long blocks to afford more direct access to nearby community facilities is desirable because of the appeal and convenience that is lent to otherwise remotely situated residential lots. Such pedestrian ways near the middle of all blocks exceeding 1,000 feet in length is recommended.

When a nearby shopping center, school, or park is so located that a large number of residents of a neighborhood are forced into circuitous routes in order that they may reach their destination, it is often desirable to provide crosswalks in shorter blocks—those over 750 feet in length. This often brings the playgrounds or grocery store as much as a quarter of a mile nearer in walking distance to the doorsteps of many homes.

BAD

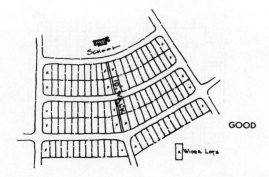

GOOD

Plan Commercial Sites
Where Needed

Local shopping centers are definite assets to a community. They should be located within convenient and safe walking distance for the residents and designed to afford adequate off-street delivery and parking facilities.

Commercial structures should be concentrated at suitable centers adjoining a major thoroughfare and be accessible by way of local connecting residential streets. They should be designed together as a group and not as a series of unrelated separate stores.

To ascertain the amount of land needed for commercial use in a community, such factors as estimated per capita sales and the volume of business per store unit must be analyzed in determining the kind and number of stores that the neighborhood can profitably sustain.

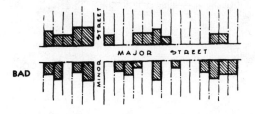

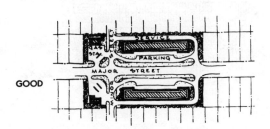

Provide School and
Church Sites

If a subdivision is large enough to warrant the consideration of all community requirements, locations should be provided for schools and churches. These sites should be centrally located for the convenience of all property owners and citizens in the vicinity. Adequate space should be provided for the parking of automobiles without interfering with private parking needs of those living near the school and church.

These buildings produce a favorable impression as to the stability of a community and, therefore, should form one of the early demonstrations of neighborhood growth. The selection of convenient sites for such facilities as schools, churches, and local shopping centers, will go far in increasing a subdivision's salability.

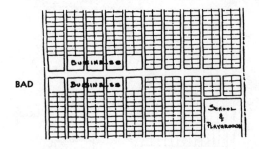

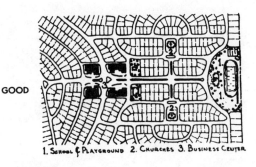

Parks Are a Definite Community Asset

Rough wooded areas that are difficult to develop into economical dwelling sites are often well adapted for recreational use. Enhanced adjoining property values may exceed the cost of developing and dedicating such public open spaces. A well-located park also may offset the sales resistance of remotely situated lots and render the entire tract more marketable.

Parks are a definite asset to a community. They are a proper place for children and adults to enjoy the out-of-doors with safety. They reserve, for all time, natural features that all property owners in the vicinity can enjoy. They are as important to neighborhood development as any other general feature.

The improvement and maintenance of park areas should be handled in the same manner as street improvements and maintenance.

Preserve Natural Features of Site for Improved Appearance

It is recommended that whenever possible all natural features of a neighborhood should be preserved to add to the beauty of the tract.

In many cases valuable tree growth has been cut down and knolls have been removed in order to fill in lower ground. Frequently this is an unnecessary expense and only results in the ruination of what might be a more valuable residential property.

A more desirable neighborhood can be created when roads are located to fit the existing lay of the ground and placed in such a manner as to preserve, as far as possible, the native tree growth. The curving of streets to fit contours of the land and the saving of valuable trees add to the beauty of a development and reduce construction cost.

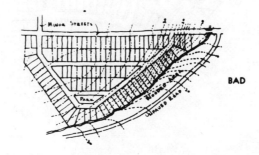
BAD

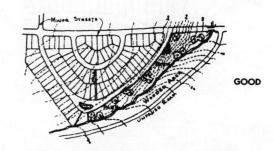
GOOD

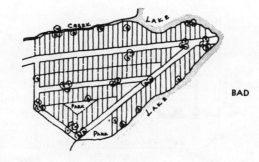
BAD

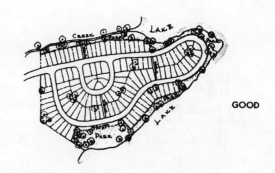
GOOD

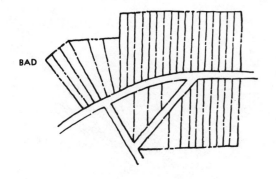

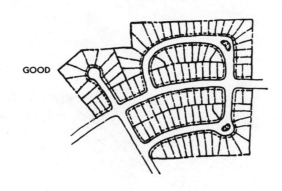

Deep Lots Are Wasteful

Great depth in a residential lot generally does not increase its salability by virtue of its large area. This type of platting materially decreases the number of lots in a subdivision. Residential lots over 150 feet in depth are usually undesirable unless they are one-quarter of an acre or more in size.

If consistent with economical land subdivision, residential lots of 50 or 60 feet in width should not greatly exceed 130 feet in depth. Lots of from 100 to 120 feet in depth will usually be found satisfactory for single-family dwellings. Lot sizes should be arrived at only after a careful study of local conditions and by an analysis of the relationship between front foot utility and street construction costs and the value of undeveloped land.

Plan Lots of Adequate Width

The well-being of a neighborhood and the economic soundness of a project rest largely on the manner in which the land is divided into lots.

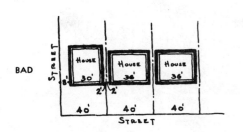

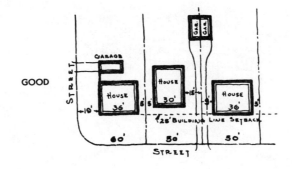

The width of these units should not be reduced beyond a minimum consistent with building coverage, and light and air requirements. Each developer should consider the question of lot width from the point of view of local regulations, the character and topography of the site, the type of dwellings contemplated and the ratio of raw (unimproved) land costs to the linear front-foot costs of local public utility improvements.

Practical building sites require lots at least 50 feet wide to provide adequate side yards for light, air, driveways, and to avoid crowding.

Avoid Sharp-angled Lots

Lots that have sharp-pointed corners are wasteful of land because the resulting wedge-shaped areas have little or no utility. Such lots also constitute poor building sites.

Sharp-angled lots can be avoided by planning streets to intersect at right angles and by making side lot lines perpendicular or radial to street lines.

In the adjacent sketches are contrasted an extravagant –though not unusual–type of subdivision plan and a suggested revised design that has 40 percent less street area, better sized and shaped lots, and eliminates hazardous traffic intersections.

Attention also is directed to the manner in which deep lots are backed against the highway bounding one side of the tract, thus permitting all houses to face into the subdivision.

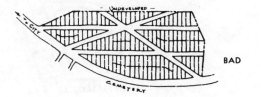
BAD

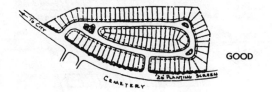
GOOD

Plan Wider Corner Lots

Every residential lot within a neighborhood should be sufficiently spacious to provide free area on all sides of the space to be covered by a dwelling. Because of the special requirements imposed upon corner lots by reason of necessary setbacks from two streets, it is recommended that corner lots be given extra width at least to the extent of the additional side yard demanded by the side street setback requirement. In the case of a normal corner lot with a side yard requirement of 15 feet, the width should be 10 feet wider than interior lots.

Regulations establishing minimum building line setbacks on the front, sides, and rear of dwellings must be considered by the subdivider at the time lot lines are established.

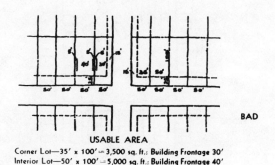
BAD
USABLE AREA
Corner Lot—35' x 100' = 3,500 sq. ft.: Building Frontage 30'
Interior Lot—50' x 100' = 5,000 sq. ft.: Building Frontage 40'

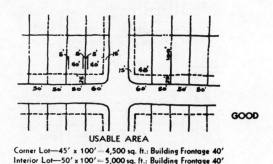
GOOD
USABLE AREA
Corner Lot—45' x 100' = 4,500 sq. ft.: Building Frontage 40'
Interior Lot—50' x 100' = 5,000 sq. ft.: Building Frontage 40'

145

Make Lot Lines
Perpendicular to Street

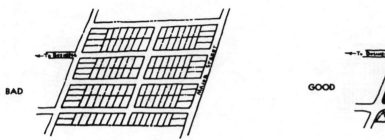

In order that maximum use be obtained from all lots, it is suggested that the lot lines be kept perpendicular or radial to street lines. When this is not done, there is a tendency to build houses on lots so that the sides of the houses are parallel with the side lot lines. This creates an unattractive sawtooth arrangement and many times causes the front of one house to face into the side or rear of a neighboring house.

If a maximum use is to be made of every square foot of the lot area, it is important that the lot be well shaped. If lines are not kept perpendicular to the street, sharp-angled corners will result. These are difficult to utilize and give the area an undesirable appearance.

Plan Lots to Face
Desirable Views

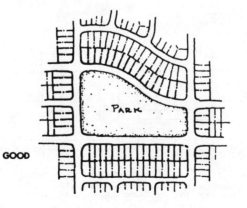

In laying out a subdivision the planner should take advantage of any natural or created beauty spot. Whenever possible, lots should be so faced that houses will look out over the park rather than face on side streets.

Developers should give consideration to the arrangement of lots so that the proposed dwellings will not overlook neighboring rear yards, face undeveloped and restricted property, or be exposed to the adverse effects of heavily traveled streets and adjacent nonconforming land uses.

Each lot within a new subdivision should not only constitute a good house site, but also be so planned as to size, shape, and orientation that it takes full advantage of such desirable natural features as views, the slope of the land, sunlight, prevailing winds, shade trees, and adjoining public spaces.

Protect Lots Against Adjacent Nonconforming Uses

Residential lots should be arranged so that they will not be seriously affected by a nonconforming use of adjoining property. Objectionable properties can be blocked off by screen planting, or the lots backed against the nonconforming land so that houses built on them front away from the objectionable use. It is suggested that where possible the subdivision boundary line be along the rear of a lot rather than the center of a street.

The appearance and value of a building site is improved when it faces a similar site across the street. Correct location of lots, well-drawn restrictive covenants and zoning ordinances are a protection against the blighting influence of adjoining nonconforming property uses.

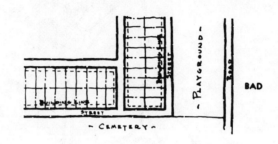

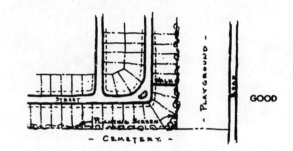

Protect Residential Lots Against Major Street Traffic

When residential lots are located on a major thoroughfare, it is suggested that the through traffic be separated from local service by a planting strip about 20 feet wide.

An 18-foot local service roadway should be located inside of this planting protecting the residences against the noise and dust of traffic, and lessening the street dangers to children. Increase in the desirability of the lots will offset the cost of added street width and the planting of trees and shrubs will add to its attractiveness.

In the past it has been the custom of developers of subdivisions to set aside all property on main thoroughfares for business or apartments because of the belief that a major highway was not a suitable place for a private dwelling. The result has been spotted developments with many vacant lots.

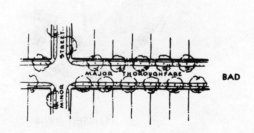

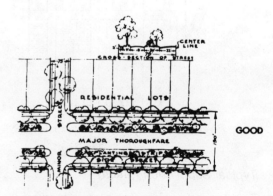

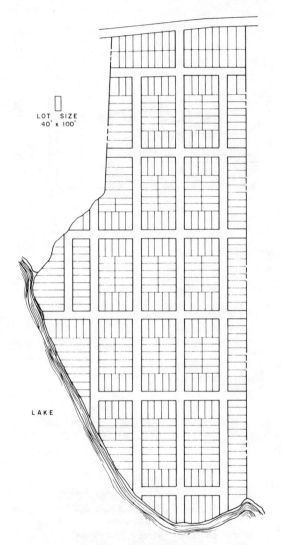

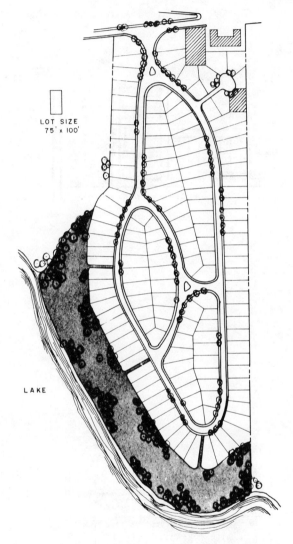

An excessive amount of street construction, the rigid and monotonous layouts of streets, the use of "butt" lots, and the subdividing of the wooded lakeshore, as shown in the original scheme, would make the project costly to develop and difficult to market.

The revised plan has overcome these objections and every lot has been made a desirable building site. Although this plan provides fewer lots, the changes permit a greater financial return and quicker sales for the developer and a better investment for the buyer.

Typical Subdivision Pattern

This type of subdivision plan is marked by excessive amounts of street construction, lots blocking the shoreline, and no open space.

SOURCE: ***Where Not to Build***, Technical Bulletin # 1, Bureau of Land Management, U.S. Dept. of the Interior, Washington, D.C., 1968

Revised Pattern

This revised plan, though of fewer building lots, provides amenities of better building lots, and preservation of the shoreline in community open space.

The subdivision on the following page provides 101 desirable building sites. A majority of the houses face east or west and will, therefore, receive sunlight into their front rooms at some time during the day. In the preparation of the plat for recording, lots should be numbered consecutively throughout the entire tract.

The street plan is adapted to the topography and provides for surface water drainage. Although the number of entrances from the major thoroughfare is limited, the street pattern facilitates the flow of traffic from the principal approach. Curved streets create greater appeal than is possible in a gridiron plan. Blocks up to 1,200 ft. long are desirable and reduce expense for cross streets. This subdivision does not require its own system of major thoroughfares. However, recognition is made of the present and planned roadway pattern of the city in which it is located.

A subdivision of this size does not require provision for complete community facilities, such as stores, schools, and churches necessary in a larger neighborhood.

Complete information regarding the site and its relation to the town or city of which it is part is essential to the planning of a desirable residential neighborhood. Not only is it necessary to have a closed, true-boundary survey, but also complete topographical data, including locations of existing trees that might be preserved. The capacity of storm and sanitary sewers should be known. The adequacy of a safe water supply system and the existence of other essential utilities, and of transportation facilities, are important factors.

Residential subdivisions should be located where they will not be adversely affected by industrial expansion and other nonconforming uses. They should be in the trend of residential development of similar type homes. To further assure stability, residential areas should be safeguarded by recorded protective covenants, and the establishment and enforcement of a zoning ordinance governing the use of the property and surrounding areas.

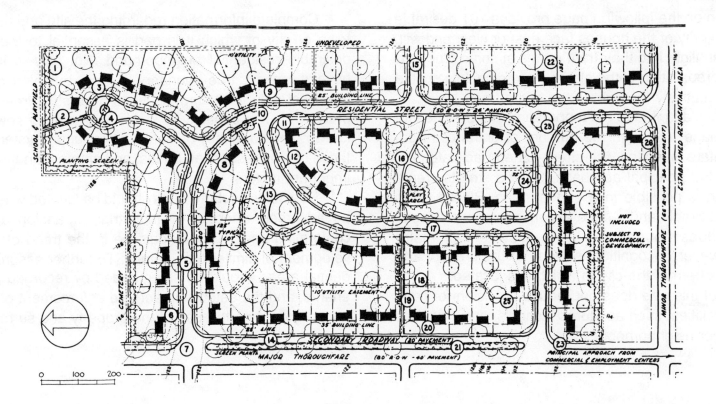

Legend

1. 15-ft. easement for planting screen to provide protection from nonresidential use.
2. 10-ft. walk easement gives access to school.
3. Cul-de-sac utilizes odd parcel of land to advantage.
4. Turnaround r.o.w. 100 ft. in diameter.
5. Street trees planted approximately 50 ft. apart where no trees exist.
6. Additional building setback improves subdivision entrance.
7. Street intersections at right angles reduce hazards.
8. Lot side line centered on street end to avoid car lights shining into residences.
9. Residences opposite street end set back farther to reduce glare from car lights.

10. Three-way intersections reduce hazards.
11. Property lines on 30-ft. radii at corners.
12. Lot lines perpendicular to street right-of-way lines.
13. "Eyebrow" provides frontage for additional lots in deeper portion of block.
14. Secondary roadway eliminates hazard of entering major thoroughfare from individual driveways.
15. Provision for access to land now undeveloped.
16. Neighborhood park located near center of tract. Adjacent lots wider to allow for 15-ft. protective side line setback.
17. Pavement shifted within right-of-way to preserve existing trees.
18. Above-ground utilities in rear line easements.

19. 10-ft. walk easement provides access to park. Adjacent lots wider to allow for 15-ft. protective side line setback.
20. Variation of building line along straight street creates interest.
21. Screen planting gives protection from noise and lights on thoroughfare.
22. Lots backing to uncontrolled land given greater depth for additional protection.
23. Low planting at street intersections permits clear vision.
24. Wider corner lot permits equal building setback on each street.
25. Platting of block end to avoid siding properties to residences across street.
26. Lots sided to boundary street where land use across street is nonconforming.

Subdivision Planning Standards, Land Planning Division, Federal Housing Division, Washington, D.C.

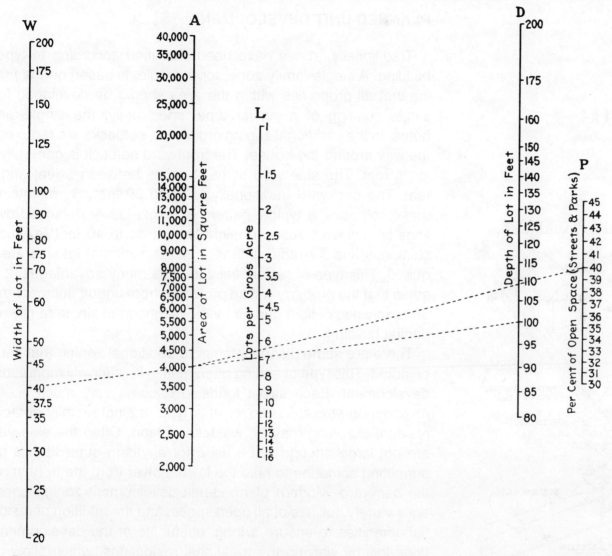

In studying a site for a possible sub-division, a critical determination is the number of lots per acre and the amount of open space for streets and park areas. The accompanying diagram provides a quick means of determining the relationship of number of lots per gross acre and percentages of open space.

It is assumed that the site is level and entirely buildable with no steep slopes, marshy land or other obstructions.

DIAGRAM FOR DETERMINING LOTS PER GROSS ACRE FOR VARYING LOT SIZES AND PERCENTAGES OF OPEN SPACE IN STREETS AND PARKS

Method of using diagram: Start with values on W and D scales; lay straight-edge between them and read area of lot on A scale; choose value on P scale; lay straight-edge between this value and determined value on A scale; read required answer on L scale.

In example shown, W = 40 feet and D = 100 feet; hence A = 4,000 square feet. With P = 40 per cent, L = 6.5 lots per gross acre.

SOURCE: NY Regional Survey of New York and Its Environs—1929

PLANNED-UNIT DEVELOPMENT

Traditionally, zones have been classified according to type of building. A single-family zone, for example, is based on the premise that all properties within the area should be developed for a single building of a similar type, specifically, the single-family home. In the traditional zoning ordinance, setbacks are required all the way around the house. The front yard setback is generally 20 to 25 feet. The side yard setback varies between 5 feet and 15 feet. The backyard traditionally is 25 to 30 feet. By maintaining these setbacks, a typical pattern of single-family detached dwellings is achieved. Also, a height limit of 30 to 40 feet (excluding chimneys and TV-radio antenna) and a minimum lot size are required. This type of residential zone has many advantages. It ensures that the property will be protected from undue encroachment and exclusion of light and air by the neighboring single-family residential building.

There are some disadvantages to traditional zoning that should be noted. This type of zoning often results in relatively monotonous development. Each street tends to become very much like the neighboring street. Moreover, this type of single-family detached residential zoning may be wasteful of land. Often the side yards are not large enough to be used for anything other than a path permitting someone to take the lawn mower from the front yard to the backyard. Modern planned-unit development zoning encourages variety, full use of all open space, and the addition of residential amenities to ensure a long, useful life of the development. It does this by waiving the traditional restrictions, which allow only single-family houses on spacious lots. Under planned-unit development zoning, the density of the area remains constant, but the developer may build an assortment of housing types—single-family units, duplexes, row houses, and apartments. This type of development, especially recommended for hilly terrain, has the added advantage of providing common parking facilities and play areas.

For example, in a 5-acre area zoned at a density of four families

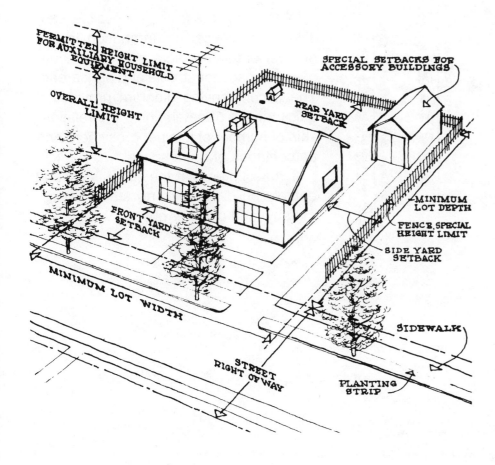

TRADITIONAL RESIDENTIAL ZONING

SOURCE: *Zoning for Small Towns and Counties*, U.S. Dept. of Commerce, Washington, D.C.—1970

per acre (approximately 10,000 square feet minimum lot size), the developer can build 20 units. He may choose to construct a row of 8 units plus 2 apartments of 6 units each, for a total of 20 units. This is the same number of units the developer could build under a traditional development of single-family homes. Under planned-unit development, however, the developer may be able to achieve substantial savings in street and utility development. More important, the housing units can be laid out so that a substantial saving in land will be achieved. Many developers add special amenities to their developments, including swimming pools, golf courses, and community centers.

The planned-unit development is usually incorporated into the zoning ordinance, not as a special zone, but as a conditional use in any of the residential zones. Usually it must conform to the density of the zone in which it is located. In some communities, a 10 or 20 percent density bonus is offered as an incentive to encourage developers to use this method of building residential areas. Usually a 5-acre minimum is required, although in some communities there is an advantage in reducing this minimum to one or two acres to encourage planned-unit development where an entire block in a built-up area is still vacant and under single ownership. The development plan is reviewed by the Board of Adjustment, which may be assisted by outside consultants. Attention should be paid to designing the zoning ordinance so that the review procedure does not discourage developers from taking advantage of the planned-unit development.

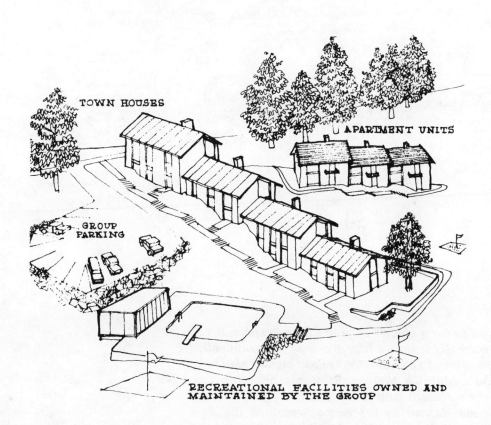

PLANNED UNIT DEVELOPMENT

TOWN HOUSES

APARTMENT UNITS

GROUP PARKING

RECREATIONAL FACILITIES OWNED AND MAINTAINED BY THE GROUP

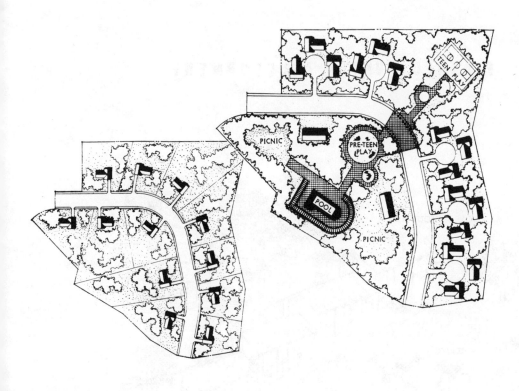

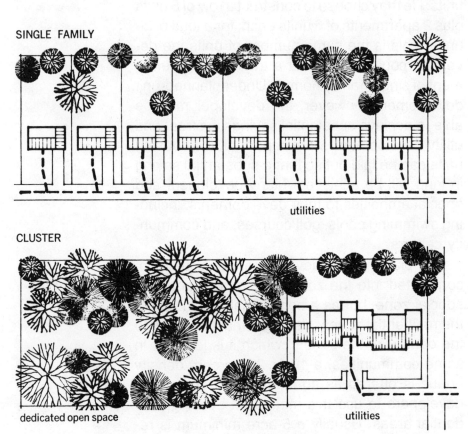

A design for a cluster zone in Poughkeepsie, N.Y., by Burt Gold, shows how the land was originally divided into 12 parcels. The revised cluster plan has three additional houses. Strategic planning releases sufficient land for a community part owned and maintained by the homeowners of the development. The recreational facilities include tennis courts, a pool, cabanas, and outdoor shower.

Single Family vs. *Cluster* comparison shows open space gained by clustering homes.

"Citizens, Computers, Clusters; A Way to Parks and Housing"—John Rahenkamp and Andrew Wolffe, *Landscape for Living, The Yearbook of Agriculture,* U.S. Dept. of Agriculture, 1972

The approach is quite simple. Open space is preserved by permitting a subdivider to develop smaller lots than specified in the zoning ordinance, coupled with the requirement that the land saved be reserved for permanent open space. No increase in the number of units is allowed, thus retaining the original density prescribed by the zoning ordinance. For this reason the technique is sometimes referred to as "density zoning" or "density averaging."

A more common term for it is "cluster development," or "cluster zoning." While this is simple and easy to remember, it can be misinterpreted to mean houses tightly packed or clustered together. While this might be appropriate in some places, it is not a necessary feature of successful open space design even though houses will be somewhat closer together than in a conventional development of the same acreage.

Still another term associated with the open space approach is "Planned Unit Development" (PUD). The U.S. Department of Housing and Urban Development uses "PUD" specifically to mean a similar kind of residential development. However, planned-unit development more commonly means a relatively large-scale development that includes commercial and public facilities, and sometimes industrial development, as well as housing, in the overall design. PUD also generally involves densities higher than permitted by existing zoning. PUD may incorporate the open-space concept in its design, but its uses are larger in scope.

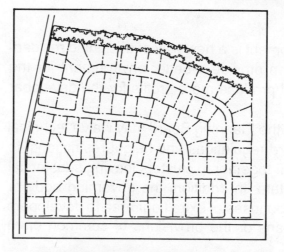

conventional development

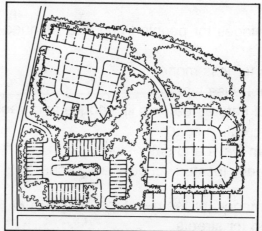

open space development

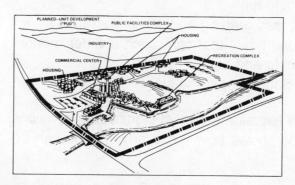

Planned Unit Development

SOURCE: Open Space Subdivision, N.Y.S.—Office of Planning Services

PUD

Planned Unit Development is a new way of designing residential neighborhoods that can provide a better environment for the people who live there and produce more profits for the developer and builder.

Under this approach, the Planning Board may waive technical requirements, such as yard regulations and height restrictions, to permit dwellings to be built together in clusters leaving substantial land areas in a natural state. In addition, the governing body or planning board can grant bonuses of extra floor area to developers in return for good site plans or the provisions of common open space.

Some of the advantages for people living in a Planned Unit Development are:

Larger houses for less money
More choice of house types
Preservation of natural features like ponds and trees
Community recreation space
Safe pedestrian ways and safer streets
More conveniently located schools and shops

Some of the advantages for the developer and builder are:
Less land used for streets
More efficient utility runs
Better drainage, less grading and site preparation
More varied house types that can reach a wider market
More dwelling units and bigger houses
The ability to include shops and stores

The following outline explains the most significant provisions of the new approach, and shows how these advantages can be obtained.

SOURCE: *Planned Unit Development* (New York, N.Y.,) N.Y.C. Planning Commission

Regulations that can be modified:

The Planning Board may authorize the following modifications to the zoning regulations, provided that the overall plan is satisfactory to the Board and is not contrary to the Master Plan.

Bulk regulations:

a. Floor area and dwelling units, rooms, or rooming units may be distributed without regard for zoning lot lines.
b. Open space may be distributed without regard to zoning lot lines.
c. Lot sizes may be reduced.
d. Yard regulations may be waived within a development.
e. Height regulations may be waived within a development, provided that regulations governing the spacing of buildings are satisfied.

Use regulations:

a. Convenience shopping, restaurants and certain other types of consumer services may be permitted within residential areas, provided that the Board is satisfied that they represent an amenity, and provided that the total area devoted to such uses is no more than 2-5 percent of the overall floor area permitted in the development.
b. Outdoor swimming pools may be provided in the common open space, provided that their use is restricted to residents of the development and that the pool is located at a reasonable distance from the development's boundary and is adequately screened from the street.

Regulations that can be modified by special permit:

The Planning Board may grant Special Permits providing for minor variations in the requirements for front or rear yards, and in the regulations governing the height of buildings, along the boundaries of a Planned Unit Development.

Bonuses given by special permit:

The Planning Board may grant bonuses of additional floor space to the developer for a good site plan with or without the provision of common open space. The bonus for a good site plan can be granted within the following limits:

1. The required open space may be reduced by 10-20 percent.
2. The required lot area per room, or the lot area required per dwelling unit, may be reduced by 5-10 percent.
3. The allowable floor area may be increased by 5-15 percent.

Larger Houses for Less Money

A large portion of the price paid for a house really goes to pay for land. Land prices in urban areas can be as much as 10 times as high as they would be in a suburb. Since Planned Unit Development permits the builder to offer houses on smaller building lots, a house in a development where this approach has been used could cost substantially less than a comparable house on a larger lot. At the same time, the easing of yard restrictions in Planned Unit Development permits the builder to construct a larger house than is now permitted on a conventional lot; so that a larger house, for less money, is a very real possibility under Planned Unit Development.

More Choice of House Types

Where conventional development tends to produce street after street of the same type of dwelling, Planned Unit Development encourages town houses, garden apartments, detached houses, and atrium houses, all of varying sizes, to be built in the same development. This means more variety of family size and income level in any given area, and allows families to move from one type and size of house to another without leaving their old neighborhood.

Preservation of Natural Features

Instead of developing a whole section with paved streets and narrow, fenced-in yards, Planned Unit Development permits as much as 30 percent of the land area to remain in its natural state, while housing the same number of families as conventional development, sometimes even more. This means that natural features, like ponds and rock outcroppings, as well as trees and streams, can be preserved near the places where people live.

At the same time, all houses continue to have their own private open space, which may well be larger than conventional backyards. The land saved for open space is land that would ordinarily have been devoted to unusable side yards and unnecessary streets.

Community Recreation Space

Open space created by Planned Unit Development can be used for recreation areas like playing fields and swimming pools, and there can easily be extra open space for schools and community facilities. The new approach allows such facilities to be designed as an integral part of the residential neighborhood, instead of being in their own separate locations.

Safe Pedestrian Ways and Safer Streets

The community open space of Planned Unit Development can also be used to create pedestrian greenways connecting houses with schools and larger open areas. Such greenways can be designed so that they cross few or no streets, providing safe routes for children to walk to school, or play space.

The intersection of two conventional "gridiron" streets creates as many as 16 potential places where a collision can take place. The neighborhood loop streets possible in Planned Unit Development can have as few as three potential collision points. In addition, the clear distinction between through-traffic streets and neighborhood streets made possible by Planned Unit Development provides a generally safer traffic pattern, with fewer cars moving more slowly, in the areas where people live.

More Convenience to Schools and Shops

In conventionally zoned areas, shops can only be placed in sections with commercial zoning. A Planned Unit Development permits small groups of shops and restaurants in the middle of residential areas, giving the kind of convenience often found in the center of cities, but seldom in outlying residential districts.

In addition, by placing a school adjacent to community open space, it is likely to be far more centrally located than would be possible under conventional conditions.

Fewer and Shorter Streets

Developers in large low-density tracts generally are responsible for building the streets themselves; therefore the fewer and shorter streets needed for Planned Unit Development mean a substantial saving for the developer. There may be as much as 30 percent less street area under Planned Unit Development, which not only means less development cost, but more valuable land available for housing.

More Efficient Utility Runs

The developer in a large tract normally must also build storm drains and the sewers for his development. Because of the more compact street system possible in Planned Unit Development, the developer is likely to realize substantial savings in providing utilities.

Better Drainage, Less Site Preparation

Conventional gridiron street systems often work against the natural contours of the land, creating steep streets to which it is hard to relate houses, and low-lying areas susceptible to flooding. Planned Unit Development, by providing streets that are only for local vehicles, allows the builder to develop those parts of his site most suitable for housing, leaving hills and flood plain areas open as part of his community open space. By not having to meet customary requirements for through and connecting streets, the builder frequently can realize a significant saving, as well as ending up with a far more satisfactory development.

More Sales Flexibility in House Types

Market conditions often change while an area is being developed. Mortgage money may become easier or harder to come by, local conditions may cause a sudden influx of a new kind of house buyer. Conventional zoning and street maps tend to lock the builder into a single type of house with a very narrow variation in price range. The variety of house types possible under Planned Unit Development allows the builder to appeal to a wider segment of the potential house market, and to switch from detached houses to garden apartments, for example, as market conditions change.

More Dwelling Units and Bigger Houses

The bonus provisions of the Planned Unit Development regulations can give the builder significantly more houses or apartments on a given piece of land, in addition to the extra buildings made possible by saving on the amount of land devoted to streets. The relaxation of yard requirements also permits bigger houses than are possible under conventional zoning, further enlarging the builder's flexibility in responding to the housing market.

Ability to Include Shops and Stores

Finally, the developer and builder benefits from the opportunity provided by Planned Unit Development to devote a portion of the floor area he builds to space for shops and restaurants. Such commercial space has a high rental value, and is not usually allowed in a residential development.

Streets

Street patterns are the most important element in establishing the character of a residential community. Most existing and mapped streets are based upon only two guiding principles: provision of maximum frontage for traditional lot size and maximum flow of all type of traffic on every street. The first step in dispelling the monotony caused by this system—particularly in low-density residential areas—is the establishment of a hierarchy of street types based on usage. Aside from expressways and highways, this hierarchy consists of three basic street types: major collector streets, local collector streets and local residential streets. Major collector streets are major arteries and interneighborhood streets; local collector streets pick up traffic from local residential streets in one neighborhood; and local residential streets are solely for the residential area served. Recommendations for specific characteristics of these three street types are:

Major Collector Streets:

Traffic characteristics: all types of vehicles, through traffic.

Pedestrian safety: limitation of pedestrian crossover to a minimum of controlled point.

Length: unlimited

Width: 60'—100'

Grades: 8 percent maximum, with other technical requirements conforming to the policies of the Department of Highways.

Local Collector Streets:

Traffic characteristics: primarily private cars and service vehicles, through traffic discouraged.

Pedestrian safety: increased through limitation of traffic, but crossover points should be designated.

Length: should be interrupted by intersections with major collector streets; intersections should be T-shaped in order to prevent local traffic from crossing major collector.

Width: 50'—60'

Grades: 10 percent maximum, with other technical requirements conforming to the policies of the Department of Highways.

Local Residential Streets:

Traffic characteristics: private cars, except that service and emergency vehicles are permitted.

Pedestrian safety: problem minimized through restriction of traffic to residents of specific residential grouping; where possible, a pedestrian should be able to pass beyond his own residential grouping without crossing any street. Furthermore, the pedestrian's path to local shops and elementary schools should cross as few streets as possible.

Length: grid and modified grid system blocks should have a continuous frontage no longer than 800', except that a 1,200' long block is permissible if a pedestrian access no narrower than 10' is provided near the midpoint of the block.

Cul-de-sacs should be no longer than 250' to the neck of the turnaround unless a connection to an adjacent street can be achieved by a 10' wide paved pedestrian walk for emergency vehicle access.

P-loop streets should have a neck no longer than 700' and a loop circumference no longer than 2,800', measured at the center line of the street. P-loop streets must have emergency vehicle access to an adjacent street.

Horseshoe-loop streets may be of varying lengths, depending on the number of dwelling units served.

Width: 40'—50'

Specifications of street and sidewalk design and construction must conform to the standards of the Department of Highways.

Sidewalks and Pedestrian Ways

Sidewalks and pedestrian ways supplement and complete street systems in establishing the character of a residential environment. The pedestrian circulation system need not parallel the street system, but the following criteria must be observed:

a. A sidewalk must be provided on at least one side of a public street except where it can be demonstrated that such a sidewalk is not desirable.
b. Pedestrian circulation systems must be provided as convenient, safe, and attractive links between residential groupings, open space areas, recreational areas, schools, and local shopping areas.
c. The width of any sidewalk must be at least 4'.
d. Alternatives to the norms of asphalt or concrete pavement construction should be considered; surface treatment and forming methods can afford an opportunity to enhance the character of a residential environment.

Utility Placement

The requirements of utility locations generally follow the street pattern; however, easements through common open space augment the flexibility of utility placement. Easement requirements are as follows: 20' unobstructed width for one storm or sanitary line; 30' for two storm or sanitary lines. The feasibility of burying electrical and telephone lines should be studied, as well as the use of existing watercourses for storm drainage.

Site Characteristics

Pre-existing site conditions have considerable importance in establishing the character of a residential development. Previous policy, again through street mapping and traditional lot sizes, has generally ignored the preservation of natural site characteristics. The Planned Unit Development amendment not only permits but encourages flexible and positive responses to the natural assets of a site. Specific site assets that should be considered in a Planned Unit Development are:

Trees:

Trees of 6″ diameter and larger are to be protected and saved wherever possible, particularly where a grouping of such trees exists; the feasibility of temporary removal and replacement of smaller trees should be considered.

Contours:

Responses to site profiles must be considered in Planned Unit Developments; ridges, rock outcroppings, slopes, and hillocks all require that special consideration be given the siting of buildings.

Water:

Existing site water, in the form of watercourses, streams, marshes, and ponds should be considered as possible resources for the establishment of viable ponds, streams, or storm drainage courses.

Orientation:

The siting of a residential development should be assessed in terms of site profiles, views, sun, prevailing wind, and water resources.

Open Space Development

All of the above considerations should be considered with a view toward developing pleasant and usable open-space patterns throughout the residential community. This open space should be related to any existing parks or park plans.

Houses and Placement of Houses on Lots

The house is the most important item for each individual homeowner in the residential community. Past practice, dictated by the inflexibilities of street mapping and subdivision, was much too limited a range of choice for homebuyers and developers alike. Typically, such practice resulted in deep, narrow houses on deep, narrow lots. The front yard in this situation is entirely given over to a paving network; sidewalks, driveways, and front walks. The side yard along which the largest dimension of the house must run is seldom much more than 8′ wide and is virtually worthless. The rear yard becomes the only usable open space, and even here, since all houses are placed in a row, it is very difficult to establish any real privacy.

Without setting down standards for houses and their placement, it is the intention of the Planned Unit Development regulations to introduce the kind of flexibility that will greatly improve the residential environment. Specifically, the individual house must be designed to relate the open area around each house to what occurs inside the house. The house has entrances for people and an entrance for automobiles; this fact has meaning both in terms of open area, and the portion of the house that serves the entrance function; and a design response to this fact is expected. The house has indoor and outdoor living functions; this requires a design that relates the two, preferably resulting in increased privacy for outdoor living because of the way adjacent buildings are placed. Similar thought and design response should be shown in the arrangement of bedrooms, internal circulation, and service spaces.

Definitions

Planned Unit: a land area that (1) has both individual building sites and common property such as a park, and (2) is designed and organized to be capable of satisfactory use and operation as a separate entity without necessarily having the participation of other building sites or other common property. The ownership of the common property may be either public or private.

Planned Unit Development:

A single planned unit as initially designed; or such a unit as expanded by annexation of additional land area; or a group of contiguous planned units, either operating as separate entities or merged into a single consolidated entity.

Homes association: an incorporated, nonprofit organization operating under recorded land agreements through which (a) each lot owner in a planned unit or other described land area is automatically a member, and (b) each lot is automatically subject to a charge for a proportionate share of the expenses for the organization's activities, such as maintaining a common property.

Common property:

A parcel or parcels of land together with the improvements thereon, the use and enjoyment of which are shared by the owners and occupants of the individual building sites in the planned unit.

The following outline explains the most significant provisions of the new approach and shows how these advantages can be obtained.

Regulations that can be modified:

The Planning Board may authorize modifications to the zoning regulations, provided that the overall plan is satisfactory to the Board and is not contrary to the Master Plan.

Table of Comparative Advantages

Table shows land use and site utilization advantages of Planned Unit Development schemes (numbered 2, 3, and 4) over conventional subdivision scheme, 1.		GROSS SITE AREA	STREET AREA	STREET AREA % OF GROSS SITE AREA	NET SITE AREA	COMMON OPEN SPACE	NUMBER OF DWELLING UNITS	ALLOWABLE FLOOR AREA PER DWELLING UNIT	ALLOWABLE COVERAGE PER DWELLING UNIT	ALLOWABLE NUMBER OF ROOMS PER DWELLING UNIT	
1		20 ACRES	6.3 ACRES	31.4%	13.7 ACRES	NONE	semi-det : 198	1400 sq. ft.	700 sq. ft.	7.5	Figures based on: typical zoning lot of 2800 sq. ft. F.A.R. (Floor Area Ratio) of .5 O.S.R. (Open Space Ratio) of 150 lot area per room of 375 sq. ft.
2		20 ACRES	5.6 ACRES	28%	14.4 ACRES	2.3 ACRES	detached: 59 semi-det: 23 townhouses: 62 garden apts: 56 total: 200	1840 sq. ft.	940 sq. ft.	9.5	Figures based on: net site area divided by number of dwelling units, and application of full bonuses resulting in: F.A.R. (Floor Area Ratio) of .575 O.S.R. (Open Space Ratio) of 120 lot area per room of 337 sq. ft.
3		20 ACRES	4.1 ACRES	20.5%	15.9 ACRES	8.6 ACRES	townhouses: 213	1900 sq. ft.	980 sq. ft.	9.8	
4		20 ACRES	5 ACRES	25%	15.0 ACRES	4.0 ACRES	townhouses: 210	1820 sq. ft.	975 sq. ft.	9.35	

SOURCE: Planned Unit Development, N.Y.C. Planning Commission

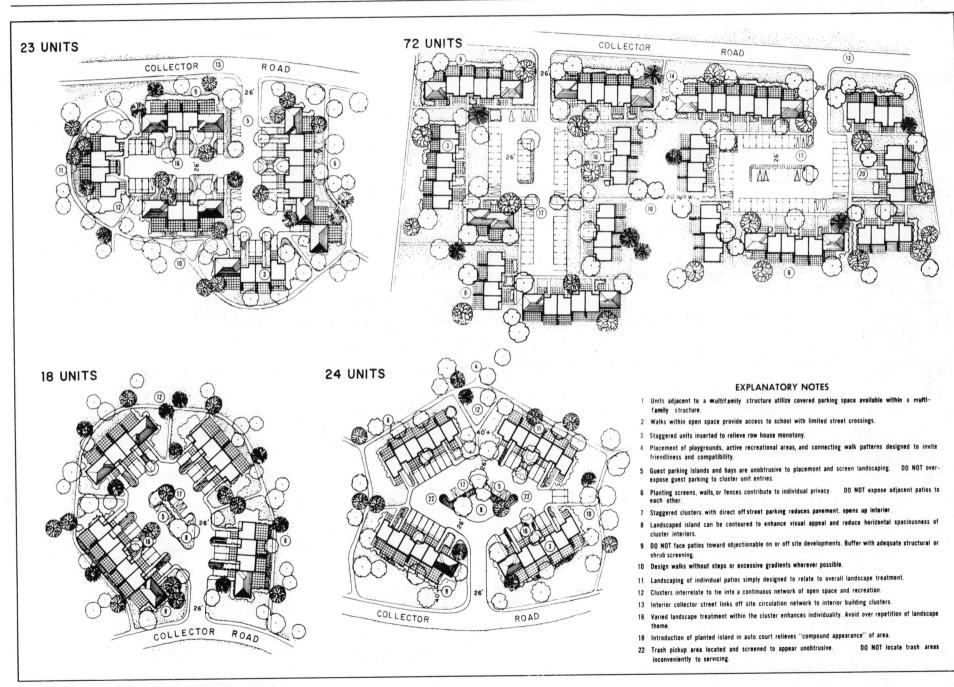

23 UNITS

72 UNITS

18 UNITS

24 UNITS

EXPLANATORY NOTES

1 Units adjacent to a multifamily structure utilize covered parking space available within a multi-family structure.

2 Walks within open space provide access to school with limited street crossings.

3 Staggered units inserted to relieve row house monotony.

4 Placement of playgrounds, active recreational areas, and connecting walk patterns designed to invite friendliness and compatibility.

5 Guest parking islands and bays are unobtrusive to placement and screen landscaping. DO NOT over-expose guest parking to cluster unit entries.

6 Planting screens, walls, or fences contribute to individual privacy. DO NOT expose adjacent patios to each other.

7 Staggered clusters with direct off street parking reduces pavement, opens up interior.

8 Landscaped island can be contoured to enhance visual appeal and reduce horizontal spaciousness of cluster interiors.

9 DO NOT face patios toward objectionable on or off site developments. Buffer with adequate structural or shrub screening.

10 Design walks without steps or excessive gradients wherever possible.

11 Landscaping of individual patios simply designed to relate to overall landscape treatment.

12 Clusters interrelate to tie into a continuous network of open space and recreation.

13 Interior collector street links off site circulation network to interior building clusters.

16 Varied landscape treatment within the cluster enhances individuality. Avoid over repetition of landscape theme.

18 Introduction of planted island in auto court relieves "compound appearance" of area.

22 Trash pickup area located and screened to appear unobtrusive. DO NOT locate trash areas inconveniently to servicing.

SOURCE: *Design Manual–Family Housing*
Dept. of the Navy, Wash., D.C.

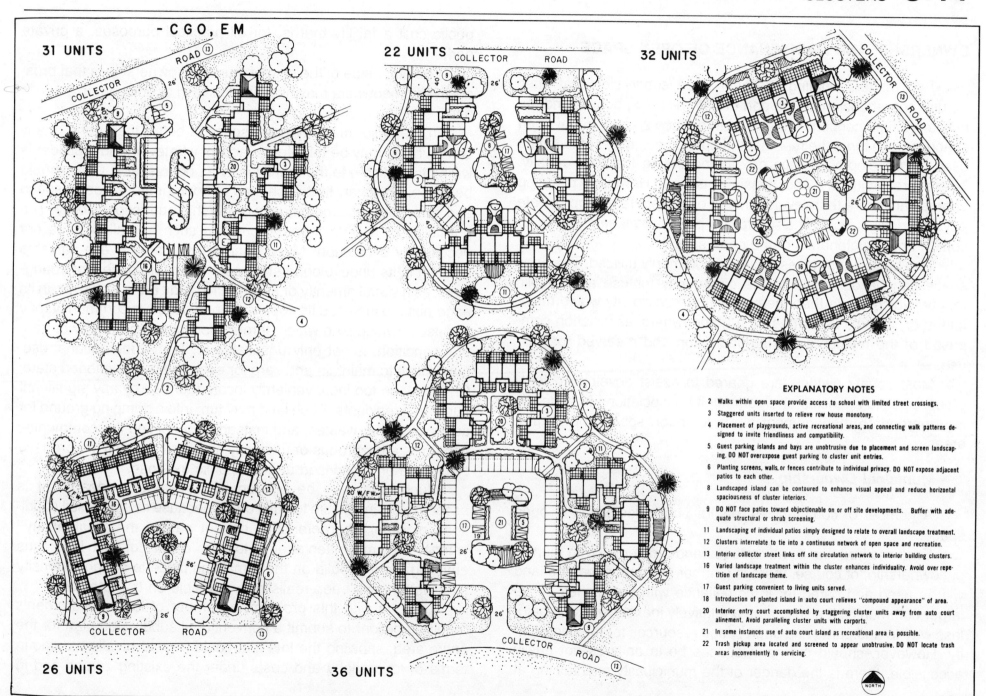

- CGO, EM

31 UNITS

22 UNITS

32 UNITS

26 UNITS

36 UNITS

EXPLANATORY NOTES

2 Walks within open space provide access to school with limited street crossings.

3 Staggered units inserted to relieve row house monotony.

4 Placement of playgrounds, active recreational areas, and connecting walk patterns designed to invite friendliness and compatibility.

5 Guest parking islands and bays are unobtrusive due to placement and screen landscaping. DO NOT overexpose guest parking to cluster unit entries.

6 Planting screens, walls, or fences contribute to individual privacy. DO NOT expose adjacent patios to each other.

8 Landscaped island can be contoured to enhance visual appeal and reduce horizontal spaciousness of cluster interiors.

9 DO NOT face patios toward objectionable on or off site developments. Buffer with adequate structural or shrub screening.

11 Landscaping of individual patios simply designed to relate to overall landscape treatment.

12 Clusters interrelate to tie into a continuous network of open space and recreation.

13 Interior collector street links off site circulation network to interior building clusters.

16 Varied landscape treatment within the cluster enhances individuality. Avoid over repetition of landscape theme.

17 Guest parking convenient to living units served.

18 Introduction of planted island in auto court relieves "compound appearance" of area.

20 Interior entry court accomplished by staggering cluster units away from auto court alinement. Avoid paralleling cluster units with carports.

21 In some instances use of auto court island as recreational area is possible.

22 Trash pickup area located and screened to appear unobtrusive. DO NOT locate trash areas inconveniently to servicing.

NORTH

OWNERSHIP AND MAINTENANCE OF OPEN SPACE

Two matters relating to open-space subdivision that often arouse apprehension on the part of both planning boards and the public are first, concern with the maintenance and control of open space, and second, the fear that the open space may someday be used for development, thus greatly increasing the total density. These are legitimate and sensitive issues. However, planning boards can insure that developers not only prepare an appropriate physical design, but can also provide proper legal safeguards for control and maintenance of the open space.

Two basic approaches are most commonly utilized. The open space can be dedicated to the community for use as a public facility, which would then mean that the municipality would maintain it; or, it could be owned by a homeowners' association comprised of the residents of the subdivision and reserved for their use.

Most county districts are geared to assist developers, local groups, public agencies and community associations in developing appropriate management plans for open space and natural areas.

Municipal Ownership

A number of communities require public dedication of open space.

Each method has its advantages and problems. With municipal ownership, of course, there is a firmer guarantee that the land will be used and cared for in compliance with the wishes of the larger community. It also can be a relatively inexpensive and painless way to add parks and open space resources for the community. However, should the open spaces be in an area not easily accessible, there is the danger of the municipality maintaining at public cost a facility that is, for all practical purposes, a private park.

The other side of the coin of municipal ownership is that prospective homeowners may not wish to live in or adjacent to a public park.

In the belief that any open space is better than none, many communities may be tempted to accept whatever land a builder is willing to dedicate to the municipality as open space. Care should be taken, however, that such land is appropriate for open space and compatible with community ownership and responsibility. The possibility of use for formal recreation such as ball fields is not necessarily a criterion. Much open space can serve a valuable function in its undeveloped state as a "wander space" for youngsters, as a visual amenity or as a nature study area. However, in its eagerness to increase its supply of open space, a community may find itself owning land which, through location, topography or general condition, is not only unsuitable for formal recreational use, but difficult to maintain and care for even in its undeveloped state. Or, it may be too inconveniently located for use by any significant number of residents. Such land may turn into a dumping ground for autos and other wastes, and instead of benefiting the community, end up as a hazardous or unsightly area that can only be properly eliminated or supervised at great public expense.

Such land may be offered by developers because it is economically infeasible to build on, or because its slope, soil conditions or other characteristics do not satisfy the "buildability" criteria. They may often attempt to gain "credit" for such land, thus enabling them to build on the remaining piece to a higher density than would have been realistically possible on the total site.

To cope with this problem, a number of local governments require a builder to submit a conventional subdivision plan for the entire area, showing the lots that could be realistically created in terms of topography and costs under the existing zoning and in compliance with the subdivision regulations. The total number of lots arrived at in compliance with these qualifications establishes the maximum density for the open-space development.

A community can protect itself against the possibility of possessing land that is a liability rather than an asset by asking that developers "finish" the land before dedicating it to the municipality. As a result, the open space received is fully equipped and laid out for baseball and for other specific recreational uses.

The Homeowners' Association

Many of the problems associated with municipal ownership may be eliminated through the use of an alternative approach to the preservation of open space—the homeowners' association.

The homeowners' association is a nonprofit corporation made up of the residents to maintain the common open spaces and facilities in an open-space development. It is, in a sense, a small neighborhood government. Such associations may be voluntary or automatic. In voluntary associations, membership is optional and, while this idea may appeal to our democratic instincts, such an approach has many shortcomings. It can lead to administrative difficulties and to inequities among members and nonmembers in the use of land and facilities.

The automatic or mandatory homeowners' association is by far the more effective approach. Such an association should be legally established before sales in a development begin. As each lot is sold, the purchaser must become a member of the association. This requirement "runs with the land"—that is, it is written into the deed of each individual lot in perpetuity.

The association is responsible for the care and maintenance of the open space and any developed facilities, such as ball fields, swimming pools or meeting rooms that may be commonly owned. A monthly or yearly service charge is assessed against each member to cover the costs involved.

The developer retains membership in the association by virtue of his ownership of the unsold lots and in the early stages will have the majority membership and thus control the community facilities and open space.

A number of such associations have been operating for many years. In Radburn, New Jersey, where an association has existed since 1930, the annual fee is based on a prearranged percentage of the real estate tax paid to the Township. In return, the Association not only cares for the recreational facilities and the open space, but also provides a library and a program of recreational and educational activities for all residents. The fee also covers the salary of a full-time manager and a small clerical staff, a necessity in a community as large as Radburn.

The municipality can require that such an association, if established, be set up by the developer according to prescribed standards. It may list a number of conditions for approval of such an association. These include the requirements that membership in the association be automatic for each lot owner and that the Homes Association gain title to all the common property and, once established, retain all responsibility for operation of the open space and common facilities.

The question of whether the open space should be municipally owned and maintained or whether it should become the property of a private homeowners' association is a decision that must be made by each municipality. Local circumstances, such as the need for public open space and the nature of existing development, will affect the decision.

Conclusion

Open-space subdivision should become an integral element of a municipality's strategy to achieve recreation and open space objectives. This subdivision technique will not, however, relieve a locality from having to acquire or in other ways obtain and preserve parklands. Though the community can facilitate, guide and encourage its use, in the final analysis Open Space Subdivision lies in the hands of private developers and is subject to the vagaries of the housing market. Yet as we have emphasized, maintaining open areas in new subdivisions is the most farsighted way of ensuring a proper balance between people and nature.

COMMUNITY FACILITIES

D-1   Introduction
        Maximum Distances for Community Facilities

EDUCATIONAL

D-2   Summary of Educational Facilities
D-3   Maximum Walking Distances for Students
D-4   Child-care Center
D-5   Nursery School
D-6   Kindergarten
D-7   Elementary School
D-8   Secondary Education
D-9   Sizes of School Sites
D-10   Summary of Facilities

SOCIAL AND CULTURAL

D-11   Religious Facilities
D-12   Public Library
D-13   Multiservice Center
D-14   Youth Center/Center for the Elderly

RECREATIONAL, LEISURE, AND OPEN SPACE

D-15   Introduction
D-16   Summary of Facilities
D-17   Playlot
D-18   Playground
D-19   Play Field
D-20   Neighborhood Areas and Facilities
D-21   Park-school Concept
D-22   Swimming Pools
D-23   Pitch and Putt Golf
D-24   Golf Courses
D-25   Recreation Center
D-26   Open-space Alternatives

NEIGHBORHOOD SHOPPING

D-27   Types of Shops
D-28   Neighborhood Community Facilities
        Land Area Requirements
D-29   Measurement of Housing Quality
D-30   Community Recreational Facilities

D

Introduction

The need for a total living environment surpassing the simple need for basic shelter has emerged as a significant development in recent years. Many housing developments and neighborhoods that appear stable and desirable are considered to owe a portion of credit to the ancillary community facilities for recreation and leisure, e.g., swimming pools, golf courses and open green areas. In addition, the quality of community life is further enhanced by the proper amount and location of educational and socio-cultural facilities.

This chapter is primarily concerned with facilities associated with neighborhood needs and design. However, a brief description is made of educational and recreational services that may serve a grouping of neighborhoods, e.g., junior and senior schools and large-scale parks. Each general grouping of facilities, educational, social and cultural, recreational and open-space, and neighborhood shopping, is presented as a self-contained unit. A summary chart of land-area requirements for the general run of facilities concludes the chapter.

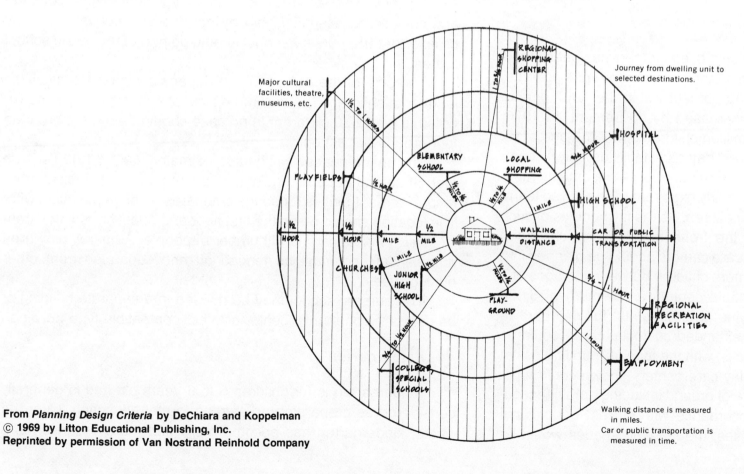

Journey from dwelling unit to selected destinations.

Walking distance is measured in miles.
Car or public transportation is measured in time.

EDUCATIONAL FACILITIES

This category includes preschool and formal school services. In general, the neighborhood components will include a child-care center, nursery schools, and kindergartens in the preschool group, and elementary schools in the latter group.

These facilities must be within safe walking distance. Ideally, the children should have walking access without having to cross any vehicular streets. The maximum distance should not exceed one-half mile. Low-density areas require modification of these standards—usually met by the use of bus transportation.

CARE CENTER

Since 1940, the number of employed mothers has been steadily rising. In 1967, four out of ten mothers were in the working force, representing an increase of 700 percent within the 1967 period, while the national population increased by 50 percent. In 1970, there were approximately 4.1 million children under the age of six with working mothers. Organized day-care facilities only accommodate one percent of this total. Educators have become increasingly aware of the importance of early exposure to structured learning for three- and four-year-old children. As the full benefits of such experiences become known, the trend toward early childhood education will accelerate. Day-care centers should be planned into developments housing fifty or more children between the ages of 3 to 5 years. These centers should contain a minimum of 5,000 gross square feet. Under varying arrangements, full day care or any portion thereof (including extended custodial care), could be provided on a twelve-month basis, with the teacher-pupil ratios not exceeding eight to one. The day-care centers shown could function adequately on ¾ of an acre of ground including ample fenced-in outdoor play spaces. In accordance with current educational practice for full day-care facilities, the learning spaces would be "open" and carpeted, and the program would follow a nongraded format. A kitchen would be included to enable every child to have a minimum of two snacks and one warm lunch each day.

Nursery School

The nursery school is for the care of children in the 4- to 5-year-old age group. The nursery school is planned for prekindergarten activities. The length of programs ranges from half-day to full-day and from several days a week to every day. Unlike the child-care center, the program is more limited in scope. The nursery school experience is also becoming increasingly common and considered essential both by parents and educators. Many believe that the nursery school should be part of the public school system.

The size of the center will be dependent upon the available number of children. The maximum size for a single group is considered to be 20-30 children. In no case should there be more than four groups per school.

The space needed will be approximately 600 to 1,000 square feet. State and Federal regulations and recommendations of other recognized authorities for space standards must be complied with. The location should be on the first floor and relatively isolated from excessive noise, cars, and number of people. A nearby play area is essential and must be fenced off and separated from other outdoor uses.

The nursery school may be housed in a separate building or be part of a community center or other compatible type building.

Kindergarten

Kindergarten is for children 5 to 6 years old and is generally considered as preparatory to starting formal education. Over the years, kindergarten has become more and more essential as a required transitional period for the child. As such, kindergarten is more often part of the public school system and integrated with the elementary school. The size of the average kindergarten class should be about 20-25 children, assuming there will be a teacher and an assistant. An outdoor play area is essential to the kindergarten.

Elementary School

The elementary school is considered one of the basic organizational elements of the neighborhood. It is required by law that such a facility be provided to meet the basic need of education. As such, it has become the logical facility around which to develop the neighborhood. The type, size, and capacity of the elementary school facilities are determined by the school boards in accordance with state standards. Since there are no national standards on the organization of the elementary school, each community will differ in some aspects. One aspect is the number of grades in the school. Most school systems operate under one of the following plans:

Elementary School	Junior High School	Senior High School
Grades 1-6	Grades 7-9	Grades 10-12
Grades 1-6	Grades 7-8	Grades 9-12
Grades 1-8	—	Grades 9-12

The most common plan is the first one, the so-called 6-3—3 plan.

The kindergarten, when it is part of the public school system, is included within the elementary school complex. The minimum size for an elementary school is that it have at least one classroom per grade. For a K-6 school, this consists of a kindergarten and six classrooms, one for each grade, plus all the other necessary facilities.

The number of pupils per classroom varies in different school districts. The generally accepted maximum number per classroom is about 30 pupils. Therefore, a minimum-sized school could contain about 180 pupils without a kindergarten, and about 210 pupils with a kindergarten. However, from the standpoint of administration, such a school may be considered too small, and the minimum size may be increased several times.

The land-area requirement for the elementary school will vary with land costs, available school board policies, and state requirements. For planning purposes, an area of 2-4 acres for larger schools would be appropriate, exclusive of outdoor recreation. Allow 5-6 acres more if the neighborhood playground is to be included.

SECONDARY EDUCATION

The junior and senior high school facilities may be part of the neighborhood pattern in high-density communities. In most suburban and moderate-to-low density areas, these facilities are normally associated with the broader community. In addition to serving the needs of the teen-age student, these buildings are generally well-suited for evening adult education and community recreational uses. The accompanying table contains general site and population served for the various school types.

Neighborhood Facilities - Educational

FACILITY	LOCATION DISTANCE	POPULATION SERVED	DESCRIPTION	FUNCTION	PLANNING CONSIDERATIONS
CHILD-CARE CENTER	CENTRAL 4 to 2 Mi.	500-1,500	A facility integrally located within the housing complex; easily and speedily reached by walking; Small-scale and residential in character.	To care for preschool-age children of 3 to 4 years of age.	Enables mothers to seek employment during the early years of motherhood. Provides a structured learning environment and social activity. Creates a mini-core of community organization and identification.
NURSERY	CENTRAL 8 to 4 Mi.	2,000-3,000	Similar to the Child-care Center; greater emphasis on social adjustment and introduction to learning process.	To serve the social and educational needs of children from 2½ to 5 years of age.	Provides: Approx. 1,000 sq. ft. per class. A fenced-in play area with equipment; 1 parking space per each 2 classes. The nursery school should be accessible by footpath from dwelling unit without crossing street and may be near an elementary school or community center.
KINDERGARTEN	CENTRAL 4 to 2 Mi.	2,000-3,000	Formal instruction to educational process.	To serve the educational needs of children from 5 to 6 years of age. Preparation for elementary school.	Usually located within the elementary school complex; requires separate entrance and play areas.
ELEMENTARY SCHOOL	CENTRAL 4 to 2 Mi.	5,000-8,000	Usually the major community facility providing the center of activity for children and mothers.	To serve the educational needs of children from 6 to 11 years of age.	Provides: 7 to 14 acres; a screened playground completely equipped for a wide range of activities; 1 parking space per class plus 3 spaces. The school should be accessible by footpath from dwelling units without crossing streets and near center of residential area, near or adjacent to other neighborhood facilities.

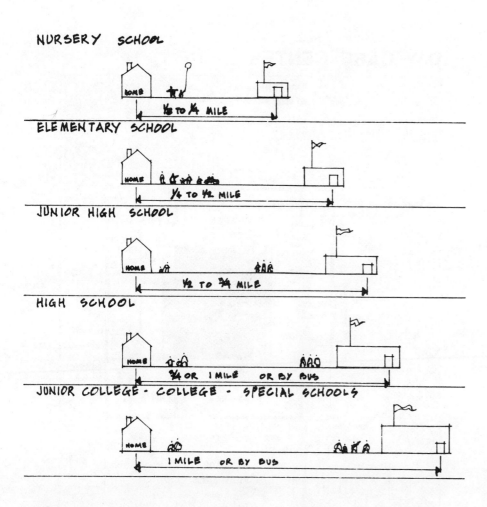

NURSERY SCHOOL

HOME — 1/8 TO 1/4 MILE

ELEMENTARY SCHOOL

HOME — 1/4 TO 1/2 MILE

JUNIOR HIGH SCHOOL

HOME — 1/2 TO 3/4 MILE

HIGH SCHOOL

HOME — 3/4 OR 1 MILE OR BY BUS

JUNIOR COLLEGE - COLLEGE - SPECIAL SCHOOLS

HOME — 1 MILE OR BY BUS

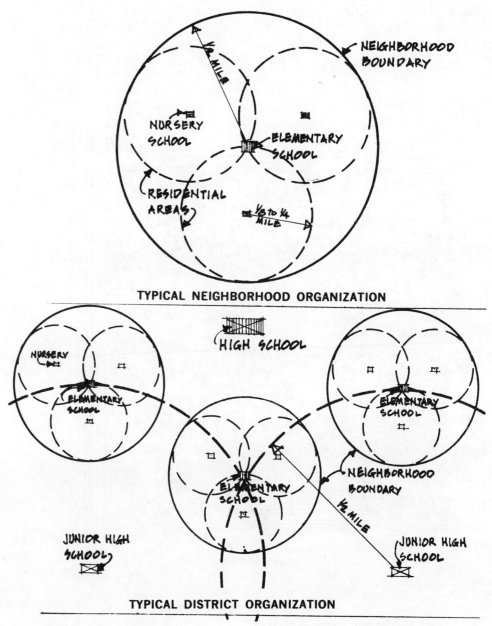

TYPICAL NEIGHBORHOOD ORGANIZATION

TYPICAL DISTRICT ORGANIZATION

- All distances given are considered to be maximum.

- In high density, urban areas most schools are located within the maximum recommended walking distances.

- In low density, rural areas many schools are located beyond maximum recommended walking distances. They must have bus service.

From *Planning Design Criteria* by DeChiara and Koppelman
© 1969 by Litton Educational Publishing, Inc.
Reprinted by permission of Van Nostrand Reinhold Company

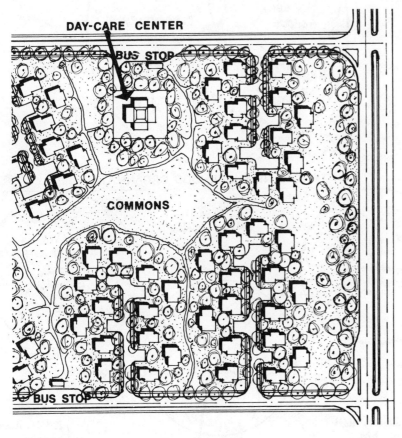

Child-care Center

Location Plan

From: *Housing with Shelter*, HUD, 1970

DAY-CARE CENTER

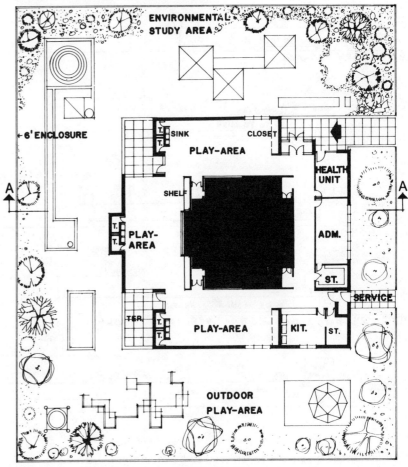

SHELTER CAPACITY: 77 PERSONS

Site Plan

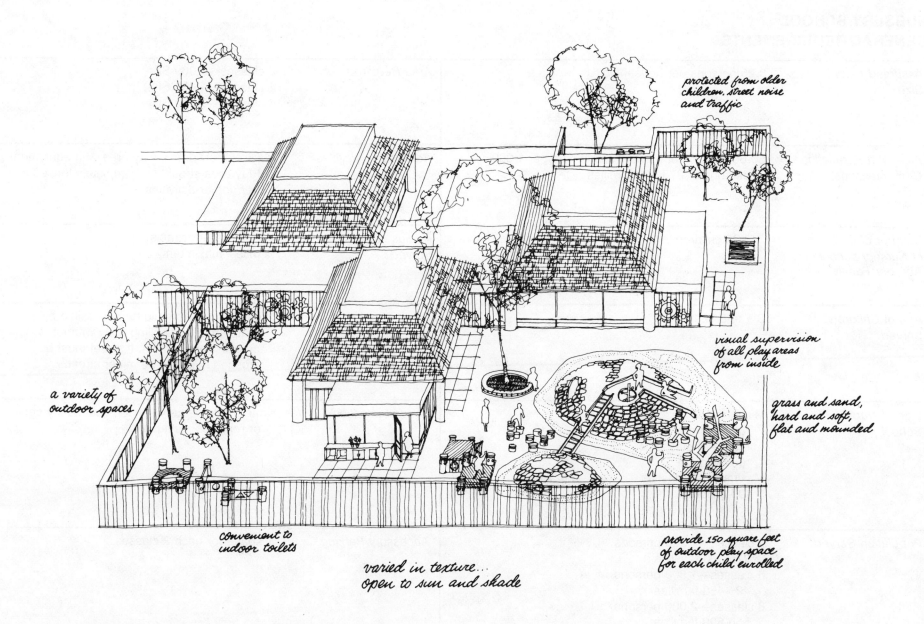

protected from older
children, street noise
and traffic

a variety of
outdoor spaces

visual supervision
of all play areas
from inside

grass and sand,
hard and soft,
flat and mounded

convenient to
indoor toilets

provide 150 square feet
of outdoor play space
for each child enrolled

varied in texture...
open to sun and shade

From *Designing the Child Development Center* by Ronald W. Haase
Project Head Start, Office of Economic Opportunity, Washington, D.C.

177

NURSERY SCHOOL
GENERAL REQUIREMENTS

Assumed Family Size	3.25 persons per household	*Area Required*	2 classes—2,000 SF 4 classes—4,000 SF 6 classes—6,000 SF
Assumed Population Characteristics	50-60 children of nursery-school age per 1,000 persons or 275-300 families	*Accessory Facilities*	Playlot or children's play area with equipment. Play area should be completely fenced in from other activities.
Number of Children of Nursery-school Age per Family	.15-.25 children	*Radius of Area Served*	1-2 blocks—desirable ⅛ mile—maximum
Age of Children Served	2½ to 5 years old	*Design Features*	Nursery school should be accessible by footpath from dwelling units without crossing any streets. If street must be crossed it should be minor street.

Size of Nursery School	Minimum—2 classes
	    (30 children)
	Average—4 classes
	    (60 children)
	Maximum—6 classes
	    (90 children)
		General Location	Near an elementary school, community center or religious institution.

Population Served	4 classes—1,000 persons
	    275-300 families
	6 classes—1,500 persons
	    425-450 families
	8 classes—2,000 persons
	    550-600 families
		Accessory Parking	1 space for each 2 classes

NOTE: These figures will vary for most areas. They are based on a full cross section of the population. Population figures should be checked for local age distribution and birth trends for any specific location.

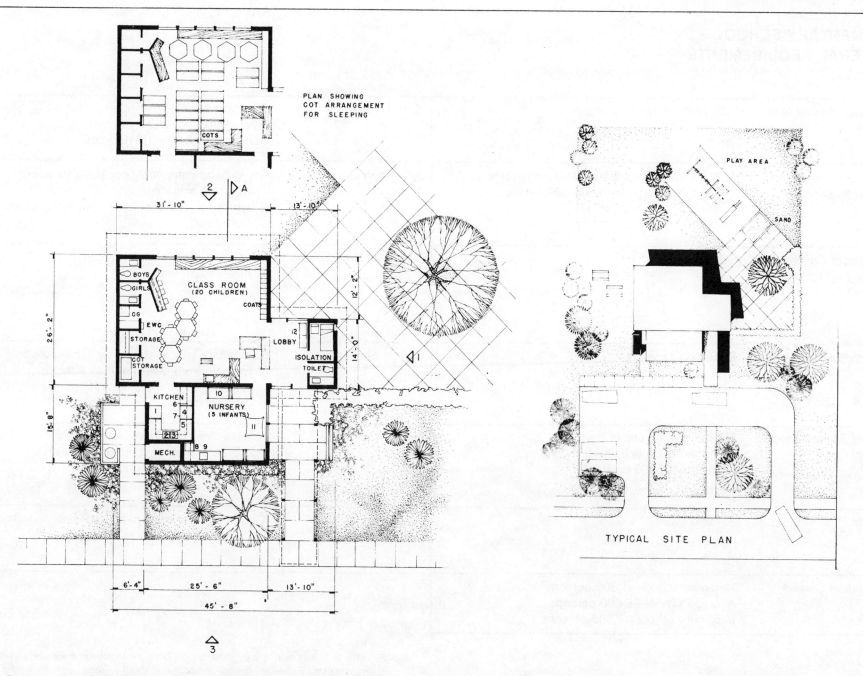

PLAN SHOWING
COT ARRANGEMENT
FOR SLEEPING

COTS

PLAY AREA

SAND

CLASS ROOM
(20 CHILDREN)

BOYS
GIRLS
CG
EWC
STORAGE
COT STORAGE

COATS

LOBBY

ISOLATION

TOILET

KITCHEN

NURSERY
(5 INFANTS)

MECH.

TYPICAL SITE PLAN

31'-10"   13'-10"

12'-2"

14'-0"

26'-2"

15'-8"

6'-4"   25'-6"   13'-10"

45'-8"

Definitive Designs—Naval Shore Facilities, Dept. of the Navy, Washington, D.C.—1962

ELEMENTARY SCHOOL
GENERAL REQUIREMENTS

Assumed Family Size	3.25 persons per household	Area Required	Minimum school—7-8 acres Average school—12-14 acres Maximum school—16-18 acres
Assumed Population Characteristics	125-175 children of elementary-school age per 1,000 persons or 275-300 families	Accessory Facilities	Playground completely equipped for a wide range of activities Playground area should be completely screened from street
Number of Children of Elementary-school age per Family	.25-.50 children	Radius of Area Served	¼ mile—desirable ½ mile—maximum
Age of Children Served	5 through 11 years	Design Features	Elementary school should be accessible by footpath from dwelling units without crossing any streets. If street must be crossed it should be a minor street
Size of Elementary School	Minimum—250 pupils Average—800 pupils Maximum—1,200 pupils	General Location	Near center of residential area, near or adjacent to other community facilities, adjacent to playground.
Size of Typical Class	30-32 pupils	Accessory Parking	One space per class plus 3 spaces
Population Served	Minimum school—1,500 persons Average school—5,000 persons Maximum school—7,000 persons		

NOTE: These figures will vary for most areas. They are based on a full cross section of the population. Population figures should be checked for local age distribution and birth trends for any specific location.

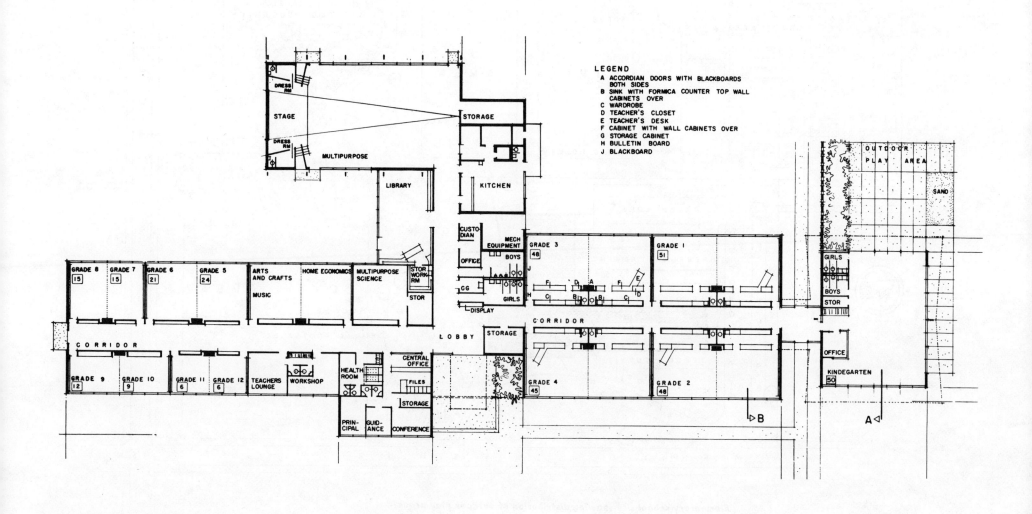

LEGEND
A ACCORDIAN DOORS WITH BLACKBOARDS BOTH SIDES
B SINK WITH FORMICA COUNTER TOP WALL CABINETS OVER
C WARDROBE
D TEACHER'S CLOSET
E TEACHER'S DESK
F CABINET WITH WALL CABINETS OVER
G STORAGE CABINET
H BULLETIN BOARD
J BLACKBOARD

Justement, Elam, Callmer, and Kidd,
William Crandall Suite,
Architects, Engineers, Washington, D.C.

181

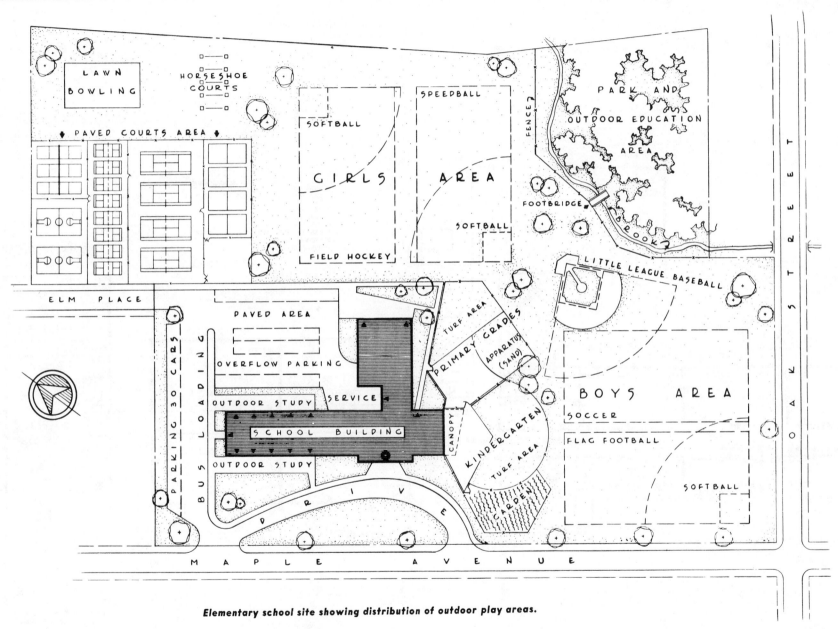

Elementary school site showing distribution of outdoor play areas.

Architects: The A. Carl Stellings Associates, Inc.

Sports and Recreation Facilities, M. Alexander Gabrielson and Coswell M. Miles, Editors. Prentice-Hall, Englewood Cliffs, New Jersey—1958

JUNIOR HIGH SCHOOL
GENERAL REQUIREMENTS

Assumed Family Size	3.25 persons per household	*Area Required*	Minimum school—18-20 acres Average school—24-26 acres Maximum school—30-32 acres
Assumed Population Characteristics	50-75 children of junior-high-school age per 1,000 persons, 275-300 families	*Accessory Facilities*	Playground and play field completely equipped for a wide range of game activities
Number of Children of Jr. High School Age per Family	.15-.20 children	*Radius of Area Served*	½ mile—desirable ¾ mile—maximum
Age of Children Served	12 to 14 years	*Design Features*	School should be away from major arterial streets; pedestrian walkways from other areas should be provided; adjacent to park
Size of Junior High School	Minimum school—800 pupils Average school—1,200 pupils Maximum school—1,600 pupils	*General Location*	Located near concentration of dwelling units or near center of residential area
Size of Typical Class	25-32 pupils	*Accessory Parking*	One space per classroom plus six spaces
Population Served	Minimum school—10,000 persons 2,750-3,000 families Average school—16,000 persons 4,500-5,000 families Maximum school—20,000 persons 5,800-6,000 families		

NOTE: These figures will vary for most areas. They are based on a full cross section of the population. Population figures should be checked for local age distribution and birth trends for any specific location.

SIZE OF SCHOOL SITES

School Type	Minimum Size	Ideal Size	Maximum Size	Site Size	Radius of Area Served
	(pupils)	(pupils)	(pupils)	(acres)	(miles)
Elementary	230	700	900	5 + 1 per 100 pupils	0.5
Junior High	750	1,000	1,500	15 + 1 per 100 pupils	1.0
Senior High	900	1,500	2,500	25 + 1 per 100 pupils	2.0
Elementary-Junior High Combination				15 + 1 per 100 pupils	1.0
Junior High-Senior High Combination				25 + 1 per 100 pupils	2.0
Elementary-Park Combination				8 + 1 per 100 pupils	0.5
Elementary-Junior High-Park Combination				20 + 1 per 100 pupils	1.0
Junior High-Senior High-Park Combination				18 + 1 per 100 pupils	1.0
Junior High-Park Combination				40 + 1 per 100 pupils	2.0
Senior High-Park Combination				35 + 1 per 100 pupils	2.0

Elementary School Site Size

SCHOOL SITE AREA	NEIGHBORHOOD POPULATION				
	1,000 persons 275 families 90 pupils	2,000 persons 550 families 180 pupils	3,000 persons 835 families 270 pupils	4,000 persons 1,100 families 360 pupils	5,000 persons 1,375 families 450 pupils
Component Uses					
1) Covered by building: square feet............................		15,300	23,000	30,600	38,200
2) Service lawn and parking: square feet............................		28,000	31,000	34,000	40,000
3) Margin for expansion (20 percent of 1 plus 2): square feet		8,600	10,800	12,900	15,600
Total Area					
4) Acres		1.2	1.5	1.8	2.2
5) Acres per 1,000 persons...................		0.6	0.5	0.45	0.44
6) Square feet per family...................		94	78	70	68

Planning the Neighborhood by the American Public Health
Association Committee on the Hygiene of Housing
Public Administration Service, Chicago, Ill. 1960

Social and Cultural Facilities

This category of institutional uses includes religious, health and public service centers, libraries, and community centers. This chart is a summary of the social and cultural *facilities relative to people served, their function, and their planning considerations.*

FACILITY	LOCATION DISTANCE	NUMBER SERVED	DESCRIPTION	FUNCTION	PLANNING CONSIDERATIONS
Church or Synagogue	Central to Congregation 1 Mi. Max.	500-2,500	A place of worship and often a social center for the congregation. If a school is included, it becomes the center for religious education.	A facility in which religious services and gatherings as well as social meetings and other neighborhood activities are held.	Should be easily accessible, on foot if possible, and located in a quiet area with sufficient space for landscaping and off-street parking.
Branch Library	Central 1 Mi. Max.	Up to 5,000	A small branch of a larger system. Should contain both children's and adult's reading rooms, and range of books, records, and magazines.	A facility to serve the limited reading and research needs of a neighborhood.	Should be easily accessible, preferably on a main thoroughfare, in a subshopping area or near a neighborhood center. Ease of parking is desirable. A minimum of 80 years expansion should be possible.
Recreation Center	¼ to ½ Mi.	Up to 5,000	A multipurpose building. Usually includes a gym, swimming pool, and game rooms. Meeting rooms and other multipurpose areas.	To serve the recreational needs of a neighborhood including small-scale outdoor activities and a full range of indoor activities.	This facility may be part of a school or located in a park. It may generate noise and should thus be somewhat separated from other quieter facilities. Ease of parking is desirable.
Social Center	¼ to ½ Mi.	Up to 5,000	A multipurpose building with emphasis upon passive activities such as game rooms, reading and meeting rooms.	A facility to be used for social activities such as dances, banquets, meetings, special-interest shows and exhibits.	This facility may be part of a school, should have some food-preparation facilities and should provide adequate off-street parking.
Health Center	Central ¼ to ½ Mi.	Up to 5,000	Small medical offices that can provide basic diagnostic and treatment services. Usually a public facility but may be private group practice.	A facility to provide minor health services, to serve as a health information center and possibly act as a referral bureau.	This facility may be part of a school, should be easily accessible on foot with the provision for off-street parking.
Multi-Service Center	Central ¼ to ½ Mi.	Up to 5,000	Group of offices or one large flexible space that can be modified as needs change.	A facility to serve primarily as an information and community-guidance center providing legal and other professional advice.	Provides a sense of contact with governmental organizations; brings the government closer to the people; provides an outlet for local participation.

185

RELIGIOUS FACILITIES

Neighborhood churches frequently play an important role not only in the religious, but also in the cultural and social activities of the community. They often serve as recreational and community centers as well.

The major problem in planning for churches and synagogues is that the religious make-up of the new community will not be known until the community is settled. If the population is of the same religious background, the problem is simplified. However, the probability is that there would be a wide variation in religious backgrounds, thereby making it almost impossible for neighborhood families to support a particular religious building. In that case, support would be required from several neighborhoods.

Membership Standards

C. A. Perry estimated that a population of 5,000 persons could probably support three churches of about 1,500 persons each. The Conference on Church Extension suggested one Protestant church for each 1,500 to 2,500 persons. It should be noted that on the national basis about 60 percent of the population may be expected to affiliate with a local church. In the western region this percentage is considerably lower. Thus, on the average, a population of 1,500 might be expected to produce a church of 900 constituents, disregarding the churching of some people outside of the neighborhood, and internal heterogeneity of the population, which may cut the degree of affiliation to one specific church.

Many urban churchmen believe that a church of about 500 members is the optimum size of a neighborhood institution, while a downtown church, to support a diversified staff and program, may need 1,500 or 2,000 or even more.

Area Requirements

There is no common uniform agreement as to the adequate size of a church site. Certainly the size of the site will depend upon the size of the church that is being projected, and the scope of the program. If an outdoor recreational program is desired, that will increase the size appreciably. If a parochial school is to be included, this will mean another appreciable increase in site needs. In most cases, landscaping and off-street parking should be provided for.

The following are some standards that have been recommended.

Source	Acres Recommended for Church Site
1. Conference on Church Extension Standards based on:[1] (below)	
0-400 membership	1 acre
400-800 membership	2 acres
800-1,200 membership	3 acres
1,200 or more members	4 acres
2. Presbyterian Board of Missions[2]	3 acres (on the average)
3. Urban Land Institute[3]	3-5 acres (preferably near a shopping center)
4. Van Osdal[4]	5-6 acres (for a 600-seat church with 150 parking spaces)
	8 acres (for a Catholic church with a parochial school)

[1]Sanderson, Ross W., condensed report, conference on church extension, 1953, N.Y. National Council of Churches.

[2]Perry, Everett L., "Selections of a Church Site," The City Church, September, 1953.

[3]Urban Land Institute, Community Builders Handbook, 1954, p. 89.

[4]Van Osdal, N. K., Jr., "The Church and the Planned Community," The City Church, May, 1952.

Church Serving One Neighborhood Only

Location of Churches Serving More Than One Neighborhood

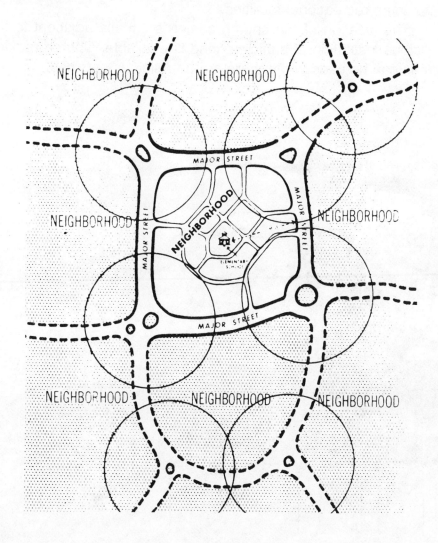

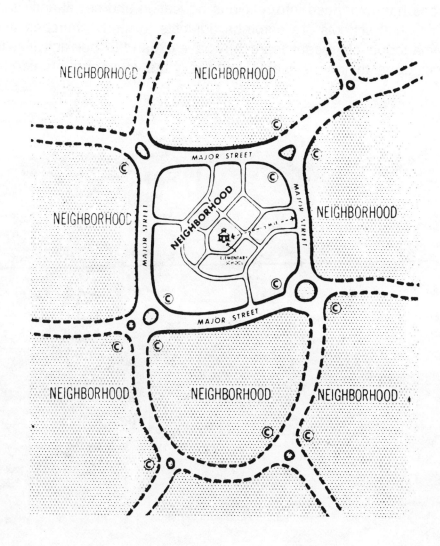

SOURCE: Robert C. Hoover and Everett L. Perry, *Church and City Planning*, Bureau of Research and Survey, National Council of the Churches of Christ in the U. S. A.

Church Centers

The church and synagogue are still vital and important community facilities for many people. The role of these religious institutions has expanded into religious education and social activities. Parochial schools are common adjuncts to many churches and synagogues. In recent years they have expanded their activities to include all their constituents, especially the youth and the elderly.

The result has been community centers built and run by the churches to meet the social and cultural needs. Such centers usually include meeting rooms, game rooms, shops, dining rooms, and some recreational facilities.

The location of the church center is usually adjacent to the religious institution, if sufficient land is available. Church parking areas can be used when there are no religious services.

M. Paul Friedberg and Associates,
Landscape Architects

Branch Library

A branch library can play an important role as a cultural center. In addition to providing books, it can provide record and tape lending, music-listening facilities, visual-aid facilities, lecture series, and act as a general information center. With such an expanded role, the library or cultural center will be an important element in the neighborhood. The general standards for small public libraries are shown on the following page.

REGARDLESS OF THE SIZE OF THE COMMUNITY, ITS LIBRARY SHOULD PROVIDE ACCESS TO ENOUGH BOOKS TO COVER THE INTERESTS OF THE WHOLE POPULATION.
1. *Libraries serving populations from 5,000 to 50,000 require a minimum of 2 books per capita.*
2. *Communities up to 5,000 persons need access to a minimum of 10,000 volumes, or 3 books per capita, whichever is greater.*

THE LIBRARY BUILDING SHOULD PROVIDE SPACE FOR THE FULL RANGE OF LIBRARY SERVICES.
All libraries should have designated areas for children's, young adult, and adult materials.

Multipurpose rooms should be provided for meeting, viewing, and listening by cultural, educational, and civic groups unless such facilities are readily available elsewhere in the community. They should be located for easy supervision so that they may be used for quiet reading and study when not needed by groups.

No single type of building is satisfactory for all public libraries. Each building is likely to be different, and its differences should be directly related to its service program.

The library building should be located in or near the community shopping center and at street level if possible. Adequate parking should be available nearby.

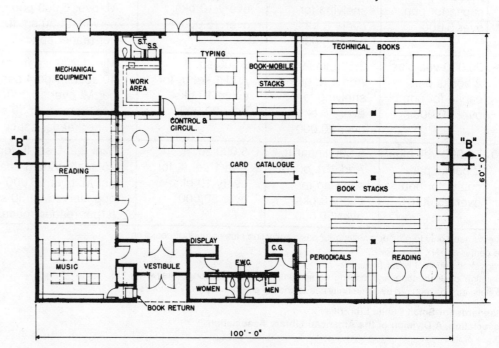

Library Buildings

D-12 SOCIAL AND CULTURAL
PUBLIC LIBRARY

Interim Standards for Small Public Libraries
Guidelines for Determining Minimum Space Requirements

POPULATION SERVED	SIZE OF BOOK COLLECTION	SHELVING SPACE (a) LINEAR FEET OF SHELVING (b)	AMOUNT OF FLOOR SPACE	READER SPACE	STAFF WORK SPACE	ESTIMATED ADDITIONAL SPACE NEEDED (c)	TOTAL FLOOR SPACE
Under 2,499	10,000 vol.	1,300 linear ft.	1,000 sq. ft.	Min. 400 sq. ft. for 13 seats, at 30 sq. ft. per reader space	300 sq. ft.	300 sq. ft.	2,000 sq. ft.
2,500-4,999	10,000 vol. plus 3 books per capita for pop. over 3,500	1,300 linear ft. Add 1 ft. of shelving for every 8 bks. over 10,000	1,000 sq. ft. Add 1 sq. ft. for every 10 bks. over 10,000	Min. 500 sq. ft. for 16 seats. Add 5 seats per M. over 3,500 pop. served, at 30 sq. ft. per reader space	300 sq. ft.	700 sq. ft.	2,500 sq. ft. or 0.7 sq. ft. per capita, whichever is greater
5,000-9,999	15,000 vol. plus 2 books per capita for pop. over 5,000	1,875 linear ft. Add 1 ft. of shelving for every 8 bks. over 15,000	1,500 sq. ft. Add 1 sq. ft. for every 10 bks. over 15,000	Min. 700 sq. ft. for 23 seats. Add 4 seats per M. over 5,000 pop. served, at 30 sq. ft. per reader space	500 sq. ft. Add 150 sq. ft. for each full-time staff member over 3	1,000 sq. ft.	3,500 sq. ft. or 0.7 sq. ft. per capita, whichever is greater
10,000-24,999	20,000 vol. plus 2 books per capita for pop. over 10,000	2,500 linear ft. Add 1 ft. of shelving for every 8 bks. over 20,000	2,000 sq. ft. Add 1 sq. ft. for every 10 bks. over 20,000	Min. 1,200 sq. ft. for 40 seats. Add 4 seats per M. over 10,000 pop. served, at 30 sq. ft. per reader space	1,000 sq. ft. Add 150 sq. ft. for each full-time staff member over 7	1,800 sq. ft.	7,000 sq. ft. or 0.7 sq. ft. per capita, whichever is greater
25,000-49,000	50,000 vol. plus 2 books per capita for pop. over 25,000	6,300 linear ft. Add 1 ft. of shelving for every 8 bks. over 50,000	5,000 sq. ft. Add 1 sq. ft. for every 10 bks. over 50,000	Min. 2,250 sq. ft. for 75 seats. Add 3 seats per M. over 25,000 pop. served, at 30 sq. ft. per reader space.	1,500 sq. ft. Add 150 sq. ft. for each full-time staff member over 13	5,250 sq. ft.	15,000 sq. ft. or 0.6 sq. ft. per capita, whichever is greater

(a) Libraries in systems need only to provide shelving for basic collection plus number of books on loan from resource center at ANY ONE TIME.
(b) A standard library shelf equals 3 linear feet.
(c) Space for circulation desk, heating and cooling equipment, multipurpose room, stairways, janitors' supplies, toilets, etc., as required by community needs and the program of library services.

From—Interim Standards for Small Public Libraries
Public Library Association, A Division of the American Library Association
Chicago, Ill. 1970.

MULTISERVICE CENTER

One of the new social institutions to emerge in the community is the multiservice center. This facility is being encouraged by the federal government in Model Cities areas. It is to be similar to a neighborhood community center housing a multitude of federal, state, and local services. Also, it is to be the headquarters of local community action groups. At this neighborhood facility, assistance can be provided in solving problems such as employment service, job training, welfare, day-care, voting, social security, and housing. In theory, each multiservice center should reflect the social, economic, and educational needs of each community. Its organization and operation must be flexible and multifunctional to adjust to constantly changing community needs. Each center, in essence, would be different from other centers.

Combined with these service facilities may be the more traditional social and recreational facilities, thereby making this center a truly community endeavor. The location, obviously, should be central and easily accessible to the entire community. Since many of the services would be for the elderly, disabled, or poor, consideration must be made for these groups. Some suggested locations would be adjacent to shopping areas, churches, or street level of multistory apartment buildings. Close proximity to bus stops and train stations would be essential.

Health Centers

Adequate medical services are essential on the local level. This should include medical, dental, and psychiatric services. This can be in the form of private and/or public facilities. A group practice providing a wide range of medical services would be one appropriate method. Medical and dental offices can easily be incorporated with the neighborhood shopping center. Provisions for accessibility to a hospital outside the neighborhood in emergencies is essential. Small preventive care and medical diagnostic facilities would also be appropriate.

COMMUNITY CENTERS

One way to provide activity space for both young and old is with a community center. It could provide meeting and recreational spaces, complete with a serving kitchen for catering. The lower (presumably more noisy) level could contain a teen-age center with separate access and include game rooms, dance halls, etc. It should not be necessary for the teen-agers to feel they must abandon the community to find activities especially suited to them; nor should their activities be in conflict with their parents' entertainment. The following floor plan depicts an arrangement that is suitable for expansion to accommodate various neighborhood sizes.

Youth Center

The youth center may consist of a variety of building types. It may be a Boys Club, a YMCA or YWCA, or a settlement house. Sometimes, it may be a church or municipally sponsored facility. Essentially it caters to the young boys and girls with a range of social and recreational facilities. This would include meeting rooms, gym, swimming pools, shops, game rooms, and lounges.

Youth centers are similar to other community centers or recreation buildings except they direct their activities to a restricted age group, usually under 21 years of age.

The location of such youth centers is very important. They should be easily accessible and convenient, preferably along major lines of circulation. The site should be large enough to provide for outdoor activities and future expansion. Adequate parking for staff and visitors is necessary. Hopefully many young people will either walk or use bicycles to get to the center.

191

Centers for the Elderly

These centers serve the senior citizens by providing them with a place to meet other people. The planned activities are primarily social. They usually include special-interest clubs, cultural groups, adult education programs, involvement in the arts, and centers for action groups. Space should be provided for passive recreation activities such as game rooms and shops.

The senior citizen center can be the location of increasing number of social, health, welfare, and employment services for the elderly in the community. By placing these services at the center, they become readily available to a group that has become far less mobile than the general population. The activities of the center are highly flexible and are limited only by the people involved.

The physical space required should be flexible to meet the changing needs of the elderly. Most appropriate would be moderate-sized meeting rooms, shops, classrooms and offices. No large specialized spaces such as gyms or swimming pools should be anticipated. The location must be considered for easy accessibility and a minimum of steps. Preferably it should be located in a separate one-story structure or the first floor of a high-rise apartment building. Parking requirements would be minimal.

M. Paul Friedberg & Associates
Brevoort Houses, Brooklyn, N.Y.

Community Center

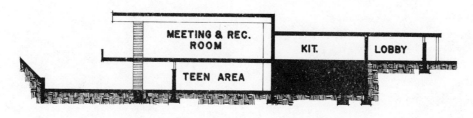

SECTION A–A

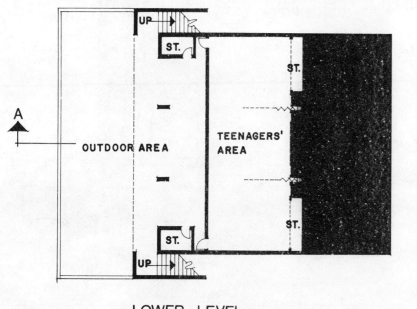

LOWER LEVEL

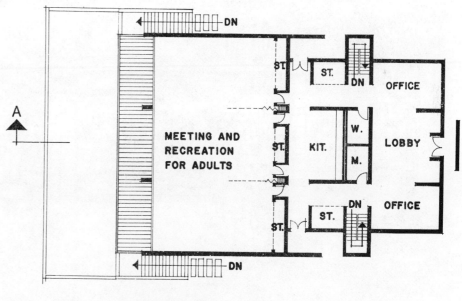

UPPER LEVEL

Housing with Shelter, HUD—1970

Lindsay-Bushwick Housing
M. Paul Friedberg and Associates

Youth Center

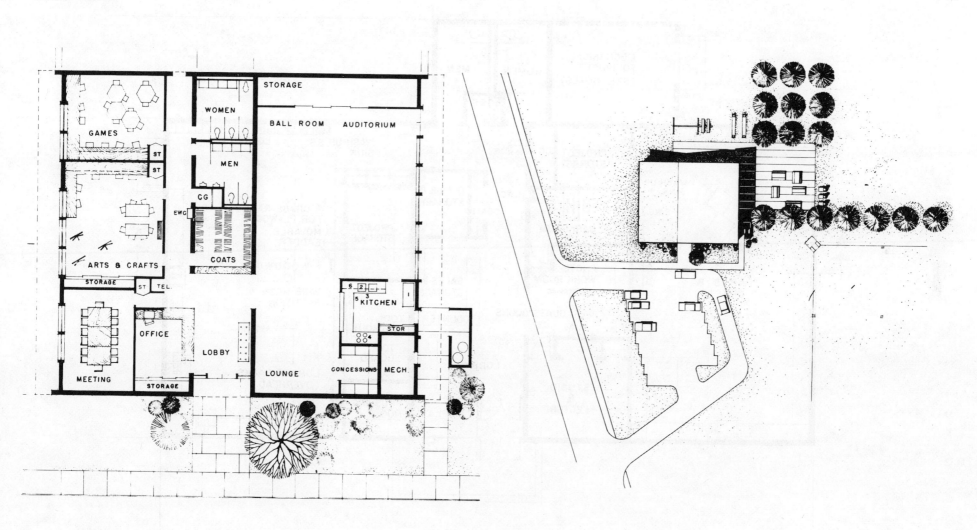

FLOOR PLAN

Arts and Crafts Shops

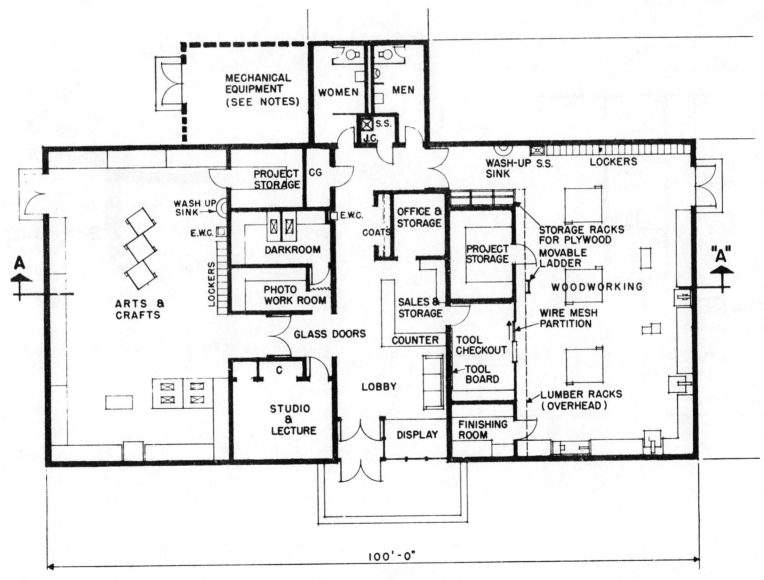

RECREATION

Every residential neighborhood requires a range of facilities for both children and adults that are easily accessible to the living units. Such facilities should include at least the following:

1. A preschool play area, usually called a playlot or a tot lot, for very young children who require close supervision. Such tot lots must be within easy reach of and visual observation from the living unit. With judicious arrangement of buildings, these spaces can usually be located between buildings or at the end of clusters, to form natural informal groups.

2. A centralized play space for grade-school children. This playground should be well-equipped and of adequate size to accommodate all the children that will use the facility.

3. Outdoor sitting areas should be provided for adults for passive activities. Such areas must be attractive and also provide a variety of visual experiences. They may include shaded areas, roof gardens, paved areas, and areas to view children at play.

4. More activity recreation areas should also be provided. These facilities can be used by a variety of age groups and require greater supervision and control. Such facilities may include tennis courts, boccie courts, bicycle riding paths, or archery ranges. The most popular facility in this category is probably the swimming pool. This can include a wading pool for young children, cabanas, and even a recreation building.

In addition, golf courses and open lands for passive recreation are desirable elements for the total community. Community recreation, where feasible, should stress year-round activities rather than limited seasonal ones.

The following pages present the salient aspects of each of the above-mentioned facilities. Section D-16 includes a summary description of the various facilities according to function, equipment, and the area served.

DESIGNATION	DESCRIPTION AND FUNCTION	FACILITIES AND EQUIPMENT	MAX. DISTANCE SERVED	NUMBER OF FAMILIES SERVED
Playlot	Generally a small area set aside for the play activity of young children under immediate adult supervision; usually located a short walking distance from the dwelling unit.	Generally includes: children's slides, seesaw, sandboxes, climbing devices, swings.. Drinking fountains and benches.	⅛ Mile	10-20
Playground	An area set aside for the play activity of children and young adults with some adult supervision; may include some quiet areas usually located a reasonable walking distance from the dwelling unit.	Generally includes: children and adult slides, seesaw, sandboxes, climbing devices, swings, tables for games. Drinking fountains and benches.	½ Mile	40-100
Play Field	A large area set aside for active play and sports with the possibility of many persons participating at one time; usually containing spectator and preparation areas. May be more than one mile from the dwelling unit.	May include: baseball and softball diamonds, football fields, tennis courts, running tracks. Parking lot Drinking fountains; spectator seating.	1 Mile Walking ½ Hour Riding	2,000-4,000
Swimming Pool	An area set aside for swimming and other low-scale water sports of all age groups with the possibility of spectators; may be more than one mile from the dwelling unit.	May include: pools, shower rooms, diving boards. Parking lot Drinking fountains; spectator seating.	1 Mile Walking ½ Hour Riding	2,000-4,000
Golf Course	An area set aside specifically for the sport of golf.	May include: up to 18-hole course, club house, driving range. Parking lot Drinking fountains	1 Mile Walking ½ Hour Riding	2,000-4,000
Waterfront Development	An area adjacent to a body of water set aside for pedestrians.	May include quiet sitting areas, bicycle paths, shops, restaurants.	1 Mile	—
Square, Mall, Plaza	An area, usually surrounded by buildings, set aside for pedestrians.	May include: quiet sitting areas, bicycle paths, shops, restaurants.	¼ Mile	—
Park	An area, often well landscaped, set aside for various levels of recreation ranging from quiet sitting to fairly active play; several of these may exist within proximity of each other.	May include: quiet sitting areas, bicycle paths, some play areas, drinking fountains, water areas.	½ Mile	40-100

PLAYLOTS

The playlot should be provided in the central open area within each block or adjoining each cluster of dwellings. In developments serving families with children, playlots should be provided for preschool children up to 6 years of age.

They are a necessary element of housing developments to complement common open-space areas. Playlots may include: (a) an enclosed area for play equipment and such special facilities as a sand area and a spray pool, and (b) an open, turfed area for active play, and (c) a shaded area for quiet activities.

Location of Playlots

Playlots should be included as an integral part of the housing area design, and are desirably located within 300 to 400 feet of each living unit served. A playlot should be accessible without crossing any street, and the walkways thereto should have an easy gradient for pushing strollers and carriages. Playlots may be included in playgrounds close to housing areas, to serve the preschool age group in the adjoining neighborhood.

Size of Playlots

The enclosed area for play equipment and special facilities should be based on a minimum of 70 square feet per child, which is equivalent to 21 square feet per family. A minimum enclosed area of approximately 2,000 square feet will serve some 30 preschool children (about 100 families). Such a size will accommodate only a limited selection of play equipment. To accommodate a full range of equipment and special facilities, including a spray pool, the minimum enclosed area should be about 1,000 square feet, which would serve up to 50 preschool children (about 165

families). Additional space is required to accommodate the elements of the playlot outside of the enclosed area. A turfed area at least 10 feet square should be provided for activity games.

Playlot Activity Spaces and Elements

A playlot should comprise the following basic activity spaces and elements:

a. An enclosed area with play equipment and special facilities including —
  (1) Play equipment such as climbers, slides, swing sets, play walls and playhouses, and play sculpture.
  (2) A sand area.
  (3) A spray pool.
b. An open, turfed area for running and active play.
c. A shaded area for quiet activities.
d. Miscellaneous elements—including benches for supervising parents; walks and other paved areas wide enough for strollers, carriages, tricycles, wagons, etc; play space dividers (fences, walks, trees, shrubs), a step-up drinking fountain, trash containers, and landscape planting.

Layout of Playlots

The specific layout and shape of each playlot will be governed by the existing site conditions and the facilities to be provided. General principles of layout can be described as follows:

a. The intensively used part of the playlot with play equipment and special facilities should be surrounded by a low enclosure with supplemental planting, and provided with one entrance-exit. This design will discourage intrusion by animals or older children, provide adequate and safe control over the children, and prevent the area from becoming a thoroughfare. Adequate drainage should be provided.

b. Equipment should be selected and arranged with adequate surrounding space in small, natural play groups. Traffic flow should be planned to encourage movement throughout the playlot in a safe, orderly manner. This traffic flow may be facilitated with walks, plantings, low walls, and benches.

c. Equipment that enables large numbers of children to play without taking turns (climbers, play sculpture) should be located near the entrance, yet positioned so that it will not cause congestion. With such an arrangement, children will tend to move more slowly to equipment that limits participation and requires turns (swings, slides), thereby modifying the load factor and reducing conflicts.

d. Sand areas, play walls, playhouses, and play sculpture should be located away from such pieces of equipment as swings and slides for safety and to promote a creative atmosphere for the child's world of make-believe. Artificial or natural shade is desirable over the sedentary play pieces, where children will play on hot days without immediate supervision. Play sculpture may be placed in the sand area to enhance its value by providing a greater variety of play opportunities. A portion of the area should be maintained free of equipment for general sand play that is not in conflict with traffic flow.

e. Swings or other moving equipment should be located near the outside of the equipment area, and should be sufficiently separated by walls or fences to discourage children from walking into them while they are moving. Swings should be oriented towards the best view and away from the sun. Sliding equipment should preferably face north, away from the summer sun. Equipment and metal surfaces should be located in available shade.

f. Spray pools should be centrally located, and step-up drinking fountains strategically placed for convenience and economy in relation to water supply and waste-disposal lines.

g. The open, turfed area for running and active play, and the shaded area for such quiet activities as reading and storytelling, should be closely related to the enclosed equipment area and serve as buffer space around it.

h. Nonmovable benches should be conveniently located to assure good visibility and protection of the children at play. Durable trash containers should be provided and conveniently located to maintain a neat, orderly appearance.

Playlot Equipment for Preschool Children

The following table indicates types, quantities, and minimum play space requirements for various types of equipment totaling about 2,800 square feet; this area, plus additional space for circulation and play space dividers, will accommodate a full range of playlot equipment serving a neighborhood containing approximately 50 preschool children (about 165 families).

Equipment	Number of Pieces	Play Space Requirements
Climber	1	10x25 feet
Junior swing set (4 swings)	1	16x32 feet
Play sculpture	1	10x10 feet
Play wall or playhouse	1	15x15 feet
Sand area	1	15x15 feet
Slide	1	10x25 feet
Spray pool (including deck)	1	36x36 feet

Smaller playlots may be developed to serve a neighborhood

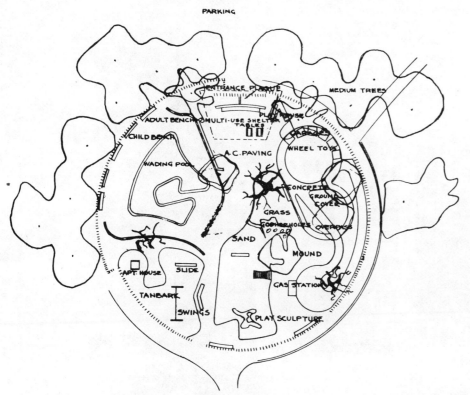

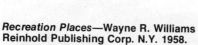

Recreation Places—Wayne R. Williams
Reinhold Publishing Corp. N.Y. 1958.

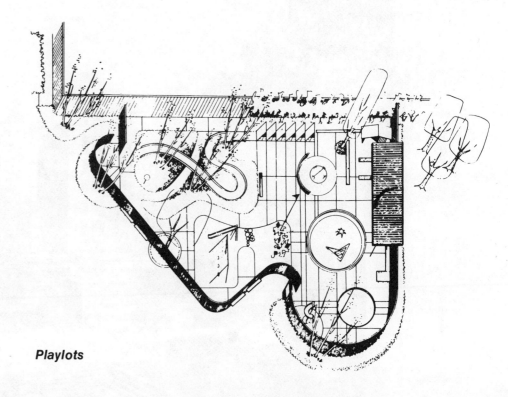

Playlots

containing some 30 children (about 100 families) using a limited selection of equipment with play space requirements totaling about 1,200 square feet; this area, plus additional space for circulation and play space dividers, should consider the following desirable priorities: (1) a sand area, (2) a climbing device such as a climber, a play wall or a piece of play sculpture, (3) a slide, and (4) a swing set. Where several playlots are provided, the equipment selections should be complementary, rather than all being the same type. For example, one playlot may include play walls or a playhouse, while another playlot may provide a piece of play sculpture. Also, such a costly but popular item as a spray pool may be justified in only one out of every two or three playlots provided.

Pebble Cove Apartments
Gruzen & Partners, Architects

PLAYGROUNDS

Each housing development that generates several hundred children between the ages of six and sixteen should provide play areas for these children.

The location of the playground should be at or near the center of the development or neighborhood so that it can be easily and safely reached from all the living units. Traditionally, the playground will be located at or adjacent to the elementary school and serve as part of the neighborhood core of activities.

The playground at every elementary school should be of sufficient size and design, and properly maintained, to serve both the elementary educational program and the recreational needs of all age groups in the neighborhood. Since education and recreation programs complement each other in many ways, unnecessary duplication of essential outdoor recreation facilities should be avoided. Only where this joint function is not feasible should a separate playground be developed.

The planning and design of the playground is critical. It must provide for a variety of activities and to serve the needs of both boys and girls of different ages. The main areas of the playground include:

a. *An apparatus area* for swings, slides, jungle gyms, and other equipment.

b. *An open area* for running, jumping and informal play.

c. *Courts and fields* for games of softball, soccer, tennis, handball, and volleyball.

d. *An area for quiet games* such as crafts, checkers, and hobbies.

e. *Wading or spray pool* for the younger children.

f. *A sitting area* both for parents to observe the children and for the children to rest from play.

The entire area should be enclosed and screened off from adjacent areas to prevent children from wandering off and to provide noise insulation for nearby living units.

The playground should be located as to receive as much sunlight as possible during the day.

Although the maximum distance generally given for a child to walk to a playground is ¼ to ½ mile, it should be located as close as possible because it is most frequently and intensely used by children who live in the immediate vicinity. Ideally, no child should be required to cross any streets to get to the playground.

Size and Number of Playgrounds

Recommended size of a playground is a minimum of 6 to 8 acres, which would serve approximately 1,000 to 1,500 families. The smallest playground that will accommodate essential activity spaces is about 3 acres, serving approximately 250 families (about 110 elementary school children). This minimum area should be increased at the rate of 0.2 to 0.4 acre for each additional 50 families. More than one playground should be provided where: a) a complete school playground is not feasible, b) the population to be served exceeds 1,500 families, or c) the distance from the housing units is too great.

Playground Activity Spaces and Elements

A playground should contain the following basic activity spaces and elements:

a. A playlot, as described in the preceding section, with its equipment and surfacing as recommended.

b. An enclosed playground equipment area with supplemental planting for elementary school children, and with equipment as recommended.

c. An open, turfed area for informal active games for elementary school children.

d. Shaded areas for quiet activities such as reading, storytelling, quiet games, handicrafts, picnicking and horseshoe pitching for both children and adults.

e. A paved and well-lighted multipurpose area large enough for:
1. Activities such as roller skating, dancing, hopscotch, four-square and captain ball.
2. Games requiring specific courts, such as basketball, volleyball, tennis, handball, badminton, paddle tennis, and shuffleboard.

f. An area for field games, preferably well-lighted (including softball, junior baseball, touch or flag football, soccer, track and field activities and other games), which will also serve for informal play of field sports and kite flying, and be used occasionally for pageants, field days, and other community activities.

g. Miscellaneous elements such as public shelter, storage space, toilet facilities, drinking fountains, walks, benches, trash containers, and buffer zones with planting.

Layout of Playgrounds

The layout of a playground will vary according to size of available area, its topography, and the specific activities desired. It should fit the site with maximum preservation of the existing terrain and such natural site features as large shade trees, interesting ground forms, rock outcrops and streams. These features should be integrated into the layout to the maximum extent feasible for appropriate activity spaces as natural divisions of various use areas, and for landscape interest. Grading should be kept to a minimum consistent with activity needs, adequate drainage and erosion control. General principles of layout are described as follows:

a. The playlot and the playground equipment area should be located adjacent to the school and to each other.

b. An open, turfed area for informal active play should be located close to the playlot and the playground equipment area for convenient use by all elementary school children.

c. Areas for quiet activities for children and adults should be somewhat removed from active play spaces and should be close to tree-shaded areas and other natural features of the site.

d. The paved multipurpose area should be set off from other areas by planting and so located near the school gymnasium that it may be used for physical education without disturbing other school classes. All posts or net supports required on the courts should be constructed with sleeves and caps that will permit removal of the posts and supports.

e. The area for field games should be located on fairly level, well-drained land with finished grades not in excess of 2.5 percent: a minimum grade of 1 percent is acceptable on previous soils having ground percolation for proper drainage.

f. In general the area of the playground may be divided as follows:
1. Approximately half of the area should be parklike, including the open, turfed areas for active play, the shaded areas for quiet activities, and the miscellaneous elements as described in g below.
2. The other half of the area should include ¾ to 1 acre for the playlot, playground equipment area, and the paved, multipurpose area, and 1¾ acres (for softball) to 1 acre (for baseball) for the field games area.

g. The playground site should be fully developed with landscape planting for activity control and traffic control, and for attractiveness. This site also should have accessible public shelter; storage for maintenance and recreation equipment; toilet facilities; drinking fountains; walks wide enough for strollers and carriages; bicycle paths; benches for adults and children; and trash containers.

Playground Equipment for Elementary School Children

The following table indicates types, quantities and minimum play space requirements totaling about 6,600 square feet; this area, plus additional space for circulation, miscellaneous elements, and buffer zones will accommodate a full range of playground equipment serving approximately 50 children at one time.

Equipment	Number of pieces	Play space requirements
Balance beam	1	15x30 feet
Climbers	3	21x50 feet
Climbing poles	3	10x20 feet
Horizontal bars	3	15x30 feet
Horizontal ladder	1	15x30 feet
Merry-go-round	1	40x40 feet
Parallel bars	1	15x30 feet
Senior swing set (6 swings)	1	30x45 feet
Slide	1	12x35 feet

Stonybrook, Long Island
M. Paul Friedberg & Associates

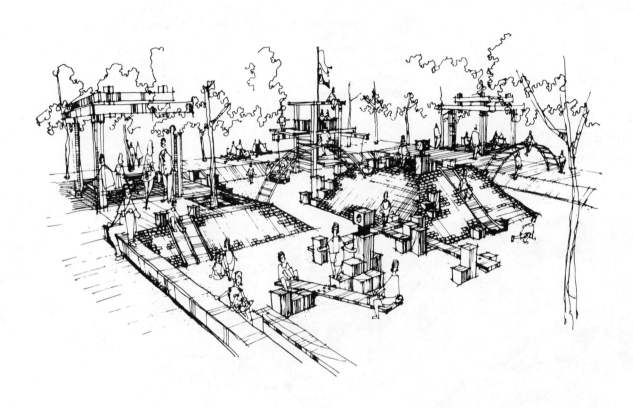

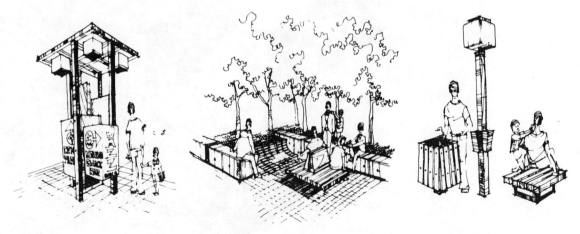

M. Paul Friedberg & Associates

M. Paul Friedberg & Associates

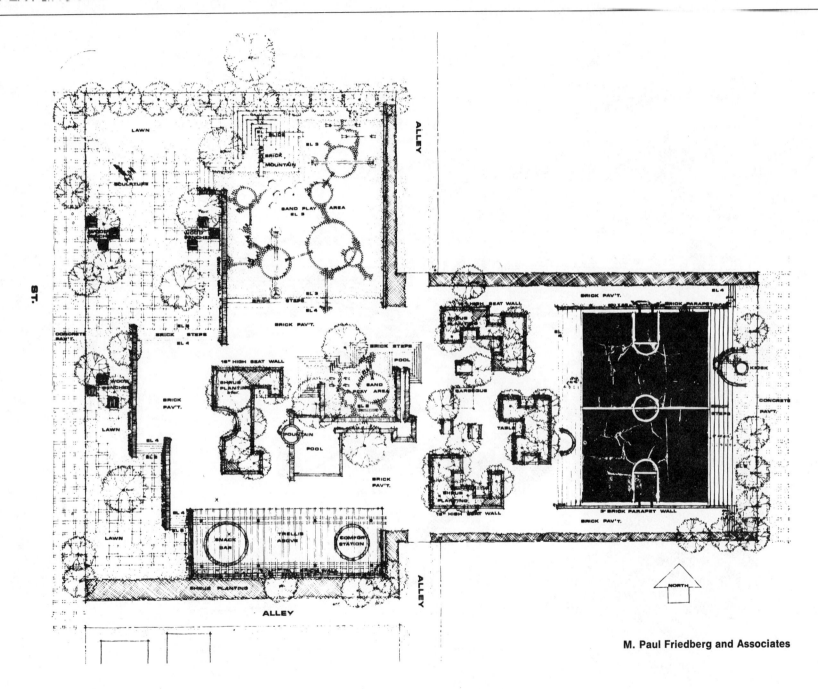

M. Paul Friedberg and Associates

PLAY FIELDS

A large housing complex or residential development that will generate from 10,000 to 20,000 people, or the equivalent of several neighborhoods, will require a play field. The play field will provide a wide range of recreational activities for teen-agers and adults.

The location of the play field should be within a half mile to one mile of every housing unit. The greater the population density, the closer the play field. Ideally, it should be easily accessible by walking or bicycle. Usually, the play field would be situated near or adacent to a high school for obvious reasons.

The area requirements for each play field will vary with the number and composition of the population to be served. The minimum area is considered to be about ten acres, or one acre for each 800-1,000 people served.

The most common recreational facilities provided in a play field are:

a. *Major sports areas* for softball, baseball, football, and soccer.

b. *Court game area* for games such as tennis, handball, and volleyball.

c. *A swimming pool complex* for general swimming and diving activities.

d. *Amphitheatre or bandshell* for concerts, rallies, and other cultural activities.

e. *A community recreation building* for indoor activities and inclement weather.

Recommended Dimensions for Game Areas*

Games	Elementary School	Junior High School	High School (Adults)	Area Size (Including Buffer Space)
Basketball	40′ x 60′	50′ x 84′	50′ x 84′	7,200 sq. ft.
Basketball (College)			50′ x 94′	8,000 sq. ft.
Volleyball	25′ x 50′	25′ x 50′	30′ x 60′	2,800 sq. ft.
Badminton			20′ x 44′	1,800 sq. ft.
Paddle Tennis			20′ x 44′	1,800 sq. ft.
Deck Tennis			18′ x 40′	1,250 sq. ft.
Tennis		36′ x 78′	26′ x 78′	6,500 sq. ft.
Ice Hockey			85′ x 200′	17,000 sq. ft.
Field Hockey			180′ x 300′	64,000 sq. ft.
Horseshoes		10′ x 40′	10′ x 50′	1,000 sq. ft.
Shuffleboard			6′ x 52′	640 sq. ft.
Lawn Bowling			14′ x 110′	1,800 sq. ft.
Boccie			15′ x 75′	1,950 sq. ft.
Tetherball	10′ circle	12′ circle	12′ circle	400 sq. ft.
Croquet	38′ x 60′	38′ x 60′	38′ x 60′	2,200 sq. ft.
Roque			30′ x 60′	2,400 sq. ft.
Handball (Single-wall)	18′ x 26′	18′ x 26′	20′ x 40′	1,200 sq. ft.
Handball (Four-wall)			23′ x 46′	1,058 sq. ft.
Baseball	210′ x 210′	300′ x 300′	400′ x 400′	160,000 sq. ft.
Archery		50′ x 150′	50′ x 300′	20,000 sq. ft.
Softball (12″ Ball)**	150′ x 150′	200′ x 200′	275′ x 275′	75,000 sq. ft.
Football			160′ x 360′	80,000 sq. ft.
Touch Football		120′ x 300′	160′ x 360′	80,000 sq. ft.
6-Man Football			120′ x 300′	54,000 sq. ft.
Soccer (Men) Minimum			165′ x 300′	65,000 sq. ft.
Maximum			240′ x 360′	105,000 sq. ft.
Soccer (Women)			120′ x 240′	40,000 sq. ft.

*Table covers a single unit; many of above can be combined.
**Dimensions vary with size of ball used.

NEIGHBORHOOD AREAS AND FACILITIES

Playlot

A playlot is a small recreation area designed for the safe play of preschool children.

Location

As an independent unit, the playlot is most frequently utilized in large housing projects or in other densely populated urban areas with high concentrations of preschool-age children. More often, it is incorporated as a vital feature of a larger recreation area. If a community is able to operate a neighborhood playground within one-quarter mile of every home, playlots should be located at the playground sites. A location near a playground entrance, close to restrooms, and away from active game areas is desirable.

Size

The space devoted to a playlot depends upon the total open space available for development on a particular site. It may vary from 2,500 to 10,000 square feet.

General Features

The playlot should be enclosed with a low fence or solid plant materials in order to assist mothers or guardians in safeguarding their children. Careful thought should be given to placement of benches, with and without shade, for ease of supervision and comfort of parents and guardians. A drinking fountain with a step for tots will serve both children and adults.

Play equipment geared to the preschool child should combine attractive traditional play apparatus with creative, imaginative equipment. Such proven favorites as chair, bucket, and glider-type swings, six-foot slides, and a small merry-go-round can be used safely. Hours of imaginative play will be enjoyed with such features as a simulated train, boat, airplane, and playhouse, and Fiberglas or concrete animals. A small climbing structure should be included as well as facilities for sand play.

NEIGHBORHOOD PARK-SCHOOL (ELEMENTARY)

The neighborhood park-school is the primary unit in planning for physical education, recreation, and health education. This is a combination of an elementary school, neighborhood park, and playground. It is planned in such a manner that all areas and facilities are used to meet the educational and recreational needs of the people living in a neighborhood. It is essential that areas and facilities be cooperatively planned for the dual purpose of instruction and recreation, and that the school and community recreation programs be coordinated for maximum use of these areas and facilities by the entire neighborhood.

The park-school concept of combining education and recreation facilities on a single site has great merit. This combination makes possible a wider variety of opportunities on less acreage and at a lower cost than do separate installations. This approach is discussed here as it applies to areas at the neighborhood, community, and city-wide levels.

Separately located recreation areas are also treated since there may be certain circumstances under which the park-school may not be possible. It must be emphasized, however, that the combined approach is highly recommended.

Location

The neighborhood park-school should service an area with a maximum radius of one-half mile and a population of approximately 8,000 people. Any deviation in the population density

Planning Areas and Facilities for Health, Physical Education, and Recreation—Rev. 1966
The Athletic Institute and American Association for Health, Physical Education, and Recreation

(larger or smaller communities) may alter the service radius and/or acreage required for this installation.

Size

The minimum area recommended for a neighborhood park-school is 20 acres.

General Features

It is suggested that this area be developed as follows:

	Acres
School building	2.0
Parking	1.0
Playlot and apparatus	1.0
Hard-surface game courts and multiple-use area	2.5
Turf field-games area	5.5
Park area, including space for drama and quiet activities	5.5
Buffer zones and circulation	2.0
Recreation service building	.2
Corner for senior citizens	.3
Total	20.0

The school building should be at the edge of the area to provide for maximum development and utilization of the site, and playground equipment should be located far enough from the building to keep noise from interfering with class instruction.

A separate building containing the recreation leader's headquarters and public restroom facilities should be provided in close proximity to hard-surface and game areas.

Hard-surface areas should be contiguous to provide a larger area for recreational, recess, physical education, and intramural activities. The field area should be large enough for baseball and softball diamonds to accommodate all age levels, for various field games, and for special events. Paths and walks between areas should be placed so as to avoid traffic over lawns, and the arrangement of facilities and landscaping should make for ease of supervision.

NEIGHBORHOOD PLAYGROUND

Designed primarily to serve children under 14 years of age, the neighborhood playground should have additional features to interest teen-agers and adults. The trend in recent years is for the neighborhood playground to become increasingly the center of activity for the wide variety of needs expressed by all residents. The more diversified interests of today's recreation consumer challenge the facility planner to provide for a broader program, with more attention devoted to multiple use by different age groups.

Modern planning for outdoor recreation at the neighborhood level places heavy emphasis on combining elementary-school needs with those of the community. This type of joint development is treated in the immediately preceding section on the neighborhood park-school.

Where elementary-school facilities are unavailable or inadequate, or joint development is impossible, a separate playground will be needed in each neighborhood.

Location

The neighborhood playground serves the recreation needs of the same population served by the neighborhood elementary school. Its maximum use radius will seldom exceed one-half mile, with most of the attendance originating within a quarter-mile distance. It should be located close to the center of the area to be served and away from heavily traveled streets and other barriers to easy and safe access.

Planning Areas and Facilities for Health, Physical Education, and Recreation—Rev. 1966
The Athletic Institute and American Association for Health, Physical Education, and Recreation

Size

In order to have the desired features, the neighborhood playground would normally require a minimum of eight acres. The particular facilities required will depend on the nature of the neighborhood, with space being allocated according to needs.

General Features

It is recommended that this area be developed as follows:

	Acres
Turf area for softball, touch football, soccer, speedball, and other field games	3.00
Hard-surface area for court games, such as netball, basketball, volleyball, and handball	.50
Open space for informal play	.50
Corner for senior citizens	.30
Space for quiet games, storytelling, and crafts	.20
Playlot	.20
Children's outdoor theater	.15
Apparatus area for elementary-age children	.25
Service building for restrooms, storage, and equipment issue, or a small clubhouse with some indoor activity space	.15
Circulation, landscaping, and buffer zones	2.00
Undesignated space	.75
Total	8.00

Depending upon the relationship of the site to school and other recreation facilities in the neighborhood, optional features such as a recreation building, a park, tennis courts, or a swimming pool might be located at the neighborhood playground. If climatic conditions warrant, a spray or wading pool should be provided. The following space for optional features should be added to the standards listed above:

	Acres
Recreation building	.2
Park area (if there is no neighborhood park)	2.0
Swimming pool	.5
Tennis courts	.4
Total	3.1

The addition of optional features may require provision for off-street parking.

Equipment

The following types of equipment are recommended:

Several pieces of equipment designed as simulated stage-coaches, fire engines, boats, locomotives, etc.

Physical-fitness or obstacle-course features, such as a scaling wall, cargo net climber, etc.

Balance beam.

Climbing structure, not to exceed 9' high.

Horizontal ladder, not to exceed 7' high.

Three horizontal bars with fixed heights, of rust-resistant metal.

Straight slide 8' high or spiral slide 10' high.

Six or more conventional swings, with low protective barriers.

Pipe equipment formed into shapes.

Sculptured forms.

Merry-go-round, safety-type.

The various apparatus groupings should be separated by plantings or attractive medium-height fencing.

NEIGHBORHOOD PARK

The neighborhood park is land set aside primarily for passive recreation. Ideally, it gives the impression of being rural, sylvan, or natural in its character. It emphasizes horticultural features, with spacious turf areas bordered by trees, shrubs, and sometimes

Planning Areas and Facilities for Health, Physical Education, and Recreation—Rev. **1966**
The Athletic Institute and American Association for Health, Physical Education, and Recreation

floral arrangements. It is essential in densely populated areas, but not required where there is ample yard space attached to individual home sites.

Location

A park should be provided for each neighborhood. In many neighborhoods, it will be incorporated in the park-school site or neighborhood playground. A separate location is required if this combination is not feasible.

Size

A separately located neighborhood park normally requires three to five acres. As a measure of expediency, however, an isolated area as small as one or two acres may be used. Sometimes the neighborhood park function can be satisfactorily included as a portion of a community or city-wide park.

General Features

The neighborhood park plays an important role in setting standards for community aesthetics. Therefore, it should include open lawn areas, plantings, and walks. Sculptured forms, pools, and fountains should also be considered for ornamentation. Creative planning will utilize contouring, contrasting surfaces, masonry, and other modern techniques to provide both eye appeal and utility.

COMMUNITY AREAS AND FACILITIES

Community Park-School (Junior High)

The community park-school (junior high), a joint development of school and community, provides an economical and practical approach to a community-wide facility for educational, cultural, social, and recreational programs. This educational and recreational center generally refers to the combination of a junior high school and a community park.

Location

It is suggested that this facility provide service for an area with a radius of ½ to 1½ miles. Such an area will normally contain 20,000 to 30,000 people, but population density may modify the size of the area served.

Size

Based upon current formulas for establishing junior-high-school and community-park sites, a minimum area of 35 acres is desirable.

General Features

It is suggested that the area be developed as follows:

	Acres
Buildings (school and community recreation)	5.00
Turf field-games area	8.00
Hard-surface games court and multiple-use area	2.75
Tennis courts	1.00
Football field with 440-yard track (220-yard straightaway)	4.00
Baseball field with hooded backstop	3.00
Playlot and apparatus	1.00
Park and natural areas	5.00
Parking	1.25
Buffer zones and circulation	4.00
Total	35.00

Planning Areas and Facilities for Health, Physical Education, and Recreation—Rev. 1966
The Athletic Institute and American Association for Health, Physical Education, and Recreation

The following may be included as standard or optional features:

Swimming pool (usually related to the building)
Nature study trails and/or center
Day-camping center

There are many optional features that may be included in the community park-school. The inclusion of these is dependent upon the section of the country, available space, topography, community needs, climate, socio-economic composition of the community, and other variables. The following may be included as optional features:

Archery range	Hard-surface area for dancing
Band shell	Horseshoe pits
Boccie courts	Ice-skating or roller-skating rink
Botanical garden	Lake for boating
Croquet courts	Lawn-bowling greens
Golf driving range	Lighted courts and fields
Golf putting course	Shuffleboard courts

In designing the community park-school, planners should consider the proper placement of apparatus and areas that serve multiple use, and also bear in mind appropriate safety features in the development of each area or facility.

COMMUNITY PARK-SCHOOL (SENIOR HIGH)

A community park-school (senior high) is planned to provide facilities for youth and adults to meet a wide range of educational and recreational needs and interests on a single site. It generally refers to a combination of a high school and a community park.

It is essential that coordination and cooperation be exercised by school and municipal authorities to insure the maximum development and use of all facilities for instruction and recreation, both during and after school hours.

Location

It is suggested that the population density of the area as well as the total population of the community determine the scope and size of the area to be served by this facility. For example, the higher the population density, the smaller the service radius.

Size

Based on current formulas, a minimum area of 50 acres is suggested.

The site size should be based upon program needs, which will include: the physical education instructional program; school-supervised games, sports, and athletics; and school and community recreation activities during out-of-school hours.

General Features

It is suggested that the area be developed as follows:

	Acres
Buildings (including a gymnasium and an aquatics center)	6.00
Turf field-games area for instruction, intramurals, interscholastic athletics practice, and recreation use	8.00
Hard-surface games court and multiple-use area	3.00
Tennis courts	1.50
Apparatus area for instructional use (optional)	.12
Recreation area	5.00
Hard-surface area (for shuffleboard and outdoor bowling)	
Turf area (for horseshoes and croquet)	
Turf area (for golf and archery)	

Planning Areas and Facilities for Health, Physical Education, and Recreation—Rev. 1966
The Athletic Institute and American Association for Health, Physical Education, and Recreation

Football field with bleachers and 440-yard track (220-yard straightaway)	6.00
Baseball field	3.50
Playlot and apparatus	.50
Park and natural areas	5.00
Recreation building with senior-citizen center	.50
Parking and driver-education range	6.00
Buffer zones and circulation	5.00
Total	50.12

For other features that may be incorporated into this facility, see the sections in this chapter devoted to the community park-school (junior high) and the city-wide or district park.

An adequate number of each kind of facility should be provided to permit full participation by the largest group that will be using the facility at any given time.

The total community park-school area should be landscaped to create a parklike setting that enhances and does not interfere with the instructional and recreational areas.

COMMUNITY PARK AND PLAYFIELD

The community park and playfield is designed to provide a variety of active and passive recreational services for all age groups of a community served by a large junior high school (20,000 to 30,000 residents). Primary requisites are outdoor fields for organized sports, indoor space for various activities, special facilities, and horticultural development.

Location

It is highly desirable that this facility be incorporated into the complex of a community park-school (junior high). Where this is not feasible, the community park and playfield should be located

Planning Areas and Facilities for Health, Physical Education, and Recreation—Rev. 1966
The Athletic Institute and American Association for Health, Physical Education, and Recreation

within ½ to 1½ miles of residents in its service area depending upon population density and ease of access.

Size

A separate community park and playfield requires an area of 15 to 20 acres. At least two-thirds of the area should be developed for active recreation purposes.

General Features

The following should be provided:

Fields for baseball, football, field hockey, soccer, and softball
Courts for tennis, basketball, boccie, volleyball, handball, horseshoes, shuffleboard, paddle tennis, and other games
Recreation building containing an auditorium, a gymnasium, and special-use rooms for crafts, dramatics, and social activities
Quiet recreation area
Hard-surface area for dodgeball and kickball
May include a neighborhood playground. (See features under Neighborhood Playground)

CITY-WIDE OR DISTRICT PARK

The city-wide or district park serves a district of a larger city, or a total community of a smaller city. This facility should serve a population of from 50,000 to 100,000. It is designed to provide a wide variety of activities.

Location

This facility should be incorporated with a high school as a park-school development. Where this is not feasible, consideration should be given to placing the park as close as possible to the center of the population to be served. The land available will be a determining factor in site selection. While the service area will vary according to population density, a normal use radius is two to four miles.

Size

The city-wide or district park may have from 50 to 100 acres.

General Features

Depending upon available acreage, topography, and natural features, the city-wide or district park will contain a large number of different components. These would include, but not be limited to, the following:

A number of fields for baseball, football, soccer, and softball
Tennis center
Winter sports facilities
Day-camp center
Picnic areas (group and family)
Bicycling paths or tracks
Swimming pool
Lake for water sports
Pitch-and-putt golf course
Recreation building
Nature-centered trails
Skating rinks (ice and roller)
Playlot and apparatus
Parking areas
Outdoor theater

The above facilities should be separated by large turf and landscaped areas. Natural areas and perimeter buffers should be provided.

SWIMMING POOLS

Because of the promotion of swimming in high schools, colleges, and clubs, competitive swimming is receiving greater recognition throughout the United States. Junior championship meets require a pool at least 75 feet long and 42 feet wide. For senior championship meets, the ideal length is 55 yards long and 56 feet wide. The official short-course record requires a pool 75 feet in length and the long-course requires a pool 165 feet long. To fully meet these requirements it is wise to build a pool one inch longer than the specified length, as the official distance cannot be even a fraction of an inch short.

The width of the pool is governed by the number and width of swimming lanes desired. The competitive pool should never have less than six lanes. The width of the lane represents the full spread of the arm in the breast stroke and widths of 6, 7, and 8 feet have been designated as satisfactory. Lanes 5 feet wide are not recommended.

The slope of the pool floor should be as follows: No sudden changes of slope should be permitted in the area where the water is less than 5 feet deep. For depths less than 6 feet, the slope should be 1 foot in each 15 feet, and from the deep area in front of the diving board, the slope must not exceed 1 foot in each 15 feet.

Standards for the depth of swimming pools have been established by the A.A.U. and these must be adhered to in connection with competitive swimming sanctioned by the organization. For the 75 foot pool, the shallow end should be at least 3 feet deep and slope not more than 1 foot each 15 feet and a minimum of 10 feet and preferably 12 feet under the diving boards. When high diving platforms (10 meters) are used, the depth must be increased to 15 feet, maintaining other dimensions given. The N.C.A.A. recommends 3½ feet of water in the shallow end of the pool.

In any public pool the depth in the shallow end should never be more than 3 feet. For all commercial, municipal, and recrea-

Planning Areas and Facilities for Health, Physical Education, and Recreation—Rev. 1966
The Athletic Institute and American Association for Health, Physical Education, and Recreation

tional pools, 80 to 85 percent of the total water area should be 5 feet or less in depth.

In planning for swimming pools, three factors must be considered. First consideration is the types of swimming pools. Second consideration is the location of the pools, and third, the size of the pools.

1. The three types of pools are: a) wading pools for young children. The maximum depth of water in a wading pool is recommended not to exceed 24 inches. Sufficient deck or circulation space for parents should be provided around the pool.

This type of pool should be separated from a regular swimming pool because of safety and consideration for older swimmers. b) General swimming pool for older children and adults. The pool may be of any size or shape but most frequently it is rectangular. The pool should be a minimum of 250 square feet with at least 25 square feet of water surface per bather at time of maximum load. The depth of the pool will vary from about 3 feet deep to about 10 feet deep. The deep end usually is used for diving. Not more than one-third of the pool area should have a water depth exceeding 5 feet.

When only one pool is possible, the general pool serves both the swimming and diving functions. The shape of the pool should be such that there is clear distinction between the two activities.

c) Diving pools are used for diving and deep-water activities. Whenever possible, this pool should be separated from the general swimming pool. The minimum depth of water in diving areas with a board one meter or less above water should be 8 feet 6 inches. If the board is over one meter, but not over three meters above the water, the depth should be 10 feet.

2. The location of pools should be such that they will receive a maximum of sunlight throughout the day. Avoid shadows from buildings and trees. The pools should have a southerly exposure. Avoid locating the pools too close to any dwelling units. An adequate buffer for noise and visual separation is essential. Avoid a location too close to the nearest lot lines.

3. The size of the pools should be sufficient to comfortably accommodate all swimmers at the peak time. After determining the maximum number of swimmers, allow at least 25 square feet per person.

Accessory facilities that are essential include a bathhouse, deck area for sunbathers and an area for games, parking, and storage. If possible, the pool can be designed for winter activities such as ice skating and hockey.

TYPICAL SHAPES AND SIZES OF POOLS

LARGE

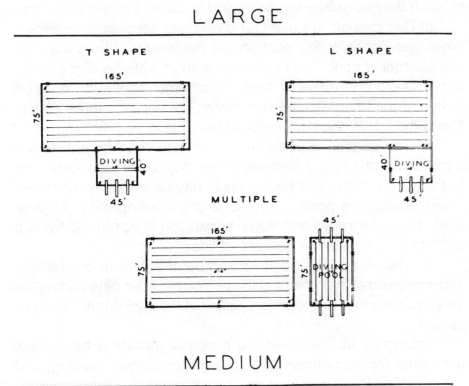

T SHAPE

165'

75'

DIVING

40

45'

L SHAPE

165'

75'

DIVING

40

45'

MULTIPLE

165'

45'

75'

75'

DIVING POOL

SMALL

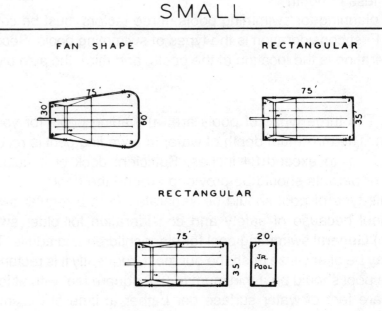

FAN SHAPE

75'

30'

60

RECTANGULAR

75'

35

RECTANGULAR

75'

35'

20'

JR. POOL

MEDIUM

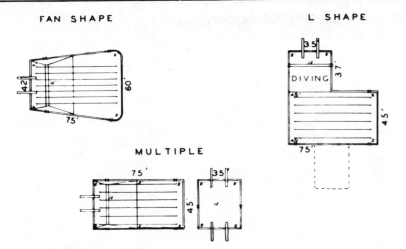

FAN SHAPE

42'

60'

75'

MULTIPLE

75'

45'

35'

L SHAPE

35'

37'

DIVING

45'

75'

IRREGULAR SHAPED POOLS
HOMES - HOTELS - CLUBS

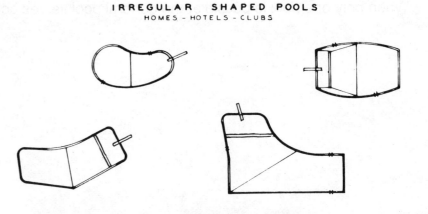

Sports and Recreation Facilities, M. Alexander Gabrielson and Coswell M. Miles, Editors. Prentice-Hall, Inc., Englewood Cliffs, New Jersey—1958.

Typical Waterfront Development with Pool

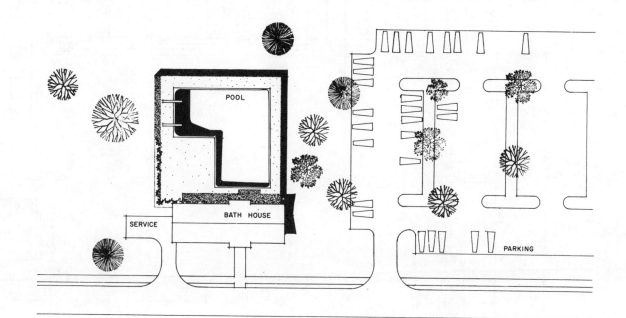

TYPICAL SITE PLAN

Justement, Elam, Callmer, and Kidd,
William Crandall Suite,
Architects, Engineers, Washington, D.C.
Dept. of the Navy, Bureau of Yards and Docks,
Washington, D.C.

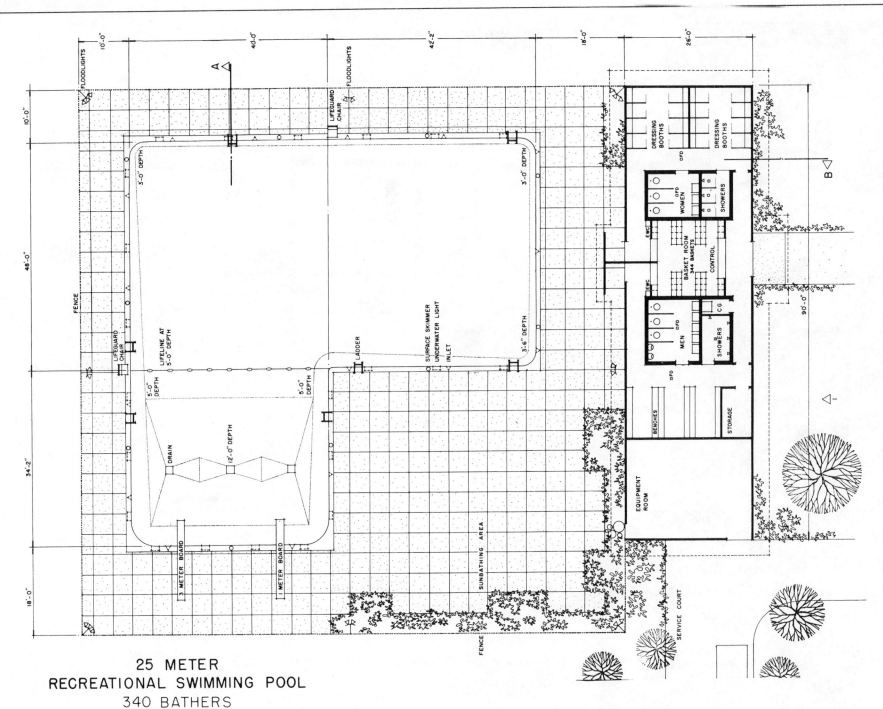

25 METER
RECREATIONAL SWIMMING POOL
340 BATHERS

PITCH AND PUTT GOLF

An undulating or steeply sloping area of land unsuitable for ordinary games can often be transformed into an excellent pitch and putt or approach course. When well laid out and maintained, this facility often proves extremely popular, particularly in densely populated urban areas. It is also one of the few games where the income can more than offset the cost of maintenance and management.

Space requirements vary according to the design of the course. Assuming, however, that only a mashie niblick and putter are to be used and the holes will not be less than 35 yards in length or more than 90 yards, 10 acres should be sufficient to provide eighteen holes or half this area for 9 holes. The minimum width of any part of the course should not be less than 70 yards and greens should be from 350 to 500 square yards in area. There should be a clear putting space of not less than 10 yards in any direction around the hole.

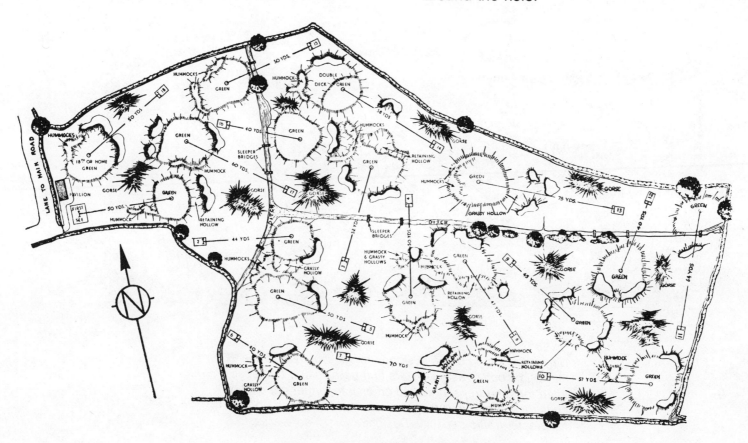

A 13-Acre Hole Pitch and Putt Golf Course

There are two general types of golf courses in use today—9-hole and 18-hole.

The 18-hole course is the standard layout. The 9-hole course is a short course with the fairways and greens smaller than those of a regulation course but similar in every other way.

The average length of an 18-hole course is 6,500 yards while a 9-hole course is less than half of this length.

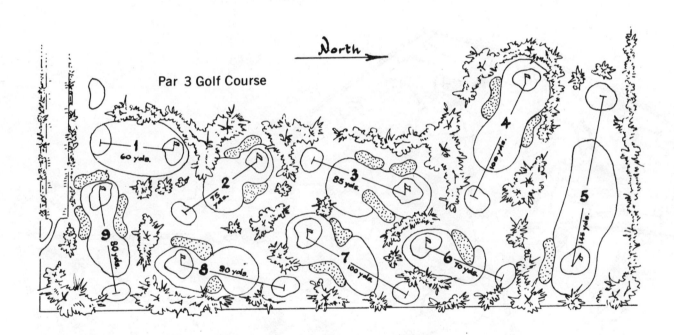

Nine-hole, par-3 course designed for maximum land use at minimum cost. Grassy bunkers and hollows can be substituted for sand traps indicated on plan to further cut cost of construction and maintenance as well as to speed up play for greater traffic capacity. Designed for 15-acre area.

SOURCE: *Golf Operators Handbook,* edited by Ben Chlevin, National Golf Foundation, Inc., 1956, p. 86.

GOLF COURSES

The use of a golf course as the main feature of the open-space area in cluster or planned-unit developments is becoming increasingly common. Golf courses are attractive because they usually present a finely manicured, permanently green, well-landscaped vista. The course can meander over rolling terrain and fit into odd shapes, incorporating ponds and rock outcroppings.

A full 18-hole course requires from 160 to 200 acres of land. A 9-hole course needs about 100 acres. A par-3 course occupies about 30 acres. One drawback is that golf courses are expensive to build and to maintain. A golf course's main asset, from a developer's standpoint, is that land values adjacent to the fairways are substantially increased. More important, from a planning standpoint, is that permanent open space is created, which enhances the aesthetic atmosphere and physical attractiveness.

The total course length ranges from 5,000 to 6,000 yards. One fairway requires a 100-yard width. One method used to conserve land is to double the fairways; that is, use two parallel fairways. This requires a width of about 150 yards, but reduces the total length. Another disadvantage in the use of a golf course is the relatively small numbers of people who can utilize it at any one time. Golf courses should be restricted to large developments where a range of other recreational facilities are available.

	MINIMUM AREA REQ.	MAXIMUM AREA REQ.	NO. OF PARKING SPACES	POPULATION SERVED	SERVICE RADIUS	AVERAGE LENGTH
9-HOLE COURSE	60 Acres	80 Acres	100 Cars	1 hole per 3,000 persons or 27,000 persons	½-¾ hour by car or public transportation	Approx. 2,250 yards
18-HOLE COURSE	120 Acres	160 Acres	200 Cars	1 hole per 1,500 persons or 25,000 persons	1 hour max. by car or public transportation	6,500 yards

RECREATION BUILDING

The recreation building is a community facility of a specialized type. It emerged as part of and usually is incorporated in the local park and recreation system. The building may contain a range of passive and active facilities from meeting rooms to gyms and indoor swimming pools. They are usually designed to function as community centers with strong citizen participation. Most recreation buildings are designed for both young and old on a year-round basis.

The programming of these facilities should be closely coordinated with existing or proposed facilities in other community buildings such as schools or private clubs. The location of the recreation building should be central to the population served and near to outdoor recreation areas. The integration of indoor-outdoor activities will provide a maximum year-round activities program. Adequate parking is essential for staff and visitors. A location near mass transit lines will remove somewhat the need for parking needs.

The building shown contains a full-sized gymnasium for regulation basketball, shower and locker rooms, storage areas, and health and administrative suites. Since the excessive height of a gymnasium might be out of scale with surrounding dwellings, the structure is shown partially recessed into the ground. The reinforced roof structure of the lower unit is flush with the adjoining grade and makes an excellent hard-surfaced play area with a backdrop wall for games such as handball. Access to the lower level is through a sunken courtyard.

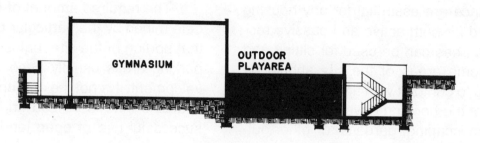

SECTION A–A

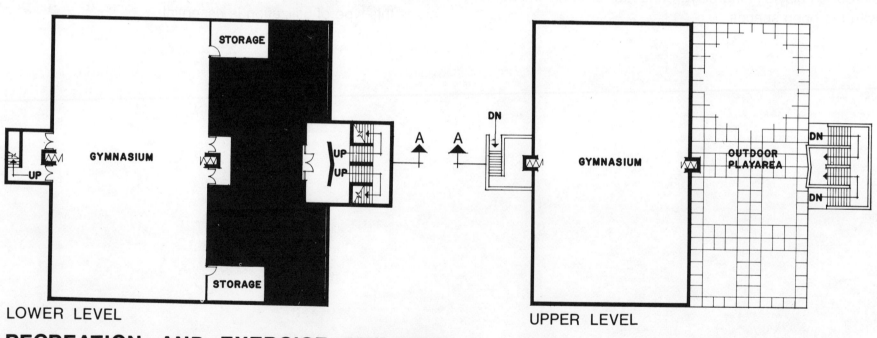

LOWER LEVEL

UPPER LEVEL

RECREATION AND EXERCISE BUILDING

OPEN-SPACE ALTERNATIVES

Parks and usable open space are essential for any housing development. These are needed for both active and passive recreation. Small parks with shade trees can be used for sitting and quiet meditation. If possible, some areas of the site should be preserved in their natural setting to contrast with and provide relief from the masonry and asphalt of the housing development. Open spaces that can be used for landscaping, gardens, or other outdoor activities are required. Natural features, when they occur, such as ponds, running brooks, and rock outcroppings, must be preserved and blended into the overall site plan.

The required playlots and playgrounds for children should be related with the open spaces.

The required amount of open space for each development is determined by the particular needs of the occupants. Realistically, that portion of the site that is not used for buildings or automobile parking areas usually becomes the open space. Often in a development, it is not the amount of land that is available, but how the available land is utilized and developed. Many fine examples of successful use of open land have been on small and restricted spaces.

In addition to the open space at ground level, additional or supplementary usable space can be provided above ground in the form of roof gardens, terraces, and balconies. In high-density areas this type of utilization is essential.

SOURCE: *Planning and Design Workbook for Community Participation*
Prepared for the State of New Jersey Dept. of Community Affairs by the
Research Center for Urban and Environmental Planning
School of Architecture & Urban Planning, Princeton University—1969

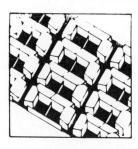

a. private open space on grade adjacent to dwelling unit; common open space reduced to access.

e. common open space shared by groups of dwelling units.

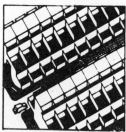

b. private open space on/in building structure, adjacent to dwelling unit; common open space reduced to access.

f. common open space, integrated with parking, shared by groups of dwelling units.

c. private open space on grade or on/in building structure, adjacent to dwelling unit; common open space shared by groups of dwelling units.

g. common open space shared by all dwelling units.

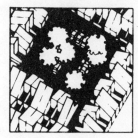

d. private open space on grade or on/in building structure, adjacent to dwelling unit; common open space, integrated with parking, shared by groups of dwelling units.

SOURCE: *Planning and Design Workbook for Community Participation*
Prepared for the State of New Jersey Dept. of Community Affairs by the
Research Center for Urban and Environmental Planning
School of Architecture & Urban Planning, Princeton University—1969

M. Paul Friedberg & Associates

M. Paul Friedberg & Associates

TYPES OF SHOPS

Shopping and other commercial space may be necessary if the development is sufficiently large to support such facilities. This usually includes retail shops for convenient goods and the supply of basic services.

The location of the neighborhood shopping center is generally located on an arterial street at the intersection of a collector street. However, it may also be located more centrally within the neighborhood and closer to the other community facilities. Vehicular access for trucks is essential for deliveries of goods and other services. However, such vehicular access must not cross or interfere with pedestrian access to the shopping area.

The neighborhood shopping center generally includes eight to fifteen stores with an average gross floor area of about 40,000 square feet. The site will vary from 1.5 to 4.0 acres, including parking area. A minimum of 800 to 1,000 families in its trade area is needed to support this center.

Stores included in this category are stationery, laundry, bakery, hardware, service station, barber and beauty shops, small restaurants, drugstore, and a food market. Frequently, professional offices are included to provide medical and dental services.

In planning such facilities, it is most important that they are not larger than required by the development. This will either result in marginal business that cannot provide proper services or attract people from outside the development, causing undesired influx of people and cars.

Limited, but adequate, parking areas must be provided. The recommended standard for the amount of parking space to floor area of stores is a 2-to-1 ratio. That is, 2 square feet of parking space for every one square foot of sales area. Some standards suggest even more parking space but this would negate the concept of pedestrian access to the center.

The location of the parking area should be between the stores and the street so that it will be away from the pedestrian access.

It is strongly recommended that the shopping center be in close proximity, not adjacent, to the school and play areas. This will encourage the multiple use of facilities and discourage the use of the automobile.

Two-story buildings may be utilized with medical, dental, or other services located there. The layout of store units should be as flexible as possible to make adjustments to meet changing community needs.

The entire complex needs sufficient buffer strips between shopping areas and adjacent residential uses. Such buffer strips for a small center should be at least 20 feet and have proper landscaping and fences. Also, it must be remembered that such shopping facilities must be clearly incidental to and compatible with the residential character of the property.

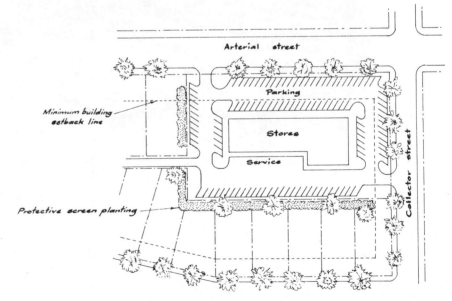

SOURCE: Land Subdivision Regulations, Housing and Home Finance Agency, Washington, D.C.

Neighborhood Shopping Center Size

POPULATION SERVED	FLOOR AREA REQUIRED (SALES AREA)	CUSTOMER PARKING AREA 2:1 RATIO	CIRCULATION, SERVICE, AND PLANTING AREAS, 25%	TOTAL SQ. FT.	TOTAL ACRES REQUIRED	SQ. FT. PER FAMILY (GROSS)	MAXIMUM WALKING DISTANCE
800 Families 2,500 Persons	20 SF/Family = 16,000 SF	32,000 SF	12,000 SF	60,000 SF	1.4 Acres	75	¼ Mile
1,600 Families 5,000 Persons	18 SF/Family = 28,800 SF	57,600 SF	36,400 SF	172,800 SF	4.0 Acres	100	½ Mile

FOOD MARKET—Should include specialty foods and delicatessen goods

BAKERY SHOP—May be included in food market

DRUGSTORE—Including reading matter, tobacco and vanity goods

RESTAURANT—Including table service and take-out orders

BARBER SHOP—Including shoeshine service

BEAUTY PARLOR—May be combined with barber shop

LAUNDRY AND DRY CLEANING STORE—Combined service, including a laundromat

HARDWARE—Should include household goods

SERVICE STATION—Including filling station, minor repairs, and auto accessories

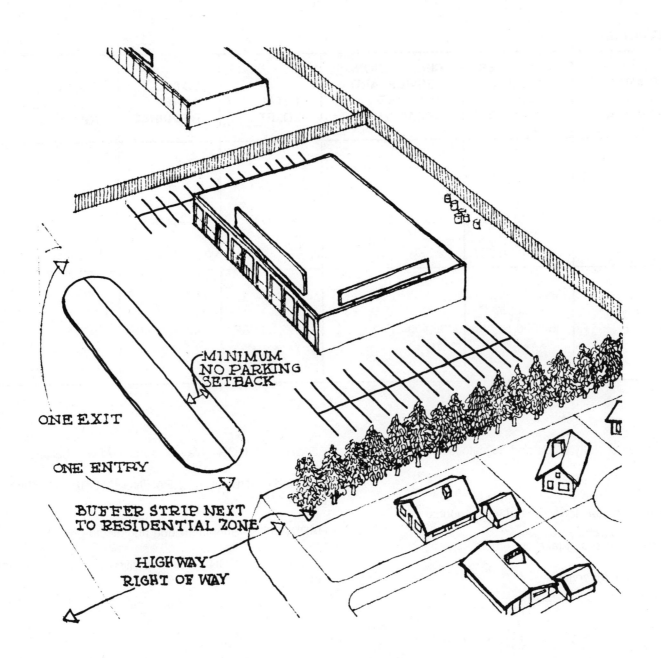

MINIMUM
NO PARKING
SETBACK

ONE EXIT

ONE ENTRY

BUFFER STRIP NEXT
TO RESIDENTIAL ZONE

HIGHWAY
RIGHT OF WAY

M. Paul Friedberg & Associates

Lindsay-Bushwick Housing
M. Paul Friedberg and Associates

LAND AREA OF ALL NEIGHBORHOOD COMMUNITY FACILITIES

Component Uses and Aggregate Area, by Type of Development and Population of Neighborhood

TYPE OF DEVELOPMENT	NEIGHBORHOOD POPULATION				
	1,000 persons 275 families	2,000 persons 550 families	3,000 persons 825 families	4,000 persons 1,100 families	5,000 persons 1,375 families
One- or Two-Family Development[a]					
Area in Component Uses					
1) Acres in school site	1.20	1.20	1.50	1.80	2.20
2) Acres in playground	2.75	3.25	4.00	5.00	6.00
3) Acres in park	1.50	2.00	2.50	3.00	3.50
4) Acres in shopping center	.80	1.20	2.20	2.60	3.00
5) Acres in general community facilities[b]	.38	.76	1.20	1.50	1.90
Aggregate Area					
6) Acres: total	6.63	8.41	11.40	13.90	16.60
7) Acres per 1,000 persons	6.63	4.20	3.80	3.47	3.32
8) Square feet per family	1,050	670	600	550	530
Multifamily Development[c]					
Area in Component Uses					
1) Acres in school site	1.20	1.20	1.50	1.80	2.20
2) Acres in playground	2.75	3.25	4.00	5.00	6.00
3) Acres in park	2.00	3.00	4.00	5.00	6.00
4) Acres in shopping center	.80	1.20	2.20	2.60	3.00
5) Acres in general community facilities[b]	.38	.76	1.20	1.50	1.90
Aggregate Area					
6) Acres: total	7.13	9.41	12.90	15.90	19.10
7) Acres per 1,000 persons	7.13	4.70	4.30	3.97	3.82
8) Square feet per family	1,130	745	680	630	610

[a]With private lot area of less than ¼ acre per family (for private lots of ¼ acre or more, park area may be omitted).

[b]Allowance for indoor social and cultural facilities (church, assembly hall, etc) or separate health center, nursery school, etc., unallocated above. Need will vary locally.

[c]Or other development predominantly without private yards.

SOURCE: *Planning the Neighborhood*, American Public Health Committee on the Hygiene of Housing, Chicago: Public Administration Service—1960

D-29 MEASUREMENT OF HOUSING QUALITY

RECREATIONAL SPACE

Goal: To provide *recreational space* appropriate in size and type to the occupancy characteristics of the development. To permit this space to be located outdoors, indoors, or in covered open space.

Program: The proposed development should provide *child-use space*, *mixed-use space* (children and adults), and *adult-use space* in relation to projected tenancy characteristics. Computation is as follows:

a. Compute the building occupancy according to the following schedule:

Apartment:	Occupancy:
Studio	1 Adult
1 BR apt.	2 Adults
2 BR apt.	2 Adults & 1 child
3 BR apt.	2 Adults & 2 children
4 BR apt.	2 Adults & 3 children

b. Compute the amount of *recreation space* required according to the following schedule:

—For **child-use space** multiply the number of children by 20 S.F.

—For **mixed-use space** multiply the total number of residents (children plus adults) by 25 S.F.

—For **adult-use space** multiply the number of adults by 100 S.F.

c. The facilities permitted to fulfill space requirements are:

Children:	Adult:	Mixed:
Tot Lot	Passive	Swimming Pool
Intermediate	Rooftop Terrace	Handball
Playground	Health Club	Tennis Courts

*Nursery Day-care (Public)
*Nursery Day-care (Private)
Terrace
*Laundry Room
Basketball
*Meeting Rooms
Volleyball
*Shops–Craft
*Shops–Automotive

*Space may be doubled for computation purposes.

All above facilities must be free to tenants. Facilities not included may be requested by the applicant. Detailed requirements for each facility are found following this section.

d. Indoor and covered recreation space are not computed as part of the floor area of the building.

Compliance:

$(B/A)100 = \%$
$(D/C)100 = \%$
$(F/E)100 = \%$

a. Child-use Space

PREFERRED (A)	PROPOSED (B)	SCALE
A = sq. ft. of **child-use** recreational space required	B = sq. ft. of **child-use space** provided	75%*

b. Mixed-use Space

PREFERRED (C)	PROPOSED (D)	SCALE
C = sq. ft. of **mixed-use space** required	D = sq. ft. of **mixed-use space** provided	60%*

c. Adult-use Space

PREFERRED (E)	PROPOSED (F)	SCALE
E = sq. ft. of **adult-use space** required	F = sq. ft. of **adult-use space** provided	50%*

*Minimum permitted

Housing Quality–A Program for Zoning Reform
Urban Design Council of the City of New York

236

CHILD		PROGRAM	TOT LOT	NURSERY/ DAYCARE—PRIVATE	NURSERY/ DAYCARE—PUBLIC	INTER. AGE PLAY-GROUND—2nd CHOICE
MIN.		Minimum Size	1,500 SF. 25' min. dim.	600 SF.	600 SF.	2,500 SF. 35' min. dim.
		Minimum Area in Sunlight	25% for 2 hours	20% for 2 hours	20% for 2 hours	25% for 2 hours
LOCATION		within Private *Outdoor* Space	Yes	not applicable	not applicable	Yes
		within Private *Open* Space	Yes	not applicable	not applicable	Yes
		within Private *Covered* Space	15% max.	not applicable	not applicable	15% max.
		within Private *Indoor* Space	not applicable	Yes	Yes	not applicable
		within Semiprivate *Outdoor* Space	No	not applicable	not applicable	No
HEIGHT ABOVE & BELOW CURB		fronting on or within Private Outdoor Space	15' max. above At level of outdoor space	15' max. above at level of outdoor space	15' max. above at level of outdoor space	15' max. above at level of outdoor space
		fronting on or within Semiprivate Outdoor Space	not applicable	not applicable	15' max. above 5' max. below	No
		within Private Indoor Space	not applicable	15' max. above at level of outdoor space	15' max. above at level of outdoor space	not applicable
ACCESS		Height above and below nearest floor	± 5'	± 5'	± 5'	± 5'
		Direct access from Private Outdoor Space	not applicable	Yes	No	not applicable
		Direct access from Lobby	Yes	Optional	No (fronting semiprivate space)	Yes
		Adjacent to Parking	Not within 30' min.	not applicable	not applicable	Not within 30' min.
WINDOWS		front on Private Outdoor Space	not applicable	Yes	Optional	not applicable
		front on Semiprivate or Public Outdoor Space	not applicable	Optional	Yes	not applicable
POLLUTION SOURCE		Air	35' min. horiz. at grade or +15' min. above grade	not applicable	not applicable	35' min. horiz. at grade or +15' min. above grade
		Noise	35' min. horiz. at grade or +15' min. above grade	No min.	No min.	35' min. horiz. at grade or +15' min. above grade
STANDARDS			1. for children 5-10 years, 2. equipment to be both kinetic—swings, slides, seesaws, etc., and static—sandboxes, wading pools, climbing apparatus, running and bike spaces, 3. benches for sitting at rate of 1/500 SF., 4. areas around equipment to be surfaced with resilient material—rubber, elastaturf, sand, grass, 5. grade differences between lobby & facility to be accomplished by ramps, 6. when adjacent to intermediate playground, facilities should not be mixed	1. same elevation as tot lot ±2', 2. grade changes by ramp, 3. child's bathroom and adult bathroom, 4. long dimension of room on exterior wall, 5. for ages 1-5 years, 6. exterior wall on private outdoor space, min. 75% transparent	1-5—see NURSERY (private) 6. exterior wall on semiprivate and/or public open space to be 50% transparent	1. for children 5-10 years, 2. equipment to be both kinetic—swings, seesaws, merry-go-round, etc., and static—climbing apparatus, running and bike space, 3. benches for sitting at the rate of 1/800 SF., 4. areas around equipment to be surfaced with resilient material, 5. grade differences between lobby and facility to be accomplished by ramps, 6. when adjacent to Tot Lot, facilities should not be mixed

Housing Quality–A Program for Zoning Reform
Urban Design Council of the City of New York

D-30 COMMUNITY RECREATIONAL FACILITIES

MIXED	PROGRAM	MEETING/SOCIAL ROOM—PRIVATE	VOLLEYBALL	BASKETBALL	SWIMMING POOL	HANDBALL
MIN.	Minimum Size	600 SF.	Single court 2,830 SF.	1,550 SF. min. for half court	800 SF.	Single court 2,250 SF.
	Minimum Area in Sunlight	No min.	No min.	No min.	When outdoors 75% + 4 hours summer solstice	No min.
LOCATION	within Private *Outdoor* Space	not applicable	Yes	Yes	Yes	Yes
	within Private *Open* Space	not applicable	Yes	Yes	Yes	Yes
	within Private *Covered* Space	not applicable	Yes	Yes	No	Yes
	within Private *Indoor* Space	Yes	Yes	Yes	Yes	Yes
	within Semiprivate *Outdoor* Space	not applicable	No	No	No	No
HEIGHT ABOVE & BELOW CURB	fronting on or within Private Outdoor Space	No limit above At level of outdoor space	Outdoors 100' max. above At level of outdoor space	Outdoors 100' max. above at level of outdoor space	Outdoors 150' max. above 10' below	Outdoor 100' max. above at level of outdoor space
	fronting on or within Semiprivate Outdoor Space	No limit above 5' max. below	Outdoors 100' max. above 5' max. below	Outdoors 100' max. above 5' max. below	Outdoors 150' max. above 10' below	Outdoors 100' max. above 5'-0" below
	within Private Indoor Space	No limit above At level of outdoor space	No limit above No limit below	No limit above No limit below	No limit above No limit below	No limit above No limit below
ACCESS	Height above and below nearest floor	± 5'	± 5'	± 5'	± 5'	± 5'
	Direct access from Private Outdoor Space	Yes	Yes when indoors and at grade ± 5'	Yes when indoors and at grade ±5'	Yes when indoors and at grade ± 5'-0"	Yes when indoors and at grade ± 5'-0"
	Direct access from Lobby	Yes	Yes when indoors	Yes when indoors	Yes when indoors	Yes when indoors
	Adjacent to Parking	not applicable	not applicable	not applicable	not applicable	not applicable
WINDOWS	front on Private Outdoor Space	Yes	Yes when indoors	Yes when indoors	Yes when indoors	Yes when indoors
	front on Semiprivate or Public Outdoor Space	Optional	Optional when indoors	Optional when indoors	Optional when indoors	Yes when indoors
POLLUTION SOURCE	Air	No min.	When outdoors 35' min. horiz. at grade or +15' min. above grade	When outdoors 35' min. horiz at grade or +15' min. above grade	When outdoors 35' min. horiz at grade or +15' min. above grade	When outdoors 35' min. horiz at grade or +15' min. above grade
	Noise	No min.	When outdoors 35' min. horiz. at grade or +15' min. above grade	When outdoors 35' min. horiz at grade or +15' min. above grade	When outdoors 35' min. horiz at grade or +15' min. above grade	When outdoors 35' min. horiz at grade or +15' min. above grade
STANDARDS		1. long dimension of room on exterior wall and to be 70% transparent, 2. transparency ratio of exterior walls to be 70%	1. minimum height throughout 20', 2. lighting level when in covered space or indoor space to meet current standards, 3. court dimensions to meet standards	1. minimum height 20' throughout, 2. lighting level in covered space or indoor space to meet current standards, 3. court dimensions to meet standards	1. when indoors at least 50% of a wall that corresponds to the long dimension of the pool area should be transparent, 2. when indoors and open to the public, separate entry should be semiprivate or public provided from outdoor space	1. back wall and ceiling to be minimum 16'-0" high, 2. lighting level in covered or indoor space to meet current standards, 3. court dimensions to meet standard

Housing Quality–A Program for Zoning Reform
Urban Design Council of the City of New York

MIXED		PROGRAM	TENNIS COURT(S)	MEETING/SOCIAL ROOM—PUBLIC
MIN.		Minimum Size	7,200 SF. for single court and enclosure	600 SF.
		Minimum Area in Sunlight	No min.	No min.
LOCATION		within Private *Outdoor* Space	Yes	not applicable
		within Private *Open* Space	Yes	not applicable
		within Private *Covered* Space	Yes	not applicable
		within Private *Indoor* Space	Yes	Yes
		within Semiprivate *Outdoor* Space	No	not applicable
HEIGHT ABOVE & BELOW CURB		fronting on or within Private Outdoor Space	Outdoors 100' max. above at level of outdoor space	No limit above At level of outdoor space
		fronting on or within Semiprivate Outdoor Space	Outdoor 100' max. above 5' max. below	No limit above At level of outdoor space
		within Private Indoor Space	No limit above No limit below	No limit above At level of outdoor space
ACCESS		Height above and below nearest floor	± 5'	± 5'
		Direct access from Private Outdoor Space	Yes when indoors and at grade ± 5'	No
		Direct access from Lobby	Yes when indoors	No (fronting semiprivate space)
		Adjacent to Parking	not applicable	not applicable
WINDOWS		front on Private Outdoor Space	Yes when indoors	Optional
		front on Semiprivate or Public Outdoor Space	Yes when indoors	Yes
POLLUTION SOURCE		Air	When outdoors 35' min. horiz. at grade or +15' min. above grade.	No min.
		Noise	When outdoors 35' min. horiz. at grade or +5' min. above grade.	No min.
STANDARDS			1. when indoors under permanent or temporary structure, minimum height at edge of court 27' and 32' at center of net, 2. when indoors and open to the public, separate entry should be provided fronting semiprivate or public outdoor space, 3. lighting level in covered or indoor space to meet current stands, 4. court dimensions to meet standard	1. long dimension of room on exterior wall and to be 70% transparent, 2. transparency ratio of exterior walls to be 70%

Housing Quality–A Program for Zoning Reform
Urban Design Council of the City of New York

D-30 COMMUNITY RECREATIONAL FACILITIES

ADULT	PROGRAM	PASSIVE SPACE	TERRACE	ROOFTOP TERRACE	HEALTH CLUB TYPE FACILITIES	SHOP—AUTOMOTIVE
MIN.	Minimum Size	None	200 SF. min.; 400 max.	Up to 25% of adult SF. requirement max. 20' min. dim.	No min.	300 SF. 10' min. dim.
	Minimum Area in Sunlight	No min.	No min.	No min.	No min.	No min.
LOCATION	within Private Outdoor Space	Yes	Yes	Yes	Yes. As adjunct to indoor uses	No
	within Private Open Space	Yes	Yes	Yes	Yes. As adjunct to indoor uses	No
	within Private Covered Space	25% max.	25% max. by structure less than 18' above	25% max.	Yes. As adjunct to indoor uses	No
	within Private Indoor Space	No	No	No	Yes	Yes
	within Semiprivate Outdoor Space	Yes	25% max. by structure less than 18' above	No	Yes. As adjunct to indoor uses	No
HEIGHT ABOVE & BELOW CURB	fronting on or within Private Outdoor Space	15' max. above At level of outdoor space	No limit above Max. 5' below	40' min. to 200' max. above curb	No limit above At level of outdoor space	unlimited above
	fronting on or within Semiprivate Outdoor Space	5' max. above At level of outdoor space	No limit above Max. 5' below	40' min. to 200' max. above curb	No limit above 10' max. below	unlimited above
	within Private Indoor Space	not applicable	not applicable	not applicable	No limit	unlimited above
ACCESS	Height above and below nearest floor	± 5'	No limit above	at same level	± 5'	± 5'
	Direct access from Private Outdoor Space	not applicable	Optional	Optional	Optional	Optional
	Direct access from Lobby	Yes	not applicable	Yes	Yes	Optional
	Adjacent to Parking	Optional	not applicable	not applicable	not applicable	Yes
WINDOWS	front on Private Outdoor Space	not applicable	not applicable	not applicable	Yes	Yes
	front on Semiprivate or Public Outdoor Space	not applicable	not applicable		Optional	No
POLLUTION SOURCE	Air	No min.	When outdoors 35' min. horiz at grade or +15' min. above grade	100' from smokestack	No min.	No min.
	Noise	No min.	When outdoors 35' min. horiz at grade or +15' min. above grade	50' from cooling tower	No min.	No min.
STANDARDS		1. the passive space is to be apportioned as follows: a. amount of passive space in semiprivate outdoor space can be no more than 25% of total Adult requirement b. and cannot be greater in area than passive space in private outdoor space	1. only 1 apartment may front on a terrace, 2. when on grade (-5'—15') there can be a direct entry to the terrace when fronting on private outdoor space, 3. when fronting on semiprivate or public outdoor space, the entry from that space must have a locked entry	1. the terrace be surfaced with a durable paving material, 2. at least 15% of the terrace be covered either permanently or with awnings, etc., 3. that following facilities be provided: a. seating b. bathrooms c. drinking fountain	1. would include such facilities as: sauna, steam baths, various types of baths, swimming pools, showers, exercise equipment and lockers, 2. have a minimum height of 12'-0" throughout, 3. exterior wall to be a minimum of 50% transparent, 4. when open to public, entrance to be provided from semiprivate or public open space, 5. exterior spaces are not counted toward interior recreation space	1. equiped with bathroom 2. appropriately equipped with benches and pit 3. must be accessible to the tenants for 12 hrs a day, 7 days a week 4. for tenants only

Housing Quality–A Program for Zoning Reform
Urban Design Council of the City of New York

240

ADULT	PROGRAM	SHOP—CRAFTS	LAUNDRY ROOM
MIN. Minimum Size		400 SF. 15' min. dim.	400 SF.
Minimum Area in Sunlight		No min.	25% min.
LOCATION within Private Outdoor Space		No	No
within Private Open Space		No	No
within Private Covered Space		No	No
within Private Indoor Space		Yes	Yes
within Semiprivate Outdoor Space		No	No
HEIGHT ABOVE & BELOW CURB fronting on or within Private Outdoor Space		No limit above / At level of outdoor space	No limit above / At level of outdoor space
fronting on or within Semiprivate Outdoor Space		No limit above / 5' max. below	No limit above / 5' max. below
within Private Indoor Space		No limit above / At level of outdoor space	No limit above / At level of outdoor space
ACCESS Height above and below nearest floor		± 5'	same level
Direct access from Private Outdoor Space		Optional	Yes
Direct access from Lobby		Yes	Yes
Adjacent to Parking		not applicable	not applicable
WINDOWS front on Private Outdoor Space		Yes	Yes
front on Semiprivate or Public Outdoor Space		Optional	Optional
POLLUTION SOURCE Air		No min.	No min.
Noise		No min.	No min.
STANDARDS		1. must have bathroom and work-sink, 2. equipped with machine tools and/or sewing/weaving, and/or pottery, 3. exterior wall on private outdoor space at least 40% transparent, 4. be accessible to tenants 12 hrs. a day, 7 days a week, 5. for tenants only	1. long dimension of room on exterior wall, 2. at least 50% transparent, 3. seating, 4. for tenants only

Housing Quality–A Program for Zoning Reform
Urban Design Council of the City of New York

SITE CONSIDERATIONS

E

E-1   Introduction: The Site Plan
       Slope Analysis
E-2   Topographic Considerations
E-3   Grades
E-4   Soil Conditions
E-5   Orientation–Sun, Breezes, and Views
E-6   Sun Orientation–Detached House
E-7   Breezes and Ventilation
E-8   Views and Vistas
E-9   Building Orientation
E-10   Room Orientation
E-11   Building Orientation to Street
E-12   Building Grouping
E-13   Circulation
E-14   Circulation–Street Parking

E-15   Circulation–Pedestrian
E-16   Streets and Highways
E-17   Street Standards
E-18   Street Classification
E-19   Typical Street Arrangements
E-20   Parking–General
E-21   Parking–Arrangement with Buildings
E-22   Curb Parking
E-23   Parking–Courts and Bays
E-24   Parking–Garages
E-25   Parking Alternatives
E-26   Requirements for Turns
E-27   Location of Utilities
E-28   Trees
E-29   Sun/Landscaping

INTRODUCTION: THE SITE PLAN

Site Planning Defined

Site planning is a broad term that embraces selection of sites; location of buildings in functional relation to each other, to the shape and topography of the site, and to the environment; provision within the site of suitable circulation routes well related to existing or proposed streets and walks; determination of land use to complement the buildings, such as private yards, parking space and recreation areas. These, and many other things are included within the scope of site planning.

There has been at least some evidence that, in the minds of inexperienced or thoughtless designers, the site plan is looked upon as the arrangement of a group of buildings into a pattern, pleasing in its two-dimensional qualities, or as a simple scattering of buildings. In either case a few details only, such as the relationship of existing topography, street grades, and sewer depths, seem to have been considered as complicating features.

The site plan is a complex thing and any underestimation of its importance risks the success of a project. The site plan is shaped by climate, by local housing customs, economic conditions and laws; by the location of the site with respect to employment, transportation, utilities, and social institutions; by the cost of the land, the relative cost of various forms of construction and the cost of utilities and maintenance; by the habits, incomes and composition of the families to be housed. It is influenced by the area, shape and topography of the site; the number of dwelling units proposed and whether these are to be apartments, flats, row or town houses; the orientation and spacing of the buildings; the method of waste collection and disposal and the landscape development and the preservation of existing trees. All of these factors must be correlated to produce a simple, livable, economical pattern of land use in which the land and buildings are integrated and so organized as to serve the needs of the families to be housed. The organization of the plan, if satisfactory, will also harmonize, not conflict, with the character of the land.

The physical site characteristics contained herein fall into five general groups. They include: natural characteristics, orientation, circulation, parking and utilities. The first group contains the major constraints vis-a-vis grades and soil conditions. Availability of potable water, energy supplies, and adequate municipal services for waste disposal are not included in this discussion, although they certainly act as constraints to site development.

Orientation is an important consideration for aesthetic and practical reasons. Despite controlled atmospheres within the dwelling unit, proper attention to placement and orientation can add greatly to the efficiency and comfort of the inhabitants.

Circulation and parking are increasing in importance as integral parts of site design for residential communities, including the higher density urban communities, due to the trend towards heavier reliance on the private automobile.

The location of utilities is also receiving increased attention commensurate with the rise in energy consumption. Placement of equipment, lines, and generating facilities are of aesthetic concern and relate directly to reliability of service as affected by storm conditions.

Reston, Conklin & Rossant—Architects

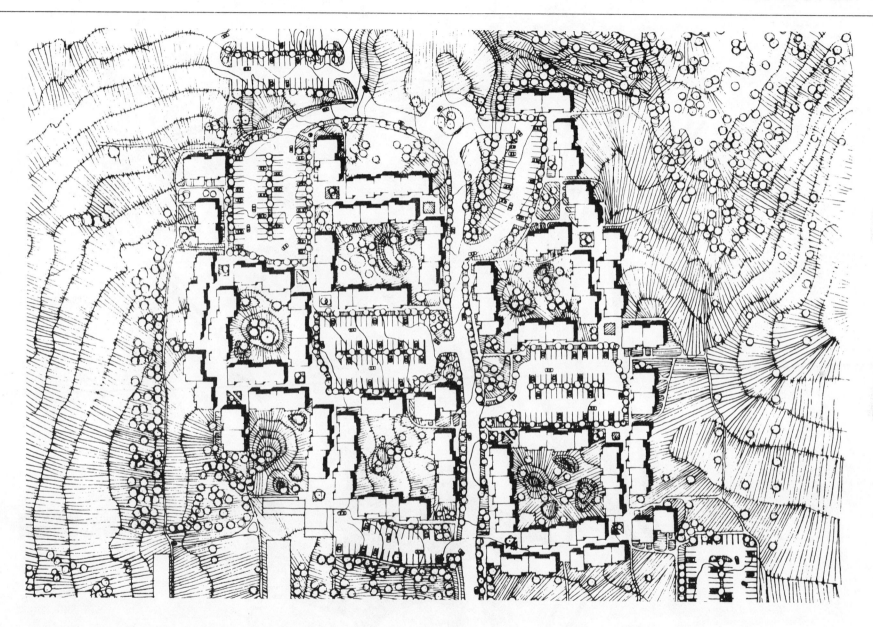

Westchester Development Corporation
Pokorny & Pertz/Architects & Planners

247

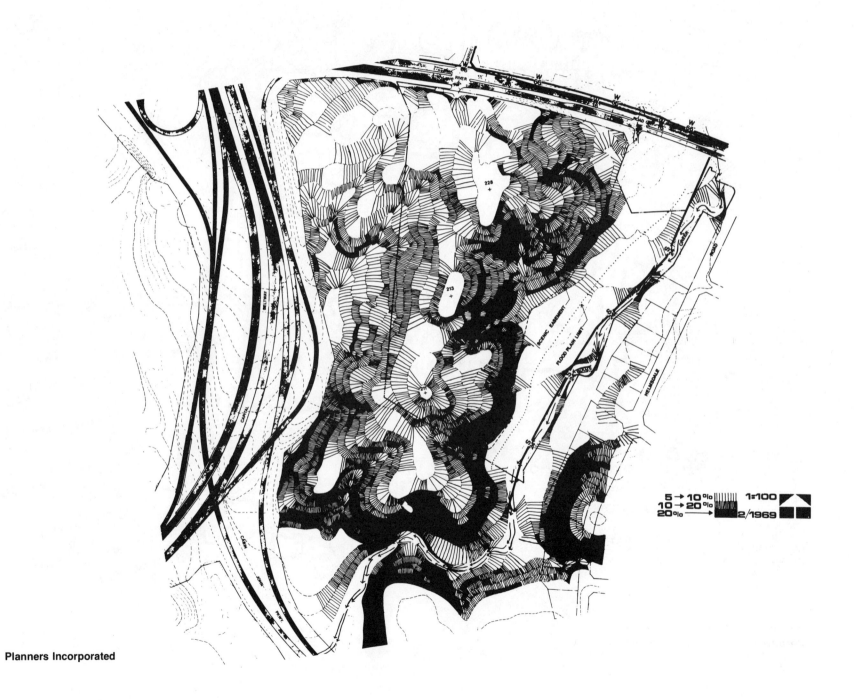

Planners Incorporated

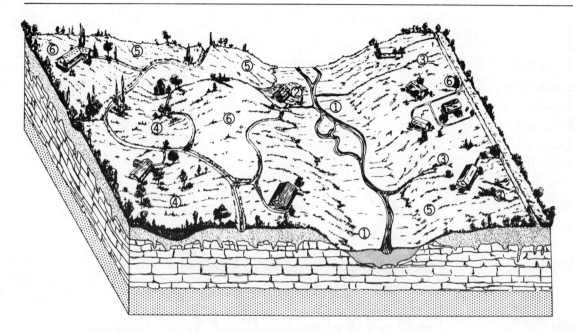

Topography

Topography is an important element in determining the acceptability or value of a site. It greatly affects the layout of buildings, how they can be placed upon it; and affects the cost of foundations and utility lines.

In order to make a proper judgment, detailed information in the form of accurate surveys showing contours are necessary. Such information must be interpreted by architects and engineers.

The best type of topography for housing is generally considered to be level or gently rolling terrain with slopes less than 10-20%. For single-family detached housing, the lot size should be increased in relation to the slope. It should also be high ground with good drainage.

However, a site should not be discarded because of rugged contours. Such features may, by careful study and imaginative design, be turned into an advantage and add features that would not be available on a level site.

Some common topographic positions:

Area 1 is a flood plain. It is subject to flooding during heavy storms.

Area 2 is an alluvial fan. The soil has been forming over the years as a result of water eroding material from the watershed above and depositing it near the mouth of the waterway. An alluvial fan can be hard hit by flash floods after heavy rains unless an adequate water-disposal system has been provided to control the runoff from the watershed above.

Area 3 is an upland waterway where water flowing from the higher surrounding land will concentrate. Natural waterways should not be used unless an adequate ditch or diversion terrace has been constructed to divert water from the site.

Area 4 is a low depressed area where water accumulates from higher surrounding areas. These soils remain wet and spongy for long periods.

Area 5 is a steep hillside. Many soils on steep slopes are shallow to rock. Some are subject to severe slippage. On all slopes, one must be careful of soil movement through gravity or by water erosion. Yet some steep hillsides can be used safely as building sites. The problem can be solved by studying the soils and avoiding the bad ones.

Area 6 is a deep, well-drained soil found on ridgetops and gently sloping hillsides. Generally these areas have the smallest water-management problems. They are the best building sites, other things being equal.

Know the Soil You Build On, Agriculture Information Bulletin 320, Soil Conservation Service, U.S. Dept. of Agriculture.

Buildable Area

No site should be given even tentative consideration unless the amount of buildable area it contains is known. If the site includes steeply sloping land, at least a sketch topography should be available. Data on soil conditions, particularly where there are areas of poor bearing due to natural conditions or to artificial fill, should also be obtained. A site engineer should cooperate with the planner in laying out topographically difficult sites. Runs and depths of sewer cuts constitute an important element of cost. Unbuildable areas of poor-bearing soil may often be used for parking or recreation areas, and thus need not cause a serious loss of useful area. Land that is unbuildable because it is so steep that construction cost becomes excessive is ordinarily of little use for other purposes, but all land may be of value to the project in giving more light and air to the houses. At the periphery of a project open area may provide useful protection against undesirable factors in the environment, acting as a miniature "green belt."

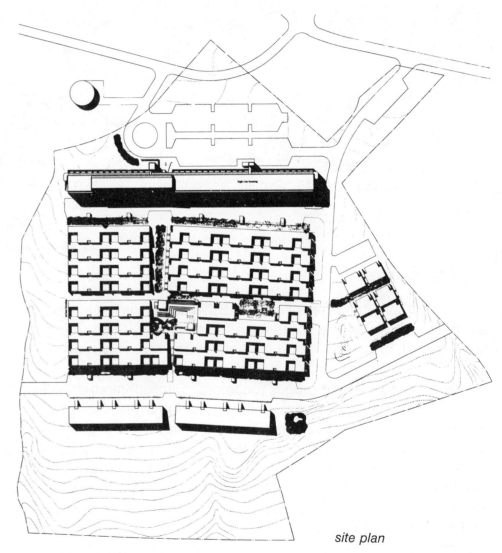

site plan

Scattered Sites Housing
Ithaca
Werner Seligmann and Associates, architects

GRADES

The table opposite gives desirable limits for slopes on different types of areas. Deviations may be warranted by especially favorable conditions, such as porous soils, mild climates, or light rainfall; also if local experience indicates that other gradients are satisfactory.

Failure to provide positive pitch away from buildings and to give open areas adequate slopes has necessitated costly regrading and reconstruction work on numerous projects. The trouble has been due in part to inaccurate construction, but incomplete or poorly conceived plans have been a contributing cause.

Of two basic design methods, one provides for drainage mainly across grassed areas, generally through "swales," until the water reaches streets, drives, or storm sewer inlets. This scheme, requiring the flow of water from walks onto lawns, is not altogether effective when slopes are inadequate and finished grading is not accurately executed, or if the turf is above the walk level. Swale drainage occasionally is carried under walks by small culverts (six- to eight-inch pipes or boxes). These are slight hazards and frequently become stopped. The other method employs walks to a considerable extent as drainage channels. This scheme has met some objection; nevertheless, it generally is more economical and practical than the use of swales, and it has been used far more widely. Moreover, when walks have been given proper cross and longitudinal slopes, with sewer inlets provided at points of concentrated storm water flow, there has been no serious inconvenience or complications.

Desirable Slopes

AREA	FUNCTION	SLOPE IN PERCENT	
		MAX.	MIN.
Streets, Service Drives, and Parking Areas		8.0	0.5
Collector and Approach Walks		10.0	0.5
Entrance Walks		4.0	1.0
Ramps		15.0	—
Paved Play and Sitting Areas		2.0	0.5
Lawn Areas		25.0	1.0
Grassed Playgrounds		4.0	0.5
Swales		10.0	1.0
Grassed Banks		3 to 1 slope (4 to 1 pref.)	
Planted Banks		2 to 1 slope (3 to 1 pref.)	

251

Soil Conditions

A thorough investigation of soil conditions is essential. The soil must be such that it can reasonably sustain the weight of the proposed buildings, and not cause any other problems. A rocky base will result in expensive foundation work, difficult site development and drainage problems. Installation of underground utility lines, such as water, gas, and sewers, would be made extremely difficult and costly.

A swampy condition will result in the use of piles to support the buildings and possible flooding conditions. Special waterproofing would be required for foundations, basements and underground garages. The nature of the soil will also determine the effectiveness of its ability to grow grass, trees and other vegetation.

Soil Conditions

DESIGNATION	VALUE AS FOUNDATION BELOW FROST LINE	POTENTIAL FROST ACTION	COMPRESSIBILITY AND EXPANSION	DRAINAGE CHARACTERISTICS	PLANNING CONSIDERATIONS
Gravel and Gravelly Soils	Good to excellent	None to medium	Almost none to slight	Excellent to practically impervious	Best location for buildings; excellent for accessory buildings, play areas, parking areas
Sand and Sandy Soils	Fair to good	None to high	Almost none to medium	Excellent to practically impervious	Good location for main buildings, accessory buildings, and active recreational areas
Low compressibility, fine-grained soils	Fair to poor	Medium to very high	Slight to high	Fair to practically impervious	Fair location for low or accessory buildings; good for play areas and parking
High compressibility, fine-grained soils	Poor to very poor	Medium to very high	High	Fair to practically impervious	Not good for building; retain as permanent green belt or open space
Peat and Other Fibrous Organic Soils	Not suitable	Slight	Very high	Fair to poor	Excavation in this material is difficult and expensive; poor location for structures; retain as open space or park area
Rock	Good to excellent	Very high	Almost none	Impervious	Excavation in this material is difficult and expensive; poor location for structures; retain as open space or park area

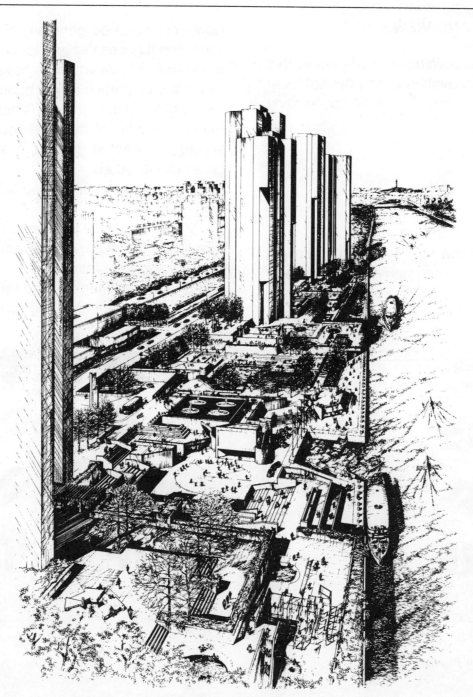

**Davis, Brody and Associates, Architects
and M. Paul Friedberg and Associates,
Landscape Architects**

ORIENTATION—SUN, BREEZES, AND VIEWS

Orientation is the placement of a building or apartment so that it may obtain the best advantages in relation to its physical location. The major consideration in orientation of a building or dwelling unit are:

1. sunlight
2. prevailing breezes
3. views

SUNLIGHT

The objective of orientation for the sun is to obtain sunlight when it is desired and to block out sunlight when it is not desired.

Since the United States has a great variety of climatic conditions, it is difficult to make universal assumptions in this respect.

However, it can be generally stated that the objective is to have sun when it is desired and to avoid it when it is not wanted. In the wintertime, it is desirable to have a maximum of sunlight. The hot summer sun, particularly at noon and late afternoon, is not desirable. Sunlight in the morning is delightful throughout the entire year. People will differ in their individual choices of how a dwelling unit should be oriented, but there are some considerations that are generally accepted:

1. Each apartment should get some sun at some time of the day.

2. Since people express a variety of desires as to amount and exposure to sunlight, it is advantageous for dwelling units to have different sun orientations.

3. No apartment should be oriented completely towards the north, because any dwelling unit facing north will get no sun.

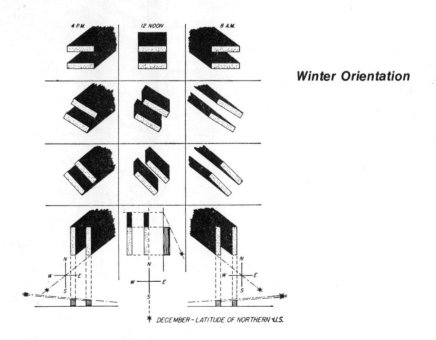

Summer Orientation

JUNE – LATITUDE OF NORTHERN U.S.

Winter Orientation

DECEMBER – LATITUDE OF NORTHERN U.S.

Apartment Houses, Abel and Severud, Reinhold Publishing Co., N.Y., 1947

Sun Orientation–Detached House

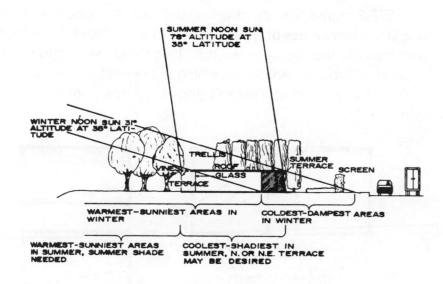

SUMMER NOON SUN
78° ALTITUDE AT
35° LATITUDE

WINTER NOON SUN 31°
ALTITUDE AT 35° LATI-
TUDE

TRELLIS

VINES
ROOF
GLASS

TERRACE

SUMMER
TERRACE

SCREEN

WARMEST-SUNNIEST AREAS IN
WINTER

COLDEST-DAMPEST AREAS
IN WINTER

WARMEST-SUNNIEST AREAS
IN SUMMER, SUMMER SHADE
NEEDED

COOLEST-SHADIEST IN
SUMMER, N. OR N.E. TERRACE
MAY BE DESIRED

ELEVATION

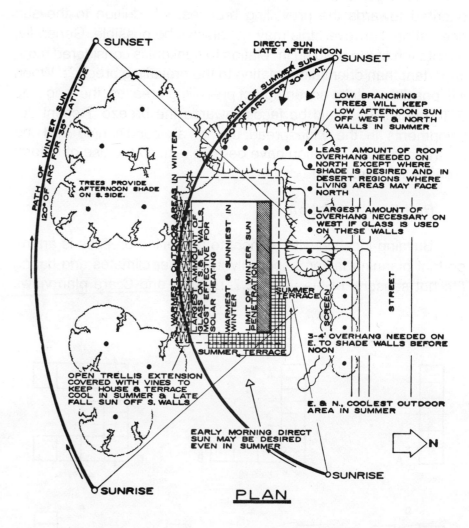

SUNSET

DIRECT SUN
LATE AFTERNOON

SUNSET

LOW BRANCHING
TREES WILL KEEP
LOW AFTERNOON SUN
OFF WEST & NORTH
WALLS IN SUMMER

PATH OF SUMMER SUN

PATH OF WINTER SUN

120° OF ARC FOR 35° LATITUDE

240° OF ARC FOR 30° LAT.

TREES PROVIDE
AFTERNOON SHADE
ON S. SIDE.

WARMEST OUTDOOR AREAS IN WINTER

LARGEST AMOUNT OF
GLASS ON S.& E. WALLS,
MOST EFFECTIVE FOR
SOLAR HEATING

WARMEST & SUNNIEST IN
WINTER

LIMIT OF WINTER SUN
PENETRATION

SUMMER
TERRACE

SCREEN

STREET

LEAST AMOUNT OF ROOF
OVERHANG NEEDED ON
NORTH EXCEPT WHERE
SHADE IS DESIRED AND IN
DESERT REGIONS WHERE
LIVING AREAS MAY FACE
NORTH

LARGEST AMOUNT OF
OVERHANG NECESSARY ON
WEST IF GLASS IS USED
ON THESE WALLS

3-4' OVERHANG NEEDED ON
E. TO SHADE WALLS BEFORE
NOON

E. & N., COOLEST OUTDOOR
AREA IN SUMMER

OPEN TRELLIS EXTENSION
COVERED WITH VINES TO
KEEP HOUSE & TERRACE
COOL IN SUMMER & LATE
FALL SUN OFF S. WALLS

SUMMER TERRACE

EARLY MORNING DIRECT
SUN MAY BE DESIRED
EVEN IN SUMMER

SUNRISE

SUNRISE

N

PLAN

BREEZES AND VENTILATION

Buildings, especially in the warmer climates, should be oriented towards the prevailing breezes, in addition to the sun orientation. However, this may not always be possible. Generally, orientation of the building in relation to sunlight is considered more important than orientation relating to the prevailing breezes. When it is possible to take advantage of prevailing breezes, the long side of the building should be faced towards the breeze. Recent developments in the widespread use of air conditioning and the awareness of air pollution have de-emphasized the use of natural breezes for ventilation.

Building Ventilation

Building location with respect to prevailing breezes is an important planning factor, especially in warmer climates and during the hot seasons of the year. E-7-1, A, B, and C are plan views

indicating the percentage of ventilation for different building arrangements, assuming they are placed perpendicular to the prevailing wind. D, E, and F show the cross section of buildings and the effect the placement to each other has on the prevailing wind.

Dwelling Unit Ventilation

E-7-2 shows how the dwelling unit layout affects ventilation. A and B are plan views of typical corner rooms. C and D are sections and indicate the result of window heights on ventilation. Plan E illustrates through-ventilation, which is the best; corner ventilation in Plan F is also good. Plans G and H indicate poor or no ventilation.

E-7-1

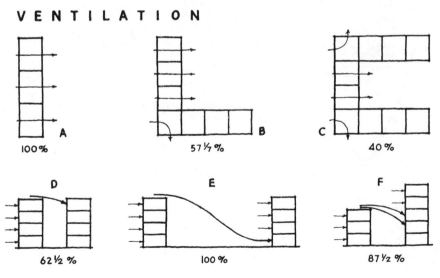

E-7-2

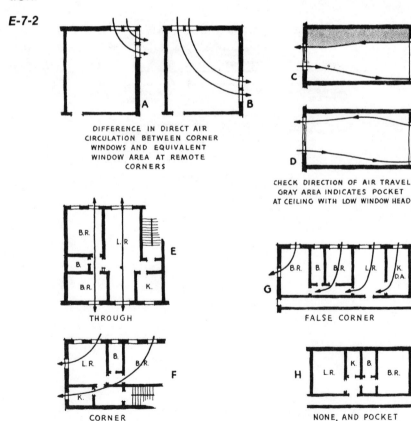

VIEWS AND VISTAS

When the situation presents itself, maximum advantage should be taken of any possible views. Natural vistas, such as rivers, mountains, parks and lakes, are the most desirable. However, many man-made views are equally interesting, such as bridges, golf courses, recreational areas. Care should be exercised in the placement of buildings to each other so that the view is not blocked by another building. Buildings should be staggered to provide maximum exposure for the most buildings.

VIEW PROTECTION

0-2% GRADE: NO VIEW EXCEPT NEIGHBORS, STREET; VARIED SETBACKS, ANGLED HOUSES AND VARIED LOT WIDTHS MIGHT DECREASE MONOTONY OF AREA

2-10% GRADE: SAME VIEW IF ALL HOMES ARE KEPT SINGLE STORY, LOW ROOF LINES; FENCING IS MODERATE; CONSIDERATION IS GIVEN TO WAIVING SETBACKS IF SUPERIOR VIEW IS GAINED.

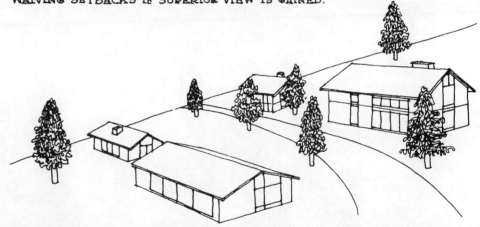

10-20% GRADE: EXCELLENT VIEW SITUATION, BUT ROADS SHOULD FOLLOW CONTOURS; VARIED SET-BACKS, 2-STORY HOMES ON HIGH SIDE PERMITTED IF LOTS ARE ADEQUATE TO INSURE MAJORITY GOOD VIEWS

BUILDING ORIENTATION

The following is a list of orientations and their resulting effects.

South Orientation

Sunlight will occur from late morning to early afternoon. During the summer months the sun will appear high in the sky and during the winter months the sun will appear low in the sky.

South orientation is the best to obtain the maximum sunlight during the day.

The hot summer sun can easily be controlled by properly designed overhangs. The low angle of the sun during the winter months will enable the rays to penetrate deep into the room.

East Orientation

Sunlight will occur only in the morning hours. During the summer months, when the sun rises in the east, the early morning hours will have sunlight. The sun will be very low in the sky and the sun will generally not be too intense. During the winter months, the sun will rise more towards the southeast, thus providing a shorter period of sunlight.

Southeast Orientation

Sunlight will occur from early morning to late morning, or possibly to noon. At midmorning the sun will be reasonably high in the sky and provide a moderately intense sunlight.

Southwest Orientation

Sunlight will occur from early afternoon to late afternoon. The sun will be reasonably high in the sky. The rays of the sun will be much more intense than the morning sun. In some areas during the winter months the sun will set in the southwest.

West Orientation

Sunlight will be present from midafternoon to late afternoon. During the summer months, the west sun will be very intense. It will set generally in the west or northwest. During the winter months, the sun will generally set in the southwest.

North Orientation

No sunlight will be obtained from a direct north orientation.

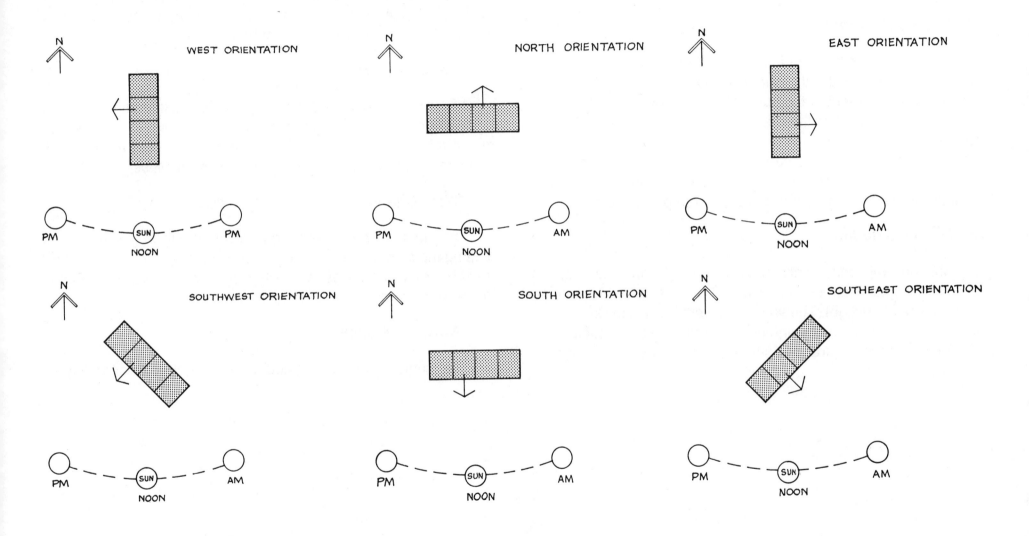

WEST ORIENTATION

NORTH ORIENTATION

EAST ORIENTATION

SOUTHWEST ORIENTATION

SOUTH ORIENTATION

SOUTHEAST ORIENTATION

ROOM ORIENTATION

Individual room orientation to the sun is, to a degree, a personal choice. However, there are generally accepted orientations for different rooms within the dwelling unit. Most frequently, it is very difficult to achieve the ideal orientation for each room and some compromises must be made. It is beneficial to obtain some sunlight in the dwelling during the day. A dwelling that is facing directly north and receiving no sunlight tends to be a cool or dreary dwelling. The accompanying chart and the following discussion for the orientation of each individual room should be used as a guide rather than a rule.

Bedrooms

Sunlight streaming into the bedroom upon waking up in the morning is a pleasant feeling. This is achieved by an easterly or southeasterly exposure. West exposure should be avoided because the west sun during the summer months is strong and heats up the room during the late afternoon and early evening.

Living Room

The living room should have a southerly exposure. In hot climates, a properly designed overhang will prevent direct sunlight from entering the room. In wintertime the low angle of the sun will allow sunlight to penetrate the depth of the room.

Dining Area

An easternly exposure will allow sunlight to enter during the morning for breakfast meals. If, however, it is desirable to view a sunset or have sunlight during the evening meal, a westernly or southwesternly exposure should be used. Since lunch is a minimal meal, this usually is not a major consideration.

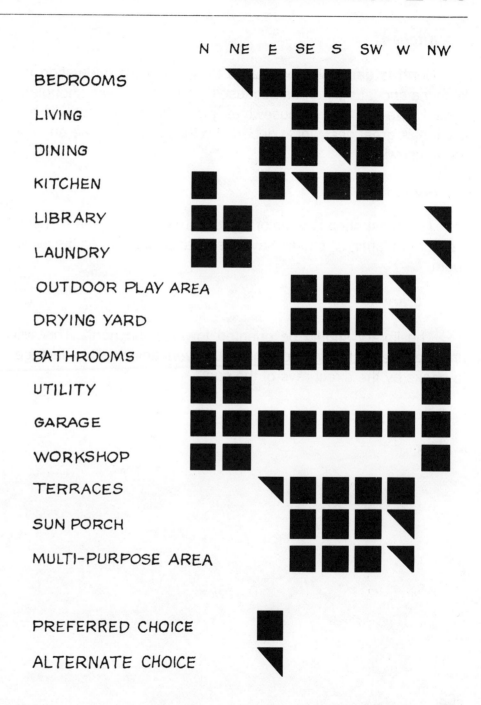

Kitchen

North is generally considered to be the best orientation for kitchens and laundry areas because it provides an even, nonglare light. However, many housewives prefer some sunlight in the kitchen. A great deal would depend on the personal preference of the housewife.

Multipurpose Area

This most often is a major activity area involving many members of the family. It should have a similar orientation as the living room.

Library

The library should be oriented towards the north. This will provide an even light source and will prevent any possible damage to books by the direct rays of the sun.

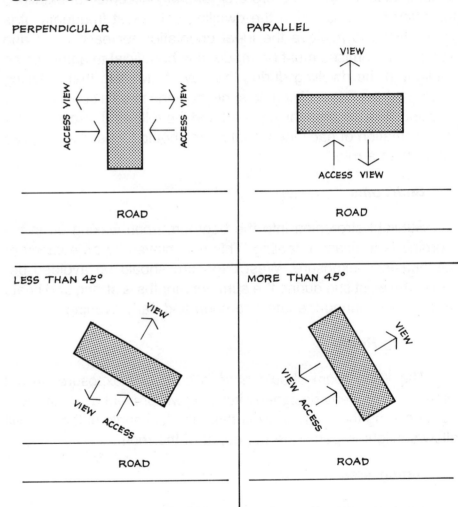

BUILDING ORIENTATION TO STREET

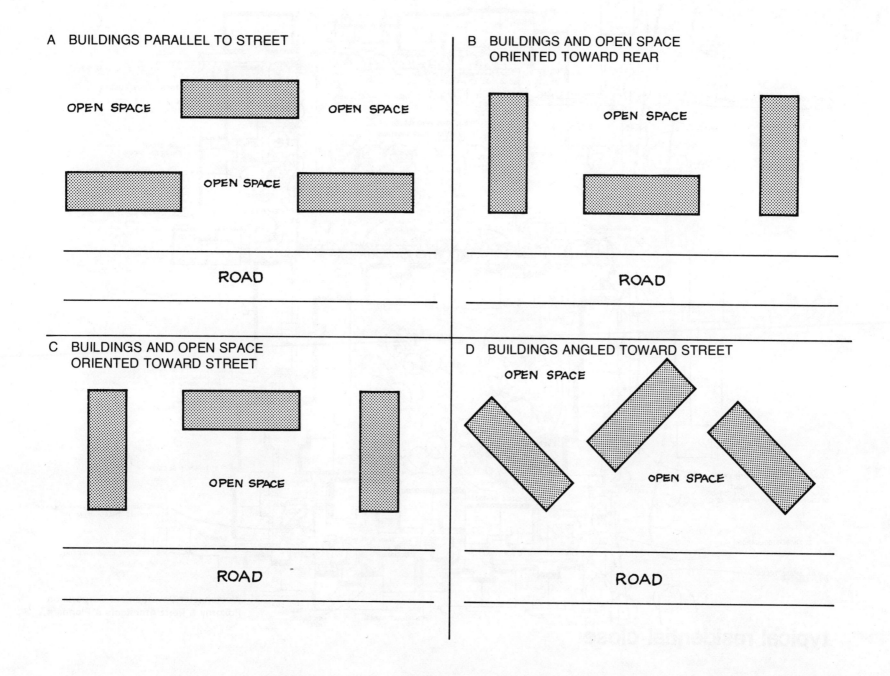

A   BUILDINGS PARALLEL TO STREET

OPEN SPACE   OPEN SPACE

OPEN SPACE

ROAD

B   BUILDINGS AND OPEN SPACE
ORIENTED TOWARD REAR

OPEN SPACE

ROAD

C   BUILDINGS AND OPEN SPACE
ORIENTED TOWARD STREET

OPEN SPACE

ROAD

D   BUILDINGS ANGLED TOWARD STREET

OPEN SPACE

OPEN SPACE

ROAD

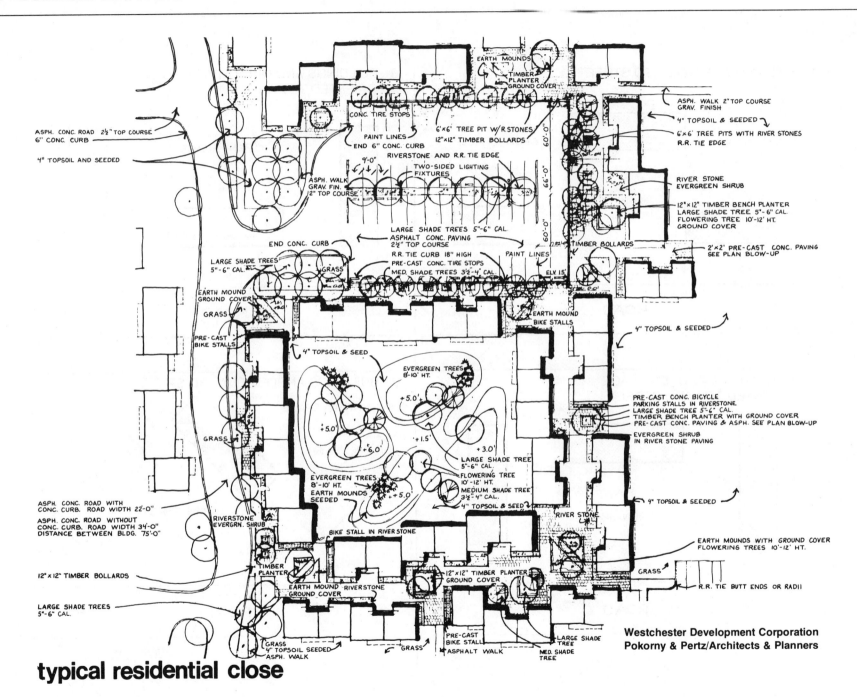

ASPH. CONC. ROAD 2½" TOP COURSE
6" CONC. CURB

4" TOPSOIL AND SEEDED

ASPH. WALK
GRAV. FIN.
2" TOP COURSE

END CONC. CURB

LARGE SHADE TREES
5"-6" CAL.

EARTH MOUND
GROUND COVER

GRASS

PRE-CAST
BIKE STALLS

GRASS

ASPH. CONC. ROAD WITH
CONC. CURB. ROAD WIDTH 22'-0"

ASPH. CONC. ROAD WITHOUT
CONC. CURB. ROAD WIDTH 34'-0"
DISTANCE BETWEEN BLDG. 75'-0"

12"x12" TIMBER BOLLARDS

LARGE SHADE TREES
5"-6" CAL.

EARTH MOUNDS

TIMBER
PLANTER
GROUND COVER

CONC. TIRE STOPS

PAINT LINES
END 6" CONC. CURB

6'x6' TREE PIT w/R.STONES
12"x12" TIMBER BOLLARDS

RIVERSTONE AND R.R. TIE EDGE

9'-0"

TWO-SIDED LIGHTING
FIXTURES

LARGE SHADE TREES 5"-6" CAL.
ASPHALT CONC. PAVING
2½" TOP COURSE
R.R. TIE CURB 18" HIGH
PRE-CAST CONC. TIRE STOPS
MED. SHADE TREES 3½"-4" CAL.

PAINT LINES

ELV. 15'

ASPH. WALK 2"TOP COURSE
GRAV. FINISH

4" TOPSOIL & SEEDED

6'x6' TREE PITS WITH RIVER STONES
R.R. TIE EDGE

RIVER STONE
EVERGREEN SHRUB

12"x12" TIMBER BENCH PLANTER
LARGE SHADE TREE 5"-6" CAL.
FLOWERING TREE 10'-12' HT.
GROUND COVER

TIMBER BOLLARDS

2'x2' PRE-CAST CONC. PAVING
SEE PLAN BLOW-UP

EARTH MOUND
BIKE STALLS

4" TOPSOIL & SEEDED

4" TOPSOIL & SEED

EVERGREEN TREES
8-10' HT.

+5.0'

+5.0'

+6.0'

+1.5'

+3.0'

EVERGREEN TREES
8-10' HT.
EARTH MOUNDS
SEEDED

LARGE SHADE TREE
5"-6" CAL.
FLOWERING TREE
10'-12' HT.
MEDIUM SHADE TREE
3½"-4" CAL.

+5.0'

4" TOPSOIL & SEED

RIVER STONE

PRE-CAST CONC. BICYCLE
PARKING STALLS IN RIVERSTONE
LARGE SHADE TREE 5"-6" CAL.
TIMBER BENCH PLANTER WITH GROUND COVER
PRE-CAST CONC. PAVING & ASPH. SEE PLAN BLOW-UP

EVERGREEN SHRUB
IN RIVER STONE PAVING

4" TOPSOIL & SEEDED

RIVERSTONE
EVERGRN. SHRUB

BIKE STALL IN RIVERSTONE

TIMBER
PLANTER

EARTH MOUND RIVERSTONE
GROUND COVER

PRE-CAST
BIKE STALL

GRASS
4" TOPSOIL SEEDED
ASPH. WALK

12"x12" TIMBER PLANTER
GROUND COVER

ASPHALT WALK

LARGE SHADE
TREE

MED. SHADE
TREE

EARTH MOUNDS WITH GROUND COVER
FLOWERING TREES 10'-12' HT.

GRASS

R.R. TIE BUTT ENDS OR RADII

**Westchester Development Corporation
Pokorny & Pertz/Architects & Planners**

GRASS

PRE-CAST
BIKE STALL

LARGE SHADE TREES
5"-6" CAL.

typical residential close

CIRCULATION—GENERAL

On housing sites it is important to plan for easy and direct movement of pedestrians and vehicles. Convenience of circulation and safety must be considered and planned together. Pedestrians generally prefer to walk in direct, straight lines. When they must use indirect or awkwardly placed walkways, they may take unauthorized routes, often trampling grass, shrubs, and other plants. Paths should follow topography and natural lines of movement, widening as traffic increases and narrowing in less-used areas. The pedestrian circulation system should also be designed to distinguish between the front and rear entrances of buildings. The quality of a multifamily dwelling appears to decrease when one entrance has to accommodate the removal of garbage and the entrance of guests, for instance. In part, this is a matter of interior space planning, but it is also a concern of site design.

Some pedestrian traffic considerations also apply to vehicular traffic: automobiles, scooters, service trucks and in some cases, bicycles. It is necessary that minor roads come close to buildings to facilitate delivery of goods, to give protection in inclement weather, and to provide access for emergency vehicles.

Vehicles should be able to approach residential buildings, but need not remain there and conflict with pedestrian movement. The ideal solution seems to be the vertical separation of pedestrians and vehicles. However, this type of separation is generally limited to central city locations where heavy traffic volume justifies the great expense. At outlying locations horizontal separation is much more common. Many of the site plans included in this book show the separation of pedestrians and vehicles and most frequently accomplish it by restricting automobiles to the periphery of a site and by allowing free pedestrian movement in the center.

CIRCULATION—VEHICULAR

A housing site should be provided with a periphery road system sufficiently wide to allow the maximum number of vehicles to move freely at all times. This road system should accommodate all through traffic that is bypassing the site and all traffic generated by the housing development.

In addition, adequate vehicular access into and out of the site is required. Such access will include delivery, service, and emergency vehicles. Access roads should be of sufficient width for all types of vehicles and also be provided with proper turning space. The following are based on FHA standards for vehicular access:

a) *Access and circulation for fire-fighting equipment, furniture moving vans, fuel trucks, garbage collection, deliveries and snow removal must be planned for efficient operation and in accordance with local custom.*

b) *Each property must be provided with vehicular access by an abutting public or private street.*

c) *Streets must be provided on the site where necessary to furnish principal trafficways for convenient access to the living units and other important facilities on the property.*

d) *The width and construction of the required street and provisions for its continued maintenance must provide safe and suitable vehicular access to and from the property at all times. Dead-end streets include adequate vehicular turning space.*

e) *The street pattern should discourage unnecessary through traffic.*

f) *The street system must connect with adjoining plotted streets except where topography does not permit or where such street connections would adversely affect the property.*

g) *The street system must provide convenient circulation by means of minor streets and properly located collector and arterial streets.*

265

h) Cul-de-sacs must be provided with adequate paved turning space, usually a turning circle of at least 80 feet in diameter (100 feet is preferable).

i) Street rights-of-way must be of adequate width to accommodate the contemplated parking and traffic load in accordance with the type of street.

j) Proper street alignment and gradients are necessary. Streets must be adapted to the topography, preserving to the extent possible the natural contour and site features. They must have a suitable alignment and gradients for safety of traffic, satisfactory surface and ground water drainage and proper functioning of sanitary and storm sewer systems.

k) Recognition of existing facilities is required. The street system must be designed to recognize existing easements, utility lines, etc., which are to be preserved, and must be designed to permit connection to existing facilities where necessary for the proper functioning of the drainage and utility systems.

l) Well-designed street intersections are essential. Street intersections must generally be at right angles. Intersections of more than two streets and offsets at junctions of less than 125 feet shall be avoided.

m) Driveways must be provided on the site where necessary for convenient access to the living units, garage compounds, parking areas, service entrances of buildings, collection of refuse and all other necessary services.

n) Driveways must be planned for convenient circulation suitable for traffic needs and safety. Cul-de-sacs must be provided with adequate paved vehicular turning space, usually a turning circle of at least 80 feet in diameter, except for short, straight-service driveways with light traffic.

STREET PARKING

Shown in the drawings are the minimum dimensions for three types of onstreet parking and two types of bay parking. Parallel, 45°, and 60° parking at curb are the most usual methods. Since it is a natural tendency for tenants to park in front of their homes, it is wise to provide for it. The dimensions indicated are for streets in average community developments. Only parallel parking is permitted on main (collector) streets. Diagonal parking is permitted on minor streets. Where traffic is heavy, streets should be increased in width. Sidewalks that are adjacent to the curb must be widened to allow for overhang of bumpers.

Parking bays, both directly off the street and within property lines, offer a solution where parking is not permitted on a public way. Parking bays directly off the street are not only more convenient for the tenants, but are less expensive to construct and more economical to maintain. These should be used, however, only on minor streets. The illustrations are for streets with two-way traffic.

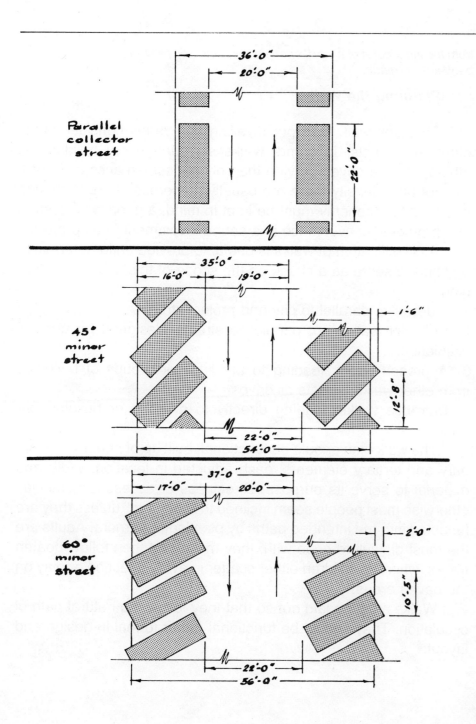

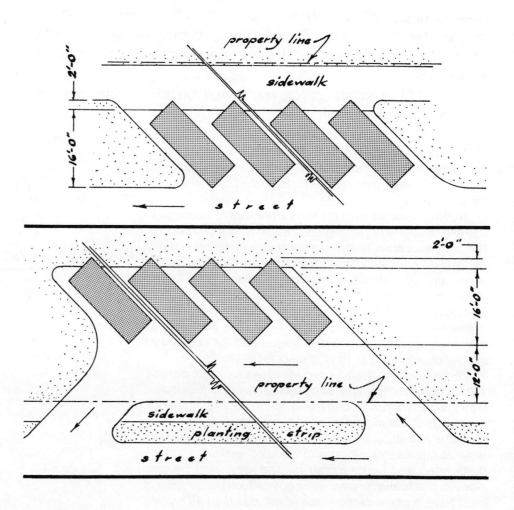

SOURCE: *Minimum Property Standards for One- and Two-Family Houses, FHA., Dept. of Housing and Urban Development, Washington D.C.*

CIRCULATION—PEDESTRIAN

A safe and convenient system of pedestrian walks is essential. It should be functionally organized and follow the natural traffic patterns of pedestrians. Walks should be wide enough to accommodate two-way traffic. Paved areas, especially at main entrances, must be of sufficient area to accommodate anticipated activities.

The following standards are based on FHA standards for pedestrian circulation:

a) Access to the dwellings and circulation between buildings and other important project facilities for vehicular and pedestrian traffic must be comfortable and convenient for the occupants.

b) Walking distance from the main entrances of buildings to a street, driveway or parking court must usually be less than 100 feet; exception to this standard should be reasonably justified by compensating advantages, such as desirable views and site preservation through adaption to topography. In no case must the distance exceed 250 feet.

c) Street sidewalks and on-site walks must be provided for convenient and safe access to all living units from streets, driveways, parking courts or garages and for convenient circulation and access to all project facilities.

d) Width, alignment and gradient of walks must provide safety, convenience and appearance suitable for pedestrian traffic, shopping carts and for moving of furniture. Small jogs in the alignment shall be avoided.

e) Steps and stepped ramps must be avoided if possible in order to facilitate servicing with wheeled vehicles.

f) An open and unobstructed passageway must be provided at grade level of each inner court. Such passageways must have a cross section area of not less than 40 square feet and sufficient headroom to permit the passage of non-vehicular fire-fighting equipment, and must be continuous from the inner court of a yard, or an unobstructed open area between buildings.

Planning the Walks

The total walk area per dwelling unit varies considerably in different projects. In some, walks surround every building; in others, service drives provide the only pedestrian access. In projects of high density there are usually numerous walks. Although the need for economy must be kept in mind, a good walk system that promotes convenience is a sound investment in all projects.

A classification of walks is useful to provide uniform terminology and to serve as a check on the scope of this feature of planning:

1. Sidewalks: parallel to city and project streets.
2. Collector walks: not parallel to streets; designed for general circulation.
3. Approach walks: leading to buildings or groups of buildings from other walks, streets or drives.
4. Entrance walks: leading directly to dwelling or building entrances.

The walk plan should be functional, built up of primary, secondary and tertiary elements, each adjusted in location, width and material to serve its purpose. Directness of access is essential, otherwise most people seem inclined to "shortcut," unless they are funneled into the intended paths by planting or barriers. Adults are the most difficult to cope with; they make and then follow beaten tracks, whereas children either scatter in every direction or play on the paved areas.

Walks must be laid out so that they follow the natural path of circulation. They should be functional rather formal in design and layout.

Streets and Highways–Types

Type of Facility	Function and Design Features	Spacing	Widths		Desirable Maximum Grades	Speed	Other Features
			R.O.W.	Pavement			
Freeways	Provide regional and metropolitan continuity and unity. Limited access: no grade crossing; no traffic stops.	Variable; related to regional pattern of population and industrial centers	200-300'	Varies; 12' per lane; 8-10' shoulders both sides of each roadway; 8'-60' median strip.	3%	60 mph	Depressed, at grade, or elevated. Preferably depressed though urban areas. Require intensive landscaping, service roads, or adequate rear lot building setback lines (75') where service roads are not provided.
Expressways	Provide metropolitan and city continuity and unity. Limited access; some channelized grade crossings and signals at major intersections. Parking prohibited.	Variable; generally radial or circumferential	200-250'	Varies; 12' per lane; 8-10' shoulders; 8-30' median strip.	4%	50 mph	Generally at grade. Requires landscaping and service roads or adequate rear lot building setback lines (75') where service roads are not provided.
Major Roads (Major Arterials)	Provide unity throughout contiguous urban area. Usually form boundaries for neighborhoods. Minor access control; channelized intersection; parking generally prohibited.	1½ to 2 miles	120-150'	84' maximum for 4 lanes, parking and median strip.	4%	35-45 mph	Require 5' wide detached sidewalks in urban areas, planting strips (5'-10' wide or more) and adequate building setback lines (30') for buildings fronting on street; 60' for buildings backing on street.
Secondary Roads (Minor Arterials)	Main feeder streets. Signals where needed; stop signs on side streets. Occasionally form boundaries for neighborhoods.	¾ to 1 mile	80'	60'	5%	35-40 mph	Require 5' wide detached sidewalks, planting strips between sidewalks and curb 5' to 10' or more, and adequate building setback lines (30').
Collector Streets	Main interior streets. Stop signs on side streets.	¼ to ½ mile	64'	44' (2-12' traffic lanes; 2-10' parking lanes)	5%	30 mph	Require at least 4' wide detached sidewalks; vertical curbs; planting strips are desirable; building setback lines 30' from right of way.
Local Streets	Local service streets. Nonconducive to through traffic.	at blocks	50'	36' where street parking is permitted	6%	25 mph	Sidewalks at least 4' in width for densities greater than 1 d.u./acre, and curbs and gutters.
Cul-de-sac	Street open at only one end, with provision for a practical turnaround at the other.	only wherever practical	50' (90' dia. turnaround)	30'-36' (75' turnaround)	5%		Should not have a length greater than 500 feet.

STREET STANDARDS

One set of design standards that can be used as a basis for a comprehensive street plan is that developed by the National Committee for Traffic Safety in 1961. These standards have been extensively used and accepted. Over the years, these standards have resulted in acceptable and functional street systems for both vehicle movement and pedestrian safety. It must be understood that these standards are minimum and should be utilized only as a guide to meet existing conditions.

Similar standards are available from the Institute of Traffic Engineers.

Recommendations of
The National Committee for Traffic Safety

(The following table is based on a maximum speed of 25 mph, determined by the Uniform Vehicle Code. Recommendations will be reasonably satisfactory even if some speeds moderately exceed 25 mph.)

Design of Residential Streets

	SINGLE-FAMILY	MULTIFAMILY
Street Width	50 feet	60 feet
Pavement Width	26 feet	32 feet
Curbs	Straight curb recommended.	Same
Sidewalks:		
Width	4 feet minimum	Same
Setback	3 feet minimum if no trees; 7 feet minimum with trees.	
Horizontal Alignment	200 feet minimum sight distance.	Same
Vertical Alignment	6-8 percent maximum grade desirable; 3-4 percent per 100 feet maximum rate of change	Same
Cul-de-sac	400-500 feet maximum length	Same
Turnarounds	40 feet minimum curb radius without parking.	Same
	50 feet minimum curb radius with parking.	Same
Pavement Surface	Nonskid with strength to carry traffic load.	Same

Design of Feeder or Collector Streets

Street Width	60 feet	Horizontal Alignment	90-degree intersections preferred; less than 60 degrees unduly hazardous
Pavement Width	36 feet		12 feet curb radius for local and feeder streets.
Curbs	Straight curb recommended		50 feet curb radius for feeder street intersecting main highway
Sidewalks:			
Width	4 feet minimum		
Setback	3 feet minimum if no trees 7 feet minimum with trees	Design of Sidewalks:	
Horizontal Alignment	Same as for local residential streets	Placement	Setback should be minimum of 7 feet where trees are planted between curb and sidewalk; minimum of 3 feet if no trees.
Vertical Alignment	Same as for local residential streets		
Pavement Surface	Same as for local residential streets	Width	4 feet minimum (4-1/2—5 feet minimum near shopping centers).
Design of Intersections:			
Sight Distance	Such that each vehicle is visible to the other driver when each is 75 feet from the intersection for 25 mph maximum speed. No building or other sight obstruction within sight triangle		
Vertical Alignment	Flat grade within intersection Flat section preferred from 50 feet to 100 feet each way from intersection, but in no case over 3-5 percent grade; 6 percent maximum between 100 and 150 feet of intersection		

STREET CLASSIFICATION

The overall street system for a housing development must conform to the circulation requirements of the master plan for the community. This will provide maximum accessibility to all parts of the community and insure proper coordination with proposed circulation changes.

Direct access to a major arterial highway is essential. Such intersections must be adequately controlled with lights or other means. The practical minimum distance between intersections on the major arterial highway should be 800 to 1,000 feet. No through streets should be provided. All circulation should be around the periphery of the development to the major arterial highway.

Each lane of traffic will carry from 600 to 800 cars per hour. Horizontal alignment of all collector, minor, loop, and access streets should provide for a minimum of 200 feet clear sight distance. The vertical alignment should not exceed 6-8% grade differential. Sidewalks, when used, should be a minimum of 4 feet wide. When trees are planted between the curb and sidewalk, the sidewalk should be set back approximately 8 feet. If no trees are used, the setback should be 4 feet.

TYPES OF STREETS

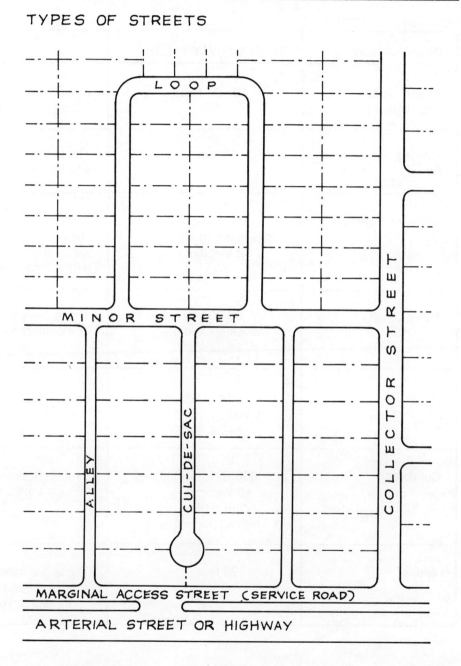

DESIGNATION	RIGHT-OF-WAY WIDTH	FUNCTION
Arterial Streets and Highways	80-120 feet	Primarily devoted to the movement of high volumes of traffic at relatively high speed; only rarely interrelated with adjacent land areas; vehicular access is almost always limited.
Marginal Access Streets	40 feet	These are minor streets that are parallel to and adjacent to arterial streets and highways; and which provide access to abutting properties and protection from through traffic.
Collector Streets	60-80 feet pavement width— 32 feet min.	These carry traffic from minor streets to the major system of arterial streets and highways, including the principal entrance streets of a residential development and streets for circulation within such a development. They permit access to adjacent land areas, but generally do not permit long-distance through traffic.
Minor Streets	50-60 feet pavement width— 24-32 feet	These carry traffic from collector streets to the individual land parcels within any given area. The primary function of these streets is to provide access to abutting properties.
Loop	50-60 feet pavement width— 24-32 feet	Same as minor street.
Cul-de-sac	800 feet max. 40 feet min. curb radius without parking	Dead-end street with proper turning radius at end. Provides quiet residential street with no through traffic. Also helps solve difficult site problems with restricted access.
Alleys	20 feet	These are minor ways that are used primarily for vehicular service access to the back or the side of properties otherwise abutting a street. May be necessary in group, row houses, or apartment developments. Not recommended in single-family developments.

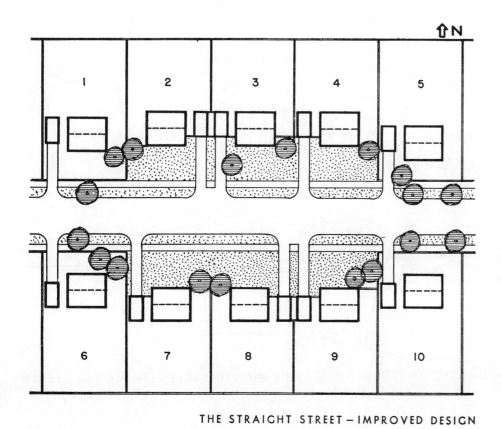

⇧N

THE STRAIGHT STREET — IMPROVED DESIGN

⇧N

THE "T" JUNCTION
IMPROVED DESIGN

V. Joseph Kostka
Planning Residential Subdivisions
Appraisal Institute of Canada

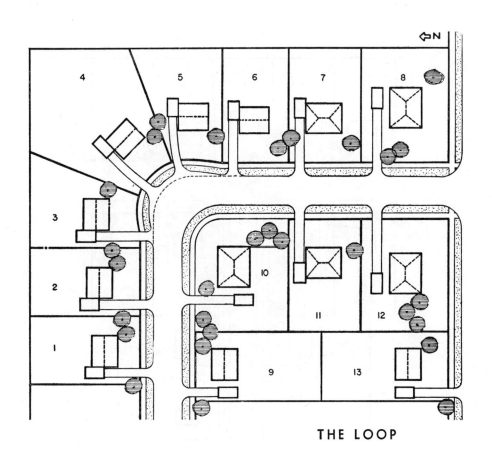

THE LOOP

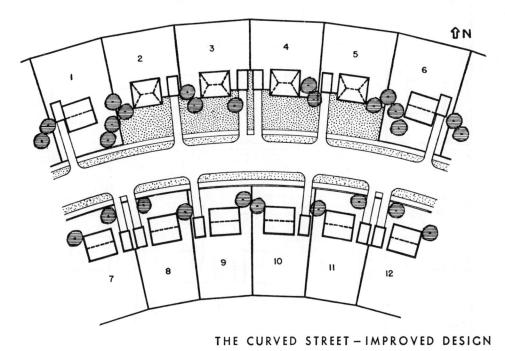

THE CURVED STREET — IMPROVED DESIGN

V. Joseph Kostka
Planning Residential Subdivisions
Appraisal Institute of Canada

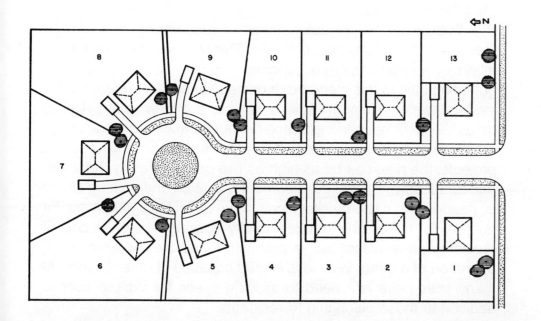

CUL-DE-SAC

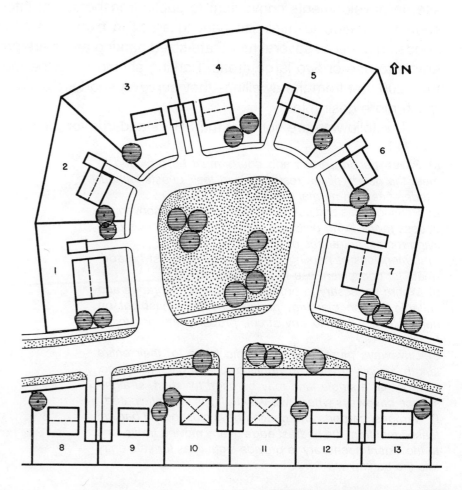

A GROUP AROUND A GREEN

V. Joseph Kostka
Planning Residential Subdivisions
Appraisal Institute of Canada

PARKING—GENERAL

Sufficient off-street parking should be provided for the housing site. In developments convenient to public transportation, efforts should be made to minimize parking areas in excess of actual needs. In general, several moderate-sized parking areas are preferable to one or two large areas. Parking should never be more than 200 feet from the dwellings they serve. A shorter distance is much more desirable.

The following are some of the FHA standards for parking:

a) Paved parking areas and courts must be provided to meet the needs of the residents and their guests without interference with normal traffic.
b) Parking areas and courts must be located for convenient access to the living units without impairing the views from living rooms, entrances or front yards.
c) Dimensions of parking areas and courts must be adequate for convenient use for occupant parking.
d) Where necessary to provide for bumper clearance and suitable screen planting, parking facilities must not be nearer than 5 feet to any street, property line or project facility.
e) Driveways must have two traffic lanes for their entire length, usually 18 feet in addition to any parking space, except that a single lane may be used for short, straight-service driveways where two-way traffic is not anticipated.
f) Garages, carports and parking bays must be set back at least 8 feet from the nearest edge of any moving traffic lane to the extent necessary to provide sight lines for safe entry into the trafficway.

AUTOMOBILE STORAGE

The tremendous increase in automobile ownership has had a profound influence on the design and location of residential districts. The problem confronting site planners is to create a balance between the allocation of space for automobile storage and for other outdoor uses. This problem is made more acute by the pressure to satisfy occupants' demands for parking as close as possible to their dwellings.

The ownership of automobiles is reaching or has already reached a ratio of one car per family. This ratio seems to prevail for all projects regardless of occupants' incomes, but many sites are not being built to this standard. If ownership of cars increases, the inadequacy of accommodations will be felt even more. Unlike other site facilities, parking space cannot be added in stages without destroying some aspect of quality. In high-income housing projects, the ratio can be as high as two cars per family. It follows that for all new housing developments, at least one parking space is needed for each dwelling unit. The exceptions might be for housing for the elderly and central-city housing where the cost of providing parking facilities is prohibitive and the ownership and operation of a motor vehicle is limited because of other factors. At many sites there is a need to allocate space for visitors' cars in addition to those belonging to residents.

If parking needs are not met on-site, crowding of adjacent streets is likely to result. However, if parking needs are met on-site, the residential buildings sometimes look as though they are built on huge parking lots. The automobile then dominates the site and infringes on privacy. The net effect is a reduction, if not the disappearance, of site quality.

The most satisfactory solution is to store cars in areas hidden from view, preferably underground. In this way, automobiles would be convenient to dwellings, greater pedestrian safety would be ensured and open space would be preserved for other uses. However, underground parking is prohibitive in cost for most developments. The next best solution is the construction of parking structures, preferably low ones whose roofs can be used for playgrounds, laundry areas, sundecks, etc. Some recent multiple housing projects have been designed with parking on lower floors and apartments on upper floors of the same structures. Solutions involving complete separation of pedestrians and automobiles, though costly, may become mandatory for central-city, high-density housing. In outlying areas and sites of lower intensity development, it is possible to satisfy parking demands without vertical separation if careful site planning is followed. Usually, parking space is provided by a number of small lots, screened from active pedestrian parts of the site. A number of small lots are aesthetically preferable to one huge paved area and, in addition, generally permit the majority of cars to be stored reasonably close to the individual living units.

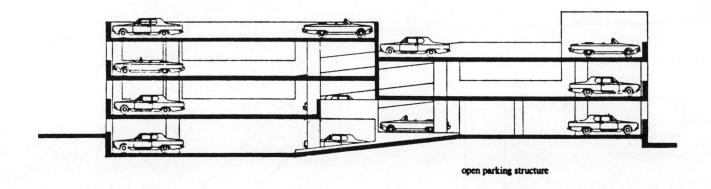

open parking structure

Building Arrangement with Parking

A

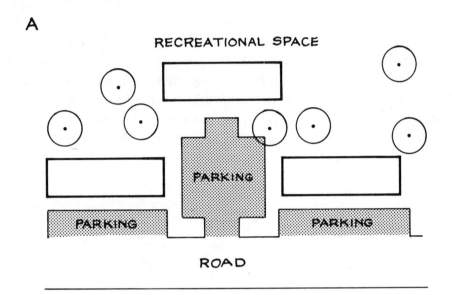

B

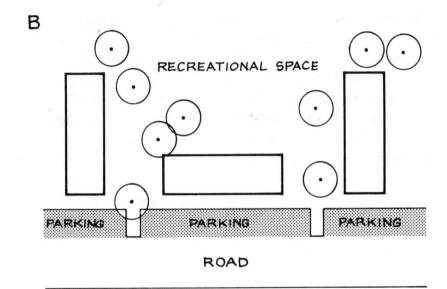

C

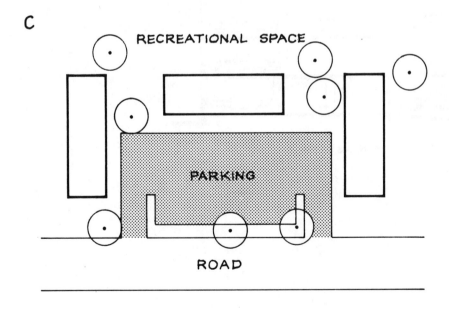

D

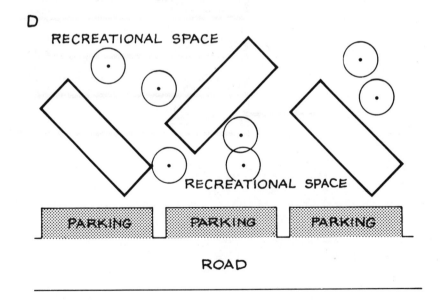

E

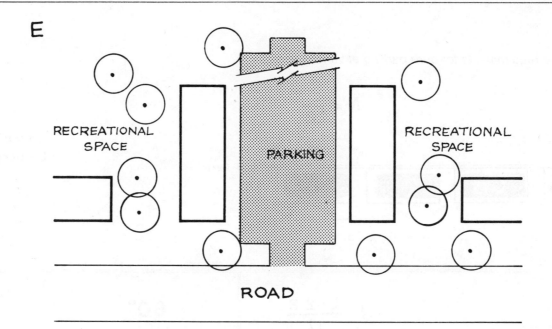

RECREATIONAL SPACE

PARKING

RECREATIONAL SPACE

ROAD

F

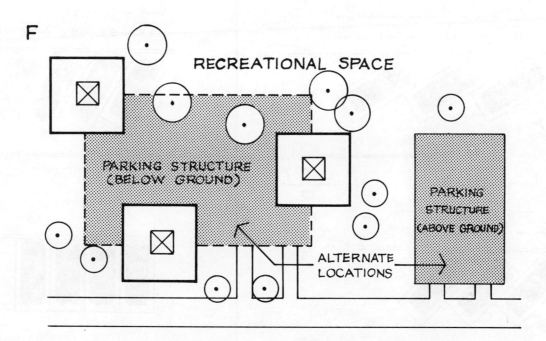

RECREATIONAL SPACE

PARKING STRUCTURE (BELOW GROUND)

PARKING STRUCTURE (ABOVE GROUND)

ALTERNATE LOCATIONS

Curb Parking–Space requirements for curb parking at various angles

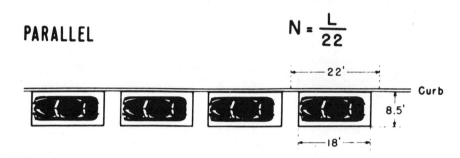

PARALLEL

$$N = \frac{L}{22}$$

N = Number of spaces
L = Curb length

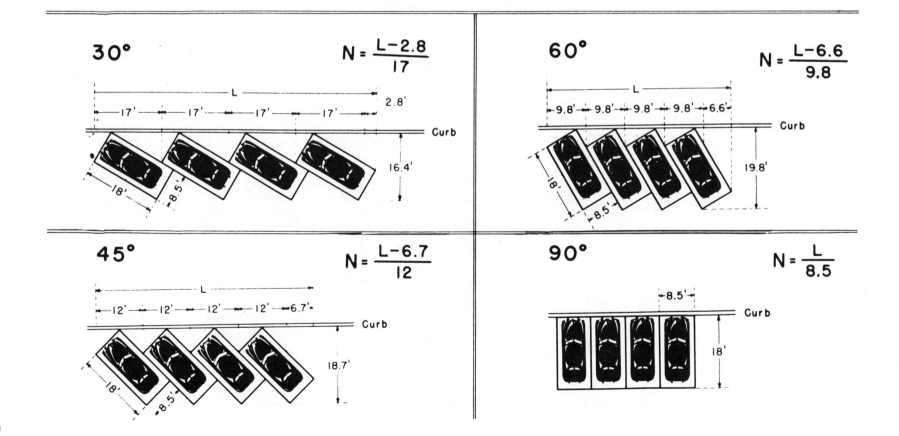

30°

$$N = \frac{L-2.8}{17}$$

60°

$$N = \frac{L-6.6}{9.8}$$

45°

$$N = \frac{L-6.7}{12}$$

90°

$$N = \frac{L}{8.5}$$

Parking

BAY

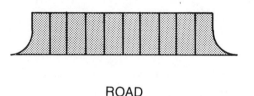

ROAD

The parking bay system is the most efficient and least expensive arrangement. It occupies a minimal area and may serve individual buildings or groups of buildings along minor residential streets. However, vehicles backing out into traffic may create hazardous conditions.

BUFFER

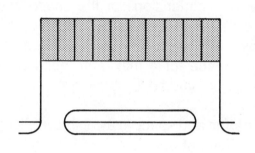

ROAD

The buffer system is similar to the parking bay, except that this arrangement separates parking maneuvering from roadway traffic. It occupies more area than the parking bay and may also serve individual buildings or groups of buildings. It may be located on a fairly active street.

PERPENDICULAR COURT

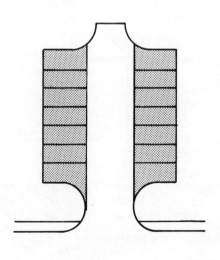

ROAD

While this is one of the safest and most attractive systems, its relatively great depth penetrates the site and may absorb area that might best be used in other ways. In some cases, buildings may be located around the parking court, thus integrating the parking space with surrounding spaces. It may be located on a fairly active street.

PARALLEL

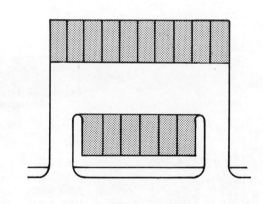

ROAD

Parallel parking is similar to the buffer system in all respects except that this design is more efficient in so far as it uses a double-loaded parking aisle. Like the parking court, it also penetrates the site fairly deeply, but may also be integrated with the open spaces around it. It may be located on a fairly active street.

PARKING—GARAGES

Using the basement of apartment buildings for parking purposes presents problems that must be weighed against each other to determine the most economical manner of providing space for the required number of cars. As is shown by the illustrations and table below, the type of parking and the number of cars that can be accommodated depend upon the dimensions of the space and location of columns in the area assigned to parking. To achieve the ideal arrangement may prove too costly and it may be more economical to use more floor space for a maximum number of cars. Each individual case must be studied to obtain the best net results.

Where local regulations permit and space is available, parking should be provided in or just off the street.

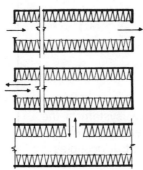

Open basement space with clear span and no columns is the most desirable but may be too costly to construct. The three diagrams illustrate three methods of circulation in open basements.

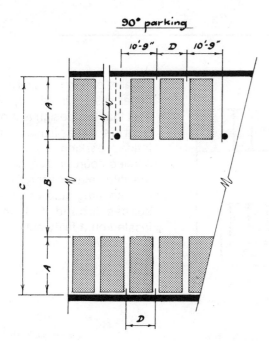

90° parking

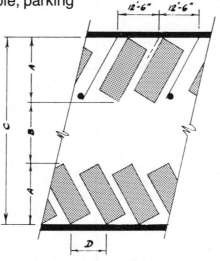

60° parking

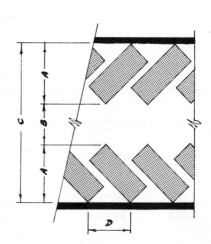

45° parking

Space	Tenant parking			Attendant parking		
	45°	60°	90°	45°	60°	90°
Stall depth perpendicular to aisle (A)	17'-6"	19'-0"	18'-0"	17'2"	18'-10"	18'0"
Aisle width .... (B)	12'-8"	18'-0"	29'-0"	12'-8"	17'-4"	22'-0"
Unit parking depth .... (C)	47'-8"	56'-0"	65'-0"	47'-0"	55'-0"	58'-0"
Stall width parallel to aisle .... (D)	12'-8"	10'-6"	9'-0"	11'-4"	9'-3"	8'-0"

Note: Where 45° and 60° parking is necessary, one way traffic should be planned.

SOURCE: *Minimum Property Requirements,* FHA, Dept. of Housing and Urban Development, Washington, D.C.

The deck of the parking garage linking the two towers provides a private plaza-garden for tenants. Natural materials such as plantings, wood, granite blocks, and a decorative pool placed in formal geometric patterns assert the man-made quality of this garden. This tightly controlled use of natural materials in counterpoint to the powerful architectural forms of the building articulates a personal statement in urban landscape.

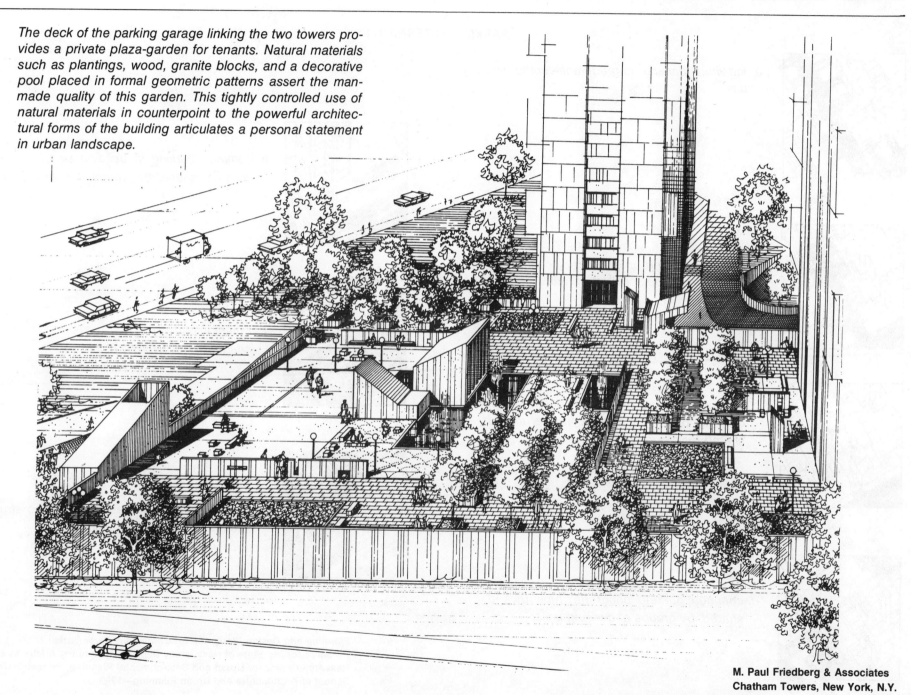

M. Paul Friedberg & Associates
Chatham Towers, New York, N.Y.

PARKING ALTERNATIVES

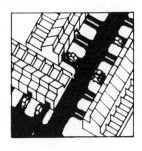

a. individual parking on grade adjacent to dwelling unit.

e. common parking in building structure below housing, shared by groups/all dwelling units.

b. common parking on grade, adjacent to and shared by groups of dwelling units.

f. common parking on grade, separate from and shared by all dwelling units.

c. common parking on grade, integrated with common open space, adjacent/near to and shared by groups of dwelling units.

g. common parking in separate building structure, shared by all dwelling units.

d. common parking on grade, near to and shared by groups of dwelling units.

Planning and Design Workbook for Community Participation
Prepared for the State of New Jersey Dept. of Community Affairs by the
Research Center for Urban and Environmental Planning, Princeton University
School of Architecture and Urban Planning—1969

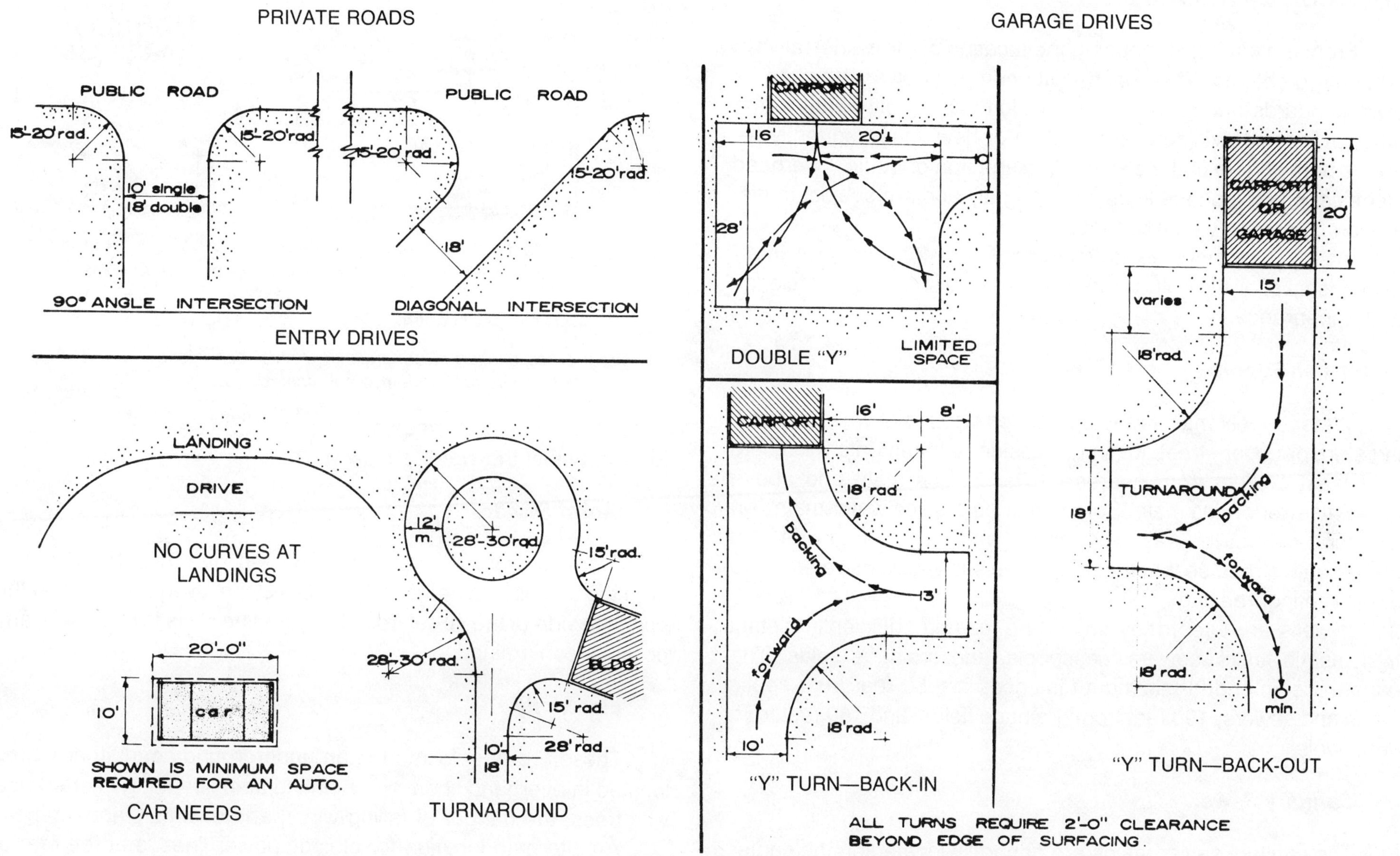

PRIVATE ROADS

GARAGE DRIVES

PUBLIC ROAD

PUBLIC ROAD

15'-20' rad.

15'-20' rad.

15'-20' rad.

15'-20' rad.

10' single
18' double

18'

90° ANGLE INTERSECTION

DIAGONAL INTERSECTION

ENTRY DRIVES

CARPORT

16'

20'

10'

28'

DOUBLE "Y"

LIMITED SPACE

LANDING

DRIVE

NO CURVES AT LANDINGS

12' m.

28'-30' rad.

15' rad.

28'-30' rad.

15' rad.

BLDG

10'
18'

28' rad.

20'-0"

10'

car

SHOWN IS MINIMUM SPACE
REQUIRED FOR AN AUTO.

CAR NEEDS

TURNAROUND

CARPORT

16'

8'

18' rad.

backing

forward

3'

10'

18' rad.

"Y" TURN—BACK-IN

CARPORT
OR
GARAGE

20'

varies

15'

18' rad.

18'

TURNAROUND

backing

forward

18' rad.

10' min.

"Y" TURN—BACK-OUT

ALL TURNS REQUIRE 2'-0" CLEARANCE
BEYOND EDGE OF SURFACING.

Landscape Development, Dept. of the Interior
Littleton, Colo.

285

LOCATION OF UTILITIES

From a planning standpoint, the location of utility lines always presents problems. First, each utility company or agency has its own standards and requirements, which very rarely relate to the other utilities. Servicing or installation of new lines frequently requires breaking up of the street and disruption of traffic. Overhead electrical and telephone lines are unsightly and are subject to disruption by severe weather conditions.

In any new housing development, the location and interrelationship of all utility lines must be carefully studied for efficiency and appearance.

Water Supply

Water supply mains may be located under sidewalk, in planting strip, or under street. Minimum design requirements will locate it at least 10 feet from nearest sewer or gas main and above highest sewer or gas main. Some engineers place water mains on the north side of the east-west street, and on the east side of a north-south street, so that the rays of the sun will be more effective in preventing freezing.

If wells are used, they should be located sufficiently distant from septic tanks, sewers, cesspools, and drainage fields. The usual recommended minimum distances are 50 feet from septic tanks and sewers, 100 feet from drainage fields, and 150 feet from cesspools.

Sanitary Sewer

The sanitary sewer mains are generally located on the center line of the road. The line is a clay tile pipe. If it were located in the planting strip the roots of the trees might cause breaks in the pipes. The center line location also locates the pipe equidistant from

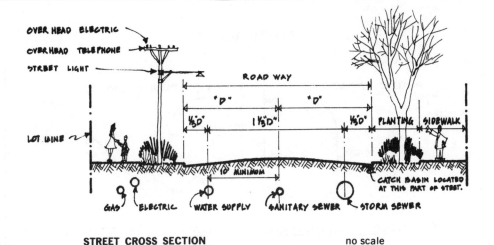

STREET CROSS SECTION   no scale

The street cross section is generalized. Actual conditions can have all or some of the elements indicated.

building lines on both sides of the street. The sewer line should be located below the water supply mains.

Storm Sewer

Storm sewers are generally located one-third the distance from the curb line to center line of street. It is always located on the opposite side of the street from the waterline. This is to prevent any possible contamination.

Electricity

These are best located in an underground conduit, are often located in overhead lines over planting strips causing interference with trees, the danger of falling wires, and unsightly appearance.

An alternate location for electric power lines is at the rear of the lots, either above or below ground, and then service lines are brought into the house. When this is done, proper easements are necessary for servicing of the lines when required.

The trend is, despite additional cost, to place electric power lines underground for two reasons. First, it reduces the chances of power failures and second, it eliminates unsightly clutter in the landscape adding to the aesthetic appeal.

Telephone, TV Cable

Similar to electric power, telephone lines can be located either above or below ground. In the past almost all lines were above ground and either utilized the electric line poles or set up an additional line. In either case, they are unsightly and subject to disruption by the weather.

Telephone lines, TV cables, and other special lines should all be located underground. Some attempts have been made to combine all electrical, telephone, and TV cables into a common underground trench that would simplify additional installations and maintenance. These lines may also be located at the rear-lot easement, if necessary.

Gas

Gas mains are generally located under sidewalk or in planting strip. They normally do not have any special requirements.

TREES

Street Trees

Goal: To assure that sidewalks are shaded and attractive, trees should be planted along the sidewalk.

Program: There should be one sidewalk tree for every 25 linear feet of sidewalk fronting on the site. Trees may be no smaller

SOURCE: *Housing Quality–A Program for Zoning Reform*
The Urban Design Council of the City of N.Y.

than 3½″-4″ caliper and must be planted in no less than a depth of 4′ of earth with a grating area of 25 sq. ft. and a minimum planting bed of 50 sq. ft. The measurement of caliper and the specifications for planting shall be in accordance with the standards and specifications of the American Society of Nurserymen.

Compliance:

PREFERRED (A)	PROPOSED (B)
A = linear feet of sidewalk fronting on site divided by 25′-0″	B = no. of street trees qualifying under this section
Built Up	Non-Built Up

50% = Minimum permitted

Landscaping Trees

Goal: To insure that *outdoor space* is shaded and attractive.

Program: Provision of trees should be based on the following schedule:

	Low Density	Medium Density	High Density
1″ caliper per X sq. ft. of site	125	300	500

Qualifying trees must:
    a. be at least 4″ caliper
    b. be planted in 4′-0″ of earth
    c. be planted in at least 200 cubic feet of soil
    d. have adequate drainage

Existing trees that remain after development may be counted if they meet qualifying conditions.

Compliance:

$(B/A)\ 100 = \%$

PREFERRED (A)
A = total caliper
required as per
schedule

PROPOSED (B)
B = total caliper
of all proposed
trees as per
specifications

50% = Minimum permitted

WINTER SUN

Goal: To maximize sunlight in *open space*.

Program: All *outdoor space* should receive sunlight between 9 A.M. and 3 P.M. during the winter solstice. Sunlight is measured as follows:

a. Measure amount of S.F. of *outdoor space* receiving sunlight at 9 A.M., 12 Noon and 3 P.M. during the winter solstice.
b. Divide by three to find the average.

Compliance:

$(B/A)\ 100 = \%$

PREFERRED (A)
A = sq. ft. of
outdoor space

PROPOSED (B)
B = average
sq. ft. of
outdoor space
receiving winter
sun, excluding
parking area

LANDSCAPING

Goal: To provide landscaped outdoor spaces and attractive buffers between recreation areas.

Program: The percent of *open space* that is landscaped should be based on the following schedule:

	Low Density	Medium Density	High Density
percentage of landscaped outdoor space	70	50	25

The standards for landscaping the *open space* are:
a. 2'-0" of soil for grass and ground cover
b. 3'-0" of soil for shrubs, bushes and low ornamental trees

Compliance:

$(B/A)\ 100 = \%$

PREFERRED (A)
A = one-half of
outdoor space
sq. ft.

PROPOSED (B)
B = sq. ft. of
landscaped
outdoor space

Housing Quality–A Program for Zoning Reform
Urban Design Council of the City of New York

TYPES OF HOUSING

F-1   General Considerations and Standards
F-2   Detached Single-family House
F-3   One-family Houses

TYPICAL HOUSE PLANS

F-4   Simple Rectangle
       "T" Plan
F-5   "H" Plan
       "U" Plan
F-6   Utility-core Plan
       In-line Plan
F-7   Split-level Plan
F-8   Court or Atrium House
F-9   Duplex (Semi-attached)
F-10   Quadruplex

F-11   Row Houses
F-12   Town Houses
F-13   Garden Apartments
F-14   Tenements
F-15   Apartment Buildings

F-16   Large-scale Developments
F-17   Dwelling Access Alternatives
F-18   Grouped Dwelling Alternatives

TYPES OF APARTMENT BUILDINGS

F-19   Center-corridor Plan
F-20   Open-corridor Plan
F-21   Skip-stop Plan
F-22   Tower Plan
F-23   Expanded Tower Plan
F-24   Cross Plan
F-25   Expanded Cross Plan
F-26   Five-wing Plan
F-27   Circular Plan
F-28   Terrace Plan
F-29   Modular Units

F-30   Apartment Building Amenities
F-31   Mobile Homes and Parks
F-32   Combination of Housing Types

GENERAL CONSIDERATIONS AND STANDARDS

The types of buildings used for housing range from detached single-family dwellings to high-rise apartment houses. Often a housing development will consist of only one type of housing, but in relatively large developments a mix or range will occur. Typical combinations would be single-family and garden apartments, or town houses and high-rise apartments.

The actual types are dictated by planning considerations such as densities, type of occupancy, economics, and community housing needs.

Housing types can be divided into several categories:

a) Single-Family Detached—are those located on a separate and independent lot. This type is generally owner-occupied.

b) Two-Family and Town Houses—are those that have two or more housing units in a group. This includes duplexes, quadruplexes, row houses, and town houses. Most frequently this type of housing is located on separate lots and also owner-occupied.

c) Garden Apartments—are clusters of apartments with higher densities and are generally rental units.

d) Low- and High-Rise Apartments—are those types of housing with the greatest densities.

No one type of housing is superior to any other. Each has an appropriate time and place for its use. In built-up urban areas, high-rise apartments are generally the most appropriate while in outlying areas, detached housing is generally more successful.

On the following pages, a review of all types of housing is given. Apartments, or multiple dwellings, obviously are more complicated structures and require greater regulation, by building codes and lending institutions.

The following analysis for each building type considers both the merits and weaknesses of each. Taken into account are the number of apartments per floor, relationship to the core area, resultant effect as to orientation and the types of apartments. Regardless of the shape or arrangement of apartments on a typical floor, the generally accepted minimum standards for safety are mandatory. Above all, each floor must be provided with the necessary passages, stairs, and exit doors so that people may quickly get out and completely away from their living unit and building in case of fire in any part of the building. This means that halls and stairs must be wide enough to accommodate all persons on a floor and also be constructed of fire-resistant materials.

For high-rise structures, two means of egress from each floor is universally accepted as being the minimum required. The stairs should be remote from each other to maximize the safety factor. Such stairs should be arranged so that they provide continuity of egress from any floor to the outside of the building at grade level. The FHA standard requires a maximum distance of travel from the entrance door of any living unit to an enclosed stairway not to exceed 100 feet for buildings of fire-resistive construction, and not more than 50 feet for other types of construction. These dimensions are illustrated below:

A. Maximum length of travel, 100 feet for type 1 construction, 50 feet for all other types—maximum distance between stairs or exterior doors equals 2 x (A).

B. Maximum length of travel, 30 feet for all construction types.

The width of corridors and hallways is another critical aspect of the safety of the occupants. The FHA requires that any public corridor serving more than six living units be a minimum of 5 feet wide. However, short corridors of less than 50 feet may be less than 5 feet, but in no case less than 3'6", if they serve less than six living units.

A type of public corridor that creates additional problems is the exterior corridor that is open to the elements. The effect of climatic factors of freezing outdoor temperatures, heavy rain, wind, sleet, and snow, must be considered. At the same time, open corridors provide the architect an opportunity to create outdoor sitting and play spaces resulting in greater livability adjacent to the apartment.

DETACHED SINGLE-FAMILY HOUSE

The single-family detached house is generally considered to be the best type of housing for families with growing children. Only the one-family house provides full use of private outdoor facilities. Another distinct advantage is the freedom to make normal amounts of noise without disturbing the neighbors. Also, the close proximity to open space, grass and trees is considered desirable and healthful.

A garage is often included, which is either attached or detached. Generally, older houses have detached garages while the new houses have attached garages.

Type of construction can be of frame, brick veneer, solid masonry, or stucco. The most common type is frame construction.

Lot sizes vary tremendously and reflect the cost of land, zoning requirements, and the general character of the neighborhood. Prior to the 2nd World War, lot sizes tended to be small, some even as small as 20' x 100'. Since then, lot sizes have increased substantially. Modest lot sizes range from 50' x 100' to half-acre lots. Lots over an acre can be considered large. Lots up to 100' front normally have depths of 100'. Lots with frontage greater than 100' usually have depths greater than 100'.

Detached Single-family House

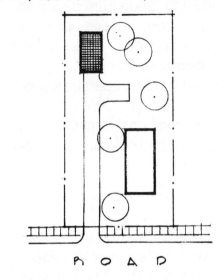

DETACHED GARAGE

ROAD

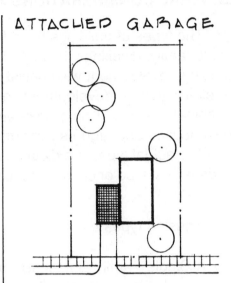

ATTACHED GARAGE

ROAD

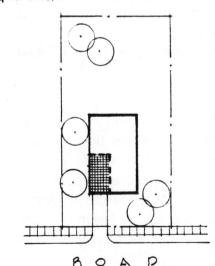

GARAGE WITHIN UNIT

ROAD

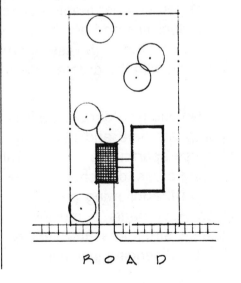

CARPORT OR SEMI-ATTACHED

ROAD

ONE-FAMILY HOUSES

Detached Single-family House

The single-family detached house is the most common type of housing in the U.S. It is characterized by being a completely independent structure and housing one family. The type of house can usually be described as a ranch, high ranch, split level, or 2-story.

Ranch

The ranch-type house is the traditional one-story house. All activities, cooking, dining, living and sleeping are on one level close to the ground. The house may or may not have a cellar, which is generally used for storage or minor activities. Older houses had high-pitched roofs for expansion. The newer houses have low-pitched roofs without provisions for expansion. This is the simplest type of construction.

High Ranch

The high ranch is similar to a ranch except that the main level is raised out of the ground allowing light and air into the basement. This lower level is then utilized as additional living space. One of the kitchen-dining-living areas can be located there, or the space can be used for additional bedrooms. The major advantage of this type of house over the traditional ranch is the utilization of the lower level for living purposes rather than storage or incidental use.

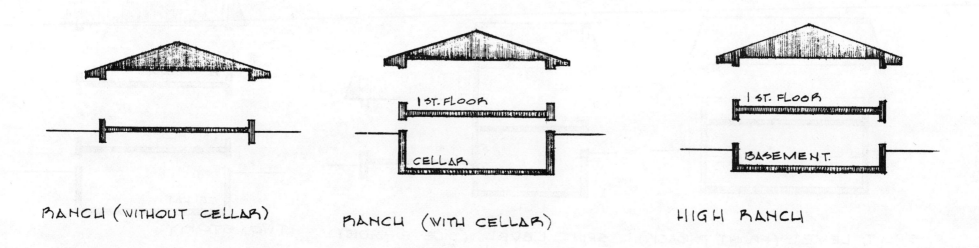

RANCH (WITHOUT CELLAR)   RANCH (WITH CELLAR)   HIGH RANCH

One-family House Types

293

Split-level

The split-level house separates the living activities into three levels. The kitchen-dining-living is the main level close to the ground. The sleeping level is located ½ level above the main level. The garage-recreation room-utility level is ½ level below the main level. The main advantage is the partial separation of activities and greater privacy. Disadvantages are the up and down stair movement and more complicated construction.

Two-Story

The two-story house is characteristic of most older houses. The lower level contains the kitchen-dining-living areas. The upper floor contains the sleeping areas. This type of house most often has a cellar for storage. The main advantage is the complete separation of living and sleeping activities for maximum privacy. The major disadvantage is the up and down stair movement. Construction is more complicated than in the ranch-type house. Also, there is less lot coverage than the other types.

A garage is most often included, which is either attached or detached. Generally, older houses have detached garages while the newer houses have attached garages.

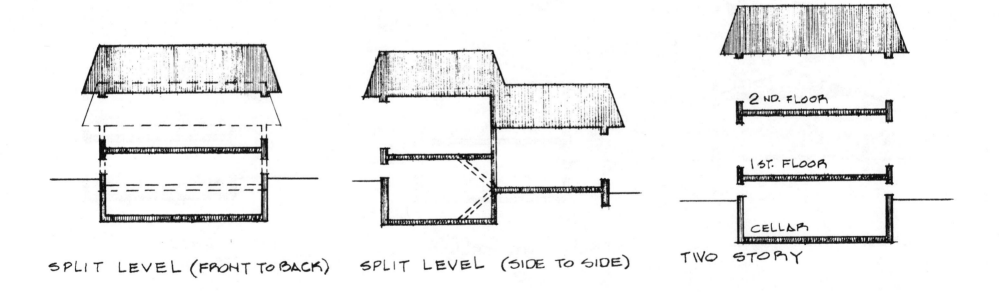

SPLIT LEVEL (FRONT TO BACK)   SPLIT LEVEL (SIDE TO SIDE)   TWO STORY

TYPICAL HOUSE PLANS

Simple Rectangle; "T" Plan

The rectangle plan is the simplest and one of the most common plan types. Most minimal or economical houses utilize this kind of plan because it encloses greater floor area per exterior wall length than other plans. Its simplicity also results in uncomplicated framing. The plan is compact, which results in a minimum of circulation space. A garage or carport is generally located alongside the kitchen or the front of the house.

Because of its compactness there is a minimum of separation between the living and sleeping activities, thereby lessening the amount of privacy. This type of house is usually referred to as a "ranch" type.

A variation on the simple rectangle plan is the offset rectangle where the living area is pushed forward.

"T" or "L" Plans

The "T" plan is the placement of the living and sleeping areas at right angles to each other. By such juxtaposition, excellent separation and privacy of the two functions is achieved. It may also be possible to achieve better orientation for both functions since they are relatively independent of each other.

The internal circulation is compact and access to all rooms direct if the entrance is located at the junction of the two wings.

This plan type is best on a flat site. If the site slopes, it is possible to locate the garage, recreation, and utility areas under one of the wings.

A variation of the "T" plan is the "L" plan. This occurs when the living area is located at the top or bottom of the sleeping wing instead of at the center.

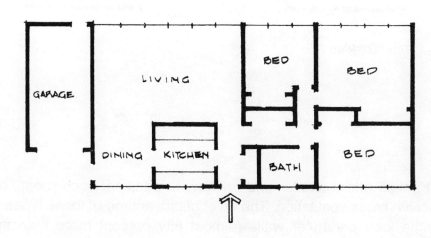

The Simple Rectangle Plan

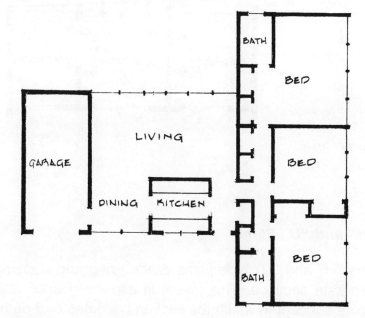

The "T" Plan

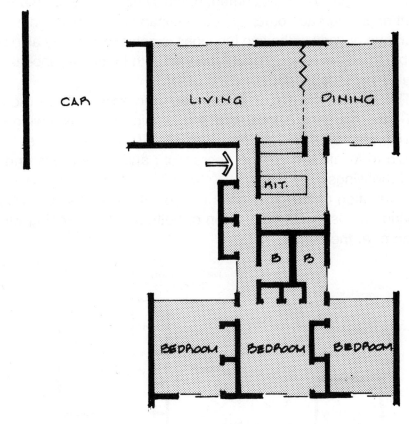

The "H" Plan

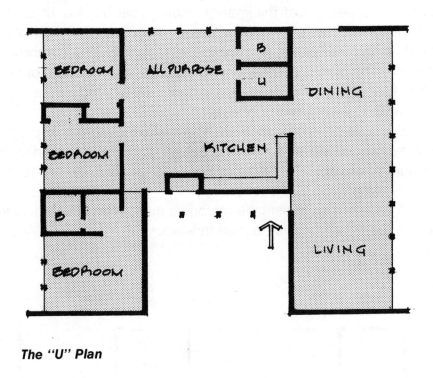

The "U" Plan

"H" and "U" Plans

The "H" and "U" type plans divide living and sleeping units into separate sections. This layout is especially applicable to a utility core concept in which the kitchen becomes part of the connecting link. Excellent separation of activities is achieved, and useful patios afford shelter and privacy. In addition, each room can receive cross ventilation. The chief disadvantage of these types is in the long perimeter walls (almost fifty percent more than the same space in a simple rectangle), resulting in higher construction cost as well as increased expense of heating and air conditioning.

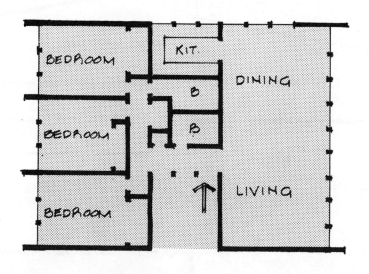

The Utility-core Plan

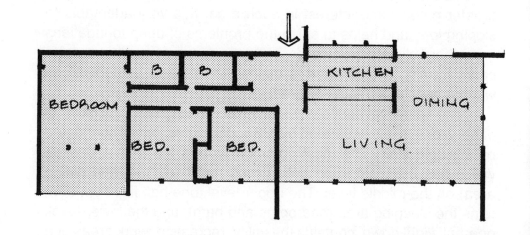

The In-line Plan

Utility-core Plan

The rectangular utility-core plan has several advantages. The house may be almost square and very compact, with a good concentration of utilities. In addition, the core acts as a buffer between the sleeping and living zones. The problems of this plan include the difficulty of properly relating the kitchen, garage and main entrances, and the excessive circulation space that is often required. This can be helped by opening up the exterior walls and actually using the lot as circulation and access in areas of mild climate.

The In-line Plan

The in-line plan is an excellent solution for many unusual site conditions. On a narrow lot it allows access to side patios and outdoor areas; on steep hillsides it allows the maximum economy of construction and land usage. It can have good circulation (at the expense of a long corridor) and the same good orientation for all the rooms.

The plan may be adapted to a two-story house, where it helps to concentrate circulation and utilities, while retaining the advantage of providing the best orientation for both floors.

The Split-level Plan

The split-level plan produces a maximum of total interior area for a house of small overall size, and its separate levels can give greater privacy and interest in each area. It is very adaptable to sloping lots, and helps to solve the problems of deep foundations in northern climates. However, it may require a somewhat complicated framing system, and is difficult to relate to outdoor areas without special terracing or grading.

The split-level house is a multilevel dwelling unit consisting of either 3 or 4 levels separated by 1/2 floor heights, but all connected by a single stair. The most common type is the 3-level design, which has the main living area (living room, kitchen, and dining area) on the middle level. The upper level, one-half flight up, contains the sleeping area (bedrooms and bath), and the lower level, one-half flight down, contains the utility, recreation, work areas or a garage. Sometimes a level below the lower level is introduced as a cellar.

The split-level house was originally designed to accommodate or take advantage of sloping terrain. Frequently, because of advantages of the split-levels, this type of house is placed on flat sites. The result is either an excessive amount of grading and retaining walls, or an awkward relationship of house to site.

The main advantage is the separation of the living, sleeping, and recreation-utility areas, yet they are more accessible than a traditional two-story house. One drawback to the split-level is that it is more complicated and costly to build than a one- or two-story house.

Section

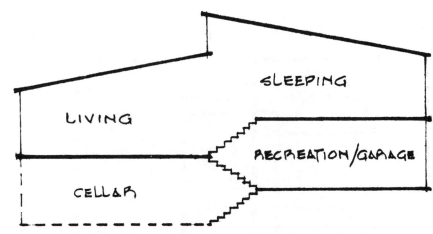

Plan

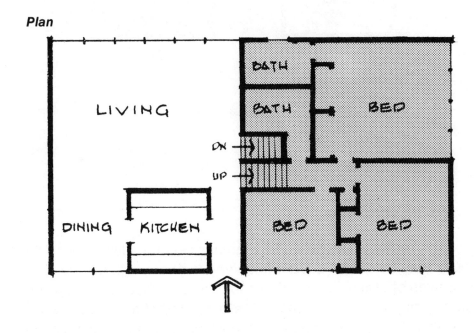

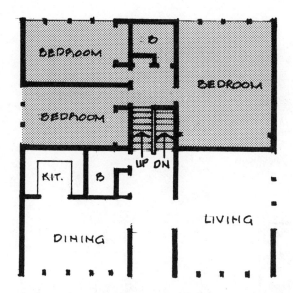

*Entry and Sleeping Level
Split-level Plan*

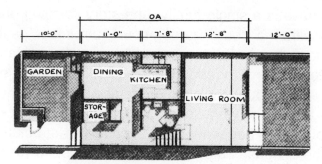

PLAN · FIRST FLOOR

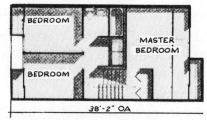

PLAN · SECOND FLOOR

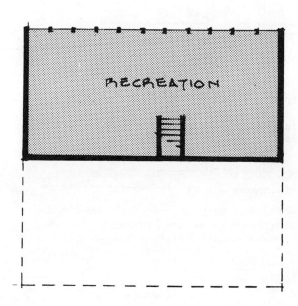

*Recreation Level
(under Sleeping Level)*

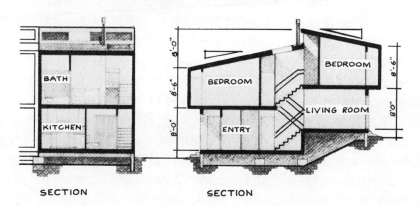

SECTION   SECTION

**Architects: Norman C. Fletcher, John C. Harkness
Architects Collaborative**

Court or Atrium House

This type of house is a single-family, one-story dwelling unit and described as either a court, garden-court, atrium or patio house. The common element is an open landscaped courtyard partially or completely surrounded by living areas. The major source of light and air is through the open garden courtyard. Sometimes it is attached, as in a row house, or clustered as in a checkerboard pattern, but most frequently it is a detached structure. Historically, this type of house dates back several thousand years to the Egyptian, Greek, and Roman houses. The open court is a variation of the Greek peristyle and the Roman atrium. All the living areas opened out into the atrium creating a secluded indoor-outdoor space. This inward-directed house provides maximum privacy and livability. A large degree of integration of the house with the landscaping can be achieved. When used as an attached house, it makes maximum use of the lot and generally can be located on a much narrower lot than a conventional detached house. When enclosed by high walls or parts of the indoor living space, the house completely shuts off the outside world and assures greater protection from intruders. A garage may be incorporated within its enclosing walls or a common parking area can be provided at the ends of the groupings or clusters.

The density of this type of housing, depending on size of units and site development, can be described as medium-density and generally will be similar to town house or row house densities. An approximate range would be from 12 units per acre for large court houses to 18 units for small ones.

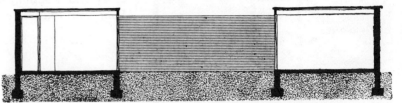

Cross section of the structure is through on-slab house. Foundation walls of basement units are carried to greater depth. Non-bearing interior walls permitted different room arrangements within identical areas.

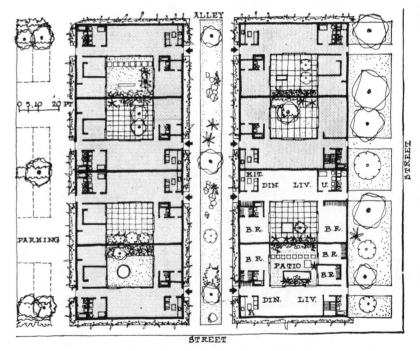

Room arrangements are varied to meet individual needs. They range from a one-bedroom-and-study layout to three-bedroom plans. Driveway, left, through the site from street to alley reduces congestion in the parking area.

House and Home, **August 1963**

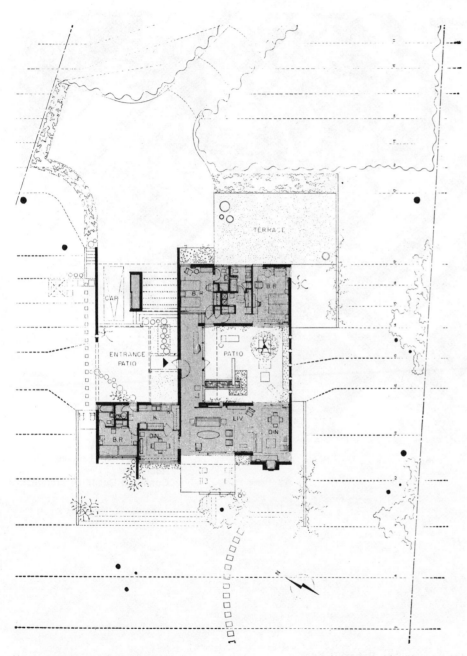

House and Home, August 1954

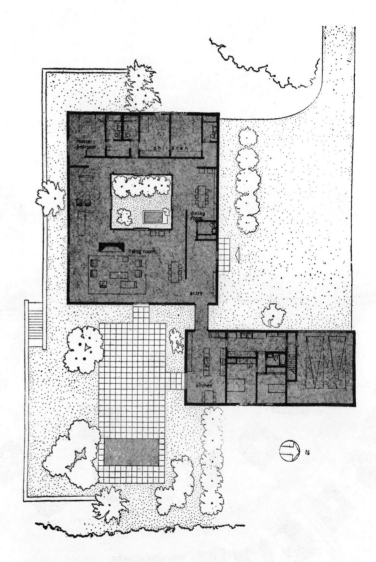

Philip Johnson—Architect
House and Home, August, 1954

Attached Houses with Courts

Genesee River Houses
Rochester
Conklin & Rossant—architects

Design of the Housing Site, Robert D. Katz
University of Illinois, 1966

Duplex (Semi-attached)

The semi-attached house is an independent lot that is attached on one side to a similar dwelling on an adjacent lot. The attachment is made along a common or "party" wall, which is jointly owned. The main advantage of this type of construction is the economy achieved in the construction of the party wall. Because one side yard is eliminated, it is also possible to build on a narrower lot than if it were a detached dwelling. This type of dwelling can be used for either one or two families. Usually this type of dwelling is two stories high, but can be one story also.

As a one-family dwelling, the living room, kitchen, dining areas are on the first floor while the sleeping areas are on the second floor. This type is usually owner-occupied.

As a two-family dwelling, each floor has a separate unit with its own independent entrance. The owner usually lives in the lower unit and rents the upper unit. Garages are either detached or incorporated into the cellar, or lowest level of the structure.

The term "duplex" refers to a single structure consisting of two separate dwelling units. It may be a two-story walk-up building in which one dwelling unit is situated over another, with access to the upper apartment by means of a private staircase. It may also be a structure having two dwelling units located side-by-side, with the individual units on one or more levels.

Duplexes are no longer as popular as they once were. They have been eclipsed by other housing—single-family houses in the suburbs, and large new apartment complexes with many conveniences on the same site.

From "duplex" has grown a whole family of "-plexes"—"triplex," "fourplex," "eightplex," and so on. The prefix identifies the number of dwelling units in the building, which is usually two stories high.

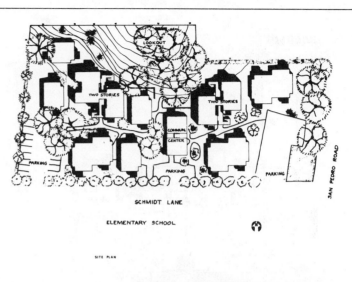

SITE PLAN

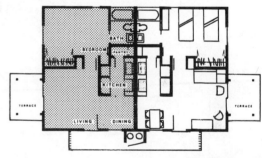

UNITS A,B,C – 1 BEDROOM

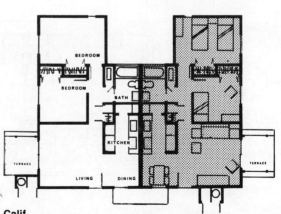

Santa Venetia Oaks, Calif.
Worley K. Wong, FAIA, Architect

UNIT D – 2 BEDROOM

Duplex (Semi-attached)

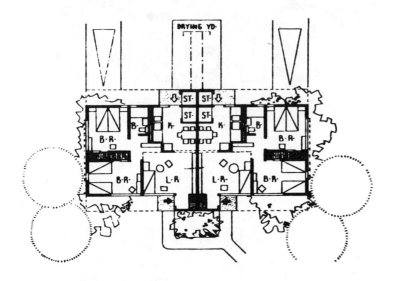

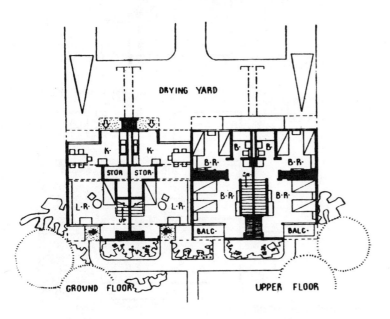

GROUND FLOOR   UPPER FLOOR

SITE PLAN

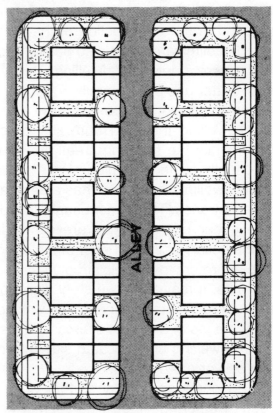

CONVENTIONAL   LAYOUT
20 UNITS

Quadruplex

The consolidation of four single-family houses into one structure utilizing common walls need not destroy the privacy of the individual dwellings. It permits greater use of the total site for outdoor living. The advantages of such an arrangement are shown on the accompanying plan. Concrete wall construction provides for better sound insulation and the back-to-back arrangement of plumbing cores. Further economies will accrue in reduced fuel costs and maintenance of shared driveways and footpaths. All utility services are combined and economically run underground rather than overhead. The elimination of rear and side yards allows maximum use of the site, while careful orientation and screening assures privacy for each residence. Automobile parking is centralized to serve the four units and thus requires less area. The amount of open land between these "quadruplexes" is greater than in many present subdivisions and can be assigned either to community functions or more dwelling units, developing higher densities without overcrowding. Abundant landscaping and the use of varied setbacks would greatly enhance the total appearance.

Adjacent to the common walls are the kitchen, bathrooms, stair hall, and power core with utility room; none of which requires a window. The bedrooms, dining and living areas, and family room have outside exposure, and in some cases they open to terraces.

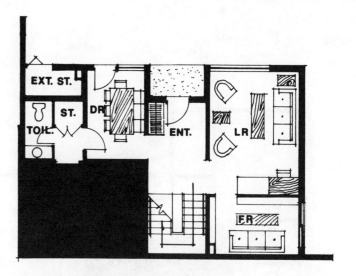

1ST FLOOR PLAN

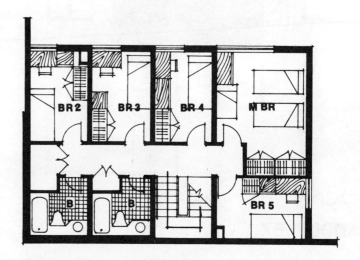

2ND FLOOR PLAN

TYPICAL QUADRANT

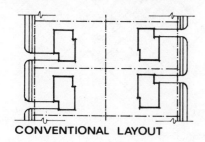

CONVENTIONAL LAYOUT

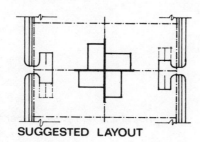

SUGGESTED LAYOUT

Quadruplex

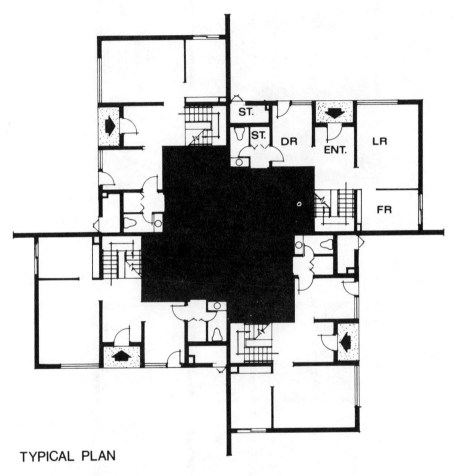

TYPICAL PLAN

QUADRUPLEX

Housing with Shelter, Dept. of Housing & Urban Development and Dept. of Defense—1970

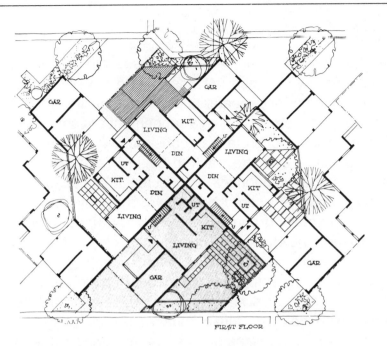

FIRST FLOOR

Plan below shows how entries, as well as patios, of units in the same building are isolated from each other.

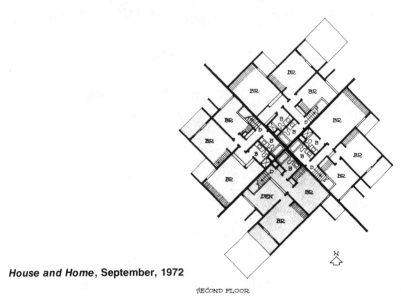

House and Home, September, 1972

SECOND FLOOR

ROW HOUSES

The row house is a standard dwelling type in many American cities. It is characterized by great economy in the use of land, moderate construction cost, and low maintenance and operating costs. It affords each family its own home and the opportunity of developing a plot of land for its own use. The economy of a row-house plan obviously derives from the length of the rows, although the per-unit saving diminishes with the length of the building. The economic advantage of a long building results in part from the elimination of end walls, but there are also savings in land utilities, and walks.

Row houses are not adaptable to steep contours except by heavy cutting; ordinarily, buildings should tend to parallel the contours, since longitudinal slopes can only be accommodated by costly breaks of floor level.

In the organization of a row-house plan an effort should be made to avoid movements of traffic in any considerable volume parallel to the rows. If the movement of vehicles is restricted to streets lying at the ends of the buildings, the space between the buildings, adjacent to the living units, is left free for the safe and comfortable use of the occupants.

Row houses may be assembled in many patterns. In general these fall into two types—court plans and parallel row plans. Each of these has advantages. A court layout may attain spaciousness of effect and esthetically satisfying enclosed areas. When the rows are predominantly parallel, the distance from row to row will be somewhat less than the average width of a court, but the longitudinal views will be longer. It is obvious that when a particular orientation to sun or prevailing wind is strongly favored, such orientation must result in predominantly parallel rows. The parallel row plan usually facilitates a simple and practical servicing scheme in which all units are handled uniformly. A court plan can seldom be arranged without streets being parallel to some of the buildings.

Two-story row houses can economically accommodate families requiring 2- and 3-bedroom units. Units with 1 bedroom or less are best handled as two-story flats or as one-story rows.

THE 20FT. ROW HOUSE

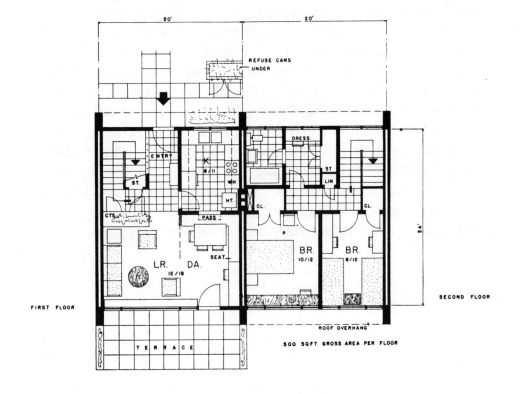

FIRST FLOOR

SECOND FLOOR

500 SQ.FT. GROSS AREA PER FLOOR

SOURCE: Technical Bulletin, HHFA, May-June, 1950

The 20-foot Row House

The 20-foot row house has a gross floor area of 1,000 square feet. Living-dining areas are combined into one room, 12 by 19 feet. This room should face south. The dining area has direct communication with the kitchen by means of a pass, and can be screened off from the living area with a curtain, bookshelves, a permanent plywood screen, or other media.

A large coat closet, 2 feet by 6 feet 6 inches, separates the stairhall from the living room. Its height can be held to 6 feet if an effect of greater spaciousness for the whole living area is desired. The space under the stairs is used for storage.

In addition to accommodating standard equipment, the kitchen provides space for a heater, water heater, and washing machine. If individual heat is planned, duct work is reduced to a minimum. If central heat is provided, the kitchen will gain 3 more feet of counter and cabinet space. On the second floor are two bedrooms, the bathroom (tub on opposite side from the window), and a small dressing alcove with a storage closet. Bedroom window sills are high so that furniture can be placed under them. All plumbing is concentrated in one wall. One flue services the heater and hot water heater. Hot water lines are short. The outdoor terrace, linking garden to living room, can be used in complete privacy.

The 25-foot Row House

The 25-foot row house has a gross floor area of 1,250 square feet. Living and dining are combined into one spacious room facing the garden side and should have south orientation. Two of the three bedrooms on the second floor will then have south orientation, also. Storage closets are ample and include a large storage space off the entry, as well as a smaller one accessible from the outside, for tools and deliveries. Mechanical installations are similar to those of the 20-foot row house.

THE 25FT. ROW HOUSE

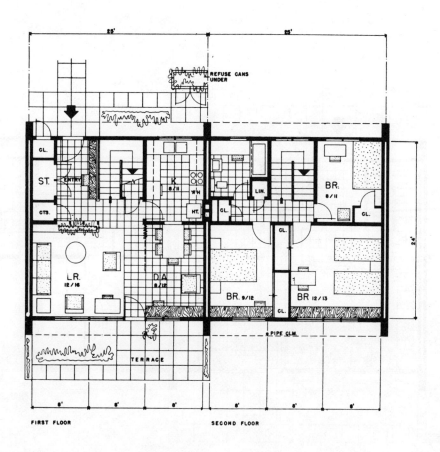

FIRST FLOOR   SECOND FLOOR

625 SQ.FT. GROSS AREA PER FLOOR

THE 30FT. ROW HOUSE

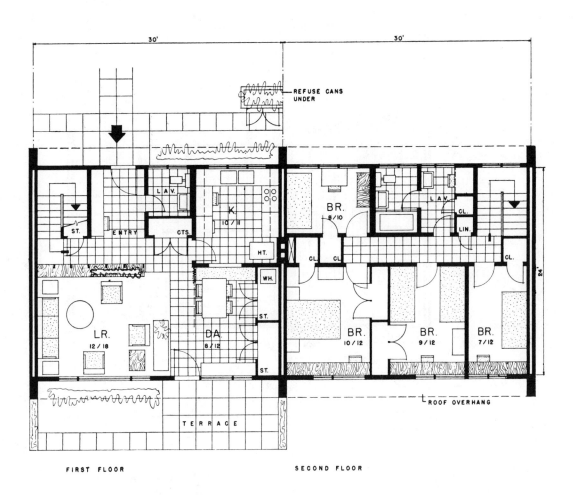

FIRST FLOOR

SECOND FLOOR

The 30-foot Row House

The 30-foot row house has a gross floor area of 1,500 square feet. The basic arrangement of rooms is similar to the preceding row house types, except for the addition of a first-floor lavatory off the entry. Three of the four bedrooms upstairs face the same direction as the living-dining combination downstairs. This direction should generally be south.

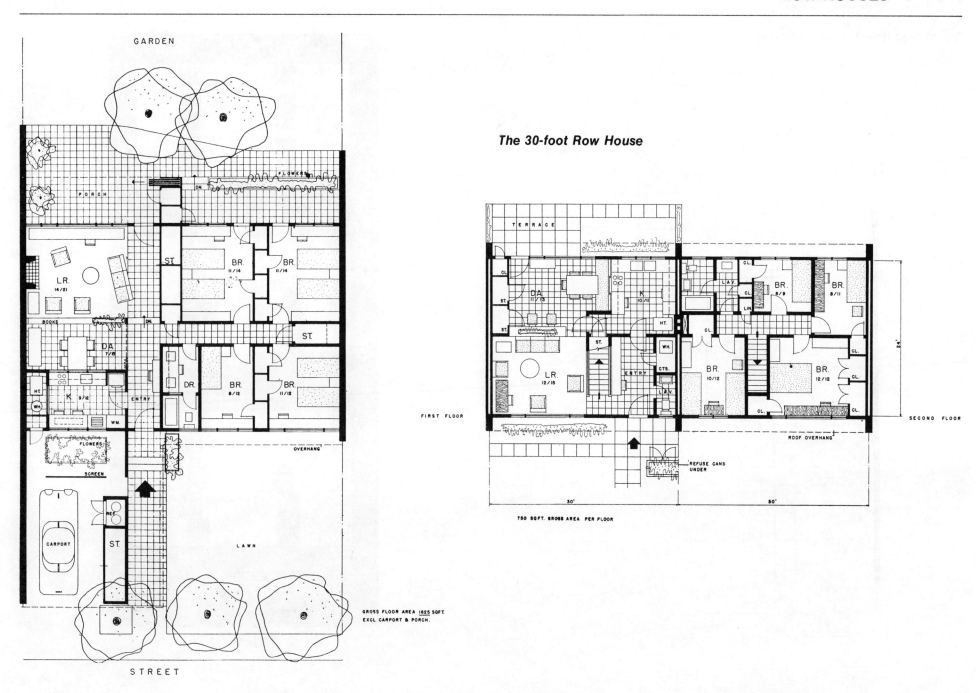

GARDEN

The 30-foot Row House

FLOWERS

DN.

PORCH

LR.
14/21

ST.

BR.
11/14

BR.
11/14

BOOKS

DN.

ST.

DA
7/5

DR.

BR.
8/12

BR.
11/12

HT.

WH.

K
9/12

ENTRY

WM.

FLOWERS

SCREEN

OVERHANG

CARPORT

ST.

LAWN

STREET

GROSS FLOOR AREA 1625 SQFT.
EXCL. CARPORT & PORCH.

TERRACE

CL.

ST.

DA
11/13

K
10/11

LAV.

CL.

BR.
8/9

BR.
8/11

ST.

HT.

LIN.

CL.

WH.

CL.

LR.
12/15

ST.

ENTRY

CTS.

BR.
10/12

BR.
12/12

LAV.

CL.

CL.

CL.

FIRST FLOOR

SECOND FLOOR

ROOF OVERHANG

REFUSE CANS
UNDER

30'

30'

750 SQFT. GROSS AREA PER FLOOR

The 40-foot Row House on One Floor

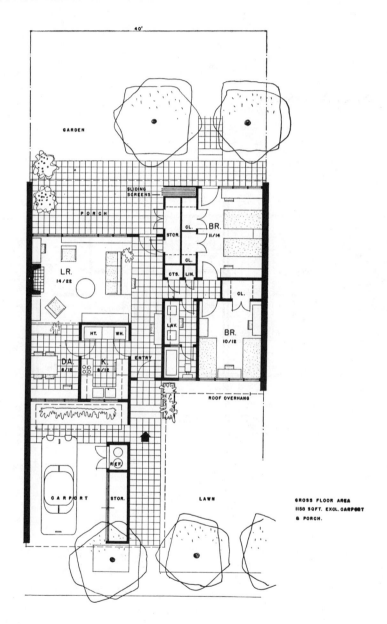

GROSS FLOOR AREA
1158 SQFT. EXCL. CARPORT
& PORCH.

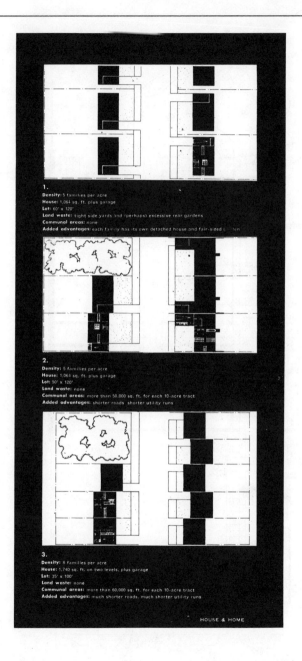

1.
Density: 5 families per acre
House: 1,064 sq. ft. plus garage
Lot: 60' x 120'
Land waste: tight side yards and (perhaps) excessive rear gardens
Communal areas: none
Added advantages: each family has its own detached house and fair-sized garden

2.
Density: 5 families per acre
House: 1,064 sq. ft. plus garage
Lot: 50' x 120'
Land waste: none
Communal areas: more than 50,000 sq. ft. for each 10-acre tract
Added advantages: shorter roads, shorter utility runs

3.
Density: 8 families per acre
House: 1,740 sq. ft. on two levels, plus garage
Lot: 35' x 100'
Land waste: none
Communal areas: more than 60,000 sq. ft. for each 10-acre tract
Added advantages: much shorter roads, much shorter utility runs

HOUSE & HOME

TOWN HOUSES

The town house, which has become popular in recent years, is similar to the old row house. It is an independent dwelling on an independent lot, which is attached on both sides to a similar dwelling on both adjacent lots. The attachment is made along two common or party walls that are jointly owned. The chief advantage of this type of construction is the economy of the party walls. Also, because no side yards are required, it is possible to build on a relatively narrow lot. Old row houses were built on lots as narrow as 16′ and 18′ wide. However, this is not recommended. Lot widths should be a minimum of 20 feet, but preferably wider.

Town houses are usually one-family dwellings with the living room, kitchen, and dining area on the lower level and the sleeping areas on the upper level. Row houses may contain two dwelling units, one above the other.

A built-in garage is desirable if it can be reasonably incorporated within the house. Alternate solutions are either a parking space in front of the house or in a group parking area close by.

The town house has long been advocated for rental housing for urban families with children as a good compromise between the desirability of a detached single-family house and the economic necessity of multifamily units. It is decidedly preferable from the viewpoint of the tenants because of greater livability. The results of surveys in both public and private housing indicate that families want to have direct access to the house, an individual yard or garden, and a place for small children to play close to the house where they can easily be supervised. These are features that the town house can provide.

From the management point of view, town house projects can be designed for maximum tenant maintenance of land area. They can also be designed for either individual heating installations or a central heating plant. Individual heating installations, though of higher operating cost to the tenant, result in lower maintenance cost to the management.

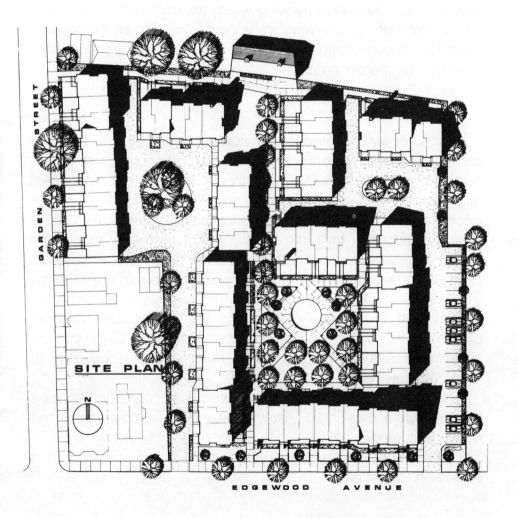

Gilbert Switzer, AIA and Associates
New Haven, Conn.

Private Garden

Privacy is an important factor in town house design. All house types show, therefore, an extension of the party walls beyond the face of the building on either side. Sitting out terraces on the garden side are separated by wing walls, approximately 6 feet long and 6 feet high. These wing walls do not have to be of masonry material, although preferably they should be of a permanent rather than of a temporary nature.

Public Access

Another arrangement that insures more privacy is the concentration of services from the front. The problem of refuse collection is solved by means of a masonry enclosure, 3 feet wide, 4 feet high, and 10 feet long for two living units. Access doors to the enclosure are from the side facing the building, away from street view. A flower box built into the top of the enclosure makes the appearance pleasing and attractive to the passer-by. A hose-bib connection facilitates cleaning and reduces odors to a minimum.

An entry space for each living unit presents another privacy feature and is absolutely necessary for service-from-the-front planning. The conventional direct entrance from the street into the living room reduces privacy and is the cause of annoyance to many housewives.

Recently in urban areas, the town house has emerged as a popular type of dwelling. The town house is usually one-family and owner-occupied.

The height is most frequently 2 stories and construction is brick or brick veneer.

The two-level town house is probably the most common, with the living activities on the first floor and the sleeping activities on the second floor. A powder room is generally provided on the lower level to minimize up and down traffic. In more elaborate developments, a second bathroom can be provided on the second floor.

The work area (kitchen) on the first floor is best located near the entrance and on the service side. This enables the living room and dining area to be oriented towards the terrace or open green areas. The bedrooms can easily be provided with a balcony.

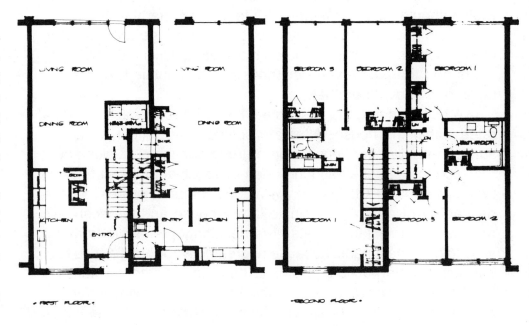

Parkway Forest, Toronto, Ontario

In this development the town houses, which are designed on 3 levels, were built on a steeply sloping site. The houses are sited in line along the existing contours. The land lends itself ideally to the provision of a walk-out basement from the family room. The main entrance to the house is on the opposite side on the first floor.

The basic house type is 3 bedrooms. Alternate schemes are shown for the 2-bedroom and 3-bedroom plan.

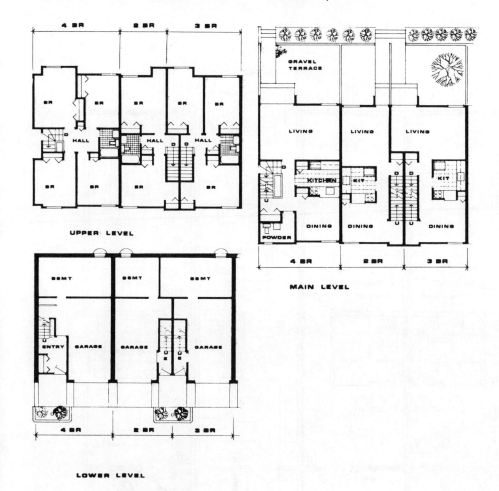

UPPER LEVEL

LOWER LEVEL

MAIN LEVEL

**Gilbert Switzer, AIA and Associates
New Haven, Conn.**

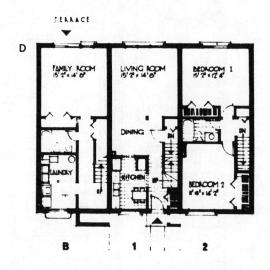

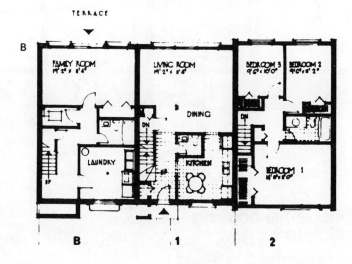

Wycliffe Hill, Toronto, Ontario, Canada, Housing Design, Canadian Housing Design Council, Ottowa, Ontario—1967

315

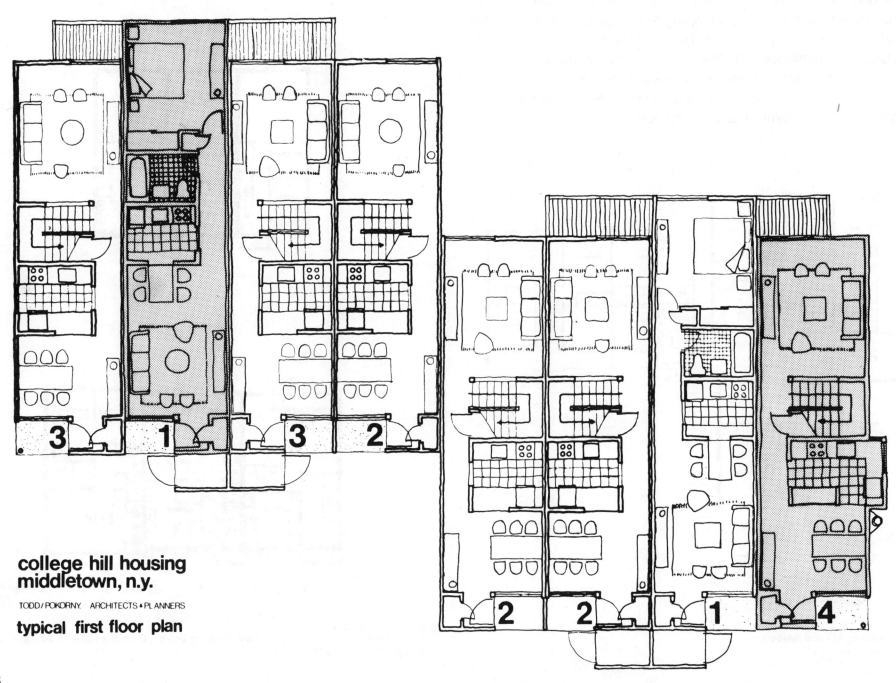

**college hill housing
middletown, n.y.**

TODD/POKORNY, ARCHITECTS & PLANNERS

typical first floor plan

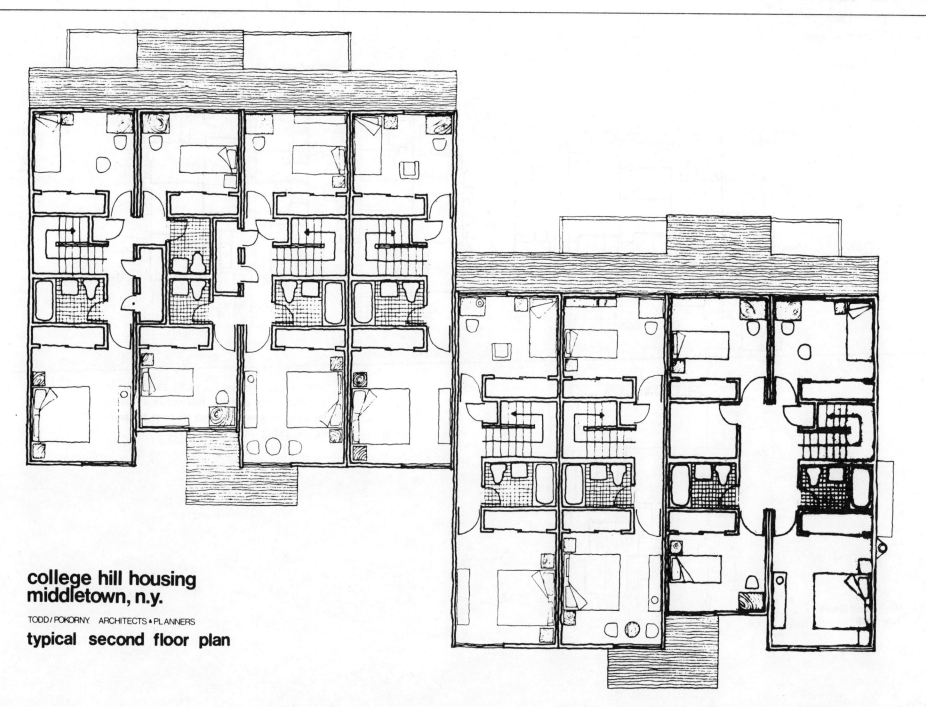

**college hill housing
middletown, n.y.**

TODD / POKORNY.   ARCHITECTS ▲ PLANNERS

typical   second   floor   plan

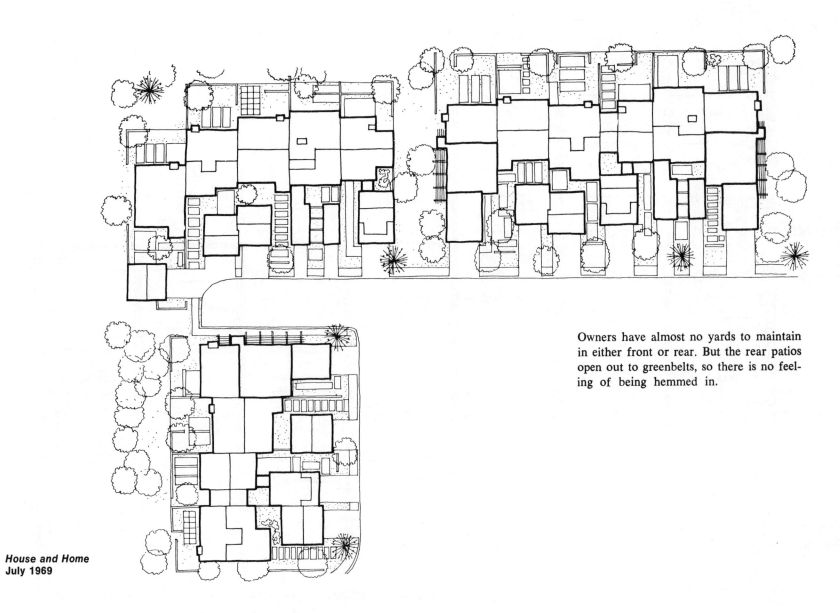

Owners have almost no yards to maintain in either front or rear. But the rear patios open out to greenbelts, so there is no feeling of being hemmed in.

House and Home
July 1969

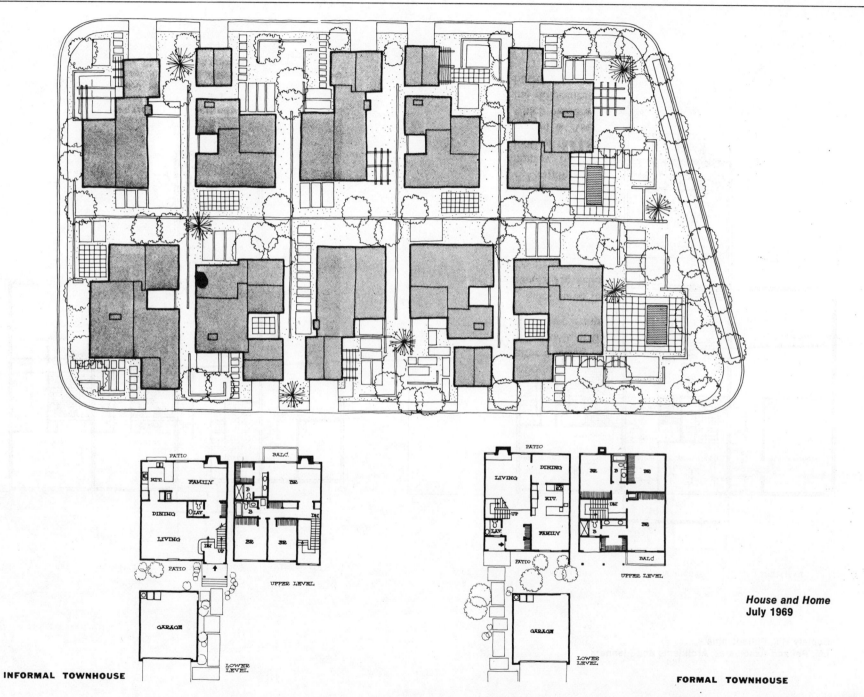

INFORMAL TOWNHOUSE

UPPER LEVEL

LOWER LEVEL

FORMAL TOWNHOUSE

UPPER LEVEL

LOWER LEVEL

House and Home
July 1969

F-12 TOWN HOUSES

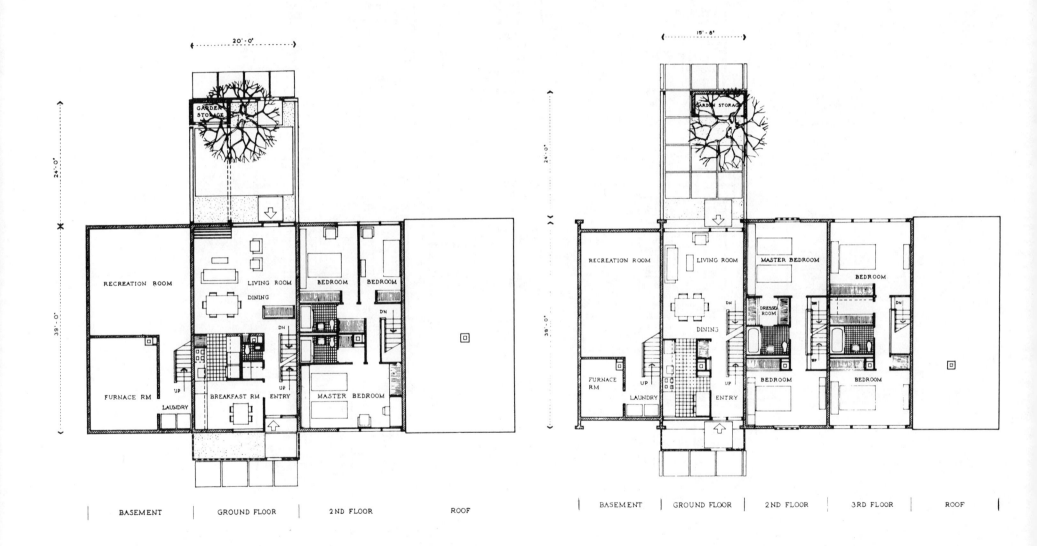

20'-0"

24'-0"

39'-0"

GARDEN STORAGE

RECREATION ROOM

LIVING ROOM

DINING

BEDROOM

BEDROOM

DN

FURNACE RM

UP

LAUNDRY

BREAKFAST RM

ENTRY

UP

DN

MASTER BEDROOM

BASEMENT | GROUND FLOOR | 2ND FLOOR | ROOF

15'-6"

24'-0"

39'-0"

GARDEN STORAGE

RECREATION ROOM

LIVING ROOM

MASTER BEDROOM

BEDROOM

DINING

DN

DRESSING ROOM

DN

FURNACE RM

UP

LAUNDRY

ENTRY

UP

BEDROOM

BEDROOM

BASEMENT | GROUND FLOOR | 2ND FLOOR | 3RD FLOOR | ROOF

Society Hill, Philadelphia
I.M. Pei and Associates, Architects and Planners

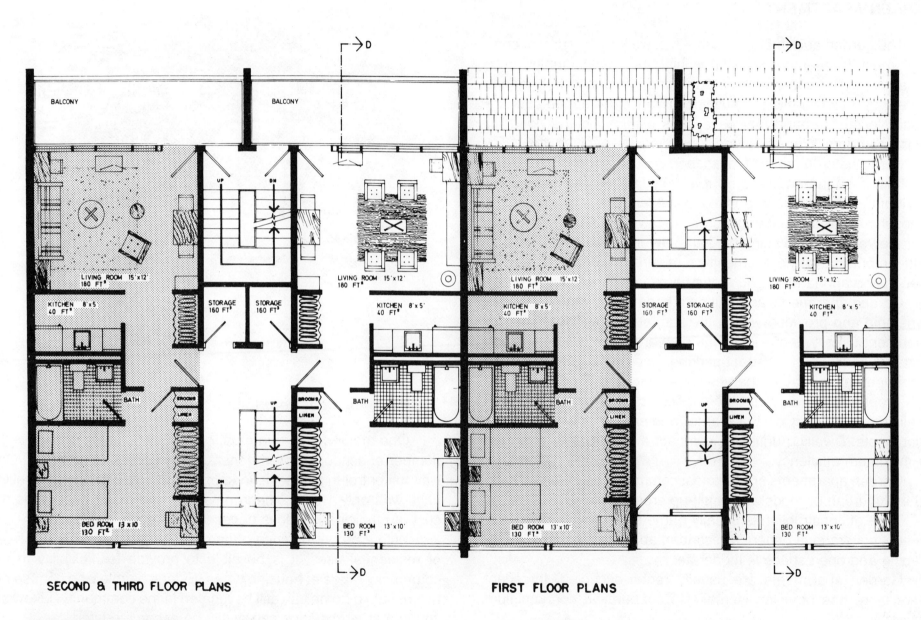

BALCONY

BALCONY

LIVING ROOM 15'x12'
180 FT²

LIVING ROOM 15'x12'
180 FT²

KITCHEN 8'x5'
40 FT²

STORAGE
160 FT³

STORAGE
160 FT³

KITCHEN 8'x5'
40 FT²

KITCHEN 8'x5'
40 FT²

BATH

BROOMS
LINEN

UP

DN

UP

DN

BED ROOM 13'x10'
130 FT²

BED ROOM 13'x10'
130 FT²

LIVING ROOM 15'x12'
180 FT²

LIVING ROOM 15'x12'
180 FT²

KITCHEN 8'x5'
40 FT²

STORAGE
160 FT³

STORAGE
160 FT³

KITCHEN 8'x5'
40 FT²

BATH

BATH

BROOMS
LINEN

BROOMS
LINEN

BATH

UP

BED ROOM 13'x10'
130 FT²

BED ROOM 13'x10'
130 FT²

SECOND & THIRD FLOOR PLANS

FIRST FLOOR PLANS

**N.Y.S. Urban Development Corp.
Charlotte Area Project, Rochester, N.Y.
Northrup, Kaelber, and Kopf, Architects**

321

GARDEN APARTMENTS

The garden apartment is generally a walk-up apartment complex, most frequently two stories high but occasionally three stories high. The apartments are grouped into separate buildings containing 8 to 16 units per building. Two to four apartments are usually located around stairways, thus eliminating the need for central corridors. When this type of building first evolved, the buildings were clustered around landscaped courts, gardens, and yards and built in suburban areas on relatively inexpensive land. As a result of the low coverage and extensive landscaping, a "garden" atmosphere was created and thereby received its name. However, over the years, due to rising land and development costs, parking requirements, and more amenities required, the percentage of open space and landscaped areas became less and less.

Garden apartments are built on a large plot of land under one ownership and provided with some community facilities. The development usually is provided with play areas for children, sitting areas for adults, and off-street parking. The parking is most often open-type parking rather than enclosed garages.

Types of units may vary from efficiency to 3- and 4-bedroom dwellings depending on the market and/or character of the developments. Dwelling units are compact and efficiently arranged for maximum efficiency.

Garden apartments are the most common type of rental housing in suburban or moderately built-up areas.

Type of construction is usually frame or brick veneer.

Lot coverage is generally less than apartment houses. Landscaping and open space is moderate.

Garden apartments are usually renter-occupied. In recent years there has been an increase in cooperative condominium ownership.

Planning Considerations

One major concern in most communities is the impact of the number of school children generated by garden apartments. One way to control this effect is to keep a large percentage of dwelling units with only 1 and 2 bedrooms. Another major concern is the cost of municipal services necessary for each new project.

With a proper balance of garden apartments with other types of residential uses, it is possible to provide for flexibility in the community range of housing types. Elderly people who choose not to maintain a home can still be located in the community. Likewise, young married couples can easily be accommodated.

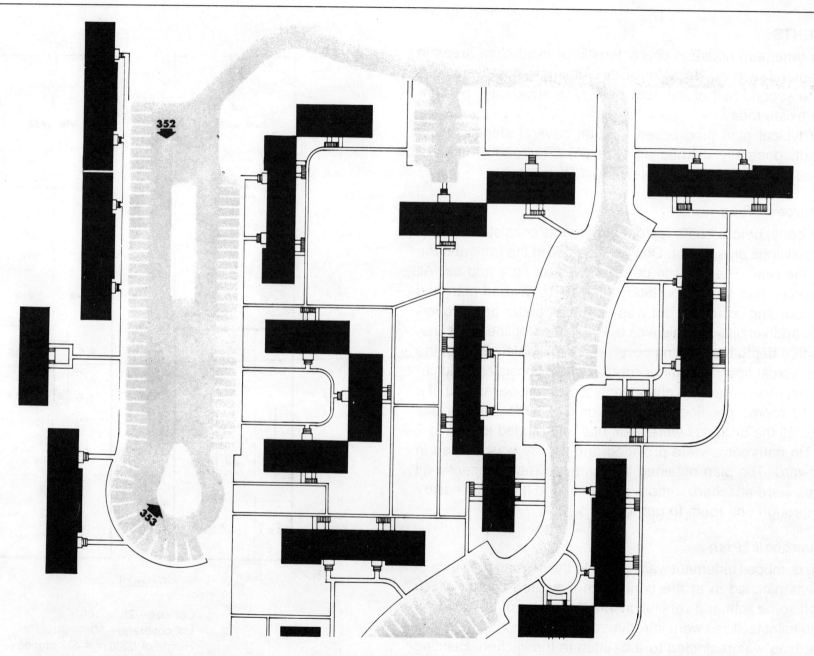

352

353

Design of the Housing Site, Robert D. Katz
University of Illinois, Urbana, Ill., 1966

TENEMENTS

The tenement house is characteristic of most slum areas in urban centers such as New York City. Although most were built during the second half of the 19th century, a substantial percentage still exists today.

The typical plan progressed through several stages of development, generally defined as type (A) "Railroad" Plan, (B) "Dumbbell" Plan, and (C) the "New-Law" Plan.

"Railroad" Plan

The early, before 1850, railroad tenements consisted of actually two buildings on each lot. One was located in the front and the other at the rear. The court in between was for light and air. All interior rooms had none. The later, after 1850, railroad plan had only one building on the lot but was not much better as to coverage, light and ventilation. This was built full from lot line to lot line. For its entire depth the building covered approximately 90% of the lot. On a typical floor, all interior rooms, which consisted of kitchens and bedrooms, had no light or ventilation whatsoever. Out of a total of 12 rooms per floor, 8 rooms or two-thirds were in this category. All the buildings were walk-ups and ranged from 5 to 7 stories. No bathrooms were provided and a privy was located in the rear yard. The plan obtained its name "railroad" because all the rooms were attached, without corridors, and it was necessary to walk through one room to get to another.

"Dumbbell" Plan

The dumbbell tenement was similar to the railroad plan except that it was pinched in at the center. This created courts, which permitted some light and ventilation into the center of the building. Common toilet facilities were introduced on each floor in the public halls. Bathing was restricted to a bathtub in the kitchen. Building coverage was between 80-90% of the lot.

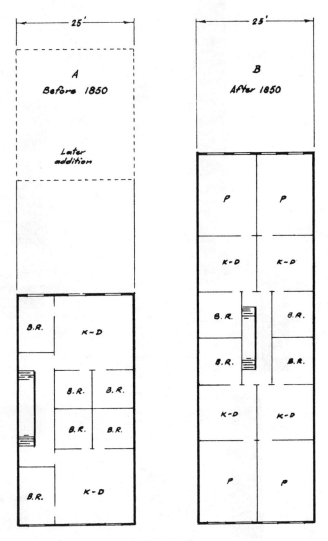

Railroad

Lot size—25' x 100'
Lot coverage—90%
Height of building—6-7 stories
Apts. per floor—4

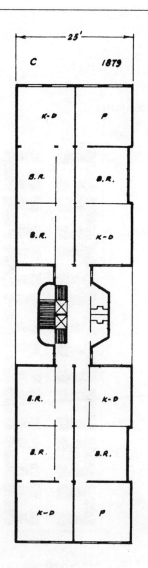

Dumbbell

Lot Size—25' x 100'
Lot coverage—80-90%
Height of building—5-7 stories
Apts. per floor—4

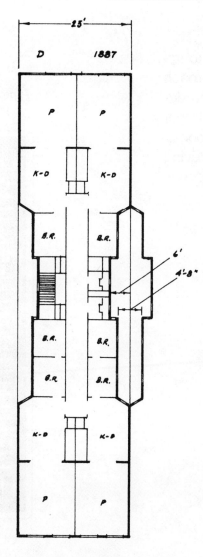

Modified Dumbbell

Same as Dumbbell

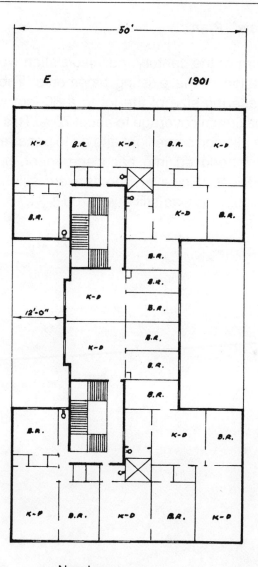

New Law

Lot size—50' x 100'
Lot coverage—70%
Height of building—5-6 stories
Apts. per floor—7-8

"New-Law" Plan

At the turn of the century, new legislation was passed to improve the design of the existing tenements. The new approach was to increase the size of the lot to a 50-foot width and to decrease the maximum coverage to about 70%. This permitted larger courts, which allowed some light and air to penetrate all the rooms. Toilets were introduced into each apartment, greatly improving sanitary conditions. However, rooms were still small and poorly laid out. The building was still a walk-up.

Typical Blocks of Tenements

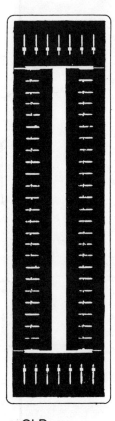

OLD
DUMBBELL

88% lot
coverage

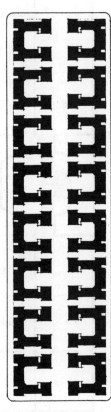

NEW
LAW

50-70% lot
coverage

APARTMENT BUILDINGS

Low-rise

The low-rise apartment building is generally considered to be a structure of 3 stories to 8 stories high. Older buildings usually are in the lower range of 3 to 5 stories and are walk-ups. Newer structures will tend to be taller and be provided with elevators.

For new buildings, the layout and design considerations are the same as for high-rise apartment buildings. In urban areas, many low-rise apartments were built on individual lots. They tend to be located in central areas, along major thoroughfares, or near railroad stations. If they are located in a commercial zone, they would generally have retail stores on the ground or street level.

One characteristic of the older, 5- and 6-story buildings, is that they are not constructed of fireproof materials. In large urban areas, low-rise apartment buildings usually will be located in districts of moderate densities. In less urbanized areas, such buildings may constitute the maximum heights designated by the community. As such, these structures would, by comparison, become high-rise buildings.

From a planning standpoint, a more current use of the low-rise apartment building is in conjunction with high-rise buildings. In large developments, when a mix of height and possibly types of building is desired, the use of low-rise buildings can be very successful. Also, a combination with town houses in a development of less density is possible.

High-rise

The high-rise apartment building is generally considered to be any structure over 8 stories. Over the years, as construction techniques improved, the height of residential building has steadily increased. Today, twenty- to forty-story buildings are not uncommon. Taller buildings can easily be constructed if necessary. All high-rise buildings are of fireproof construction with steel or reinforced concrete. The most common type of buildings are the tower and the slab. Such type of construction is usually necessitated by high land cost in central urban areas.

Most of the structures are relatively new and are provided with good room layouts, adequate light and air, and proper vertical circulation.

High-rise buildings can be constructed individually on their own lots or in large developments such as urban-renewal projects. When they are built on individual lots, they usually are constructed to their maximum limits as to height, coverage, and floor area. Care must be exercised that such large structures do not overwhelm adjacent areas. When built as part of a large project, sufficient controls are usually invoked to provide adequate open space and a good relationship to other structures.

In recent years, many planners have advocated the use of high-rise apartment buildings in suburban and outlying areas. Such use would be strictly controlled and limited to care areas that would form the center of future development resulting from the decentralization of the central cities.

F-15 APARTMENT BUILDINGS

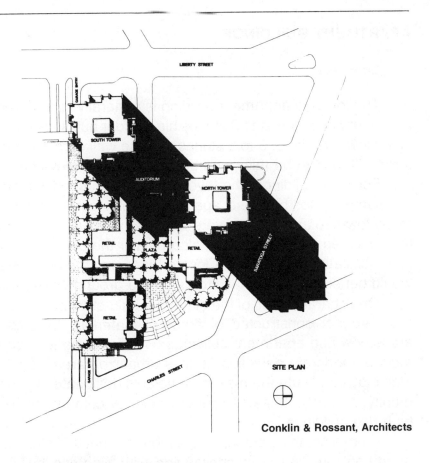

Conklin & Rossant, Architects

Low-rise Apartment Building

Common type of multiple dwelling. It is provided with adequate light and air.

Construction is usually nonfireproof with brick exterior.

Height is often 5-8 stories; building is provided with an elevator. Lot coverage is moderate (50%-70%).

Located on an individual lot. Sometimes may have stores located at the lowest (street) level.

High-rise Apartment Building

Type of construction necessitated by high land costs in built-up urban areas.

Range in height from 6 to 40 stories.

Construction is fireproof with steel frame or poured concrete.

Lot coverage generally less than low-rise apartment house.

Most of these structures are relatively new and are provided with good room layouts, light and air, and several elevators.

LARGE-SCALE DEVELOPMENTS

A project involves more than one building on a large site, usually a superblock. The type of housing can be either low- or high-rise. The site is characterized by low land coverage (20-40%) and provisions for basic community facilities, such as play areas and sitting areas. Construction is dependent upon height of building. Because of low lot coverage, the project often has extensive landscaping and open areas.

The project usually is under one ownership and the dwelling units are rented. In recent years there has been an increase in cooperative and condominium ownership.

The Superblock

The superblock is a relatively large area, usually containing one or more common open spaces, and bounded on all sides by major arterial roads. Secondary and cul-de-sac streets branch out from the major arterial road to provide internal access and service to the residential and nonresidential elements. No through traffic is permitted. Many variations on the superblock are possible. The area of the superblock frequently is used as the basis for the physical organization of the neighborhood or subneighborhood. The superblock is characterized by an articulated street system that will provide proper circulation and access to all buildings, service areas, and parking facilities. Another characteristic of the superblock is the provision of a variety of open spaces and their integration with the residential uses. This would include play lots, playgrounds, and sitting areas. Another important element is a functional layout of pedestrian walks and paths, one that will provide for the complete separation of vehicular and pedestrian circulation.

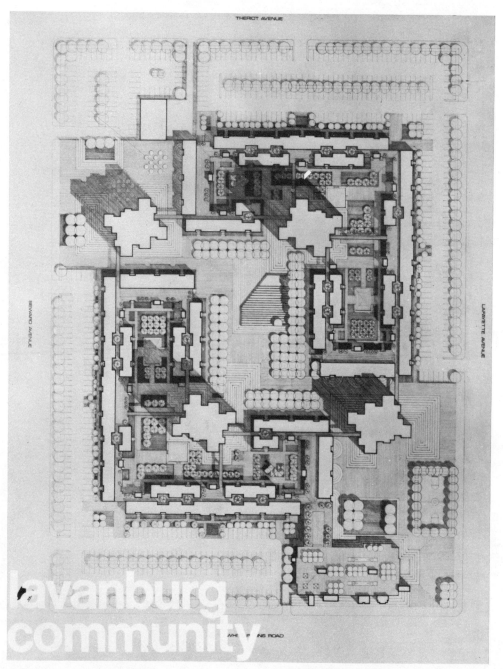

Conklin & Rossant, Architects

Dwelling Access Alternatives

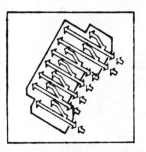

a. direct grade access.

b. stair, exterior gallery access.

c. stair, interior corridor access.

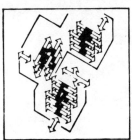

d. stair, interior/exterior core access.

e. elevator, exterior gallery access.

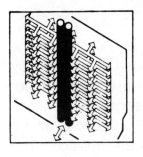

f. elevator, interior corridor access.

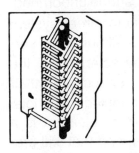

g. elevator, interior core access.

Planning and Design Workbook for Community Participation
Prepared for the State of New Jersey Dept. of Community Affairs by the
Research Center for Urban and Environmental Planning, Princeton University
School of Architecture and Urban Planning—1969

Grouped Dwelling Alternatives

a. direct access units forming a row.

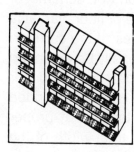

e. exterior access stacked units forming a slab.

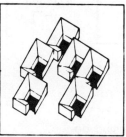

b. direct access or stacked units forming a court.

f. interior access stacked units forming a slab.

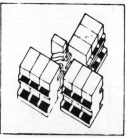

c. direct access or stacked units forming a cluster.

g. interior access stacked units forming a tower.

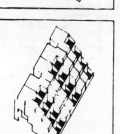

d. interior/exterior access stacked units forming a terrace.

Planning and Design Workbook for Community Participation
Prepared for the State of New Jersey Dept. of Community Affairs by the
Research Center for Urban and Environmental Planning, Princeton University
School of Architecture and Urban Planning—1969

Center-corridor Plan

The center-corridor scheme, or interior-corridor scheme or double-loaded corridor, is the most common type of floor plan. It is characterized by having apartments on both sides of the corridor, thereby making it economical. The corridor can easily be extended allowing a maximum number of apartments per floor and per elevator/stair core. In fact, the building length can be extended indefinitely, provided adequate exit stairs are located at proper intervals to meet local code requirements. The total width of the building is limited to the depth of two apartments plus the corridor, or approximately 50 to 80 feet. The result of this is a narrow width and long length making a building configuration called a "slab" as opposed to a "tower."

One drawback is that it does not provide for through or cross-ventilation except for the four corner apartments. Another limitation is orientation of the building. If the building is facing south, half of the apartments will have good orientation while the other half will be facing north, which is not desirable. The compromise orientation is east-west, which is acceptable, but not considered the best. Also, all apartments, except the corners, have only one exposure. One planning consideration for this type of building is the placement of these slablike buildings on the site. If they are too long, or placed parallel to each other, such buildings tend to visually create a "Chinese-wall" effect.

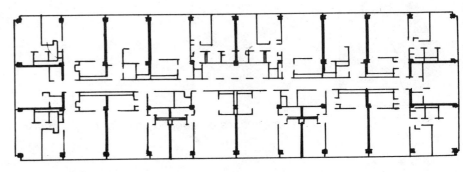

Typical floor

With respect to orientation, in high-rise housing developments, the largest apartments should ideally go in the corners for two-way orientation.

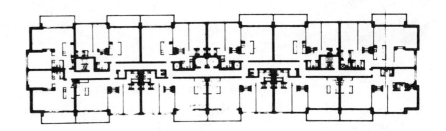

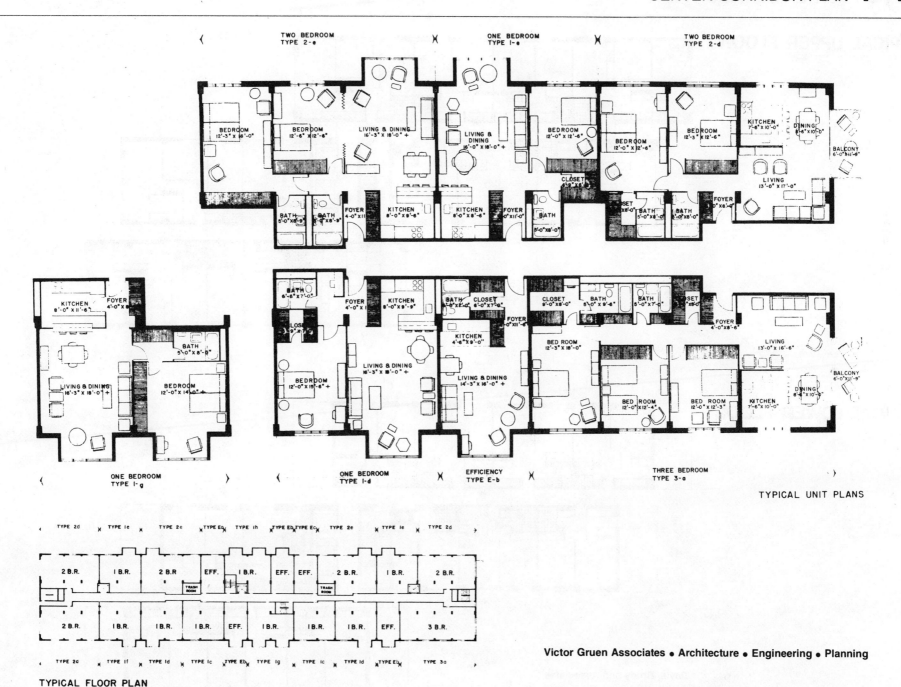

TWO BEDROOM
TYPE 2-e

ONE BEDROOM
TYPE 1-e

TWO BEDROOM
TYPE 2-d

ONE BEDROOM
TYPE 1-g

ONE BEDROOM
TYPE 1-d

EFFICIENCY
TYPE E-b

THREE BEDROOM
TYPE 3-a

TYPICAL UNIT PLANS

TYPICAL FLOOR PLAN

Victor Gruen Associates ● Architecture ● Engineering ● Planning

333

TYPICAL UPPER FLOOR

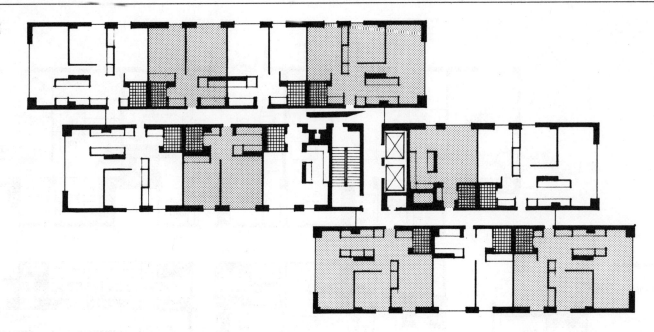

TYPICAL LOWER FLOOR

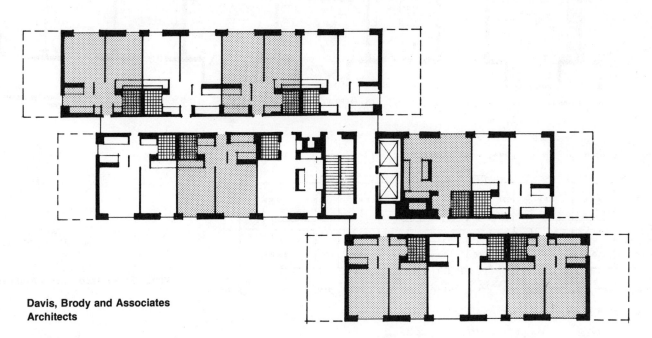

Davis, Brody and Associates
Architects

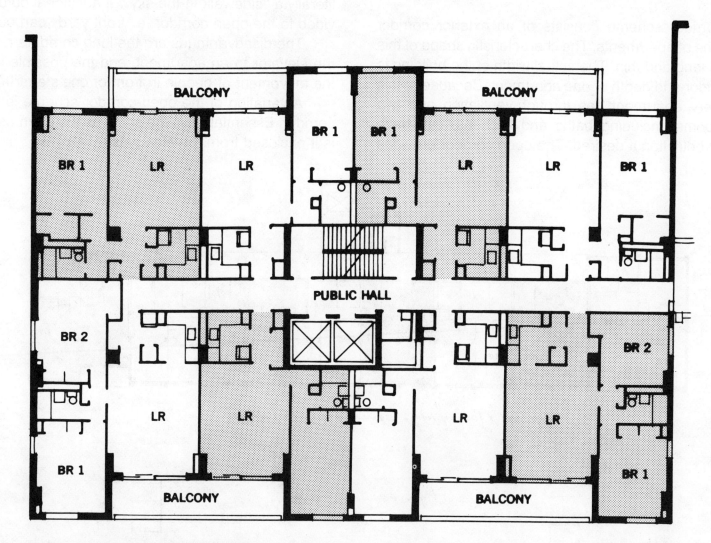

TYPICAL FLOOR PLAN—NORTH TOWER

Riverbend—Davis, Brody & Associates, Architects

Open-corridor Plan

The open-corridor scheme consists of an exterior corridor serving a single line of apartments. The characteristic shape of this type of building is long and thin. The actual width of the building is limited to the corridor and depth of one apartment. Because of this arrangement, every apartment has through-ventilation and two exposures. All rooms, including baths and kitchens, can have natural light and ventilation if desired. The open corridor provides literally a "sidewalk-in-the-sky." If additional outdoor space is provided to the open corridor, a "front yard" can be created.

The disadvantages are the long corridors and distances from the elevator to an apartment, and the possible loss of privacy by the movement of people in front of one's apartment.

A variation of the open-corridor scheme is the single-loaded corridor. Essentially it is the same as the open-corridor except that is it enclosed from the elements.

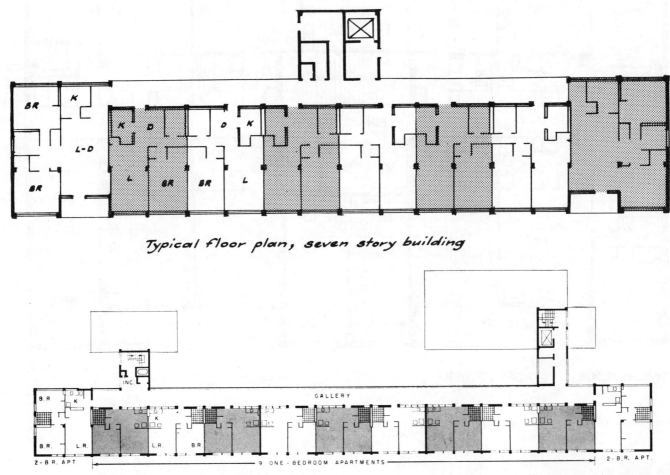

Typical floor plan, seven story building

Archer Courts: Everett F. Quinn & Associates, Architects
Alfred L. Mell, Associate Architect

Skip-stop Plan

A variation of the center-corridor scheme is the so-called "skip-stop" plan. In this arrangement, the elevator stops only on alternate floors and eliminates completely the public corridor on the nonstop floors. The objective is to eliminate nonliving floor area and reduce the number of elevator doors thereby reducing construction costs and making the building more efficient.

By using duplex apartments, through-ventilation can be achieved on the noncorridor level. Also, apartments will have two exposures, which will simplify the problem of orientation.

The main objection to the skip-stop scheme is that each apartment is required to have an interior stair to the alternate level. This may create serious problems for elderly and handicapped people. Another problem is providing two means of egress from each floor, which most building codes require. Exit through common balconies is sometimes accepted as meeting this requirement. A more extreme variation of the skip-stop is to have the elevator stop on every third level. People would walk either up or down to the level of their apartment.

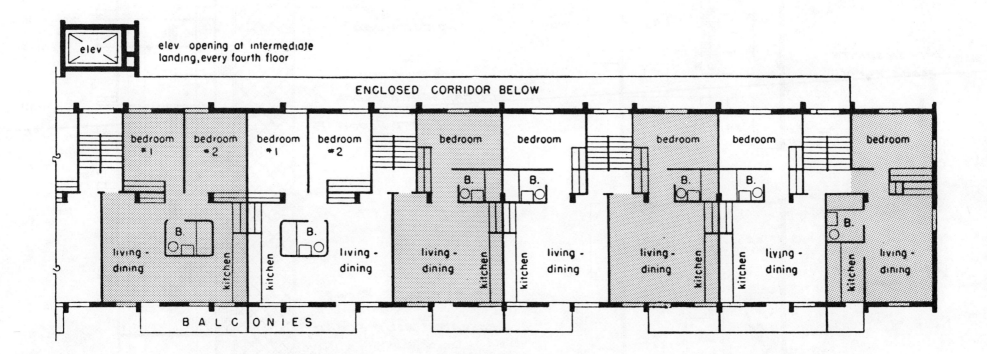

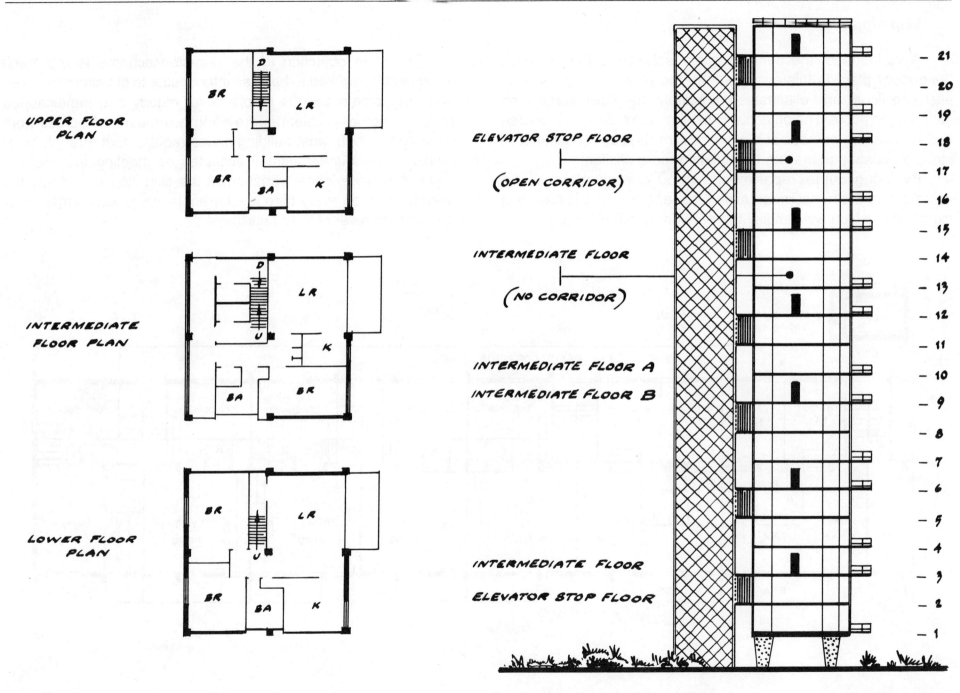

UPPER FLOOR
PLAN

INTERMEDIATE
FLOOR PLAN

LOWER FLOOR
PLAN

ELEVATOR STOP FLOOR

(OPEN CORRIDOR)

INTERMEDIATE FLOOR

(NO CORRIDOR)

INTERMEDIATE FLOOR A

INTERMEDIATE FLOOR B

INTERMEDIATE FLOOR

ELEVATOR STOP FLOOR

338

Tower Plan

The tower scheme consists of a central core with apartments wrapped compactly around it. The overall plan configuration is, or approximates, a square. This provides maximum floor area with minimum exterior perimeter. The usual number of apartments per floor is limited to four or six. The tower scheme has a number of advantages and one serious disadvantage. The most significant advantage is the reduction of lengthy and expensive public corridors. The tower scheme provides cross-ventilation and two exposures for each apartment, which enhances its attractiveness and livability. The tower scheme is also advantageous in site planning. The square plan results in a greater feeling of openness than a slab building. It is also easier to situate on an irregular site or a site with topographical difficulties.

The main disadvantage of the tower scheme is the small number of apartments per core. If a typical floor is limited to only four apartments for each elevator and stair core, this becomes inefficient. Most often the same core can serve up to eight or ten apartments per floor. This drawback has usually restricted the tower to middle income or luxury type of development.

Another minor disadvantage is that one side of the building usually is facing north, which is not ideal. However, since each apartment has two exposures, this is not critical.

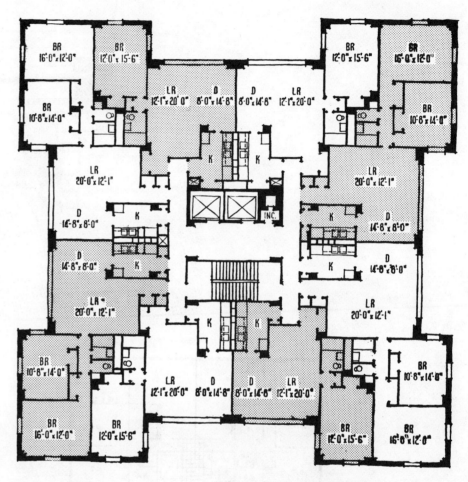

Fordham Hill, Bronx, N.Y.
Leonard Schultze and Associates, Architects

339

Waterside—Davis, Brody & Associates, Architects

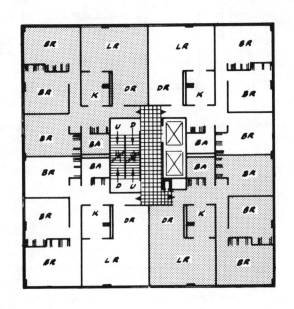

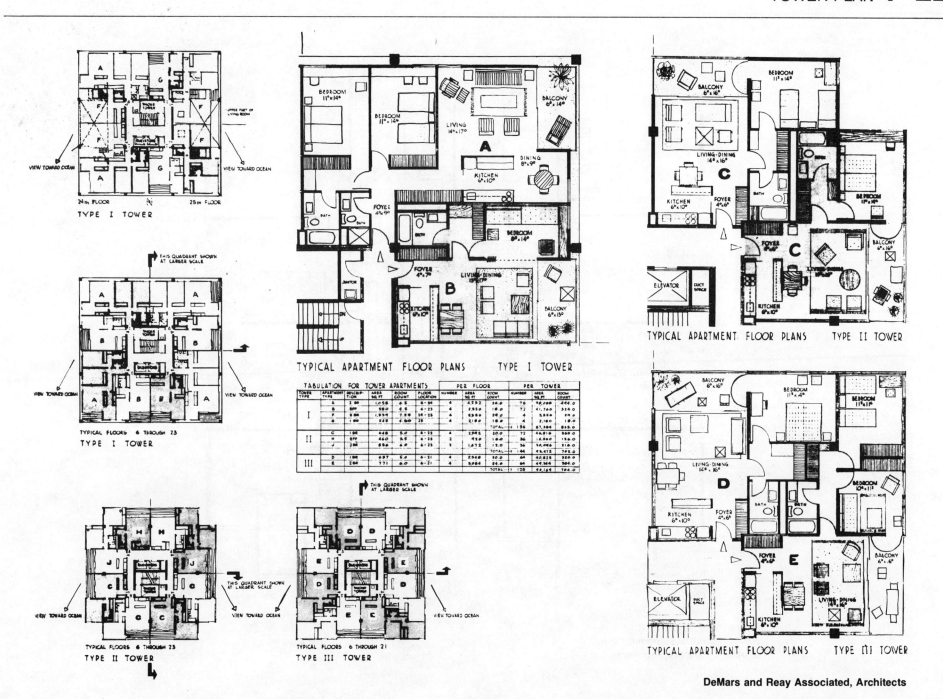

TYPE I TOWER

24TH FLOOR   25TH FLOOR
VIEW TOWARD OCEAN   VIEW TOWARD OCEAN

TYPICAL FLOORS 6 THROUGH 23
TYPE I TOWER

TYPICAL FLOORS 6 THROUGH 23
TYPE II TOWER

TYPICAL FLOORS 6 THROUGH 21
TYPE III TOWER

TYPICAL APARTMENT FLOOR PLANS   TYPE I TOWER

TYPICAL APARTMENT FLOOR PLANS   TYPE II TOWER

TYPICAL APARTMENT FLOOR PLANS   TYPE III TOWER

DeMars and Reay Associated, Architects

341

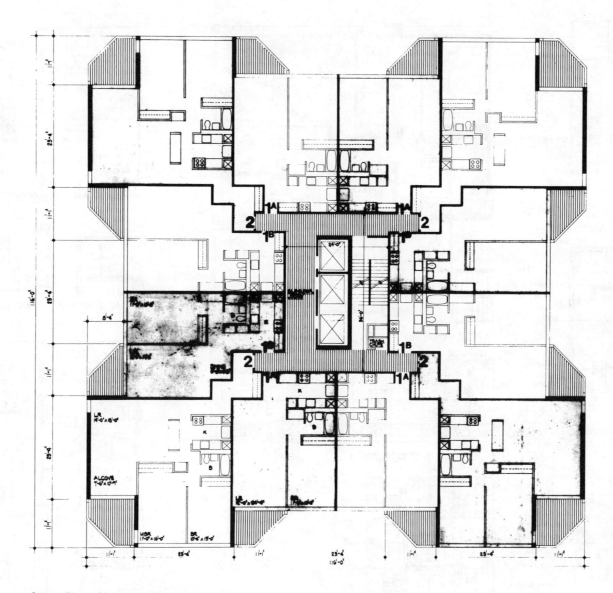

Seven Pines, Yonkers, N.Y.
N.Y.S. Urban Development Corp.
Gruzen & Partners, Architects

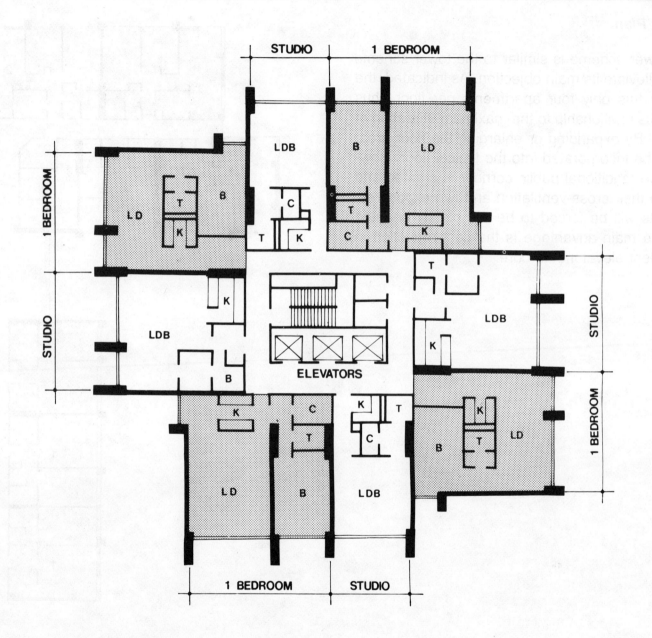

STUDIO | 1 BEDROOM

1 BEDROOM

STUDIO

STUDIO

1 BEDROOM

LDB B LD

LD B

C

T T K

T K C

K

LDB

K T

B

ELEVATORS

LDB

K C

K T

K C T

LD C B

LD B LDB B LD

T

1 BEDROOM | STUDIO

Charles Towers—Conklin & Rossant, Architects

Expanded Tower Plan

The expanded tower scheme is similar to the tower scheme except it attempts to alleviate its main objection. As indicated, the tower scheme usually has only four apartments per floor, thus making it inefficient in its relationship to the maximum utilization of the elevator/stair core. By expanding or enlarging the floor area, more apartments can be incorporated into the typical floor. However, when this is done, additional public corridor is created and some apartments lose their cross-ventilation and two exposures. Also, some apartments will be forced to be completely oriented towards the north. The main advantage is the cost reduction in providing a more efficient elevator/stair core.

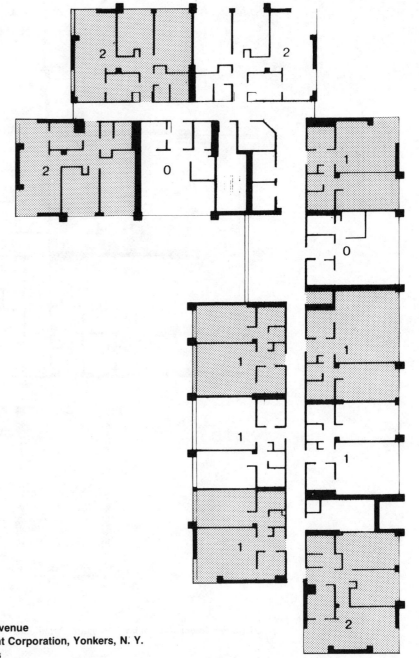

Warburton Houses at Ashburton Avenue
New York State Urban Development Corporation, Yonkers, N. Y.
Louis Sauer Associates, Architects

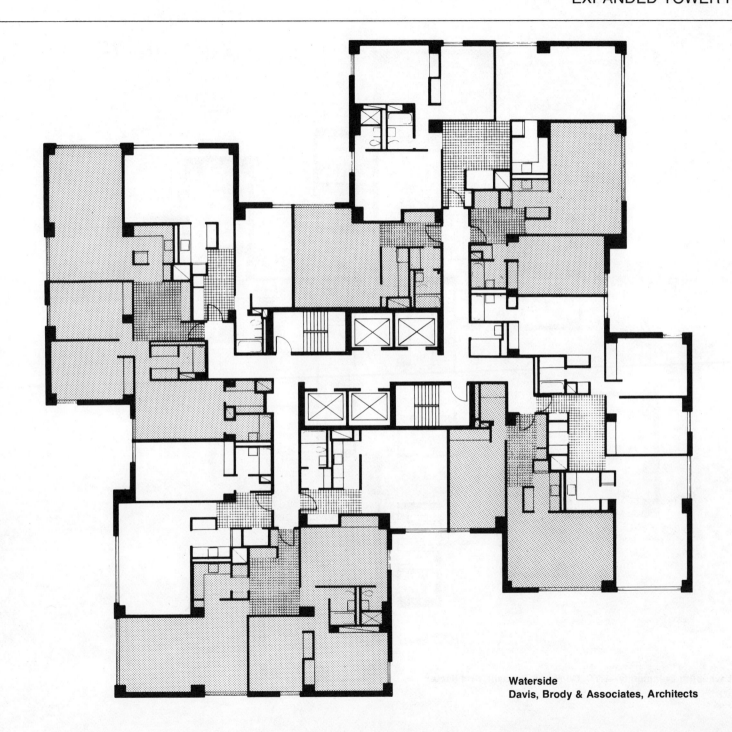

Waterside
Davis, Brody & Associates, Architects

Lavanburg Community—NYC, Conklin & Rossant, Architects

Cross Plan

The cross scheme has four equal wings extending out from a central service core. The most common apartment arrangement is to have two apartments per wing for a total of eight. The amount of corridor space is compact and access to the apartments is directly off the elevator. Since each wing has two apartments, each apartment has some cross-ventilation at the bend of the apartment and two exposures. Because of the configuration, the typical floor has an extensive perimeter, which permits practically all rooms to have windows. Each apartment is situated at a 90 degree angle with the opposite apartment, which is acceptable.

One major difficulty with the cross plan is orientation. No matter which direction the building is facing, some apartments will have unacceptable orientations, while other will have good ones. For example, if the building is placed on a north-south axis, two apartments will face each of the four compass points.

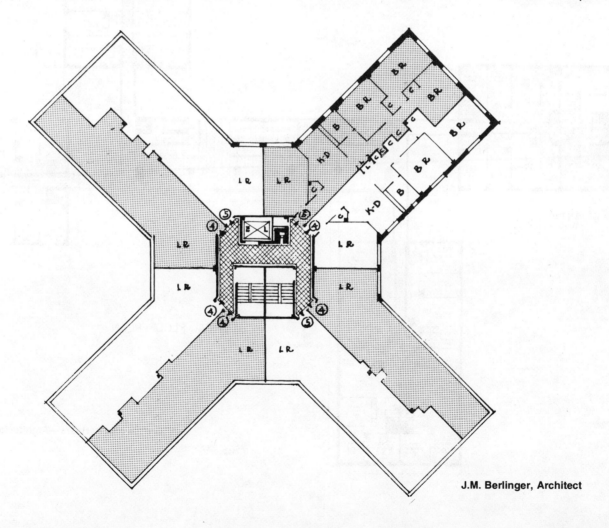

J.M. Berlinger, Architect

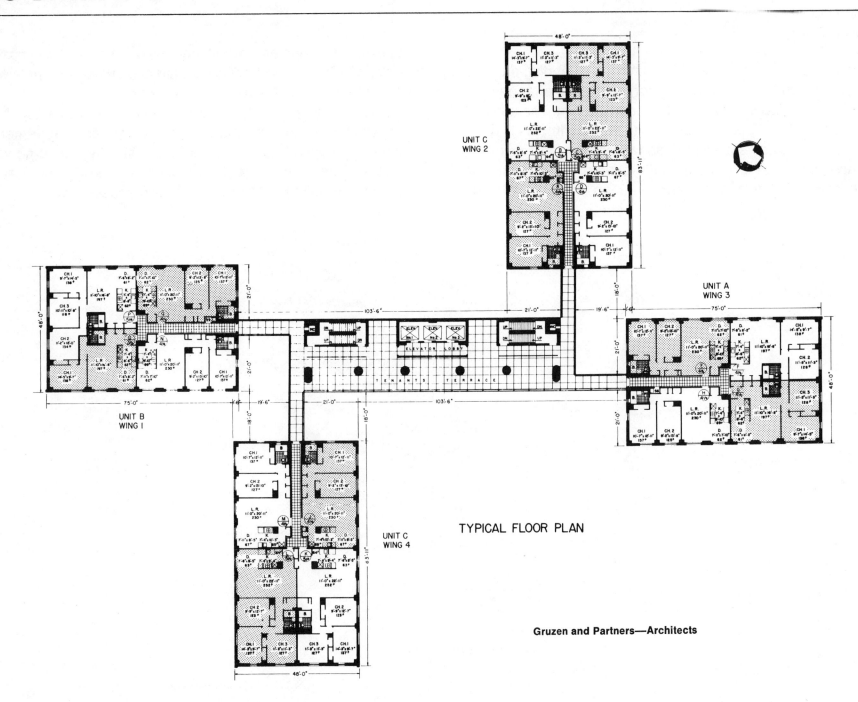

UNIT C
WING 2

UNIT A
WING 3

UNIT B
WING 1

UNIT C
WING 4

TYPICAL FLOOR PLAN

Gruzen and Partners—Architects

Five-wing Plan

The five-wing radial scheme is similar to the cross scheme except that it has an additional wing. Access to the apartments is direct from the service core. Each wing has two apartments making a total of ten apartments per floor. The motivating factor for this scheme is the larger number of apartments per elevator/stair core.

Each apartment has some cross-ventilation at the end of the unit. Also, two exposures are achieved. The length of building perimeter is more extensive and complicated than the simple cross plan. The cost savings in providing ten apartments per service core can easily be offset by the complications in the perimeter construction. The orientation limitations are even more severe than in the cross plan. No matter which direction the building is facing, more apartments will have unacceptable or poor orientations. More critical, however, is the fact that each wing is only 72° to each other. This results in apartments that can partially face each other and thereby reduce privacy.

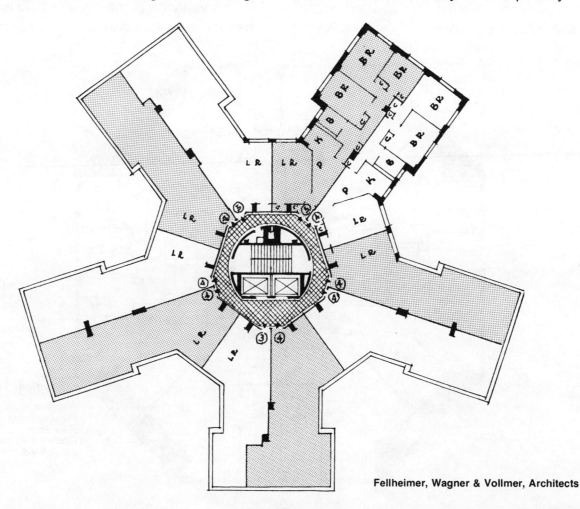

Fellheimer, Wagner & Vollmer, Architects

Circular Plan

The circular scheme is similar to the tower. It contains a central service core with apartments wrapped around it. The number of apartments possible depends upon the size of the apartments and the diameter of the building. Access to the apartments is directly off a corridor at the center.

The major advantage is that, as any circle, the plan encompasses the largest floor area with the minimum amount of perimeter. Also, the service core area is minimal and located at the center, which is undesirable as living space.

A drawback of this plan is in orientation. One side is always facing north while the other sides have the full range of orientations. Through- or cross-ventilation is not possible.

Like the tower plan, the circular plan is advantageous in site planning. It creates a greater feeling of openness and spaciousness than the slab. It is also easier to situate on irregular sites or those with topographical difficulties.

A variation of the circular plan is the spiral. The spiral scheme has a continuous corridor from bottom to top.

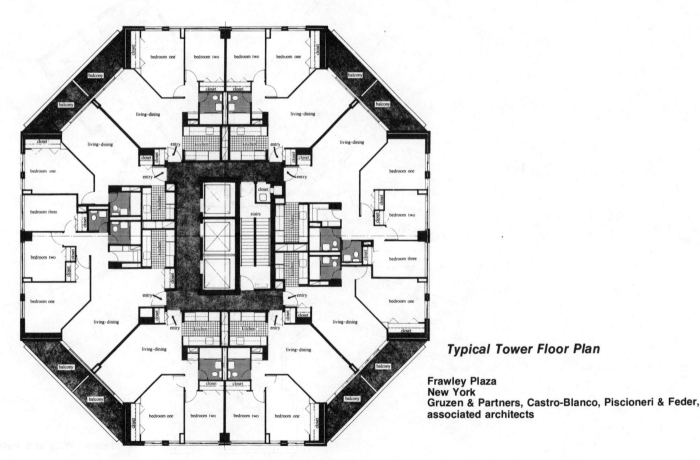

Typical Tower Floor Plan

Frawley Plaza
New York
Gruzen & Partners, Castro-Blanco, Piscioneri & Feder,
associated architects

Terrace Plan

The terrace plan is generally a single-loaded corridor arrangement with each succeeding floor set back from the floor below. This creates an extensive terrace area that can be utilized as an extension of the adjacent apartment. The building is usually oriented towards a view or the sun.

As a single-loaded corridor scheme it has the same characteristics. It can have through-ventilation and a good orientation for all or most of its apartments. The terrace area is expensive to build but its cost can be offset by the added livability it creates. One major difficulty is the vertical alignment of stairs, elevators, and utility lines. In the best of schemes, these elements would be in direct vertical alignment. With a terrace scheme, this is difficult to achieve, and therefore creates serious problems.

The ideal siting for this type of building is along a steeply sloping terrain where it would naturally take advantage of the physical conditions.

Residential Court

M. Paul Friedberg and Associates

Habitat—Rochester
Architect—Safdie
PA, June, 1971

MODULAR UNITS

The modular scheme is based upon the prefabricated modular housing unit. The module, which is contructed in a factory and delivered to the site as one unit, can be arranged in many ways. They can be simply stacked, terraced, or oriented in different directions. Heights of each group can be varied to create greater interest.

With such a system, the advantage is the flexibility that is possible. Maximum advantage of orientation can easily be achieved. One disadvantage is that with greater complexity of arrangement, it becomes more difficult to resolve the problems of circulation, elevators, structure, and utility lines.

Innovative building systems can be identified and grouped under three structural types:

1. Post and beam systems
2. Slab systems
3. Box systems

The groupings of building systems into three structural categories is intended to facilitate comparative evaluations of different systems, rather than to suggest that innovation in building systems may be only structural. Such innovation of necessity concerns the total process of design, production, assembly and maintenance of a nonstructural subsystem, as well as the structural frame.

The following discussion will identify the attributes of each structural type, describe the examples, and evaluate their potential for use.

SOURCE: *Developing New Communities*, Dept. of Housing and Urban Development, Washington, D.C., 1968

Post and Beam (Frame) Systems

The example shown here is a model of the Neal Mitchell system, which is a post and beam system.

Post and beam systems usually consist of premanufactured columns and beams and infill panels of either a structural or nonstructural nature. When lightweight concrete is used as a structural material, the building components are frequently light enough to allow placement without elaborate construction machinery. This kind of system is quite versatile with respect to site design and interior planning.

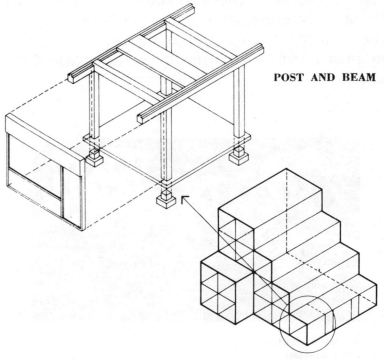

POST AND BEAM

Neal Mitchell System

Slab or Panel Systems

Slab or panel systems are almost universally made of reinforced concrete, the variations occurring primarily in the degree to which other components and assemblies are integrated into the slab, and its structural functions. The majority of European systems are of the slab variety, and hence slab systems have been subject to more use and experimentation than other system types. These systems make extensive use of off-site fabrication yards and factories, specialized moving and handling equipment, and automated scheduling systems. The amount of plant required is frequently so extensive that small building projects cannot be undertaken using slab systems. Key factors in the use of these systems are the definitions of a large and fairly homogeneous market to amortize the cost of equipment, and its location within a specified economic radius of operation. The illustration indicates typical structural characteristics of slab systems.

Slab systems have a poor record of adaptability to varying site conditions and interior space requirements. Interior planning arrangements are usually dictated by the spans of structural components. Most slab systems utilize longitudinal bearing walls, thus resulting in a minimum of variation. Scandinavian systems are more versatile in that they utilize core bearing walls, leaving the building facade free for a variety of architectural treatments. In general, slab systems are notable for their speed of erection and control of quality of component. However, past experience has shown their design versatility to be somewhat limited. It seems to be a reasonable assumption that considerable modification of European slab systems must be made in order to meet American standards.

The intermediate box system is usually a monolithic element designed to be dropped into place in a space grid of similar cells. Elements in this system are often whole rooms, such as bedrooms and living rooms, and frequently include mechanical, electrical, and utility subsystems.

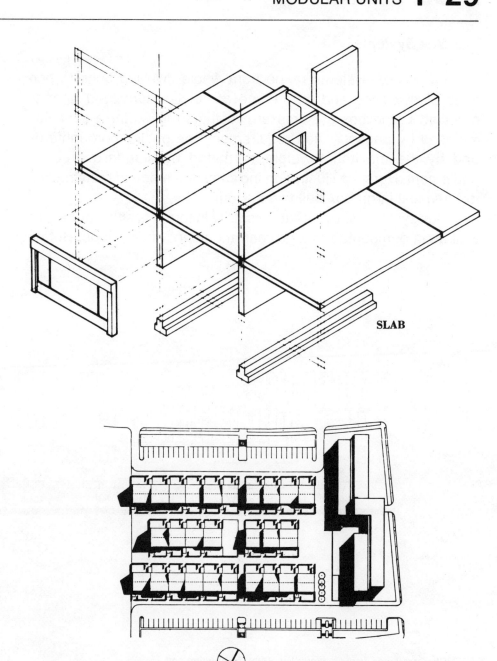

SLAB

Fort Lincoln Project
Harry Weese—Architect

SOURCE: *Developing New Communities*, Dept. of Housing and Urban Development, Washington, D.C., 1968

353

Box Systems

Large box systems range from whole dwelling units to portions of dwellings and may come completely furnished prior to erection. Large box systems are restricted in width, a limitation imposed by transportation requirements on public thoroughfares and by the maximum weight permitted by standard erection equipment. Here the illustration indicates the mode of construction for a typical large box building system.

Box systems show great versatility in terms of site planning as well as in demountability and rearrangement of dwellings. But no solution to cost increases resulting from deviations from straight stacking has yet been found. In addition, unconventional stacking has another drawback: Often it forms a structure of mixed uses (e.g. parking, access and egress), which leads, in turn, to conflicts with conventional code regulations. The mobile home is a unique example of a large box system that has met the financial and mobility needs of a large segment of the American housing market, and has therefore become the focus of attention on the part of industrialized building advocates as an element to be used in stacked systems.

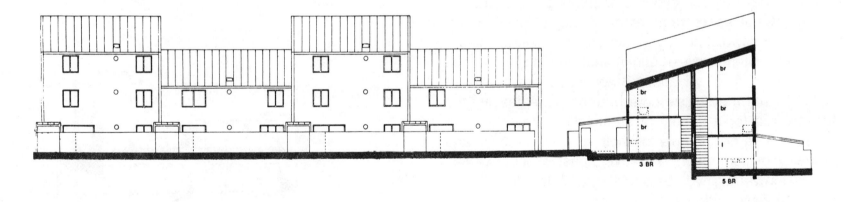

Fort Lincoln Project
Harry Weese—Architect

SOURCE: *Developing New Communities*, Dept. of Housing and
Urban Development, Washington, D.C., 1968

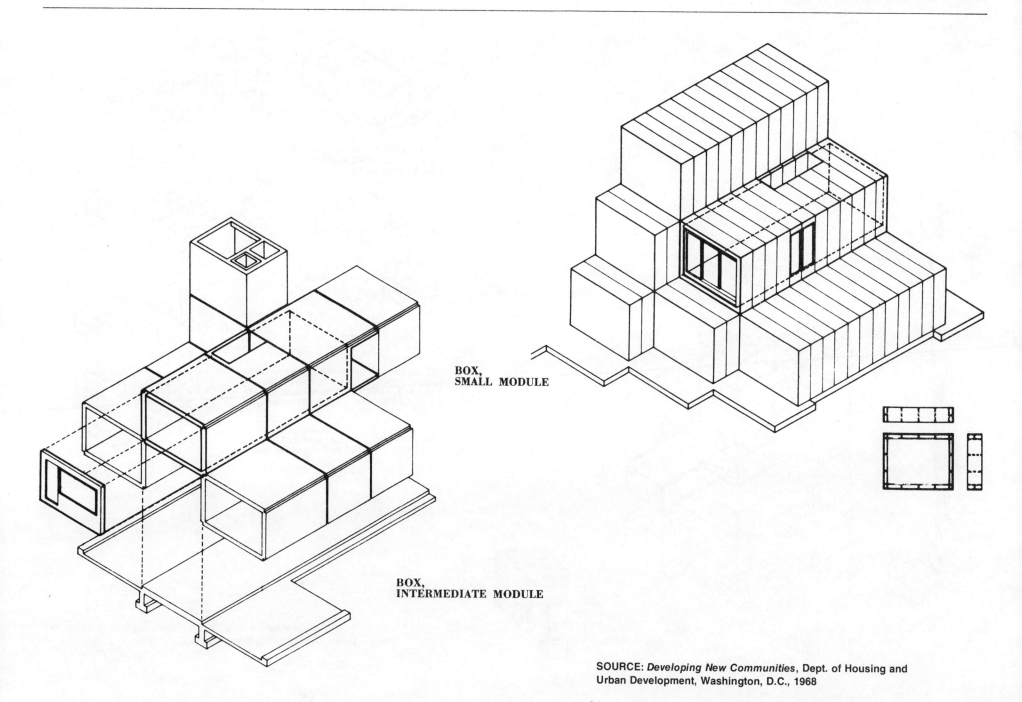

BOX,
SMALL MODULE

BOX,
INTERMEDIATE MODULE

SOURCE: *Developing New Communities*, Dept. of Housing and
Urban Development, Washington, D.C., 1968

355

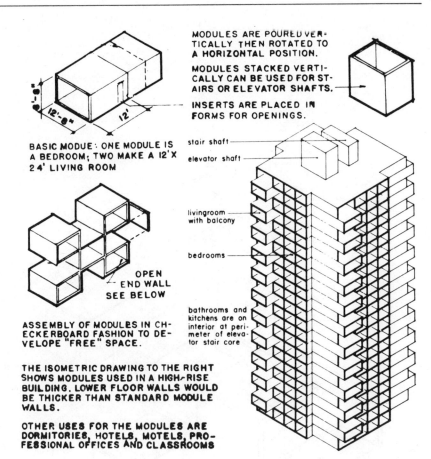

MODULES ARE POURED VERTICALLY THEN ROTATED TO A HORIZONTAL POSITION.

MODULES STACKED VERTICALLY CAN BE USED FOR STAIRS OR ELEVATOR SHAFTS.

INSERTS ARE PLACED IN FORMS FOR OPENINGS.

BASIC MODUE: ONE MODULE IS A BEDROOM; TWO MAKE A 12'X 24' LIVING ROOM

OPEN END WALL SEE BELOW

ASSEMBLY OF MODULES IN CHECKERBOARD FASHION TO DEVELOPE "FREE" SPACE.

THE ISOMETRIC DRAWING TO THE RIGHT SHOWS MODULES USED IN A HIGH-RISE BUILDING. LOWER FLOOR WALLS WOULD BE THICKER THAN STANDARD MODULE WALLS.

OTHER USES FOR THE MODULES ARE DORMITORIES, HOTELS, MOTELS, PROFESSIONAL OFFICES AND CLASSROOMS

stair shaft
elevator shaft
livingroom with balcony
bedrooms
bathrooms and kitchens are on interior at perimeter of elevator stair core

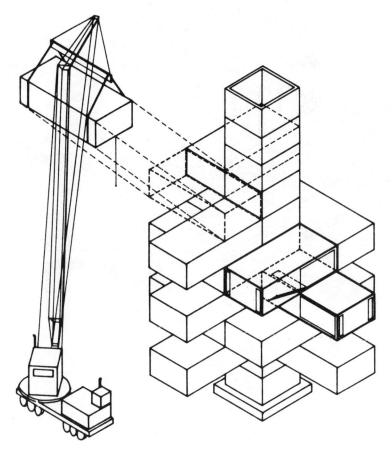

BOX, LARGE MODULE

SOURCE: *Developing New Communities*, Dept. of Housing and Urban Development, Washington, D.C., 1968

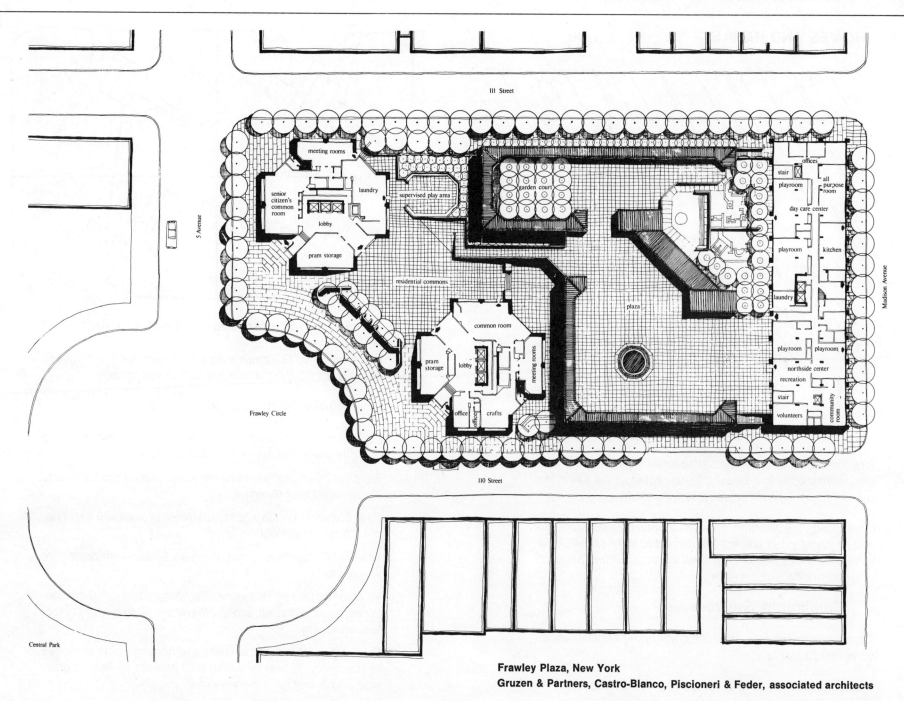

Frawley Plaza, New York
Gruzen & Partners, Castro-Blanco, Piscioneri & Feder, associated architects

MOBILE HOMES AND PARKS

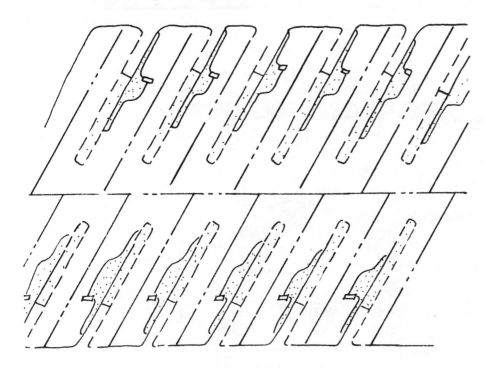

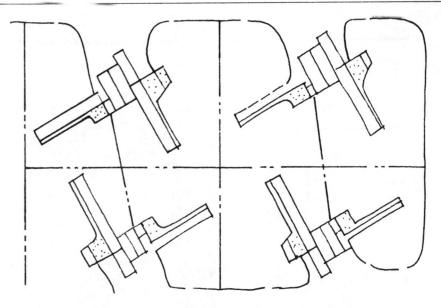

Parallel Arrangement–Zoning

Site should be in a residential zone if mobile home courts are permitted; or in a heavier zone provided the site is not subject to unhealthful or adverse influences.

If unzoned, the location chosen should be such that the mobile home court will not be subject to unhealthful or adverse influences and will not itself adversely affect adjacent neighborhoods.

Community Facilities

Accessible to schools, churches, shopping facilities as for other residential uses.

Reasonable commuting distance to employment.

Perpendicular Arrangement–Lot Area

Lot area of 3,000 square feet or larger for each mobile home, with possibly a few lots somewhat smaller.

Mobile Home Stand

To accommodate modern mobile homes, the stand where home is placed should be 10 feet by 50 feet.

From mobile home stand to the stand line on opposite side of street, 60 feet minimum.

To a common parking area, roadway or walk, 20 feet typical, 10 feet minimum.

To a public highway or major street, 50 feet with protective screening.

To other boundary of the mobile home court, 25 feet if adjoining uses are compatible; otherwise, 50 feet with protective screening.

Sum of side yards at entry side and nonentry side of mobile home stand, 32 feet minimum with at least 15 feet on entry side and 5 feet on nonentry side.

Major growth of the mobile home industry began after World War II and was spurred by the housing shortage that existed at that time. In 1947, 60,000 mobile homes were produced. These units had an average size of 8 feet wide by 27 feet long, comparable to the size of travel trailers now produced.

Between 1947 and 1954, primarily because of market demand, lengths increased and in 1954 the first 10-foot wide units were produced. Since 1954 the size of mobile homes has steadily increased until currently almost 18 percent of the mobile homes produced are 12 or more feet wide and 55 or more feet long. It is now possible to transport separately two full-size elements, connect them on the lot to form a single mobile home, and obtain floor areas of up to 1,800 square feet.

Production figures indicate that about 1,600,000 mobile homes were produced in the period from World War II through 1964. It is estimated that about 70 percent of these mobile homes were in use in 1964 as dwelling units. To accommodate these units, there were more than 20,200 mobile home parks in the United States containing approximately 880,000 lots.

Mobile homes constitute an increasing percentage of the new housing supply each year. In 1960, shipments of new mobile homes accounted for 9.6 percent of all new private, nonfarm, single-family housing units. By 1963, the percentage had increased to 13.4 percent and even further increases are indicated.

The number of Americans living in mobile homes is likewise increasing. In 1956, approximately 2 million people lived in mobile homes and by 1963 the number increased to 4 million.

SITE PLANNING

Location and Area of Site

Sites selected for mobile home parks should be well-drained and free from topographical or geographical hindrances or other conditions unfavorable to a proper residential environment.

Sites should not be located near swamps, marshes or other breeding places for insects and rodents, or heavy industrial zones with objectionable odors or noise. The site should have good natural drainage, or a storm-drainage system should be provided. Drainage from the park should not endanger any water supply. The site should be graded to eliminate depressions and provide a uniform ground surface. Steep slopes should be graded as much as possible to minimize the hazards they present.

Because mobile homes are for residential use, they should preferably be placed in residentially zoned districts rather than in commercial or industrial districts. Wherever possible, mobile home parks should be so located as to be accessible to public water and sewage systems.

The area of a mobile home park must be sufficient to accommodate (1) the desired number of mobile home lots (it is recommended that a minimum of 50 mobile home lots be constructed in any new park to obtain a better designed, more economical plan), (2) parking areas for motor vehicles, (3) access roads and walkways, and (4) recreation facilities. Additional area must be provided for management buildings, service buildings, or other structures to be included.

Experience has shown that mobile home park designs should be based on local conditions since neither the repetitious application of one lot design nor any arbitrary conglomeration of various modules will result in good planning. Local conditions that might affect a particular site plan include: the size, shape, and topography of the site and surrounding area; land costs; local codes and ordinances; the uses of adjacent property; the availability of water supply and sewage disposal facilities; and the needs of any special groups in the park, such as the elderly.

The best designs are those that make effective use of existing topographical conditions and properly blend in an adequate amount of open area, recreation area, and other common-use area. See illustrations for possible modules and arrangements of mobile homes.

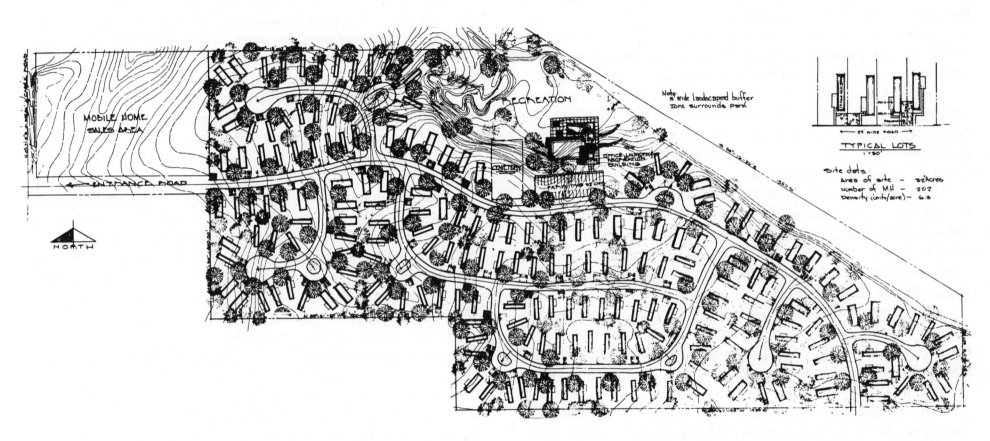

SOURCE: Land Development Division, Mobile Homes Manufacturers Association

Before land is acquired for a mobile home park, the health authority should be consulted regarding the compliance of the proposed site with existing health regulations. Other local agencies, such as zoning or planning commissions, should also be consulted.

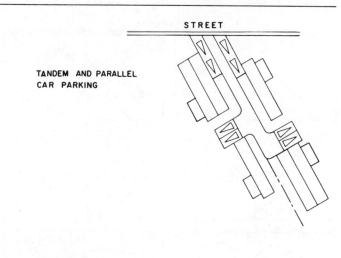

TANDEM AND PARALLEL
CAR PARKING

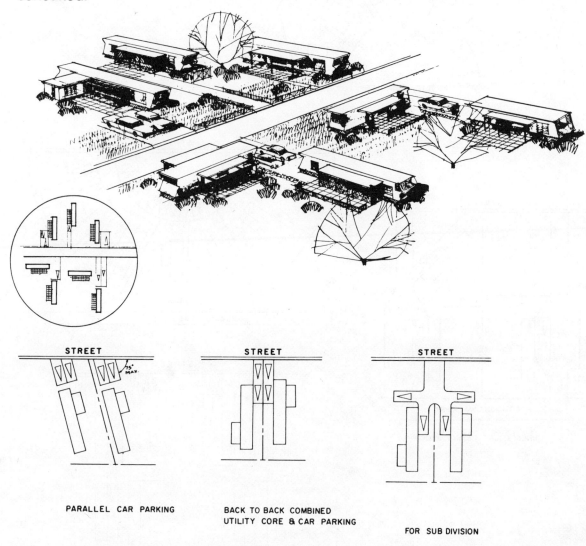

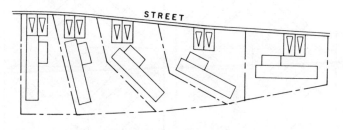

TRANSITION OF MOBILE HOME STAND

STREET

PARALLEL CAR PARKING

STREET

BACK TO BACK COMBINED
UTILITY CORE & CAR PARKING

STREET

FOR SUB DIVISION

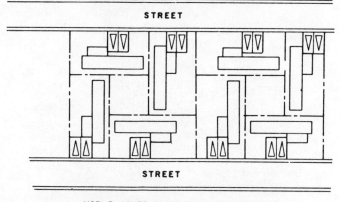

MOBILE HOMES PARALLEL & PERPENDICULAR
TO STREET.

SOURCE: Land Development Division, Mobile Homes Manufacturers Association

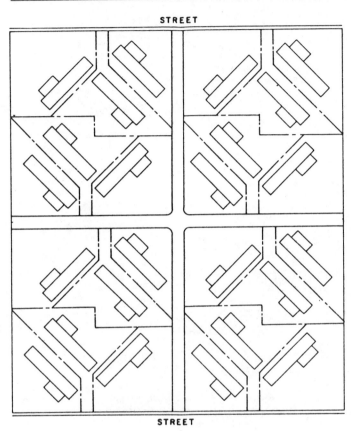

THREE UNITS FOR INTERIOR BLOCKS.

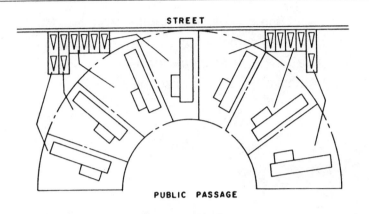

PUBLIC PASSAGE

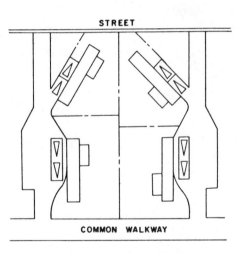

COMMON WALKWAY

INNER COURT NEIGHBORHOOD

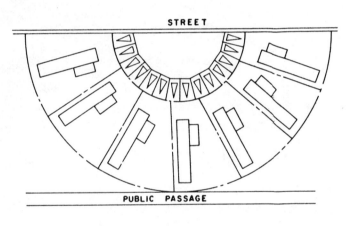

PUBLIC PASSAGE

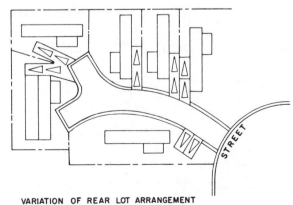

VARIATION OF REAR LOT ARRANGEMENT

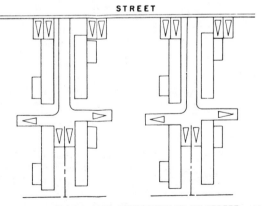

MOBILE HOMES PERPENDICULAR TO STREET

SOURCE: Land Development Division, Mobile Homes Manufacturers Association

Roads and Parking Facilities

All roads in mobile home parks should provide for convenient vehicular circulation. Pavements should be of adequate widths to accommodate anticipated parking and traffic loads.

Entrance streets that connect the internal streets of a mobile home park to a public street or road should have a minimum width of 34 feet if parking is permitted along both sides or 27 feet if parking is permitted on only one side. If parking is not allowed, the width can be reduced to 24 feet provided the entrance street is more than 100 feet long and does not provide access to abutting mobile home lots within the first 100 feet.

All typical internal streets should have a minimum width of 24 feet. However, the width of minor internal streets can be reduced to 18 feet if parking is prohibited on both sides. Minor streets are (1) two-way streets that are less than 500 feet in length and serve less than 25 mobile homes and (2) one-way streets, of any length, that provide access to abutting mobile home lots on one side only. Cul-de-sacs should be limited in length to 1,000 feet and should be provided with a surface turning circle of at least 60 feet in diameter.

The proper design of street intersections is an important safety consideration. Within 100 feet of intersections, streets should be at approximately right angles. Street intersections should be at least 150 feet apart and the intersection of more than two streets at one point should be avoided.

Street grades should not be excessive, especially at intersections. It is suggested that grades be less than eight percent whenever possible; however, short runs of up to 12 percent can be used if necessary.

All streets should be provided with a smooth, hard, and dense surface that is properly drained and durable under normal use and weather conditions.

Off-street parking, in the form of parking bays or individual parking spaces on each lot, should be provided to reduce traffic hazards and improve the appearance of the mobile home park. Parking spaces should be provided in sufficient number to obtain a ratio of at least five spaces per every four mobile home lots in order to accommodate two-car tenants and guests. Every parking space should be designed and located so as to be convenient for use and should be within 200 feet of the mobile home it is to serve.

Walkways

All mobile home parks should be provided with walkways where pedestrian traffic is expected to be concentrated, such as around recreation, management, or service areas and between individual mobile homes. It is recommended that these common walks be at least 3½ feet wide.

Walks should be provided on each individual lot to connect the mobile home with a common walk, street, or paved surface. Such walks should be at least 2 feet wide.

Mobile Home Lots

Every mobile home lot should contain at least 2,500 square feet of area to accommodate modern mobile homes and their appurtenances and to assure adequate clearances between mobile homes and other structures. Many of the mobile homes presently being manufactured are between 50 and 60 feet long and 10 and 12 feet wide. Some are as large as 70 feet long and 24 feet wide. These larger units require correspondingly larger lots. Lot sizes of 3,000 square feet and more are frequently used to accommodate the larger mobile homes and provide more privacy to residents. Some other advantages of larger lots are that they facilitate later changes in design, such as the addition of carports or other accessory structures to mobile homes, and they also provide assurance against premature obsolescence of the mobile home park. All lots within any mobile home park should not be the same size and shape if different-sized mobile homes are to be accommodated and if effective use is to be made of the available space.

It is generally agreed that small lots contribute to overcrowding and create an undesirable appearance, especially when used to accommodate the larger mobile homes. A practical program to eliminate undersized lots should be developed by the local governmental agency having authority that is agreeable to all organizations concerned, including mobile home park operators and owners, the local health authority, and other involved groups. Once adopted, such a program should be enforced to assure that all mobile home lots not meeting established minimum space requirements will be eliminated.

There should be a clearance of at least 15 feet between adjacent mobile homes and between mobile homes and other structures except that mobile homes placed end-to-end need a clearance of only 10 feet when opposing rear walls are staggered. Mobile homes should be at least 25 feet from any park property line abutting upon a public street or highway, 15 feet from all other park property lines, and 10 feet from any area such as a park street, a common parking area, or common walkway. When determining clearances, any accessory structure that has a horizontal area exceeding 25 square feet, located within 10 feet of a window on a mobile home, should be considered as part of the mobile home if the accessory structure has an opaque top or roof higher than the window.

If driveways are provided for individual mobile home lots, they should be at least 8 feet wide, with an individual 2 feet added if they also serve as walks. The on-lot parking space served by the driveway should have dimensions of 9 feet wide by 20 feet long.

It may be desirable to provide storage facilities for each lot in order to discourage the storing of objects under mobile homes. Many mobile homes presently built do not contain ample space for storing equipment such as rakes, shovels, garden hose, lawn chairs, and other similar items. The storage of such items under a mobile home is undesirable since they can provide a potential harborage for rodents, snakes, insects, and other pests.

Recreation Areas

Mobile home parks that accommodate 25 or more mobile homes should be provided with at least one easily accessible recreation area. When several different age groups are to be provided for, it may be desirable to have two or more separate areas to serve the varied interests.

For safety reasons, recreation areas should always be located where they are free of traffic hazards. It may also be desirable to provide some sort of buffer zone around the area such as trees, bushes, or other vegetative growth. A recreation area can be located adjacent to recreation or service buildings, if provided for efficient construction, use, and maintenance of both the area and the structure.

Recreation areas should be provided in a ratio of at least 100 square feet of space per each mobile home lot. However, many planners will provide more recreational space than the minimum, depending on the availability of recreational facilities in the neighborhood of the mobile home park. Swimming pools, recreation buildings and child play areas can be considered as fulfilling part of the total requirement for recreational area. Each outdoor recreation area should contain at least 2,500 square feet of area to assure adequate space for all activities.

Swimming pools should be constructed and operated in accordance with all applicable State and local requirements and regulations.

Service Buildings and Other Structures

Every mobile home park should be provided with a service building containing emergency sanitary facilities consisting of at least one lavatory and one flush toilet for each sex per each 100 mobile home lots. Where feasible, the consolidation of sanitary, laundry, management, and other service facilities in a single building and location is recommended if the single location will adequately serve all mobile home lots. Consolidation is preferable for efficient construction, use, and maintenance of all facilities.

Service Areas

Where areas for the outdoor drying of clothes are necessary, it has been found that approximately 2,500 square feet per 100 mobile home lots is adequate with rotated use. It may be desirable to locate the drying yard near the service or laundry building, if provided, and as far as possible from roadways or traveled areas. It has been found practical to provide clothes-drying facilities on the individual mobile home lots provided that the drying units are standardized and are properly located and installed. Where the clothes-drying facilities are permitted on the individual mobile home lots, it is suggested that they be provided as a part of the basic facilities to assure that the same type of unit, located in the same general area of each mobile home lot, is used throughout the park. Umbrella-type lines in permanent sockets are recommended. The use of individual drying facilities also requires that the owner or operator develop and enforce rules that permit clothes drying only on the facilities provided. All clothes-drying areas, whether centrally located near the service building or on the individual mobile home lot, should be adequately screened from view so as not to detract from the appearance of the mobile home park or be objectionable to residents on adjacent property.

If desired, car-wash and other general-purpose facilities can be provided as a service to residents of the mobile home park. Any such facilities should be properly constructed and preferably screened from view.

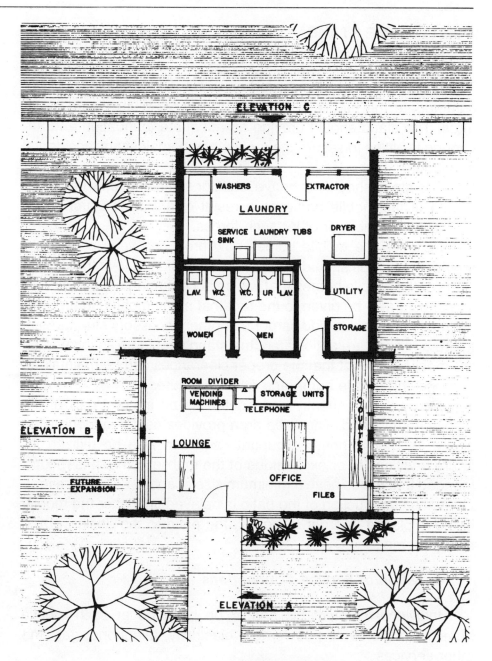

FLOOR PLAN

MOBILE HOME STAND
General

A stand should be provided on every mobile home lot to accommodate the mobile home and its attached accessory structures. The stand should provide an adequate foundation and anchoring facilities to secure the mobile home against any accidental movement.

The stand should not heave, shift, or settle unevenly under the weight of the mobile home as a result of any frost action, poor drainage, vibration, or other such forces.

Because the mobile homes now produced vary in size and shape, the stands should be individually designed to fit the dimensions of the mobile homes that will be accommodated. Consideration should also be given to the fact that many mobile home owners may later want to add carports or other accessory structures. If future additions are anticipated, the stand should be so located on the mobile home lot that the proper clearances can be maintained between the mobile home and other structures.

Patios are frequently constructed as an integral part of the mobile home stand. The patio area provides useful outdoor living space for mobile home occupants and can also be utilized for future additions to or expansions of the mobile home. It is recommended that patios have a minimum size of about 180 square feet. Often the construction of the patio is delayed until after the mobile home is placed in order to best fit the patio to the design of the mobile home.

Location of Service Connections

Individual connections should be provided at each mobile home stand for water, sewerage, electricity, telephone, gas and other services.

WATER SUPPLY
General

An adequate and safe supply of water under pressure should be provided to each mobile home lot. The source and distribution system should be satisfactorily constructed and approved by the health authority having jurisdiction.

Sewage Treatment

If possible, the sewerage system of a mobile home park should be connected to a public sewerage system. If public sewers are not available within a reasonable distance of the mobile home park, adequate treatment facilities must be installed to dispose of the sewage. Where the sewerage system of the mobile park is not connected to a public sewer, any proposed sewage disposal facilities should be approved by the health authority prior to construction. The effluent from such treatment facilities should not be discharged into any body of water without approval.

REFUSE HANDLING
General

Public health problems are often associated with improper storage, collection, and disposal of refuse. There are significant relationships between the incidence of certain diseases in humans and animals and improper refuse handling. It is also common knowledge that many hazards and nuisances, such as fire, smoke, odors, and unsightliness, are created by poor refuse handling practices. Experience has shown that application of the basic principles of sanitation to refuse handling results in substantial reductions in insects, rodents, and related health problems.

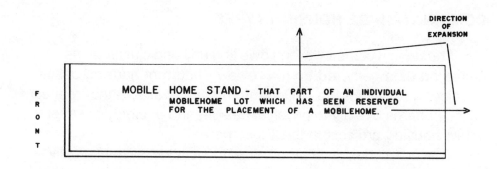

MOBILE HOME STAND — THAT PART OF AN INDIVIDUAL MOBILEHOME LOT WHICH HAS BEEN RESERVED FOR THE PLACEMENT OF A MOBILEHOME.

FRONT

DIRECTION OF EXPANSION

Notes

DESIGN CRITERIA FOR MOBILE HOME STAND IS 14' x 60'. (MOST STATES ALLOW 14' FEET WIDE MOVEMENT FOR MOBILE HOME. MOST DOUBLE WIDE UNITS ARE 24' WIDE.

USE LANDING MATS OR SIMILAR MEANS FOR EASY AND ACCURATE PLACEMENT OF MOBILE HOME ON MOBILE HOME STAND.

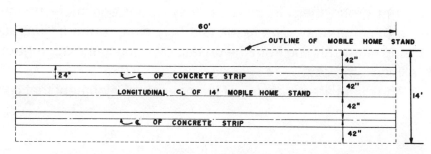

60'

OUTLINE OF MOBILE HOME STAND

24" ℄ OF CONCRETE STRIP

LONGITUDINAL C$_L$ OF 14' MOBILE HOME STAND

℄ OF CONCRETE STRIP

42" 42" 42" 42"   14'

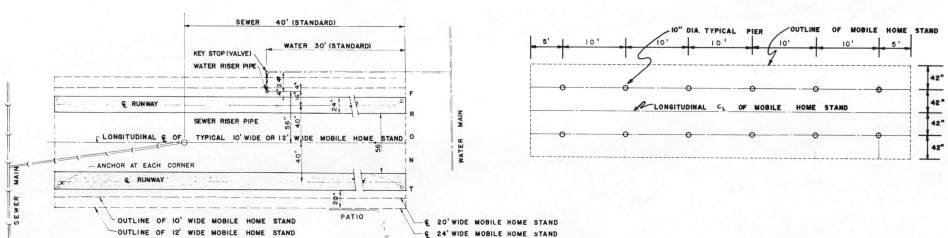

LOCATION OF WATER & SEWER RISER PIPES

SEWER 40' (STANDARD)

WATER 30' (STANDARD)

KEY STOP (VALVE)
WATER RISER PIPE

℄ RUNWAY

SEWER RISER PIPE

LONGITUDINAL ℄ OF TYPICAL 10' WIDE OR 12' WIDE MOBILE HOME STAND

ANCHOR AT EACH CORNER

℄ RUNWAY

OUTLINE OF 10' WIDE MOBILE HOME STAND
OUTLINE OF 12' WIDE MOBILE HOME STAND

SEWER MAIN

WATER MAIN

FRONT

PATIO

℄ 20' WIDE MOBILE HOME STAND
℄ 24' WIDE MOBILE HOME STAND

10" DIA. TYPICAL PIER   OUTLINE OF MOBILE HOME STAND

5' 10' 10' 10' 10' 10' 5'

LONGITUDINAL C$_L$ OF MOBILE HOME STAND

42" 42" 42" 42"

COMBINATION OF HOUSING TYPES

The design of the following dwelling unit and cluster plans was based on data gathered from a review of current housing design practice, a review of the limited information available that relates social patterns directly to physical design, and a survey of several public housing projects in the Boston area.

The urban design method was to develop systematically a range of dwelling unit plans, combine them into buildings and clusters and group them in progressively larger and more complex levels of community. The result is a fully dimensioned, illustrative housing study ranging from the private dwelling to the aggregate of dwellings—the city.

The plans are examples of the type of development that could take place in tho city. The actual housing design and grouping are matters for careful architectural study. The urban design study has established the probable limits within which architectural development could take place as well as providing an expression of urban design intent. The summary illustrates a few representative examples selected from two dozen building types applied in the development of the demonstration plans.

The primary considerations in the distribution of population throughout the city as a whole, and within the several residential areas, have included proximity to transportation facilities, to commercial activity, to open space, to education facilities and to the quality of the specific sites for containing people. The result is a range of net residential density from 83 p/acre to 282 p/acre. The gross density, including the recreation areas is about 40 p/acre.

New Communities: One Alternative
New Communities Project, Graduate School of Design, Harvard University, Cambridge, Massachusetts, 1968.

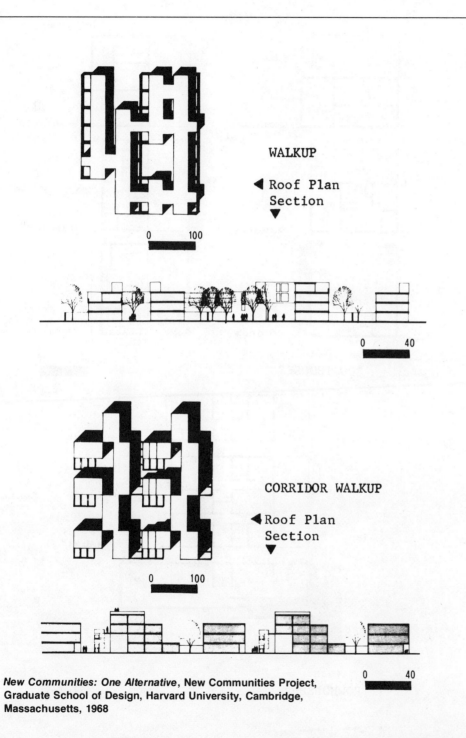

WALKUP

◀ Roof Plan
Section ▼

0   100

0   40

CORRIDOR WALKUP

◀ Roof Plan
Section ▼

0   100

0   40

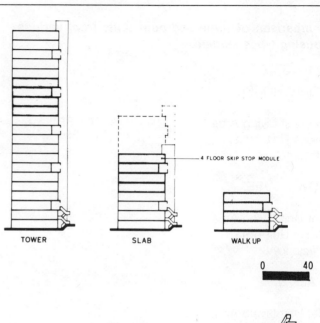

TOWER   SLAB   WALK UP

4 FLOOR SKIP STOP MODULE

0   40

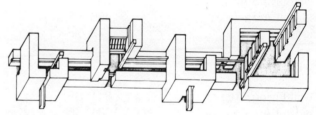

▲
ILLUSTRATIVE HIGHRISE SPINE
Composed with 4 Floor Modules

SKIP STOP SYSTEMS
▼

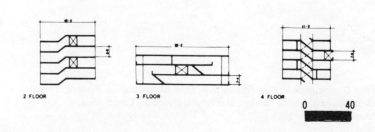

2 FLOOR   3 FLOOR   4 FLOOR

0   40

New Communities: One Alternative, New Communities Project,
Graduate School of Design, Harvard University, Cambridge,
Massachusetts, 1968

Comparison of three-bedroom units from various housing types studied

COURTHOUSE

Net Unit Living Area	722	SF
Gross Unit Area	1016	SF
Efficiency	71	%

ROW HOUSE

Net Unit Living Area	697	SF
Gross Unit Area	1030	SF
Efficiency	68	%

WALK-UP

Net Unit Living Area	698	SF
Gross Unit Area	966	SF
Efficiency	73	%

CORRIDOR WALK-UP

Net Unit Living Area	811	SF
Gross Unit Area	1024	SF
Efficiency	79	%

SKIP-STOP SYSTEM

Net Unit Living Area	781	SF
Gross Unit Area	1070	SF
Efficiency	73	%

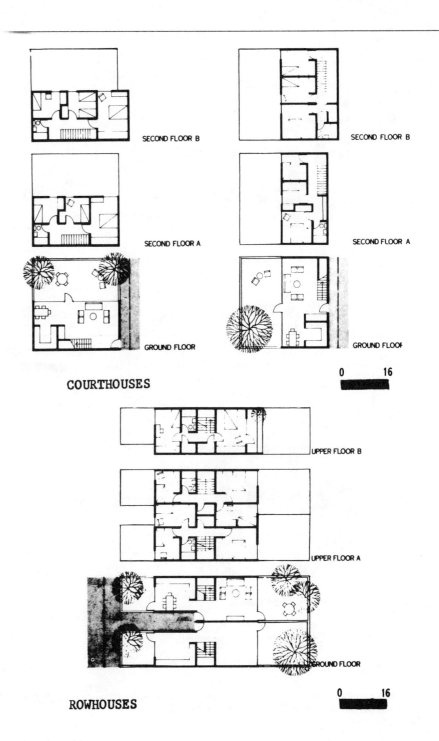

COURTHOUSES

ROWHOUSES

New Communities: One Alternative, New Communities Project, Graduate School of Design, Harvard University, Cambridge, Massachusetts, 1968

Comparison of typical clusters of housing types studied

COURTHOUSE CLUSTER

Dwelling Units per Acre	40
Building Coverage	50 %
Floor-Area Ratio	.91

ROW HOUSE CLUSTER

Dwelling Units per Acre	34
Building Coverage	43.5 %
Floor-Area Ratio	.81

WALK-UP CLUSTER

Dwelling Units per Acre	69
Building Coverage	49 %
Floor-Area Ratio	1.63

CORRIDOR WALK-UP CLUSTER

Dwelling Units per Acre	73
Building Coverage	41.6 %
Floor-Area Ratio	1.66

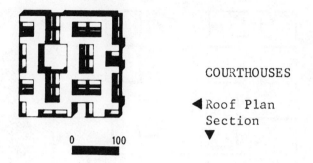

COURTHOUSES

◀ Roof Plan
Section
▼

0   100

0   40

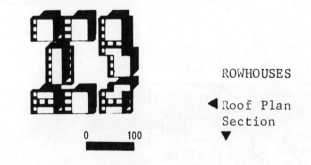

ROWHOUSES

◀ Roof Plan
Section
▼

0   100

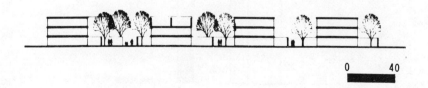

0   40

New Communities: One Alternative, New Communities Project, Graduate School of Design, Harvard University, Cambridge, Massachusetts, 1968

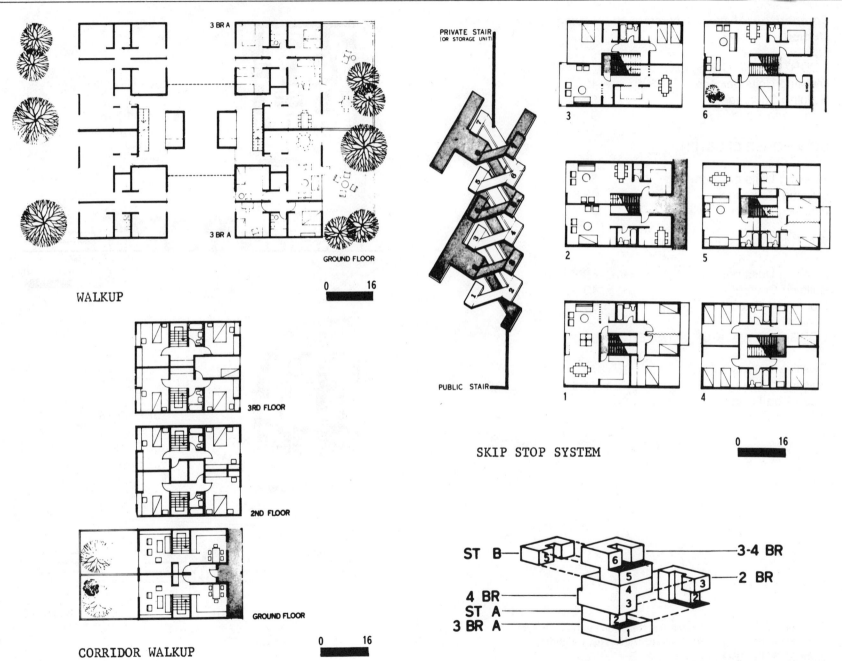

3 BR A

GROUND FLOOR

WALKUP

0   16

3RD FLOOR

2ND FLOOR

GROUND FLOOR

CORRIDOR WALKUP

0   16

PRIVATE STAIR
(OR STORAGE UNIT)

3

6

2

5

1

4

PUBLIC STAIR

SKIP STOP SYSTEM

0   16

ST B
3-4 BR
5
6
5
2 BR
4 BR
4
3
2 BR
ST A
2
3 BR A
1

New Communities: One Alternative, New Communities Project,
Graduate School of Design, Harvard University, Cambridge,
Massachusetts, 1968

TYPES OF APARTMENTS

G

G-1   Introduction

G-2   General Considerations and Standards:
       Floor Area, Dwelling Units
       Space Standards

G-3   Summary of Apartment Types

G-4   Efficiency Apartment

G-5   One-bedroom Apartment

G-6   Two-bedroom Apartment

G-7   Three-bedroom Apartment

G-8   Four-bedroom Apartment

G-9   Five-bedroom Apartment
       Six-bedroom Apartment

G-10   Simplex Apartment/Flat

G-11   Duplex Apartment

G-12   Triplex Apartment

G-13   Kitchen Arrangements

G-14   Kitchen/Dining Area

G-15   Bathroom Arrangements

G-16   Living Rooms

G-17   Dining Rooms

G-18   Bedrooms

G-19   Outdoor Living Space

G-20   Combination of Dwelling Unit Types

INTRODUCTION

Most aspects of apartment unit design today reflect the need to comply with basic minimum standards. Such standards are enforced by building and housing codes, and by administrative requirements set by governmental agencies that approve housing proposals. Generally, these standards deal with minimal floor areas, access, privacy, ventilation, sanitation, food preparation, safety, utilities, and construction.

These requirements provide adequate space for typical family activities, e.g., relaxation, sleeping, preparation of meals, eating and for maintaining sanitary conditions and storage.

It is recognized that all of the criteria relative to selection of apartment types cannot be met completely on any one development. Since many factors in the problem may be in some degree opposed to a number of the others, a well-balanced compromise is often the best solution that can be obtained. For instance, dwelling types that naturally lend themselves to the physical nature of the site may not be well suited to the special needs of the tenants; types that are best fitted to the general economic level of the tenants may not be in accord with the zoning regulations in effect, or may be incongruous with the existing neighborhood pattern or its trend.

Many such conflicts between the several factors might be cited. Moreover, there are no rules whereby any single criterion can be met with assurance that the right answer has been found.

All of the factors listed, however, have proved significant and worthy of full consideration in this phase of project development. Hasty decisions or rigid adherence to preconceived ideas as to types of housing may not only jeopardize the success of a project but may work an injury to the orderly and proper development of the community of which it is a part.

Food Preparation

A food preparation center is required that will allow normal food preparation and serving activities for the number of occupants of the living unit. For the smaller units, efficiency and one bedroom, a kitchenette would be adequate; for the larger units a full kitchen is required.

The food preparation center must be equipped with at least a sink, range, refrigerator, and full complement of storage space including wall and base cabinets, counters, and broom closet. Optional equipment may include a dishwasher, washing machine, clothes dryer, and a separate freezer.

Bathrooms

Every living unit must have at least one private bathroom equipped with a water closet, lavatory, and bathtub. Larger units with two or three bedrooms should have an additional compartment equipped with a water closet and lavatory. Other requirements include a medicine cabinet, a clothes hamper, and other accessories.

Apartment Layout and Privacy

All parts of the dwelling unit should be so arranged that each may function properly without interfering with any other. Specifically, the arrangement of rooms should be such that no person need walk through one room to get to another room. To walk through a bedroom or a living room to get to another bedroom is unacceptable. The bathroom must be accessible to all bedrooms without entering any other room intended for sleeping purposes. Also, the bathroom must not open directly off the kitchen, living room, dining area, or bedroom.

The following table shows the room arrangements that are not acceptable by FHA standards:

Only access from	To	Shall not be through
a. Habitable room (1)	Bathroom	Bedroom
b. Habitable room	Habitable room	Bedroom
c. Habitable room (2)	Habitable room	Bathroom
d. Bedroom (3)	Bathroom	Another bedroom
e. Bedroom	Bathroom	Habitable room

(1) In one-bedroom living units only, access to the bathroom from the living room may be through the bedroom.

(2) A required bathroom opening directly into a kitchen is not acceptable.

(3) An only bathroom shall not be located on a separate floor (full story height) from all bedrooms of a living unit.

Even exterior spaces such as balconies or porches must be provided with privacy. This can easily be achieved by physical separation or adequate visual screening from each other.

Storage

Every dwelling must be provided with adequate closet and storage facilities for a variety of uses. This should include provision for a normal amount of frequently used personal and household items. The following types of locations of closets are considered to be minimal.

The FHA requires the following minimum amounts of general storage if it is located entirely within the living unit. If storage is provided outside the unit, the total volume must be increased by approximately 100 percent.

Schedule of General Storage

OBR and 1 BR	= 100 cu. ft.
2 BR	= 140 cu. ft.
3 BR	= 180 cu. ft.
4 BR	= 200 cu. ft.

Storage Outside Living Unit

Each development or building requires central storage spaces for individual tenant storage. This area would be for baby buggies and wheeled toys. Adequate protection and ready accessibility is essential. These needs require management control and security with locks and other devices. If space is located in basement areas, ramps or elevators are required.

Coat Closet

Each living unit requires one coat closet near the front entrance of the unit, preferably off the foyer. The length should be sufficient to hold all the outer garments of the family.

Linen Closet

A linen closet is needed to store all kinds of linens that are used daily. The best location is usually considered to be near the bedrooms or near the bathroom. The greater the number of bedrooms, the larger the linen closet should be.

Storage within Living Unit

Each living unit requires at least one separate closet for general storage purposes. It should be located in a conveniently accessible place within the unit. Sometimes it can be combined with clothes closets or coat closets.

Light and Ventilation

Each living unit must be provided with an adequate amount of light and ventilation. The purpose of this requirement is to prevent the accumulation of unpleasant odors and provide adequate fresh air for healthful living.

The generally accepted standard for natural light is that each habitable room must be provided with a minimum window area of at least 10 percent of the floor area of the room.

For natural ventilation, each habitable room must be provided with a minimum ventilation area of at least 5 percent of the floor area of the room. In most cases this is achieved by having half of the window area open to get the required ventilation. Only in kitchens or bathrooms may mechanical ventilation be substituted for natural ventilation. For bathrooms, mechanical ventilation is generally considered to be more effective because a positive movement of air is achieved. For kitchens, both natural and mechanical ventilation are used. For obvious reasons, mechanical ventilation does remove cooking odors much more effectively than natural ventilation, and is preferable in most cases.

The ideal arrangement of rooms in a living unit for natural ventilation is to achieve through-ventilation; that is, air enters at one end of the unit and exits at the other end. If the building is properly oriented towards the prevailing breezes, through-ventilation can easily be obtained with the proper floor layout.

The next best arrangement of rooms is to have the living unit face in two different directions at a minimum of 90 degrees. This will achieve cross-ventilation through the living unit. In recent years, with the installation of air conditioning in most luxury and middle-income housing, the need to depend on natural ventilation has lessened. Also, the poor quality of our air in urban areas reinforces the desire to utilize mechanical ventilation or air conditioning rather than natural ventilation.

Utilities

a) *Water*—All living units must have hot and cold running water.

b) *Electricity*—All living units must have enough current capacity in the electrical system to allow the use of normal electric lights and appliances.

c) *TV*—Provisions must be made for the installation of a master antenna, amplifier and distribution system to an outlet in each apartment.

d) *Heat*—A system of heating must be provided that is adequate for the maintenance of a temperature of 70 degrees when the outside temperature is 0 degrees Fahrenheit.

e) *Garbage and Trash Removal*—An adequate system for the storage, removal or disposal of trash and garbage must be provided. This includes temporary storage within easy reach of the living unit, a method of collection, and incineration or compaction.

The balance of this chapter is devoted to a description and illustration of apartment floor plans ranging from the efficiency unit to the triplex layout. In addition, specific bathroom and kitchen arrangements are depicted.

GENERAL CONSIDERATIONS AND STANDARDS

The minimum requirements insure sufficient space to allow the placement of normal furniture in all the rooms. In addition, reasonable allowances are made for circulation between and around the furniture and to have access to all drawers, cabinets, and work spaces.

These standards are defined as (a) minimum room dimensions and as (b) minimum floor areas. The most widely used standards are Federal Housing Administration standards, which are given below. Many states, cities, and housing authorities have adopted variations on these standards. The first table indicates the minimum room sizes and dimensions for individual rooms. The second table indicates the minimum room sizes and dimensions for combined spaces. To insure adequate volume for each space, the FHA requirement for ceiling height is 8 feet, which is considered to be the absolute minimum for all habitable rooms. Halls, public corridors, toilets, and storage areas may have slightly less height.

A safety requirement is that the distance of travel within a living unit and the door of any room leading to the doorway of an exit corridor must not exceed 50 feet.

Floor Areas

Total net floor areas per dwelling unit, as shown in the table, are calculated at the principal floor level and measured between the inner finished faces of exterior walls in detached dwellings, and to the centerline of partitions.

Light and Ventilation

A. Method of measurement. Measurements in this section are based on distance between finished floor surface and ceiling surface (if finished) and between finished wall or partition surface.

B. Minimum ceiling heights. (1) Basements: 7 feet clear under joists; for basement dwelling units, 7 feet, 6 inches. (2) For all dwelling units on floors above basement, 7 feet, 6 inches.

C. Living space in basements. In rooms used for living, sleeping, or eating, or dwelling units, the finished floor should be not more than 2 feet 6 inches below the outside finished grade at required windows.

D. Habitable rooms. Provide light and ventilation in rooms used for living, sleeping, eating, and cooking, as indicated below. In computing the floor area of rooms with sloping ceilings, the area with less than 5 feet of headroom should not be included.

1. Total glass area—not less than 10 percent of floor area of room.

2. Ventilating area—not less than 4 percent of floor area of room.

3. If windows open on covered porches and terraces, or are in rooms any portion of which is more than 18 feet from a window, the glass area should be not less than 15 percent of the floor area of the room.

4. Unless separately lighted and ventilated by windows that provide the required glass and ventilating area, include any alcove adjoining a habitable room as part of that room in computing required glass and ventilating area.

5. An alcove may receive light and ventilation from the window of an adjoining habitable room only when the common wall between the alcove and the habitable room contains an opening, the area of which is not less than 80 percent of the area of the entire wall on the alcove side.

E. Bathrooms. Provide light and ventilation in bathrooms.

Minimum and maximum floor areas per dwelling unit[2]
[Square foot net areas]

Dwelling type structures	Number of stories	Number of bedrooms[1]									
		0-BR		1-BR		2-BR		3-BR		4-BR	
		Min.	Max.	Min.	Max.	Min.	Max.	Min.	Max.	Min.	Max.
Detached, semidetached and rows	1	445	545	580	750	765	950	985	1,200	1,185	1,400
		50	70	70	90	80	110	90	130	100	140
	1½ and 2	X	X	X	X	815	1,050	1,040	1,275	1,245	1,450
						80	110	90	130	100	140
Flats[3]	2	440	520	575	715	750	910	960	1,075	1,150	1,250
Apartments[4]	2 or more	410	470	535	650	685	825	875	975	1,070	1,150

[1]As a minimum, 1 bathroom should be provided for each unit of 3 or less bedrooms, and a bathroom-and-a-half for units of 4 bedrooms. As a maximum, units of 2 or less bedrooms should have no more than 1 bathroom, units of 3 bedrooms may include a bathroom-and-a-half, and units of 4 bedrooms may have 2 bathrooms.

[2]Areas should be reduced by these amounts if the dwelling has a basement or if facilities for laundry washing and drying, home repairs, and heating are provided outside the unit.

[3]Flats are dwelling units which occupy a single floor in a 2-story building, or a portion of a building, and in which the entrance and exit facilities (such as the stairs to the units on the second floor) are designed for one family's exclusive use. The areas shown for flats are based on the use of a space heater in each flat. If central heating is used, deduct 15 square feet per dwelling unit from the areas given. If a heater room is required, the areas for flats should be increased by 30 square feet. If space for laundry washing and drying is not provided in basement space, or on a community basis, the minimum areas for flats should be increased by from 15 square feet for 0-bedroom units, to 30 square feet for 4-bedroom units, and the maximum areas by from 50 to 75 square feet for the same range of unit sizes.

[4]Areas for apartments do not include space for laundry washing and drying, or heating, since these facilities are customarily provided outside of individual dwelling units. Areas are for walk-up structures and include space for one stair, for walk-up structures with two stairs, increase the area by 30 square feet per unit. Areas do not include corridor space in corridor-type apartment structures. Storage space in basements or elsewhere should be provided, ranging from a minimum of 20 square feet to a maximum of 60 square feet per unit, in accordance with the size of the unit.

Design Standards for Federal Personnel, Housing and Home Finance Agency, Bureau of the Budget, Washington, D.C.—1953

GENERAL CONSIDERATIONS AND STANDARDS
G-2
SPACE STANDARDS

Minimum Floor Space Required for Household
Activities, Furniture, Equipment and Storage
In Square Feet

FOR BASIC ACTIVITIES	NUMBER OF PERSONS					
	1	2	3	4	5	6
Sleeping and dressing	74	148	222	296	370	444
Personal cleanliness and sanitation	35	35	35	70	70	70
Food preparation and preservation	8	76	97	97	118	118
Food service and dining	53	70	91	105	119	146
Recreation and self-improvement	125	164	221	286	357	383
Extra-familial association	17	17	34	34	51	51
Housekeeping	48	91	110	127	146	149
Care of the infant or the ill	—	124	124	124	124	124
Circulation between areas	20	20	35	35	45	45
Operation of utilities	—	20	20	20	20	20
Total Basic Dwelling Unit Area	380	765	989	1159	1450	1550

FOR OTHER ACTIVITIES						
Laundry	36	48	65	80	96	112
Household Maintenance	—	42	42	42	42	42
Circulation, two story	—	32	32	32	32	32
Total With Other Activities	416	887	1128	1313	1590	1736

"Planning a Home for Occupancy"
Standards for Healthful Housing
Public Administration Service, 1950
American Public Health Association, Committee on the Hygiene of Housing

380

Maximum Allowable Dwelling Unit Areas

	Elderly		Non-elderly					
	Effic. 0-BR	1-BR	1-BR	2-BR	3-BR	4-BR	5-BR	6-BR
Occupancy (persons)	1	2	2	2	6	8	10	12
Room Count	3	3 1/2	3 1/2	4 1/2	5 1/2	6 1/2	7 1/2	8 1/2
Maximum Area within perimeter walls—gross sq. ft.	400	525	550	720	900	1120	1320	1540

These areas do not include stairs and stair landings inside unit, general storage and circulation outside unit, public facilities (stair, elevators, etc.), or space for heating equipment.

For heating equipment, add 15 sq. ft. for equipment operated by tenant; add 30 sq. ft. for heater room for gas equipment; add 45 sq. ft. for heater room for coal or oil equipment.

Guide to Maximum Space Areas (not mandatory)

	Effic. 0-BR	1-BR	1-BR	2-BR	3-BR	4-BR	5-BR	6-BR
Living Room minimum dimension 10'6"			145	155	160	165	170	175
Living Room—Dining Room combination	120	120	170	185	205	220	230	240
Kitchen	40	40	50	60	75	90	100	110
Kitchen—Dining Room combination			70	90	110	130	150	170
Guest Coat Closet		4	4	6	8	10	12	14
Linen Closet	2	3	4	5	6	7	8	9
Kitchen work top (countertop)	4	4	4	6	8	9	9	9
Kitchen shelving	20	20	30	36	42	54	60	60
General Storage (20% should be near kitchen)	10	20	25	30	35	40	45	50
*Bedroom #1 minimum width 8'6"	65	120	125	125	125	125	125	125
Bedroom #1 closet	6	8	10	10	10	10	10	10
*Bedroom #2				100	100	100	100	100
Bedroom #2 closet				8	8	8	8	8
*Bedroom #3					90	100	100	100
Bedroom #3 closet					8	8	8	8
Additional Bedrooms						90	90	90

*All Bedrooms 100 SF or larger shall accommodate twin beds

"Low-Rent Housing Manual"—221.1, Housing Assistance Administration
Department of Housing and Urban Development, September, 1967

Maximum Areas

(1) The total floor area of the unit, measured between the linear finish of enclosing exterior walls and between partitions separating units, shall not exceed the following:

Occupancy (persons)	1	2	4	6	8	10	12
Description	Efficiency	1BR	2BR	3BR	4BR	5BR	6BR
Room Count	3	3½	4½	5½	6½	7½	8½
Area sq. ft.	360	550	720	900	1120	1320	1540

(2) These areas do not include stairs and stair landings inside unit, general storage and circulation outside unit, public facilities (stairs, elevators, etc.)

Furnishability Requirements

A dwelling unit must contain space so planned as to accommodate the following furniture, facilities, and equipment, and permit free circulation with due allowance for heating devices, door swings, accessibility to electric outlets, etc. Such furnishability shall be demonstrated on the dwelling plans.

(1) *Living Space*
  Couch, 3'0" x 6'9"
  Large Chairs, 2'6" x 3'0"
    1 for 1 person unit—2 for all others
  Desk, 2' x 2' x 3'4"
    None required for efficiency unit
  TV, 1'4" x 2'8"

(2) *Dining Space*
  Table, 1 or 2 persons, 2'6" x 2'6"
  Table, 4 persons, 2'6" x 3'2"
  Table, 6 persons, 3'4" x 4'0"
  Table, 8 persons, 3'4" x 6'0" or 4'0" x 4'0"
  Table, 10 persons, 3'4" x 8'0" or 4'0" x 6'0"
  Table, 12 persons, 4'0" x 8'0"
  Chairs, 1'6" x 1'6"

(3) *Sleeping Spaces (per 2 persons)*
  Twin beds, 3'6" x 6'9" or double bed, 4'6" x 6'9"
    (Single bed for efficiency unit)
  Dresser, 1'10" x 3'6" (one for efficiency unit)
  Chair, 1'6" x 1'6"
  Crib, 2'4" x 4'5" (for first bedroom of family unit)

"Low Rent Housing Manual"—207.1, Housing and Urban Development Housing Assistance Administration, September, 1963.

Minimum Room Sizes and Allowable Room Count for Separate Rooms

Minimum Area (Square Feet)

Name of Space (1)	Room Count	LU with 0-BR	LU with 1-BR	LU with 2-BR	LU with 3-BR	LU with 4-BR	Least Dimension
LR	1	NA	160	160	170	180	12'0"
DR or DA	1	NA	100	100	110	120	8'4"
K	1	NA	60	60	70	80	5'4"
Kitchenette	1/2	40	40	NA	NA	NA	3'6"
BR (primary)	1	NA	120	120	120	120	9'4"
BR (secondary)	1	NA	NA	80	80	80	8'0"
Total area, BR's	—	NA	120	200	280	380	—
OHR	1	NA	80	80	80	80	8'0"
Bathroom	1/2	—	—	—	—	—	—
Half-Bathroom	1/4	NA	—	—	—	—	—
Foyer	1/4	25	25	25	25	25	4'0"
Balcony or Porch	1/4	70	70	70	70	70	6'0"
Terrace	1/4	120	120	120	120	120	8'0"

Notes:
(1) Abbreviations:
LU=Living Unit
LR=Living Room
DR=Dining Room
DA=Dining Area
K=Kitchen
K'ette=Kitchenette
NA=Not Applicable
BR=Bedroom
OHR=Other Habitable Room
0-BR=LU with no separate Bedroom

Minimum Room Sizes and Allowable Room Count for Combined Spaces

Combined Space (1) (2)	Comb. Room Count	LU with 0-BR	LU with 1-BR	LU with 2-BR	LU with 3-BR	LU with 4-BR
LR—DA	1-1/2	NA	200	200	220	230
LR—DA (DR size)	2	NA	240	240	260	270
LR—DA—BR (3)	2	240	NA	NA	NA	NA
LR—DA—K	2-1/2	NA	260	270	290	310
LR—BR	1-1/2	190	NA	NA	NA	NA
K—DA (2)	1-1/2	100	110	110	120	140
K—DA (DR size) (2)	2	NA	150	150	160	180
K'nette—DA	1	80	80	NA	NA	NA

Notes:
(2) For two adjacent spaces to be considered a combined space, the clear horizontal opening between spaces shall be at least 8 feet wide, except for a combined K-DA. For 1-1/2 room count of K-DA, the least dimension shall be 6'0" and the clear opening at least 4'0". For 2 room count of K-DA, the least dimension shall be 10'0" and the clear opening at least 6'0". All requirements having to do with light and ventilation shall be complied with.

Adapted from Federal Housing Administration, *Minimum Property Standards*

G-3 SUMMARY OF APARTMENT TYPES

Summary of Apartment Types

	EFFICIENCY	ONE-BEDROOM	TWO-BEDROOM
GENERAL CHARACTERISTICS	Minimal apartment with cooking and bathroom facilities. Desired by people who will occupy premises for short periods of time or only for sleeping. Meals will be simple and few.	Smallest apartment having separate living and sleeping accommodations. Contains adequate cooking facilities and dining areas.	Apartment having adequate space for family living. Contains full cooking and bathing facilities. May have separate dining room. Requires storage space for many activities.
ELEMENTS	Combined living, sleeping, dining area; minimal cooking facilities; bathroom; minimal storage space.	Combined living-dining area, kitchenette, separate bedroom, bathroom.	Living room, dining room, kitchen, master bedroom, bedroom, bathroom, small outdoor area.
TOILET FACILITIES	Full bathroom plus storage and dressing	1 bathroom (3 fixtures)	1 bathroom (4 fixtures)
SITE	Minimum area permitted—150 sq. ft.-300 sq. ft.	400 sq. ft.-600 sq. ft.	600 sq. ft.-800 sq. ft.
NUMBER OF OCCUPANTS	1 or 2 persons	2 persons	3 or 4 persons
TYPE OF OCCUPANCY	Single persons Young couples Elderly Temporary personnel or transients	Young couples Elderly Families with one child	Family with 1 or 2 children Couple with older or younger relatives
PLANNING CONSIDERATIONS	Generates the least number of children per dwelling unit. Fastest turnover in occupancy. Minimum requirements for community facilities.	Generates a small number of children per dwelling unit. Provides flexibility for variety of dwelling unit types in a community. Relatively stable type of occupancy.	Adequate school facilities required for children. Adequate facilities for recreation required. Generally stable type of occupancy.
PARKING REQUIREMENTS	One car per dwelling unit. Elderly people may require less.	One car per dwelling unit.	1¼-1½ cars per dwelling unit.

THREE-BEDROOM	FOUR-BEDROOM	FIVE-BEDROOM
Apartment for average-sized family.	Apartment for large-sized family or occupancy with different generations living in the same household.	Apartment for extremely large family or with several generations living in the same household.
Living room, separate dining room, kitchen, master bedroom, 2 smaller bedrooms, bathrooms, outdoor area.	Living room, separate dining room, kitchen, family room, master bedroom, 3 smaller bedrooms, bathrooms, outdoor area.	Living room, separate dining room, kitchen, family room, master bedroom, 4 smaller bedrooms, bathrooms, outdoor area.
1½ or 2 bathrooms	2 bathrooms	2½-3 bathrooms
800 sq. ft.-1,100 sq. ft.	1,100 sq. ft-1,500 sq.ft.	Minimum area—1,400 sq. ft.
4-6 persons	6-8 persons	8-12 persons
Family with 2 to 4 children Family with elderly persons or relatives	Family with 3 to 6 children Family with elderly persons or relatives	Family with 6 or more children Family with elderly persons or relatives
Generates a variety of school needs and recreational facilities.	Generates a variety of school needs and recreational facilities.	Generates a variety of school needs and recreational facilities. May require facilities for the elderly.
1½-2 cars per dwelling unit.	2 cars per dwelling unit.	2-3 cars per dwelling unit.

EFFICIENCY APARTMENT

Elements

The efficiency apartment consists mainly of a one large room combining living, eating and sleeping activities. An alcove may be provided for a kitchenette with minimum facilities. It is also provided with a full bathroom.

Design

The essential design feature is the flexibility of the main space to be used alternatively for living, sleeping, and dining. Most often, a convertible sofa-bed is used to achieve this flexibility and entry foyer can be used as a dining area. A critical problem is storage of clothes and a dressing area, which is often less than minimum.

Size

The size of an efficiency can range from approximately 200 sq. ft. to 500 sq. ft. The FHA minimum requirement for an efficiency apartment is approximately 300 sq. ft. One way to add to the spaciousness of the apartment is to provide a terrace with an all-glass wall.

Type of Occupancy

Efficiency apartments are generally occupied by single persons, young married couples without children, or elderly couples. Maximum number of occupants should be two persons.

Planning Implications

Because of the type of occupancy, no or few children are generated from this size apartment. This can easily avoid the need for new schools or the addition to an existing one. Single persons and young married couples are a relatively mobile group because of changes in status or arrival of children. As a result, this type of occupancy will see a faster turnover than older families. The elderly tend to be stable in family size.

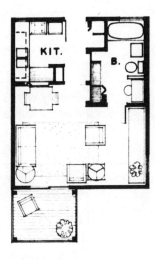 

Homestead Terrace
Mill Valley, Calif.
Worley K. Wong, FAIA, Architect

Studio

When the efficiency unit increases substantially in size beyond the minimum size, it usually is referred to as a "studio" apartment. This type of unit occupies as much space as a one-bedroom apartment or more. However, it still is arranged as an efficiency apartment but with a feeling of openness and spaciousness. This type of apartment is usually restricted to luxury-type housing and has a special appeal for professional use such as for artists and photographers.

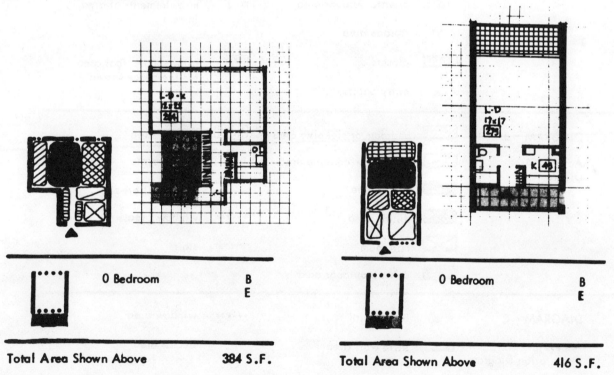

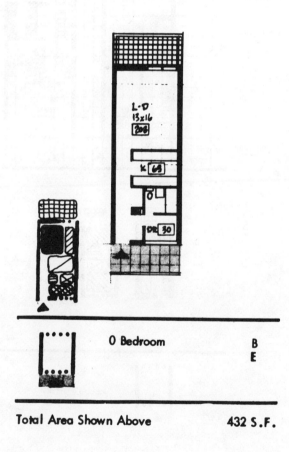

| | 0 Bedroom | B E |
| Total Area Shown Above | | 384 S.F. |

| | 0 Bedroom | B E |
| Total Area Shown Above | | 416 S.F. |

| | 0 Bedroom | B E |
| Total Area Shown Above | | 432 S.F. |

Planning & Design Workbook for Community Participation
Prepared for the State of New Jersey Dept. of Community Affairs by the
Research Center for Urban and Environmental Planning, Princeton University
School of Architecture and Urban Planning—1969

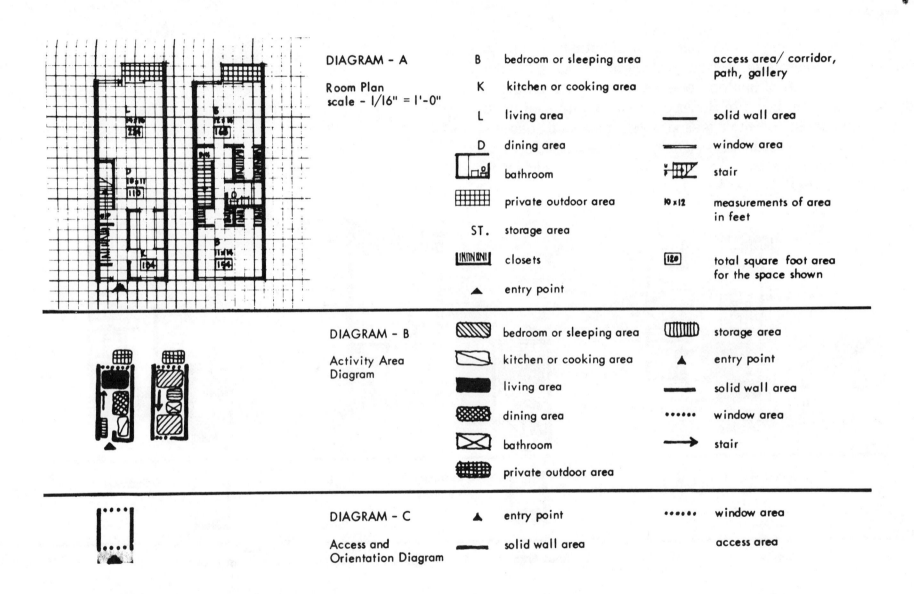

DIAGRAM - A

Room Plan
scale - 1/16" = 1'-0"

B	bedroom or sleeping area	access area/ corridor, path, gallery
K	kitchen or cooking area	
L	living area	——— solid wall area
D	dining area	=== window area
	bathroom	stair
	private outdoor area	10 x 12 measurements of area in feet
ST.	storage area	
	closets	120 total square foot area for the space shown
▲	entry point	

DIAGRAM - B

Activity Area
Diagram

	bedroom or sleeping area		storage area
	kitchen or cooking area	▲	entry point
	living area	———	solid wall area
	dining area	······	window area
	bathroom	⟶	stair
	private outdoor area		

DIAGRAM - C

Access and
Orientation Diagram

▲	entry point	······	window area
———	solid wall area		access area

Planning & Design Workbook for Community Participation
Prepared for the State of New Jersey Dept. of Community Affairs by the
Research Center for Urban and Environmental Planning, Princeton University
School of Architecture and Urban Planning—1969

ONE-BEDROOM APARTMENT

Elements

The one-bedroom consists of (a) a living-dining room (a separate dining room is very rare), (b) kitchen area, (c) bedroom, (d) bathroom, (e) an outdoor terrace, which is optional.

Design

The main object of a one-bedroom apartment is its compactness. A full range of activities is anticipated within a minimal area. The foyer is frequently used as a dining space. The kitchen is often minimal.

Size

The size of a one-bedroom apartment can range from 400 sq. ft. to 600 sq. ft. The FHA minimum requirement for a one-bedroom apartment is approximately 500 sq. ft. The addition of an outdoor terrace will add to the spaciousness of the apartment.

Type of Occupancy

One-bedroom apartments are occupied by 2 or 3 persons. This could include a wide range of individuals, such as, young married couples with or without a child, elderly persons, or unrelated single persons sharing an apartment. Whether the occupancy is stable or has a quick turnover will be directly related to the type of occupancy.

Planning Implications

The one-bedroom apartment can be expected to yield a greater number of children than the efficiency. Also, this type of apartment can be used as a transition between home-ownership and relocation to a different community by elderly persons.

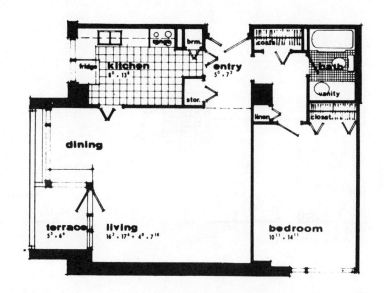

**House and Home,
September, 1972**

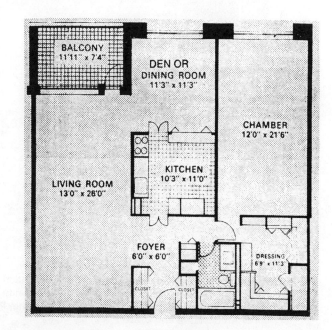

G-5 ONE-BEDROOM APARTMENT

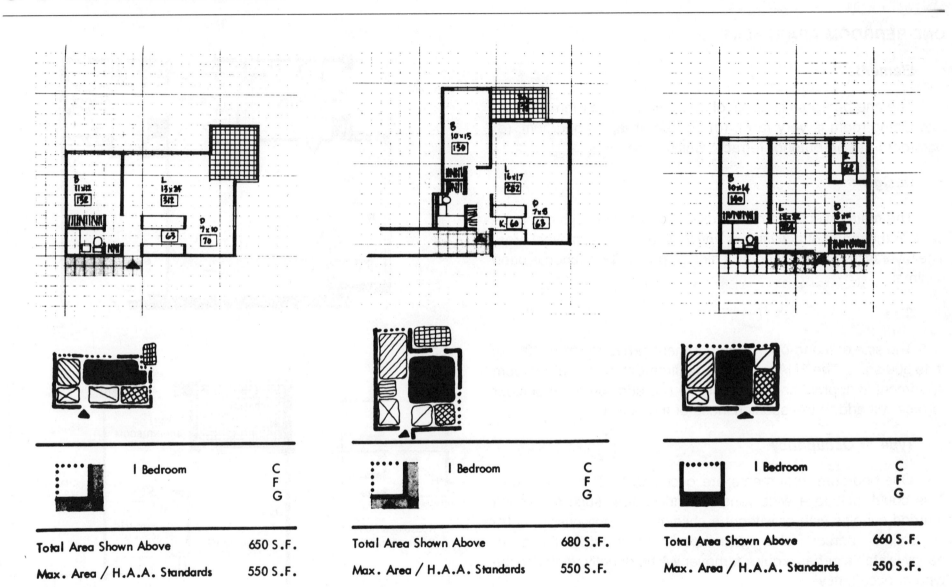

	I Bedroom	C F G
Total Area Shown Above	650 S.F.	
Max. Area / H.A.A. Standards	550 S.F.	

	I Bedroom	C F G
Total Area Shown Above	680 S.F.	
Max. Area / H.A.A. Standards	550 S.F.	

	I Bedroom	C F G
Total Area Shown Above	660 S.F.	
Max. Area / H.A.A. Standards	550 S.F.	

Planning & Design Workbook for Community Participation
Prepared for the State of New Jersey Dept. of Community Affairs by the
Research Center for Urban and Environmental Planning, Princeton University
School of Architecture and Urban Planning—1969

390

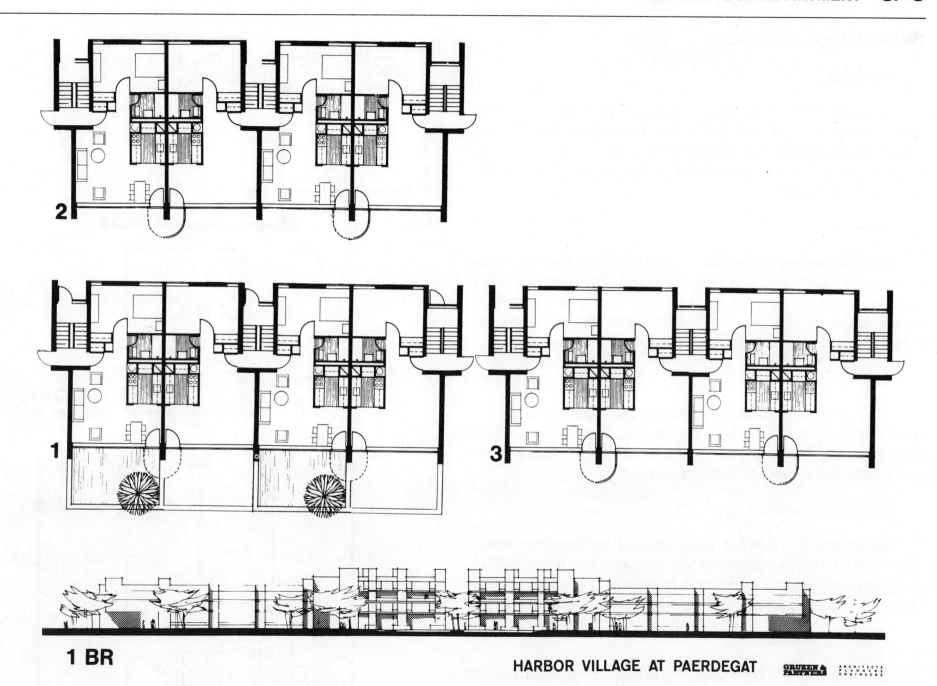

1 BR

HARBOR VILLAGE AT PAERDEGAT   GRUZEN & PARTNERS   ARCHITECTS PLANNERS ENGINEERS

TWO-BEDROOM APARTMENT

Elements

The two-bedroom apartment consists of two bedrooms, living room, dining area (usually part of the living room), full kitchen, bathroom and possibly an outdoor terrace. In luxury apartments, an additional half-bath, consisting of a water closet and washbasin, may be included.

Design

The two-bedroom apartment is considered the average size for a typical family with one or two children. The range of family activities is anticipated within the dwelling unit. The arrangement of rooms should be such to permit a reasonable separation of living activities (kitchen, dining, living) from sleeping activities.

Size

The size of a two-bedroom apartment will range from 500 sq. ft. to 1,000 sq. ft. The FHA minimum requirement for such an apartment is approximately 650 sq. ft. An outdoor terrace is important to add to the livability of the apartment.

Type of Occupancy

As stated, the average occupancy of two-bedroom apartments will be a family with one or two children. Often a third child or an older relative would be included. Number of occupants will be a minimum of three persons and maximum of 4 persons.

Planning Implications

Due to the type of occupancy, the two-bedroom apartment will yield one or two children of school age. Also, as an average family, they will require a full range of municipal services.

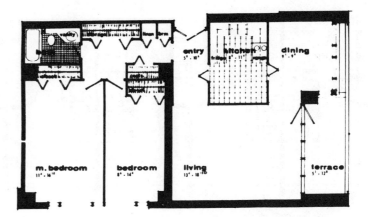

House and Home,
September, 1972

two bedroom/two bath

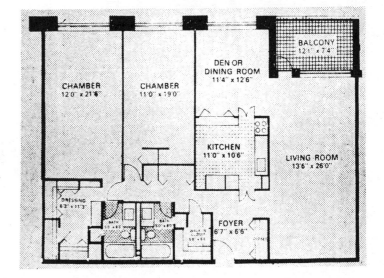

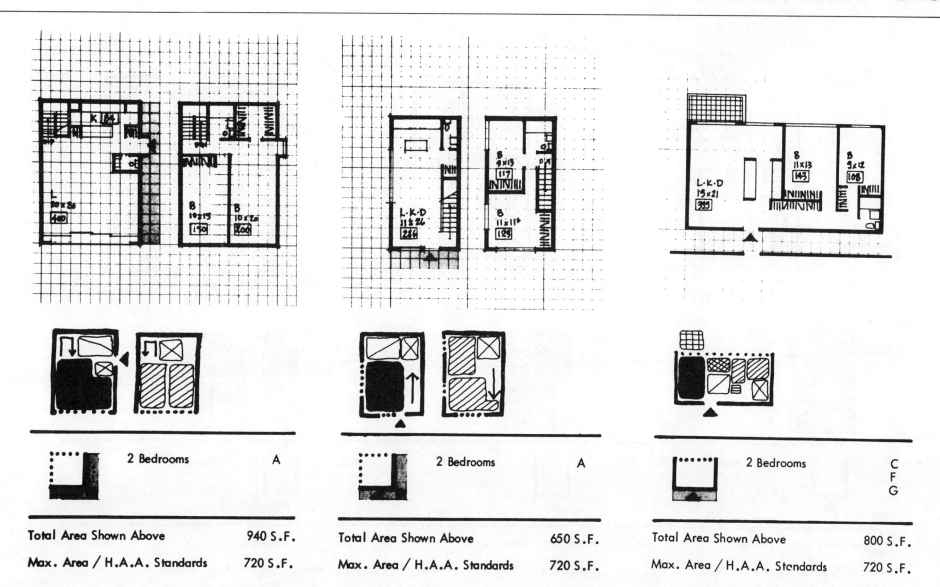

	2 Bedrooms	A
	2 Bedrooms	A
	2 Bedrooms	C F G

Total Area Shown Above	940 S.F.
Max. Area / H.A.A. Standards	720 S.F.

Total Area Shown Above	650 S.F.
Max. Area / H.A.A. Standards	720 S.F.

Total Area Shown Above	800 S.F.
Max. Area / H.A.A. Standards	720 S.F.

Planning & Design Workbook for Community Participation
Prepared for the State of New Jersey Dept. of Community Affairs by the
Research Center for Urban and Environmental Planning, Princeton University
School of Architecture and Urban Planning—1969

G-6 TWO-BEDROOM APARTMENT

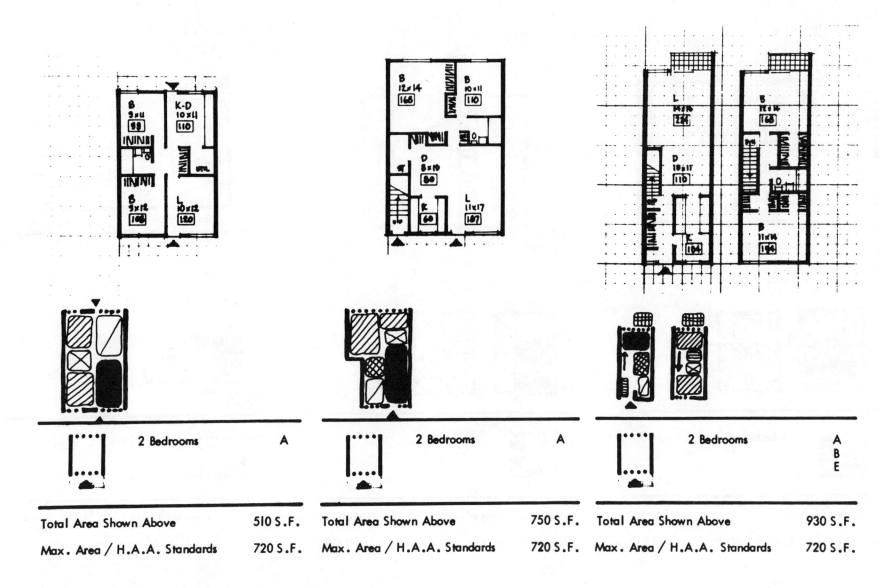

	2 Bedrooms	A
	2 Bedrooms	A
	2 Bedrooms	A B E

| Total Area Shown Above | 510 S.F. | Total Area Shown Above | 750 S.F. | Total Area Shown Above | 930 S.F. |
| Max. Area / H.A.A. Standards | 720 S.F. | Max. Area / H.A.A. Standards | 720 S.F. | Max. Area / H.A.A. Standards | 720 S.F. |

Planning & Design Workbook for Community Participation
Prepared for the State of New Jersey Dept. of Community Affairs by the
Research Center for Urban and Environmental Planning, Princeton University
School of Architecture and Urban Planning—1969

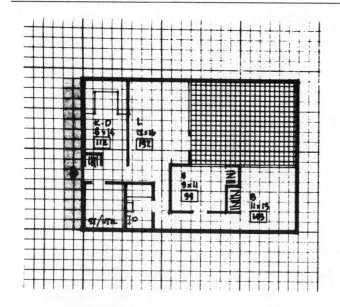

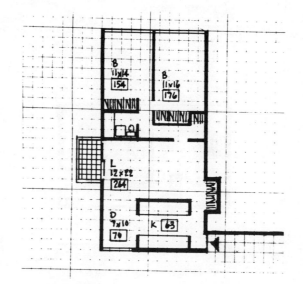

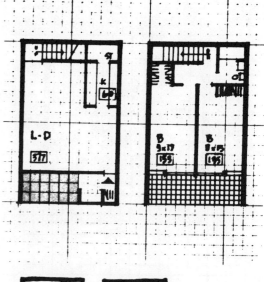

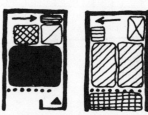

	2 Bedrooms	A

Total Area Shown Above	840 S.F.
Max. Area / H.A.A. Standards	720 S.F.

	2 Bedrooms	C F G

Total Area Shown Above	840 S.F.
Max. Area / H.A.A. Standards	720 S.F.

	2 Bedrooms	A

Total Area Shown Above	1040 S.F.
Max. Area / H.A.A. Standards	720 S.F.

Planning & Design Workbook for Community Participation
Prepared for the State of New Jersey Dept. of Community Affairs by the
Research Center for Urban and Environmental Planning, Princeton University
School of Architecture and Urban Planning—1969

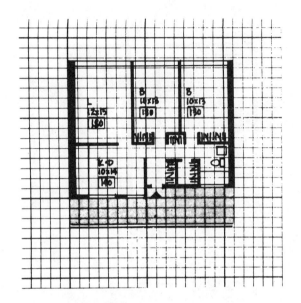

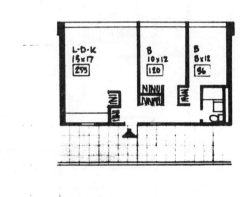

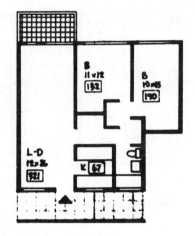

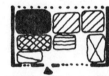

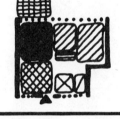

	2 Bedrooms	A B E
Total Area Shown Above	720 S.F.	
Max. Area / H.A.A. Standards	720 S.F.	

	2 Bedrooms	A B E
Total Area Shown Above	610 S.F.	
Max. Area / H.A.A. Standards	720 S.F.	

	2 Bedrooms	A B E
Total Area Shown Above	805 S.F.	
Max. Area / H.A.A. Standards	720 S.F.	

Planning & Design Workbook for Community Participation
Prepared for the State of New Jersey Dept. of Community Affairs by the
Research Center for Urban and Environmental Planning, Princeton University
School of Architecture and Urban Planning—1969

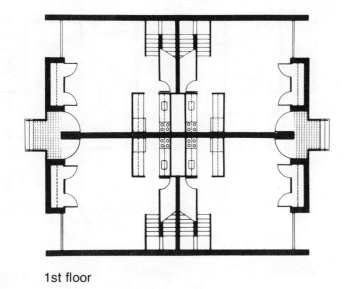

1st floor

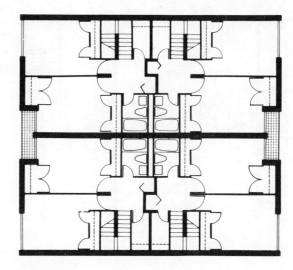

2nd floor

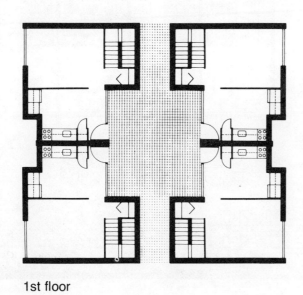

1st floor

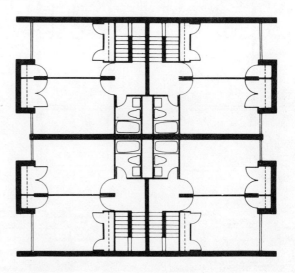

2nd floor

Lavanburg Community, NYC. Conklin & Rossant, Architects

G-6 TWO-BEDROOM APARTMENT

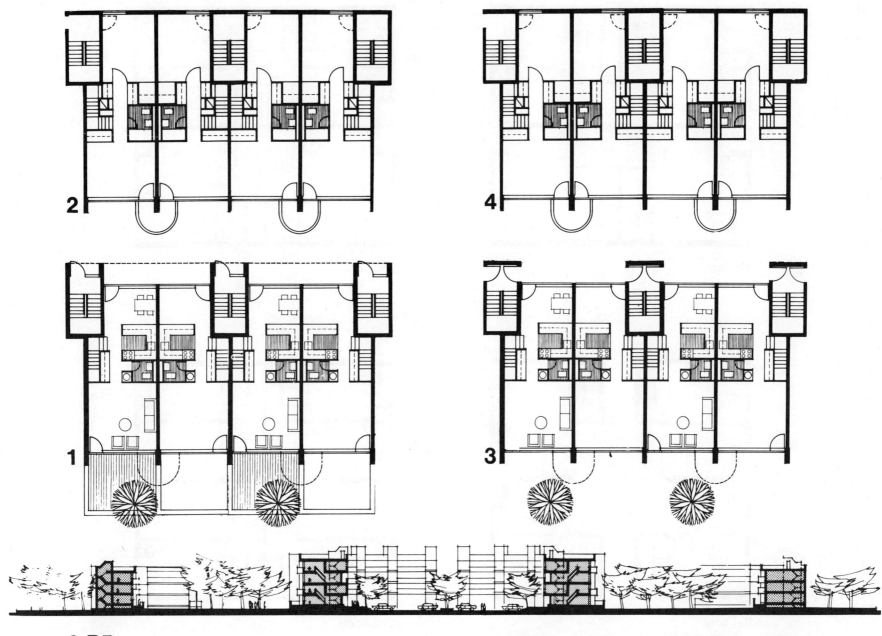

2 BR

HARBOR VILLAGE AT PAERDEGAT   GRUZEN & PARTNERS   ARCHITECTS PLANNERS ENGINEERS

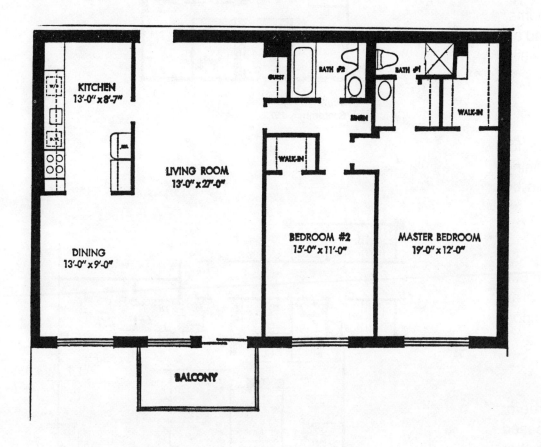

Hampshire House, White Plains, New York

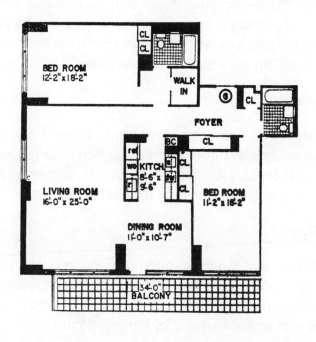

Riviera Towers, West New York, New Jersey

THREE-BEDROOM APARTMENT

Elements

The three-bedroom apartment consists of three bedrooms, living room, dining area, full kitchen, one to two bathrooms, and an outdoor terrace. Luxury apartments will have two bathrooms, while public housing may still have only one.

Design

The three-bedroom apartment is generally considered for large families with three or more children. A larger living and dining area is necessary for the larger family. Consideration should be given for the greater privacy for each member of the family.

Size

The size of the three-bedroom apartment will range from 600 sq. ft. to 1,200 sq. ft. The FHA minimum requirement for such an apartment is approximately 800 sq. ft. An outdoor terrace is important to add to the livability of the apartment.

Type of Occupancy

Occupancy is expected to be for a large family with three or more children. Frequently, however, family size may be increased by other family members, such as in-laws or grandparents, rather than more children.

Planning Implications

The additional children will definitely add to the school population. Elderly persons will also require additional services.

House and Home,
September, 1972

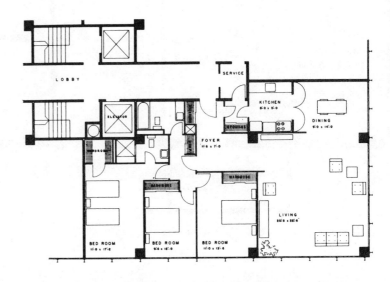

Apartments and Dormitories, McGraw-Hill Book Co., Inc. 1962
Lake Shore Drive Apartments, Chicago, Illinois
Mies Van der Rohe—Architect

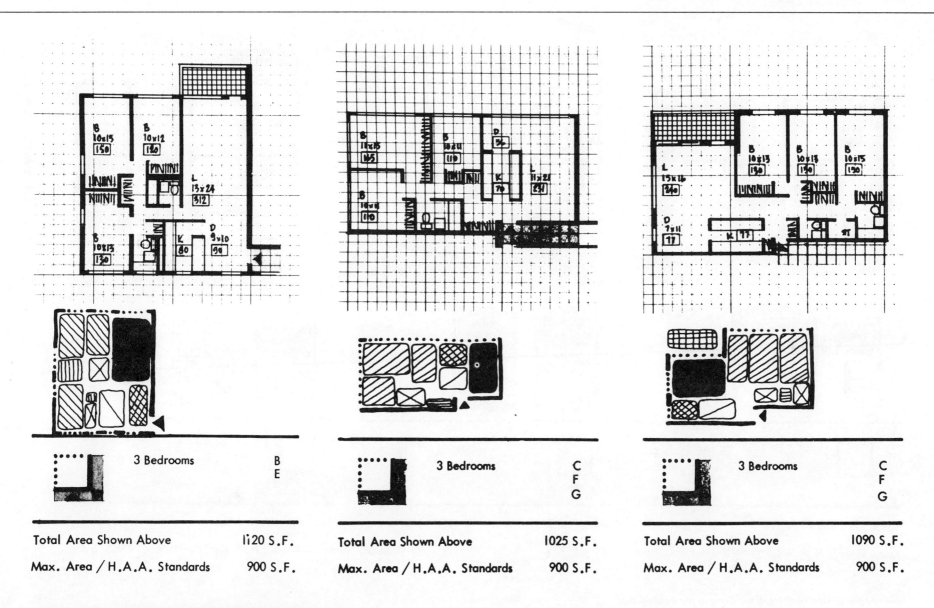

3 Bedrooms		B E
Total Area Shown Above	1120 S.F.	
Max. Area / H.A.A. Standards	900 S.F.	

3 Bedrooms		C F G
Total Area Shown Above	1025 S.F.	
Max. Area / H.A.A. Standards	900 S.F.	

3 Bedrooms		C F G
Total Area Shown Above	1090 S.F.	
Max. Area / H.A.A. Standards	900 S.F.	

Planning & Design Workbook for Community Participation
Prepared for the State of New Jersey Dept. of Community Affairs by the
Research Center for Urban and Environmental Planning, Princeton University
School of Architecture and Urban Planning—1969

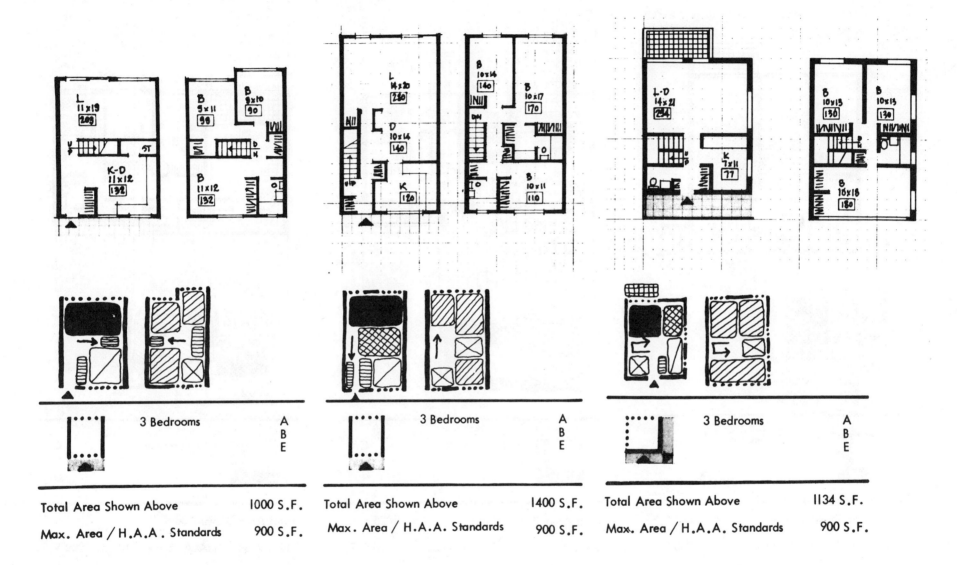

| Total Area Shown Above | 1000 S.F. | Total Area Shown Above | 1400 S.F. | Total Area Shown Above | 1134 S.F. |
| Max. Area / H.A.A. Standards | 900 S.F. | Max. Area / H.A.A. Standards | 900 S.F. | Max. Area / H.A.A. Standards | 900 S.F. |

Planning & Design Workbook for Community Participation
Prepared for the State of New Jersey Dept. of Community Affairs by the
Research Center for Urban and Environmental Planning, Princeton University
School of Architecture and Urban Planning—1969

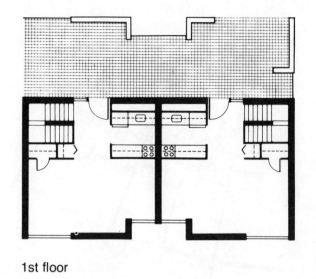

1st floor

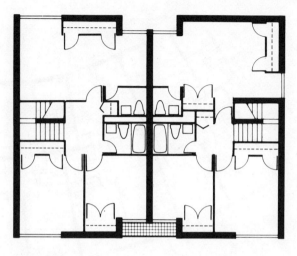

2nd floor

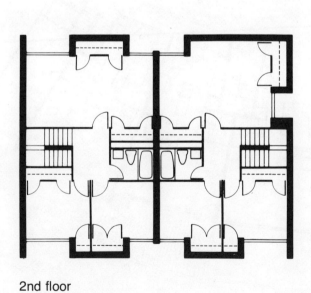

2nd floor

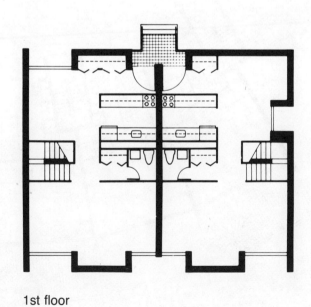

1st floor

Lavanburg Community, NYC. Conklin & Rossant, Architects

G-7 THREE-BEDROOM APARTMENT

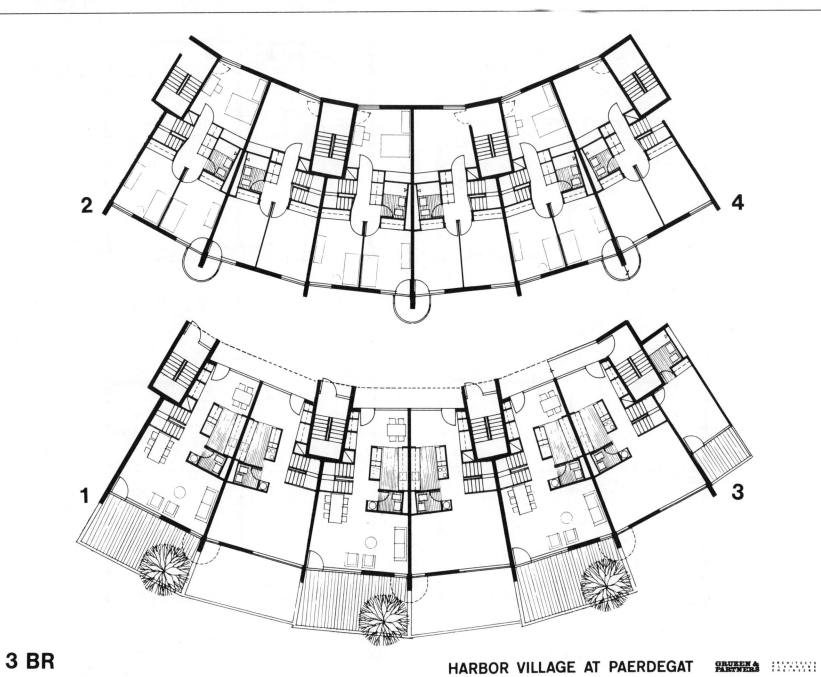

3 BR

HARBOR VILLAGE AT PAERDEGAT   GRUEN & PARTNERS   ARCHITECTS PLANNERS ENGINEERS

404

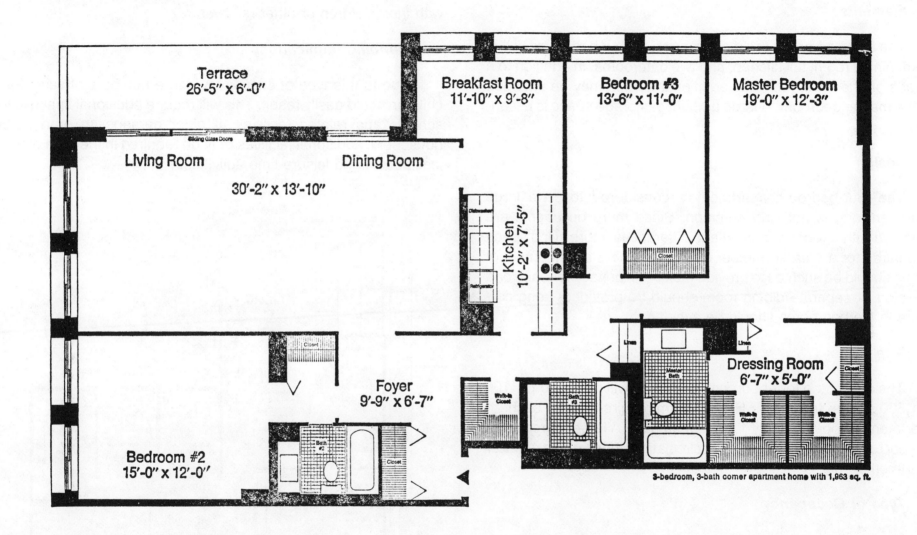

Terrace
26'-5" x 6'-0"

Breakfast Room
11'-10" x 9'-8"

Bedroom #3
13'-6" x 11'-0"

Master Bedroom
19'-0" x 12'-3"

Sliding Glass Doors

Living Room

Dining Room
30'-2" x 13'-10"

Dishwasher

Kitchen
10'-2" x 7'-5"

Refrigerator

Closet

Closet

Linen

Linen

Master Bath

Dressing Room
6'-7" x 5'-0"

Closet

Foyer
9'-9" x 6'-7"

Walk-In Closet

Bath #3

Walk-In Closet

Walk-In Closet

Bath #2

Closet

Bedroom #2
15'-0" x 12'-0"

3-bedroom, 3-bath corner apartment home with 1,963 sq. ft.

Winston Towers, Fort Lee, New Jersey

FOUR-BEDROOM APARTMENT

Elements

The four-bedroom apartment consists of four bedrooms, living room, dining room, full kitchen, and two bathrooms. In addition to a terrace off the living room, an additional terrace may be provided off the master bedroom. A large amount of storage space is essential.

Design

The four-bedroom apartment is considered to be a large apartment and is not very common. Since more occupants are expected with a wider spread of age differences, more living space is required for a greater number of activities. This arrangement of rooms should be such as to provide maximum privacy for each one grouping. A separate dining room should be provided. Long corridors to the bedrooms should be avoided.

Size

The size of the four-bedroom apartment will range from 1,100 to 1,500 square feet. The FHA minimum requirement for such an apartment is approximately 1,200 square feet. A larger percentage of floor area will be utilized for circulation than in the smaller apartments.

Type of Occupancy

The number of occupants can range from five to eight persons. The most typical would be a normal family with three to six children. The minimum occupancy would be one child per bedroom plus the parents in the master bedroom. The maximum would be two children per bedroom. Another fairly common type of occupancy would be occupancy by three generations, that is, grandparents, parents and children. As the life expectancy increases, some other people are sharing housing accommodations with their children or other relatives.

Planning Implications

Due to this type of occupancy, large numbers of school-age children could easily result. This will require additional space in the schools and related facilities. If older persons are part of the household, additional facilities may be required in the form of medical, social, and leisure-time activities.

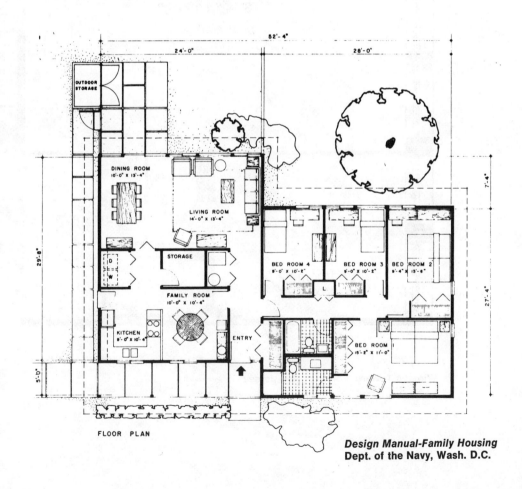

FLOOR PLAN

Design Manual-Family Housing
Dept. of the Navy, Wash. D.C.

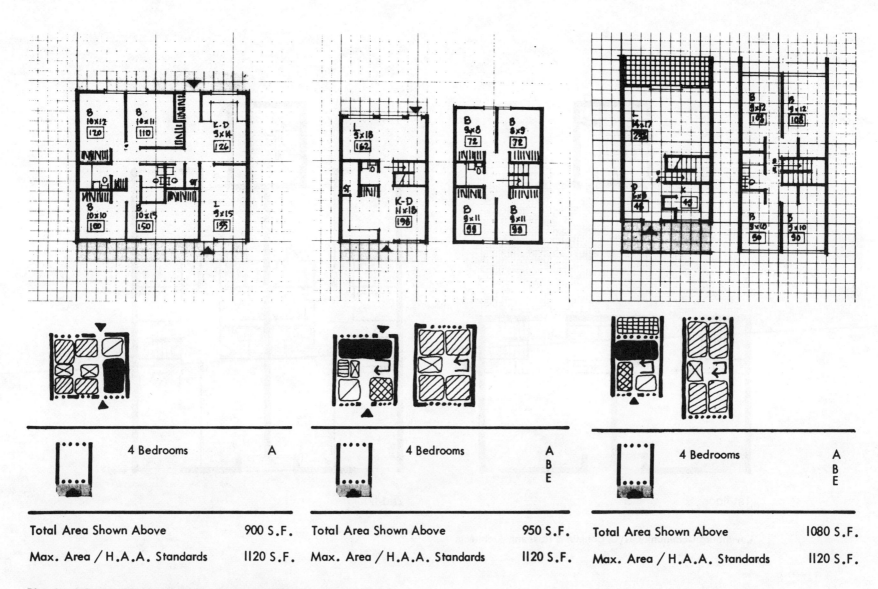

4 Bedrooms		A
Total Area Shown Above	900 S.F.	
Max. Area / H.A.A. Standards	1120 S.F.	

4 Bedrooms		A B E
Total Area Shown Above	950 S.F.	
Max. Area / H.A.A. Standards	1120 S.F.	

4 Bedrooms		A B E
Total Area Shown Above	1080 S.F.	
Max. Area / H.A.A. Standards	1120 S.F.	

Planning & Design Workbook for Community Participation
Prepared for the State of New Jersey Dept. of Community Affairs by the
Research Center for Urban and Environmental Planning, Princeton University
School of Architecture and Urban Planning—1969

G-8 FOUR-BEDROOM APARTMENT (DUPLEX)

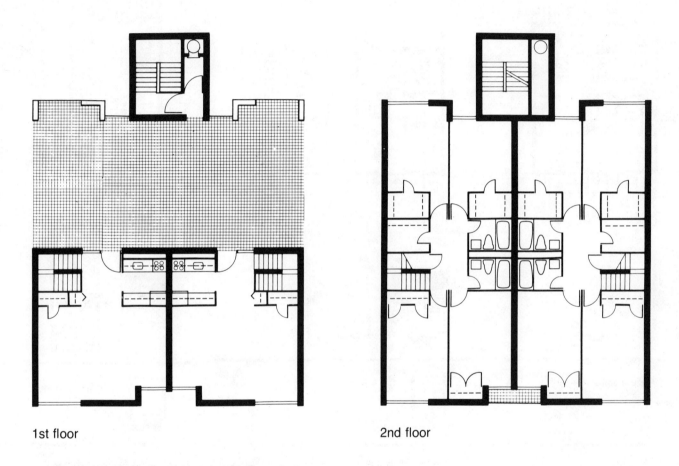

1st floor   2nd floor

Lavanburg Community, NYC. Conklin & Rossant, Architects

FIVE-BEDROOM APARTMENT

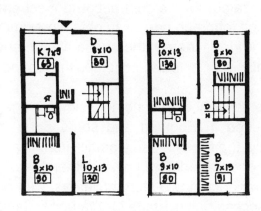

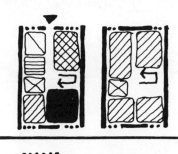

	5 Bedrooms	A B E
Total Area Shown Above		1280 S.F.
Max. Area / H.A.A. Standards		1320 S.F.

SIX-BEDROOM APARTMENT

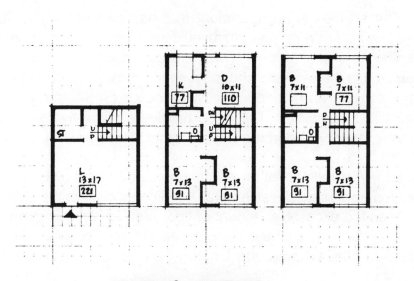

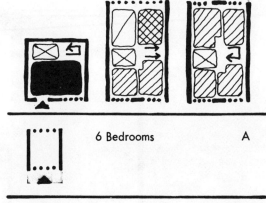

	6 Bedrooms	A
Total Area Shown Above		1360 S.F.
Max. Area / H.A.A. Standards		1540 S.F.

Planning & Design Work for Community Participation
Prepared for the State of New Jersey Dept. of Community Affairs by the
Research Center for Urban and Environmental Planning, Princeton University
School of Architecture and Urban Planning—1969

SIMPLEX APARTMENT/FLAT

The simplex is an apartment that has all its rooms on one level. The size may range from an efficiency up to a multi-bedroom unit. The simplex apartment is the most common type of apartment because it is the simplest and most economical to build. Because both the living and sleeping activities occur on the same level, circulation is simplified. The close proximity of the two activities, however, may be disturbing to each other if they are not properly zoned.

It may be located either in a high-rise apartment building or in a garden apartment development. A major criticism of the simplex has been the excessive amount of floor area required in corridors or stairs in order to gain access to the apartment. For example, in a central-corridor scheme, the length of public corridor is approxi-

mately equal to the length of the apartment. The configuration or shape of the apartment will be determined by the type of building in which it will be located. With a central-corridor scheme, the apartment shape will be long and narrow to obtain maximum perimeter. With an open-corridor scheme, the shape would tend to be deep and narrow, while with a tower scheme, the shape tends to be square.

A flat is another way of describing a simplex apartment. It is a common term used in England and some parts of the United States. Generally, the flat refers to a small simplex apartment such as an efficiency or one-bedroom unit. Another use of the term was to describe apartments in two-story buildings, with one flat above the other. The access hall or stairs for the upper flat is often incorporated into the living unit and is maintained by the tenant. The flats are usually grouped continuously in one building.

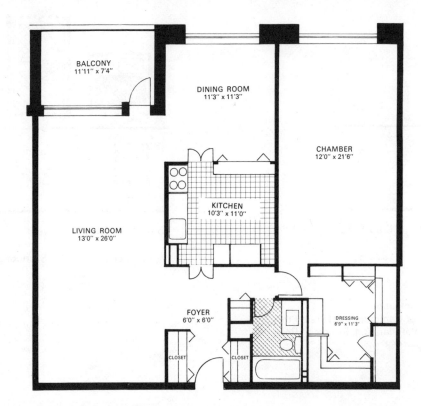

Scarborough Manor
Westchester, N.Y.

DUPLEX

The typical duplex apartment is located on two levels with the living room, kitchen, and dining area on one level and the sleeping area on the other level connected by an interior stair. The illustrations shown are for a typical duplex apartment with an open-corridor building, and one utilized with a center-corridor building type.

The major economic advantage of the duplex apartment is the elimination of a corridor and elevator doors on every other floor. However, this saving is partially offset by the need for an interior stair for each apartment. From a livability standpoint, the main advantage is the separation of the living activities from the sleeping activities. This separation approximates the relationship in a typical two-story, one-family house. It provides greater privacy and feeling of more space.

The duplex apartment, whether located in a center-corridor scheme or open-corridor scheme has the added advantage of through-ventilation for the upper level and two exposures, which permits better building orientation. With an open-corridor plan, both levels can have through-ventilation. The major disadvantage for the duplex is the need for the interior stair. For handicapped people or for the elderly, this may be a severe problem. Another advantage, which is less tangible, is the fact that a duplex apartment generally has more prestige or value than an equal simplex apartment. This can be seen in the development over the past years of greater numbers of duplex apartments in middle-income and luxury-type buildings.

A variation of the traditional duplex is the use of two levels separated by only one-half flight of stairs. This arrangement reduces the separation of the two levels and reduces the number of stairs a person needs to go up and down. Also the inter-relationship of levels allows for more imaginative and exciting use of space.

This kind of separation of levels, however, tends to be more expensive than conventional construction.

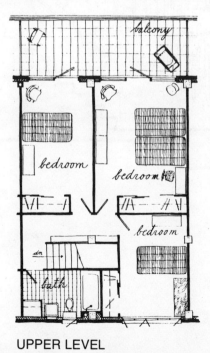

Apartment Houses, Abel and Severud,
Reinhold Publishing Co., 1947

LOWER LEVEL

UPPER LEVEL

411

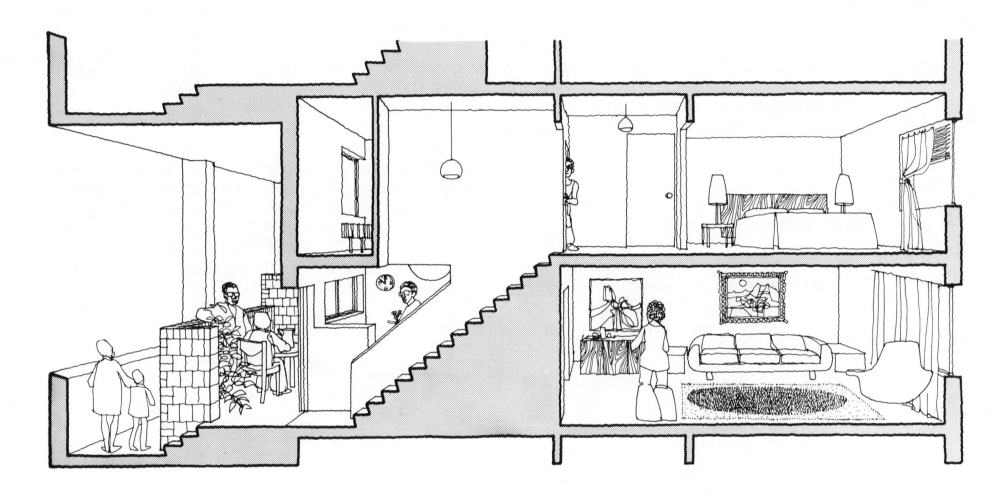

Riverbend—Davis, Brody & Associates, New York City, Architects

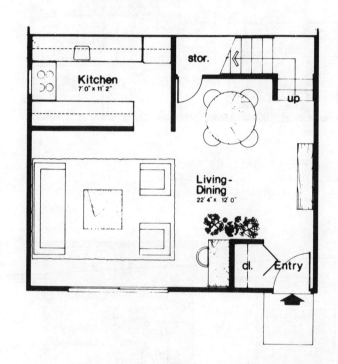

First Floor

Kitchen
7' 0" x 11' 2"

stor.

up

Living-
Dining
22' 4" x 12' 0"

cl.

Entry

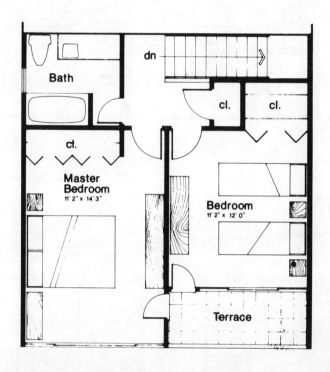

Second Floor

Bath

dn

cl.

cl.

ct.

Master
Bedroom
11' 2" x 14' 3"

Bedroom
11' 2" x 12' 0"

Terrace

G-11 DUPLEX APARTMENT

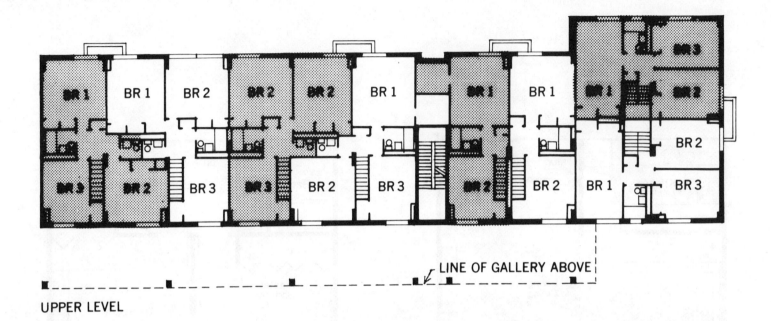

LINE OF GALLERY ABOVE

UPPER LEVEL

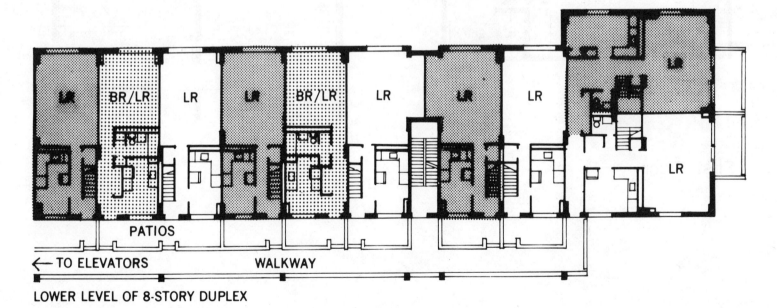

PATIOS

← TO ELEVATORS   WALKWAY

LOWER LEVEL OF 8-STORY DUPLEX

Riverbend—Davis, Brody & Associates, New York City, Architects

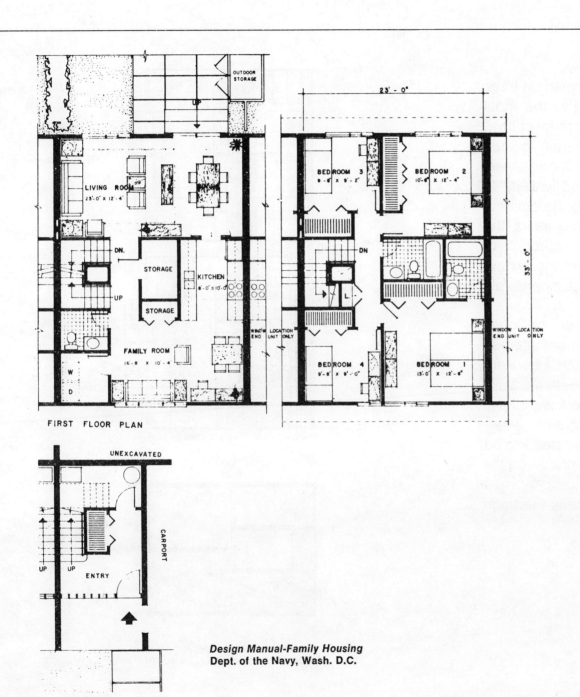

FIRST FLOOR PLAN

LIVING ROOM
23'-0" X 12'-4"

STORAGE

KITCHEN
8'-0" x 10'-0"

FAMILY ROOM
16'-8" X 10'-4"

OUTDOOR STORAGE

UP

DN.

UP

W
D

23'-0"

35'-0"

BEDROOM 3
9'-6" x 9'-2"

BEDROOM 2
10'-6" X 12'-4"

BEDROOM 4
9'-8" x 9'-0"

BEDROOM 1
13'-0" X 12'-6"

DN

L.

WINDOW LOCATION
END UNIT ONLY

WINDOW LOCATION
END UNIT ONLY

UNEXCAVATED

CARPORT

UP   UP   ENTRY

GROUND FLOOR PLAN

Design Manual-Family Housing
Dept. of the Navy, Wash. D.C.

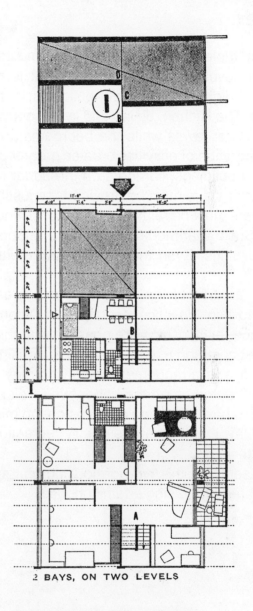

2 BAYS, ON TWO LEVELS

Apartment Houses, Abel and Severud
Reinhold Publishing Co., N.Y., 1947

415

TRIPLEX

The triplex apartment is, as its name imples, located on three different levels. This type of aprtment is restricted to the most luxurious high-rise apartment buildings, or to the three-level town houses. The kitchen, dining and living rooms are generally located on the lower levels while the bedrooms are on the upper levels. The separation of activities creates greater privacy and livability. In high-rise buildings, corridors on the upper levels may be omitted, but interior stairs must be provided. To justify the use of stairs, the apartment must be relatively large consisting of three bedrooms or more. Such apartments can only be supported in private luxury-type buildings. Even then triplex apartments are not extensively used.

A variation of the triplex utilizing three half-levels or floors, similar to a split-level house, is shown. A compact unit and interesting space relationships are possible with this approach. However, the most common use of this type of housing unit is with the town house. In this arrangement, the living may be at the lowest level and the bedrooms on the upper two levels. An alternate arrangement is to have the living activities on the middle level, sleeping on the top level, and a garage, family recreation room, or den on the lowest level.

Essentially, this type of housing unit approximates the traditional three-story, single-family house.

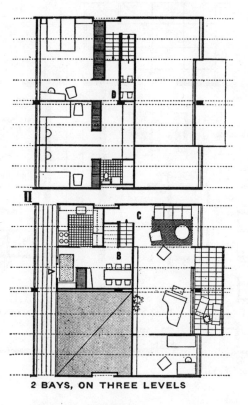

2 BAYS, ON THREE LEVELS

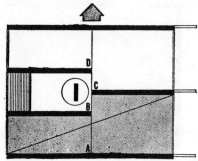

Apartment Houses, Abel and Severud
Reinhold Publishing Co., N.Y., 1947

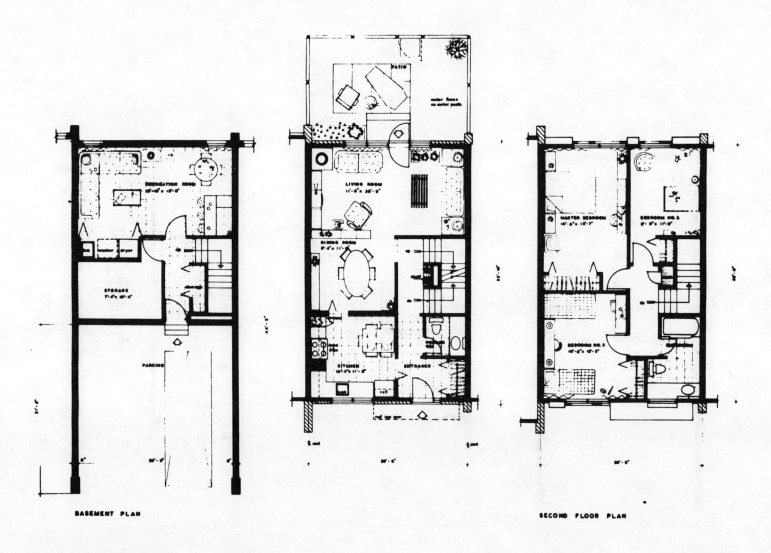

BASEMENT PLAN

SECOND FLOOR PLAN

Ottawa, Ontario—Herongate

417

G-12 TRIPLEX APARTMENT

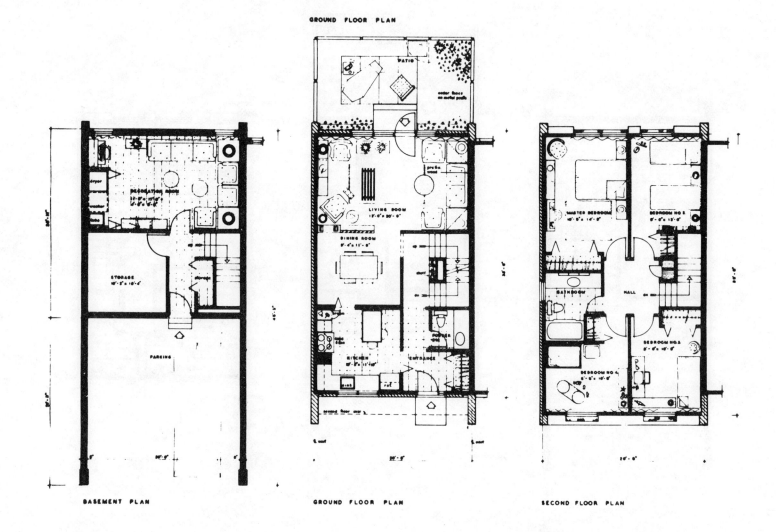

GROUND FLOOR PLAN

BASEMENT PLAN   GROUND FLOOR PLAN   SECOND FLOOR PLAN

Ottawa, Ontario—Herongate

KITCHEN ARRANGEMENTS

Kitchens and Kitchenettes

The most common type of kitchen arrangements are the (a) straight-line or galley, (b) the parallel, (c) the "U" type, or (d) the "L" type. The galley-type arrangement is used for kitchenettes that require a minimum of equipment. The parallel and "U" arrangements are considered the most efficient in regard to movement and working relationships. The "L" is more common when used in a large kitchen, which makes possible an eating area.

Kitchen

The kitchen is an area where many different functions occur. These normally include:

a. Food preparation and cleanup
b. Food storage
c. Utensil and general storage
d. Eating
e. Laundry
f. Other, miscellaneous activities.

The kitchen receives intensive use by most families, whether it is in a single-family house or a high-rise apartment.

Food Preparation

The food-preparation function has received a great deal of study and analysis. The sink, the range, and the refrigerator have been the traditional elements of food preparation and cleanup. Over the years, each of these elements has become increasingly more extensive. For example, from a simple sink it follows into a double sink, disposal units, and a dishwasher. The range has evolved into a wall oven, double oven, grille, barbecue pit, rotis-serie, and infrared oven. The refrigerator has evolved into a large-sized refrigerator, separate freezer and ice-making equipment.

The development of the sink disposal units and compactors have greatly helped in the cleanup of the food preparation. The increasing use of a large battery of mechanical appliances, such as mixers, blenders, and slicers, are adding to the complexities of the kitchen.

This constant evolution of the food preparation area of the kitchen is expected to continue and become more complicated.

Food Storage

Over the years, the type and packaging of foods available on the market has changed considerably. There has been a tremendous increase in prepackaged and semiprepared foods. All kinds of frozen foods are now available.

It can be reasonably anticipated that additional storage space for frozen foods will be needed. Sufficient storage for canned goods and other foods not requiring refrigeration is also needed.

Utensil and General Storage

Space for utensils includes storage for dishes, pots and pans, utensils, and appliances. With the increased use of such electrical appliances, their storage becomes a significant problem. General storage requires space for linens, towels, and kitchen supplies. Included in this category are brooms, mops, and other cleaning equipment and supplies.

Laundry

The laundry activities are often assigned as part of the kitchen or directly related to it. The laundry function requires a clothes washer, dryer, sink, ironing board, and storage for both dirty and clean laundry.

Minimum Kitchen Storage Required

40 to 60 sq. ft. area—Kitchenette (2)

Item	0-BR Liv. Unit (1) (sq. ft.)	1-BR Liv. Unit (sq. ft.)
Total Shelving in Wall and Base Cabinets	24	30
Shelving in Either Wall or Base Cabinets	10	12
Drawer Area	4	5
Countertop area	5	6

(1) Kitchen unit assemblies serving the kitchen function and occupying less than 40 sq. ft. area in 0-BR Living Units shall not be less than 5 feet in length and shall provide at least 12 sq. ft. of total shelving in wall and base cabinets. Drawer and countertop space shall also be provided. No room count is allowable for this type facility.

60 sq. ft. area and over—Kitchen

Item	1-BR and 2-BR Living Units (sq. ft.)	3-BR and 4-BR Living Units (sq. ft.)
Total Shelving in Wall and Base Cabinets	48	54
Shelving in Either Wall or Base Cabinets	18	20
Drawer Area	8	10
Countertop Area	10	12

a. An area occupied by sink basin(s) and by cooking units shall not be included in countertop area.

b. Usable storage space in or under ranges, or under wall ovens, when provided in the form of shelving or drawers, may be included in the minimum shelf or drawer area.

c. The shelf area of revolving base shelves (lazy susan) may be counted as twice its actual area in determining required shelf area provided the clear width of opening is at least 8-1/2 inches.

d. Drawer area in excess of the required area may be substituted for required base shelf area up to 25 percent of total shelf area.

e. At least 60 percent of required shelf space shall be enclosed by cabinet doors.

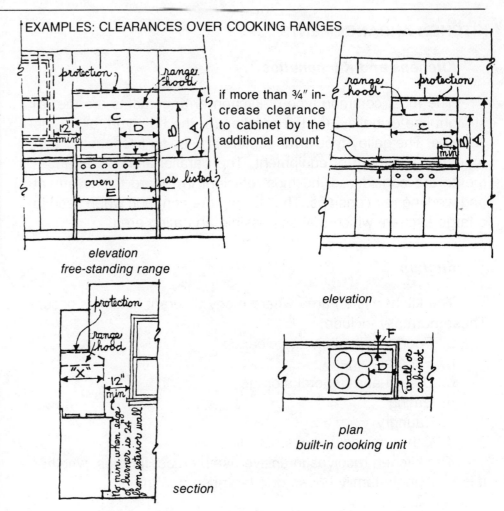

EXAMPLES: CLEARANCES OVER COOKING RANGES

if more than ¾″ increase clearance to cabinet by the additional amount

elevation
free-standing range

elevation

plan
built-in cooking unit

section

A   2′6″ min. clearance between top of range and bottom of unprotected wood or metal cabinet,
or—2′0″ min. when bottom of wood or metal cabinet is protected.

B   2′0″ min. when hood projection "X" is 18″ or more,
or—1′10″ min. when hood projection "X" is less than 18″.

C   Not less than width of range or cooking unit.

D[2]   10″ min. when vertical side surface extends above countertops.

E[2]   When range is not provided by builder, 40″ min.

F[2]   Min. clearance shall be not less than 3″.

[1]cabinet protection shall be at least ¼″ asbestos millboard covered with not less than 28 ga. sheet metal (.015 stainless steel, .024 aluminum, or .020 copper).
[2]clearance for D, E, or F shall be not less than listed UL or AGA clearances.

Kitchen Storage

Each kitchen or kitchenette shall have: (1) accessible storage space for food and utensils; (2) sufficient space for the average kitchen accessories; (3) sufficient storage space for those items of household equipment normally used and for which storage is not elsewhere provided.

width (w) in feet, times the depth (d) in feet, times the number of full-depth drawers equals area of drawer space

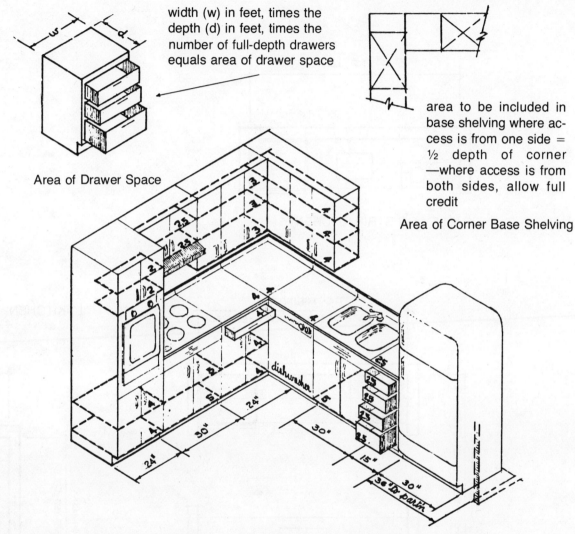

shelving that does not project past 60° may be included as required shelving

28″ min.—sink
15″ min.—other
range—see detail of previous figure

Area of Drawer Space

area to be included in base shelving where access is from one side = ½ depth of corner —where access is from both sides, allow full credit

Area of Corner Base Shelving

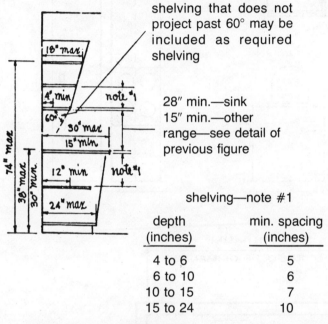

shelving—note #1

depth (inches)	min. spacing (inches)
4 to 6	5
6 to 10	6
10 to 15	7
15 to 24	10

Height, Depth, and Spacing
of Shelving and Countertop

wall shelving			base shelving			countertop			drawers		
2 s. ft.	x 2 =	4 s. ft.	4 s. ft.	x 4 =	16 s. ft.	4 s. ft.	x 3 =	12 s. ft.	4 s. ft.	x 1 =	4 s. ft.
2.5	x 2 =	5	5	x 3 =	15	2.5	x 1 =	2.5	2.5	x 4 =	10
3	x 3 =	9	2	x 2 =	4	total		14.5 s. ft.	total		14 s. ft.
4	x 3 =	12	total		35 s. ft.						
total		30 s. ft.									

EXAMPLE: MEASUREMENT OF SHELF AND COUNTERTOP AREAS

5'-0" TO 12'-0"

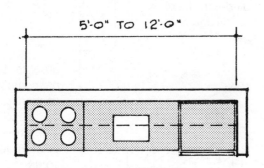

GALLEY OR STRIP KITCHEN

7'-0" TO 9'-0"

7'-0" TO 9'-0"

"L" KITCHEN

7'-0" MINIMUM
10'-0" TO 12'-0" RECOMMENDED

7'-0" MINIMUM
8'-0" RECOMMENDED

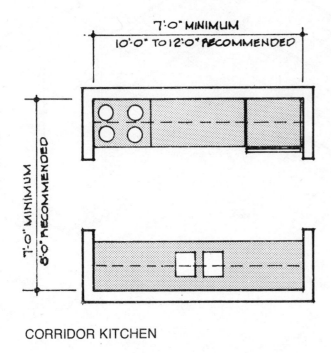

CORRIDOR KITCHEN

7'-0" MINIMUM
10'-0" TO 12'-0" RECOMMENDED

7'-0" MINIMUM
8'-0" RECOMMENDED

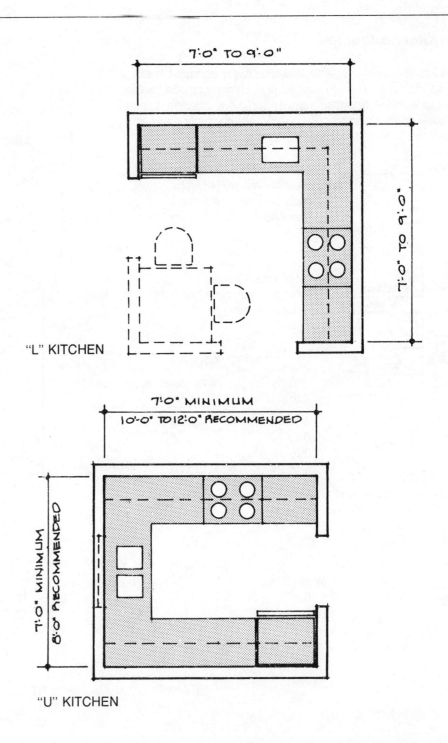

"U" KITCHEN

Eating

One of the primary functions of the kitchen has been to provide a place for informal or family eating. This is different than guest or formal dining in a separate dining room or area. The informal dining generally consists of breakfast, lunch, snacks, or just serving coffee to a neighbor. This eating area should be clearly defined as a separate functional area.

A frequent and desirable arrangement is the combined kitchen-dining area. The following sketches show the various possible arrangements. Another arrangement is the kitchen-family room.

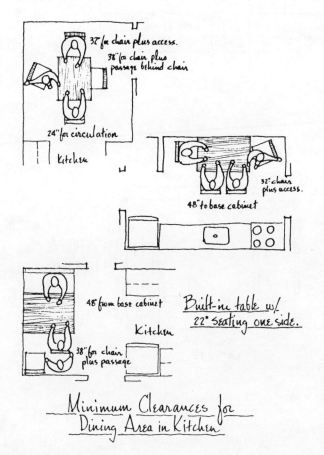

Minimum Clearances for Dining Area in Kitchen

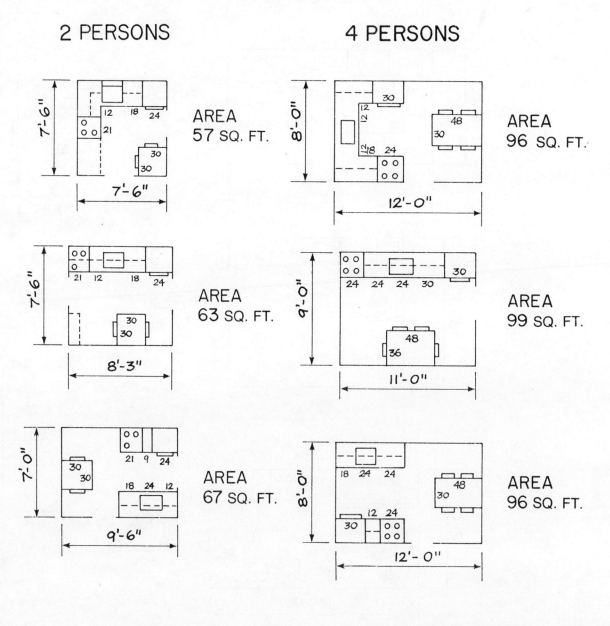

2 PERSONS

AREA
57 SQ. FT.

AREA
63 SQ. FT.

AREA
67 SQ. FT.

4 PERSONS

AREA
96 SQ. FT.

AREA
99 SQ. FT.

AREA
96 SQ. FT.

6 PERSONS

8 PERSONS

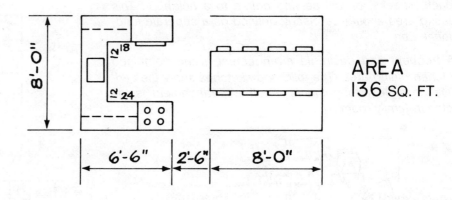

AREA
116 SQ. FT.

AREA
136 SQ. FT.

AREA
132 SQ. FT.

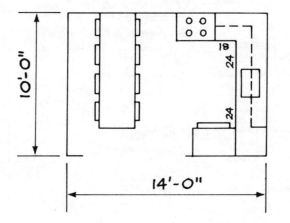

AREA
140 SQ. FT.

AREA
118 SQ. FT.

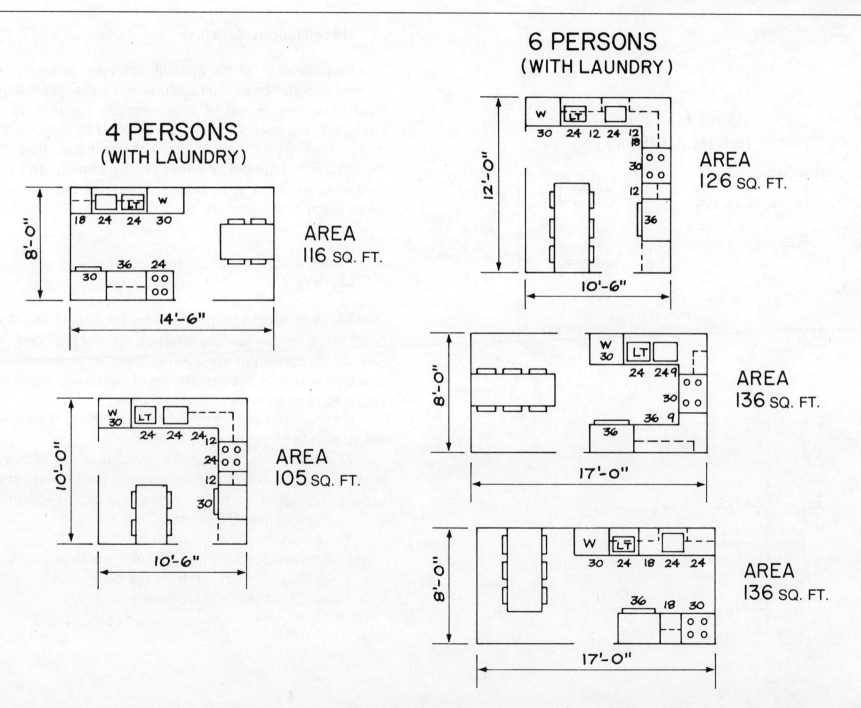

6 PERSONS
(WITH LAUNDRY)

W 30 LT 24 12 24 12 18 30 12 36

AREA
126 SQ. FT.

12'-0"
10'-6"

4 PERSONS
(WITH LAUNDRY)

18 24 LT 24 W 30 36 24 30

AREA
116 SQ. FT.

8'-0"
14'-6"

W 30 LT 24 24 24 12 24 12 30

AREA
105 SQ. FT.

10'-0"
10'-6"

W 30 LT 24 24 9 30 36 9 36

AREA
136 SQ. FT.

8'-0"
17'-0"

W LT 30 24 18 24 24 36 18 30

AREA
136 SQ. FT.

8'-0"
17'-0"

8 PERSONS
(WITH LAUNDRY)

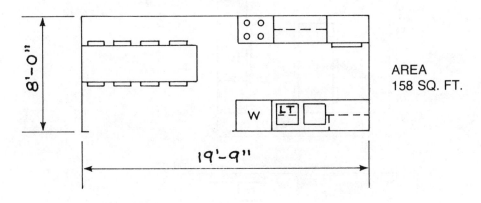

AREA
158 SQ. FT.

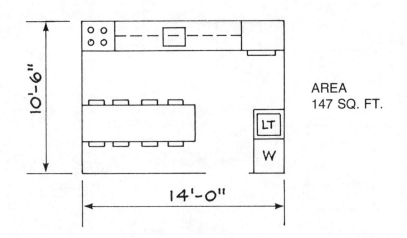

AREA
147 SQ. FT.

Miscellaneous Activities

In addition to all the specific functions indicated above, the kitchen also serves as the headquarters for a wide variety of other family activities. Some of those include entertaining, children's study and homework center, children's recreation area, ironing and clothes drying, sewing, care of the baby, shop for making repairs on household articles, hobby center, and conference center. In essence, a large percentage of the real family living takes place in the kitchen.

Laundry

Facilities should be provided for household laundry needs.

Where central laundry facilities are not provided, each living unit should contain at least a laundry tray, or a combination sink and tray fixture, or the installation of water and waste piping and space for a clothes-washing machine.

Artificial light should be provided. Clothes dryers, where provided, should be adequately vented.

The laundry facility may be located in the kitchen or family room but its location in a utility room or bathroom is preferable in order to provide more noise control and improved sanitation.

Laundry Space Allowances:

1—laundry tray, 24″ frontage x 20″
1—combination sink and tray, 42″ frontage x 21″
1—clothes washer, 30″ frontage x 30″
1—clothes dryer, 30″ frontage x 30″

Each dwelling unit should have a bathroom with enough area to accommodate a lavatory, a water closet, and a bathtub or shower. Arrangement for fixtures should provide for comfortable use of each fixture and permit at least a 90 degree door swing unless sliding doors are used.

The bathroom should be convenient to the bedroom zone, and accessible from the living and work areas. Linen storage should be accessible from the bathroom, but not located within the bathroom.

Each complete bathroom should be provided with the following:

(a) Grab-bar and soap dish at bathtub
(b) Toilet paper holder at water closet
(c) Soap dish at lavatory (may be integral with lavatory)
(d) Towel bar
(e) Mirror and medicine cabinet or equivalent enclosed shelf space
(f) In all cases where shower head is installed, provide a shower rod or shower door

Each half-bath should be provided with Items b, c, d and e as listed above.

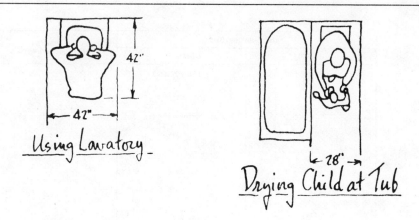

Using Lavatory

Drying Child at Tub

Bath with Tub

Bath with Shower

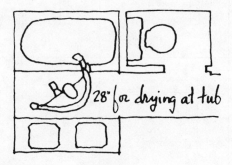

Bath with Water Closet in Separate Compartment

Minimum Clearances for Bathrooms

*Guide Criteria for the Evaluation of Operation Breakthrough—
Housing Systems,* HUD, Dept. of Commerce, National Bureau of Standards, Wash., D.C.

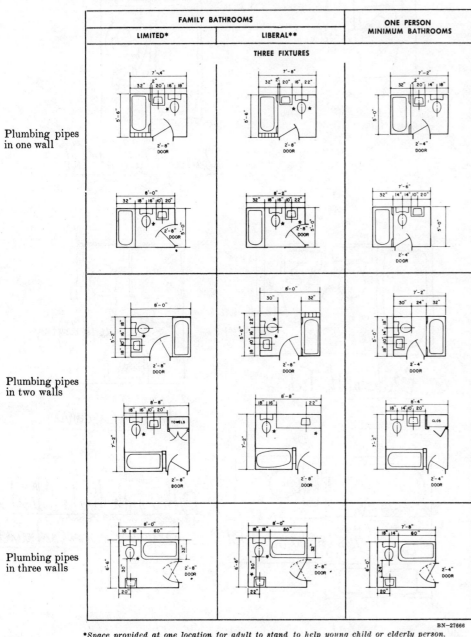

FAMILY BATHROOMS — LIMITED* — LIBERAL** — ONE PERSON MINIMUM BATHROOMS

THREE FIXTURES

Plumbing pipes in one wall

Plumbing pipes in two walls

Plumbing pipes in three walls

BN-27666

Plumbing pipes in three walls

Two lavatories, one tub, and one toilet

Two lavatories, two toilets, and one tub

Toilet, lavatory, and shower stall

FAMILY BATHROOMS — LIMITED* — LIBERAL** — ONE PERSON MINIMUM BATHROOMS

THREE FIXTURES

COMPARTMENTED BATHROOMS

FOUR FIXTURES

FIVE FIXTURES

BATHROOMS WITH SHOWER STALLS

BN-27671

*Space provided at one location for adult to stand to help young child or elderly person.
**Space provided at two locations for adult to stand to help young child or elderly person.

*Space provided at one location for adult to stand to help young child or elderly person.
**Space provided at two locations for adult to stand to help young child or elderly person.

LIVING ROOMS

The size of the living room should reflect the size of the dwelling unit and the economic status of the occupants. A living room for a three- or four-bedroom dwelling unit requires more space for its occupants than one for a one- or two-bedroom dwelling unit. Luxury units will necessarily need more space to accommodate more furnishings. In any case, the minimum living room with no dining facilities should be approximately 180 square feet but preferably around 200 square feet. A and B show two living rooms with typical furniture groupings (no dining facilities).

C shows a living room with one end used for dining. This area often is arranged in an "L" shape to achieve greater definition or privacy from the living activities. Dwelling units with three or more bedrooms should have separate dining rooms or clearly defined dining areas.

The range of living activities generally includes a conversation area (sitting area), relaxation area (books, T.V. and music center), a work area (sewing machine, desk and chair), and an entertainment area (bar, card table, terrace). Often it is the center of child-play if there is no space in the kitchen.

The minimum width of a living room should be 11'0" to 12'0". The recommended width is 14'0". There should be no through traffic in the living room. Preferably, the living room should be a dead-end space with all traffic handled at one end.

The major problem is to provide for the necessary flexibility in order to achieve the various activities. Separation and some degree of privacy is required. When the living room is combined with dining area, the dining area should be offset into an alcove or be clearly identified as such.

A

for 1- and 2-bedroom apartments
12'6" x 16'0"
200 sf.

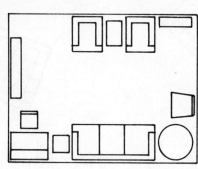

B

for 3-bedroom apartments
12'6" x 20'0"
250 sf.

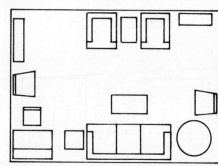

C

for 3-bedroom apartments
12'6" x 22'0"
275 sf.

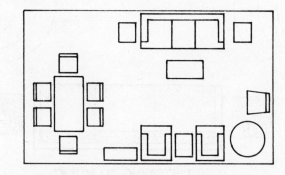

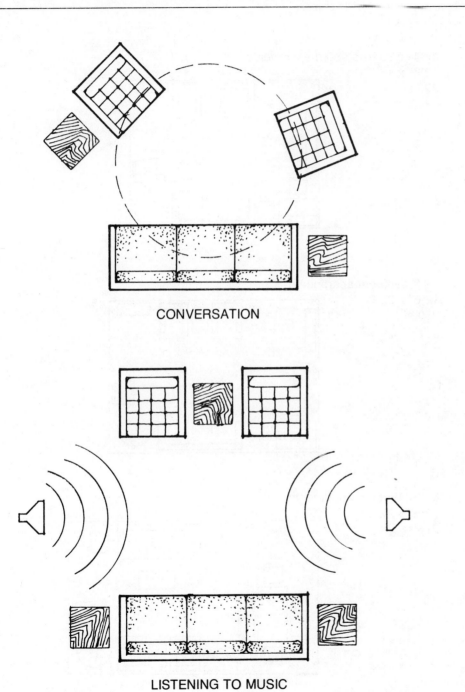

CONVERSATION

LISTENING TO MUSIC

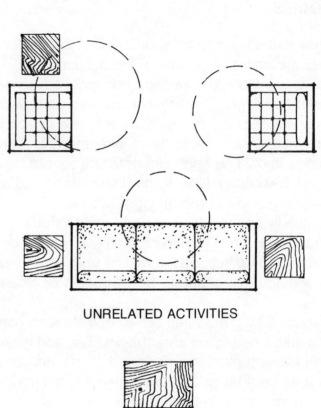

UNRELATED ACTIVITIES

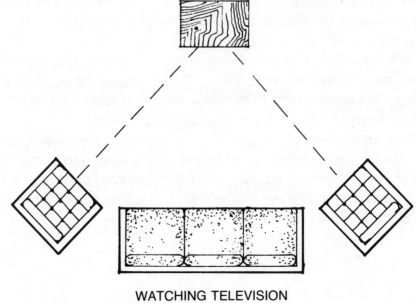

WATCHING TELEVISION

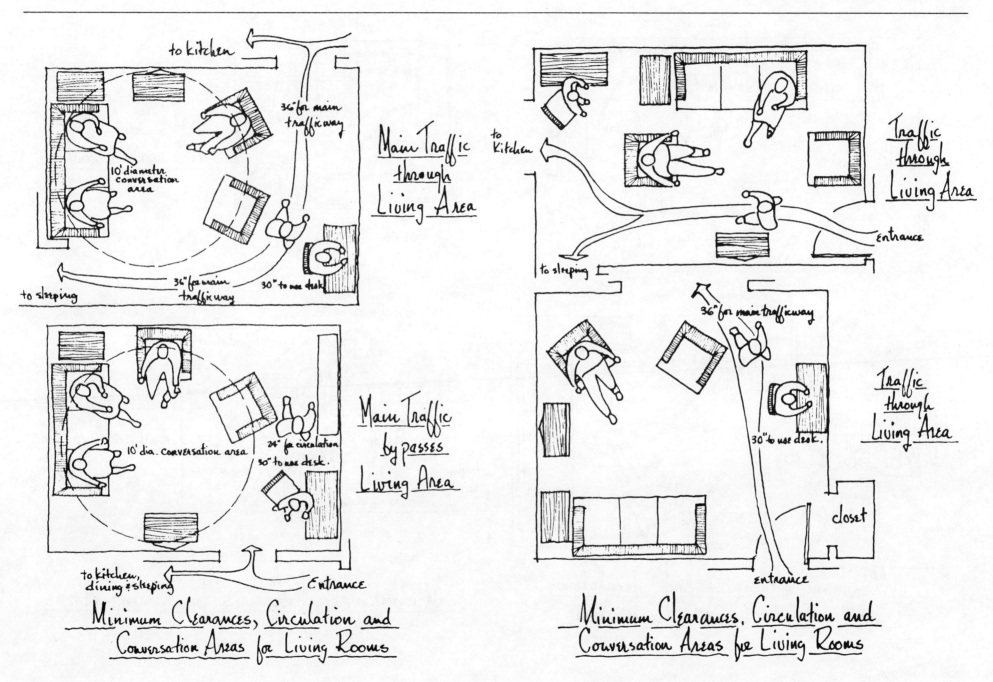

to kitchen

36" for main trafficway

10' diameter conversation area

Main Traffic through Living Area

36" for main trafficway

30" to use desk

to sleeping

Traffic through Living Area

to kitchen

to sleeping

entrance

10' dia. conversation area

24" for circulation

30" to use desk.

Main Traffic bypasses Living Area

to kitchen, dining & sleeping

Entrance

Minimum Clearances, Circulation and Conversation Areas for Living Rooms

36" for main trafficway

30" to use desk.

Traffic through Living Area

closet

entrance

Minimum Clearances, Circulation and Conversation Areas for Living Rooms

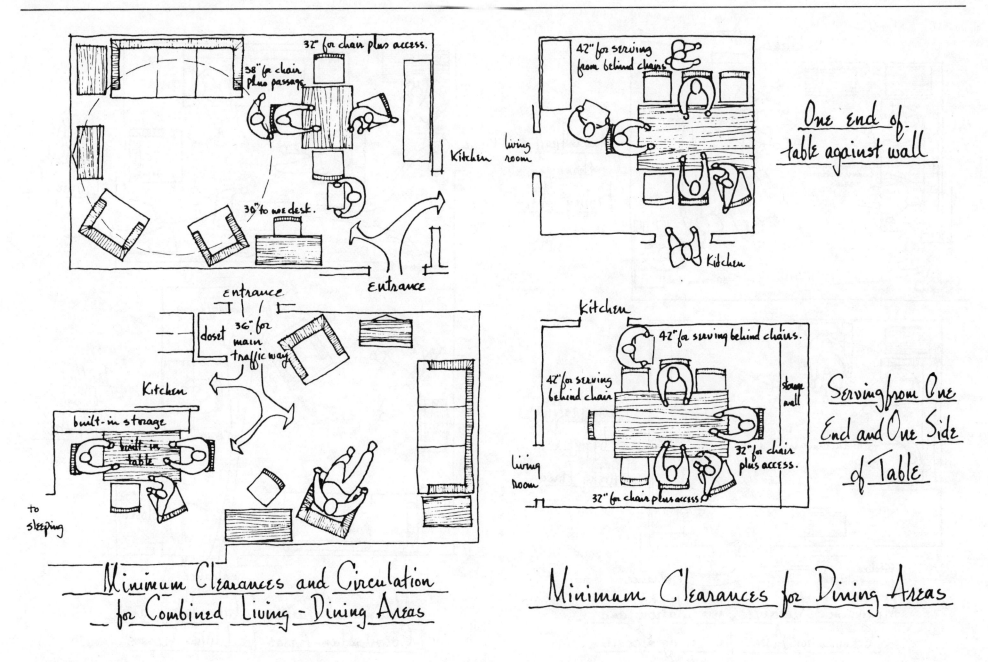

32" for chair plus access.

38" for chair plus passage

30" to use desk.

Entrance

42" for serving from behind chairs

living room

Kitchen

One End of table against wall

Kitchen

entrance

closet

36" for main traffic way

Kitchen

built-in storage

built-in table

to sleeping

Minimum Clearances and Circulation for Combined Living - Dining Areas

Kitchen

42" for serving behind chairs.

42" for serving behind chair

storage wall

living room

32" for chair plus access.

32" for chair plus access

Serving from One End and One Side of Table

Minimum Clearances for Dining Areas

DINING ROOMS

The dining area should be large enough to accommodate comfortably all members of the household. In addition, provisions for occasional guests are necessary. If no cabinets or breakfronts are used, the minimum size should be 10'0" x 10'0". If some furniture is used, the minimum size should be 12'0" x 12'0".

Table Sizes[1]

The following are minimum table sizes for eating purposes. (Sizes are based on individual spaces with a frontage of 24 inches and an area of approximately 240 square inches.) Tables must also be large enough to accommodate serving dishes, and other table utensils.

	Seating on 2 sides	Seating on 4 sides	
	(dimensions in inches)		
For 2 persons	30 x 30		
3-4 persons	30 x 48	30 x 38	
5-6 persons	30 x 72	40 x 48	48" round
7-8 persons	30 x96	40 x 72	60" round

Clearance:

For chairs plus access thereto:	26 inches
For chairs plus access and passage:	30 inches
From table to wall for passage:	30 inches
From table to base cabinet or appliances:	48 inches (36" for kitchen in 2 person households)

The tables designated for seating on two sides are generally larger than those specified for seating on four sides. However, seating on two sides almost invariably requires less room space, as can be seen in the illustration.

The 26-inch clearance specified for "chairs plus access thereto" provides the space necessary to edge into the seating after the chairs have been moved back from the table. This is *not* sufficient clearance for an individual to pass behind the chair once it is occupied.

[1]Adapted from *Performance-Based Space Criteria for Low-Cost Housing,* Rudyard A. Jones and William H. Kapple, A.I.A.

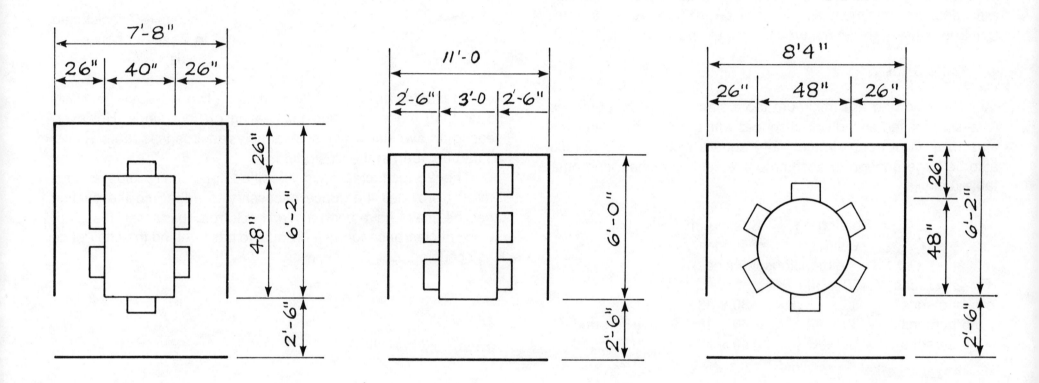

The Performance Concept: A Study of Its Application to Housing—Vol. III,
John P. Eberhard, Institute of Applied Technology, Wash. D.C. 1969

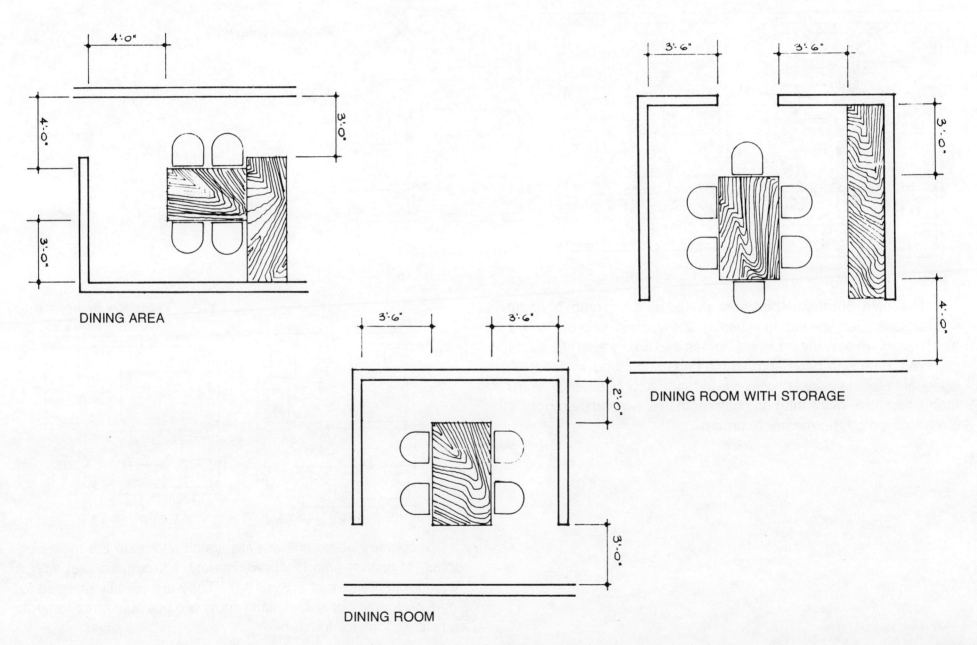

DINING AREA

DINING ROOM

DINING ROOM WITH STORAGE

G-18 BEDROOMS

BEDROOMS

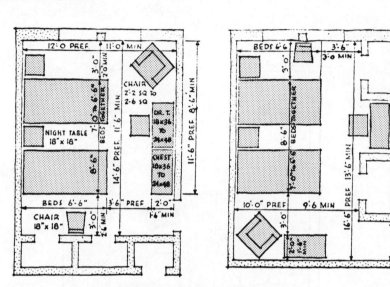

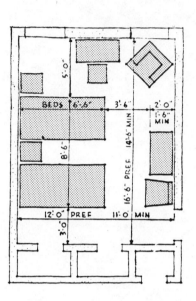

The main, or master, bedroom should be a minimum of about 125 square feet, excluding closets. Many main bedrooms are much larger, especially in private homes and luxury apartments. In planning, both twin beds and double beds should be considered; adequate closet space is required. In many new houses or apartments that have more than one bathroom, the second bathroom is often located off the master bedroom.

Secondary Bedrooms

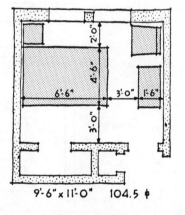

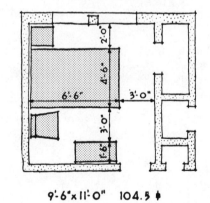

Secondary bedrooms are always smaller than the main bedrooms. Minimum size is approximately 100 square feet with a minimum dimension of 8'6" to 9'0". They are usually planned for single or double beds. The plans show two possible arrangements and clearances for furniture.

The bedroom, in addition to being a place to sleep, may contain other activities. These include relaxation (terrace, lounge chair), work area (desk, sewing machine), entertainment (radio, books, T.V. and music center), dressing (closets, dressing table), and children's recreation and study areas.

The major characteristic of the bedroom is the privacy it provides and the complete separation from other parts of the dwelling. Bedrooms may have single or double occupancy. More than two persons per room is considered overcrowding.

The minimum size of a bedroom, not including closets, should not be less than 10'0" x 10'0". A recommended minimum should be 10'0" x 12'0". Larger bedrooms should not be less than 12'0" x 16'0".

A larger proportion of the bedroom floor area is occupied by furniture than is the case with any other room; windows and doors account for a large percentage of the wall and partition space. These two factors complicate the planning of bedrooms, especially when the rooms are small.

Because of the room layout, some bedrooms with smaller areas better meet the needs than larger ones. The location of doors, windows, and closets must be properly planned to allow the best placement of the bed and other furniture.

Privacy, both visual and sound, are desirable for the bedroom. Children's bedrooms should be located away from the living room, because conversation in the living room prevents the children from sleeping. Closets should be used between all bedrooms wherever possible.

Each child needs a space that is his own to develop a sense of responsibility and a respect for the property rights of others. The ideal plan would provide a bedroom for each child, but since this is not always possible, there should be a bed for each.

The minimum room width shall be determined by the space required for the bed, activity space and any furniture facing the bed. Widths less than 9'0" will usually require extra area to accommodate comparable furniture.

Aside from sleeping, the bedroom is the center of dressing and undressing activities. An interrelationship exists between dressing, storage of clothes and the bedroom.

Inevitably, in a small apartment, it is not only economical but necessary to plan the use of the bedroom for more than one activity. It is essential to incorporate in the bedroom other functions such as relaxation, work or entertainment.

G-18 BEDROOMS

Master Bedroom–Minimum Furniture Requirements

Parents' or master bedrooms must be larger than others, because their possessions are larger, and the rooms sometimes accommodate the baby. Following is the recommended furniture:

Bed:
  1 double bed 4'6" x 6'6"
  or single beds 3'3" x 6'6" each

  1 crib 2'4" x 1'5"

Storage furniture:
  1 dresser 3'6" x 1'10"
  1 chest of drawers 2'6" x 1'10"

Chairs:
  1 or 2   1'6" x 1'6" each

Two night tables

Desk or table for sewing machine or other work 1'6" x 3'0"

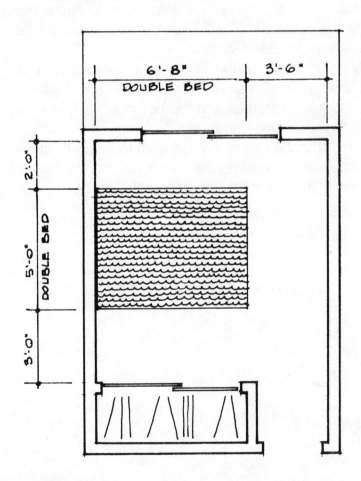

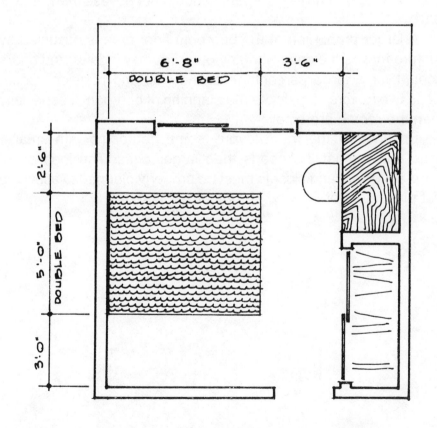

Bedroom for Two Children–Minimum Furniture Requirements

Beds:
  2 single beds (each 3′3″ x 6′6″)
  or 1 double bed 4′6″ x 6′6″

Storage Furniture:
  1 dresser 3′6″ x 1′10″
  1 chest or desk 1′6″ x 2′6″ for children's toys and for play

Chairs:
  1 or 2   1′6″ x 1′6″ each

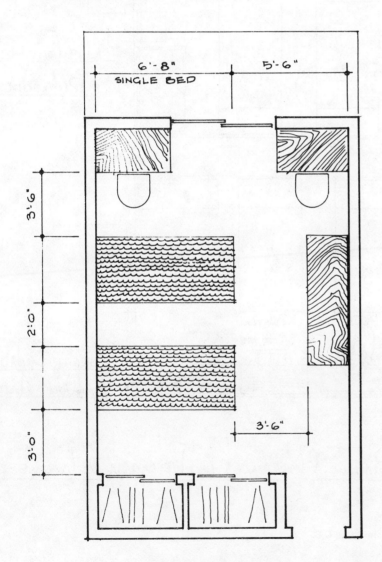

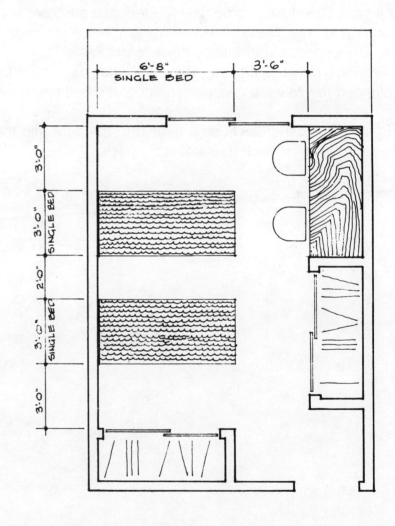

Location

(a) The bedroom or sleeping area of the living unit should be located away from the living and working areas for privacy.

(b) In the analysis of the bedroom area, there should be a regard for the make-up of the family. With preschool children, it is convenient if the master bedroom is located close to children's bedrooms. With teenage children, separation of the master bedroom from other bedrooms wherever possible to reduce noise is desirable.

(c) The location of doors, windows, and closets should be planned to allow the best placement of the bed and other furniture.

(d) Placement of the closet so it is next to the door into the bedroom minimizes the use of wall space.

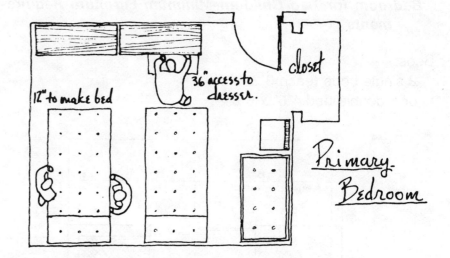

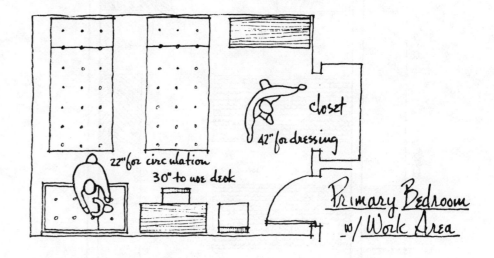

Minimum Clearances in Primary Bedrooms

HUD—Washington, D.C.

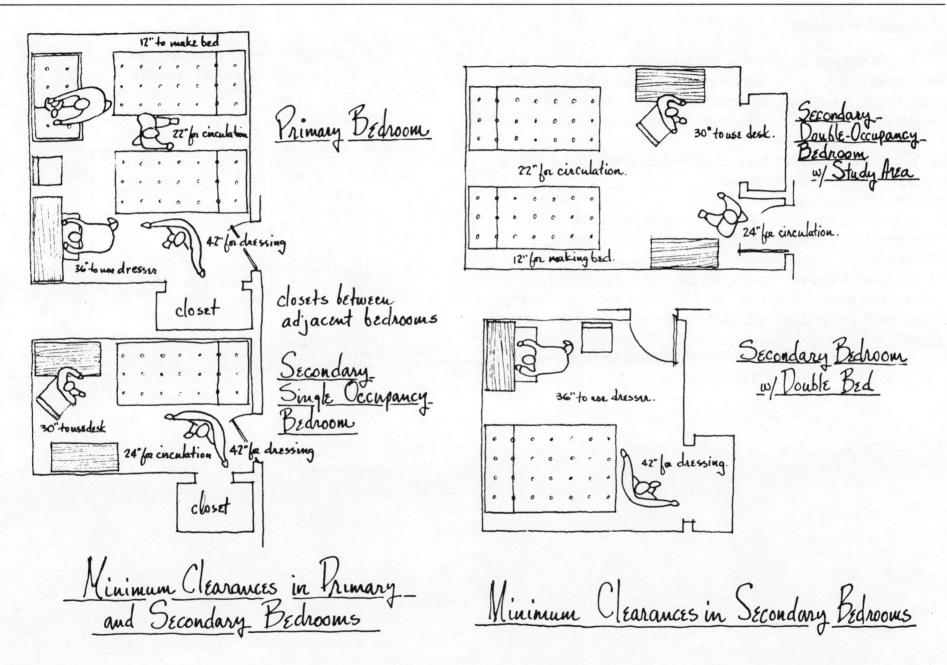

12" to make bed

22" for circulation

Primary Bedroom

36" to use dresser

42" for dressing

closets between adjacent bedrooms

30" to use desk

24" for circulation

42" for dressing

Secondary Single Occupancy Bedroom

closet

Minimum Clearances in Primary and Secondary Bedrooms

30" to use desk.

22" for circulation.

12" for making bed.

Secondary Double-Occupancy Bedroom w/ Study Area

24" for circulation.

36" to use dresser.

42" for dressing.

Secondary Bedroom w/ Double Bed

Minimum Clearances in Secondary Bedrooms

HUD—Washington, D.C.

Bedroom Closets

Ample storage is essential. Each bedroom requires at least one clothes closet. For master bedrooms, at least five linear feet of closet length is needed. For secondary bedrooms, at least three linear feet is needed. Clothes closets require a clear depth of two feet.

Each bedroom shall have at least one closet that meets or exceeds the following standards:

a. Depth—2 feet, clear
b. Length—(For Primary Bedroom)—5 linear feet clear
   Length—(For Secondary Bedroom)—3 linear feet clear
c. Height:
   (1) At least 5'4" clear hanging space
   (2) Lowest shelf shall not be over 6'2" above the floor of room.
d. One shelf and rod with at least 12 inches clear space above shelf.
e. At least one-half the closet floor shall be level and not more than 12 inches above floor of adjacent room.

EXAMPLE: MINIMUM DIMENSIONS
OF REQUIRED CLOSETS

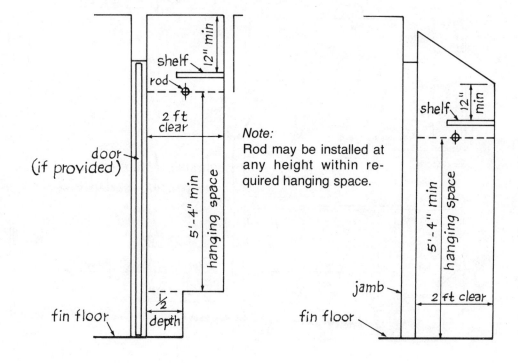

Note:
Rod may be installed at any height within required hanging space.

OUTDOOR LIVING SPACE

Space for living, dining, or just relaxing need not be confined to the interior of a dwelling unit. Full advantage of outdoor living areas should be taken, especially where the climate permits it for more than a few months of the year. By properly designing and integrating the indoor-outdoor areas, the entire living space can be greatly enhanced at a minimum of cost. The most common methods used are the:

Balcony—Usually designed as an extension of an apartment unit in a high-rise building. In the past, most have been constructed for limited use and inadequately sheltered. Since the balcony is above the ground and in close proximity to other balconies, privacy and protection is most essential. Also, because of the construction cost, balconies have tended to be minimal in size.

Terrace—Generally related to the extension of the first floor at grade level of the living-dining area. Because of the simplicity of the slab on grade, terraces have tended to be more expansive than balconies. Terraces related to multipurpose rooms or even bedrooms are not uncommon.

Patios—Patios are similar to terraces and always located on the lowest levels on grade.

Enclosed porch—The enclosed porch is not truly an outdoor space because it usually has a roof overhead and is partially enclosed. However, it does serve as a transitional or in-between area of the indoors and the outdoors.

All outdoor spaces should have ample space to properly function, be adequately screened and sheltered for privacy, and be functionally integrated with the adjacent living area.

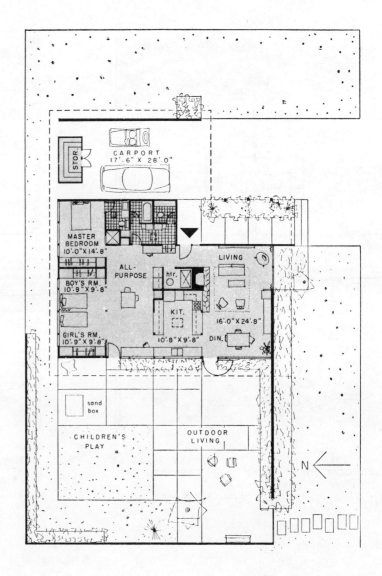

House and Home, **August, 1954**

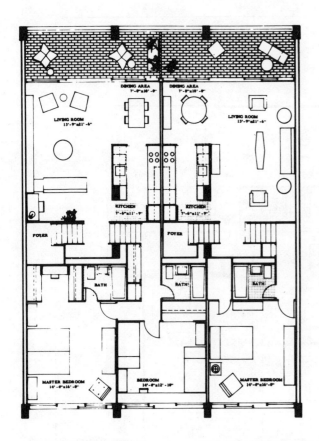

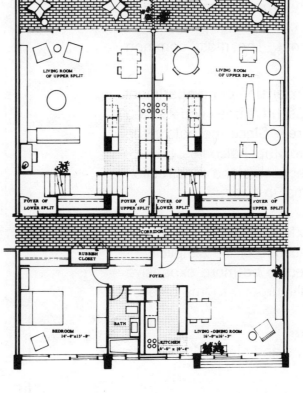

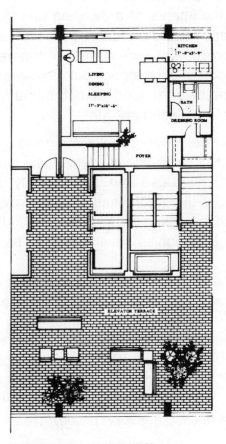

LOWER SPLIT LEVEL
2 BEDROOM UNIT

6 1/2 ROOMS

LOWER SPLIT LEVEL
1 BEDROOM UNIT

5 ROOMS

1 BEDROOM FLAT

4 3/4 ROOMS

O BEDROOM APARTMENT

3 1/4 ROOMS

KELLY & GRUZEN   ARCHITECTS
Robert E. Alexander, F.A.I.A. and Associates

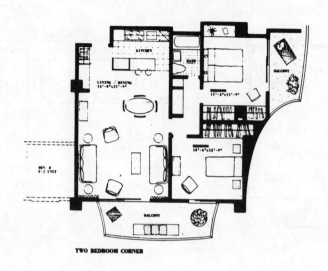

TWO BEDROOM CORNER

ONE BEDROOM & DEN

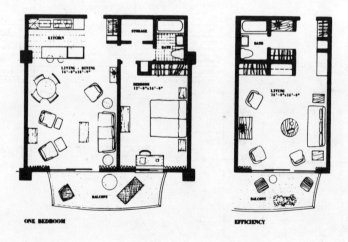

ONE BEDROOM   EFFICIENCY

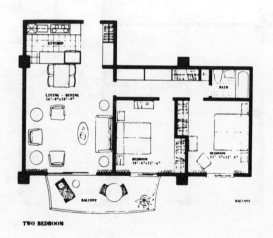

TWO BEDROOM

Ladd & Kelsey—Architects

TYPICAL HIGH RISE LIVING UNITS

TWO BEDROOM TYPE 2-b

EFFICIENCY TYPE E-a

TWO BEDROOM TYPE 2-c

TWO BEDROOM TYPE 2-a

ONE BEDROOM TYPE 1-a

TYPICAL UNIT PLANS

TYPICAL FLOOR PLAN
SCALE: 1/16" = 1'-0"

TABULATION

APARTMENT TYPE	TOTAL NO. IN PROJECT	PER. UNIT			PER. FLOOR		PER. BLDG.	
		AREA (SQ.FT)	F.H.A. ROOM COUNT		UNITS	F.H.A. ROOM COUNT	UNITS	F.H.A. ROOM COUNT
EFFICIENCY			LR-DA-BR 2 / K ½ / BATH ½ / FOYER ¼					
Ea	95	580	3½		1	3¼	19	61¾
TOTAL EFFICIENCY	—	—	—		1	3¼	19	61¾
I BEDROOM			LR-DA 2 / K 1 / BR 1 / BATH ½ / FOYER ¼					
1a	190	940	4¾		2	9½	38	180½
			LR-DA 1½ / K 1 / BR 1 / BATH ½ / FOYER ¼					
1b	190	775	4¼		2	8½	38	161½
TOTAL I BEDROOM	—	—	—		4	18	76	342
2 BEDROOM			LR-DA 2 / K 1 / BR'S(2) 2 / BATH ½ / FOYER ¼					
2a	190	1190	5¾		2	11½	38	218½
			LR-DA 2 / K 1 / BR'S(2) 2 / BATHS(2) ½ / FOYER ¼					
2b	190	1250	6¼		2	12½	38	237½
			LR-DA 2 / K 1 / BR'S(2) 2 / BATHB(2) 1 / FOYER ¼					
2c	95	1175	6¼		1	6¼	19	118¾
TOTAL 2 BEDROOM	—	—	—		5	30¼	95	574¾
TOTAL UNITS & ROOM COUNTS-UPPER LEVELS	—	—	—		10	51½	190	978½
GROUND LEVEL UNITS	30	—	—		—	—	6	43
TOTALS	—	—	—		—	—	196	1021½
GROSS BLDG. AREA	—	—	—		11,335 SQ.FT.		238,035 SQ.FT.	

THE TOWER BUILDING
21 STORY

Victor Gruen Associates ● Architects ● Engineering ● Planning

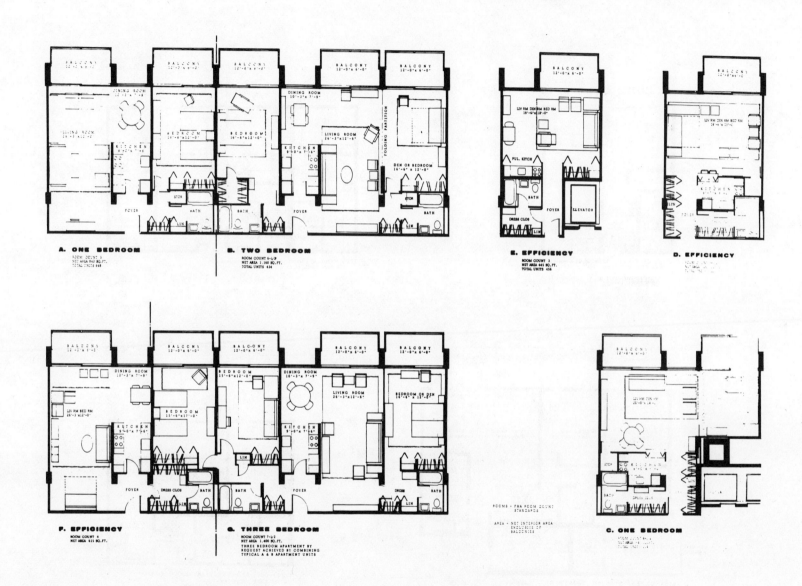

A. ONE BEDROOM
ROOM COUNT 3
NET AREA 842 SQ.FT.
TOTAL UNITS 948

B. TWO BEDROOM
ROOM COUNT 6-U.P
NET AREA 1,160 SQ.FT.
TOTAL UNITS 434

E. EFFICIENCY
ROOM COUNT 3
NET AREA 645 SQ.FT.
TOTAL UNITS 456

D. EFFICIENCY

F. EFFICIENCY
ROOM COUNT 4
NET AREA 615 SQ.FT.

G. THREE BEDROOM
ROOM COUNT 7-U.2
NET AREA 1,400 SQ.FT.
THREE BEDROOM APARTMENT BY
REQUEST ACHIEVED BY COMBINING
TYPICAL A & B APARTMENT UNITS

ROOMS - FHA ROOM COUNT
STANDARDS

AREA - NET INTERIOR AREA
EXCLUSIVE OF
BALCONIES

C. ONE BEDROOM

Architects: Milton Schwartz and Associates
Planning Consultants: Simon Eisner and Associates

447

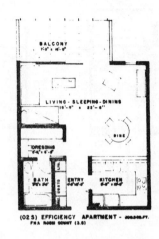

(02 S) EFFICIENCY APARTMENT - 200,000 SQ.FT.
FHA ROOM COUNT (3.0)

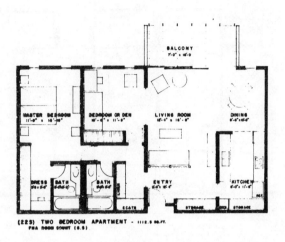

(22 S) TWO BEDROOM APARTMENT - 1112.5 SQ.FT.
FHA ROOM COUNT (6.5)

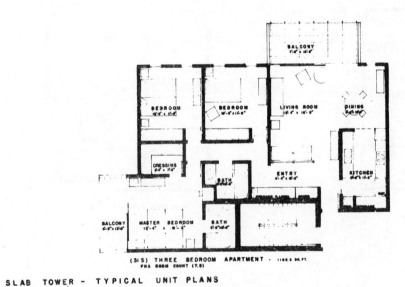

(31 S) THREE BEDROOM APARTMENT - 1160.5 SQ.FT.
FHA ROOM COUNT (7.5)

SLAB TOWER - TYPICAL UNIT PLANS

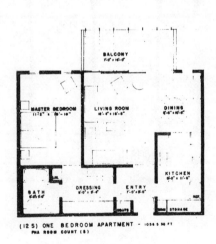

(12 S) ONE BEDROOM APARTMENT - 1056.5 SQ.FT.
FHA ROOM COUNT (5)

Maynard Lyndon, A. Quincy Jones, Frederick E. Emmons, Associated Architects

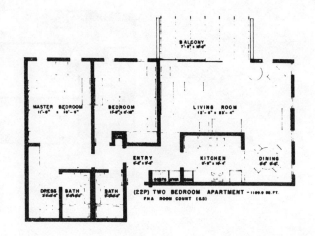

(22P) TWO BEDROOM APARTMENT - 1199.0 SQ. FT.
FHA ROOM COUNT (6.5)

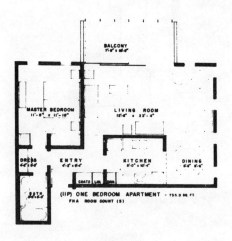

(11P) ONE BEDROOM APARTMENT - 735.0 SQ. FT.
FHA ROOM COUNT (5)

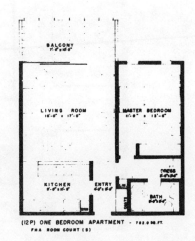

(12P) ONE BEDROOM APARTMENT - 782.0 SQ. FT.
FHA ROOM COUNT (5)

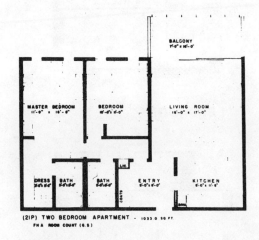

(21P) TWO BEDROOM APARTMENT - 1033.0 SQ. FT.
FHA ROOM COUNT (6.5)

POINT TOWER - TYPICAL UNIT PLANS

Maynard Lyndon, A. Quincy Jones, Frederick E. Emmons, Associated Architects

449

G-20 COMBINATION OF DWELLING UNIT TYPES

0 BEDROOM

1 BEDROOM

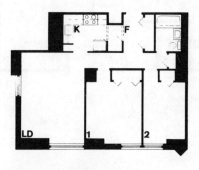

2 BEDROOM

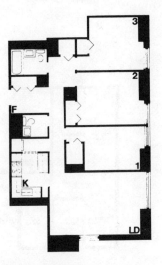

3 BEDROOM

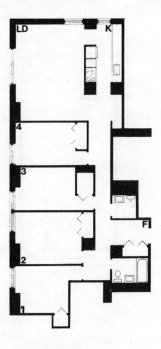

4 BEDROOM

Harlem River Park Housing
Davis, Brody and Associates, Architects

0 BEDROOM

1 BEDROOM

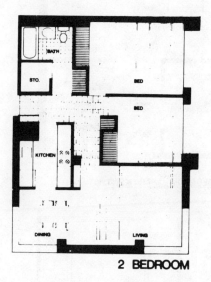

2 BEDROOM

Warburton Houses at Ashburton Avenue
New York State Urban Development Corporation, Yonkers, N.Y.
Louis Sauer Associates, Architects

G-20 COMBINATION OF DWELLING UNIT TYPES

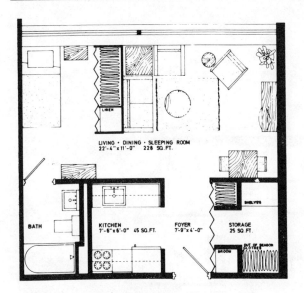

TYPICAL ZERO BEDROOM APARTMENT

GROSS AREA 483 SQ. FT.

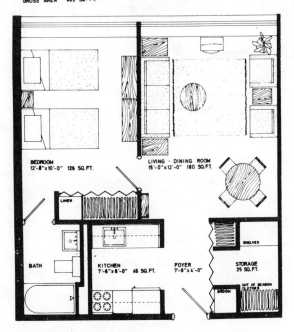

TYPICAL ONE BEDROOM APARTMENT

GROSS AREA 575 SQ. FT.

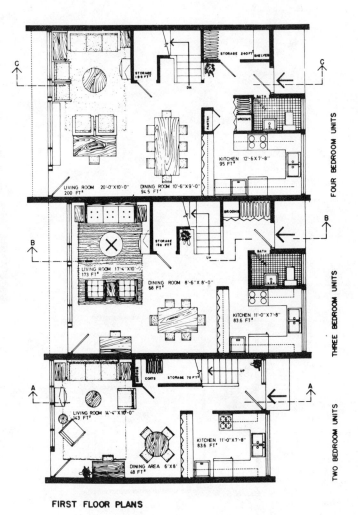

FIRST FLOOR PLANS

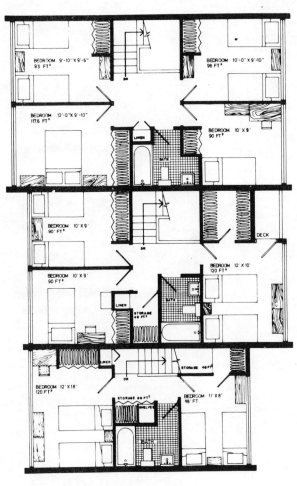

SECOND FLOOR PLANS

Charlotte Area Project, Rochester, New York
New York State Urban Development Corporation
Northrup Kaelber and Kopf, Architects and Engineers
Rochester, N.Y.

452

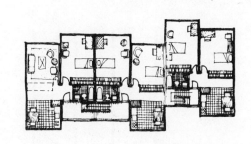
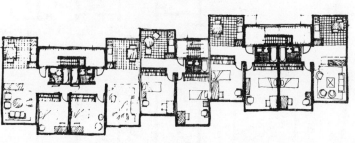

second floor plan

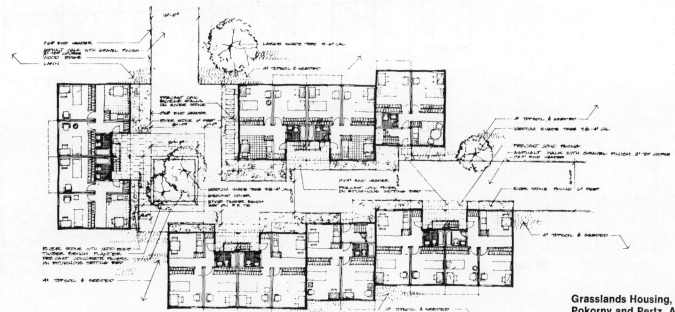

first floor plan

**Grasslands Housing, Westchester
Pokorny and Pertz, Architects**

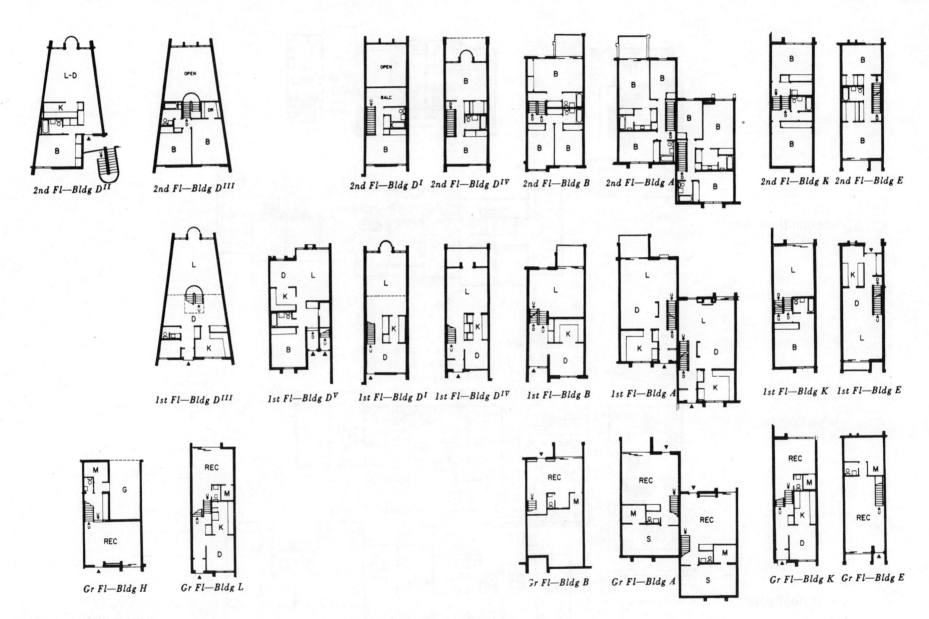

2nd Fl—Bldg D^{II}   2nd Fl—Bldg D^{III}   2nd Fl—Bldg D^{I}   2nd Fl—Bldg D^{IV}   2nd Fl—Bldg B   2nd Fl—Bldg A   2nd Fl—Bldg K   2nd Fl—Bldg E

1st Fl—Bldg D^{III}   1st Fl—Bldg D^{V}   1st Fl—Bldg D^{I}   1st Fl—Bldg D^{IV}   1st Fl—Bldg B   1st Fl—Bldg A   1st Fl—Bldg K   1st Fl—Bldg E

Gr Fl—Bldg H   Gr Fl—Bldg L   Gr Fl—Bldg B   Gr Fl—Bldg A   Gr Fl—Bldg K   Gr Fl—Bldg E

Reston, Virginia
Conklin & Rossant, Architects

454

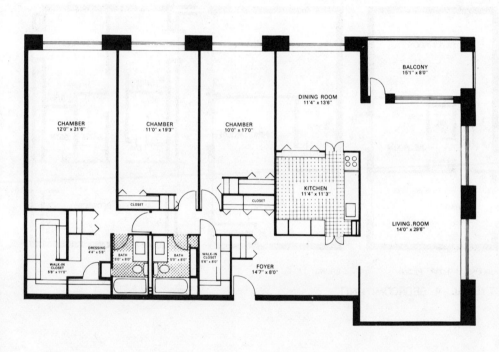

CHAMBER
12'0" x 21'6"

CHAMBER
11'0" x 19'3"

CHAMBER
10'0" x 17'0"

DINING ROOM
11'4" x 13'6"

BALCONY
15'1" x 8'0"

KITCHEN
11'4" x 11'3"

CLOSET

CLOSET

LIVING ROOM
14'0" x 29'6"

DRESSING
4'4" x 5'6"

BATH
5'0" x 8'0"

BATH
5'0" x 8'0"

WALK-IN
CLOSET
5'6" x 8'0"

FOYER
14'7" x 8'0"

WALK-IN
CLOSET
5'8" x 11'0"

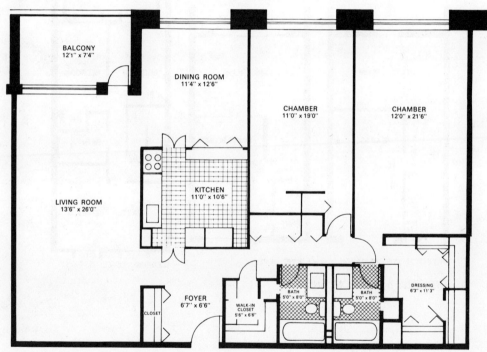

BALCONY
12'1" x 7'4"

DINING ROOM
11'4" x 12'6"

CHAMBER
11'0" x 19'0"

CHAMBER
12'0" x 21'6"

LIVING ROOM
13'6" x 26'0"

KITCHEN
11'0" x 10'6"

FOYER
6'7" x 6'6"

CLOSET

WALK-IN
CLOSET
5'6" x 6'6"

BATH
5'0" x 8'0"

BATH
5'0" x 8'0"

DRESSING
6'3" x 11'3"

**Scarborough Manor
Westchester, N.Y.**

455

G-20 COMBINATION OF DWELLING UNIT TYPES

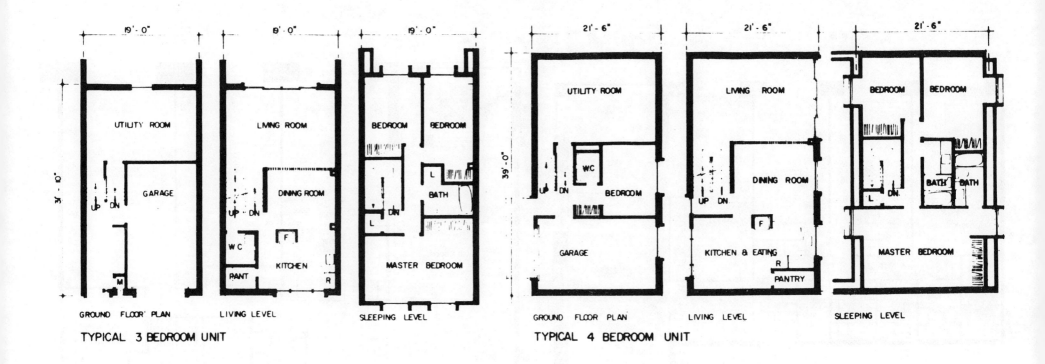

19'-0"　　　19'-0"　　　19'-0"

UTILITY ROOM

GARAGE

UP DN

M

GROUND FLOOR PLAN

LIVING ROOM

DINING ROOM

UP DN

F

WC

PANT

KITCHEN

R

LIVING LEVEL

BEDROOM　BEDROOM

L

BATH

DN

L

MASTER BEDROOM

SLEEPING LEVEL

TYPICAL 3 BEDROOM UNIT

21'-6"　　　21'-6"　　　21'-6"

39'-0"

UTILITY ROOM

WC

UP DN

BEDROOM

GARAGE

GROUND FLOOR PLAN

LIVING ROOM

DINING ROOM

UP DN

F

KITCHEN & EATING

R

PANTRY

LIVING LEVEL

BEDROOM　BEDROOM

L DN

BATH BATH

MASTER BEDROOM

SLEEPING LEVEL

TYPICAL 4 BEDROOM UNIT

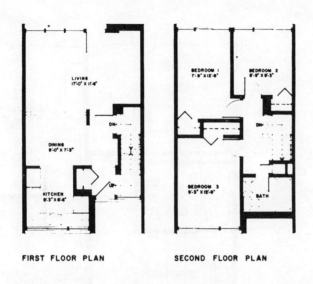

FIRST FLOOR PLAN SECOND FLOOR PLAN

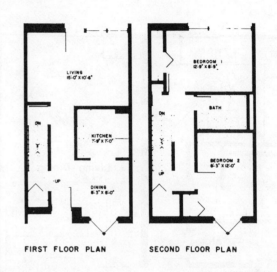

FIRST FLOOR PLAN SECOND FLOOR PLAN

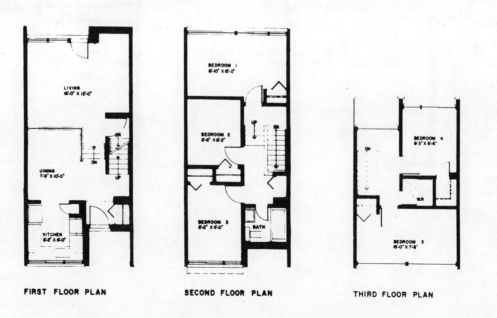

FIRST FLOOR PLAN SECOND FLOOR PLAN THIRD FLOOR PLAN

G-20 COMBINATION OF DWELLING UNIT TYPES

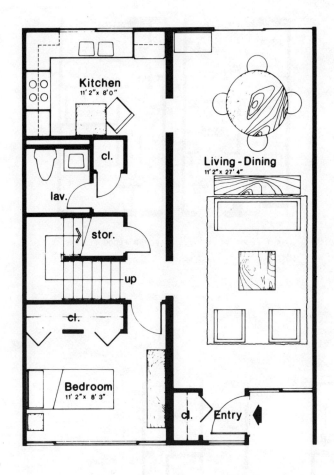

Kitchen
11' 2" x 8' 0"

cl.

lav.

stor.

up

cl.

Living - Dining
11' 2" x 27' 4"

Bedroom
11' 2" x 8' 3"

cl. Entry

First Floor

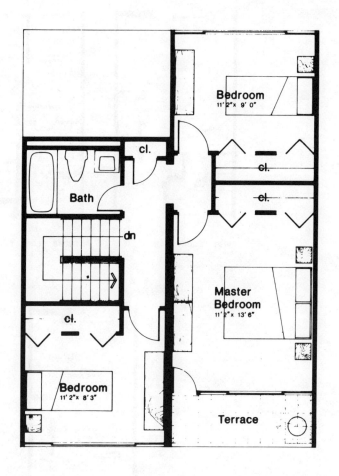

Bedroom
11' 2" x 9' 0"

cl.

cl.

Bath

cl.

dn

Master Bedroom
11' 2" x 13' 6"

cl.

Bedroom
11' 2" x 8' 3"

Terrace

Second Floor

HOUSING CONTROLS

H

H-1   Introduction
H-2   Codes and Regulations
H-3   Types of Zoning Lots
H-4   Yard Definitions
H-5   Building Heights
H-6   Angle of Light Obstruction
H-7   Sky Exposure Plane
H-8   Floor Area
H-9   Floor Area Ratio
H-10   Zoning–The Legislative Document
H-11   Evaluation of Zoning Elements
H-12   Density Considerations
H-13   Density and Housing Types
H-14   Cumulative Zoning
H-15   Transition Zoning
H-16   Flexibility Devices
H-17   Architectural Review
H-18   Sample Ordinance
H-19   Signs and Nonconforming Uses
H-20   Advertising and Business Signs

H-21   Mapping Deficiencies
H-22   Zoning Ordinance Outline
H-23   Zoning Administration
H-24   Regional Considerations
H-25   Regional Planning with Local
       Zoning Implications
H-26   Building Codes
H-27   Mobile Home Park Ordinance
H-28   Area for Light Access
H-29   Housing Code
H-30   Noise, Vibration Standards
H-31   Smoke, Odorous Matter
H-32   Explosives, Hazards, Glare
H-33   Evaluation of Site Exposure to
       Aircraft Noise
H-34   Evaluation of Site Exposure to
       Roadway Noise
H-35   Summary of Housing Controls
Bibliography

INTRODUCTION

The Housing Act of 1965 recognized the role of "building laws, standards, codes and regulations," and their impact on housing and building costs ... and what methods might be adopted to promote more uniform building codes. . . .[1] The Douglas Commission in examining these issues sought to achieve a "more rational building system" and concluded that in place of the multitude of codes applying to the construction industry, we should seek a set of national standards.[2] Such standards still do not exist. It is not the intent in this chapter to suggest such a single document nor to be all-inclusive relative to the broad range of approaches, regulatory devices, or existing practices. The intent rather is to discuss the major concepts that can be implemented by various levels of municipal governments in achieving some degree of rationality as applied to the construction and maintenance of sound housing inventories within the respective jurisdictions. In some instances, such as architectural control and subdivision regulations, the authors have relied on personal experience in meeting these needs. This does not infer a panacea for planners and housers generally, but at least the material can serve as a starting point for beginners, or as a comparative guide for other practitioners.

The major and most prevailing regulatory devices used by local government fall in four general groupings: zoning ordinances, subdivision regulations, building codes, and housing codes. In addition there are a number of supplementary codes and regulations that are often administered outside the major ones, although some codes, such as fire, electrical and plumbing, are included under a general building code. Site design architectural review, and sign ordinances are sometimes found within zoning and subdivision regulations. Most environmental control devices normally fall under the jurisdiction of county health agencies rather than with local municipal control, except in the case of cities that operate city health or environmental control agencies. The chart on the following page outlines a general array of codes and the typical administrative agencies and functions. Since the prime focus of this book is towards planning agencies, emphasis in this chapter is placed on zoning and subdivision practice. Brief mention is included at the end of the chapter of building, housing, and health codes, as well as the inclusion of a general bibliography of the representative literature.

Zoning's main concern is with the definition of the interrelationships among buildings, public facilities, and activities. Zoning ordinances generally include standards for the regulation of land uses; population density; building heights, setbacks and yard clearances; minimum house sizes; and off-street parking. Pages H-3—H-9 define and illustrate zoning lots, yards, building heights, and floor area ratios. This is followed by a discussion of zoning as a legislative document including such elements as: density ranges; cumulative zoning; flexibility devices; transition zoning; sign control; zoning deficiencies; a model ordinance outline; zoning administration; and regional zoning implications.

---

[1] Section 301, Housing and Urban Development Act of 1965.

[2] *Building the American City,* Report of the National Commission on Urban Problems to the Congress and to the President of the United States (Washington, D.C., U.S. Government Printing Office, Dec. 1968, p. 254.

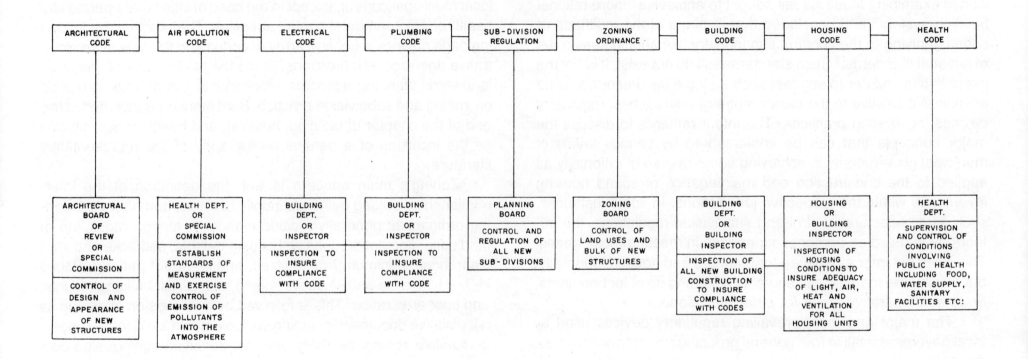

ARCHITECTURAL CODE	AIR POLLUTION CODE	ELECTRICAL CODE	PLUMBING CODE	SUB-DIVISION REGULATION	ZONING ORDINANCE	BUILDING CODE	HOUSING CODE	HEALTH CODE
ARCHITECTURAL BOARD OF REVIEW OR SPECIAL COMMISSION CONTROL OF DESIGN AND APPEARANCE OF NEW STRUCTURES	HEALTH DEPT. OR SPECIAL COMMISSION ESTABLISH STANDARDS OF MEASUREMENT AND EXERCISE CONTROL OF EMISSION OF POLLUTANTS INTO THE ATMOSPHERE	BUILDING DEPT. OR INSPECTOR INSPECTION TO INSURE COMPLIANCE WITH CODE	BUILDING DEPT. OR INSPECTOR INSPECTION TO INSURE COMPLIANCE WITH CODE	PLANNING BOARD CONTROL AND REGULATION OF ALL NEW SUB-DIVISIONS	ZONING BOARD CONTROL OF LAND USES AND BULK OF NEW STRUCTURES	BUILDING DEPT. OR BUILDING INSPECTOR INSPECTION OF ALL NEW BUILDING CONSTRUCTION TO INSURE COMPLIANCE WITH CODES	HOUSING OR BUILDING INSPECTOR INSPECTION OF HOUSING CONDITIONS TO INSURE ADEQUACY OF LIGHT, AIR, HEAT AND VENTILATION FOR ALL HOUSING UNITS	HEALTH DEPT. SUPERVISION AND CONTROL OF CONDITIONS INVOLVING PUBLIC HEALTH INCLUDING FOOD, WATER SUPPLY, SANITARY FACILITIES ETC:

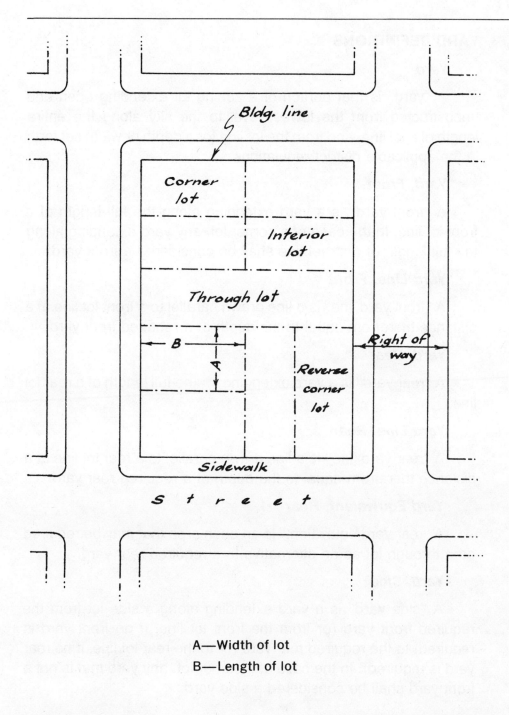

A—Width of lot
B—Length of lot

TYPES OF ZONING LOTS

Zoning Lot

A "zoning lot" is either:

a. A lot of record existing on the effective date of the zoning ordinance or any applicable subsequent amendment thereto, or

b. A tract of land, either unsubdivided or consisting of two or more contiguous lots of record located within a single block in single ownership.

Lot, Interior

An "interior lot" is any zoning lot that is neither a corner lot nor a through lot.

Lot, Corner

A "corner lot" is either a zoning lot bounded entirely by streets, or a zoning lot that adjoins the point of intersection of two or more streets and in which the interior angle formed by the extensions of the street lines in the directions they take at their intersections with lot lines other than street lines forms an angle of approximately 135 degrees or less.

Lot, Through

A "through lot" is any zoning lot, not a corner lot, that adjoins two street lines opposite to each other and parallel or within 45 degrees of being parallel to each other. Any portion of a through lot that is not or could not be bounded by two such opposite street lines and two straight lines intersecting such street lines shall be subject to the regulations for an interior lot.

Reverse Corner Lot

A "reverse corner lot" is a corner lot that reverses the depth from the normal pattern of interior lots on a street. The front of the lot also changes from one street to the other.

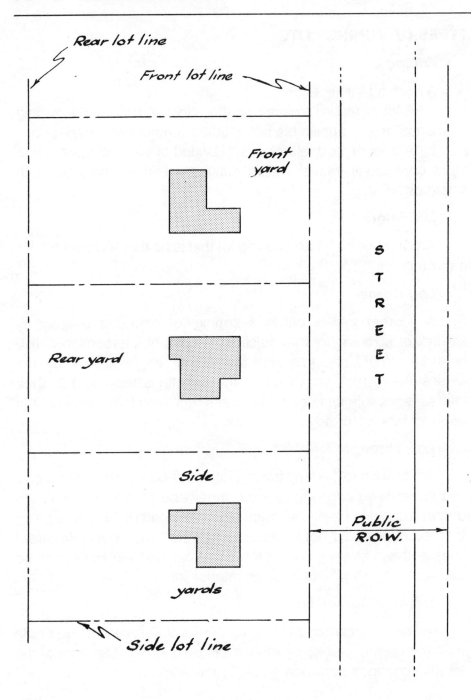

YARD DEFINITIONS

Yard

A "yard" is that portion of a zoning lot extending open and unobstructed from the lowest level to the sky along the entire length of a lot line, and from the lot line for a depth or width set forth in the applicable district regulations.

Yard, Front

A "front yard" is a yard extending along the full length of a front lot line. In the case of a corner lot, any yard extending along the full length of a street line shall be considered a front yard.

Yard Line, Front

A "front yard line" is a line drawn parallel to a front lot line at a distance therefrom equal to the depth of a required front yard.

Yard, Rear

A "rear yard" is a yard extending for the full length of a rear lot line.

Yard Line, Rear

A "rear yard line" is a line drawn parallel to a rear lot line at a distance therefrom equal to the depth of a required rear yard.

Yard Equivalent, Rear

A "rear yard equivalent" is an open area that may be required on a through lot as an alternative to a required rear yard.

Yard, Side

A "side yard" is a yard extending along a side lot from the required front yard (or from the front lot line, if no front yard is required) to the required rear yard (or to the rear lot line, if no rear yard is required). In the case of a corner lot, any yard that is not a front yard shall be considered a side yard.

BUILDING HEIGHTS

Building height is the vertical distance measured from the established grade to the highest point of the roof surface for flat roofs; to the deck line of mansard roofs; and to the average height between eaves and ridge for gable, hip and gambrel roofs.

Story

A "story" is that part of a building between the surface of a floor (whether or not counted for purposes of computing floor area ratio) and the ceiling immediately above. However, a cellar is not a story.

Basement

A "basement" is a story (or portion of a story) partly below curb level, with at least one-half of its height (measured from floor to ceiling) above curb level. On through lots the curb level nearest to a story (or portion of a story) shall be used to determine whether such story (or portion of a story) is a basement.

Cellar

A "cellar" is a space wholly or partly below curb level, with more than one-half of its height (measured from floor to ceiling) below curb level. On through lots the curb level nearest to such space shall be used to determine whether such space is a cellar.

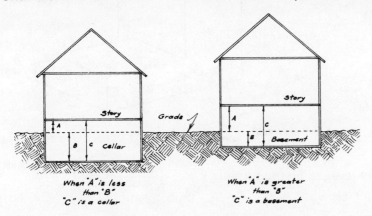

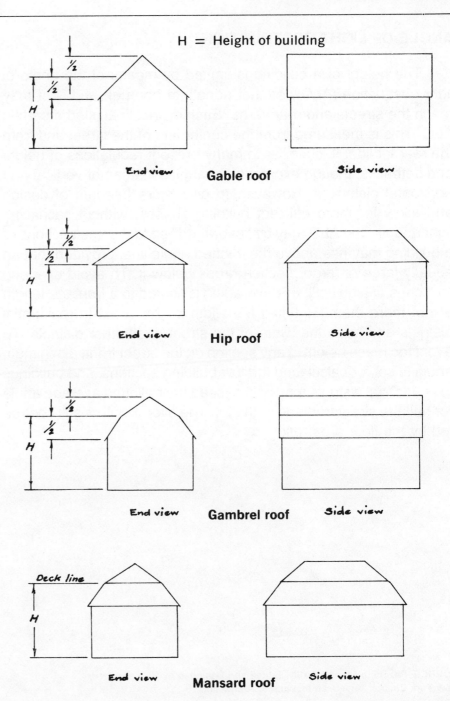

H = Height of building

End view Gable roof Side view

End view Hip roof Side view

End view Gambrel roof Side view

End view Mansard roof Side view

ANGLE OF LIGHT OBSTRUCTION

The height of a building is limited by means of the angle of light obstruction (ALO), so that adequate open air and light may reach the streets and rear yards. Each district is allotted a certain ALO. This is measured from the center line of the street and from the rear lot line. It is similar to many present regulations of height and setbacks, though expressed in angles instead of vertical and horizontal distances. However, to give more freedom of design and allow for more efficient building shapes, without sacrificing light and air, the ALO may be "averaged" so that some sections of a building may rise above the allotted angle line, provided that an equally large or larger section drops below it. To avoid overlong stretches of high wall, this averaging is limited to a frontage length of not more than 1½ times the width of the street in residential districts and twice the width of the street in all other districts. To avoid too much height in any section on the street front, a minimum angle is set for calculating the low building sections, and buildings in residential districts may only exceed their allotted average angle for half the street frontage of the lot. The overall bulk is still controlled by the floor area ratio.

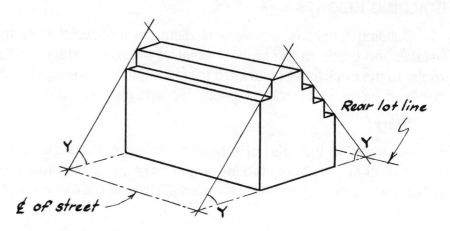

The Angle of Light Obstruction Y may be kept constant along the whole street frontage,

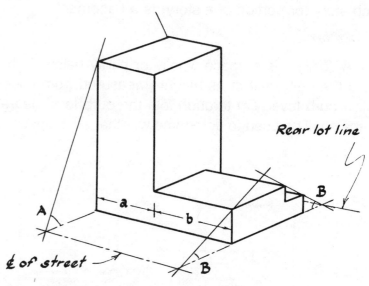

or averaged by the formula $Y = \dfrac{Aa + Bb}{a + b}$

SOURCE: *Rezoning New York City*, Edited and Designed by Baker-Funaro, New York Chapter, American Institute of Architects.

SKY EXPOSURE PLANE

A "sky exposure plane" is an imaginary inclined plane beginning above the street line at a set height and rising over a zoning lot at a ratio of vertical distance to horizontal distance.

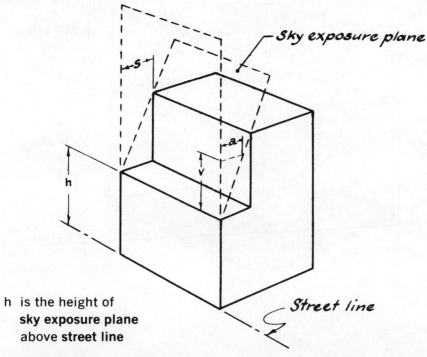

h is the height of
sky exposure plane
above **street line**

s is the **initial
setback distance**

v is the vertical distance

a is the horizontal distance

ILLUSTRATION OF SKY EXPOSURE PLANE

$$\text{Sky Exposure Plane} = \frac{\text{Vertical Distance}}{\text{Horizontal Distance}}$$

SOURCE: *New York City Zoning Resolution—1961*

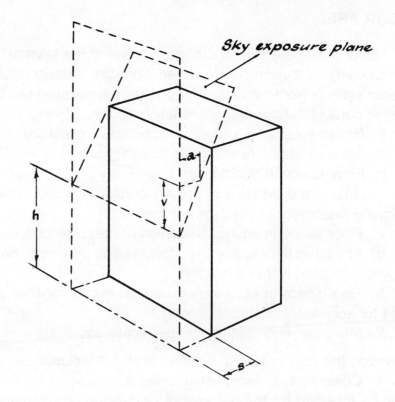

h is the height of
sky exposure plane
above **street line**

s is the depth of the
optional front open area

v is the vertical distance

a is the horizontal distance

ILLUSTRATION OF ALTERNATE SKY EXPOSURE PLANE

On narrow streets, the slope will be less than on wide streets.
The height (h) should relate to the general scale of the neighboring structures.

467

FLOOR AREA

"Floor area" is a sum of the gross areas of the several floors of a building or buildings, measured from the exterior faces of exterior walls or from the center lines of walls separating two buildings. In particular, floor area generally includes:

a. Basement space, except as specifically excluded

b. Elevator shafts or stairwells at each floor

c. Floor space in penthouses

d. Attic space (whether or not a floor has been laid) providing structural headroom of eight feet or more

e. Floor space in interior balconies or mezzanines

g. Any other floor space used for dwelling purposes, no matter where located within a building

h. Floor space in accessory buildings, except for floor space used for accessory off-street parking

k. Any other floor space not specifically excluded.

However, the floor area of a building shall not include:

a. Cellar space, except that cellar space used for retailing shall be included for the purpose of calculating requirements for accessory off-street parking spaces and accessory off-street loading berths

b. Elevator or stair bulkheads, accessory water tanks, or cooling towers

c. Uncovered steps

d. Attic space (whether or not a floor actually has been laid) providing structural headroom of less than eight feet

h. Floor space used for mechanical equipment.

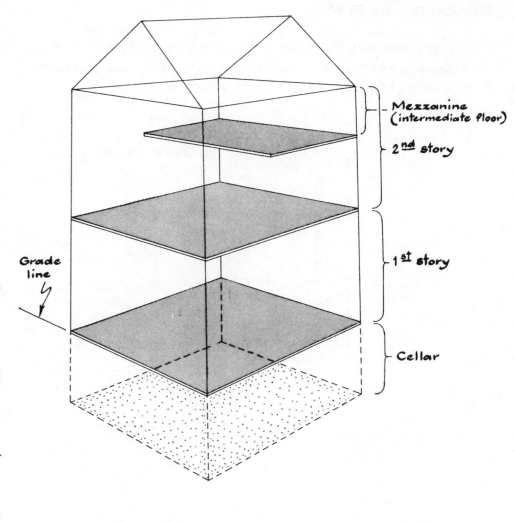

 Floor area included

Floor area excluded

FLOOR AREA RATIO (F.A.R.)

A FAR OF 1.
ONE STORY, 100%
LOT COVERAGE

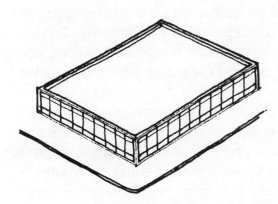

OR A FAR OF 1.
4 STORIES, 25%
LOT COVERAGE

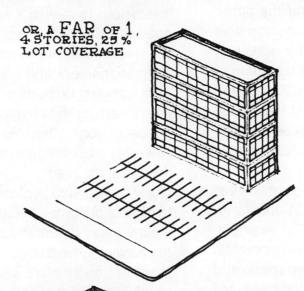

$$FAR = \frac{total\ floor\ area}{total\ lot\ area}$$

Floor area ratio is the total floor area on a zoning lot, divided by the lot area of that zoning lot.

OR A FAR OF 1.
2 STORIES, 50%
LOT COVERAGE

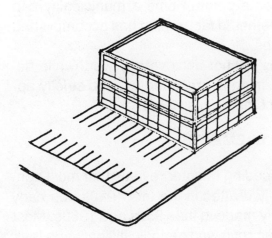

OR, A FAR OF 1.
8 STORIES, 12.5%
LOT COVERAGE

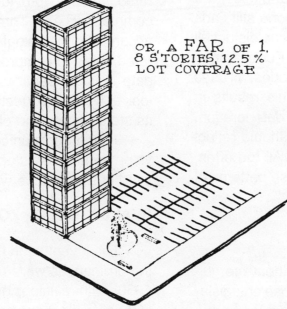

ZONING—THE LEGISLATIVE DOCUMENT

Zoning is the most generally applied legal tool for the public regulation of private land. The original rationale for zoning was based on the desire to avoid overcrowding, provide for adequate light, air and privacy, avoid mixed uses, and preserve the value of real estate. The first zoning ordinance adopted in the United States—by the City of New York in 1916—attempted to achieve these aims by creating districts in which the height, bulk, and use of buildings, the use of land, and the density of population was set forth.

The majority of current ordinances are based on this early code. Many improvements in concept have developed but unfortunately are not reflected in general current practice. For example, the provision for cluster zoning and planned unit developments, which are attempts to promote the preservation of open space and the creation of planned communities with balanced land uses, are rarely included in local zoning ordinances. Instead, one still finds evidence of "pyramidal" zoning that allows within a zone district all uses that are considered "higher" in the list of uses. For example, in the progression from residential to industrial categories, all uses before industrial are allowable within that zone. This results in unplanned mixed uses leading to eventual blight and deterioration. Perhaps the greatest drawback to zoning is that it should reflect the goals and objectives of a comprehensive plan. All too often, zoning codes merely reflect and reinforce the land-use patterns of an earlier unplanned growth.

Zoning in Accordance with a Plan

Most zoning ordinances have been devised without the guidance of a comprehensive plan. A statement of purpose or legislative intent at the beginning of an ordinance usually serves as the comprehensive plan summarized into a sentence or paragraph that embodies some broad goals. While these statements serve as the rationale to cover legal interpretation by the courts, they are insufficient to devise a sound ordinance based on logical growth policies. Ordinances that are drafted without the guidance of a plan are destined at the outset to be weak and consequently open to mismanagement and ineffectiveness.

A zoning ordinance is a legislative document constituting the law governing the physical development of a community. The language of zoning laws is prohibitive and restrictive requiring considerable planning forethought before the prohibitions and restrictions are imposed.

The first step in planning is the formulation of goals and objectives; this becomes the antecedent of zoning intent. It is clear from the inventory that many zoning ordinances have a single purpose: to maintain the status quo of purely residential communities. Needed services are generally left up to neighboring unincorporated areas to provide, especially in the case of industrial and commercial uses. Through this process, the smaller municipalities accomplish their single-purpose goals, thereby forcing unincorporated areas to compromise and alter their objectives to accommodate residual services. At some point in time a municipality can look at itself and question whether in fact zoning has accomplished its stated goals and objectives.

The larger municipalities cannot achieve any worthwhile development patterns unless zoning is preceded by, and strictly applied in accordance with, a comprehensive plan.

EVALUATION OF ZONING ELEMENTS

The inventory in the preceding chapter reveals that most zoning ordinances were originally drafted in the late 1920s and early 1930s with revisions generally made in the 1950s and 1960s. Most of these ordinances have been reviewed periodically between their inception and their latest date of revision (intermediate revisions are not reflected in the inventory). Revisions have varied from minor changes in the wording of the text to complete recodification. The motivations for these revisions are usually a result of crisis conditions or fear of them, rather than a desire for methodical periodic review. As a rule, zoning ordinances should be reviewed every five years in the more developed municipalities and every two years in municipalities with high growth potentials. The reviews should be comprehensive in scope including definitions, district descriptions, dimensional requirements, permitted uses, etc. Mapping reviews should be preceded by a land-use inventory updated to determine land use quantities developed and future land uses needed. Hypothetically, a municipality may find that commercial development has occurred primarily on rezoned land rather than on land originally designated for commercial uses. The municipality can then systematically rezone commercial land to another category to maintain a balance. This affords an excellent method of eliminating zoned strip commercial, if the inequalities of land values can be reasonably compensated.

A primary advantage of the periodic review is the opportunity for the inclusion of innovations such as performance standards, planned unit developments and clustering of all land uses. These techniques, which are discussed in more detail in section C, have particular applicability to new community design.

DENSITY CONSIDERATIONS

The nature of urban growth is such that as vacant land becomes scarce, its value is increased and the value of the improvements on the land must yield a higher investment return. Economic factors such as these must be taken into account in the density considerations of a zoning ordinance. The fact that some municipalities have upzoned vacant land toward off growth results in further inefficiencies in development patterns. Upzoning of residential land should be accompanied by mandatory clustering with density controls.

Most zoning ordinances represent density by requiring minimum lot sizes without regard to soil conditions, topography, ground water supply or natural coverage. There is a tendency to adhere strictly to minimum lot sizes when an applicant applies for a building permit and to exhibit reticence when anyone questions the basic derivation of the minimum lot size.

Once the constitutional guarantees of health, safety and welfare are satisfied and the zoning precepts of adequate light and air are considered, transportation and environmental factors are the only remaining justification for rigid density controls. Zoning does not usually reflect attention to traffic conditions, water supply, or sanitary facilities.

Keeping in mind environmental factors, choice, and overall efficiency, reasonable density ranges recommended for the suburban areas are as follows:

1 Du/acre or less i.e., low-density, single-family
2-4 Du/acre i.e., single-family
5-10 Du/acre i.e., town houses
15-25 Du/acre i.e., apartments

The application of all of these density ranges, with some imagination in housing types, can alter the present wasteful pattern of suburban sprawl in new growth areas as well as the rehabilitative areas.

Use District Variations

There has been a proliferation of special-use districts for such diverse uses as amusement-commercial, golden age communities, urban renewal and the like. The reasons for the application of the special-use district device lie in part with the rigidity of zoning theory, and in part with the overwhelming number of new development proposals. Perhaps the best example of creating a special-use district is the retirement community proposal. Developers seeking potential sites usually select the lowest density

DENSITY (Families Per Acre)	GROSS AREA Per Family (Acre assumed to be 40,000 SF)		NO. OF PERSONS Per acre (4 Persons Per Family)	SUGGESTED Housing Type	DENSITY (Families Per Acre)	GROSS AREA Per Family (Acre Assumed to be 40,000)	NO. OF PERSONS Per Acre (4 Persons Per Family)	SUGGESTED Housing Type
1	40,000	SF	4	1 Family, Detached	50	800 SF	200	Low-Rise Multi-Family Apts. (6 Stories Max.)
2	20,000	SF	8	,, ,,	60	660 SF	240	,,
3	14,000	SF	12	,, ,,	70	580 SF	280	,,
4	10,000	SF	16	,, ,,	80	500 SF	320	,,
5	8,000	SF	20	,, ,,				
6	6,600	SF	24	,, ,,				
7	5,800	SF	28	,, ,,	100	400 SF	400	Medium-Rise Multi-Family Apartments (6-20 Stories)
8	5,000	SF	32	,, ,,				
10	4,000	SF	40	1 Family, Attchd. 2 Family, Detchd.	120	330 SF	480	,,
					140	280 SF	560	,,
12	3,300	SF	48	,, ,,	160	250 SF	640	,,
16	2,500	SF	64	,, ,,	180	220 SF	720	High-Rise Multi-Family Apts. (Over 20 Stories)
20	2,000	SF	80	Row Houses Or Garden Apts.				
					200	200 SF	800	,,
25	1,600	SF	100	,, ,,	300	150 SF	1200	,,
30	1,330	SF	120	,, ,,	400	100 SF	1600	,,
40	1,000	SF	160	,, ,,				

zoning areas available with corresponding low land values. The developers then approach the municipality with a model golden age or retirement district, which in effect represents a downzoning to permit a greater number of dwelling units than the present zoning allows. The rationale for the downzoning is that the senior citizens who will buy or rent the units do not create a tax deficit since they will need less municipal services, particularly schools. Also, the downzoning to small parcels makes it economically feasible for the senior citizens to carry and maintain their retirement dwelling. The municipality, wanting some guarantee that the development will not fall into the hands of young people with children, accepts an age restriction clause that only permits retired persons (for example, age fifty-five or older) and their families. Hence, the retirement community special-use district is created, which leaves the municipality happy because of the tax picture; the developer is pleased over the high yield; and the senior citizens are satisfied because they can purchase an inexpensive dwelling tailored to their income and needs. Planners are generally unhappy because zoning is being used for exclusionary purposes to segregate people by age. Aside from the misuse of zoning for the aged, there are social pros and cons that have preoccupied sociological thinking for the past two decades both in this country and abroad. Retirement housing satisfying the needs of senior citizens and the fiscal concerns of municipalities can be accomplished by clustering in any residential district.

Other special-use districts are created for different reasons, which usually do not come under the purview of zoning. The inventory shows landmark districts for historical preservation purposes, power-generating districts to apply specific controls, research office districts to allow only sophisticated office facilities and a long list of other special uses and the reasons why the districts were created. The overall effect is cumbersome zoning ordinances, complex requirements, and confusion on the part of zoning administrators and recipients.

The special-use district is a useful tool when applied with discretion and moderation. It should not be applied as a substitute for other legal instruments, such as local ordinances or special controls, which have direct jurisdiction. The notion that special-use districts are a panacea for zoning all unusual development proposals will prove faulty when considering the infinite number of unusual proposals that loom in the not-too-distant future.

CUMULATIVE ZONING

Cumulative zoning was widespread in the early 1920s when residential uses were considered the highest and best uses, commercial the next highest and industrial as the lowest use. The cumulative zoning method automatically permitted a higher use in a lower use zone, but prohibited the reverse. Thus, an ordinance containing total cumulative zoning would allow residential uses in commercial and industrial districts and commercial uses in industrial districts, while prohibiting both industrial and commercial uses in residential zones. This method of zoning is archaic. For instance, light industry today, especially ratables, is considered an asset to the tax base, with municipalities willing to make concessions to attract them. Industrial zones are no longer located on residual land but are located with adequate accessibility, an amenity that traditionally had only been associated with residential uses.

While it can be recommended that all ordinances be revised to eliminate cumulative zoning, there are, on the planning horizon, theories to allow a careful mixing of all uses governed by sensitive urban design. Research industries that do not create traffic problems and are environmentally inoffensive can coexist with residential areas in planning unit developments or specially designed urban redevelopment projects. The pendulum of cumulative zoning has thus taken a full swing. Nevertheless, those ordinances that have cumulative aspects should be reviewed in terms of modern development patterns, and revised accordingly.

TRANSITION ZONING

This is applied at the boundary between residential and non-residential districts to prevent this becoming a no-man's land, undesirable for residences yet so zoned that it cannot be used for anything else. The zoning resolution should provide curbs upon business signs, show windows and entrances to stores adjoining residential districts. Three examples are shown:

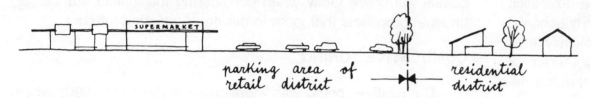

1. In retail and commercial districts parking areas which adjoin a residential zone must be shielded by walls, shrubs, or trees along the boundary line.

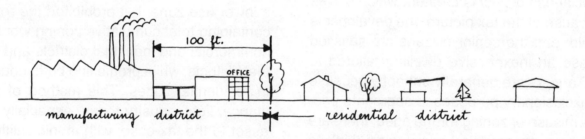

2. In industrial districts adjoining a residential zone a 100 ft. wide strip along the boundary line cannot be used for actual manufacture but must be reserved for less objectionable uses, for example, an administration building or a parking lot.

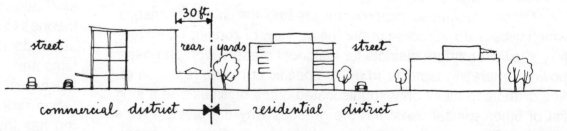

3. In non-residential lots which are back to back with residential, 30 ft. deep rear yards are prescribed, though a single story rising not more than 23 ft. above curb level may extend to the rear lot line.

SOURCE: *Rezoning New York City*, edited and designed by Baker-Funaro, New York City Chapter, American Institute of Architects.

474

FLEXIBILITY DEVICES

There are many ways of providing flexibility in zoning to ease its restrictiveness and to foster wider latitude in interpretation. The most prevalent flexibility devices are special permits or special exceptions, floating zones, variances, and transition zones.

Most municipal zoning ordinances include special permits for such uses as gas stations, two-family dwellings, model homes, signs, and mining excavations. The special permit premise is based on the need for particular land uses which, because of their inherent characteristics, are generally undesirable in an area unless additional restrictions are imposed. These additional restrictions or requirements, such as mandating additional buffer planting for gasoline stations abutting residential zones or high solid fencing for outdoor storage uses, are normally handled on an ad hoc basis. The imposition of additional requirements should be guided by standards particularly when the power to grant such permits is delegated to the zoning board of appeals. Many municipalities, however, retain the special permit authority within the legislative function, and as a result, standards are either omitted or vaguely stated, leaving them open to broad interpretation. Nearly all special permit provisions include filing fees and some specify the term of the permit, i.e., annual renewal. Requiring both a fee and a specific time period, in essence, constitutes a form of taxation that is clearly not within the purview of zoning.

The special permit device has become a "dumping ground" for controversial land uses primarily because individual zoning ordinances usually do not follow the recommendations of the land-use plan.

Another flexibility device is the so-called "floating zone," which implies the existence of a district by inclusion in the ordinance, but is not mapped. The most commonly used floating zone district is for garden apartments because of the appreciable increase in land value to the parcel zoned for such use. The floating zone devices have been upheld by the courts, but, in terms of planning for high-density residential uses, this device has resulted in chaotic density patterns, poorly located apartment complexes, inadequate services, and traffic congestion. Since the location of a floating zone requires a legislative act amending the zoning map preceded by a public hearing, the zones, usually for apartments, end up in remote areas where little or no public opposition is expected.

The floating zone concept will serve as an excellent device for implementing planned unit developments (PUD). A planned unit development district would allow a developer of a large tract of land wide latitude in designing an open-space community including residential, commercial, industrial and institutional uses. The district restrictions would include the percentage of land devoted to each use as well as the minimum acreage of the site. Approval for a proposed PUD floating zone would be based on complete site plans of all intended land uses.

Two other flexibility devices (flexible in an interpretive rather than a discretionary sense) are the variance and transition provisions. The criticism of these devices is directed more toward their administrative handling than to their zoning legality, therefore they will be covered under the zoning administration section of this study.

One aspect of variance and transition provisions that deserves mention here is the general lack of standards to guide the decisions of boards of appeals. Enabling legislation is quite explicit in describing conditions that merit the use of variances or transition devices. The term "hardship" associated with variances is too often interpreted as self-incurred hardship or deprivation of maximum capital gain. If standards had been applied to control the consistency of decisions and to uphold the original intent of these devices, a considerable number of undesirable zoning precedents could have been avoided.

Quality Controls

Four quality-control categories have emerged as controversial zoning jurisdictions: architectural review, performance standards, sign controls, and amortization of nonconforming uses. These quality controls, stemming from a broadened interpretation of zoning theory, imply exclusionary practices that interfere with free enterprise, or, as with performance standards, are based on unscientific judgments. There is little doubt that quality controls, in spite of their controversial nature, are necessary for orderly growth, and protection of the environment from physical and visual pollution. The method of handling such critical issues, as in all zoning matters, requires an understanding of planning and design principles related to human need.

ARCHITECTURAL REVIEW

One form of review is an appointed Architectural Review Board that reviews all architectural drawings for all types of construction within the boundary of the municipality. A second form of review is carried out by stipulating in the zoning ordinance that no "excessively similar buildings" are allowed within the boundary of the municipality. A third common form of architectural review relates to the minimum distance requirement between buildings of similar architecture. Generally, zoning theorists classify architectural review as either "look-alike" or "look-different" provisions in the ordinance. "Look-alike" provisions require that architectural harmony be preserved, e.g., insistence on colonial motif. "Look-different" provisions are directed toward preventing "cookie-cutter" or assembly-line developments characteristic of much of the housing built in the 1950s and 1960s.

The most important part of the review process is the site plan approval requirements that appear in zoning ordinances either separately or in conjunction with architectural review. The site plan indicates the treatment of bulk structures with neighboring structures and is sensitive to topography and natural cover. Properly administered, site plan review is one of the most significant zoning requirements available to help achieve the desirable in the area's growth.

Industrial quality controls have increased in importance during the past decade with considerable concern given to air pollution, noise, glare and other environmental factors. Monitoring devices for performance standards present the single most important weakness of these quality controls since they are generally not standardized or scientifically sophisticated. Present technology can provide the instruments for careful monitoring; and a county or regional agency can provide the administration. A county or regional agency is suggested because the affected environment is not usually confined to local municipal boundaries.

Zoning control of signs has been justified on the basis of safety. Signs, by their very nature and intent, are designed to catch the eye or attention of the observer. There are two types of signs: advertisement and information. Advertising signs are the target of most sign controls because they are considered manifestations of competition, which if uncontrolled, could blight an area as well as create traffic hazards. The belief that signs tend to cheapen an area has motivated many municipalities to revise controls to more stringent levels. Some municipalities have taken bold steps to prohibit large, distracting, obstrusive signs and to amortize, with mandatory removal of existing signs that exceed current requirements. An excellent method of controlling the undesirable effect of signs is to impose a ten-year amortization on all metal billboard signs, and a five-year amortization on all wood signs. The amortization procedure is an equitable solution to a highly competitive situation; while the present indiscriminate method of granting sign variances allowing larger and higher signs tends to set a precedent resulting in chaos.

SAMPLE ORDINANCE

Purpose—Section 1

The municipal legislative body finds that excessive uniformity, dissimilarity, inappropriateness or poor quality of the design and location of buildings and appurtenant structures, including signs, adversely affect the desirability of the immediate and neighboring areas and thereby impair the benefits of occupancy of existing property and the stability and value of both improved and unimproved real property in such areas, prevent the most appropriate development of such areas, produce degeneration of property and destroy the proper relationship between the taxable value of real property in such areas and the cost of municipal services provided therefore. It is the intent of this Section to establish procedures and design criteria necessary to avoid such results and to preserve and enhance the character, historical interest, beauty and general welfare of the municipality and to insure that the location and design of buildings, structures and open spaces in the municipality shall aid in creating a balanced and harmonious composition of the whole as well as in the relationship of its several parts.

The Board of Architectural Review— Section 2

A Board of Architectural Review is hereby created consisting of five (5) members appointed by the municipal legislative body. Of the original members one each shall be appointed for terms of one, two, three, four and five years. All members shall be residents of the municipality.

The municipal legislative body may remove any member for cause after a public hearing.

If a vacancy shall occur, otherwise than by expiration of a member's term, it shall be filled by an interim appointment for the remainder of the former member's unexpired term.

The members of the Board of Architectural Review shall designate a chairman, an acting chairman and a secretary.

The Board shall adopt Rules of Procedure as it may deem necessary to the proper exercise of its responsibilities with regard to architectural review.

All meetings of the Board shall be open to the public.

Every decision of the Board shall be by resolution and shall contain a full record of the findings of the Board in the particular case. A quorum shall consist of three (3) members.
The Board shall officially designate a registered architect to advise and take part in its deliberations, but without a vote, unless a registered architect be a member of the Board. The municipal legislative body shall fix the compensation of such registered architect and pay other expenses of the Board.

Application and Public Hearing Procedure—Section 3

Preliminary plans, elevations, sketches and/or proposals may be submitted to the Board of Architectural Review by the owner, or the architect or other agent of the owner, for consultation prior to filing an application for a building permit.

Every application for a building permit for the construction of any building or structure shall be referred to the Board of Architectural Review by the Building Inspector for consideration. All those for one- and two-family dwellings and accessory structures to residential buildings shall be reviewed by a committee of one member of the Board to determine whether or not consideration of the full Board shall be appropriate. In addition to those one- and two-family dwellings so determined to be appropriate for consideration by the Board, all those for three- or more family dwellings and for nonresidential buildings and structures shall be considered by the full Board as set forth herein.

Meetings of the Board shall be held at the request of the Building Inspector or at the call of the chairman or of any two (2) members of the Board, and at such times as the Board may determine.

In addition to a public notice of such meetings published once in the official newspaper at least five (5) days prior to the meeting date, the municipal legislative body shall require the applicant to notify all property owners within 200 feet of the subject premises, as shown on the latest completed tax roll, measured along the street frontage on both sides of the street, and to all other property owners located within 200 feet of the boundaries of the premises, by certified mail, return receipt requested.

The failure of the Board to hold a hearing on any application that may have been referred to it, within thirty (30) days, or to render its decision within ten (10) days of the closing of the hearing thereon, shall entitle the applicant to prompt issuance of a building permit provided that all other applicable requirements have been satisfied.

No building permit shall be issued by the Building Inspector on any application that has been referred to the Board unless the Board shall have approved the building or structure in writing.

The Board may require changes in plans as a condition of their approval. The Board may direct that the execution of landscaping and planting be made a part of a plan before approval thereof.

Criteria–Section 4

The Board of Architectural Review is charged with the duty of maintaining the desirable character of the municipality and of disapproving the construction, reconstruction and alteration of buildings that are designed without consideration of the harmonious relation of the new or altered building to such buildings as already exist and the environs in which they are set.

The Board is charged with the duty of exercising the sound judgment and of rejecting plans that in its opinion, based upon study and advice, are not of harmonious character because of proposed style, materials, mass, line, color, detail, or placement upon the property or in relation to the spaces between buildings or the natural character of landscape and planting or because the plans do not provide for the location and design of structures and open spaces so as to create a balanced and harmonious composition as a whole and in relation to its several parts and features to each other.

Remedies–Section 5

Any person aggrieved by a decision of the Board of Architectural Review in disapproving a building permit application and of the Building Inspector in denying such permit because of such disapproval may appeal therefrom to the Board of Appeals in the same manner as is provided for other zoning appeals.

Violation–Section 6

Any violation of the approvals established by the Board of Architectural Review shall be deemed a violation of this Ordinance, punishable under the provisions of Sections of applicable law.

SIGNS AND NONCONFORMING USES

The elimination of nonconforming entities has become a controversial issue especially when long-established businesses are involved. Most ordinances provide for the rehabilitation and extension of nonconforming uses. In urbanizing areas, these provisions have run into serious conflict, particularly when the use is incompatible with surrounding uses. The quality control aspect of nonconforming uses has been resolved by amortizing the use over a reasonable period of time after which the certificate of occupancy is revoked and the facility must be either removed or made to conform to the ordinance. Amortization of nonconforming entities is included in six of the region's one hundred seven ordinances. While many municipalities have no nonconforming uses, the rapidly urbanizing municipalities will be facing serious issues as zoning changes and development continues.

A review of zoning ordinances revealed many statements, restrictions, and regulations of entities that are clearly not within the purview of zoning. Such nonzoning aspects as the minimum age of residential occupants, minimum value of improvement, and taxation considerations have been justified on grounds broadly interpreted as constitutional guarantees of health, safety, welfare and morals. It is doubtful that today's courts will uphold such broad interpretations, when in fact the actual intents are to provide for a particular group of persons, preserve the tax base, and maintain the economic status of the community. Some of these issues are in accord with long-range planning goals, but the instrument for their regulation and subsequent implementation is not the zoning ordinance.

ADVERTISING AND BUSINESS SIGNS

Sign

A "sign" is any writing (including letter, word, or numeral); pictorial representation (including illustration or decoration); emblem (including device, symbol, or trademark); flag (including banner or pennant); or any other figure of similar character, that:

a. Is a structure or any part thereof, or is attached to, painted on, or in any other manner represented on a building or other structure, and

b. Is used to announce, direct attention to, or advertise, and

c. Is visible from outside a building. A sign shall include writing representation, or other figure of similar character within a building only when illuminated and located in a window.

Sign, Advertising

An "advertising sign" is a sign that directs attention to a business, profession, commodity, service, or entertainment conducted, sold, or offered elsewhere than upon the same zoning lot.

Sign, Business

A "business sign" is an accessory sign that directs attention to a profession, business, commodity service, or entertainment conducted, sold, or offered upon the same zoning lot.

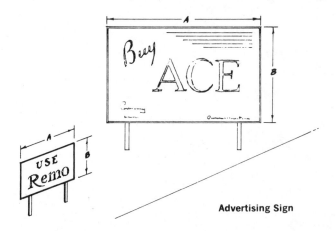

Advertising Sign

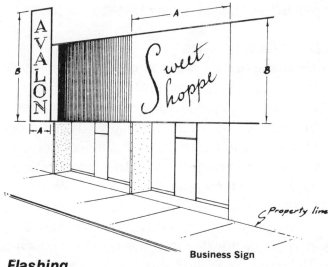

Business Sign

Sign, Flashing

A "flashing sign" is any illuminated sign, whether stationary, revolving or rotating, that exhibits changing light or color effects, provided that revolving or rotating signs exhibiting no changing light or color effects other than those produced by revolution or rotation shall be deemed flashing signs only if they exhibit sudden or marked changes in such light or color effects.

Sign, Illuminated

An "illuminated sign" is a sign designed to give forth any artificial light or reflect such light from an artificial source.

Sign, Surface Area of

The area of the face of the sign is A x B, as shown in the illustration.

Sign with Indirect Illumination

A "sign with indirect illumination" is any illuminated non-flashing sign whose illumination is derived entirely from an external artificial source and is so arranged that no direct rays of light are projected from such artificial source into residences or streets.

MAPPING DEFICIENCIES

Most criticism of zoning ordinance formats is directed toward the text and mapping, although the administration and clerical work related to the ordinance also deserves examination. The following inadequacies were found in the handling of actual zoning documents:

1. Inadequate supply of ordinances and maps.
2. Lack of responsible personnel in charge of maintaining the document.
3. Amendments scattered, lost, or unattached to the document.
4. In a few instances, exorbitant fees charged for the document.
5. Preceding editions discarded with no historical record of original ordinances.
6. Dating of amendments, revisions and current ordinances omitted.
7. Lack of written requirements or formal procedures for zoning applications.

Analyses of the text of local zoning ordinances reveal that they are generally complex, confusing, incomplete, redundant and, in many cases, contradictory. The primary reason for these deficiencies is a disorderly arrangement of the elements that make up the text. Numerous ordinances begin with an elaborate metes and bounds description of each district. Anyone using the ordinance must read the latter half first and then wade back to the beginning to decipher the district.

Many ordinances do not contain a definition of terms section but resort to defining each term after it is used in the ordinance. As a result, the description paragraphs become cumbersome, wordy, and confusing. Oftentimes a term is used but not defined, which leaves the ordinance incomplete and subject to individual interpretation.

The tendency to repeat the definition of terms or procedures for zoning action results in useless redundancy, which adds bulk to the ordinance with no appreciable substantive benefit. Separate sections on definitions and procedures would greatly simplify zoning documents. Many ordinances have, in fact, been revised to include zoning schedules and dimension tables. This has further simplified the codes by eliminating repetitious restrictions on permitted uses and dimensional requirements. Excellent examples of tabular summaries are included in many ordinances for regulations regarding minimum lot sizes, front, rear and side yard dimensions, parking, coverage, uses permitted by special permit, height and other entities that can be summarized.

Perhaps the most serious inadequacies observed in the zoning research were the contradictions. It is not difficult to understand why contradictions appear since zoning ordinances are continuously subjected to amendments, partial revisions and recodification. Some contradictions are obvious, such as dimension envelopes that do not relate to district restrictions. Others are less obvious, such as contradictions between the stated intent and the results of the district regulation. Aside from administrative embarrassment, contradictions weaken the ordinance, leaving the municipality on the defense in possible litigation. Ordinances without separability clauses can be declared invalid in their entirety as a result of dubious contradictions.

Critical mapping deficiencies exist in almost all of the region's 107 ordinances. Zoning maps are part of the legal documentation of a zoning ordinance. It is apparent that this fact is not clearly understood by some municipalities that treat maps as ancillary or supplemental clarifications of the ordinance text. Maps should be dated, officially endorsed, and referenced pursuant to local zoning law. Amendments and revisions of the map should be properly posted, referenced, and endorsed. All outdated map editions should be revised and amended maps reissued.

Most mapping deficiencies noted below pertain to graphics and descriptive clarity:

1. Street names and district boundary descriptions omitted.

2. Map scales and legends omitted or unclear.

3. Orientation registers such as north arrows omitted.

4. Similar graphic patterns used to distinguish districts.

5. For multimap ordinances, key map or adjacent map references omitted.

6. Hamlet or community names omitted.

Metes and bounds descriptions, which are included in some ordinances, should be replaced by carefully drawn maps. There is no need for both verbal district boundary descriptions and zoning maps in the ordinance. Zoning changes, which in the language of the law are described by metes and bounds, can be translated into graphical representation making the verbal description part of the ancillary legal proceedings.

ZONING ORDINANCE OUTLINE

Recommendations

The zoning ordinance, with all its appurtenances, is a legislative document requiring careful treatment. The following additional recommendations are suggested for local consideration, which would improve zoning in general, place it in the proper context of modern development, and direct it toward the goal of healthy regional growth:

Recommendation 1.

That local zoning ordinances be revised or updated in accordance with the following model format suggested by New York State:

Illustrative Outline for an Ordinance

Article I	*Purposes*
Section 1.	*Purposes*
Article II	*Definitions*
Section 2.	*Definitions*
Article III	*Establishment of Districts*
Section 3.	*Establishment of Districts*
Section 4.	*Zoning Map*
Section 5.	*Interpretation of District Boundaries*
Article IV.	*Regulations*
Section 6.	*Application of Regulations*
Section 7.	*District Regulations*
(Alternate Section 7.	*Schedule of Regulations)*
Section 8.	*Standards for Special Permits*
Section 9.	*Supplementary Regulations*
Section 10.	*Nonconforming Uses*
Article V.	*Administration*
Section 11.	*Enforcement*
Section 12.	*Board of Appeals*
Section 13.	*Violations*
Article VI.	*Amendments*
Section 14.	*Procedure for Amendments*
Article VII.	*Miscellaneous*
Section 15.	*Interpretation*
Section 16.	*Separability*
Section 17.	*Repealer*
Section 18.	*Short Title*
Section 19.	*When Effective*

Recommendation 2.

That local ordinances, particularly in the urbanizing areas of Suffolk County, include a planned unit development district according to the following model:

Planned Unit Development District (PUD)

Purpose

To encourage flexibility and variety in housing design, to preserve open space and to control environmental factors. The PUD district also provides for the planning of commercial services, community facilities, and employment as part of the total plan for a site.

Requirements

a. Minimum site area (not less than 100 contiguous acres recommended).
b. Minimum open space (not less than 30 percent recommended).
c. Maximum commercial land use (as a percent of total site).
d. Maximum industrial land use (as a percent of total site).
e. Community facilities (expressed as a function of population).
f. Utilities (based on prerequisite design standards).

Use Regulations

Listing of allowable uses with specific controls on each use.

Design and Density Standards

Prerequisite design standards for the following:

a. Topographic treatment with respect to drainage and soil stabilization.
b. Natural features, particularly vegetation and water bodies.
c. Water supply.
d. Sanitary sewers.
e. Views and vistas.

Prerequisite Density Specifications to Allow For

a. Variety in housing types for detached houses, town houses, and apartments.
b. Maximum floor areas for commercial uses.

c. Maximum floor areas as well as performance standards for industrial uses.
d. Coverage limitations for all uses.
e. Height restrictions for all uses.

PUD District Application Procedures

a. Preliminary site plans showing proposed land uses and roads, as well as a natural features map. After approval of preliminary site plan, action for the zone change can be initiated. After the change of zone, the application submits:
b. Detailed plans of the entire development including architectural plans, utility systems, landscaping designs, paving plans, etc. Approval of this final submission remains in effect for a specific period of time (recommended not to exceed one year) after which the district reverts back to original zoning. Within the specified period the applicant must obtain building permits and initiate the project.

Recommendation 3.

That all municipalities include in their ordinance a mandatory site plan review by the local planning agency.

The site plan review section of the ordinance should specify the purpose and intent of the regulation as well as the planning agency review powers.

Recommendation 4.

That all major ordinance recodifications include standardized district descriptions, abbreviations and symbols as recommended in the publication, *Zoning in New York State*.[3]

Standardization of district descriptions, abbreviations, and symbols will facilitate coordination among local municipalities and

[3]*Zoning in New York State*, Office of Planning Coordination, Revised, 1968.

respective counties and will provide quick comprehension of any ordinance in the region without destroying the integrity of individual ordinances.

Recommendation 5.

That all zoning maps be standardized in symbols, nomenclature, and scales and orientation.

It is recommended that a scale of one inch to a thousand feet be used for base maps, and a scale of one inch to five hundred feet be used for insets showing intensely developed areas and central business districts.

ZONING ADMINISTRATION

A poorly devised zoning ordinance without planning guidance will more assuredly result in chaotic growth. But, even a well-devised zoning ordinance drafted in accordance with sound planning principles will not insure orderly and efficient growth. The success or failure of local zoning depends primarily on the performance of the local zoning administration.

Local government has a functional role in zoning administration by way of the direct powers of the legislative body and the quasi-judicial board of appeals. In some municipalities planning boards have advisory functions related to decision making, but do not have direct powers. General public involvement is direct, through applications for zoning action, or indirect, through participation at mandatory public hearings.

Theoretically, the roles of each individual, private interest group or official agency involved in day-to-day zoning administration are distinct and understandable. In actuality, politics, social concerns, taxation, economic prosperity, conservation and other vital preoccupations play havoc with rational zoning administration.

Town and village boards in the region have the legal respon-

sibility for zoning administration and to this extent are charged with adapting, modifying, changing or updating the legal document. Governing decisions not influenced by a plan are vulnerable to suspicions of unethical practices. This is especially so when the issue involves changes in zoning classifications to permit more lucrative uses, e.g., gas stations, multiple dwellings, nearly all permitted uses other than low-density residential uses. Some avid critics even attack governing board decisions that are based on a master plan claiming part of the plan to be a premeditated violation of the public trust. Unfortunate dilemmas such as these can be avoided by widespread, long-term public exposure to the master plan together with legislative sanctioning and zoning modifications in accordance with the plan's recommendations.

Local zoning boards of appeals are charged with the responsibility of interpreting the zoning document, rendering judgments in cases of conflict, and granting variances from zoning restrictions that impose unnecessary hardships on recipients. Many ordinances in the region do not mandate standards to guide board of appeals judgments, resulting in serious abuse of their delegated powers. The abuses run the full gamut ranging from no action on legitimate hardship issues to rote endorsement of all variance requests. Inconsistent or irresponsible decisions on the part of local zoning boards of appeals represent a very destructive force undermining the integrity of a zoning ordinance.

Zoning ordinances that include comprehensive standards for the guidance of boards of appeals limit discretionary judgments to equitable treatment of each application. Standards should provide guidance for special permits, variances, and performance standards for industrial as well as some commercial uses.

Local planning boards are gradually becoming more involved in zoning administration mainly by providing active advisory capabilities. The planning board review of certain zoning actions essentially amounts to comparing proposals with local planning goals and determining their consistency, if any. The board makes recommendations to the appropriate agency having jurisdiction, which, in turn, either respects the board's position or formulates reasons to reject the recommendations. Some municipalities have delegated powers to their planning boards through a mandatory site plan review for any zoning application. In these cases, the planning board's functions are strengthened because proposed zoning actions are not considered without the planning board's site plan approval. The unfortunate deterrent to increased planning board involvement in local affairs is the fact that very few municipalities have active planning boards supported by professional staffs. Local boards need staff that can research zoning proposals and place them in the proper planning context for sound recommendations.

Zoning is the most effective instrument for the implementation of a plan, yet oftentimes planning and zoning are administratively divorced resulting in a dichotomy of policy for future growth. The relationship of planning and zoning must be reinforced, if not through enabling legislation, then by local administration processes.

Local citizens play an important role in zoning administration through petitions and public hearings. Aside from the possible influence exercised through the right of general petitions, New York State enabling legislation provides for mandatory recognition by governing bodies or zoning boards of appeals of petitions against specific zoning changes affecting subject properties or adjacent properties. Sections 179 and 265 of the General Municipal Law concerning village and town zoning require a favorable vote of at least two-thirds or three-fourths (depending on the size of the governing body) of the village or town board to pass a proposed zoning change opposed by a petition signed by twenty percent of the owners or adjacent owners within specified distances. This represents the only formal power delegated to local citizens.

Public hearings are perhaps the most interesting and entertaining part of zoning administration. Public hearings, prescribed by law and imbued with the principle of direct democracy, are milieus of emotion encompassing the old cliches of "stand up and be counted," "united we stand," and "get involved" on the public's side and "salesmanship" on the applicant's side. Whenever zoning officials are lonely, they merely have to schedule a public hearing re: a high-rise, or garden apartment, or public housing, or nuisance industry rezoning, that will surely end all loneliness and boredom. It is at controversial public hearings that the people of a community get together and display remarkable unity and strength, not to mention a sense of humor and in many cases rhetorical genius. Tactics used by the opposing public include packing the hearing, verbally threatening political officials, and loud, raucous debating. The purpose of the organized disorder at hearings is to make the zoning officials decide the issue on the basis of mass opposition and noise decibels rather than substantive information.

Zoning officials conducting public hearings act in a quasi-judicial capacity having to distinguish, among all verbal attacks and rebuttals, what are the revelant statements regarding the issue. In small municipalities, a massive crowd at the public hearing may only represent the voice of a very small minority—but an affected minority. All sorts of procedures are used throughout the region to determine consensus, from a show of hands to verbal votes accompanied by names and addresses. The opinions of prominent citizens and civic leaders in large municipalities are informally given an edge over the opinions of others.

REGIONAL CONSIDERATIONS

Zoning applicants at public hearings are automatically on the defensive concerning their proposal. Since zoning changes often represent large expenditures of money for attorneys, architects, engineers, and expert testimony, as well as filing fees, applicants weigh the odds very carefully by feeling out the opposition before formulating their request. Many applicants have learned that "the best way to run a war is to avoid a fight" and have sought to rezone parcels in remote areas that will generate little or no opposition. The unfortunate result of such applications is that zoning officials are prone to endorse the proposal on the sole basis of no opposition in lieu of sound planning principles.

Public hearings are necessary for reasons other than meeting the candidates, enjoying an evening of decent entertainment, and a wholesome crack at togetherness. The public hearing serves to allow the applicant to fully explain his proposal and permits citizens to state their disagreements with it. A public hearing is not a matter of consensus, influence, personalities, threats, or noise decibels. The decision on the proposal and the responsibility for that decision is in the hands of the zoning officials who must base their decision on planning criteria, e.g., physical, economic and social factors.

Recommendations

Recommendation 1.

That municipalities place greater emphasis on planning review of all zoning action.

Recommendation 2.

That comprehensive standards guiding the boards of appeals be adopted in all ordinances, including performance standards for industrial and certain commercial uses.

REGIONAL PLANNING WITH LOCAL ZONING IMPLEMENTATION

Within the last decade or so, public attention has broadened to include awareness of environmental problems that transcend municipal boundaries. Earlier preoccupation focused on economic prosperity manifested by industrialization through a system that measured benefits in terms of rising employment, growing family incomes and heightening standards of living. The costs of prosperity were rarely measured, and for the most part ignored. Now, approaching the last quarter of a century marked by industrial and technological progress, the costs to the environment have emerged to top all priorities for government action.

Environmental problems requiring regional solutions are air pollution, ground water pollution, pollution of recreation water bodies, destruction of ecologically sensitive wetlands, and elimination of natural vegetation and topographic features. Other regional problems such as traffic congestion, unbalanced tax structures, housing shortages, and exorbitant real property taxes have pointed to the critical need for intercoordination through planning. All of these broadened concerns are the subject of regional planning directed toward sound solutions for existing problems and formulation of policy for the orderly growth of the entire region.

Like widespread public concern for the environment, regional planning is a relative newcomer, following in the wake of long-established local zoning practices that are primarily responsible for the physical pattern of the region today. In fact, most local zoning ordinances have preceded respective local master plans. The situation, therefore, is a reversal of what is considered the logical planning process, described as follows:

1. Formulation of the regional plan as a general guide.
2. Development of local master plans with specific detailed recommendations.
3. Formulation and enactment of the legal and fiscal instruments for implementation (zoning, subdivision regulation, capital programs, etc.).

Since planning and development are continuous processes,

the foregoing order can be instituted through proper administrative handling, as follows:

1. Formulation of the regional plan as a general guide.
2. Revision of the local master plan reflecting the recommendations of the regional plan.
3. Amendment of legal and fiscal instruments for implementation reflecting the regional considerations and recommendations of the revised local master plan.

Experience has indicated that strip commercial zoning is inefficient in terms of traffic handling, hazardous because of the greatly increased interaction points, and in most cases, visually distasteful. This form of strip commercial has regional implications since the primary function of arterial roads is to serve intercommunity travel. Strip commercial zoning should be minimized with commercial activities concentrated around selected nodes. Local master plans should be revised to reflect this basic recommendation detailing the selected geographical areas and parcels that would accomplish this goal. Local zoning ordinances should be amended in accordance with the plan and supported by strict administrative adherence to the basic policy. Admittedly, this action will arouse controversy since the reclassification of commercial land will involve a decrease in land value. However, not to take such action will require huge capital expenditures in road improvements and traffic controls.

The reasons just cited are some of the many intermunicipal and environmental problems that could only be analyzed within a regional framework. In most cases, the methodology of handling regional considerations through local zoning remains the same.

BUILDING CODES

The first regulatory device based on the exercise of the police power, i.e., the right of government to control private activities based on the "general welfare" clause of the Constitution, to be widely used was the building code. Although the underlying concept is one of protecting the safety of the public, including provisions for electrical, heating, plumbing, fire, industrial hazards, elevators, and so on, additional factors have been included such as requirements for adequate ventilation and light access. This latter concern is often included in zoning ordinances as mentioned on pages H-6 and H-7. However, provision is sometimes found in building codes as shown on H-6 and H-28.

Building codes generally contain a series of standards and specifications designed to establish minimum safeguards in the erection and/or reconstruction of buildings. Over the years, four basic model codes have been developed to serve as guides to municipalities throughout the country. They are:

1. "The Basic Building Code"—The Building Officials' Conference of America (B.O.C.A.)
2. "The Uniform Building Code"—The International Conference of Building Officials (I.C.B.O.)
3. "The Southern Standard Building Code"—The Southern Standard Building Code Conference (S.S.B.C.C.)
4. "The National Building Code"—The American Insurance Association (A.I.A.)

Numerous problems are cited about codes and the enforcement thereof: ". . . .lack of qualified administrative and enforcement personnel, lack of uniformity in the requirements of codes, slow response to technical innovation, lengthy time required to revise local ordinances, lack of performance standards."[4] Two major recommendations to overcome these deficiencies would be the adoption of one of the four national performance codes and new educational and vocational programs in code administration and enforcement on a national scale. However, a major obstacle is becoming more prevalent in regard to mobile homes. Although the

---

[4]*LOGA* National Association of Home Builders of the United States (Washington, D.C., Vol. 2, No. 1, Spring 1971), p. 4.

installation, alteration, materials and equipment of mobile homes must comply with code provisions, many communities are reticent about providing for them due, in part, to the difficulties involved with enforcement. The New York State Office of Planning Services found that, contrary to conventional housing, the mobile homes arise from outside the state ready for occupancy without the opportunity for local inspectors to determine if the units comply with local regulations.[5] On the following pages are reproduced a sample ordinance for mobile home parks.[6] This ordinance, in effect, is a composite building, housing, health and subdivision code. It is included here even though general building codes are only referred to, since local communities have not had as much exposure to mobile home issues. A representative bibliography is included at the end of this chapter. Particular attention should be given to the array of excellent literature prepared by Frederick H. Bair, Jr.

[5]*Facts on Mobile Homes,* N.Y.S. Office of Planning Services (Albany, N.Y., No. 6 Regulations and Controls, August 1971), pp. 2-3.

[6]*Environmental Health Guide for Mobile Home Parks,* United States Department of Health, Education and Welfare (Washington, D.C., January 1966), pp. 27-35.

MOBILE HOME PARK ORDINANCE

(TITLE: The following is a suggested title; the actual title should conform to local requirements.)

AN ORDINANCE enforcing MINIMUM STANDARDS for mobile home parks; establishing requirements for the design, construction, alteration, extension and maintenance of mobile home parks and related utilities and facilities; authorizing the issuance of permits for construction, alteration and extension of mobile home parks; authorizing the licensing of operators of mobile home parks; and authorizing the inspection of mobile home parks; and fixing penalties for violations.

Be it, therefore, ordained by the (name of municipality) as follows:

SECTION 1: DEFINITIONS

As used in this ordinance:

a. HEALTH AUTHORITY means the legally designated health authority or its authorized representative of (name of municipality).

b. LICENSE means a written license issued by the health authority allowing a person to operate and maintain a mobile home park under the provisions of this Ordinance and regulations issued hereunder.

c. MOBILE HOME means a transportable, single-family dwelling unit suitable for year-round occupancy and containing the same water supply, waste disposal and electrical conveniences as immobile housing.

d. MOBILE HOME LOT means a parcel of land for the placement of a single mobile home and the exclusive use of its occupants.

e. MOBILE HOME PARK means a parcel of land under single ownership, which has been planned and improved for the placement of mobile homes for nontransient use.

f. MOBILE HOME STAND means that part of an individual lot that has been reserved for the placement of the mobile home, appurtenant structures or additions.

g. PERMIT means a written permit issued by the health authority permitting the construction, alteration and extension of a mobile home park under the provisions of this Ordinance and regulations issued hereunder.

h. PERSON means any individual, firm, trust, partnership, public or private association or corporation.

i. SERVICE BUILDING means a structure housing toilet, lavatory and such other facilities as may be required by this Ordinance.

j. SEWER CONNECTION means the connection consisting of all pipes, fittings and appurtenances from the drain outlet of the mobile home to the inlet of the corresponding sewer riser pipe of the sewerage system serving the mobile home park.

k. SEWER RISER PIPE means that portion of the sewer lateral that extends vertically to the ground elevation and terminates at each mobile home lot.

l. WATER CONNECTION means the connection consisting of all pipes, fittings and appurtenances from the water riser pipe to the water inlet pipe of the distribution system within the mobile home.

m. WATER RISER PIPE means that portion of the water supply system serving the mobile home park that extends vertically to the ground elevation and terminates at a designated point at each mobile home lot.

SECTION 2: PERMITS

2.1

It shall be unlawful for any person to construct, alter or extend any mobile home park within the limits of (name of municipality) unless he holds a valid permit issued by the health authority in the name of such person for the specific construction, alteration or extension proposed.

2.2

All applications for permits shall be made to the health authority and shall contain the following:

(a) Name and address of applicant.

(b) Interest of the applicant in the mobile home park.

(c) Location and legal description of the mobile home park.

(d) Complete engineering plans and specifications of the proposed park showing:

1. The area and dimensions of the tract of land;

2. The number, location, and size of all mobile home lots;

3. The location and width of roadways and walkways;

4. The location of service buildings and any other proposed structures;

5. The location of water and sewer lines and riser pipes;

6. Plans and specifications of the water supply and refuse and sewage disposal facilities;

7. Plans and specifications of all buildings constructed or to be constructed within the mobile home park; and

8. The location and details of lighting and electrical systems.

2.3

All applications shall be accompanied by the deposit of a fee of .... dollars.

2.4

When, upon review of the application, the health authority is satisfied that the proposed plan meets the requirements of this Ordinance and regulations issued hereunder, a permit shall be issued.

2.5

Any person whose application for a permit under this Ordinance has been denied may request and shall be granted a hearing on the matter before the health authority under the procedure provided by Section 5 of this Ordinance.

SECTION 3: LICENSES

3.1

It shall be unlawful for any person to operate any mobile home park within the limits of (name of municipality) unless he holds a valid license issued annually by the health authority in the name of such person for the specific mobile home park. All applications for licenses shall be made to the health authority, who shall issue a license upon compliance by the applicant with provisions of this Ordinance and regulations issued hereunder and of other applicable legal requirements.

3.2

Every person holding a license shall give notice in writing to the health authority within twenty-four hours after having sold, transferred, given away, or otherwise disposed of interest in or control of any mobile home park. Such notice shall include the name and address of the person succeeding to the ownership or control of such mobile home park. Upon application in writing for transfer of the license and deposit of a fee of .... dollars, the license shall be transferred if the mobile home park is in compliance with all applicable provisions of this Ordinance and regulations issued hereunder.

3.3

(a) Application for original licenses shall be in writing, signed by the applicant, accompanied by an affidavit of the applicant as to the truth of the application and by the deposit of a fee of .... dollars, and shall contain: the name and address of the applicant; the location and legal description of the mobile home park; and a site plan of the mobile home park showing all mobile home lots, structures, roads, walkways, and other service facilities.

(b) Applications for renewals of licenses shall be made in writing by the holders of the licenses, shall be accompanied by the deposit of a fee of .... dollars and shall contain any change in the information submitted since the original license was issued or the latest renewal granted.

3.4

Any person whose application for a license under this Ordinance has been denied may request and shall be granted a hearing on the matter before the health authority under the procedure provided by Section 5 of this Ordinance.

3.5

Whenever, upon inspection of any mobile home park, the health authority finds that conditions or practices exist that are in violation of any provision of this Ordinance or regulations issued hereunder, the health authority shall give notice in writing in accordance with Section 5.1 to the person to whom the license was issued that unless such conditions or practices are corrected within a reasonable period of time specified in the notice by the health authority, the license shall be suspended. At the end of such period, the health authority shall reinspect such

mobile home park and, if such conditions or practices have not been corrected, he shall suspend the license and give notice in writing of such suspension to the person to whom the license is issued. Upon receipt of notice of such suspension, such person shall cease operation of such mobile home park except as provided in Section 5.2.

3.6

Any person whose license has been suspended, or who has received notice from the health authority that his license will be suspended unless certain conditions or practices at the mobile home park are corrected, may request and shall be granted a hearing on the matter before the health authority under the procedure provided by Section 5 of this Ordinance; provided that when no petition for such hearing shall have been filed within ten days following the day on which notice of suspension was served, such license shall be deemed to have been automatically revoked at the expiration of such ten-day period.

3.7

A temporary license, upon written request therefore, shall be issued by the health authority for every mobile home park in existence upon the effective date of this Ordinance, permitting the mobile home park to be operated during the period ending 180 days after the effective date of this Ordinance in accordance with such conditions as the health authority may require.

3.8

The term of the temporary license shall be extended, upon written request, for not to exceed one additional period of 180 days, if (1) the licensee shall have filed application for a license in conformity with Section 3.3 of this Ordinance within 90 days after the effective date of this Ordinance; (2) the plans and specifications accompanying the application for license comply with all provisions of this

Ordinance and all other applicable ordinances and statutes; (3) the licensee shall have diligently endeavored to make the existing mobile home park conform fully to the plans and specifications submitted with application; and (4) failure to make the existing mobile home park conform fully to such plans and specifications shall have been due to causes beyond the control of the licensee.

SECTION 4: INSPECTION OF MOBILE HOME PARKS

4.1

The health authority is hereby authorized and directed to make such inspections as are necessary to determine satisfactory compliance with this Ordinance and regulations issued hereunder.

4.2

The health authority shall have the power to enter at reasonable times upon any private or public property for the purpose of inspecting and investigating conditions relating to the enforcement of this Ordinance and regulations issued hereunder.

4.3

The health authority shall have the power to inspect the register containing a record of all residents of the mobile home park.

4.4

It shall be the duty of the owners or occupants of mobile home parks, and mobile homes contained therein, or of the person in charge thereof, to give the health authority free access to such premises at reasonable times for the purpose of inspection.

4.5

It shall be the duty of every occupant of a mobile home park to give the owner thereof or his agent or employee access to any part of such mobile home park or its premises at reasonable times for the purpose of making such repairs or alterations as are necessary to effect com-

pliance with this Ordinance and regulations issued pursuant to the provisions of this Ordinance.

SECTION 5: NOTICES, HEARINGS AND ORDERS

5.1

Whenever the health authority determines that there are reasonable grounds to believe that there has been a violation of any provision of this Ordinance, or regulations issued hereunder, the health authority shall give notice of such alleged violation to the person to whom the permit or license was issued, as hereinafter provided. Such notice shall (a) be in writing; (b) include a statement of the reasons for its issuance; (c) allow a reasonable time for the performance of any act it requires; (d) be served upon the owner or his agent as the case may require: Provided: That such notice or order shall be deemed to have been properly served upon such owner or agent when a copy thereof has been sent by registered mail to his last known address, or when he has been served with such notice by any method authorized or required by the laws of this state; (e) contain an outline of remedial action, which, if taken, will effect compliance with the provisions of this Ordinance and regulations issued hereunder.

5.2

Any person affected by any notice that has been issued in connection with the enforcement of any provision of this Ordinance, or regulation issued hereunder, may request and shall be granted a hearing on the matter before the health authority: Provided: That such person shall file in the office of the health authority a written petition requesting such hearing and setting forth a brief statement of the grounds therefore within ten days after the day the notice was served. The filing of the request for a hearing shall operate as a stay of the notice and of the suspension except in the case of an order issued under Section 5.5. Upon receipt of such petition, the health authority shall set a time and place for such hearing and shall give the petitioner written notice thereof. At such hearing the petitioner shall be given an opportunity to be heard and to show why such notice should be modified or withdrawn. The hearing shall be commenced not later than ten days after the day on which the petition was filed: Provided: That upon application of the petitioner the health authority may postpone the date of the hearing for a reasonable time beyond such ten-day period when in his judgment the petitioner has submitted good and sufficient reasons for such postponement.

5.3

After such hearing the health authority shall make findings as to compliance with the provisions of this Ordinance and regulations issued hereunder and shall issue an order in writing sustaining, modifying or withdrawing the notice that shall be served as provided in Section 5.1(d). Upon failure to comply with any order sustaining or modifying a notice, the license of the mobile home park affected by the order shall be revoked.

5.4

The proceedings at such a hearing, including the findings and decision of the health authority, and together with a copy of every notice and order related thereto shall be entered as a matter of public record in the office of the health authority but the transcript of the proceedings need not be transcribed unless judicial review of the decision is sought as provided by this Section. Any person aggrieved by the decision of the health authority may seek relief therefrom in any court of competent jurisdiction, as provided by the laws of this State.

5.5

Whenever the health authority finds that an emergency exists that requires immediate action to protect the public health, he may without notice or hearing issue an order reciting the existence of such an emergency and requiring that such action be taken as he may deem necessary to meet the emergency including the suspension of the permit or license. Notwithstanding any other provisions of this Ordinance, such order shall be effective immediately. Any person to whom such an order is directed shall comply therewith immediately, but upon petition to the health authority shall be afforded a hearing as soon as possible. The provisions of Sections 5.3 and 5.4 shall be applicable to such hearing and the order issued thereafter.

SECTION 6: ADOPTION OF REGULATIONS BY THE HEALTH AUTHORITY

6.1

The health authority is hereby authorized to make and, after public hearing, to adopt such written regulations as may be necessary for the proper enforcement of the provisions of this Ordinance. Such regulations shall have the same force and effect as the provision of this Ordinance, and the penalty for violation of the provisions thereof shall be the same as the penalty for violation of the provisions of this Ordinance, as hereinafter provided.

SECTION 7: ENVIRONMENTAL, OPEN SPACE AND ACCESS REQUIREMENTS

7.1
General Requirements

Condition of soil, ground water level, drainage and topography shall not create hazards to the property or the health or safety of the occupants. The site shall not be exposed to objectionable smoke, noise, odors or other adverse influences, and no portion subject to unpredictable and/or sudden flooding, subsidence or erosion shall be used for any purpose that would expose persons or property to hazards.

7.2
Soil and Ground Cover Requirements

Exposed ground surfaces in all parts of every mobile home park shall be paved, or covered with stone screenings, or other solid material, or protected with a vegetative growth that is capable of preventing soil erosion and of eliminating objectionable dust.

7.3
Site Drainage Requirements

The ground surface in all parts of every mobile home shall be graded and equipped to drain all surface water in a safe, efficient manner.

7.4
Park Areas for Nonresident Uses

(a) No part of any park shall be used for nonresidential purposes, except such uses that are required for the direct servicing and well being of park residents and for the management and maintenance of the park.

(b) Nothing contained in this Section shall be deemed as prohibiting the sale of a mobile home location on a mobile home stand and connected to the pertinent utilities.

7.5
Required Separation Between Mobile Homes

(a) Mobile homes shall be separated from each other and from other buildings and structures by at least 15 feet; provided that mobile homes place end-to-end may have a clearance of 10 feet where opposing rear walls are staggered.

(b) An accessory structure that has a horizontal area exceeding 25 square feet, is attached to a mobile home or located within 10 feet of its window, and has an opaque top or roof that is higher than the nearest window shall, for purposes of all separation requirements, be considered to be part of the mobile home.

7.6
Required Recreation Areas

(a) In all parks accommodating or designed to accommodate 25 or more mobile homes, there shall be one or more recreation areas that shall be easily accessible to all park residents.

(b) The size of such recreation areas shall be based upon a minimum of 100 square feet for each lot. No outdoor recreation area shall contain less than 2,500 square feet.

(c) Recreation areas shall be located as to be free of traffic hazards and should, where the topography permits, be centrally located.

7.7
Required Setbacks, Buffer Strips and Screening

(a) All mobile homes shall be located at least 25 feet from any park property boundary line abutting upon a public street or highway and at least 15 feet from other park property boundary lines.

(b) There shall be a minimum distance of 10 feet between an individual mobile home and adjoining pavement of a park street, or common parking area or other common areas.

(c) All mobile home parks located adjacent to industrial or commercial land uses shall be provided with screening such as fences or natural growth along the property boundary line separating the park and such adjacent nonresidential uses.

7.8
Park Street System

(a) GENERAL REQUIREMENTS: All mobile home parks shall be provided with safe and convenient vehicular access from abutting public streets or roads to each mobile home lot. Alignment and gradient shall be properly adapted to topography.

H-27 MOBILE HOME PARK ORDINANCE

(b) ACCESS: Access to mobile home parks shall be designed to minimize congestion and hazards at the entrance or exit and allow free movement of traffic on adjacent streets. The entrance road connecting the park streets with a public street or road shall have a minimum road pavement width of 34 feet where parking is permitted on both sides, or a minimum road pavement width of 27 feet where parking is limited to one side. Where the primary entrance road is more than 100 feet long and does not provide access to abutting mobile home lots within such distance, the minimum road pavement width may be 24 feet, provided parking is prohibited at both sides.

(c) INTERNAL STREETS: Surfaced roadways shall be of adequate width to accommodate anticipated traffic, and in any case shall meet the following minimum requirements:

1. All streets, except minor streets ....24 feet
2. Minor streets, no parking.......................18 feet (Acceptable only if less than 500 feet long and serving less than 25 mobile homes or of any length if one-way and providing access to abutting mobile home lots on one side only.)
3. Dead-end streets shall be limited in length to..........1,000 feet and shall be provided at the closed end with a turn-around having an outside roadway diameter of at least 60 feet.

(d) REQUIRED ILLUMINATION OF PARK STREET SYSTEMS: All parks shall be furnished with lighting units so spaced and equipped with luminaries placed at such mounting heights as well provided the following average maintained levels of illumination for the safe movement of

pedestrians and vehicles at night:
1. All parts of the park street systems: 0.6 footcandle, with a minimum of 0.1 footcandle.
2. Potentially hazardous locations, such as major street intersections and steps or stepped ramps: individually illuminated, with a minimum of 0.3 footcandle.

(e) STREET CONSTRUCTION AND DESIGN STANDARDS:
1. PAVEMENT: All streets shall be provided with a smooth, hard and dense surface, which shall be durable and well drained under normal use and weather conditions. Pavement edges shall be protected to prevent raveling of the wearing surface and shifting of the pavement base. Street surfaces shall be maintained free of cracks, holes and other hazards.
2. GRADES: Grades of all streets shall be sufficient to insure adequate surface drainage, but shall be not more than eight percent. Short runs with a maximum grade of 12 percent may be permitted, provided traffic safety is assured by appropriate paving, adequate leveling areas and avoidance of lateral curves.
3. INTERSECTIONS: Within 100 feet of an intersection, streets shall be at approximately right angles. A distance of at least 150 feet shall be maintained between center lines of offset intersecting streets. Intersections of more than two streets at one point shall be avoided.

7.9
Required Off-Street Parking Areas

(a) Off-street parking areas shall be provided in all mobile home parks for the use of park occupants and guests. Such areas shall be fur-

nished at the rate of at least 1.25 car spaces for each mobile home lot.

(b) Required car parking spaces shall be so located as to provide convenient access to the mobile home, but shall not exceed a distance of 200 feet from the mobile home that it is intended to serve.

7.10
Walks

(a) GENERAL REQUIREMENTS: All parks shall be provided with safe, convenient, all-season pedestrian access of adequate width for intended use, durable and convenient to maintain, between individual mobile homes, the park streets and all community facilities provided for park residents. Sudden changes in alignment and gradient shall be avoided.

(b) COMMON WALK SYSTEM: A common walk system shall be provided and maintained between locations where pedestrian traffic is concentrated. Such common walks shall have a minimum width of three and one-half feet.

(c) INDIVIDUAL WALKS: All mobile home stands shall be connected to common walks, to paved streets, or to paved driveways or parking spaces connecting to a paved street. Such individual walks shall have a minimum width of two feet.

7.11
Mobile Home Stands

The area of the mobile home stand shall be improved to provide an adequate foundation for the placement and tie-down of the mobile home, thereby securing the superstructure against uplift, sliding, rotation and overturning.

(a) The mobile home stand shall not heave, shift or settle unevenly under the weight of the mobile home due to frost action, inadequate drainage, vibration or other forces acting on the superstructure.

(b) The mobile home stand shall be provided with anchors and tie-downs such as cast-in-place concrete "dead men," eyelets imbedded in concrete foundations or runways, screw augers, arrowhead anchors, or other devices securing the stability of the mobile home.

(c) Anchors and tie-downs shall be placed at least at each corner of the mobile home stand and each shall be able to sustain a minimum tensile strength of 2,800 pounds.

SECTION 8: WATER SUPPLY

8.1
General Requirements

An accessible, adequate, safe, and potable supply of water shall be provided in each mobile home park. Where a public supply of water of satisfactory quantity, quality, and pressure is available, connection shall be made thereto and its supply used exclusively. When a satisfactory public water supply is not available, a private water supply system may be developed and used as approved by the health authority.

8.2
Source of Supply

(a) The water supply shall be capable of supplying a minimum of 150 gallons per day per mobile home.

(b) Every well or suction line of the water supply system shall be located and constructed in such a manner that neither underground nor surface contamination will reach the water supply from any source. The following minimum distances between wells and various sources of contamination shall be required.

Building Sewer	50
Septic Tank	50
Disposal Field	100
Seepage Pit	100
Dry Well	50
Cesspool	150

(c) No well-casings, pumping machinery or suction pipes shall be placed in any pit, room or space extending below ground level nor in any room or space above ground that is walled in or otherwise enclosed, unless such rooms, whether above or below ground, have free drainage by gravity to the surface of the ground.

(d) The treatment of a private water supply shall be in accordance with applicable laws and regulations.

8.3
Water Storage Facilities

All water storage reservoirs shall be covered, watertight and constructed of impervious material. Overflows and vents of such reservoirs shall be effectively screened. Manholes shall be constructed with overlapping covers, so as to prevent the entrance of contaminated material. Reservoir overflow pipes shall discharge through an acceptable air gap.

8.4
Water Distribution System

(a) The water supply system of the mobile home park shall be connected by pipes to all mobile homes, buildings, and other facilities requiring water.

(b) All water piping, fixtures and other equipment shall be constructed and maintained in accordance with state and local regulations and requirements and shall be of a type and in locations approved by the health authority.

(c) The water piping system shall not be connected with nonpotable or questionable water supplies and shall be protected against the hazards of backflow or back siphonage.

(d) The system shall be so designed and maintained as to provide a pressure of not less than 20 pounds per square inch, under normal operating conditions, at service buildings and other locations requiring potable water supply.

8.5
Individual Water Riser Pipes and Connections

(a) Individual water riser pipes shall be located within the confined area of the mobile home stand at a point where the water connection will approximate a vertical position.

(b) Water riser pipes shall extend at least four inches above ground elevation. The pipe shall be at least three-quarter inch. The water outlet shall be capped when a mobile home does not occupy the lot.

(c) Adequate provisions shall be made to prevent freezing of service lines, valves and riser pipes and to protect risers from heaving and thawing actions of ground during freezing weather. Surface drainage shall be diverted from the location of the riser pipe.

(d) A shutoff valve below the frost line shall be provided near the water riser pipe on each mobile home lot.

(e) Underground stop and waste valves shall not be installed on any water service.

SECTION 9: SEWAGE DISPOSAL

9.1
General Requirements

An adequate and safe sewerage system shall be provided in all mobile home parks for conveying and disposing of all sewage. Such system shall be designed, constructed and maintained in accordance with state and local laws.

9.2
Sewer Lines

All sewer lines shall be located in trenches of sufficient depth to be free of breakage from traffic or other movements and shall be separated from the park water supply system at a safe distance. Sewers shall be at a grade that will insure a velocity of two feet per second when flowing full. All sewer lines shall be constructed of materials approved by the health authority, shall be adequately vented, and shall have watertight joints.

9.3
Individual Sewer Connections

(a) Each mobile home stand shall be provided with at least a four-inch diameter sewer riser pipe. The sewer riser pipe shall be so located on each stand that the sewer connection to the mobile home drain outlet will approximate a vertical position.

(b) The sewer connection (see definition) shall have a nominal inside diameter of at least three inches and the slope of any portion thereof shall be at least one-fourth inch per foot. The sewer connection shall consist of one pipe line only without any branch fittings. All joints shall be watertight.

(c) All materials used for sewer connections shall be semirigid, corrosive resistant, nonabsorbent and durable. The inner surface shall be smooth.

(d) Provision shall be made for plugging the sewer riser pipe when a mobile home does not occupy the lot. Surface drainage shall be diverted away from the riser. The rim of the riser pipe shall extend at least four inches above ground elevation.

9.4
Sewage Treatment and/or Discharge

Where the sewer lines of the mobile home park are not connected to a public sewer, all proposed sewage disposal facilities shall be approved by the health authority prior to construction. Effluents from sewage treatment facilities shall not be discharged into any waters of the State except with prior approval of the health authority.

SECTION 10: ELECTRICAL DISTRIBUTION SYSTEM

10.1
General Requirements

Every park shall contain an electrical wiring system consisting of wiring, fixtures, equipment and appurtenances that shall be installed and maintained in accordance with applicable codes and regulations governing such systems.

10.2
Power Distribution Lines

(a) Main power lines not located underground shall be suspended at least 18 feet above the ground. There shall be a minimum horizontal clearance of three feet between overhead wiring and any mobile home, service building or other structure.

(b) All direct burial conductors or cable shall be buried at least 18 inches below the ground surface and shall be insulated and specially designed for the purpose. Such conductors shall be located not less than one foot radial distance from water, sewer, gas or communication lines.

10.3
Individual Electrical Connections

(a) Each mobile home lot shall be provided with an approved disconnecting device and overcurrent protective equipment. The minimum service per outlet shall be 120/240 volts AC, 50 amperes.

(b) Outlet receptacles at each mobile home stand shall be located not more than 25 feet from the overcurrent protective devices in the mobile home and a three-pole, four-wire grounding type shall be used. Receptacles shall be of weatherproof construction and configurations shall be in accordance with American Standard Outlet Receptacle C-73.1.

(c) The mobile home shall be connected to the outlet receptacle by an approved type of flexible cable with connectors and a male attachment plug.

(d) Where the calculated load of the mobile home is more than 50 amperes, either a second outlet receptacle shall be installed or electrical service shall be provided by means of permanently installed conductors.

10.4
Required Grounding

All exposed noncurrent carrying metal parts of mobile homes and all other equipment shall be grounded by means of an approved grounding conductor with branch circuit conductors or other approved method of grounded metallic wiring. The neutral conductor shall not be used as an equipment ground for mobile homes or other equipment.

SECTION 11: SERVICE BUILDING AND OTHER COMMUNITY SERVICE FACILITIES

11.1
General

The requirements of this Section shall apply to service buildings, recreation buildings and other community service facilities such as:

(a) Management offices, repair shops and storage areas;
(b) Sanitary facilities;
(c) Laundry facilities;
(d) Indoor recreation areas;
(e) Commercial uses supplying essential goods or services for the exclusive use of park occupants.

11.2
Required Community Sanitary Facilities

Every park shall be provided with the following emergency sanitary facilities;
For every 100 mobile home lots,

or fractional part thereof, there shall be one flush toilet and one lavatory for each sex.

The building containing such emergency sanitary facilities shall be accessible to all mobile homes.

11.3
Structural Requirements for Buildings

(a) All portions of the structure shall be properly protected from damage by ordinary uses and by decay, corrosion termites and other destructive elements. Exterior portions shall be of such materials and be so constructed and protected as to prevent entrance or penetration of moisture and weather.

(b) All rooms containing sanitary or laundry facilities shall:

1. Have sound-resistant walls extending to the ceiling between male and female sanitary facilities. Walls and partitions around showers, bathtubs, lavatories and other plumbing fixtures, shall be constructed of dense, nonabsorbent, waterproof material or covered with moisture-resistant material.

2. Have at least one window or skylight facing directly to the outdoors. The minimum aggregate gross area of windows for each required room shall be not less than 10 percent of the floor area served by them.

3. Have at least one window that can be easily opened, or a mechanical device that will adequately ventilate the room.

(c) Toilets shall be located in separate compartments equipped with self-closing doors. Shower stalls shall be of the individual type. The rooms shall be screened to prevent direct view of the interior when the exterior doors are open.

(d) Illumination levels shall be maintained as follows: (1) general seeing

tasks—5 footcandles; (2) laundry room work area—40 footcandles; (3) toilet room, in front of mirrors—40 footcandles.

(e) Hot and cold water shall be furnished to every lavatory, sink, bathtub, shower and laundry fixture, and cold water shall be furnished to every water closet and urinal.

11.4
Barbecue Pits, Fireplaces, Stoves and Incinerators

Cooking shelters, barbecue pits, fireplaces, woodburning stoves and incinerators shall be so located, constructed, maintained and used as to minimize fire hazards and smoke nuisance both on the property on which used and on neighboring property. No open fire shall be permitted except in facilities provided. No open fire shall be left unattended. No fuel shall be used and no material burned that emits dense smoke or objectionable odors.

SECTION 12: REFUSE HANDLING

12.1

The storage, collection and disposal of refuse in the mobile home park shall be so conducted as to create no health hazards, rodent harborage, insect breeding areas, accident or fire hazards or air pollution.

12.2

All refuse shall be stored in flytight, watertight, rodentproof containers, which shall be located not more than 150 feet from any mobile home lot. Containers shall be provided in sufficient number and capacity to properly store all refuse.

12.3

Refuse collection stands shall be provided for all refuse containers. Such container stands shall be so designed as to prevent containers from being tipped, to minimize spillage and container deterioration and to facilitate cleaning around them.

12.4

All refuse containing garbage shall be collected at least twice weekly. Where suitable collection service is not available from municipal or private agencies, the mobile home park operator shall provide this service. All refuse shall be collected and transported in covered vehicles or covered containers.

12.5

Where municipal or private disposal service is not available, the mobile home park operator shall dispose of the refuse by incineration or transporting to a disposal site approved by the health authority.

12.6

Refuse incinerators shall be constructed in accordance with engineering plans and specifications that shall be reviewed and approved by the health authority or other authority having jurisdiction.

12.7

Incinerators shall be operated only when attended by some person specifically authorized by the owner or operator of the mobile home park.

SECTION 13: INSECT AND RODENT CONTROL

13.1

Grounds, buildings and structures shall be maintained free of insect and rodent harborage and infestation. Extermination methods and other measures to control insects and rodents shall conform with the requirements of the health authority.

13.2

Parks shall be maintained free of accumulations of debris that may provide rodent harborage or breeding places for flies, mosquitoes and other pests.

13.3

Storage areas shall be so maintained as to prevent rodent harborage;

lumber, pipe and other building material shall be stored at least one foot above the ground.

13.4

Where the potential for insect and rodent infestation exists, all exterior openings in or beneath any structure shall be appropriately screened with wire mesh or other suitable materials.

13.5

The growth of brush, weeds and grass shall be controlled to prevent harborage of ticks, chiggers and other noxious insects. Parks shall be so maintained as to prevent the growth of ragweed, poison ivy, poison oak, poison sumac and other noxious weeds considered detrimental to health. Open areas shall be maintained free of heavy undergrowth of any description.

SECTION 14: FUEL SUPPLY AND STORAGE

14.1
Natural Gas System
(a) Natural gas piping systems shall be installed and maintained in accordance with applicable codes and regulations governing such systems.
(b) Each mobile home lot approved with piped gas shall have an approved manual shutoff valve installed upstream of the gas outlet. The outlet shall be equipped with an approved cap to prevent accidental discharge of gas when the outlet is not in use.

14.2
Liquified Petroleum Gas Systems
(a) Liquified petroleum gas systems shall be installed and maintained in accordance with applicable codes and regulations governing such systems.
(b) Systems shall be provided with

safety devices to relieve excessive pressures and shall be arranged so that the discharge terminates at a safe location.
(c) Systems shall have at least one accessible means for shutting off gas. Such means shall be located outside the mobile home and shall be maintained in effective operating condition.
(d) All LPG piping outside of the mobile homes shall be well supported and protected against mechanical injury. Undiluted liquified petroleum gas in liquid form shall not be conveyed through piping equipment and systems in mobile homes.
(e) Liquified petroleum gas containers installed on a mobile home lot shall be securely but not permanently fastened to prevent accidental overturning. Such containers shall not be less than 12 or more than 60 U. S. gallons gross capacity.
(f) No liquified petroleum gas vessel shall be stored or located inside or beneath any storage cabinet, carport, mobile home, or any other structure, unless such installations are approved by the health authority.

14.3
Fuel Oil Supply Systems
(a) All fuel oil supply systems shall be installed and maintained in accordance with applicable codes and regulations governing such systems.
(b) All piping from outside fuel storage tanks of cylinders to mobile homes shall be permanently installed and securely fastened in place.
(c) All fuel oil storage tanks or cylinders shall be securely fastened in place and shall not be located inside or beneath any mobile home or less than five feet from any mobile home exit.

(d) Storage tanks located in areas subject to traffic shall be protected against physical damage.

SECTION 15: FIRE PROTECTION

15.1

The mobile home area shall be subject to the rules and regulations of the (name of municipality) fire prevention authority.

15.2

Mobile home parks shall be kept free of litter, rubbish and other flammable materials.

15.3

Portable fire extinguishers of a type approved by the fire prevention authority shall be kept in service buildings and at all other locations designated by such fire prevention authority and shall be maintained in good operating condition.

15.4

Fires shall be made only in stoves, incinerators and other equipment intended for such purposes.

15.5
(a) Fire hydrants shall be installed if the park water supply system is capable to serve them in accordance with the following requirements:
1. The water supply system shall permit the operation of a minimum of two one and one-half inch hose streams.
2. Each of two nozzles, held four feet above the ground, shall deliver at least 75 gallons of water per minute at a flowing pressure of at least 30 pounds per square inch at the highest elevation point of the park.
(b) Fire hydrants, if provided, shall be located within 500 feet of any mobile home, service building or other structure in the park.

SECTION 16: MISCELLANEOUS REQUIREMENTS

16.1
Responsibilities of the Park Management
(a) The person to whom a license for a mobile home park is issued shall operate the park in compliance with this Ordinance and regulations issued hereunder and shall provide adequate supervision to maintain the park, its facilities and equipment in good repair and in a clean and sanitary condition.
(b) The park management shall notify park occupants of all applicable provisions of this Ordinance and inform them of their duties and responsibilities under this Ordinance and regulations issued hereunder.
(c) The park management shall supervise the placement of each mobile home on its mobile home stand, which includes securing its stability and installing all utility connections.
(d) The park management shall maintain a register containing the names of all park occupants. Such register shall be available to any authorized person inspecting the park.
(e) The park management shall notify the health authority immediately of any suspected communicable or contagious disease within the park.

16.2
Responsibilities of Park Occupants
(a) The park occupant shall comply with all applicable requirements of this Ordinance and regulations issued hereunder and shall maintain his mobile home lot, its facilities and equipment in good repair and in a clean and sanitary condition.
(b) The park occupant shall be responsible for proper placement of his mobile home on its mobile home stand and proper installation of all

utility connections in accordance with the instructions of the park management.

(c) No owner or person in charge of a dog, cat or other pet animal shall permit it to run at large or to commit any nuisance within the limits of any mobile home lot.

16.3
Restrictions on Occupancy

A mobile home shall not be occupied for dwelling purposes unless it is properly placed on a mobile home stand and connected to water, sewerage and electrical utilities.

SECTION 17: PENALTIES[1]

Any person who violates any provision of this Ordinance shall upon conviction be punished by a fine of not less than .... dollars nor more than .... dollars; and each day's failure of compliance with any such provision shall constitute a separate violation.

SECTION 18: CONFLICT OF ORDINANCES: EFFECT OF PARTIAL INVALIDITY

18.1

In any case where a provision of this Ordinance is found to be in conflict with a provision of any other ordinance or code of this (name of municipality) existing on the effective date of this Ordinance, the provision that, in the judgment of the health authority, establishes the higher standard for the promotion and protection of the health and safety of the people shall prevail. In any case where a provision of this Ordinance is found to be in conflict with a provision of any other ordinance or code of this (name of municipal-

ity) existing on the effective date of this Ordinance that establishes a lower standard for the promotion and protection of the health and safety of the people, the provisions of this Ordinance shall be deemed to prevail, and such other ordinances or codes are hereby declared to be repealed to the extent that they may be found in conflict with this Ordinance.

18.2

If any section, subsection, paragraph, sentence, clause or phrase of this Ordinance should be declared invalid for any reason whatsoever, such decision shall not affect the remaining portions of this Ordinance, which shall remain in full force and effect; and to this end the provisions of this Ordinance are hereby declared to be serviceable.

SECTION 19: EFFECTIVE DATE[2]

This Ordinance shall be effective on and after the .... day of ...., 19.....

---

[1]Since the penalties that may be prescribed for violations will be governed by state constitutional or statutory limitations, which vary from state to state, blank space in the Penalty Section of this Ordinance must be filled in by local authorities.

[2]In many states a local ordinance cannot become effective until it has been published or until a specific period of time after adoption has elapsed, etc. Even in the absence of such requirements, however, it will probably be considered advisable to prescribe an effective date that is at least 30 to 60 days later than the date of adoption of this Ordinance to give ample time for compliance.

AREA FOR LIGHT ACCESS

All windows that are needed to satisfy the ventilation requirements of the Building Code will have to give upon a certain minimum of open space known as the area for light access (ALA). This can be easily and quickly measured with a graphic device marked off in a series of wedge-shaped sections.

The required ALA may be within the lot upon which the building is placed or on the street, or on the required open yard of an adjoining lot. The area for light access is measured by a series of wedges marked out within the segments of a circle.

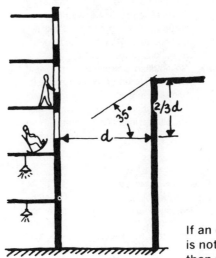

If an obstruction in front of the window is not higher (from the sill line) than two-thirds the distance from that window, it is not considered an obstruction when checking the window for Units of Light Access.

All windows which are needed to satisfy the ventilation requirements of the Building Code and the Multiple Dwelling Law will have to give upon a certain minimum of open space known as the Area for Light Access. This can be easily and quickly measured with a graphic device marked off in a series of wedge-shaped sections.

The required ALA may be within the lot upon which the building is placed, or on the street, or on the required open yard of an adjoining lot.

The Area for Light Access is measured by a series of wedges marked out within the segments of a circle.

For residential buildings
the wedges are within the band between 40 and 60 ft. from the window.
Eight wedges (six of them contiguous) must be unobstructed.

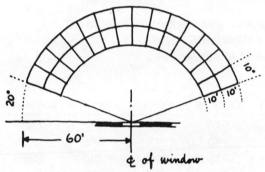

The window at **a** satisfies the requirements for residential buildings: a minimum of eight Units of Light Access, at least six of which are contiguous.

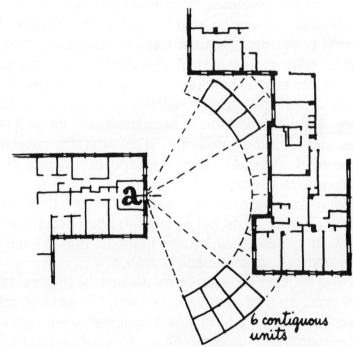

6 contiguous units

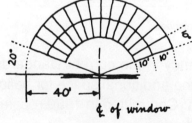

For low-bulk commercial buildings the wedges are within the band between 20 and 40 ft. from the window. Eight wedges (six of them contiguous) must be unobstructed.

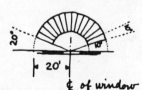

For high-bulk commercial and manufacturing buildings the wedges are within the band between 10 and 20 ft. from the window. Eight wedges (all contiguous) must be unobstructed.

SOURCE: *Rezoning New York City*, Edited and Designed by Baker-Funaro, New York Chapter, American Institute of Architects.

HOUSING CODE

A housing code is one of a series of ordinances created to protect health, safety and general welfare through the exercise of the police power. It is primarily a regulatory device designed to effect the preservation of acceptable dwellings and the rehabilitation of salvageable units. It is also used, on occasion, to obtain temporary minimal improvement of severely deteriorated or dilapidated dwellings in an urban renewal area pending their ultimate demolition. Unlike most housing-related legislation, such as building, plumbing, electrical, and fire-prevention codes, which deal with structural or design standards and are prospective in nature, housing codes deal with permissible conditions of occupancy of already existing dwellings. A comprehensive housing code normally specifies the required living space per person, minimum standards for lighting and ventilation, structural soundness and safety, fire protection, basic equipment and the provision of services, and spells out, preferably in considerable detail, the maintenance responsibilities of owners and occupants. In effect, the housing code attempts to influence the life style of residents by requiring "owners and occupants to conduct themselves and to order their lives so as not to create undue accumulations of filth and trash, to keep their houses in repair, and to keep their walls, floors and ceilings in a clean condition."[7]

The housing code generally defines the precise conditions for legal occupancy of dwelling units and, in most but not all cases, prescribes the manner in which compliance with locally adopted requirements is to be obtained.

Dwelling Unit Occupancy Requirements

Similarly to building codes, four basic model housing codes have been developed. They are:

1. "Recommended Housing Maintenance and Occupancy Ordinance" American Public Health Association (APHA)
2. "The Basic Housing Code"–The Building Officials' Conference of America (BOCA)
3. "The Southern Standard Housing Code"–The Southern Standard Building Code Conference (S.S.B.C.C.)
4. "Housing Code"–The International Conference of Building Officials (I.C.B.O.)

In general there is a reasonable uniformity among most of the codes relative to occupancy requirements as shown on the following table in terms of habitable floor area/person.

Dwelling Unit Occupancy Requirements, 4 National Model Housing Codes
(Floor area in square feet)

Code	1 person	2 persons	3 persons	4 persons	5 persons
APHA-PHS	150	250	350	450	550
BOCA	150	250	350	450	550
ICBO	200[1]	200[1]	290	330	380
Southern	150	250	350	450	525

[1]150 is not prohibited, but the higher standard is recommended.
Source: Model housing codes by organizations named.

However, there is great discrepancy in the current standards for the total floor area requirements (the additional space for halls, foyers, bathrooms, etc.). The A.P.H.A. Committee in 1950 recommended the following minimum standards.[8]

Minimum Total Floor Area

For 1 person	400
For 2 persons	750
For 3 persons	1,000
For 4 persons	1,150
For 5 persons	1,400
For 6 persons	1,550

[7]Frank P. Grad, *Legal Remedies for Housing Code Violations,* The National Commission on Urban Problems. Research Report No. 14, U.S.G.P.O. Washington D.C. 1968, p. 3.

[8]op. cit. Douglas, p. 278.

Misunderstanding of the uses and limitations of code enforcement has led to considerable disillusionment among those who regarded it as a cure-all for urban and suburban housing ills. It is in fact only one of several tools—among them, publicly assisted housing, urban renewal, improved services, and enforcement of a full range of codes—that must be employed simultaneously if real progress is to be achieved.

Promulgation and enforcement of a housing code does not automatically insure the creation of safe and sanitary dwellings, but it may very well prevent the onset or spread of blight in neighborhoods where units were originally of sound construction, and, on rare occasions, may even foster the reconstruction of badly deteriorated or dilapidated houses. In a suburban area with manageable housing problems it can help to preserve sound dwellings and to secure the upgrading of all but the poorest units with a minimum expenditure of public funds. By slowing or even halting the unnecessary attrition of sound dwellings, it can help public authorities and nonprofit corporations engaged in the construction of new low- and middle-income units to begin to catch up with the backlog of unfilled housing needs. The prerequisites for the successful use of a housing code appear to be the widespread if not enthusiastic public acceptance of code enactment and enforcement as an appropriate activity of local government, adequate funding of the enforcement operation, the existence of a sufficient supply of housing for temporary relocation, and the availability of financial aids to assist low-income owners and tenants otherwise unable to bear the higher costs of improved housing. Unfortunately, the housing code is least effective when and where it is most needed. A "tight" housing market, with little or no new construction at prices low- and middle-income families can afford, necessarily reduces the options of the enforcing agency. The fact that the housing code applies to existing and already occupied houses, apartments, or rooms means that the forced vacation of a substandard dwelling resulting from efforts to protect the public health and safety through code enforcement frequently produces increased hardship for those obliged to live in such units.

Housing code enactment and enforcement is a relatively new development in suburban areas. Although it is somewhat early to judge its effectiveness, it is already evident that legislative changes and administrative modifications, such as those discussed in the Douglas Report,[9] must be introduced to permit the housing code to serve the purpose for which it was intended. A major fault is that virtually none of the existing codes established standards for a suitable living environment, i.e., standards for open space, housing density, or schools and their location.

Nothing is said, in the typical housing code, about private nonresidential properties, such as stores and factories–how they are mixed in with homes; how much noise, smoke, dust, or glare they make, how many signs they put up; how well they are maintained and landscaped. Nothing is said in the typical housing code about the adequacy of public lands such as parks and playgrounds; public structures such as schools, libraries, fire and police stations; or even public facilities such as right-of-way for access, paving for streets, exclusion of nonneighborhood traffic, sidewalks, storm sewers, street lights, street trees, and street signs.[10]

It is true that many of these elements are provided for by municipalities by inclusion in comprehensive plans, zoning ordinances, subdivision regulations, or through special statutes. However, housing codes differ from the other regulatory procedures in that housing codes apply to already existing structures, whereas the other ordinances and regulations apply at the initiation of new facilities.

An adequate code should also contain sufficient provisions to insure that implementation of the purpose of the code can be achieved. For example:

[9]op. cit. Douglas, p. 287.

[10]op. cit. Douglas, p. 287.

1. The power to enter and inspect buildings at reasonable times.
2. Written notice served on the owner naming the specific violations found.
3. Mechanics for formal conferences with the owner.
4. The power to make repairs or demolish the building if the owner is unwilling or otherwise incapable.
5. Maximum fines and/or prison terms should be specified.

As increased urbanization takes place, the issues of incompatibility and environmental degradation resulting from non-residential activities will become more pressing. Noise from aviation activities over residential communities and noise, glare and fumes from upwind industrial activities can render residential life unpalatable.

NOISE, VIBRATION STANDARDS

Noise

A "decibel" is a unit of measurement of the intensity of sound (the sound pressure level).

A "sound level meter" is an instrument standardized by the American Standards Association that is used for measurement of the intensity of sound and is calibrated in decibels.

An "octave band" is one of a series of eight bands that covers the normal range of frequencies included in sound measurements. Such octave bands serve to define the sound in term of its pitch components.

An "octave band analyzer" is an instrument used in conjunction with a sound level meter to measure sound in each of eight octave bands.

An "impact noise analyzer" is an instrument used in conjunction with the sound level meter to measure the peak intensities of short-duration sounds.

Method of Measurement

For the purpose of measuring the intensity or frequency of sound, the sound level meter, the octave band analyzer, and the impact noise analyzer shall be employed.

The "C" network and the "slow" meter response of the sound level meter shall be used. Sounds of short duration, as from forge hammers, punch presses, and metal shears, which cannot be measured accurately with the sound level meter, shall be measured with the impact noise analyzer as manufactured by the General Radio Company, or its equivalent, in order to determine the peak value of the impact.

Maximum Permitted Decibel Levels

The sound pressure level resulting from any activity, whether open or enclosed, shall not exceed, at any point on or beyond any lot line, the maximum permitted decibel levels for the octave band as set forth in the following table.

MAXIMUM PERMITTED SOUND PRESSURE LEVEL
(in decibels)

Octave band (cycles per second)	
20 to 75	79
75 to 150	74
150 to 300	66
300 to 600	59
600 to 1,200	53
1,200 to 2,400	47
2,400 to 4,800	41
Above 4,800	39

Vibration

"Steady state vibrations" are earth-borne oscillations that are continuous. Discrete pulses that occur more frequently than 100 times per minute shall be considered to be steady state vibrations.

"Impact vibrations" are earth-borne oscillations occurring in discrete pulses at or less than 100 pulses per minute.

A "frequency" is the number of oscillations per second of a vibration.

A "three-component measuring system" is a device for recording the intensity of any vibration in three mutually perpendicular directions.

Maximum Permitted Steady State Vibration Displacement

No activity shall cause or create a steady state vibration, at any point on any lot line, with a displacement in excess of the permitted steady state vibration displacement for the frequencies as set forth in the following table.

MAXIMUM PERMITTED STEADY STATE VIBRATION DISPLACEMENT
(in inches)

Frequency (cycles per second)	
10 and below	.0008
10—20	.0005
20—30	.0003
30—40	.0002
40—50	.0001
50—60	.0001
60 and over	.0001

Maximum Permitted Impact Vibration Displacement

No activity shall cause or create an impact vibration, at any point on any lot line, with a displacement in excess of the permitted impact vibration displacement for the frequencies as set forth in the following table.

MAXIMUM PERMITTED IMPACT VIBRATION DISPLACEMENT
(in inches)

Frequency (cycles per second)	M1
10 and below	.0016
10—20	.0010
20—30	.0006
30—40	.0004
40—50	.0002
50—60	.0002
60 and over	.0002

SMOKE, DUST, AND OTHER PARTICULATE MATTER

"Particulate matter" is any finely divided liquid or solid matter capable of being air- or gas-borne.

"Dust" is solid particulate matter capable of being air- or gas-borne.

"Process weight" is the total weight of all materials used in any process that discharges dust into the atmosphere. Such materials shall include solid fuels, but not liquid or gaseous fuels or combustion air.

"Combustion for indirect heating" is the burning of fuel in equipment, such as steam boilers, water or air heaters, stills, or brew kettles, where there is no contact between the products of combustion and the materials being heated.

"Standard Smoke Chart numbers" are the numbers on the Standard Smoke Chart indicating graduations of light-obscuring capacity of smoke.

"Smoke" is any visible emission into the open air from any source, except emissions of an uncontaminated water vapor.

A "smoke unit" is a measure of the quantity of smoke being discharged and is the number obtained by multiplying the smoke density in a Standard Smoke Chart number by the time of emission in minutes. For example, the emission of Standard Smoke Chart number 1 for one minute equals one smoke unit.

Maximum Permitted Emission of Smoke

The density of emission of smoke during normal operations shall not exceed Standard Smoke Chart number 2, and the quantity of smoke shall not exceed a maximum of 10 smoke units per hour per stack.

Maximum Permitted Emission of Dust

a. Related to Combustion for Indirect Heating

The emission into the atmosphere of dust related to combustion for indirect heating from any source shall not exceed the maximum number of pounds of dust per million British thermal units heat input per hour as set forth herein:

The maximum permitted emission shall be 0.50 pounds per minimum-size plants producing a heat input of 10 million or less British thermal units per hour and 0.15 for maximum-size plants producing a heat input of 10,000 million or more British thermal units per hour. All intermediate values shall be determined from a straight line plotted on log graph paper.

b. Related to Processes

The emission into the atmosphere of process dust or other particulate matter that is unrelated to combustion for indirect heating or incineration shall not exceed 0.50 pounds per hour for 100 pounds of process weight or 50 pounds per hour for 100,000 pounds of process weight. All intermediate values shall be determined from a straight line plotted on log graph paper.

Odorous Matter

The emission of odorous matter in such quantities as to be readily detectable at any point along lot lines or to produce a public nuisance or hazard beyond lot lines is prohibited.

Toxic or Noxious Matter

"Toxic or noxious matter" is any solid, liquid, or gaseous matter, including but not limited to gases, vapors, dusts, fumes, and mists, containing properties that by chemical means are:
a. Inherently harmful and likely to destroy life or impair health, or
b. Capable of causing injury to the well-being of persons or damage to property.

Regulation of Toxic or Noxious Matter

The emission of such matter shall be so controlled that no concentration at or beyond lot lines shall be detrimental to or endanger the public health, safety, comfort, and other aspects of the general welfare, or cause damage or injury to property.

Radiation Hazards

"Fireproof containers" shall include steel or concrete containers and shall not include lead or other low-melting metals or alloys, unless the lead or low-melting metal or alloys are completely encased in steel.

Maximum Permitted Quantities of Unsealed Radioactive Material

Unsealed radioactive materials shall not be manufactured, utilized or stored (unless such materials are stored in a fireproof container at or below ground level) in excess of one million times the quantities set forth in Column 1 of the table in Section 38-2 of the Industrial Code Rule No. 14 of the New York State Department of Labor relating to Radiation Protection.

EXPLOSIVES, HAZARDS, GLARE

Maximum Permitted Quantities of Fissionable Materials

No one of the following fissionable materials shall be assembled at any one point, place, or work area on a zoning lot in a quantity equal to or in excess of the amount set forth herein:

Material	Quantity
Uranium-233	200 grams
Plutonium-239	200 grams
Uranium-235	350 grams

Fire and Explosive Hazards

"Slow-burning" materials are materials that will not ignite nor actively support combusion during an exposure for 5 minutes to a temperature of 1,200°F. and which, therefore, do not constitute an active fuel.

Moderate Burning

"Moderate-burning" materials are materials that in themselves burn moderately and may contain small quantities of a higher grade of combustibility.

Free Burning

"Free-burning" materials are materials constituting an active fuel.

Intense Burning

"Intense-burning" materials are materials that by virtue of low ignition temperature, high rate of burning, and large heat evolution, burn with great intensity.

Flammable or Explosive

"Flammable or explosive" materials are materials that produce flammable or explosive vapors or gases under ordinary weather temperature, including liquids with an open cup flash point of less than 100°F.

The "open cup flash point" is the temperature at which a liquid sample produces sufficient vapor to flash but not ignite when in contact with a flame in a Tagliabue open cut tester.

Original Sealed Containers

"Original sealed containers" are containers with a capacity of not more than 55 gallons.

Classifications

Materials are divided into four classifications or ratings based on the degree of fire and explosive hazard. The rating of liquids is established by specified open cup flash points.

a. Class I includes slow-burning to moderate-burning materials. This shall include all liquids with an open cup flash point of 182°F. or more.

b. Class II includes free-burning to intense-burning materials. This shall include all liquids with an open cup flash point between 100°F. and 182°F.

c. Class III includes materials that produce flammable or explosive vapors or gases under ordinary weather temperature. This shall include all liquids with an open cup flash point of less than 100°F.

d. Class IV includes materials that decompose by detonation, including but not limited to all primary explosives.

Regulations Applying to Class I Materials or Products

Class I materials or products may be stored, manufactured, or utilized in manufacturing processes or other production.

Regulations Applying to Class II and Class III Materials or Products

Class II materials or products may be stored, manufactured, or utilized in manufacturing processes or other production only in accordance with the following provisions:

1. Such storage, manufacture or utilization shall be carried on only within buildings or other structures that are completely enclosed by incombustible exterior walls;

2. Such buildings or other structures shall either be set back at least 40 feet from any lot lines, or in lieu thereof, all such buildings shall be protected throughout by an automatc fire extinguishing system.

Humidity, Heat, or Glare

Any activity producing excessive humidity in the form of steam or moist air, or producing intense heat or glare, shall be carried out within an enclosure and in such a manner as not to be perceptible at or beyond any lot line.

EVALUATION OF SITE EXPOSURE TO AIRCRAFT NOISE

If NEF or CNR contours are available, locate the site by referring to the marked scale. Also locate a point roughly in the center

TABLE I.

SITE EXPOSURE TO AIRCRAFT NOISE

Distance from Site to the Center of the Area Covered by the Principal Runways	Acceptability Category
Outside the NEF-30 (CNR-100) contour, at a distance greater than or equal to the distance between the NEF-30 and NEF-40 (CNR-100, CNR-115) contours	Clearly Acceptable
Outside the NEF-30 (CNR-100) contour, at a distance less than the distance between the NEF-30 and NEF-40 (CNR-100, CNR-115) contours	Normally Acceptable
Between the NEF-30 and NEF-40 (CNR-100, CNR-115) contours	Normally Unacceptable
Within the NEF-40 (CNR-115) contour	Clearly Unacceptable

TABLE II.

DISTANCES FOR APPROXIMATE NEF CONTOURS

Effective Number of Operations	Distances to NEF 30 Contour		Distances to NEF 40 Contour	
	①	②	①	②
0 – 50	1000 ft	1 mile	0	0
51 – 500	1/2 mile	3 miles	1000 ft	1 mile
501 – 1300	1 1/2 miles	6 miles	2000 ft	2 1/2 miles
More than 1300 or any supersonic jet operations	2 miles	10 miles	3000 ft	4 miles

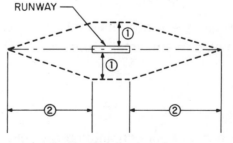

Construction of Approximate NEF Contours Using the Distances in Table II.

NEF—Noise Exposure Forecast
CNR—Composite Noise Rating

Noise Assessment Guidelines
U.S. Dept. of Housing and Urban Development
Wash. D.C. 1971

of the area covered by the principal runways. If the site lies outside the NEF-30 (CNR-100) contour, then draw a straight line to connect these two points. Measure along this line the distances between (1) the NEF-40 (CNR-115) and NEF-30 (CNR-100) contours and (2) the NEF-30 (CNR-100) contour and the site. Now use Table I to elevate the site's exposure to aircraft noise.

If NEF or CNR contours are not available, determine the effective number of operations for the airport as follows. Multiply the number of nighttime jet operations by 17. Then add the number of daytime jet operations to obtain an effective total. *Any* supersonic jet operation automatically places an airport in the largest category of Table II, which governs noise acceptability.

On a map of the area that shows the principal runways, mark the locations of the site and of the center of the area covered by the principal runways. Then, using the distances below, you can construct approximate NEF-40 and NEF-30 contours for the major runways and flight paths most likely to affect the site. Again use Table I to evaluate the site's exposure to aircraft noise.

Example 1: The illustration at the top shows two sites located on a map that has NEF contours. We draw a line from each of these sites to a point roughly in the center of the area covered by the principal runways.

Measuring along these lines, we find that Site #1 lies outside the NEF-30 contour at a distance greater than that between the NEF-30 and NEF-40 contours and that Site #2 lies outside the NEF-30 contour at a distance less than that between the NEF-30 and NEF-40 contours.

Therefore, the exposure of Site #1 to aircraft noise is Clearly Acceptable and the exposure of Site #2 is Normally Acceptable.

Example 2: The illustration at the bottom of the page shows an airport for which NEF or CNR contours are not available. The airport has 20 nighttime and 125 daytime jet operations.

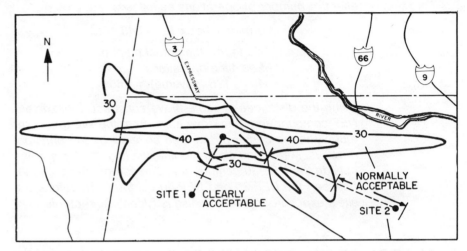

Example of NEF Contours

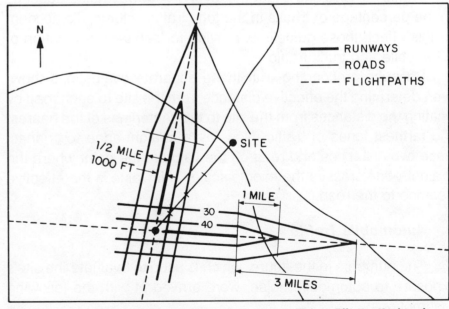

Example of Approximate NEF Contours Drawn for An Airport With An Effective Number of Operations Between 51 and 500.

There are no supersonic flights and so we determine the effective number of operations as follows:

20 (nighttime) x 17 = 340

Add to this the actual number of daytime operations:
340 + 125 (daytime) = 465

Using the distances in Table II, we construct approximate NEF contours and then draw a line from the site to a point roughly in the center of the area covered by the principal runways. Measuring along this line, we find that the site lies outside the NEF-30 contour at a distance greater than that between the NEF-30 and NEF-40 contours. Therefore, the site's exposure to aircraft noise is Clearly Acceptable.

EVALUATION OF SITE EXPOSURE TO ROADWAY NOISE

Traffic surveys show that the level of roadway noise depends on the percentage of trucks in the total traffic volume. To account for this effect, these guidelines provide for separate evaluation of automobile and truck traffic.

Because proceeding with these separate evaluations, however, determine the effective distance from the site to each road by locating the distances from the site to the centerlines of the nearest and farthest lanes of traffic. Now lay a straight-edge to connect these two distances and read off the value at the point where the straight-edge crosses the middle scale. This value is the effective distance to the road.

Automobile Traffic

The numbers in the figure, which is used to evaluate the site's exposure to automobile noise, were arrived at with the following assumptions:
- There is no traffic signal or stop sign within 800 ft. of the site.
- The mean automobile traffic speed is 60 mph.

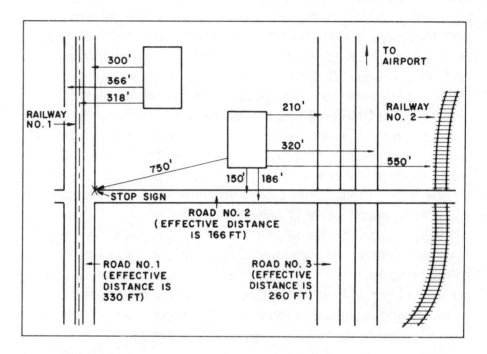

Plan view of site showing how distances should be measured from the location of the dwelling nearest to the source.

Noise Assessment Guidelines,
U.S. Dept. of Housing & Urban Development
Washington, D.C., 1971.

- There is line-of-sight exposure from the site to the road, i.e., there is no barrier that effectively shields the site from the road.

If a road meets these three conditions, proceed to the figure for an immediate evaluation of the site's exposure to the automobile noise from that road. But if any of these conditions are different, make the necessary adjustment(s) and *then* use the figure for the evaluation.

Adjustments for Automobile Traffic

Stop-and-go Traffic: If there is a traffic signal or stop sign within 800 ft. of the site, multiply the total number of automobiles per hour by 0.1.

Mean Traffic Speed: If there is no traffic signal or stop sign within 800 ft. of the site *and* the mean automobile speed is other than 60 mph, multiply the total number of automobiles by the appropriate adjustment factor.

Mean Traffic Speed	Adjustment Factor
20 (mph)	0.12
25	0.18
30	0.25
35	0.32
40	0.40
45	0.55
50	0.70
55	0.85
60	1.00
65	1.20
70	1.40

Barrier Adjustment: This adjustment affects distance and applies equally to automobiles and trucks on the same road. Therefore, instructions for this adjustment appear after those for truck traffic.

Truck Traffic

The numbers in Figure 3, which is used to evaluate the site's exposure to truck noise, were arrived at with the following assumptions:

- There is a road gradient of less than 3%.
- There is no traffic signal or stop sign within 800 ft of the site.
- The mean truck traffic speed is 30 mph.
- There is line-of-sight exposure from the site to the road, i.e., there is no barrier that effectively shields the site from the road.

If a road meets these four conditions, proceed to Figure 3 for an immediate evaluation of the site's exposure to truck noise from that road. But if any of the conditions are different, make the necessary adjustment(s) listed below and *then* use Figure 3 for the evaluation.

Adjustments for Truck Traffic

Road Gradient: If there is a gradient of 3% or more, multiply the number of trucks per hour in the uphill direction by the appropriate adjustment factor.

% of Gradient	Adjustment Factor
3-4%	1.4
5-6%	1.7
More than 6%	2.5

Add to this adjusted figure the number of trucks per hour in the downhill direction.

Stop-and-go Traffic: If there is a traffic signal or stop sign within 800 ft. of the site, multiply by 5 the total number of trucks.

Mean Traffic Speed: Make this adjustment only if there is no traffic signal or stop sign within 800 ft. of the site *and* the mean speed is not 30 mph.

If the mean truck speed differs with direction, treat the uphill and downhill traffic separately. Multiply each by the appropriate adjustment factor.

Mean Traffic Speed (mph)	Adjustment Factor
20	1.60
25	1.20
30	1.00
35	0.88
40	0.75
45	0.69
50	0.63
55	0.57
60	0.50
65	0.46
70	0.43

Examples

The site shown is exposed to noise from three major roads: Road #1 has four lanes, each 12 ft. wide, and a 30-ft. wide median strip that accommodates a rapid transit line. Road #2 has four lanes, each 12 ft. wide. Road #3 has six lanes, each 15 ft. wide, and a median strip 35 ft. wide.

Example 1: Road #1–The distance from the site to the centerline of the nearest lane of traffic is 300 ft. The distance to the centerline of the farthest lane of traffic is 366 ft. Figure 1 shows that the effective distance from the site to this road is 330 ft.
Road #2–The distance to the centerline of the nearest lane of traffic is 150 ft. The distance to the centerline of the farthest lane of traffic is 186 ft. Figure 1 shows that the effective distance from the site to this road is 166 ft.
Road #3–The distance to the centerline of the nearest lane of traffic is 210 ft. The distance to the centerline of the farthest lane of traffic is 320 ft. Figure 1 shows that the effective distance from the site to this road is 260 ft.

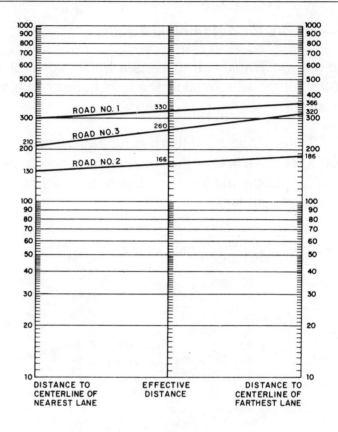

Example of how Figure 1 is used to determine effective distances.

Example 2: Road #1 meets the three conditions that allow for an immediate evaluation. In obtaining the information necessary for this evaluation, we found that the hourly automobile flow is 800 vehicles. On Figure 2, we locate on the vertical scale the point representing 800 vehicles/hr. and on the horizontal scale the point representing 330 ft. (Note that we must estimate the location of this point.) Using a straight-edge, we draw lines to connect these two values and find that the site's exposure to automobile noise from this road is Normally Acceptable.

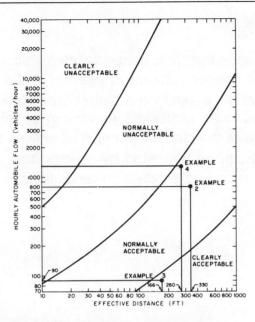

Example of how Figure 2 is used to evaluate site exposure to automobile noise.

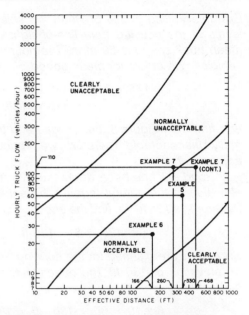

Example of how Figure 3 is used to evaluate the site's exposure to truck noise.

Example 3: Road #2 has a stop sign at 750 ft. from the site. The hourly automobile flow is reported as being 900 vehicles. We adjust for stop-and-go traffic

900 x 0.1 = 90 vehicles

and find from Figure 2 that the exposure to automobile noise is Clearly Acceptable.

Example 4: Road #3 is a depressed highway. There is no traffic signal or stop sign and the mean speed is 60 mph. The hourly automobile flow is 1,200 vehicles. The road profile shields all residential levels of the housing from line-of-sight to the traffic. The only adjustment that can be made is the barrier adjustment. This adjustment is necessary, however, only when the site's exposure to noise has been found Clearly or Normally Unacceptable. Figure 2 shows that the exposure to automobile noise is Normally Acceptable. Therefore, no adjustment for barrier is necessary.

Example 5: Road #1 meets the four conditions that allow for an immediate evaluation. The hourly truck flow is 60 vehicles. Figure 3 shows that the site's exposure to truck noise from this road is Normally Acceptable.

Example 6: Road #2 has a stop sign at 750 ft. from the site. There is also a road gradient of 4%. No trucks are allowed on this road, but 4 buses per hour are scheduled, 2 in each direction.

We adjust first for gradient:

	2 x 1.4=
uphill:	*2.8 vehicles*
downhill:	*2.0 vehicles*
total flow:	*4.8 vehicles*

And then adjust for stop-and-go traffic

4.8 x 5 = 24 vehicles (per hour)

Figure 3 shows that the exposure to truck (bus) noise from this road is Normally Acceptable.

509

Example 7: The profile of Road #3 shields all residential levels of the housing from line-of-sight to the traffic. The mean truck speed is 50 mph. The hourly truck flow is 175 vehicles. We adjust for mean speed

$$175 \times 0.63 = 110.25$$
$$= 110 \text{ vehicles}$$

and find from Figure 3 that exposure to truck noise is Normally Unacceptable. Therefore, we proceed with the barrier adjustment.

Road #3 has been depressed 25 ft. from the 150 ft. elevation of the natural terrain. The actual road elevation, therefore, is 125 ft. We find the effective road elevation to be

$$125 + 5 = 130 \text{ ft.}$$

Six stories are planned for the housing, which is located at an elevation of 130 ft. The effective site elevation for the highest story is:

$$6 \times 10 = 60 + 130 - 5 = 185 \text{ ft.}$$

CONCLUSION

In this chapter the basic concepts, elements, standards, sample ordinances, and/or references thereto, to the four basic regulatory tools for the creation and maintenance of a sound housing inventory have been discussed in varying detail. The following table summarizes the nine substantive objectives and the specific elements of each, as regulated by building and housing codes, zoning ordinances, and subdivision regulations.

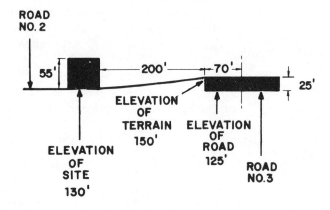

Detail of site showing the measurements necessary for a barrier adjustment.

IMPLEMENTATION OF OBJECTIVES THROUGH SEPARATE DEVELOPMENT INSTRUMENTS—EXAMPLES OF THE INTERRELATIONSHIP OF STANDARDS AMONG BUILDING CODES, HOUSING CODES, ZONING ORDINANCES, AND SUBDIVISION REGULATIONS				
Principal partici-pants in devel-oping standards and codes	Building codes Engineers-architects	Housing codes Health specialists	Zoning ordinances Planners-engineers	Subdivision regulations Engineers-planners
ELEMENTS REGULATED				
Subject of objective: 1. Natural light (penetration, quality, location).	Windows, yards, courts, light wells, habitable room size, building separations.	Windows, habitable room size	Courts, yards (front, side, rear), building height.	
2. Access and egress	Access to streets, corridors, stairs, doors; exits; access to bath-rooms and bedrooms.	Corridors, stairways, doors, exits; access to bathrooms and bed-rooms.	Required access to streets	Required access to streets.
3. Occupancy	Room dimensions (area, least di-mension, ceiling height); mini-mum area per person.	Room dimensions (area, least di-mension, ceiling height); mini-mum area per person, minimum area per dwelling unit.	Minimum area per dwelling unit	
4. Air supply	Windows; air conditioning	Windows; air conditioning	Windows, yards, courts	
5. Water supply	Sizes, materials, and construction; fixtures.	Materials, temperature, fixtures, maintenance.	Relation of uses to water supply	Sizes, materials, construction.
6. Air pollution (dis-charge into air).	Vents and venting systems, blowers and exhaust systems, incinera-tors.	Vents and venting systems, blowers and exhaust systems, incinera-tors.	Industrial performance standards; land use locations.	
7. Water pollution	Plumbing systems, septic tanks	Maintenance and functioning of plumbing and fixtures.	Industrial performance standards; land use locations.	Water courses, ground cover, grading.
8. Heating	Design and construction	Design and maintenance		
9. Fire safety	Construction and materials, build-ing separations, access and egress.	Maintenance requirements for in-teriors, exitways, and heating equipment.	Land use locations and relation-ship, building separations, access.	Access.

BIBLIOGRAPHY

Anderson, Robert M. *American Law of Zoning.* (4 volumes.) The Lawyers Cooperative Publishing Company, Rochester, N.Y. 1968.

Babcock, Richard F. *The Zoning Game.* The University of Wisconsin Press. Madison, 1966.

Bair, Frederick H. *Zoning Ordinance Checklist.* ASPO Planning Advisory Service Report No. 248, July 1969.

Bair, Frederick H. and Bartley, Ernest R. *A Model Zoning Ordinance.* American Society of Planning Officials, Chicago, 1966.

Faraci, Piero. *The Authority of the Zoning Administrator.* American Society of Planning Officials Report No. 226, September, 1967.

Goodman, William I. (ed.) and Freund, Eric C. (assoc. ed.). *Principles and Practices of Urban Planning.* International City Managers Association, Washington, D.C., 1968.

Haar, Charles M. *Land-Use Planning: A Casebook on the Use, Misuse, and Re-use of Urban Land.* Little, Brown & Company, Boston, 1959.

Krasnowiecki, Jan; Babcock, Richard F.; and McBride, David N. *Legal Aspects of Planned Unit Residential Development.* Technical Bulletin No. 52. Urban Land Institute, Washington, D.C., 1965.

Mandelker, David R. *Controlling Planned Residential Developments.* American Society of Planning Officials, Chicago, 1966.

McLean, Mary. *Local Planning Administration.* The International City Managers Association, Chicago, 1959.

Office of Planning Coordination. *Control of Land Subdivision.* New York, 1968.

Office of Planning Coordination. *Local Planning and Zoning.* New York, 1969.

Office of Planning Coordination. *Zoning in New York State.* New York, 1968.

Raymond & May Associates. *Residential Market Analyses (Progress Report).* Nassau-Suffolk Regional Planning Board, September, 1968.

Regional Plan Association. *Spread City.* Bulletin 100. New York, September, 1962.

Suffolk County Planning Commission. *A Plan for Open Space in Suffolk County.* Happauge, New York, 1964.

Sussna, Stephen. *New Developments in Zoning Law.* Stephen Sussna Associates, Planning Consultants, Trenton, N.J.

Toll, Seymour, I. *Zoned America.* Grossman Publishers, New York, 1969.

Ward, Richard C. "Site Plan Review in Zoning," *Land Use Quarterly,* Vol. 3, #2 American Society of Planning Officials, Spring 1969. (pp. 1-21).

Wolffe, Leonard L. *New Zoning Landmarks in Planned Unit Development.* Technical Bulletin No. 62. Urban Land Institute, Washington D.C., 1968.

Bair, Frederick H., Jr. *Local Regulation of Mobile Home Parks, Travel Trailer Parks and Related Facilities.* Mobile Homes Manufacturers Association, 1965. A manual on standards and regulations that deals with treatment zoning, accessory uses, state regulations and model zoning provisions.

Bair, Frederick H., Jr. "Mobile Homes—A New Challenge," *Law and Contemporary Problems,* XXXII, Spring, 1967, pp. 286-304.

Bair, Frederick H., Jr. *Mobile Homes and the General Housing Supply–Past, Present and Outlook.* Chicago: Mobile Homes Manufacturers Association, 1970. Discusses trends in construction techniques, sizes, and the mobile home as a growing proportion of housing production.

Bair, Frederick H., Jr., and Bartley, Ernest R. *Mobile Home Parks and Comprehensive Community Planning.* Studies in Public Administration No. 19. Gainesville, Florida: University of Florida, 1960. A comprehensive discussion of a broad range of issues, making this publication a good source to start with for municipalities dealing with mobile homes for the first time.

Bair Frederick H., Jr. "Modular Housing, Including Mobile Homes: A Survey of Regulatory Practices and Planners' Options." *American Society of Planning Officials Planning Advisory Service,* Report No. 165, January 1971.

Bair, Frederick H., Jr. *Regulation on Modular Housing with Special Emphasis on Mobile Homes,* American Society of Planning Officials Planning Advisory Service, Report No. 271, July-August 1971.

Edwards, C. M. "Dwelling Costs: A Comparison Made of Apartments, Mobile Homes, and Houses." *Mobile Home/Recreation Vehicle Dealer Magazine,* November 5, 1968.

Edwards, C. M. "Taxation and Mobile Homes." *Mobile Home/Travel Trailer Dealer,* May, 1965.

Edwards, C. M. "Trailer Topics Presents a Survey of the Mobile Home Consumer." *Trailer Topics Magazine,* 1970. Provides information on mobile home owners and prospective owners—family descriptions, occupations, income, educational achievement, etc.

Hades, Barnet, and Roberson, G. Gale. *The Law of Mobile Homes.* Chicago: Commerce Clearing House Inc., 1965.

"How to Gather Tax Data in Your Community." *Mobile Home Park Management,* February/March, 1967. Cost-revenue implications of mobile home parks are discussed with particular reference to comparison with single-family subdivisions.

Mobile Homes: A Selected List of References, 1964-69. Washington: National Housing Center, February, 1969.

Mobile Homes Manufacturers Association. *Mobile Home Minimum Body and Frame Design and Construction Standards.* Chicago, 1967.

Mobile Homes Manufacturers Association. *New Housing Systems Concepts.* Chicago, 1967.

Municipal Regulation of Mobile Homes and Mobile Home Parks. Bureau of Governmental Research and Services in cooperation with the Association of Washington Cities. Seattle: University of Washington Press, 1964.

Randall, William J. *Appraisal Guide for Mobile Home Parks.* Chicago: Mobile Homes Manufacturers Association, 1966.

U.S. Department of Health, Education, and Welfare, U.S. Public Health Service, Division of Environmental Engineering. *Environmental Health Guide for Mobile Home Parks, with a Recommended Ordinance,* 1966.

U.S. Department of Housing and Urban Development. *Mobile Home Court Development Guide: A HUD Guide.* Washington: Superintendent of Documents, U.S. Government Printing Office, 1970.

Wehrley, Max S. "The Evolution of the House Trailer: A Promising Approach to Low Cost Housing." *Urban Land News and Trends,* XXVI, No. 3, March, 1967, pp. 3-11.

GOVERNMENTAL PROGRAMS

I-1   Introduction
I-2   Federal Housing Administration
I-3   Housing Assistance Administration
I-4   Farmers Home and Veterans Administration
I-5   Department of Housing and
        Urban Development
I-6   FHA–Section 203
I-7   FHA–Sections 207, 213
I-8   FHA–Sections 213, 220
I-9   FHA–Section 221
I-10   FHA–Sections 221, 222, 233, 234
I-11   FHA–Sections 231, 232, 233, 234
I-12   FHA–Sections 235, 236

I-13   Adjusted Family Income Scale for
        Sections 235 and 236 Occupancy
I-14   Summary of Sales Programs
I-15   Summary of Rental Programs
I-16   Farmers Home Administration

HUD PROGRAMS

I-17   Grants; Neighborhood Facilities
I-18   Transportation, Open-space
I-19   Grants; Urban Renewal; Planning Assistance
I-20   Loans; College Housing; Rehabilitation
I-21   Loans; Public Works, Land Development

Although some of these programs have been curtailed or terminated, they are included for several reasons. The potential increase in revenue-sharing will allow states and municipalities to adopt a stronger role in housing initiative. The past federal approaches are a guide to local action.

It is also feasible that future Congressional action will be built upon current programs.

Furthermore, these programs are of educational interest to students and others involved in public housing.

I-1 INTRODUCTION **FEDERAL HOUSING ADMINISTRATION I-2**

INTRODUCTION

There are three general approaches that may be taken for the financing of existing or proposed housing.

1. *Conventional–housing entirely financed by private sources.*
2. *Governmental–entrepreneurial–housing built with governmental financial assistance ranging from mortgage insurance to outright subsidization.*
3. *Governmental–housing owned or leased and operated by public housing authorities.*

This chapter is designed as a guide, for builders, housing planners, and public officials, to the vast array of programs available from the federal government. It is also an attempt to clarify the essential differences in seemingly overlapping and competing programs. The concentration herein will therefore be related to the second and third class of approaches.

Three separate federal agencies are involved in housing programs. They are the Department of Housing and Urban Development (HUD), the Department of Agriculture, and the Veterans Administration (VA). The overwhelming majority of programs and number of housing units constructed may be attributed to HUD through the activities of the Federal Housing Administration and the Housing Assistance Administration.

The granting of departmental status under the Housing and Development Act of 1965 was an explicit indication of the importance Congress and the President placed on the responsibility of the government to provide assistance for housing and development of the nation's communities. The Department, in addition to assisting the private market in the production and rehabilitation of housing, also administers assistance programs for the development of new communities, colleges and hospital housing, nonprofit hospitals, group medical practice facilities, and nursing homes. It is also worth mentioning (even though it is tangential to the specific nature of this chapter) that HUD provides its community assitance by means of grants and/or loans for comprehensive planning, urban renewal, community facilities, open space acquisition, land acquisition for new communities, and urban beautification.

FEDERAL HOUSING ADMINISTRATION

The Federal Housing Administration, created in 1934, has made home ownership possible for millions of American families through the use of low downpayment, long-term mortgages for construction, purchase and rehabilitation purposes. F.H.A.'s primary role is the insurance of loans made by private lending institutions. The Administration also runs a number of programs specifically designed to aid moderate- and low-income families to obtain housing by means of rent supplements, below-market rental units (Section 221 (d) (3)), and by monthly subsidies to the lending institutions to reduce the interest rates to as low as 1%.

Sections 1-6 through 1-16 describe the various F.H.A. programs for sale and rental housing for middle-, moderate- and low-income families, the elderly, the handicapped, and certified servicemen. Several of the very limited programs have been omitted. Two other notes of caution. First, the numbering system indicated on the charts refers to the sections of the original Housing Act of 1934, as amended. The numbers of new or changed programs have been interjected over the years and do not connote any necessary consecutive program substance. Second, these various programs are often altered, modified or amended. Since this chapter becomes static once committed to the printer, the information contained herein should be considered as a guide and not as gospel.

Although the F.H.A. has been enlarging its role in assisting low-income families to receive suitable housing by rental or purchase by means of Sections 221 (d) (2), 221 (d) (3), 235 and 236, low-income public housing is the responsibility of the Housing Assistance Administration.

HOUSING ASSISTANCE ADMINISTRATION

The passage of the Housing Act of 1937 provided for low-rent housing programs for low-income families. The rentals are based on ability to pay and include eligibility for senior citizens and handicapped persons, in addition to family units. For almost three decades, public housing has been in the form of new construction built by private builders for public ownership and operation by local public housing authorities. This practice was amended in 1965 to allow public authorities to expand the supply of low-cost housing by means of leases of private housing and the acquisition of suitable existing nonpublic housing. A further innovation in the Act was the initiation of a rent supplement program. The concept is to enable HUD to make payments on behalf of eligible tenants to owners of certain multifamily housing projects. The eligible projects include:

1. *Housing built under Section 221 (d) (3) (market interest rate), which covers proposed or rehabilitation of multifamily housing projects by private nonprofit, limited-distribution, or cooperative housing mortgagors if the mortgage was insured after August 10, 1965.*
2. *Experimental housing built under Section 221 (d) (3) (below market-interest rate), and;*
3. *Section 231 housing, which covers proposed or rehabilitation of a project by a nonprofit mortgagor.*

In order to qualify, a tenant must be an individual or family that has been determined to have assets and income below the established maximums and must be one of the following: an individual or family; displaced by government action, 62 years of age or older, or whose spouse is 62 years or older, physically handicapped, occupying substandard housing, or housing affected by a natural disaster. (Nonassisted tenants may also rent units in the project.)

The amount of the rent supplement payable for an individual or family is the difference between the rental for the unit and one-fourth of the tenant's income except that the payment cannot exceed seventy percent or be less than five percent of the unit rental.

An additional innovation was the development of a new method—"turnkey housing." Emphasis is now being placed on the rehabilitation or construction of projects for use as low-rent public housing with major reliance on the private housing enterprise. Local housing authorities may now contract to buy housing that meets acceptable design standards. This approach also allows for the management of low-rent projects by private tenant organizations or management firms. HUD is also promoting home ownership among public tenants and eligible families as a result of other provisions within the Housing Act of 1968. Families who can build an equity through self-maintenance and monthly payments related to income are eligible for ownership assistance. This may occur in private housing or through the sale of existing public housing units. (See Sections 235, 236 also)

Most of the families and individuals included under rent supplements are also eligible for public housing. Both rent supplement and public housing have the same income limits, but there are stricter eligibility requirements for supplement aid. It appears likely—subject to the availability of funding —that the interest subsidies of Sections 235 and 236 render these programs to be the most active means for private enterprise to supply low-cost housing.

FARMERS HOME AND VETERANS ADMINISTRATIONS

The Housing Act of 1949 (Title V) authorized the granting and insuring of rural loans for farmers and rural inhabitants in towns of less than 5,500 population for applicants who are unable to obtain credit from other sources. In 1961 the program was amended to provide insured loans to farm labor, farm associations, states and political jurisdictions, and public or private nonprofit associations. In 1962 provision was included for senior citizen rental housing loans. In 1964 grants were made possible for the financing of low-rent housing for domestic farm workers by public agencies and qualified private nonprofit sponsors. In 1966 further expansion transferred to the Department the Federal National Mortgage Association.

Purpose

The declaration of purpose of the Department of Housing and Urban Development Act declares that "the general welfare and security of the Nation and the health and living standards of our people require, as a matter of national purpose, sound development of the Nation's communities and metropolitan areas in which the vast majority of its people live and work.

"To carry out such a purpose, and in recognition of the increasing importance of housing and urban development in our national life, the Congress finds that establishment of an executive department is desirable to achieve the best administration of the principal programs of the Federal Government which provide assistance for housing and for the development of the Nation's communities; to assist the President in achieving maximum coordination of the various Federal activities that have a major effect upon urban community, suburban, or metropolitan development; to encourage the solution of problems of housing, urban development, and mass transportation through State, county, town, village, or other local and private action, including promotion of interstate, regional and metropolitan cooperation; to encourage the maximum contributions that may be made by vigorous private homebuilding and mortgage lending industries to housing, urban development, and the national economy; and to provide for full and appropriate consideration, at the national level, of the needs and interests of the Nation's communities and of the people who live and work in them."

Organization

The Secretary of Housing and Urban Development established the organization of the Department and assigned programs and functions to the respective organization units in Secretary's Organization Order 1, dated February 24, 1966. The internal structure is shown in the organization chart.

PURPOSE—The overall purpose of the Department of Housing and Urban Development is to assist in providing for sound development of the nation's communities and metropolitan areas.

As stated in the Department of Housing and Urban Development Act, the Department was created to administer the principal programs that provide assistance for housing and for the development of the nation's communities; to assist the President in achieving maximum coordination of the various Federal activities that have a major effect upon urban, community, suburban, or metropolitan development; to encourage the solution of problems of housing and urban development through state, county, town, village or other local and private action, including promotion of interstate, regional and metropolitan cooperation; to encourage the maximum contributions that may be made by vigorous private home-building and mortgage-lending industries to housing, urban development, and the national economy; and to provide for full and appropriate consideration at the national level of the needs and interests of the nation's communities and of the people who live and work in them.

Office of the Secretary

SECRETARY—The department is administered under the supervision and direction of the Secretary, who is responsible for the administration of all programs, functions, and authorities of the Department; for the general regulation of the Federal National Mortgage Association; and for advising the President on Federal policy, programs, and activities relating to housing and urban development. The Secretary also serves as Chairman of the Board of Directors of the New Communities Development Corporation.

The Under Secretary assists the Secretary in the discharge of his duties and responsibilities, and serves as Acting Secretary in the absence of the Secretary.

provided for cooperatively owned and/or rental housing for non-senior citizen rural families. The Housing and Urban Development Act of 1968 authorized interest credit programs for low-income families. In this instance, the Farmers Home Administration exercises certain responsibilities in connection with Federal Housing Administration programs under Sections 235 and 236 in accord with an agreement reached between the Secretaries of HUD and and Agriculture. In regard to Section 235, the Farmers Home Administration carries out the functions normally handled by HUD except that the funds are advanced by the Federal Housing Administration and the loans are serviced by the mortgagee. In regard to Section 236, the Farmers Home Administration assists the applicants by counseling them in obtaining 236 aid from HUD. The Act also created a new authority to make loans to nonprofit sponsors to buy land and subdivide it into individual building sites for families who use the self-help method to construct their homes. Section I-16 is a summary of the most applicable programs.

Veterans' Administration Home Loan Guarantee Program

The Serviceman's Readjustment Act of 1944, as amended over the years, included provisions for credit assistance to veterans for the purchase or construction of homes. The extension of favorable credit terms by private lenders for the purchase, construction, rehabilitation, or improvement of homes to be occupied by veterans purchasers is the major objective of the program. The Federal Government guarantees the loan, thereby making it feasible for private lenders to extend longer term mortgages with minimal downpayment requirements. This is particularly beneficial to many veterans who cannot qualify for conventional mortgages. Home loans may be guaranteed up to 60 percent of the loan, not to exceed $12,500. Some of the main features of the program include:

1. *The home has to be occupied by the veteran.*
2. *The payment terms must relate to the veteran's present*

and anticipated ability to qualify as a satisfactory credit risk.
3. *The maximum loan term is 40 years.*
4. *No downpayment is required by the V.A.*
5. *The interest rate cannot exceed that set by the V.A.*

There are also provisions for direct loan credit to veterans in rural and semirural areas where private credit is unavailable. In these cases the loan may be up to $17,500 for a 30-year period.

The main deterrent to the V.A. program lies in the difficulty to find interested private lenders during periods of high interest rate requirements.

The balance of the chapter, Sections I-17—I-21, contains a brief description of the ancillary general HUD programs for community development including:

1. *Grants for: neighborhood facilities, advance acquisition of land, basic water and sewer facilities, urban mass transportation, urban renewal and urban planning assistance.*
2. *Loans for: college housing, rehabilitation aids and programs, advances for public works planning, public facilities, and land development and new communities.*

DEPARTMENT OF HOUSING AND URBAN DEVELOPMENT

Creation and Authority

The Department of Housing and Urban Development was established by the Department of Housing and Urban Development Act of September 9, 1965 (79 Stat. 667; 5 U.S.C. 642). The act, which became effective November 9, 1965, transferred to and vested in the Secretary of Housing and Urban Development all of the functions, powers, and duties of the Housing and Home Finance Agency (including the Community Facilities Administration and the Urban Renewal Administration), of the Federal Housing Administration and the Public Housing Administration, and

DEPARTMENT OF HOUSING AND URBAN DEVELOPMENT

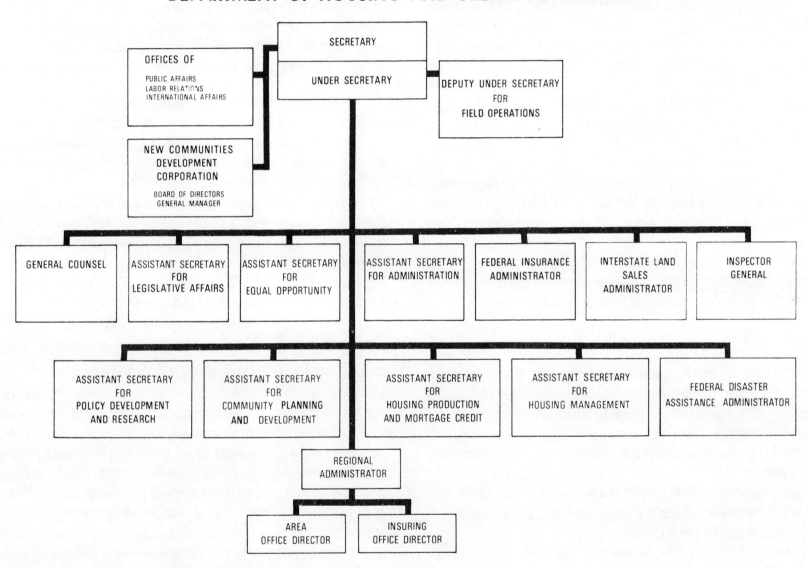

SOURCE: U.S. Government Organization Manual, 1972/73

POLICY ANALYSIS AND PROGRAM EVALUATION—The Deputy Under Secretary for Policy Analysis and Program Evaluation performs functions with respect to program formulation and evaluation, and makes comprehensive studies and analyses of developments, trends, and problems relating to national housing and community development goals.

GENERAL ASSISTANT SECRETARY—The General Assistant Secretary provides general assistance to the Secretary in the pursuance of the objectives of the Department, and advises on policies and programs. He is also the Assistant Secretary for Community Planning and Management.

STAFF—The Office of the Secretary also contains offices having Department-wide responsibility in specialized functional areas such as congressional relations, public affairs, labor relations, and international affairs.

The Secretary is assisted in performing the functions of the Department by Assistant Secretaries and other officials who have responsibilities in specific functional and program areas.

Functional Areas

ADMINISTRATION—The Assistant Secretary for Administration is the principal adviser to the Secretary and the chief officer on administrative management, including budget, organization, methods, and directives systems; automatic data processing; accounting and financial management; personnel administration; and regional liaison.

GENERAL COUNSEL—The General Counsel is the chief law officer of the Department and is the legal adviser to the Secretary and other principal staff of the Department.

INSPECTOR GENERAL—The Inspector General (IG) has primary responsibility for reviewing the integrity of the conduct of the Department's operations. IG is the central authority concerned with the quality, coverage, and coordination of the audit, investigation, and security services of the Department.

EQUAL OPPORTUNITY—The Assistant Secretary for Equal Opportunity is the principal adviser to the Secretary on all matters relating to civil rights and equal opportunity in housing and related facilities, employment and business opportunity. He is also responsible for assuring that all departmental policies, procedures, issuances, and activities effect and promote equal opportunity for all.

The responsibilities assigned to the Department concerning equal opportunity include administering the fair housing program authorized by the Civil Rights Act of 1968; assuring that the programs and activities of the Department operate affirmatively to further the goals of equal opportunity; coordinating planning, monitoring, and reviewing programs to increase training, employment, and economic opportunities for low-income and minority-group project area residents in HUD-assisted activities; and developing standards, procedures, and guidelines for implementing Executive Order 11478 of August 8, 1969, providing for equality of employment opportunity within the Department.

Program Areas

COMMUNITY PLANNING AND MANAGEMENT

The Assistant Secretary for Community Planning and Management is responsible for the following programs and activities:

COMPREHENSIVE PLANNING ASSISTANCE—HUD provides grant assistance to State and local governments and areawide multijurisdictional organizations to encourage State, local and areawide officials to improve executive planning, decision making, and management capability; encourage community planning and management as a continuous process; and assist State and local governments and areawide organizations in dealing with community development and growth for urban and rural areas.

Comprehensive planning assistance under this program means a continuing process whereby State and local governments and areawide planning organizations formulate and coordinate community strategies and management decisions. It spans the broad range of governmental activities, services, and investments for which assisted governments are responsible.

Grants may be made to states for statewide planning, assistance to cities with less than 50,000 population and counties of all sizes, metropolitan planning, assistance to nonmetropolitan areawide planning organizations (including Economic Development Districts and Local Development Districts), and to cities with populations in excess of 50,000.

Special grants are also available to assist innovative projects; planning related to new communities, urban growth, and Operation Breakthrough; and systems analysis techniques as applied to public facilities and services under the Urban Systems Engineering Program.

COMMUNITY DEVELOPMENT TRAINING PROGRAMS—HUD may make matching grants to states to assist in programs to provide special training in skills needed for economic and efficient community development to persons employed by a governmental or public body or a private nonprofit organization that has responsibility for housing and community development programs; and supporting State and local research needed in connection with housing programs and needs and other similar community development problems.

URBAN STUDIES FELLOWSHIP PROGRAM—HUD provides fellowships to candidates for graduate training in accredited universities in such fields as urban economics, housing and urban renewal, community organization, urban sociology, urban geography, urban engineering and systems design, urban transportation, and new communities.

STATE AND LOCAL MANAGEMENT ASSISTANCE—This program area includes technical assistance to states, areawide agencies, and communities in planning and management through such activities as: aid to City Demonstration Agencies (Model Cities) to assist such agencies in planning, developing, and administering comprehensive city demonstration programs; assisting State and local governments, as well as Indian tribal bodies, in comprehensive planning, including transportation planning; encouragement of planning and assistance on a unified regional district, or metropolitan basis; and management assistance to states and State agencies to aid in comprehensive coordinated planning and planning related activities.

WORKABLE PROGRAM FOR COMMUNITY IMPROVEMENT—Under this program a community designs its own plan of action for disciplining its development and using appropriate private and public resources to eliminate and prevent slums and blight, addressing locally determined needs, goals, and objectives as well as federally determined requirements.

ESSENTIAL ELEMENTS OF A WORKABLE PROGRAM are the adoption of modern codes and their enforcement, comprehensive planning and programming, provisions for housing and relocation, and provisions for citizen involvement, as well as provisions for equal opportunity in housing. Recertification is based on review of progress submitted by the community to HUD every 2 years. The localities' Workable Program must be (re)certified by HUD before the community can become eligible for Federal renewal assistance, for HUD-FHA mortgage insurance for housing to be built or rehabilitated in renewal areas, and for rehabilitation loans and grants in specified areas.

PROJECT REVIEW—Under title II of the Demonstration Cities and Metropolitan Development Act of 1966, applications for Federal loans or grants to assist in carrying out open-space land projects or for the planning or construction of hospitals, airports, libraries, water supply and distribution facilities, law enforcement facilities, and water development and land conservation projects within any metropolitan area shall be submitted for review to an areawide agency designated to perform the metropolitan or regional planning for the area in which the assistance is to be used, and recommendations shall be reviewed by HUD for the purpose of assisting in determining whether the application is in accordance with the provisions of Federal law that governs the making of the loans or grants.

RELOCATION—HUD develops and administers relocation policies and requirements for the fair and equitable treatment of persons who are displaced or have their property taken as a result of activities planned or carried out by local agencies with HUD assistance.

ENVIRONMENT—Environmental quality and planning activities are conducted by the Department, such as clearinghouse and coordinating functions in the evaluation, review, and coordination of Federal and federally assisted programs and projects; development and coordination of HUD environmental activities with other Federal departments and agencies, and with the Council on Environmental Quality; and monitoring of HUD activities in response to national environmental policies and guidelines.

GUARANTEES—This grant program enables developers to obtain financing on favorable terms by pledging the full faith and credit of the United States for obligations issued to help finance new community land acquisition and development, and construction of public facilities. Eligible for this assistance are public land development agencies, if income from the obligations guaranteed is not exempt from Federal taxation, and private developers. For public land development agencies the guarantee may cover up to 100 percent of the value of the development cost. For private developers the guarantee covers up to 80 percent of the value of the real property before development and 90 percent of the development cost; not more than 50 million dollars principal amount of outstanding obligations may be guaranteed for a single program.

SUPPLEMENTARY GRANTS—These grants assist new community projects by providing additional grants supplementing 13 existing Federal programs. Eligible are agencies that have received basic grant approval for facilities serving an eligible new community. These include public land development agencies and any other State or local public body or agency. The amount granted is not to exceed 20 percent of the cost of the total project. Total Federal contribution to the project cannot exceed 80 percent of total cost.

SURPLUS LAND FOR COMMUNITY DEVELOPMENT PROGRAM—Surplus Federal real property may be: sold for fair market value to a local public agency that certifies that such land is within the area of an urban renewal project being planned by it; or sold or leased to public or private developers at its fair value for use in providing housing for families and individuals of low or moderate income, including necessary related public, commercial and industrial facilities.

Housing Production and Mortgage Credit

The Assistant Secretary for Housing Production and Mortgage Credit, who is also the Federal Housing Commissioner, administers the programs and functions of the Department that assist in the production and financing of housing and in the conservation and rehabilitation of the housing stock.

These programs include the insurance, under the National Housing Act, of mortgages and loans made by private lending institutions for the purchase, construction, rehabilitation, repair, and improvement of single-family and multifamily housing, the low-rent public housing program, and the homeownership assistance, interest-reduction, rent supplement, and college housing programs. With respect to these programs, the functions assigned to the Assistant Secretary for Housing Production and Mortgage Credit are those required from preapplication through construction completion and the execution and closing of the contract or mortgage or other credit financing instrument, as well as actions that are a direct extension of the construction and production phase that may occur after final endorsement.

APPLICATIONS—All applicants who wish to participate in a

mortgage insurance program must submit their applications through the mortgage lender who is financing the home or project. However, in the case of subsidized multifamily projects, the applicants submit to the Department a request for feasibility determination prior to formal application for a firm commitment. The Department then determines if the applicant and the project meet certain eligibility criteria, and a study is made to determine the feasibility of the project. The applicant then submits, through the mortgage lender, a formal application.

INSURANCE—Mortgages and loans are insured under the terms of the National Housing Act for the purchase of single-family housing, private residences, rental housing, cooperative housing, condominiums, and mobile homes. Mortgage insurance also is provided for housing for the elderly, nursing homes and intermediate care facilities, nonprofit hospitals, and group practice medical facilities. Special programs are provided for yield insurance on equity investments in rental housing; loan and mortgage insurance for land development, mobile home parks, experimental housing, housing in urban renewal areas, armed services housing, and single-family housing for homeownership subsidized by interest assistance payments and multifamily housing subsidized through interest assistance payments and rent supplements.

LOANS AND ASSISTANCE—The Department is authorized to provide, or contract with public or private organizations to provide, advice and technical assistance to nonprofit sponsors of low- and moderate-income housing. In addition, interest-free loans are authorized to cover up to 80 percent of the preconstruction costs incurred by nonprofit sponsors in planning a federally assisted, low-and-moderate income housing project.

The low-rent public housing program, authorized by the United States Housing Act of 1937, provides Federal loans and annual contributions to assist local housing authorities in providing low-rent housing by construction, by rehabilitation of existing structures, by purchase from private builders or developers (the Turn-

key method), and through leasing from private owners. Special provisions allow for purchase of such housing by low-income families.

The College Housing Program provides loans and debt service grants to colleges and eligible hospitals to finance the construction, rehabilitation, or purchase of housing and related facilities.

MORTGAGE CREDIT—The Assistant Secretary for Housing Production and Mortgage Credit also directs the administration of the Government National Mortgage Association (GNMA). Under the direct leadership of a president, the Association carries out the following programs of the Department in accordance with the general policies of the Secretary and title III of the National Housing Act; the provision of special assistance in the financing of eligible types of federally underwritten mortgages; the mortgage-backed security program; the management and liquidation of the portfolio of mortgages held by GNMA; the management of the Government Mortgage Liquidation Trust, Small Business Obligations Trust, Federal Assets Liquidation Trust, and Federal Assets Financing Trust; and the guaranty of timely payments of principal and interest on such trust certificates or other securities as shall be backed by trusts or pools composed of mortgages insured by HUD or guaranteed by the Veterans Administration.

Community Development

The responsibilities of the Assistant Secretary for Community Development are the administration of the various programs concerning the community, which are now grouped to eliminate duplication of programmatic efforts and facilitate packaging of HUD community development assistance at the area office level.

MODEL CITIES—Funding and technical assistance is provided to a selected number of cities throughout the country for a com-

I-5 HUD

prehensive program to deal with social, economic, and physical problems in slum and blighted areas. The Model Cities program involves concentration and coordination of Federal, State, and local public and private resources. Residents of designated Model Cities areas as well as other interested citizens are involved in the planning and implementation of local Model Cities programs.

PLANNED VARIATIONS—Selected Model Cities participate in the developing and testing of procedures to strengthen local capacities in dealing with urban problems, thereby serving as a guide for other communities as they orient their governmental processes to handle new community development programs and other revenue-sharing resources.

URBAN RENEWAL—Loans and grants are provided for slum clearance and urban renewal including neighborhood development, interim assistance for blighted areas, concentrated code enforcement, demolition projects, general neighborhood renewal plans and feasibility surveys.

REHABILITATION LOANS AND GRANTS—This is a program of loans and grants for rehabilitation projects, not including servicing and disposition. Individuals who qualify may receive loans and grants for rehabilitation purposes.

OPEN SPACE LAND AND RELATED PROGRAMS—Grants are available for the acquisition and development of open space land, and urban beautification and improvement. Historic preservation grants are made to public bodies.

COMMUNITY FACILITIES—Grants are provided for basic water and sewer facilities and neighborhood facilities, and loans for public facilities.

Housing Management

The Assistant Secretary for Housing Management directs the administration of departmental programs and activities in the following areas:

Provision of assistance is given the local housing authorities in management and modernization of low-rent public housing projects including support of resident and community services in these projects, and the necessary special family and other operating subsidies.

HUD-insured and Government-held mortgages are managed and serviced for all mortgage insurance programs under the National Housing Act, including nursing homes, intermediate care facilities, mobile homes and mobile home courts, hospitals, group practice facilities and land development.

Management and administration of assistance is offered for contracts for interest-reduction payments and rent supplements, homeownership for low- and middle-income families, operation, and forbearance agreements and assignments of mortgages.

Loans are serviced and managed for housing assisted by Department lending and grant programs; real and related property conveyed to or in the custody of the Secretary is managed, rehabilitated, rented, and disposed.

Direction is given to resident and homeownership counseling to low- and middle-income families; private market financing through the sale of notes and bonds; local financing for urban renewal; defense planning, disaster relief and economic stabilization activities; and liquidating programs.

Research and Technology

The Assistant Secretary for Research and Technology is the principal adviser on scientific and technological matters of concern to the Department. The Office of the Assistant Secretary for Research and Technology conducts action research (applied research including experiments, demonstrations, and pilot implementations) to provide a better understanding; improved methods, services and facilities; improved Federal programs; and solutions to housing and community problems of our growing population.

Operation Breakthrough has as its primary objective breaking

526

through the barriers of unimproved methods and design, production, land use, marketing technology, and management in housing. To meet this objective HUD has entered into a cooperative effort with local and State government, industry, labor, financial institutions, and community groups to improve the entire housing process.

In meeting the goal of providing housing to meet national needs, research and technology programs include projects in the areas of improved operation and management of the existing stock of housing, assisting families to obtain housing through housing allowance subsidies, assembling housing statistics and economics information, encouraging new and improved building technology, and fair housing and equal opportunity practices. In addition, experiments to test the components of the program for preventing the spread of abandonment and neighborhood decay are being developed. Further, research related to practical demonstrations of waste disposal systems, energy systems including the utilization of waste heat, noise abatement methods, advanced communication systems, utility installation and geological problems in community development are supported.

The Municipal Information Systems program initiated in 1970 as an aid in improving and modernizing the information-gathering capabilities of municipalities to assist in their management and decision-making processes, is managed within the Office of the Assistant Secretary for Research and Technology.

Federal Insurance

The Administrator of the Federal Insurance Administration (FIA) is the principal adviser to the Secretary on insurance matters, particularly on those administered by the FIA. In all insurance programs, the Administration utilizes the cooperation of other Federal agencies, State and local governments, and the private insurance industry. The FIA conducts studies and makes recommendations of alternative programs of insurance and financial assistance in meeting natural and other disasters and similar occurrences.

FLOOD INSURANCE—The National Flood Insurance Program is designed to enable persons to purchase insurance against losses resulting from physical damage to or loss of real or personal property arising from floods or mudslides occurring in the United States. Communities having flood or mudslide hazards put into effect land-use and control measures meeting FIA standards and apply for eligibility to the Administrator. After the community has been designated as eligible, insurance policies may be purchased from any licensed insurance agent or broker.

RIOT INSURANCE—The Riot Reinsurance Program is designed to assist property owners in urban areas to obtain essential insurance protection, particularly on property located in areas possibly subject to civil disturbances. Federal reinsurance is available for companies participating in Fair Access to Insurance Requirements (FAIR) Plans under the supervision of the state's insurance authority. These companies agree to provide coverage based on the insurability of the property regardless of location. Property owners in FAIR Plan jurisdictions who cannot obtain insurance coverage in the private market are referred to the FAIR Plan headquarters, the property is inspected and the rate determined, and the policy is issued.

CRIME INSURANCE—The Federal Crime Insurance Program is designed to enable businessmen and residents of homes and apartments to purchase crime insurance in states where crime insurance is difficult to obtain or excessively costly. The Administrator reviews the market situation in the several states to determine where the Federal program is needed. Citizens of the states so designated may purchase the Federal policy through any licensed insurance agent or broker.

Interstate Land Sales Registration

The Interstate Land Sales Administration exercises the Department's responsibilities under the Interstate Land Sales Full

Disclosure Act. The Administrator heads the Office of Interstate Land Sales Registration, which administers and enforces registration and disclosure requirements that apply to developers who sell land through the use of any means of interstate commerce or the mails. Pursuant to the regulations, developers of all nonexempt subdivisions containing 50 or more lots must file a Statement of Record with the Office of Interstate Land Sales Registration and furnish each purchaser with a printed Property Report in advance of the time that they sign the sales contract. Developers who do not comply with the statutory and regulatory requirements may be subject to administrative proceedings, civil proceedings to enjoin the acts or practices, and criminal prosecution.

Field Structure

The field operations of the Department are carried out through a series of regional, area, and insuring offices.

The regional offices of the Department have regional boundaries and headquarters locations prescribed by the Secretary as indicated on the map. Each regional office is headed by a Regional Administrator who is responsible to the Secretary and the Under Secretary for the execution of the Department's programs assigned his region, the overall management of the regional office, and the supervision and direction of regional office staff, and of the area and insuring office in his region.

Area offices of the Department are operational in the locations listed below. For information concerning the address or detailed jurisdiction of an area office, the indicated regional office should be consulted.

Field activities of the Federal Housing Administration are carried out through the area offices or insuring offices indicated below.

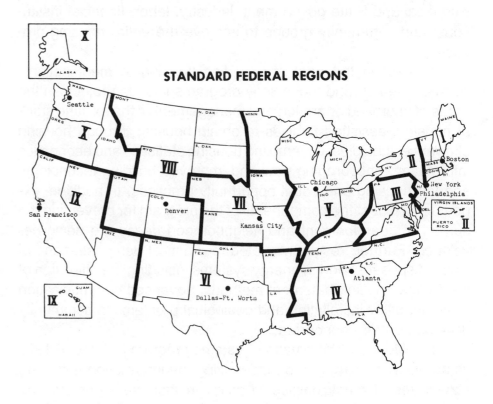

STANDARD FEDERAL REGIONS

SOURCE: U.S. Government Organization Manual, 1973/74

FHA MORTGAGE LOANS

HOMES—TITLE II—SEC. 203

Section of Act	Purpose of Loan	Amount Insurable	Loan-Value Ratio	Term of Loan	Interest Rates

Section 203(b)
1
2
3
4
	Finance proposed or existing 1-4 family housing	Occupant mortgagor:
		$33,000 1-family
		$33,750 2- or 3-family
		$41,250 4-family
		$12,500 if property meets only Minimum Property Standards for low-cost housing
		
		Nonoccupant mortgagor:
		$25,500 1-family
		$27,600 2- or 3-family
		$31,800 4-family
		$10,600 if property meets only Minimum Property Standards for low-cost housing
			Occupant mortgagor:
			  Proposed construction or completed more than 1 year: 97% of $15,000 of appraised value + 90% of value above $15,000 but not over $20,000 + 80% above $20,000; limits for 1-family housing for veterans are 100% of $15,000 of appraised value, or sum of such value not in excess of $15,000 and items of prepaid expense, less $200, but not over $20,000 + 85% of value above $20,000.
			
			  Under construction or completed less than 1 year: 90% of $20,000 of appraised value + 80% of value above $20,000; limits for 1-family housing for veterans are 90% of $20,000 of appraised value + 85% of value above $20,000.
			
			Nonoccupant mortgagor: 85% of amount computed under any of above formulae.
				Occupant or nonoccupant mortgagor, except operative builder: 30 years, except 35 years if mortgagor is unacceptable under 30-year term, for housing built under FHA or VA inspection, or 3/4 of remaining economic life, whichever is less.
				
				Operative builder: 20 years, or 3/4 of remaining economic life, whichever is less.
					8-1/2% + 1/2% mortgage insurance premium

Section 203(h) 1 2 3	Finance proposed or existing 1-family housing for occupant-mortgagor victim of natural disaster	$14,400 occupant mortgagor	Appraised value	30 years, except 35 years if mortgagor is unacceptable under a 30-year term, for housing built under FHA or VA inspection, or 3/4 of remaining economic life, whichever is less.	8-1/2% + 1/2% m.i.p.

Section 203(i)
1
2
3
5
	Finance proposed or existing 1-family nonfarm housing or farm housing on 5 or more acres adjacent to highway	$16,200 occupant mortgagor
		$10,600 operative builder
			Occupant mortgagor:
			  Proposed construction or completed more than 1 year: 97% of appraised value.
			  Under construction or completed less than 1 year: 90% of appraised value.
			
			Operative builder:
			  85% of appraised value.
				Occupant mortgagor: 30 years, except 35 years if mortgagor is unacceptable under 30-year term, for housing built under FHA or VA inspection, or 3/4 of remaining economic life, whichever is less.
				
				Operative builder: 20 years, or 3/4 of remaining economic life, whichever is less.
					8-1/2% + 1/2% m.i.p.

Section 203(k) 6 7 8	Finance proposed alteration, repair, or improvement of existing 1-4 family housing not within urban renewal areas	$10,000 1-family $20,000 2-family $30,000 3-family $37,500 4-family 9	Amount of loan plus debt on property cannot exceed dollar limitations insurable under Section 203(b).	20 years, or 3/4 of remaining economic life, whichever is less.	8-1/2% + 1/2% m.i.p.

[1] Certification to mortgagor of FHA appraisal amount required in 1- or 2-family dwellings.

[2] Builder warranty required on proposed construction.

[3] Eligible for open-end advances.

[4] If borrower is 62 years of age or older, downpayment, settlement charges, and prepaid expenses may be borrowed from approved corporation or individual.

[5] Downpayment, settlement charges, and prepaid expenses may be borrowed from approved corporation or individual.

[6] Housing must be at least 10 years old, unless loan is primarily to make major structural improvements, or correct faults not known when structure was completed or caused fire, flood, or other casualty, or construct civil defense shelter.

[7] Loan proceeds may be used to pay municipal assessments or similar charges for water sewer, sidewalk, curb, or other public improvements.

[8] An insured loan may be made to lessee if term of lease will run more than 10 years beyond maturity of loan.

[9] Limits may be increased up to 45% in high-cost construction areas.

SOURCE: Digest of Insurable Loans, Federal Housing Administration, Dept. of Housing and Urban Development, Washington, D.C., 1966

FHA MORTGAGE LOANS

MULTIFAMILY TITLE II—SEC. 207, 213

Section of Act	Purpose of Loan	Amount Insurable	Loan-Value Ratio	Term of Loan	Interest Rate

Section 207
1
	Proposed or rehabilitation of detached, semi-detached, row, walk-up, or elevator-type rental housing—8 or more units.	$20,000,000 private mortgagor
		$50,000,000 public mortgagor
		
		Elevator type:
		$10,500 No bedroom
		$15,000 1-bedroom
		$18,000 2-bedroom
		$22,500 3-bedroom
		$25,500 4-bedroom or more
		
		All other types:
		$ 9,000 No bedroom
		$13,750 1-bedroom
		$16,500 2-bedroom
		$20,350 3-bedroom
		$23,100 4-bedroom or more 2
			Proposed construction: 90% of estimated value
			  Rehabilitation: 90% of appraised value after rehabilitation, subject to following limitations:
			Property to be acquired: 90% of estimated rehabilitation cost + 90% purchase price or appraised value before rehabilitation, whichever is less
			  Property owned: estimated rehabilitation cost + debt on property or 90% of appraised value before rehabilitation, whichever is less
			  Five times estimated rehabilitation cost
				Satisfactory to FHA Commissioner (usually 40 years, or 3/4 of the remaining economic life, whichever is less)	8-1/2% + 1/2% mortgage insurance premium

Section 207, Mobile-Home Courts 1	Finance proposed or rehabilitation of mobile-home courts—50 or more spaces	$1,000,000 $2,500 per space 3	90% of estimated value after construction or rehabilitation	40 years, or 3/4 of the remaining economic life, whichever is less	8-1/2% + 1/2% mortgage insurance premium
Section 213, Management 1	Finance proposed, existing or rehabilitation of detached, semidetached, row, walk-up, or elevator-type housing by a nonprofit cooperative or acquisition from investor sponsor—5 or more units	Same as Section 207, except $25,000,000 public mortgagor 2	Proposed construction: 97% of estimated replacement cost Existing construction: 97% of appraised value Rehabilitation: 97% of estimated value after rehabilitation	40 years, or 3/4 of the remaining economic life, whichever is less	8-1/2% + 1/2% mortgage insurance premium
Section 213(i) Management Supplementary Loans 1	Finance improvement or repair of existing Section 213, Management, housing; construction of community facilities; or resale of cooperative memberships	Estimated cost of improvements, repairs, and facilities and/or amount needed to finance resales, except supplementary loan plus debt on property plus other loan balances may not exceed original mortgage.		Remaining term of mortgage	8-1/2% + 1/2% mortgage insurance premium
Section 213, Sales	Finance proposed single-family detached, semidetached, or row housing for sale to members of nonprofit cooperative—5 or more units	$12,500,000, or sum of separate maximum mortgages on single-family housing that meet limits insurable for occupant-mortgagors under Section 203(b), whichever is less.		35 years, or 3/4 of the remaining economic life, whichever is less	8-1/2%
Section 213, Investor Sponsored 1 2	Finance proposed or rehabilitation of detached, semidetached, row, walk-up, or elevator-type housing by corporation intending to sell to nonprofit cooperative—5 or more units	Same as Section 213, Management	Proposed construction: 90% of estimated replacement cost Rehabilitation: 90% of appraised value after rehabilitation	40 years, or 3/4 of the remaining economic life, whichever is less	8-1/2% + 1/2% mortgage insurance premium

[1] Cost certification is required.

[2] Limits per family unit may be increased up to 45% in high-cost construction areas.

[3] Limit per space may be increased up to 25% in high-cost construction areas.

FHA MORTGAGE LOANS
HOME TITLE II—SEC. 213, 220

Section of Act	Purpose of Loan	Amount Insurable	Loan-Value Ratio	Term of Loan	Interest Rate
Section 213, Individual Sales 1	Finance individual mortgage on housing released from cooperative project-sales mortgage	Unpaid balance of project mortgage allocable to individual property		30 years, except 35 years if mortgagor is unacceptable under 30-year term	8-1/2% + 1/2% mortgage insurance premium
Section 220 1 2 3	Finance proposed or rehabilitation of 1-11 family housing in approved urban renewal areas or purchase of existing 1-11 family housing constructed or rehabilitated pursuant to approved urban renewal plan	Occupant mortgagor: $33,000 1-family $35,750 2- or 3-family $41,250 4-family $7,000 per family over 4 Mortgagor: Property held for rental purposes: $27,900 1-family $30,200 2- or 3-family $34,800 4-family $6,500 per family over 4 Property held for sale to owner-occupant: $25,500 1-family $27,600 2-family	Occupant mortgagor: Proposed construction or completed more than 1 year: 97% of $15,000 of estimated replacement cost + 90% of cost above $15,000 but not over $25,000 + 80% of cost above $25,000 Under construction or completed less than 1 year: 90% of estimated replacement cost + 75% of cost above $20,000 Rehabilitation: Constructed under FHA or VA inspection or completed more than 1 year: 97% of $15,000 of estimated rehabilitation cost + estimated value before rehabilitation + 90% of such sum above $15,000 but not over $20,000 + 75% of such sum above $20,000, or estimated rehabilitation cost + amount required to refinance debt on property, whichever is less Not constructed under FHA or VA inspection or completed less than 1 year: 90% of $20,000 of estimated rehabilitation cost + estimated value before rehabilitation + 75% of such sum above $20,000, or estimated rehabilitation cost + amount required to refinance debt on property, whichever is less Property held for rental purpose: 93% of amount under any of above formulae, but not to exceed estimated rehabilitation cost + amount required to refinance debt on property Property, 1- or 2-family, held for sale to owner-occupant: 85% of amount under any of above formulae, but not to exceed estimated rehabilitation cost+ amount required to refinance debt on property, or amount available to occupant mortgagor under any of above formulae, subject to at least 15% escrow or refinancing + minimum cash-investment requirements, whichever is less	30 years, except 35 years if mortgagor is unacceptable under 30-year term for housing built under FHA or VA inspection, or 3/4 of remaining economic life, whichever is less	8-1/2% + 1/2% m.i.p.
Section 220(h) Improvement Loans 4 5 6	Finance alteration, repair, or improvement of existing 1-11 family structure in approved urban renewal areas	$10,000 1-family $20,000 2-family $30,000 3-family $37,500 4-family $40,000 5-11 family 7 8	Loan plus debt on property cannot exceed dollar limitations for home mortgages insurable under Section 220	20 years, or 3/4 of remaining economic life, whichever is less	8-1/2% + 1/2% m.i.p.

1 Eligible for open-end advances.
2 Certification to mortgagor if FHA appraisal amount or estimate of replacement cost is required on 1- or 2-family housing.
3 Builder warranty is required on proposed construction of 1- to 4-family housing.
4 Cost certification is required if 5-family units or more.
5 Loan proceeds may be used to pay municipal assessments or similar charges for water, sewer, sidewalk, curb, or other public improvements.

6 Structure must be at least 10 years old, unless loan is primarily to make major structural improvements, correct faults not known when housing was completed or caused by fire, flood, or other casualty, or construct civil defense shelter.
7 Limits may be increased up to 45% in high-cost construction areas.
8 Application for loans to improve 5- to 11-family housing may be purchased as home or multifamily improvement loans.
9 Insured loan may be made to lessee if term of lease is more than 10 years beyond maturity of loan.

FHA MORTGAGE LOANS
MULTIFAMILY TITLE II—SEC. 221

Section of Act	Purpose of Loan	Amount Insurable	Loan-Value Ratios	Term of Loan	Interest Rate

Section 221(d) (3) (below-market rate) 1 2 3	Finance proposed or rehabilitation of rental or cooperative detached, semidetached, row, or walk-up housing for low- or moderate-income families or individuals 62 or older or handicapped, with priority in occupancy to those displaced by urban renewal or other governmental action
	Refinance existing housing in urban renewal areas—5 or more units
		$12,500,000 per project
		Walk-up:
		$ 9,200 No bedroom
		$12,937 1- bedroom
		$15,525 2-bedroom
		$19,550 3-bedroom
		$22,137 4-bedroom or more
		
		Elevator:
		$10,925 No bedroom
		$15,525 1-bedroom
		$18,400 2-bedroom
		$23,000 3-bedroom
		$26,162 4-bedroom
		4
			Public, nonprofit, cooperative, builder-seller, or investor-sponsor mortgagor:
			  Proposed construction: estimated replacement cost
			  Rehabilitation: estimated rehabilitation cost + estimated value before rehabilitation, subject to following limitations:
			  Property to be acquired: estimated rehabilitation cost + the lesser of purchase price or estimated value before rehabilitation
			  Property owned: estimated rehabilitation cost + existing debt on property or estimated value before rehabilitation, whichever is less
			  5 times estimated cost of rehabilitation
			  Refinancing: debt on property or appraised value, whichever is less
			
			Limited-distribution mortgagor:
			  Proposed construction: 90% of estimated replacement cost
			  Rehabilitation: 90% of estimated rehabilitation cost + 90% of purchase price or estimated value before rehabilitation, whichever is less
			  Property owned: estimated rehabilitation cost + debt on property or 90% of estimated value before rehabilitation, whichever is less
			  5 times estimated cost of rehabilitation
			  Refinancing: debt on property or 90% of appraised value, whichever is less
			Builder-seller or investor-sponsor mortgagor subject to 10% escrow
				Satisfactory to FHA Commissioner (usually 40 years, or 3/4 of remaining economic life, whichever is less)	8-1/2% which is reduced at final endorsement of mortgage of insurance to 3% or rate determined by the Secretary of the Treasury, whichever is lower

Section 221(d) (3) (market rate program) requirements same as below-market rate, except 1/2% insurance premium and no reduction in interest rate at time of final endorsement—5 or more units 3					

Section 221(d)(4) 1 2	Finance proposed or rehabilitation of detached, semidetached, row, walk-up, or elevator-type rental housing for low- or moderate-income families or persons 62 or older or handicapped, with priority in occupancy to those displaced by urban renewal or other governmental action—5 or more units	$12,500,000
		Elevator type:
		  $10,925 No bedroom
		  $15,525 1-bedroom
		  $18,400 2-bedroom
		  $23,000 3-bedroom
		  $26,162 4-bedroom or more
		
		All other types:
		  $ 9,200 No bedroom
		  $12,937 1-bedroom
		  $15,525 2-bedroom
		  $19,550 3-bedroom
		  $22,137 4-bedroom or more
		4
			Private profit-motivated mortgagor:
			  Proposed construction: 90% of estimated replacement cost
			  Rehabilitation: 90% of estimated rehabilitation cost + 90% of estimated value before rehabilitation, subject to following limitations:
			  Property to be acquired: 90% of estimated rehabilitation cost + 90% of purchase price or estimated value before rehabilitation, whichever is less
			  Property owned: estimated rehabilitation cost + debt on property or 90% of estimated value before rehabilitation, whichever is less
			  5 times estimated cost of rehabilitation
				Satisfactory to FHA Commissioner (usually 40 years, or 3/4 of remaining economic life, whichever is less)	8-1/2% +1/2% mortgage insurance premium

[1] Cost certification required.

[2] Property must be located in community certified by Secretary, Department of Housing and Urban Development.

[3] Data on Rent Supplement Program.

[4] Limits per family unit may be increased up to 45% in high-cost construction areas.

FHA MORTGAGE LOANS
HOMES TITLE II—SEC. 221, 222, 233, 234

Section of Act	Purpose of Loan	Amount Insurable	Loan-Value Ratio	Term of Loan	Interest Rate
Section 221(d)(2) 1 2 3	Finance low-cost 1- to 4-family proposed, existing, or rehabilitated housing for families displaced by urban renewal or other governmental action or 1-family housing for other low- or moderate-income families	Occupant mortgagor: Displaced family: $18,000 1-family $24,000 2-family $32,400 3-family $39,600 4-family Other family: $11,000 1-family Operative builder: $9,350 1-family 4	Displaced family: Proposed construction or completed more than 1 year: appraised value or appraised value + prepaid expenses, minus $200 per unit, whichever is less Construction completed less than 1 year: 90% of appraised value Rehabilitation: appraised value before rehabilitation + estimated cost of rehabilitation or appraised value + prepaid expenses, minus $200 per unit, whichever is less Other low- or moderate-income family: Proposed construction or completed more than 1 year: appraised value or 97% of appraised value + prepaid expenses, whichever is less Construction completed less than 1 year: 90% of appraised value Rehabilitation: appraised value before rehabilitation + estimated rehabilitation cost, appraised value after rehabilitation, or 97% of sum of appraised value + prepaid expenses, whichever is less Operative builder: Proposed construction: 85% of appraised value Rehabilitation: least of 85% of appraised value before rehabilitation, 5 times estimated cost of improvements, or 85% of sum of purchase price of property or appraised value before rehabilitation, whichever is less, + estimated rehabilitation cost	Displaced family: 30 years, except 35 or 40 years if mortgagor is unacceptable under 30-year term Other occupant mortgagor: Housing built under FHA or VA inspection: 30 years, except 35 or 40 years if mortgagor is unacceptable under 30-year term Existing construction: 30 years All maturities limited to not more than 3/4 of remaining economic life.	8-1/2% + 1/2% m.i.p.
Section 222 1 2 3 5	Finance proposed or existing 1-family housing for mortgagors certified as servicemen by Secretary of Treasury; not available for refinancing existing mortgages executed or assumed by servicemen	Property meetings eligibility criteria of Section 203(b), $30,000 Property meeting eligibility criteria of Section 203(i), $12,500 Property meeting eligibility criteria of Section 221(d)(2), $11,000 or up to $15,000 in high-cost construction areas	Proposed construction or completed more than 1 year: 97% of $15,000 of appraised value + 90% of value above $15,000 but not over $20,000+ 85% of value above $20,000	30 years, except 35 years if mortgagor is unacceptable under 30-year term, for housing built under FHA or VA inspection, or 3/4 of the remaining economic life, whichever is less	5-1/2%
Section 233, Experimental Housing 1 2 3	Finance proposed or rehabilitation of housing using advanced technology or experimental neighborhood design	Type of construction, mortgage limit, loan ratio, term, interest rate, and fees are governed by eligibility requirements of applicable home mortgage or improvement programs under Sections 203, 213, 220, 221, or 234; under all sections prescribed loan ratios will be applied to estimated replacement cost for proposed construction or for rehabilitation estimated value before rehabilitation plus estimated cost of improvements, using comparable conventional design, material, and construction or advanced technology or experimental property standards, whichever is less			
Section 234(c), Condominium Individual Units 3 5 6 7	Finance detached, semi-detached, row, walk-up or elevator-type individually owned family unit in project, containing 5 or more units, that is or was insured under any multifamily program, except Section 213, management or sales type	$33,000 occupant mortgagor $25,500 nonoccupant mortgagor	Occupant mortgagor: 97% of $15,000 of appraised value + 90% of value above $15,000 but not over $25,000 + 80% of value above $25,000 Nonoccupant mortgagor: 85% of amount computed under above formula	30 years, except 35 years if owner-occupant mortgagor is unacceptable under 30-year term, or 3/4 of remaining economic life, whichever is less	8-1/2% + 1/2% mortgage insurance premium

[1] Certification to mortgagor of FHA appraisal amount required on 1- or 2-family housing.

[2] Builder's warranty required on proposed construction.

[3] Eligible for open-end advances.

[4] Limits may be increased in high-cost construction areas up to $21,000, 1-family; $30,000, 2-family; $38,400, 3-family; and $45,600, 4-family.

[5] Certificate to mortgagor of FHA appraisal amount required.

[6] Mortgagor may not own more than 4 insured units.

[7] If mortgagor is 62 years of age or older, downpayment, settlement charges, and prepaid expenses may be borrowed from approved corporation or individual.

FHA MORTAGE LOANS
MULTIFAMILY TITLE II—SEC. 231, 232, 233, 234

Section of Act	Purpose of Loan	Amount Insurable	Loan-Value Ratio	Term of Loan	Interest Rate
Section 231 Housing for Elderly Persons 1	Finance proposed or rehabilitation of detached, semidetached, row, walk-up, or elevator-type rental housing designed for occupancy by elderly or handicapped individuals—8 or more units 2	$12,500,000 private mortgagor $50,000,000 public mortgagor Elevator type: $10,450 No bedroom $14,850 1-bedroom $17,600 2-bedroom $22,000 3-bedroom $25,025 4-bedroom or more All other types: $ 8,800 No bedroom $12,375 1-bedroom $14,850 2-bedroom $18,700 3-bedroom $21,175 4-bedroom or more 3	Nonprofit mortgagor: Proposed construction: estimated replacement cost Rehabilitation: estimated value after rehabilitation, subject to following limitations: Property to be acquired: estimated rehabilitation cost + actual purchase price or estimated value before rehabilitation, whichever is less Property owned: estimated rehabilitation cost + debt on property or estimated value before rehabilitation, whichever is less 5 times estimated cost of rehabilitation Profit mortgagor: Proposed construction: 90% of estimated replacement cost Rehabilitation: 90% of estimated value after rehabilitation, subject to following limitations: Property to be acquired: 90% of estimated rehabilitation cost + 90% of purchase price or 90% of estimated value before rehabilitation, whichever is less Property owned: 100% of estimated rehabilitation cost + debt on property or 90% of estimated value before rehabilitation, whichever is less 5 times estimated cost of rehabilitation	Satisfactory to FHA Commissioner (usually 40 years, or 3/4 of remaining economic life, whichever is less)	8-1/2% +1/2% mortgage insurance premium
Section 232, Nursing homes 1	Finance proposed or rehabilitation of facilities, accommodating 20 or more patients, for care and treatment of convalescents or other individuals who are not acutely ill and not in need of hospital care but require skilled nursing care and related medical services.	$12,500,000	Proposed construction: 90% of estimated value Rehabilitation: 90% of estimated value after rehabilitation, subject to following limitations: Property to be acquired: 90% of estimated rehabilitation cost + 90% of purchase price or 90% of estimated value before rehabilitation, whichever is less Property owned: estimated rehabilitation cost + debt on property or 90% of estimated value before rehabilitation, whichever is less 5 times estimated cost of rehabilitation	Satisfactory to FHA Commissioner (usually 20 years, or 3/4 of remaining economic life, whichever is less)	8-1/2% + 1/2% m.i.p.
Section 233, Experimental Housing 1	Finance proposed or rehabilitation of rental housing, using advanced technology or experimental property standards for neighborhood design	Type of construction, mortgage limit, loan ratio, term, interest rate, and fees are governed by eligibility requirements of applicable mortgage or improvement loan insurance programs under Sections 207, 220, 221, 231, or 234; under all Sections prescribed loan ratios will be applied to estimated replacement cost for proposed construction or for using comparable conventional design, materials, and construction or advanced technology or experimental property standards, whichever is less 3			
Section 234(d) Condominium 1	Finance proposed or rehabilitation of detached, semidetached, row, walk-up, or elevator-type housing by sponsor intending to sell individual units as condominiums —5 or more units	$20,000,000 private mortgagor $25,000,000 public mortgagor Elevator-type: $11,550 No bedroom $16,500 1-bedroom $19,800 2-bedroom $24,750 3-bedroom $28,050 4-bedroom or more All other types: $ 9,900 No bedroom $13,750 1-bedroom $16,500 2-bedroom $20,350 3-bedroom $23,100 4-bedroom or more	Proposed construction: 90% of replacement cost or sum of unit mortgage amounts computed under Section 234(c) assuming mortgagor to be owner occupant, whichever is less Rehabilitation: 90% of estimated rehabilitation cost + 90% of estimated value before rehabilitation or sum of unit mortgage amounts computed under Section 234(c) assuming mortgagor to be an owner occupant, subject to following limitations: Property to be acquired: 90% of estimated rehabilitation cost + 90% of purchase price or estimated value before rehabilitation, whichever is less Property owned: estimated rehabilitation cost + debt on property or 90% of estimated value before rehabilitation, whichever is less 5 times estimated cost of rehabilitation	Blanket mortgage: Satisfactory to Commissioner (usually 39 years, or 3/4 of remaining economic life, whichever is less)	8-1/2% +1/2% mortgage insurance premium

[1] Cost certification is required.

[2] Limits per family unit may be increased up to 45% in high-cost construction areas.

[3] Data covering Rent Supplement Program.

FHA MORTGAGE LOANS
MULTIFAMILY TITLE II—SEC. 235, 236

Section of Act	Purpose of Loan	Amount Insurable	Loan-Value Ratio	Term of Loan	Interest Rate
Section 235	To provide direct payments to the lending institution to reduce the effective rate of interest from the market rate to as low as 1% in order to keep monthly mortgage or monthly rental payments to not more than 20% of family income or not more than 25% for rental.		80% interest-free loans to cover preconstruction expenses 100% of estimated value after construction	40 years maximum, in general should not exceed 35 years or the term of the mortgage	8-1/2% + 1/2% for mortgage insurance premium. 1% minimum.
Section 235(j)	To assist eligible moderate and lower income families to purchase rehab housing from private nonprofit organizations and public bodies.	$18,000 per dwelling unit $25,000 per 2-family units	100% of estimated value	40 years or the remaining economic life, whichever is less	8-1/2% + 1/2% for mortgage insurance premium. May be reduced to 1% by assistance payments.
Section 235(i) 1	To assist lower income families to purchase homes by providing direct monthly payments to lenders	$18,000-21,000 per 1 family $24,000-30,000 per 2 family	100% of estimated value	30 years, except 35-40 years for mortgagor ineligible under 30-year term	8-1/2% + 1/2% for mortgage insurance premium. May be reduced by 1% by assistance payments.
Section 236	To eventually replace Section 221 (d) (3). It is a below-market-interest-rate program for nonprofit organizations, cooperative, or limited-dividend types as permitted under 221 (d) (3) for rental and cooperative housing. 2	$12,500,000 per project Elevator-type: $10,925 No bedroom $15,525 1 bedroom $18,400 2 bedroom $23,000 3 bedroom $26,162 4 bedroom or more All Other Types: $ 9,200 No bedroom $12,937 1 bedroom $15,525 2 bedroom $19,550 3 bedroom $22,137 4 bedroom	Same as for 221 (d) (3)	40 years or 3/4 of remaining economic life whichever is less	8-1/2% + 1/2% for mortgage insurance premium. May be reduced to 1%.

1 Families needing benefits of Section 235 may be sold units on the same subdivision where units are sold to families without need of assistance.
2 See following page for adjusted family income units.

ADJUSTED FAMILY INCOME FOR SECTIONS 235 AND 236 OCCUPANCY

Under the law a family's "adjusted income" is derived by deducting (a) $300 per year for each child, (b) any unusual income, (c) an allowance for social security withholding and similar payroll deductions, (d) any unusual overtime pay, etc. annual gross income.

Such "adjusted income" cannot exceed 135% of that of the same sized family eligible for admission to local public housing. These limits are determined—and revised periodically —by HUD. Current admission limits can be obtained from the local FHA insuring office.

Here are some representative adjusted income limits by city as of February, 1970.

LOCALITY	\multicolumn{8}{c}{NUMBER OF PERSONS IN FAMILY}
	1	2	3	4	5	6	7	8
Austin, Texas	4,050	4,860	5,400	5,670	5,940	6,075	6,210	6,345
Atlanta, Georgia	4,320	5,265	5,535	5,805	6,075	6,480	6,615	6,750
Baltimore, Md.	4,455	4,995	5,265	5,535	5,805	6,075	6,345	6,615
Birmingham, Ala.	4,455	5,130	5,805	6,210	6,480	6,615	6,750	6,885
Boston, Mass.	5,670	6,210	7,020	7,695	7,965	8,235	8,505	8,505
Buffalo, New York	5,510	5,995	6,690	7,695	7,695	8,750	8,750	9,775
Charlotte, N.C.	4,455	5,265	5,670	5,940	6,210	6,480	6,615	6,750
Chicago, Illinois	5,670	6,480	7,290	8,100	8,910	9,720	10,530	11,340
Cincinnati, Ohio	4,590	6,210	7,020	7,425	7,830	8,100	8,370	8,640
Cleveland, Ohio	4,860	6,480	7,290	7,695	8,100	8,370	8,640	8,910
Columbus, Ohio	3,375	4,995	5,535	5,940	6,345	6,750	7,020	7,290
Dallas, Texas	4,455	5,130	5,670	5,670	6,210	6,210	6,210	6,210
Dayton, Ohio	4,860	6,750	7,425	7,830	8,235	8,505	8,775	9,045
Denver, Colorado	5,535	5,535	6,480	6,480	7,155	7,155	8,100	8,100
Detroit, Mich.	4,860	6,480	7,020	7,425	7,830	8,235	8,240	9,045
Dist. of Columbia	4,320	4,725	4,995	5,265	5,535	5,805	6,075	6,345
Ft. Lauderdale, Fla.	4,590	5,670	6,075	6,345	6,615	6,885	7,020	7,155
Fort Worth, Texas	4,590	5,130	5,940	5,940	6,480	6,480	6,480	6,480
Honolulu, Hawaii	5,400	5,670	6,345	6,345	7,155	7,155	7,425	7,425
Indianapolis, Ind.	4,390	5,670	6,210	6,615	7,020	7,425	7,830	8,235
Kansas City, Mo.	4,995	4,995	5,940	5,940	6,615	6,615	6,615	6,615
Los Angeles, Calif.	4,050	4,860	6,345	6,750	7,290	7,695	8,100	8,505
Louisville, Ky.	4,050	4,995	6,075	6,210	6,615	6,750	6,885	7,020
Memphis, Tenn.	4,185	5,670	5,940	6,210	6,480	6,615	6,750	6,885
Miami, Fla.	4,860	5,670	5,940	6,075	6,345	6,480	6,615	6,750
Milwaukee, Wis.	4,050	5,940	6,275	6,615	6,950	7,290	7,625	7,965
Minneapolis, Minn.	3,240	5,400	6,750	6,750	8,100	8,100	9,450	9,450
Nashville, Tenn.	4,455	5,130	5,400	5,400	5,940	5,940	5,940	5,940
New Orleans, La.	4,050	4,050	4,725	4,725	5,400	5,400	5,400	5,400
New York, N.Y.	5,835	7,390	8,555	8,555	10,095	10,095	10,660	10,660
Oklahoma City, Okla.	4,050	4,455	4,860	5,265	5,265	5,265	5,265	5,265
Omaha, Nebraska	3,240	5,940	6,480	7,020	7,965	8,910	9,180	9,450
Philadelphia, Pa.	4,320	4,860	5,130	5,130	5,400	5,400	5,670	5,670
Phoenix, Arizona	4,455	4,860	5,265	5,670	6,075	6,480	6,885	7,290
Pittsburgh, Pa.	5,740	6,750	7,425	7,425	7,765	7,765	8,100	8,100
Portland, Oregon	4,725	4,725	5,130	5,130	5,535	5,535	5,535	5,535
Providence, R.I.	5,670	5,670	6,750	7,290	7,695	8,100	8,505	8,505
Richmond, Virginia	4,185	4,185	4,590	4,590	4,995	4,995	4,995	4,995
Rochester, N.Y.	4,860	5,940	6,245	6,750	7,155	7,695	8,235	8,775
Sacramento, Calif.	4,455	5,400	5,940	6,345	6,750	7,020	7,290	7,560
St. Louis, Mo.	5,265	5,265	6,750	6,750	8,640	8,640	8,640	8,640
San Antonio, Texas	5,400	5,940	6,345	6,345	6,885	6,885	6,885	6,885
San Bernardino, Calif.	5,130	5,130	5,400	5,400	5,805	5,805	5,805	5,805
San Diego, Calif.	4,590	5,130	5,940	6,480	6,750	7,155	7,560	7,830
San Francisco, Calif.	4,320	5,400	6,076	6,615	7,155	7,695	8,235	8,775

PROGRAMS FOR HOME SALES

Section	Purpose	Income Level	Page Reference
203 (h)	To finance purchase of 1-family housing to victims of natural disaster.	middle	I-6
203 (i)	To finance 1-family housing on 5 or more acres adjacent to highway.	middle	I-6
213	To finance individual sales in cooperatives.	middle	I-8
222	To finance 1-family housing for certified servicemen.	middle	I-10
234 (c)	To finance individual comdominium units that were originally financed under other rental programs.	middle	I-10
234 (d)	To finance individual condominium units.	middle	I-11
235 (i)	To finance home purchase with monthly subsidy.	low	I-12
235 (j)	To finance purchase of rehabilitated units from nonprofit sponsors and governmental bodies.	low	I-12
203 (b)	In case of 1-family occupant mortgagor unit, this section is for sales.	middle	I-6
221 (d) (2)	In case of 1-family, this section is for sales.	low	I-10

PROGRAMS FOR RENTAL HOUSING

Section	Purpose	Income Level	Page Reference
203 (b)1 1	To finance proposed or existing 1-4 family housing.	middle	1-6
203 (k) 1	To finance proposed alteration, repair or improvement of existing 1-4 family housing not within urban renewal areas.	middle	1-6
207	To finance proposed or rehabilitation of 8 or more units.	middle	1-7
207 mobile home	To finance proposed or rehabilitation of 50 or more unit mobile home courts.	middle	1-7
213 2	To finance proposed, existing or rehabilitation of 5 or more units by a nonprofit cooperative.	middle	1-7
213 (j)	To finance improvement or repair of existing Section 213 housing.	middle	1-7
213 sales	To finance proposed housing of 5 or more units to members of a nonprofit cooperative.	middle	1-7
220	To finance proposed or rehabilitation of 1-11 family housing in urban renewal areas.	middle	1-8
220 (h)	To finance alteration, repair or improvement of existing 1-11 family housing in approved urban renewal areas.	middle	1-8
221 (d) (3)	To finance rental or cooperative housing of 5 or more units with priorities for those displaced by urban renewal projects or other governmental action; or to refinance existing housing within urban renewal areas.	low elderly or handicapped	1-9
221 (d) (4)	Similar to above except only for rental and mortgagor is private profit-motivated.	low	1-9
221 (d) (2) 3	To finance 1-4 family housing for families displaced by urban renewal.	low	1-10
231	To finance 8 or more units for elderly or handicapped.		1-11

[1] Section 203 1-family occupant-mortgagor is actually sales housing.
[2] See Page I-7, investor sponsored.
[3] May be used to finance 1-family housing for other low- or moderate-income families.

FARMERS HOME ADMINISTRATION
SEC. 502, 504, 516, 524, 515, 521

				Term of Loan	Interest Rate
Section 502 low- to moderate-income loans	Finance construction, purchase or rehabilitation of homes and farm service buildings and the purchase of building sites. May also be used to refinance debts on existing buildings with guaranteed and insured loans.	Average initial direct loan $4,000; insured $10,000			5-1/8% may be reduced for low-income families with interest credit to 1% Interest is the same as in FHA for above moderate-income families
Sections 514, 516 Labor housing	Finance low-rent housing and related facilities for domestic farm laborers, by farmers, nonprofit organizations and public bodies by loans and grants.	Average initial loan $100,000 Average initial grant $300,000	66-2/3% of development cost	33 years	
Section 524 Self-help housing-site loans	Finance purchase of land for subdivision for sale on nonprofit basis to eligible low- and moderate-income families and cooperatives by public or private nonprofit organizations.	$100,000 limit	n.a.	n.a.	n.a.
Sections 515, 521 rental housing low- to moderate-income	Finance rental and cooperative housing for rural residents to individuals, cooperatives, nonprofit organizations for low-moderate rural residents, senior citizens, or low-moderate income urban residents working in a rural area.	Initial average loan $50,000, average subsequent loan $30,000	up to 50 years	n.a.	5-1/8% may be reduced to 1%

HUD PROGRAMS—GRANTS; NEIGHBORHOOD FACILITIES

Grants for Neighborhood Facilities

PURPOSES: To provide neighborhood facilities needed for programs carrying out health, recreation, social or similar necessary community services in the area.

SPECIFIC USES: Finance specific projects, such as neighborhood or community center, youth centers, health stations and other public buildings to provide health or recreational or similar social services.

TERMS: Grants can cover up to two-thirds of the project cost, or 75 percent in redevelopment areas designated under the Public Works and Economic Development Act of 1965, or any act supplemental to it.

WHO MAY APPLY: A local public body or agency. (In some circumstances, projects may be undertaken by a local public body or agency through a nonprofit organization.)

SPECIFIC REQUIREMENTS: Emphasis will be placed on projects that are so located as to be available for use by a significant portion of the area's low- or moderate-income residents, and on those that will support a community action program under the Economic Opportunity Act.

Grants for Advance Acquisition of Land

PURPOSES: To encourage communities to acquire, in a planned and orderly fashion, land for future construction of public works and facilities.

TERMS: Grants may not exceed the interest charges on a loan incurred to finance the acquisition of land for a period of not more than 5 years.

WHO MAY APPLY: Local public bodies and agencies.

SPECIFIC REQUIREMENTS: The facility for which the land is to be used must be started within a reasonable period of time, not exceeding 5 years after the grant is approved. Construction of the facility must contribute to the comprehensively planned development of the area.

RELATED PROGRAMS: Grants for basic sewer and water facilities, advances for public works planning, urban planning assistance, and public facility loans.

Grants for Basic Sewer and Water Facilities

PURPOSES: This program is designed to assist and encourage the communities of the nation to construct adequate basic water and sewer facilities to promote their efficient and orderly growth and development.

SPECIFIC USES: Provides grants to local public bodies and agencies to finance up to 50 percent of the cost of improving or constructing basic water and sewer facilities. Where there is no existing system, the project must be so designed that it can be linked with other independent water and sewer facilities in the future.

TERMS: Terms will be determined shortly.

WHO MAY APPLY: Local public bodies and agencies.

SPECIFIC REQUIREMENTS: A grant may be made for any project if it is determined that the project is necessary to provide adequate water or sewer facilities for the people to be served, and that the project is:

1. designed so that an adequate capacity will be available to serve the reasonably foreseeable growth needs of the area,

2. consistent with a program for a unified or officially coordinated area-wide water or sewer facilities system as part of the comprehensively planned development of the area, and

3. necessary to orderly community development.

No grant shall be made for any sewer facilities unless the Secretary of Health, Education, and Welfare certifies to the Secretary of the Department of Housing and Urban Development that any waste material carried by such facilities will be adequately treated before it is discharged into any public waterway so as to meet applicable Federal, State, interstate, or local water quality standards.

RELATED PROGRAMS: Public facility loans program, public works planning advances, urban planning grant program and grants for advance land acquisition.

HUD PROGRAMS—GRANTS, TRANSPORTATION, OPEN-SPACE

Urban Mass Transportation Grants

PURPOSES: To help localities provide and improve urban mass transportation facilities and equipment; encourage planning and establishment of area-wide urban transportation systems; and aid financing of such systems.

Federal grants may be made for up to two-thirds of the cost of facilities and equipment that cannot reasonably be financed by revenues. Local grants are required for the other one-third.

Federal loans for a maximum period of 40 years may be made for the entire cost of capital improvements, where financing is not available privately on reasonable terms.

WHO MAY APPLY: Qualified State or local public bodies or agencies, including those of one or more states, or more municipalities or other political subdivisions of a single state.

SPECIAL REQUIREMENTS: All projects must be needed for carrying out a program for a unified or officially coordinated transit system as part of the comprehensively planned development of the urban area. However, until July 1, 1967, loans and grants may be made on an emergency basis with less strict planning requirements, but grants are limited to one-half rather than two-thirds of net project cost. The full grant would be available upon completion of the full planning requirements within three years.

RELATED PROGRAMS:

Mass Transportation Demonstration Program: Federal grants up to two-thirds of the cost of projects to test and demonstrate new ideas and new methods for improving mass transportation systems and service.

Urban Planning Assistance: Federal grants help finance comprehensive planning for urban areas, including mass transportation planning.

Public Works Planning Advances: Interest-free advances for engineering surveys, designs and plans for specific public works, including public transportation facilities.

Open-Space Land and Urban Beautification Grants

PURPOSES: To assist communities in acquiring and developing land for open-space uses and in carrying out urban beautification programs.

SPECIFIC USES: Provide parks and other recreation, conservation, and scenic areas or preserve historic places. Urban beautification and improvement includes such activities as street landscaping, park improvements, tree planting, and upgrading of malls and squares. Relocation payments are provided for individuals, families and businesses displaced by land acquisition.

TERMS: Federal assistance has been increased from 20 and 30 percent to a single level of 50 percent to help public agencies acquire and preserve urban lands having value for park, recreation, scenic, or historic purposes. Where necessary to provide open space in built-up urban areas, grants can cover up to 50 percent of the cost of acquiring and clearing developed land. Fifty percent assistance is also available to assist in developing lands acquired under the open-space land program.

A grant for urban beautification can be up to 50 percent of the expenditures for urban beautification. However, grants of up to 90 percent are authorized to carry out projects of special value for demonstrating new and improved methods and materials for urban beautification.

WHO MAY APPLY: State and local public bodies.

SPECIFIC REQUIREMENTS: Assisted open-space activities must be part of an area-wide open-space acquisition and development program, which, in turn is consistent with area-wide comprehensive planning. Developed lands in built-up areas are eligible only if open-space needs cannot be met with existing undeveloped or predominantly undeveloped land. Beautification activities must have significant, long-term benefits to the community and must be part of a local beautification program. Such programs must (1) represent significant and effective efforts, involving all available public and private resources for urban beautification and improvement, and (2) be important to the comprehensively planned development of the locality.

RELATED PROGRAMS: Urban renewal; urban planning assistance; outdoor recreation and parks programs of Department of Interior; neighborhood facilities program of HUD; small watershed program of Department of Agriculture; landscaping activities under Federal highway program—FHA Land Development Program.

HUD PROGRAMS—GRANTS; URBAN RENEWAL, PLANNING ASSISTANCE

Urban Renewal

PURPOSE: To assist cities undertaking local programs for the elimination and prevention of slums and blight, whether residential or nonresidential, and the elimination of the factors that create slums and blight. Urban renewal is a long-range effort to achieve better communities through planned redevelopment of deteriorated and deteriorating areas by means of a partnership among local governments, private enterprise, citizens, and the Federal Government.

SPECIFIC USES: Community-wide renewal programs that identify needs and resources and establish schedules and priorities for accomplishing the work to be done; plan and carry out urban renewal projects for the rehabilitation and redevelopment of blighted areas; and undertake programs of concentrated code enforcement and demolition of buildings that are substandard and constitute a hazard to public health and welfare.

TERMS: Activities and projects are financed with Federal advances and loans, Federal grants, and local contributions. Federal grants generally pay up to two-thirds of net project cost, but may be as much as three-fourths in some instances. Local contributions may include cash or noncash grants in aid. Also available are special rehabilitation loans and grants, and housing assistance programs for low-income, elderly, and handicapped individuals and families who reside in project areas.

WHO MAY APPLY: Local public agencies authorized by State law to undertake projects with Federal assistance. LPAs may be separate public agency, local housing authority, or a department of the city government.

SPECIFIC REQUIREMENTS: Community must certify that it cannot carry out its urban renewal plans with local resources alone; must adopt and have certified by the Department of Housing and Urban Development a Workable Program for Community Improvement; and must have a feasible plan for the relocation of families and individuals displaced as a result of governmental action into decent, safe, and sanitary housing at prices or rentals within their means. A renewal project must conform to a general plan for the development of the community as a whole.

Urban Planning Assistance Program

PURPOSES: To foster good community, metropolitan area, regional and state-wide planning.

SPECIFIC USES: Preparation of comprehensive development plans, including planning for the provision of public facilities; transportation facilities, and long-range fiscal plans. Programming and scheduling of capital improvements.

TERMS: Federal grants of two-thirds of the cost of the work; local contribution of one-third. In some instances, Federal grants may amount to as much as three-fourths.

WHO MAY APPLY: Cities and other municipalities with less than 50,000 population, counties, and Indian reservations, through their State Planning Agencies.

Official State, metropolitan, and regional planning agencies. Metropolitan organizations of public officials. Cities and counties in redevelopment areas, without regard to size. Official governmental planning agencies for Federally impacted areas. Localities that have suffered a major disaster and areas that have suffered a decline in employment as a result of decline in Federal purchases may apply directly to the Department of Housing and Urban Development.

HUD PROGRAMS—LOANS; COLLEGE HOUSING; REHABILITATION

College Housing

PURPOSES: To help colleges and hospitals expand their facilities to absorb the increasing influx of students.

SPECIFIC USES: The loans must be used for the construction of college residence halls, faculty and married student housing, dining facilities, college unions and housing for student nurses and interns.

TERMS: Loans may be repaid over periods as long as 50 years, at an interest rate of 3 percent.

WHO MAY APPLY: Public or private nonprofit colleges and universities, if they offer at least a two-year program acceptable for full credit toward a bachelor's degree. Public or private nonprofit hospitals, if approved by the appropriate State authority to operate a nursing school beyond the high school level, or approved for internship and residencies by the American Medical Association or American Osteopathic Association.

SPECIFIC REQUIREMENTS: Each institution develops its own plans, subject to local zoning and building codes. Engineering plans are reviewed by HUD. Competitive bidding is required.

Rehabilitation Aids and Programs

OBJECTIVE: To effect rehabilitation and renewal of housing, buildings and communities by repairing, remodeling and restoring rather than by clearance and demolition.

Major grant, loan and mortgage insurace programs are:

Direct grants of up to $1,500 to enable low-income homeowners in urban renewal areas and areas of concentrated code enforcement to bring their homes up to required standards.

Direct loans with maximum interest rate of 3 percent and maximum terms of 20 years to property owners for rehabilitation of residential or business structures in urban renewal areas and areas of concentrated code enforcement. Structures are to be brought up to local code requirements or standards set by an urban renewal plan.

FHA insurance of loans made by private lenders for repairs of existing housing, with special provisions for major repairs of housing in urban renewal areas and areas of concentrated code enforcement. The special loans can be up to $10,000 (45% higher in high-cost areas) per dwelling unit. Interest rate is 6 percent plus ½ percent mortgage insurance premium and terms can be up to 20 years.

FHA mortgage insurance for low-cost rehabilitated housing for sale or rent to moderate-income families, including the elderly and those displaced by government action. Mortgage amount can be up to 100 percent of the value of rehabilitated structures; interest rate at 5¼ percent plus ½ percent mortgage insurance premiums; terms to 30 years.

FHA-insured below-market interest rate loans for rehabilitated rental and cooperative housing for low- and moderate-income families. Mortgage amount can be up to 100 percent of value for nonprofit sponsors, at maximum interest rate of 3 percent. Terms are usually the lesser of 40 years or ¾ of the remaining economic life of the structure.

Local housing authorities under 1965 legislation are enabled to purchase, lease and rehabilitate existing housing, which can be rented to low-income families.

The Department can make grants to cities for the cost of planning and carrying out programs of concentrated code enforcement in deteriorated or deteriorating areas. This program is not limited to urban renewal areas. Grants can also be made for planning rehabilitation projects and for city-wide surveys and rehabilitation needs.

HUD PROGRAMS—LOANS; PUBLIC WORKS, LAND DEVELOPMENT

Advances for Public Works Planning

PURPOSES: Provides interest-free advances to assist planning for individual local public works and for area-wide and long-range projects that will help communities deal with their total needs.

SPECIFIC USES: All types of public works, except public housing, are eligible. Examples include water and sewer systems, school buildings, recreational projects, public buildings, irrigation projects, health facilities, bridges, and a variety of other public works.

TERMS: The advance is repayable to HUD promptly upon start of construction of the planned public work.

WHO MAY APPLY: States, municipalities and other public agencies.

SPECIFIC REQUIREMENTS: An applicant must show that it intends to start construction within a reasonable period of time

considering the nature of the project and that financing of such construction is feasible. The public work must conform to a State, local or regional plan, as appropriate, approved by a competent State, local, or regional authority.

RELATED PROGRAMS: Grants for basic water and sewer facilities, urban planning assistance, public facility loans, and grants for advance acquisition of land.

Public Facility Loans

PURPOSES: This program provides long-term loans for the construction of needed public facilities such as sewer or water facilities.

SPECIFIC USES: A variety of public works may be financed under this program. When aid is available from other Federal agencies, such as for airports, highways, hospitals and sewage treatment facilities, HUD assists only with those parts of the project not covered by other Federal programs.

TERMS: Term of loan may be up to 40 years. It will be governed by the applicant's ability to pay and by the estimated useful life of the proposed facility. The interest rate for fiscal year to be determined.

WHO MAY APPLY: Local units of government or State instrumentalities. Private nonprofit corporations for sewer and water facilities needed to serve a small municipality if there is no existing public body able to construct and operate the facilities.

SPECIFIC REQUIREMENTS: The population of the applicant community must be under 50,000 with two exceptions. In those communities near a research or development installation of the National Aeronautics and Space Agency, the population requirement does not apply. In the case of communities located in redevelopment areas so designated under the Public Works and Economic Development Act of 1965, the population limit is 150,000.

RELATED PROGRAMS: Grants for basic water and sewer facilities, public works planning advances, urban planning assistance and grants for advance acquisition of land.

Land Development and New Communities Loans

PURPOSES: Finance purchase of land and development of building sites, including water and sewage systems, streets, or the development of new communities.

TERMS: The maximum mortgage amount for any single undertaking is $25 million, or 75 percent of value of the developed land, or 50 percent of land value before development and 90 percent of the estimated development cost. The maximum term is 50 years at 8½% interest.

WHO MAY APPLY: Qualified private developers.

SPECIFIC REQUIREMENTS: The development must be characterized by sound land-use patterns and consistent with a comprehensive plan or planning for the area in which the land is situated. In the case of a new community, the development must make a substantial contribution to sound economic and physical planning of the region.

INDEX

Accessibility criteria 56
Advertising signs 480
Air rights 68, 69
Amenities, apartment building 357
Apartment buildings 327-372
Apartment building complex 119, 120
Apartment buildings, types:
    center corridor 332-335
    circular plan 350
    cross plan 347, 348
    five-wing plan 349
    modular 353-356
    open-corridor 336
    skip-stop 337, 338
    terrace 351
    tower 339-346
Apartment, garden 322, 323
Apartment types 386, 387
Apartments:
    duplex 411-415
    efficiency 384, 386-388
    five-bedroom 385, 409
    flat 410
    four-bedroom 385, 406-408
    one-bedroom 384, 389-391
    simplex 410
    six-bedroom 409
    three-bedroom 385, 401-405
    triplex 416-418
    two-bedroom 384, 392-399
Apportionment method 18
Architectural review, zoning 476
Arts and crafts shops 196
Automobile turning requirements 285

Bathroom arrangements 427, 428
Bay, parking 281
Beautification grants, H.U.D. programs 451
Bedrooms 436-442
Breezes, orientation 254-256

Buildable area 250
Building bulk 78
Building coverage 77
Building grouping 263-264
Building heights 465
Building, parking 278-279
Building orientation 259-260
Building ventilation 256
Business signs 480

Center-corridor plan 332-335
Central facilities, housing site 58
Census items, 1970 ....8, 9
Census reports, housing 7
Child-care center 172, 174, 176, 177, 237
Church 185-188
Circular plan 350
Circulation:
    pedestrian 268
    vehicular 265-267
Classification, street 271, 272
Cluster development 155
Cluster of neighborhoods 121
Clusters 154, 164, 165
Codes:
    building 487, 488, 511
    housing 462, 498, 499, 511
College housing loans, H.U.D. 543
Communities, new, H.U.D. loans 545
Community 51
Community center 191, 193
   (see Multiservice center)
Community facilities:
    accessibility 56
    cultural 185-196
    educational 172-184
    maximum distances 171
    recreation, leisure, and open space 197-229
    social 185-196
Community park 215

Community pattern, a design prototype 43
Community playfield 215
Community recreational facilities 237-241
Community renewal study 6
Compatibility with housing, land uses 54, 55
Corridor plan:
    center 332-335
    open 336
Costs, subdivision 133
Court house 300-302
Courts, parking 281
Cultural facilities, accessibility 56
Cultural facilities, housing site 59
Cumulative zoning 473

Deficient housing units 24-28
Densities, neighborhood 109-115
Density, measures of 74, 80, 81
Density ranges 79
Density, residential 72-78
Density, zoning 471, 472, 473
Design considerations 138-150
Design, land subdivision 122-125
Design prototype 37, 38
    community pattern 43
    existing land use 39
    existing neighborhood pattern 41
    proposed land use 40
    proposed neighborhood pattern 42
    regional pattern 44
Development over water, housing 70, 71
Dining areas 425, 428
Dining rooms 432-435
Drainage, subdivisions 132
Duplex apartment 411-415
Duplex house (semi-attached) 303, 304
Dwelling access alternatives 330
Dwelling unit areas 282-285
Dwelling unit, neighborhood 117
Dwelling unit types, combinations 444-458

Dwelling unit ventilation 256

Educational facilities 172-184
    child-care center 172, 174, 176, 177
    elementary . . .173, 174, 175, 180-182, 184
    high school .175, 184
    junior high school 175, 183, 184
    kindergarten 172, 174, 179
    nursery 172, 174, 175, 179
    size of school sites 184
Efficiency apartment 384, 386-388
Elderly, centers for the 192, 195, 196
Elementary school . .173-175, 180-182, 184, 210,
. . . . 211
Employment facilities, housing site 57
Explosives, zoning 503
Exposure plane, sky 467

Family cycle 90, 91
Farmers Home and Veterans Administration
. 518-519
Federal Housing Administration 517
FHA mortgage loans 529-539
Five-bedroom apartment 385, 409
Flat 410
Flexible devices, zoning 475
Floor area 468
Floor area ratio .78, 469
Floor area, apartment 378, 379
Four-bedroom apartment 385, 406-408

Garages, parking 282, 283
Garden apartments 322, 323
Garden city 101
Glare, zoning 503

Golf course 198, 223
Golf, pitch and putt 221, 222
Governmental agencies:
    Farmers Home and Veterans Administration
    . . . . .518, 519
    Housing Assistance Administration 518
    Housing and Urban Development,
    Department of 519-528
Grades 251
Grants, H.U.D. programs 540-543
    neighborhood facilities 540, 541
    open-space 541, 542
    planning assistance 542, 543
    transportation .541
    urban renewal .542
Grouped dwelling access alternatives 331

Handball courts 238
Hazards, zoning 503
Health center .185, 191
Health club facilities 240
Heights, building 465
High school 175, 214, 215
Highways 269, 270
High-rise apartment building 327, 328
Homeowners association, P.U.D. 167
Homes, mobile 360, 369
Houses, types:
    atrium 300-302
    court 300-302
    duplex 303, 304
    garden apartments 322, 323
    "H" plan 296
    in-line plan 297
    quadruplex 305, 306
    ranch 293
    rectangle 295
    row houses 307-312
    town houses 313-321

Houses, types: (cont.)
    "T" plan 295
    two-story 294
    "U" plan 296
    utility core plan 297
Housing and Urban Development 519-528
Housing Assistance Administration 518
Housing Census reports 7
Housing codes 462, 498, 499, 511
Housing data, tract reports 16, 17
Housing element, case study 23
Housing element, required 22
Housing location 53
Housing quality, measurement of 236
Housing regulation 462, 498, 499, 511
Housing site:
    air rights .68, 69
    central facilities 58
    cultural 59
    employment .57
    inland considerations 62
    pollution factors 67
    recreational .59
    shore considerations 62
    site comparison 64
    site configuration 63
    topographic considerations 60, 61
    utilities 65, 66
    water, over 70, 71
Housing study 4
Housing types, combination 368-372
Housing types, standards 291
Housing units, deficient 28-29
Housing welfare recipients 29-36
Howard, Ebenezer 101
H.U.D. Programs 540-545

Inland considerations, housing site 62
Intensity, land use 83-88

Junior high school 175, 183, 213

Kindergarten 172, 174, 179
Kitchen arrangements 419-426

Land area requirements, community facilities 235
Land development, and loans 544
Land use, design prototype:
    existing 39
    proposed 40
Land-use intensity 83-88
Land uses, compatibility with housing 54
Landscaping 288
Laundry room, housing 241
Library, public 185, 189, 190
Light access, area for 496, 497
Light, apartment 377, 378
Light obstruction, angle of 466
Linear development 108
Living rooms 429-431
Living space, outdoor 443
Loans, H.U.D. programs 543-545
    college housing 543
    land development 544
    new communities 545
    public works 544
    rehabilitation 544, 545
Loans, mortgage, F.H.A. 529-539
Location, housing 53
Location of utilities 286, 287
Lot area per gross acre 151
Lot layout, subdivisions 127-131
Lots, type of zoning 463
Low-rise apartment building 327, 328

Mall 198

Mapping deficiencies, zoning 481
Master plan, subdivisions 122
Mathematical method 20, 21
Maximum distances:
    community facilities 171
    educational 175
    recreational 198
Meeting rooms 238, 239
Migration/natural increase method 19
Mobile homes 358-367
Mobile home park ordinance 489-495
Modular units 353-356
Mortgage loans, F.H.A. 529-539
Multiservice center 185, 191-194

Neighborhood 51, 121
Neighborhood center 107
Neighborhood concept 103
Neighborhood densities 109-115
Neighborhood facilities, H.U.D. programs ...540
Neighborhood park 212, 213
Neighborhood park-school 210, 211
Neighborhood pattern:
    existing 41
    proposed 42
Neighborhood, physical elements 116
Neighborhood playground 211, 212
Neighborhood shopping 230-235
Neighborhood sizes 113
Neighborhood, types of 92-98
Neighborhood unit 102-108
Noise, aircraft 504
Noise, roadway 505-510
Noise standards 500
Nonconforming uses 479
Nursery 172, 174, 175, 178

Occupancy, types of 91

Odorous matter, zoning 501, 502
One-bedroom apartment 384, 389-391
One-family houses 292-299
Open-corridor plan 336
Open-space grants, H.U.D. programs ..541-542
Open space, planned-unit development 155, 161,
..................................166
Open space, recreational 226-229
Open-space standards, density 82
Orientation 253-261
    breezes 254-256
    building 259, 260
    building to street 262, 263
    room 261
    sun 254, 255
    views and vistas 254, 255, 257
Ordinance, mobile home park 439-495
Ordinance, zoning 477, 478
Outdoor living space 443

Park 198
Park, city-wide, district 215, 216
Park, mobile home 360-367
Park-school, community 213-215
Park-school, neighborhood 210, 211
Parking 276-284
Parking alternatives 284
Parking arrangement to building 278, 279
Parking, courts and bays 281
Parking garages 282, 283
Parking, street 266, 267, 280
Passive recreational space 240
Pedestrian circulation 268
Perry, Clarence 102
Pitch and putt golf 221, 222
Planned unit development 152-168
Planning Assistance Grants, H.U.D. ...542, 543
Planning units, types 51
Playfield 198, 209, 215
Playground 198, 203-208, 211, 212, 237

Playlot 198-202, 210
Plaza 198
Pollution factors, housing site 67
Pools 198, 216-220
Population data, tract report 10-15
Population projection:
    apportionment method 18
    mathematical method 20, 21
    migration/natural increase method 19
Population study 5
Preliminary plat 133-134, 136
Public works loans, H.U.D. 544

Quadruplex 305, 306

Radburn 104, 105
Ranch house 293
Recreation 197, 198
Recreation center 185, 224, 225
Recreational facilities accessibility 56
Recreational facilities, community 237-241
Recreational facilities, housing site 59
Recreational space, passive 240
Recreational spaces, alternatives 226-229
Regional pattern, design prototype 44
Regulations, housing 462, 511
Rehabilitation loans, H.U.D. 544, 545
Renewal study, community 6
Residential density 72-78
Room orientation 261
Row houses 307-312

School accessibility 56
School district 51
Semi-attached house 303, 304
Shopping, neighborhood 230-235

Shops, types of 231, 240, 241
Shore considerations, housing site 62
Signs 479
Simplex 410
Single-family house 292-299
Site characteristics, subdivisions 126, 127
Site comparison, housing 64
Site configuration 63
Site plan 245-248
Site planning 245
Six-bedroom apartment 409
Skip-stop plan 337-338
Sky exposure plane 467
Slope analysis 248
Slopes, desirable 251
Smoke, zoning 501
Social center 185, 238
Soil conditions 252
Space standards, apartments 280-283
Split-level house 294, 298, 299
Square 198
Standards, floor area, apartment 280-283
Standards, street 270
Stein, Clarence 104, 105
Streams, subdivisions 132
Street arrangements 273, 274, 275
Street classification 271, 272
Street layout, subdivisions 127-130
Street orientation, building 262
Street parking 266, 267, 280
Street standards 270
Streets 269, 270
Studies:
    community renewal 6
    housing 4
    housing element, case study 23
    population 5
Subdivision plat 134, 137
Subdivisions 122-150
Sun orientation 254, 255, 288
Superblocks 329
Swimming pool 198, 216-220, 238

Synagogue 185-188

Tenements 324-326
Tennis courts 239
Terrace 240
Terrace plan 351
Three-bedroom apartment 385, 401-405
Topographic considerations 249-251
Topographic considerations, housing site .60, 61
Tot lot (see also Playlot) 237
Tower plan 339-346
Town houses 313-317
Tract report, census:
    housing data 16-17
    population data 10-15
Transition zoning 474
Transportation grants, H.U.D. 541
Trees 287
Triplex apartment 416-418
Two-bedroom apartment 384, 392-399
Types of neighborhoods 92-98
Types of occupancy 89

Urban Renewal Grants, H.U.D. 542
Utilities, apartment 379
Utilities, housing site 65, 66
Utilities, location 286, 287

Vehicular circulation 265-267
Ventilation 256
Ventilation, apartment 377, 378
Vibration standards 500, 501
Views, orientation 254, 255, 257
Vistas 257, 258
Volleyball 238

INDEX

Wading pools 217
Waterfront development 198, 219
Welfare recipients, housing 29-36

Yards 464
Youth center 191, 195, 196

Zoning:
    architectural review 476

Zoning: (*cont.*)
    area for light access 496, 497
    building heights 465
    cumulative 473
    density 471-473
    explosives, hazards, glare 503
    flexible devices 475
    floor area 468
    floor area ratio 469
    light obstruction 466
    lots 463
    mapping deficiencies 481

Zoning: (*cont.*)
    noise 500, 504-510
    nonconforming use 479
    odorous matter 501, 502
    signs 479, 480
    sky exposure plane 467
    smoke 501
    transition 474
    vibration 500, 501
    yards 464
Zoning ordinance, sample ...477, 478, 482-485
Zoning, planned unit development 152, 153